THE
ANNUAL REGISTER
Vol. 223

Rex Features

THE SPIRIT OF POLAND
The group of three crosses in Gdansk, which commemorate the workers killed in anti-government riots in 1960, became a focus of aspiration for freedom in 1981.

THE
ANNUAL REGISTER

A Record of World Events
1981

Edited by
H. V. HODSON

Assisted by
VERENA HOFFMAN

FIRST EDITED IN 1758
BY EDMUND BURKE

LONGMAN

1982

LONGMAN GROUP LIMITED
Longman House, Burnt Mill, Harlow, Essex CM20 2JE, UK

© Longman Group 1982

First published 1982

British Library Cataloguing in Publication Data:
The annual register.
    1981
    1. History—Periodicals
    909.82′8′05   D410
    ISBN 0 582 50303 5

Set in Times Roman and
PRINTED IN GREAT BRITAIN AT
THE PITMAN PRESS LTD BATH

CONTENTS

   ILLUSTRATIONS

   The Spirit of Poland. The group of three crosses in Gdansk,   Frontispiece
   which commemorate the workers killed in anti-government
   riots in 1960, became a focus of aspiration for freedom in
   1981.

   The Prince of Wales and Lady Diana Spencer on the day   *between pp. 174–175*
   their engagement was announced; they were married in St
   Paul's Cathedral amid great public rejoicing on 29 July 1981.

viii   CONTENTS

On 30 March 1981 an attempt was made on the life of
President Reagan on a Washington street. Above, the
President immediately after he had been shot and wounded;
a secret service agent hustles him into his motor car. Below,
the scene as the would-be assassin is overpowered; encircled
is the colonel carrying the black box with the code that could
launch nuclear war.

The extraordinary scene immediately after the assassination
of President Sadat at a military parade in Cairo on 6
October 1981. All but one or two flee the saluting base as
gunmen pour bullets into their victim.

Pope John Paul II, seriously wounded by a Turkish gunman
in St Peter's Square, Rome, on 15 May 1981, sinks into the
arms of his aides.

Colonel Antonio Tejero Molina, gun in hand and supported
by armed civil guards, declaims from the rostrum of the
Spanish Cortes, which they had seized in an abortive coup
attempt on 23 February 1981.

A new British political party is formed: the 'gang of four'   *between pp. 366–367*
ex-Labour Cabinet Ministers (left to right: Mr Roy Jenkins,
Dr David Owen, Mr William Rodgers, Mrs Shirley Williams)
launch the Social Democratic Party on 26 March 1981

A picture that scarcely needs a caption: Korchnoi
unsuccessfully challenges Karpov for the world chess
championship, November 1981.

Four European political figures prominent in the news of
1981: above, Andreas George Papandreou and François
Mitterrand, socialist victors in the Greek and French
elections; below, General Jaruzelski, Prime Minister of
Poland, and President Orho Kekkonen of Finland, who
resigned on 27 October after 26 years in office.

Among the eminent people who died in 1981 were, above,
President Ziaur Rahman of Bangladesh and President Anwar
Sadat of Egypt, both assassinated; below, Cardinal Stefan
Wyszynski, Primate of Poland, and Moshe Dayan, Israeli
soldier and statesman.

Triumph and disaster: above, the American space shuttle
Columbia makes a perfect landing, 14 April 1981; below, a
Soviet submarine aground near the Swedish naval base of
Karlskrona, 29 October 1981.

ABBREVIATIONS

ACP	Africa—Caribbean—Pacific
AID	Agency for International Development
ASEAN	Association of South-East Asian Nations
AR	Annual Register
AWACS	Advanced Warning and Communication Systems
CAP	Common Agricultural Policy
CARICOM	Caribbean Common Market
CBI	Confederation of British Industry
CIA	Central Intelligence Agency
COMECON	Council for Mutual Economic Assistance
ECA	Economic Commission for Africa (UN)
ECE	Economic Commission for Europe (UN)
ECOSOC	United Nations Economic and Social Council
EEC	European Economic Community (Common Market)
EFTA	European Free Trade Association
EMS	European Monetary System
ESCAP	Economic and Social Commission for Asia and the Pacific (UN)
EURATOM	European Atomic Energy Community
FAO	Food and Agriculture Organization
GATT	General Agreement on Tariffs and Trade
GDP/GNP	Gross Domestic/National Product
IBRD	International Bank for Reconstruction and Development
ICAO	International Civil Aviation Organization
ICBM	Inter-Continental Ballistic Missile
IDA	International Development Association
ILO	International Labour Organization
IMF	International Monetary Fund
LDCs	Less Developed Countries
MBFR	Mutual and Balanced Force Reductions
MDCs	More Developed Countries
NATO	North Atlantic Treaty Organization
OAS	Organization of American States
OAU	Organization of African Unity
OECD	Organization for Economic Cooperation and Development
OPEC	Organization of Petroleum Exporting Countries
PLO	Palestine Liberation Organization
SALT	Strategic Arms Limitation Talks
TUC	Trades Union Congress
UN	United Nations
UNCTAD	United Nations Conference on Trade and Development
UNDP	United Nations Development Programme
UNESCO	United Nations Educational, Scientific and Cultural Organization
UNRWA	United Nations Relief and Works Agency
VAT	Value Added Tax
WEU	Western European Union
WHO	World Health Organization

CONTRIBUTORS

Africa, North:
Sudan

AHMED AL-SHAHI, D.PHIL
(Lecturer in Social Anthropology, Department of
Social Studies, University of Newcastle-upon-
Tyne)

Libya, Tunisia, Western
Sahara, Algeria, Morocco

DR ROBIN BIDWELL
(Secretary, Middle East Centre, University of Cambridge)

Africa, Equatorial:
Ethiopia, Somalia, Djibouti

CHRISTOPHER CLAPHAM, MA, D.PHIL
(Senior Lecturer in Politics, University of Lancaster)

Kenya, Tanzania, Uganda

WILLIAM TORDOFF, MA, PH.D
(Professor of Government, University of
Manchester)

Ghana

D. G. AUSTIN
(Professor of Government, University of
Manchester)

Nigeria

MARTIN DENT
(Senior Lecturer, Department of Politics, University
of Keele)

Sierra Leone, The Gambia,
Liberia

ARNOLD HUGHES, BA
(Lecturer in Political Science, Centre of West
African Studies, University of Birmingham)

Senegal, Mauritania, Mali,
Guinea, Ivory Coast, Upper
Volta, Togo, Benin, Niger,
Equatorial Guinea, Chad,
Cameroon, Gabon, Congo,
Central African Republic

KAYE WHITEMAN
(Editor, *West Africa*)

Africa, Central and Southern:
Zaïre, Rwanda and Burundi,
Guinea-Bissau and Cape Verde,
São Tome and Principe,
Mozambique, Angola,
Zambia, Malawi

ROBIN HALLETT, MA
(Writer and lecturer on African affairs)

Zimbabwe

R. W. BALDOCK, BA, PH.D
(Director of Academic Publishing, Weidenfeld and
Nicolson; writer on African affairs)

Botswana, Lesotho, Swaziland,
South Africa, Namibia

GERALD SHAW, BA (Hons.)
(Chief Assistant Editor, *The Cape Times*)

Albania

ANTON LOGORECI, B.SC (ECON)
(Writer and broadcaster on communist affairs)

Arab States of the Middle East:
Egypt, Jordan, Syria, Lebanon,
Iraq

CHRISTOPHER GANDY
(Formerly UK Diplomatic Service; writer on Middle
Eastern affairs)

CONTRIBUTORS

xi

Saudi Arabia, Yemen	R. M. BURRELL, (Lecturer in the Contemporary History of the Near and Middle East, School of Oriental and African Studies, University of London)
Gulf States	DR ROBIN BIDWELL (see Africa, North)
Australia	GEOFFREY SAWER, BA, LL.M (Emeritus Professor of Law, Australian National University)
Austria	ANGELA GILLON (Researcher in West European affairs)
Bangladesh	PETER LYON, PH.D (see India)
Benelux countries	J. D. MCLACHLAN (Managing Director, The Financial Times Business Publishing Ltd.)
British Indian Ocean Territory	JANE DAVIS (see Defence Negotiations)
Bulgaria	RADA NIKOLAEV (Head of Bulgarian research section, Radio Free Europe)
Canada	BRUCE THORDARSON, BA, MA (Writer on Canadian affairs)
Caribbean	NEVILLE C. DUNCAN, PH.D (Head, Department of Government and Sociology, University of the West Indies)
China	MICHAEL YAHUDA (Professor of East Asian Studies, The University of Adelaide)
Cyprus	ANNE KERNAHAN (Staff reporter, Middle East Media Operations)
Czechoslovakia	VLADIMIR V. KUSIN, PH.D (Senior Analyst, Radio Free Europe, Munich)
France	MARTIN HARRISON (Professor of Politics, University of Keele)
Germany, West and East	H. N. CROSSLAND (Bonn correspondent, *The Economist*)
Greece	RICHARD CLOGG, MA (King's College, University of London)
Hong Kong	A. S. B. OLVER, MA (Specialist in South East Asian affairs)
Hungary	GEORGE SCHÖPFLIN (Joint Lecturer in East European Political Institutions at the London School of Economics and the School of Slavonic and East European Studies)
India, Nepal, Afghanistan	PETER LYON, PH.D (Reader in International Relations and Secretary, Institute of Commonwealth Studies, University of London)
Iran	KEITH MCLACHLAN, BA, PH.D (Senior Lecturer in Geography with reference to the Near and Middle East, School of Oriental and African Studies, University of London)

Ireland, Northern   A. T. Q. STEWART, MA, PH.D
                           (Reader in Irish History, Queen's University,
                           Belfast)
Ireland, Republic of   LOUIS MCREDMOND, MA, BL
                           (Head of Information in Radio Telefis Eireann, the
                           Irish broadcasting service)
Israel   The Hon. TERENCE PRITTIE, MBE, MA
                           (Director, Britain and Israel)
Italy   MURIEL GRINDROD, OBE
                           (Writer on Italian affairs; formerly Assistant Editor,
                           The Annual Register)
Japan   REGINALD CUDLIPP
                           (Director, Anglo-Japanese Economic Institute)
Korea   RICHARD SIM (Consultant and political analyst on
                           Far Eastern Affairs)
Latin America   PETER CALVERT, AM, MA, PH.D
                           (Reader in Politics, University of Southampton)
Malagasy, Comoro State   KAYE WHITEMAN
                           (Editor, *West Africa*)
Malaysia, Singapore, Brunei MICHAEL LEIFER, BA, PH.D
                           (Reader in International Relations, London School
                           of Economics and Political Science)
Malta, Gibraltar   D. G. AUSTIN
                           (Professor of Government, University of
                           Manchester)
Mauritius   DAVID KINGSLEY
                           (Partner, Kingsley and Kingsley, consultants)
Mongolia   ALAN SANDERS, FIL
                           (Soviet Regional Editor, BBC Monitoring Service)
New Zealand   RODERIC ALLEY, PH.D
                           (School of Political Science and Public Administra-
                           tion, Victoria University of Wellington)
Nordic States   HILARY ALLEN, B.SC (ECON), D.PHIL
                           (Writer on Nordic affairs)
Pakistan   SALMAN A. ALI
                           (Formerly Pakistan Diplomatic Service)
Papua New Guinea   G. P. KING
                           (Professor, Political Studies Department, University
                           of Papua New Guinea)
Poland   Z. J. BLAZYNSKI
                           (Writer and broadcaster on Polish and communist
                           affairs)
Portugal   G. A. M. HILLS, BA, D.LIT
                           (Writer and broadcaster on Iberian current affairs
                           and history)
Romania   GEORGE FODOR
                           (East European Service, BBC)
Scandinavian States *see* Nordic States
Scotland   MAURICE BAGGOTT
                           (Principal, Scottish Industrial Communications)

Seychelles	H. V. HODSON (see U.K.)
South-East Asian States (except Malaysia, Singapore, Brunei)	A. S. B. OLVER, MA (Specialist in South-East Asian affairs)
South Pacific	RODERIC ALLEY, PH.D (see New Zealand)
Spain	G. A. M. HILLS (see Portugal)
Sri Lanka	JAMES JUPP, M.SC (ECON), PH.D (Principal Lecturer in Politics, Canberra College of Advanced Education, Australia)
Switzerland	HERMANN BÖSCHENSTEIN, D.PH (Historian and Editor)
Taiwan	BRIAN HOOK (Senior Lecturer in Chinese Studies, University of Leeds)
Turkey	A. J. A. MANGO, BA, PH.D (Orientalist and writer on current affairs in Turkey and the Near East)
United Kingdom	H. V. HODSON, MA (Formerly Editor, *The Sunday Times*)
USA	JAMES BISHOP (Editor, *The Illustrated London News*)
USSR	PHILIP HANSON, MA, PH.D (Reader in Soviet Economics, Centre for Russian and East European Studies, University of Birmingham)
Wales	PETER STEAD (Lecturer in History, University College of Swansea)
Yugoslavia	F. B. SINGLETON, MA (Formerly Chairman, Post-Graduate School of Yugoslav Studies, University of Bradford)

INTERNATIONAL ORGANIZATIONS AND CONFERENCES

African Conferences and Institutions	KAYE WHITEMAN (Editor, *West Africa*)
Cancún Summit	CAROL GELDART (Research Officer, Institute of Commonwealth Studies, University of London)
Caribbean Organizations	NEVILLE C. DUNCAN, PH.D (Head, Department of Government and Sociology, University of the West Indies)
Comecon	MICHAEL KASER, MA (Reader in Economics, Oxford, and Professorial Fellow of St Antony's College, Oxford)
Commonwealth	EVAN CHARLTON (Editor, *The Round Table* 1979-81; formerly Editor, *The Statesman,* Calcutta and New Delhi)
Council of Europe	SIR JOHN RODGERS, Bt, MA, DL, FRSA (Former President, Political Affairs Commission, Council of Europe and Vice-President of the Assembly of Western European Union)

Defence Negotiations and   JANE DAVIS
  Organizations   (Lecturer, Department of International Politics, The
                                University College of Wales, Aberystwyth)
European Community   CHARLES HODSON
                                (BBC Radio News, Brussels)
Non-Aligned Movement   PETER WILLETTS, PH.D
                                (Lecturer in International Relations, The City Uni-
                                versity, London; author of *The Non-Aligned in
                                Havana*)
Nordic Council   HILARY ALLEN, B.SC (ECON), D.PHIL
                                (Writer on Nordic affairs)
North Atlantic Assembly   RT. HON. SIR GEOFFREY DE FREITAS, KCMG
                                (Former President, North Atlantic Assembly)
Organization of American States PETER CALVERT, AM, MA, PH.D
                                (Reader in Politics, University of Southampton)
South-East Asian Conferences and A. S. B. OLVER, MA
  Institutions   (Specialist in S.E. Asian affairs)
United Nations   MARY ALLSEBROOK, BA
                                (Writer on international and UN matters)

RELIGION   GEOFFREY PARRINDER, MA, PH.D, DD, D.LITT (HON)
                                (Emeritus Professor of the Comparative Study of
                                Religions, University of London)

SCIENCE

Science, Medicine, and Technology JOHN NEWELL, B.SC
  Technology   (Assistant Editor, Science, Industry and Agri-
                                culture, BBC External Services)
Environment   TONY SAMSTAG
                                (General reporter, *The Times*)

LAW

International Law   MAURICE MENDELSON, MA, D.PHIL
                                (Fellow of St John's College, Oxford)
European Community Law   N. MARCH HUNNINGS, LL.M, PH.D
                                (Editor, *Common Market Law Reports*)
Law in the United Kingdom   W. A. MCKEAN, PH.D
                                (Fellow of St John's College, Cambridge)

THE ARTS

Architecture   GEORGE MANSELL, RIBA
                                (Architectural writer)
Art   LADY (MARINA) VAIZEY
                                (Art Critic, *The Sunday Times*)
Ballet   G. B. L. WILSON, MA
                                (Ballet critic of *The Jewish Chronicle* and *Dancing
                                Times,* London, and *Dance News,* New York;
                                author of the *Dictionary of Ballet*)

Cinema	ROGER MANVELL, PH.D, D.LITT, LITT.D (HON) (Director, British Film Academy 1947-59; Visiting Fellow, University of Sussex; University Professor and Professor of Film, Boston University)
Fashion	ANNE PRICE (Fashion Editor, *Country Life*)
Literature	DAVID HOLLOWAY (Literary Editor, *The Daily Telegraph*)
Music	FRANCIS ROUTH (Composer and author; founder/director of the Redcliffe Concerts of British Music)
Opera	RODNEY MILNES (Associate Editor, *Opera*)
Television and Radio	RICHARD LAST (Television critic, *The Daily Telegraph*)
Theatre	BENEDICT NIGHTINGALE (Theatre Critic, *The New Statesman*)
New York Theatre	EDWARD G. GREER (Associate Professor, Drama Department, Syracuse University, USA)

SPORT	DOUG GARDNER (Sports journalist, *United Newspapers*)

ECONOMIC AFFAIRS	
International, UK and USA Economic Developments	PETER RIDDELL (Political Editor, *The Financial Times*)
Economic and Social Data	SUE COCKERILL (Statistical Department, *The Financial Times*)

INDEX	ELIZABETH WALLIS (Registrar, Society of Indexers)

THE ANNUAL REGISTER 200, 150, 100, 50 years ago	W. N. MEDLICOTT, D.LITT, MA, FRHistS (Stevenson Professor of International History Emeritus, University of London)

PREFACE

THE WORLD suffered great strain, both economically and politically, in 1981. The imposition of martial law in Poland was but the most dramatic of a number of incidents threatening peaceful relations between East and West. While the major powers all proclaimed policies of negotiated limitation of armaments, their actions were in the opposite direction. The determination of the Reagan Administration to increase defence spending in order to achieve at least Western equality with the USSR in all elements, thus threatening a new arms race, caused some disarray in the Atlantic alliance, whose European members were under pressure for budgetary economy and beset by a tide of public opinion opposed to nuclear arms. The other side of American and Nato policy, a fresh effort for balanced reduction of armaments, made no headway in the adverse political atmosphere. Attitudes of the United States towards events in Poland and elsewhere also conspicuously differed from those of some Western European countries behind a nominal common front.

American defence policy had serious economic reactions too. Its cost, as a threat of inflation, was countered by a monetary control involving high interest rates which strained other economies. Unemployment rose almost everywhere. The West drew what comfort it could from the fact that not only Poland but indeed the whole communist bloc including the USSR was experiencing equally grave economic problems.

Yet the Western democratic world showed remarkable political stability. The advent of Socialist Governments in France and Greece was accomplished with *sang froid* both nationally and internationally.

In the rest of the world the pattern of previous years was little altered. The problems of Afghanistan and Kampuchea were unalleviated but not worsened. In Africa economic difficulties heightened the characteristic political unrest. Human rights were scarcely better observed in those parts of Latin America and Asia where they had suffered gravely in the past. South Africa continued to defy world opinion on apartheid.

Altogether it was a restless, disappointed and dangerous world, eating the bitter fruits of past errors and continuing enmities, that is recorded in the Annual Register 1981.

Editorially the only major change in the contents is a revision and consolidation of the statistical section.

ACKNOWLEDGEMENTS

The Advisory Board again gratefully acknowledges its debt to the Royal Institute of International Affairs and other institutions for their help with sources, references, documents, figures and maps. The Board, and the bodies which nominate its members, disclaim responsibility for any opinions expressed or the accuracy of any facts recorded in this volume.

200 years ago

19 October 1781. *Surrender of Yorktown.* It would have been cruelty in the extreme to have sacrificed such gallant, and in every respect deserving troops, to a point of honour, which the improved state of civilization has wisely exploded, that of standing an assault, which could not in the nature of things but prove successful. Lord Cornwallis accordingly wrote a letter to Gen. Washington on . . . the 17th, proposing a cessation of arms for 24 hours, and that commissioners might be appointed on both sides for settling the terms of capitulation.

150 years ago

1831. *The plague in Eastern Europe.* The evils of war in this part of eastern Europe, were accompanied by, and assisted in propagating, a much more mortal and extensive calamity, which had gradually been moving westward from the interior of the Russian empire. A pestilential disease, denominated *cholera morbus* . . . had appeared at Moscow towards the close of the preceding year, and, outliving the winter, again manifested itself in the spring, and spread, not only to the capital, but into Poland, Moldavia, Gallicia, and Hungary. In all of these countries, where the lower orders of the people live on scanty food, and amid uncleanly habits, the mortality was great . . . In some of the infected countries, the physical malady was attended by a moral pestilence still more deplorable [in the form of] the idea, that the pretended disease was the result of a conspiracy of the upper classes to sweep away by poison their miserable inferiors. In Hungary, where the disease was most violent, and the ignorance of the people profound, the peasantry, under the influence of this extravagant notion, rose in open insurrection, sacked the castles of the nobility, imprisoned and outraged their persons, and perpetrated the most brutal excesses and atrocious murders.

100 years ago

1881. *Irish enigma.* Neither the suppression of the Land League nor the application of the Land Act succeeded in allaying the agitation and disturbance in Ireland. The outrages that had existed before the arrest of the national leaders existed still. The lawless districts were no less lawless because the Land League had been forcibly put to death, and the year ended, unfortunately, as it had begun, in hostility and disaffection. . . It seems the very irony of fate that an English Government coming into office pledged and eager to give satisfaction to Irish demands, and a body of representative Irishmen trusted in by the majority of their countrymen, should make between them so hopeless a business of their common purposes.

50 years ago

November 1931. *Statute of Westminster.* In the meanwhile the House of Commons had embarked on the discussion of the so-called Statute of Westminster Bill, which sought to put into legal form the resolutions adopted by the Imperial Conferences of 1926 and 1930 for determining the relations between the constituent parts of the British Commonwealth . . . Mr. Churchill's regrets at the passing of the old imperialistic order were not shared even by so staunch a Conservative as Mr. Amery, who declared that the Empire could not be held on the foundation of the former legislative supremacy, but only on that of free co-operation. Nevertheless, the Bill had not so easy a passage as the Government expected, since many members besides Mr. Churchill cherished misgivings with regard to Ireland, and they did not scruple to demand consideration for them, going so far, in spite of Mr. Churchill's advice, as to move the rejection of the second reading . . . After due consideration, the Government decided that it would be unwise to make any alteration in the Bill [which was] subsequently read a third time without a division.

ANNUAL REGISTER

FOR THE YEAR 1981

EDITORIAL

IN 1981 politicians and other leaders of opinion in the industrialized countries of the world began to perceive, or to acknowledge they perceived, that mass unemployment was not a trouble created only by mistaken national policies or one that could be banished by recovery from cyclical world depression. Even political oppositions were claiming for their rival economic strategies rather a reversal of the upward trend than an early return to 'full employment'.

The total of unemployed in the 15 industrialized countries belonging to the Organization for Economic Cooperation and Development (OECD) rose in the third quarter of 1981 to over 20 million, or 6·7 per cent of the work-force. In the EEC the ratio was nearly 8 per cent, and in Belgium and the United Kingdom over 11 per cent. There could be a cheerful way of looking at those figures; when even nine out of ten of all those available for work (including many very young, elderly or handicapped) were in paid employment the economic machine had hardly come to a stop. That view gained legitimacy if the Western situation was compared with that in many countries of Asia, Africa and Latin America. Beside their countless millions living unemployed, or miserably under-employed, in dire poverty, the out-of-work in the richer countries, with their social security benefits and other cushions, were to be envied rather than pitied.

Nevertheless, 20 million men and women out of work in fifteen chief non-communist nations—a group excluding several European countries and all industrialized Latin America—could only be seen as a massive social and human defect, not just a dead statistic but a living swamp of hardship and misery. High unemployment in 1981 presented social, political, regional and sometimes inter-racial problems which threatened national solidarity, social stability and even public order.

* * *

Unemployment has four main components: residual, transitional, structural and cyclical. They merge and overlap but in cause and character are distinct. *Residual* unemployed range from the constructively unemployable, through degrees of inadequate competence or willingness for steady work, to a variable layer whose work ability is simply below the marginal value of labour at the going rates of wages. *Transitional* unemployed are those people, capable of doing work worth marginal pay for their degree of skill or lack of it, who are nevertheless out of a job for reasons peculiar to their locality, their personal circumstances or the fortunes of their past employers, and who are hopefully seeking jobs; they include, initially, most school-leavers. *Structural* unemployed are those thrown out of work, or unable to get work, by reason of changes in the national or international economic structure—for instance, a decline of old industries, mechanization and automation, heightened international competition, or major changes in government policy on public expenditure. *Cyclical* unemployed are those not belonging to the other three categories whose loss of opportunity to work is due to depression of the general curve of activity in the world economy.

Clearly the scale of each of the four components may vary, and their thresholds may change. Thus the marginal value of labour in money terms, which indicates the upper threshold for residual unemployment, can move up or down. The fact that inflation can temporarily lower that upper threshold and reduce the number of residual unemployed has been a temptation to governments who have aimed at too low a level of total unemployment, too low in that it under-estimated the economic minimum and so could not be sustained in competitive conditions once the initial inflationary impulse had expired. (Britain in 1971-73 was a notable example). The threshold of transitional unemployment alters with the speed of economic change, with the degree of mobility of labour and inter-changeability of skills, and with the strength of individual motive to find work quickly. Factors affecting the threshold of structural unemployment include labour mobility, policies of national or regional protection, the volume of government employment, major shifts in consumer demand, and the availability both of capital and of key skills for new or expanding sectors.

As for cyclical unemployment, its threshold is all but arbitrary. For when a recession strikes the capitalist economies generally, whatever its initiating cause, all the other categories of unemployment are worsened. When markets shrink, profit margins fall and the good-time hoarding of labour is reversed, employment falls most sharply among the least employable, those whom hard-pressed companies get rid of first, and among those in structurally declining segments of the economy or in jobs whose technological redundancy is exposed in the chillier climate. The average period of transitional unemployment is prolonged. It could indeed be argued that all supposed cyclical unemployment is really either transitional or structural (including jobs lost through government economy measures). But this would be to ignore the fact of decline in the real output of industry and commerce overall, not only that of particular segments. Such decline in output is the real measure of cyclical recession;

to take unemployment as the measure is to fall into the trap of attempted cure by inflation.

* * *

The cyclical ups and downs of the Western economies in the last three decades show a clear tendency for the level of unemployment, both in the troughs and in the peaks, to rise with each succeeding wave. In the seven leading industrial countries of the West the low point of unemployment in the affluent 1960s was 2·6 per cent in 1966; in the next decade it was 3·4 per cent in 1973. The 1979 recovery brought the percentage down to 4·9 before it resumed its rise. Likewise the successive 'depression' figures were 2·9 per cent in 1967-68, 5·4 per cent in 1975-78 and 6·4 per cent in 1981. Those figures tell their own tale; while cyclical unemployment has certainly afflicted the industrialized world of late, it has been only of the order of 1½ per cent of the work-force from peak to trough of business activity, or less than 4 million of the 20 million out-of-work in 1981 in the OECD group. So 'recovery' from the current economic recession would leave heavy unemployment still with us.

It may be protested that the fluctuations since 1973, with their symptom of continuous high unemployment, were quite untypical of the historic business cycle and that no such long-term conclusions can be drawn from them. The multiplication of oil prices from the end of 1973 onwards required real standards to fall in the importing countries if it was to be absorbed without damage; but since union power prevented any cut in money wages—indeed the United Kingdom suffered a wage explosion just when the opposite should have happened—in greater or less degree the Western countries took the alternative path of inflation. When the consequence became too menacing, they imposed deflationary policies which—again through the rigidity of the wage structure—inevitably caused unemployment. That account, however, does not invalidate the previous argument. The rigidities that have made unemployment so prompt and so large an outcome of deflation after an inflationary bout are a fact of life which will not go away when the business cycle enters another phase. In the analysis used here, it is a structural fact, which has to be countered by structural means. So 'reflation', apart from its inherent risks, would not and could not by itself 'cure unemployment'.

Nor would 'economic growth'* by itself cure unemployment. Unemployment has persisted, and fluctuated, within periods of fairly continuous economic growth, and has been statistically high in some countries, like the United States, with above-average growth rates. Economic growth, besides being linked to rising material standards, is obviously necessary to maintain the scale of employment where the population of

* Usually measured by increase in the real gross national product, the sum of output of goods and service in money terms corrected overall for general price changes.

working age is increasing. Between the third quarters of 1975 and 1981 the total available labour force of OECD countries (excluding Japan, a special case) rose by 21½ million, of whom 17½ million were absorbed into employment. Nevertheless, at the end of those six years 4 million more of the labour force were unemployed than at the beginning, although meanwhile many people had dropped out of the labour market. Had growth been sustained in 1980-81, the numbers employed in OECD would probably have been about 2½ million higher than they were, but normal growth alone would not have provided jobs for the rest of those out of work.

*   *   *

It is evidently necessary to seek reasons for large-scale unemployment in Western economies (above, that is to say, an average of about 3 per cent) beyond the downward phase of the trade cycle and the consequent faltering of economic growth. Reverting to the other three components of unemployment, structural change is manifestly a very big contributor, especially in the United Kingdom and indeed in all countries with ship-building, steel, heavy engineering, textile and footwear industries and, on a rather different footing, motor manufacture. The causes include changes in final demand (e.g., ships and steel, in which there was over-capacity even in a buoyant market), automation (including micro-chip technology) and the competition of newly industrialized countries (NICs). Without protectionism—which would have deleterious effects on living standards and growth—a great deal of former European and North American production of ships, automobiles, electronic equipment, textiles, clothing and footwear was likely to be permanently lost to NICs in Asia (following in the wake of Japan) and in parts of South America whose industrial potential had not yet been realized.

It is often argued, in respect of technological developments in industry and commerce, that loss of employment in some industries and occupations is balanced by gains in others that replace them, directly or indirectly. There is evidence that historically this has been the case. But much depends on the nature of the new industries; if, as in the current industrial revolution, the replacing employment is generally more skilled than that which it replaces, a given turnover requires fewer workers at higher pay. Indirectly the compensating effect may take time to work out, and its bearing on employment will depend on where the diverted spending power goes. What is certain is that all such change enhances transitional unemployment, which may be so prolonged as to be classed as structural.

The upper threshold of residual unemployment has also been heightened by current forces. Where trade union power has raised acceptable minimum wages above the economic margin in the prevailing market conditions, more people of low work capacity have been ren-

dered effectively unemployable. It has had that effect particularly in relation to the employment of untrained labour (including school leavers)
and minority communities. Increasing taxes on employment (like the
British national insurance surcharge) works in the same way.

*   *   *

In the rest of the non-communist world the same components of unemployment exist, but in poor, highly populated countries their proportions are very different. Cyclical unemployment is relatively small.
Residual unemployment, on the other hand, is vast, including as it does
chronic under-employment of millions in rural areas and on the fringes
of city life. Structural unemployment has displayed a dominating
feature, the flow of people to the cities and large towns from rural areas
because the latter could not sustain the natural increase of population
and indeed tended to employ fewer workers with modern methods of
agriculture and rural transport. While rural unemployment and under-
employment have remained as a grave blot, their aspect and social consequences have been softened by relics of an imagined golden age in which
everyone in a village or town had his appointed role, and if many went
hungry none went without work. But in the cities millions have congregated who had no such traditional structure to support them.

People in more affluent countries often ask how do these workless,
apparently income-less, people survive, with no unemployment pay or
cash welfare benefits to support them. The answer lies in a sort of
sharing of poverty. Where the rule of family responsibility is strong, one
income may have to maintain not one nuclear family but two or more.
Begging from poor as well as better-off neighbours brings virtue to both
giver and receiver. For the rest, an unmeasurable 'grey economy' yields
some money income from odd jobs and petty trading. This is a phenomenon too little acknowledged in Western industrialized countries themselves. A few hours of casual labour, uncontracted part-time work (often
at night or weekends), self-employment in decorating, gardening, house
cleaning and the like, eke out recorded income and in some cases make
altogether a tolerable way of life. Such earnings moderate the social
impact of unemployment and discount global figures of the workless as a
measure of people without economic activity or any earned income. The
grey economy is a kind of sharing of economic benefit between those
with regularly paid or profitable occupation and those without. It offers
little value in places where almost everyone is poor and the ratio of
unemployment is high.

The newly industrialized countries are a different case. Expanding industry, with export markets, has created thousands of jobs both directly
and in associated commerce, transport, building and retail trade, jobs
which did not previously exist. They have been filled by men and women
who in the past would have lived as peasants or in non-industrial and

often irregular employment. It is not only technical and managerial skills that have made expanding industry possible but also the existence of a pool of available labour, including women who in previous circumstances were not in the labour market. Once an industrial urban proletariat appears in this fashion, the possibility of classic unemployment appears with it. Successful in manufacture and export as countries like South Korea or Taiwan have been, after a while they, too, may be afflicted with substantial levels of urban unemployment.

Such a world-wide economic phenomenon seems to imply a need for world-wide approaches to its mitigation. That was the philosophy of the Brandt Commission, whose report (see AR 1980, pp. 492-9) was the subject of the summit conference at Cancún, Mexico, in October 1981. The Brandt report was concerned rather with poverty than with unemployment in the Third World, but unemployment and under-employment were of course major causes of that poverty. A basic Brandt theme was that an acute need for capital for development in the Third World ('the South') confronted unused capacity both of labour and of other resources in the industrialized countries ('the North'): that capacity, it was argued, could be activated by a concerted development programme, which would soon create an expanding market for the North's industrial exports. Whatever the substance of that theme, it was too crude a diagnosis when applied to the world-wide sickness of unemployment. Much of the capital needed by the poorer countries to give more employment was required for the development (directly or through improvement of infrastructure) of industries competing with those of the older industrial economies, while much employment in the latter was in industries making products increasingly manufactured in the Third World. The Brandt proposition could almost be turned on its head: it was not merely the rich who needed the poor to prosper, but equally the poor who needed the rich to prosper. A booming market in the West would do more for Third World economies than any likely transfer of resources.

That might suggest that a world-wide reflation was the right prescription for world-wide unemployment. But its defects would be the same globally as nationally: it would leave structural unemployment unaltered; it would achieve through price inflation a lowering of real wages —which in itself would cut residual unemployment for a while, but in the worst way, whereby the strong would gain and the weak would suffer. That argument does not oppose an expansion of credit to finance international trade, or global cooperation to smooth out the waves of the business cycle and the fluctuation of exchange rates which checks international trade where its finance is weakest.

*   *   *

Even so, unemployment would, it seemed certain, remain high even at the peaks of the cycle unless there were other changes. Must then the industrialized countries, in particular, be resigned to the permanence of much higher levels of unemployment than they have thought tolerable in the past? The pace of technical and market change, which has fomented a new industrial revolution, with all its consequences for unemployment, is unlikely to slacken. The conclusion must be that, if such levels were held insufferable for social and political reasons, unemployment must be tackled directly, not as just a symptom of general economic conditions.

It may prove that the world—or at least the Western industrialized world—was emerging in 1981 into a new phase of economic policies and objectives. In such a phase, if it eventuated, no longer would 'economic growth' be the guiding talisman, but rather a concept of economic welfare which prominently included a minimization of unemployment for its own social, human and political sake.

I HISTORY OF THE UNITED KINGDOM

Chapter 1

A QUEEN APPARENT

ON 29 July, 1981, the Prince of Wales was married in St Paul's Cathedral to Lady Diana Spencer, daughter of the 7th Earl Spencer. In a year of economic gloom and political dissension in the United Kingdom, the occasion proved a unique display of national joy and devotion to the Crown. Moreover, of all British events in the year it was the one that most caught the world's attention. It was estimated that 700 million people in all continents watched the ceremony, with its attendant processions and royal appearances, on television.

The British people had reason to rejoice. The heir to the throne, himself popular with all classes, was marrying a young and beautiful English girl who had already earned universal respect and affection for her discreet yet charming behaviour in face of all the harassment and publicity that afflicted her both before and after the engagement was announced by Her Majesty the Queen 'with the greatest pleasure' on 24 February, the media having anticipated it for months beforehand (see AR 1980, p. 39). A future King had chosen a future Queen whom everyone took to their hearts. Her good taste matched her personal charm and freshness, and her choice of clothes was a model for a generation which seemed almost not to care about dress or femininity.

The celebrations, which were blessed with fair weather, began with a firework display in Hyde Park on the eve of the wedding. The gorgeous carriage processions from Buckingham Palace to St Paul's and back again were watched by crowds almost as great as at a Coronation. The most moving and memorable demonstration of public happiness, however, occurred after the married couple and the Royal Family had returned to the palace. As the tail of the procession clattered forward, thousands of people who had been lining the streets poured at its heels into the Mall, filling the avenue from end to end and presenting an immense sea of faces to the television cameras. They could not have too many appearances of the Queen and the Duke of Edinburgh, the bride and bridegroom and others of the Royal Family on the palace balcony. Young people predominated; there seemed to be relatively few immigrants or foreigners. Complete orderliness prevailed; no such incidents occurred as many had feared in an age of violent protest.

The couple spent their honeymoon at the Mountbatten 'stately home' in Hampshire and on a cruise of the Mediterranean and Egypt on the royal yacht. The affair of the King of Spain's declining an invitation to the wedding because the Prince and Princess were embarking at Gibraltar wrung no British withers. From Northern Ireland, Mr Ian Paisley, MP, stayed away on the grounds that the participation of a Roman Catholic archbishop was a betrayal of the Protestant Reformation.

The Prince and Princess of Wales were enthusiastically received on a tour of the Principality in October (see p. 50), and the Princess's immense popularity was further reflected in the attention paid by the media to all her public appearances, not least at the state opening of Parliament on 4 November, the day before it was announced, to national joy, that Her Royal Highness was expecting a baby in June.

Chapter 2

RIOTS, RACE AND THE POLICE

ON 11 April grave rioting broke out in the inner London area of Brixton, and continued in waves for the next two days. Brixton had a population of mixed races, and most of the young rioters were black, but white youths were also engaged, the targets being primarily the police and secondarily shop property, some of it black-owned, to which severe damage was done. Middle-aged and white people took part in looting. Firemen and their vehicles and even ambulances were attacked. By the evening of 12 April there had been some 250 reported casualties, of whom over 200 were policemen, and probably many more unreported. The trigger had been an incident on 10 April when a crowd of some hundred black youths attacked police officers who were questioning a black boy found with stab wounds. Strong police reinforcements heightened the tension, but eventually dispersed the mobs.

The riots shocked the nation not only by their violence and presumed racial implications but also by their demonstration that police forces could not control or even contain mobs throwing petrol bombs and other lethal missiles and attacking them with petrol bombs, crowbars or the like in confined city streets, even in the metropolis. On 13 April, the Home Secretary announced an immediate and far-ranging inquiry into the events and their causes by Lord Scarman, a highly respected Lord of Appeal. This decision relieved the tension, and not long afterwards a 'Brixton Defence Committee', largely representing the racial minority, called off its initial boycott of the inquiry when it saw with what energy, sympathy and frankness Lord Scarman was setting about his task. The Home Secretary also banned all political demonstrations in London for a month, the second such ban during the year.

On 20 April and 21 June there was some more rioting of a not dissimilar kind in two other London districts, Finsbury Park and Peckham, but it was on a smaller scale and seemed more an expression of mob action by young hooligans gathered together for some event than anything deeper. An outbreak of street violence in Southall, a West London suburb largely inhabited by Asians, on 3 July had been provoked by an invasion by National Front racists.

However, rioting even worse than that at Brixton began next day in the depressed Liverpool district of Toxteth. On the evening of Saturday 4 July policemen who were investigating a stolen car were set upon by a mob of youths, black and white, estimated at 150, who thereupon took over the district's main thoroughfare, Upper Parliament Street, wrecking cars, looting and burning shops and attacking the police with bricks, bottles and petrol bombs. On the Sunday evening, after a lull, a much larger mob charged lines of police, wielding scaffold poles, hosepipes, stolen milk floats and other weaponry, forcing the police to retreat, destroying more property, burning shops and offices and preventing firemen from putting out the fires. Rioting was resumed on the Monday, when a hospital was looted and doctors were attacked. After three days Upper Parliament Street was left a ruin.

Nor was this all. As if by infection—and that may have been so—on 8 July hundreds of youths, mostly black, rampaged through the Manchester district of Moss Side, smashing windows, looting shops and attacking the police. In the next few days more rioting followed in Brixton, Southall and other parts of London, in Reading, Liverpool, Hull and Preston, all of much the same nature—young people defying police and opening the way to destruction and looting in which some older people took part.

While Lord Scarman conducted his investigation, many explanations of the disorders were loudly voiced. The Government's economic policies and consequent high unemployment were blamed by Labour critics; the added charge of neglecting the social and economic plight of the decayed inner cities had to be directed at previous Governments as well. Others stressed the heavy preponderance of blacks among the miscreants. The far-right Monday Club, after Brixton, called for repatriation of 50,000 immigrants each year and repeal of all race relations laws. The Prime Minister reassured the immigrant communities: 'British citizenship', she said, 'once granted, cannot be taken away'. The fact was that the worst incidence of unemployment was within the 16 to 20 age-group and heaviest among coloured people congregated in certain city areas.

Still others, including some police chiefs, calling the riots 'just hooliganism', laid the blame on parents and school-teachers for failure to inculcate discipline and respect for order in their children and charges, citing as evidence the numbers of boys and girls too young to have left school who took part in the rioting. Speaking on television on 8 July Mrs Thatcher declared: 'A free society will survive only if we, its citizens, obey the law and teach our childen to do so.' Next day the Home Secretary, in a by-election speech, said the Government would legislate to enable courts to require parents to pay fines imposed on offenders under 17 unless they could prove this to be unreasonable. Weakness of parental control and home discipline in West Indian families was generally suspected. An inquiry into the education of ethnic minorities disclosed evidence of very poor performance by West Indian children by comparison not only with white but also with Asian children, who on average did as well as white pupils; it laid the blame on racist sentiment, negative attitudes on the part of teachers and inappropriate curricula, the element of home influence being skated over.

Some police officers and politicians alleged political instigation from extreme groups like the Workers' Revolutionary Party. But, whatever the force of those allegations, the outstanding fact common to all the major disorders was open warfare between young people, mainly black, and the police. The causes of such total estrangement had to be found. Much of the evidence to the Scarman inquiry concentrated on this aspect. The police were accused of persistent harassment. They replied that their duty was to uphold the law, to prevent crime and to apprehend offenders. (The notorious 'sus' law, enabling citizens to be apprehended on suspicion of intent to commit crime, was repealed, to be replaced by a Criminal Attempts Law which came into force on 24 August, making it an arrestable offence to try to do that which, if successful, would constitute a crime.) They defended themselves against charges of racial bias by protesting that in districts like Brixton the majority of crimes like theft were demonstrably committed by blacks. A Brixton residents' group claimed that increasing the number of policemen in an area actually raised the crime rate. The controversy over police methods turned in some cases into breaches between chief constables and the police committees of their local councils, thus sharpening debate over the public accountability of police forces. Impartial, outside determination of complaints against the police was also widely demanded.

The principal Government reaction, apart from setting up the Scarman inquiry, was predictably to stand firmly behind the forces of law and order. Visiting Liverpool after the Toxteth riots, where she met a hostile reception, Mrs Thatcher promised strong support for the police, including the supply of better anti-riot equipment and a review of the Public Order Acts. A few days later she said the police could have anything they wanted—not only better defensive equipment but, if they asked, rubber bullets, which it was averred had proved deadly in Northern Ireland. The Government's response was not, however, entirely defensive. After Toxteth, a special task force of Ministers and civil servants headed by Mr Michael Heseltine, Secretary of State for the Environment, was despatched to Merseyside to investigate the causes and possible solution of the troubles. Mr Heseltine's report to the Cabinet was not published but he was known to have recommended certain remedial measures of redevelopment in Merseyside, and some administrative reforms, aimed at directing and co-ordinating expenditure by different departments in inner-city areas.

On the racial front a happier note was struck when the Notting Hill Carnival, a primarily West Indian celebration over the August bank holiday weekend, which had provoked violence in the past, proved cheerful and peaceable bar some hooligan violence as it ended.

Lord Scarman's report (*The Brixton Disorders 10-12 April 1981.* Cmnd. 8427) was published on 25 November. An important chapter dealt with the predetermining social conditions in Brixton and in other disturbed areas. Although the position of ethnic minorities appeared to have improved, they suffered more acutely the deprivations common to all in inner cities.

Unemployment and poor housing bear on them very heavily; and the educational system has not adjusted itself satisfactorily to their needs. Their difficulties are intensified by the sense they have of a concealed discrimination against them, particularly in relation to job opportunities and housing. . . . In addition, they do not feel politically secure. Their sense of rejection is not eased by the low level of black representation in our elective political institutions. . . . The accumulation of these anxieties and frustrations . . . encourages them to protest on the streets and it is regrettably true that some are tempted by their deprivations into crime, particularly street crime. . . . The recipe for a clash with the police is therefore ready-mixed; and it takes little, or nothing, to persuade them that the police, representing an establishment which they see as insensitive to their plight, are their enemies.

None of these features can perhaps be usefully described as a *cause* of the disorders, either in Brixton or elsewhere. . . . But taken together they provide a set of *conditions* which create a predisposition towards violent protest. . . . Moreover, many of them [young blacks in Brixton] believe with justification that violence, though wrong, is a very effective means of protest; for by attracting the attention of the mass media of communication they get their message across to the people as a whole.

In a controversial passage Lord Scarman averred that 'a policy of direct co-ordinated attack on racial disadvantage inevitably means that the ethnic minorities will enjoy for a time a positive discrimination in their favour'. He enjoined such an attack, and recommended particularly improvements in the education of ethnic minorities. In later statements Lord Scarman denied that by positive discrimination he implied discrimination against anyone else; equal opportunity required removing unequal disadvantage.

The bulk of his report, however, dealt with the events of the April riots and the conduct of the police and the public. He found that save in one or two respects the police 'acted wisely, coolly and with commendable restraint in a testing, dangerous and alarming situation'. 'They stood between our society and a total collapse of law and order in the streets of an important part of the capital. For that, they deserve, and must receive, the praise and thanks of all sections of our community.'

But Lord Scarman strongly criticized as an error of judgment a plan of saturating the district with police to combat minor offences, and he recommended a number of reforms, including the establishment of statutory consultative committees to make the police more accountable to local communities, greater independent oversight of procedure in complaints against police behaviour, improved training of recruits in relations with the public and coping with disorder, more recruitment of black and Asian policemen, and making racially prejudiced conduct by police an offence punishable with dismissal. Despite its criticism the report was generally well received by the police authorities as well as by politicians, the press and public generally. Some black community and far left spokesmen attacked it as whitewashing the police and ignoring the crucial issues. The Home Secretary said that the Government accepted most of the recommendations but he avoided instant specific commitments.

When the House of Commons debated the report on 10 December, Mr Whitelaw continued to show caution. Recruitment of coloured people to the police forces, he said, would be eased by new tests to be devised, free of cultural ties. Improvements would be made to police training after further examination. He could not endorse an automatic penalty of dismissal for conduct showing racial bias but he sought the support of police organizations for demonstration that such conduct would not be tolerated. On relations between police authorities and community leaders he would aim to produce national guidelines. He did not rule out a statutory framework for consultation either in London or elsewhere if the advice he received pointed that way. Financial help would be given to local authorities with special needs for education and other services to minorities. (A day earlier Mr Heseltine had announced an addition of £95 million in grants for creating jobs and improving the environment in inner cities.) The Government would give a lead to public and private employers by introducing ethnic monitoring in the civil service. Opposition spokesmen thought the Home Secretary's statement too tepid. In particular, Mr Roy Hattersley called for radical changes in the set-up of the Metropolitan Police, now responsible directly to the Home Secretary; they should be made accountable to a democratic body.

Chapter 3

POLITICAL DRAMA

A GOVERNMENT halfway through its parliamentary term, having a powerful leader and a big Commons majority, would seem on its face a classic prescription for a period of political quiescence. Yet 1981 was a year of extraordinary excitement in British politics, which at its end were in a state wholly different from that of the previous year. A new major party had been born, and an inter-party alliance formed in the centre which seemed to exceed in electoral popularity either of the two main traditional parties. Of those, the Labour Party had endured a devastating internal struggle, while the Conservatives were far from unanimous in supporting their own Government's economic policies. The three major developments were closely connected. The Labour rift was the result of a campaign by the militant left to change both the party's main policies and its internal structure, proceeding so successfully that some leading party members, and many previous Labour voters, saw salvation only in the creation of a new moderate party. The centre being already occupied by the Liberals, the latter and the new party had the choice between splitting the middle vote and allying to unite it. Suddenly a centre coalition appeared as a viable alternative Government, and as an electoral haven not only for moderate Labour voters but also for Tory voters dissatisfied with the Government's economic record. Consequently some Conservative MPs began to vocalize the criticism of the Government's economic severity that had been growing among them as unemployment mounted.

The formation of a new Social Democratic Party had been foreshadowed in 1980 by a speech by Mr Roy Jenkins, whose term as President of the European Commission was about to expire, and by the professions of three other former Labour Cabinet Ministers—the 'gang of three'—Mrs Shirley Williams, Dr David Owen and Mr William Rodgers (see AR 1980, pp. 16-17). On 21 January Mr Michael Foot, the Leader of the Opposition, in a radio interview, pleaded passionately with such dissidents to 'argue their case within the party', but that cause was dealt a fatal blow by the special Labour Party conference held at Wembley on 24 January to settle the question of an electoral college to choose the party leader (see AR 1980, p. 18). Mr Foot had wanted at least one-half of the college votes to be assigned to the parliamentary party, but on a third ballot, after some very curious manoeuvring by the big unions whose vote was decisive, that figure was rejected in favour of giving only 30 per cent of the college voting power to the parliamentarians, 30 per cent to constituency parties and 40 per cent to the trade unions. The prospect of having the party's parliamentary leader, and thus the potential Prime Minister, nominated by the manipulation of a caucus of constituency militants and union bosses was too much for the 'gang of four' (Owen, Rodgers and Williams, now joined by Jenkins). The next day they announced jointly that they were setting up a Council for Social Democracy (CSD) with the avowed aim of later launching a new party, though they would remain in the Labour Party meanwhile.

Their goal was 'more, not less radical changes, but with greater stability of direction'.

Mr Foot continued to beg the dissidents to stay with Labour, but their impulse to separate was greatly encouraged by the indication of opinion polls that a centre alliance of Liberals and Social Democrats would be highly popular with the electors. Thus a poll published in *The Times* on 9 February showed 39 per cent of the sample willing to vote for such an alliance, 27 per cent for Labour and 21 per cent for the Conservatives. Some Liberals, however, were dubious; Mr Cyril Smith, MP, wrote in a party newspaper that he would be extremely apprehensive about any electoral pact which enabled a fourth party to gain life: such a move would be fatal to the Liberal Party. Mrs Thatcher called the Social Democrats trimmers and 'slow-motion socialists'. Mr Foot prognosticated that they would have little effect.

Nevertheless the movement continued to gather momentum. On 5 February the CSD published in a newspaper advertisement the names of a hundred committed supporters, including four more former Labour Cabinet Ministers and five former junior Ministers, along with distinguished economists, scientists and other academics and one union leader, Mr Frank Chapple of the electricians' union. After Mr Tony Benn had pronounced 'I do not think it is moral for someone to sit in the highest echelons of one party in order to get enough time to prepare another party', Mrs Williams, who had lost her parliamentary seat at the general election, resigned from Labour's National Executive Committee (NEC) on 9 February, declaring that 'the party I loved and worked for no longer exists'. On 2 March Dr Owen and Mr Rodgers renounced the Labour whip, along with ten other Labour MPs and nine Labour peers. In vain did Mr Foot challenge the defecting MPs to resign their seats, branding their refusals as 'acts of dishonour'. A Social Democratic parliamentary committee was formed with Dr Owen as chairman, and on 3 March linked with the Liberals in a joint consultative committee to co-ordinate parliamentary tactics. On 16 March a Conservative MP, Mr Christopher Brocklebank-Fowler, crossed the floor to sit with the Social Democrats below the gangway, declaring that the Thatcher Government had 'knocked the stuffing out of British industry'.

On 26 March the 'gang of four' launched the new Social Democratic Party (SDP). No leader or method of electing one was named, Mr Jenkins being nominated only as co-ordinator of policy. A steering committee of 14 included seven defecting Labour members and two well-known former MPs, Mr Dick Taverne and Mr David Marquand. Twelve tasks for Social Democrats were proclaimed. The first was 'breaking the mould'—a favourite phrase of the new evangel:

Britain needs a reformed and liberated political system without the pointless conflict, the dogma, the violent lurches of policy and the class antagonisms that the two old parties have fostered.

Other 'tasks', or objectives, included proportional representation, a consistent economic strategy including a large investment programme based on oil revenues, a mixed economy with both management and unions aware of their national responsibility, a fair distribution of wealth without taking reward from enterprise, decentralization of government and reform of the second chamber of Parliament, improved health and welfare services, protection of the environment at some economic cost, fuller equality for women, no racial discrimination, international cooperation through continued membership of the European Community and Nato, multilateral disarmament and more help to the Third World.

The launching, at eight simultaneous press conferences in London and provincial, Scottish and Welsh cities, was a highly successful public relations exercise. Phone-in arrangements for would-be supporters were made in 21 centres and were reported to have yielded a massive response; only a fortnight after the launching over 43,000 subscribers (at an average of £9 a head) had been enlisted.

The SDP declared it would not fight as a national party in the local government elections due in May, but a number of individual candidates stood in social democrat colours. Mrs Williams advised electors to vote Liberal where no such candidate appeared. This may have helped the Liberals to make a net gain of some 250 county council seats in an election whose main feature was a big swing from Conservative to Labour. The Labour Party gained or kept control of 21 councils in 54 counties in England and Wales, including London and all the other five metropolitan councils, against 19 held by the Conservatives and one by the Liberals, the remainder being in control of Independents or of no single group. The four-year oscillation of the local government pendulum had been expected to produce such a swing, but a striking aspect in May 1981 was its far greater amplitude in the north than in the south—12½ per cent in London, for instance, but 73 per cent in Manchester.

In the capital, the militant left majority in the Labour group ousted the previous moderate leader in favour of Mr Ken Livingstone, an extremist whose eccentric utterances on such matters as the police or Irish terrorism often embarrassed the centre and right of the party.

On 16 June the SDP and the Liberal Party issued a joint statement of policy entitled 'A Fresh Start for Britain'. While skating over such divisive issues as incomes policy and nuclear power, it was firm in advocating support for Nato and the EEC, proportional representation, parliamentary reform, administrative devolution, freedom of information, protection of individual rights, industrial partnership and 'a more balanced economy'.

The first real electoral test for the SDP, and for its constituency relations with the Liberal Party, occurred in a by-election on 16 July in the

Cheshire industrial constituency of Warrington, previously held by Labour with a 10,000 majority. A Liberal candidate was in the field but Mrs Williams was strongly favoured to fly the SDP-Liberal banner. After some wavering, which somewhat tarnished her image as a leader, she declined, and the challenge was taken up by Mr Roy Jenkins, the Liberal contender being then persuaded to withdraw. Mr Jenkins's courage in staking his reputation on so unpromising a tourney was wholly vindicated. Standing for the SDP with Liberal support he secured 12,521 votes against 14,280 for Labour; the Labour vote fell by 5,000 and the Tory vote by 7,000 compared with the 1979 general election, when the Liberal candidate had taken fewer than 3,000 votes. Mr Jenkins described this, the first parliamentary election he had lost, as 'by far the greatest victory in which I have participated'. For Mr Steel it proved that a Liberal SDP alliance could form the next Government. Mr Healey reflected that as the main opposition to 'the most unpopular government in history' Labour was doing 'not well enough to win a general election'. The successful left-wing Labour candidate's description of the SDP as 'a media-created party that has been sold like soap-flakes' sounded like sour grapes.

Through the summer the SDP made progress both in organizing itself and in furthering its yet unratified alliance with the Liberals. On 16 September the annual Assembly of the Liberal Party at Llandudno voted overwhelmingly for the alliance, only 112 out of some 1,600 delegates being recorded as against it. In his winding-up speech Mr Steel declared: 'This assembly has seen the Liberal Party discard its role of eternal opposition and face up to the realities of power.' The alliance, which would call for a high degree of vision, trust and forbearance on both sides, was 'an alliance for Britain, between management and labour, young and older, black and white, the private and public sectors of the economy'. On one issue at least the Liberals were not in the middle of the road: defying the leadership, the Assembly voted by a majority for unilateral British renunciation of nuclear arms. Its other most important policy decision was in favour of a statutory incomes policy.

In its first annual conference the SDP deliberately presented the likeness of a rolling band-wagon. Successive sessions were held during the week to 10 October in Perth (Scotland), Bradford and London with train journeys in between like an American presidential campaign. No motions were put, nor votes taken, so the trend of policy could be gauged only by platform speeches and the tenor of debates. The alliance with the Liberals was endorsed by acclamation. On the divisive question of election of a leader the groundswell of opinion seemed to favour a poll of all party members, the solution favoured by Dr Owen and Mrs Williams, against a choice by MPs only, preferred by Mr Jenkins and Mr Rodgers.

An outline constitution, published on 22 September, emphasized party democracy, exercised at three levels—area, regional and national— whereby members would be consulted on all important issues. A Council for Social Democracy, some 400 strong, would be 'the parliament of the party'; not more than one-quarter of its members should be MPs and one-third should be women.

On policy the leaders promised a Scottish Assembly with taxing powers, a big investment in economic infrastructure including a Channel Tunnel, less government interference with industry but an expansion of the National Enterprise Board, 'integration' of the public and private sectors of school education without compulsion but with a review of the charitable status of independent schools, a six-point crash programme costing up to £3,000 million per annum to cut unemployment by one million within two years, and an anti-inflation plan to tax employers on wage settlements above a nationally fixed norm. Much breath was spent on denouncing what Mr Jenkins called the 'doctrinaire and incompetent monetarism' of the Thatcher Government and on rebutting the imputa- tion that the SDP was a 'Mark II Labour Party'. 'We have a different and constantly growing constituency,' he said. However, to the public gaze the party's pale red complexion was heightened by the enlistment of four more Labour MPs during the conference, making a total of 21 SDP members in the Commons (all save one ex-Labour), compared with 13 Liberals. Further defections from Labour raised the number to 27 by the end of the year.

When, in July, the Tory-held seat of Croydon NW, a middle-class London suburban constituency, became vacant, Mrs Williams had indi- cated her willingness to stand, and her candidature was openly backed by Mr Steel. The local Liberals, however, thought otherwise and re-adopted their candidate, with the historic name of William Pitt, who had received declining percentages of the vote in 1974 (two elections) and 1979, when he had polled only 4,239 votes against 19,928 for the Conservative and 16,159 for Labour. Since it was, after Warrington, 'the Liberals' turn', nothing more could be said. The by-election was held on 22 October. Mr Pitt, standing as a Liberal with SDP support but with the word 'Alliance' on the ballot paper, was returned with 13,800 votes against 10,546 for the Conservative, a good Labour candidate being beaten into third place with 8,967 votes. Some Liberal spokesmen claimed that Mr Pitt could have won on the Liberal ticket alone.

On 13 October the Liberal and SDP leaders reached a pact on appor- tionment of seats to fight at the next general election: each party would field candidates in about half the constituencies, the details to be worked out regionally. Implementing the pact, however, caused some bitter disputes, not least in cases where an established Liberal candidate faced a sitting ex-Labour MP now flying SDP colours. In an end-of-year message to Liberal candidates Mr Steel complained that progress had been 'painfully slow', and the omens were poor for universal amity between the two parties at constituency level.

Meanwhile, in by-elections, the uncovenanted alternation continued. Local Liberals in Crosby, a middle-class Merseyside constituency, where a by-election was called for 26 November, voted overwhelmingly to withdraw in favour of Mrs Shirley Williams. To begin with, even the SDP were daunted by the Tory majority of over 19,000 in 1980, but in the event Mrs Williams triumphed, with 28,118 votes against 22,829 for the Conservatives. The Bennite Labour candidate polled only 5,450 votes and lost his deposit, as did six other candidates receiving 900 votes between them, including one representing the Cambridge University Raving Loony Society who secured the franchise of 223 Crosby citizens. To have lost one of their previously safest seats in the country was a severe blow to the Conservative Party, but most commentators thought the result even worse for Labour. In the sequence of by-elections, Warrington, Croydon, Crosby, the Conservatives suffered a declining loss of votes from the general election, the Labour Party a less but increasing one, despite the Government's unpopularity.

The overall pattern of the three elections was repeated in local authority by-elections. In 214 of these between July and Christmas, the centre alliance gained 100 seats. Opinion polls showed the alliance still growing in support at the expense of the Conservative and Labour Parties. On this ground SDP leaders were claiming an allowance of time for party political broadcasts equal to that of either of those parties; it had none of the established basis of votes at the previous general election. Such was the measure of the change in the political scene in a single year.

The rise of the SDP evidently owed much to troubles and dissensions in the two major parties. In the Labour Party, after the Wembley conference, these largely centred on a bitterly-fought contest for election of a deputy leader under the new electoral college system. By previous custom the existing office-holder, Mr Denis Healey, would have been returned unopposed, but in November 1980 Mr Tony Benn had declared that he would stand and he confirmed that intention in April. Mr Foot urged him to withdraw, prophesying that the promised six-month campaign 'can only distract attention from the party's main purpose, which is to defeat the Tories'. But Mr Benn claimed as his aim to commit the parliamentary leadership to the fundamental and irreversible socialist policies adopted by the party conference, including abolition of the second chamber and immediate withdrawal from the EEC and allied nuclear defence.

Indeed the Labour movement was rent through the spring and summer by war of words conducted both in public and in private. After Mr

Benn, on 20 May, had defied the party leader and the Shadow Cabinet by voting, with 74 unilateralist colleagues, for a Commons motion denouncing the Government's White Paper on defence, when Mr Foot had carefully drafted a motion on which the party could unite, Mr Healey accused his rival of 'kicking Michael Foot in the stomach'. Mr Benn retorted (31 May) that the whole Shadow Cabinet was collectively responsible for implementing the policies agreed by the party. On 3 June Mr Foot declared that Mr Benn's 'only honest course' was to stand against himself as leader. Mr Benn declined. From 4 to 17 June he was in hospital with a muscular infection known as the Guillain–Barré syndrome, and was out of public action for several weeks. Meanwhile several left-dominated constituency executives had voted down sitting moderate Labour MPs in the reselection process, to the anger of the right: Mr Roy Hattersley vainly called on Mr Benn to condemn the 'bullying and blackmail'. Mr Foot's contribution was to declare that 'MPs must not be Hon. midgets or Right Hon. marionettes but real men and women exercising their own independent powers and judgement'. When the Labour election agent at Barnsley joined the SDP on 15 June he declared that constituency general management committees were a farce, a mere vehicle for ramming down left-wing doctrine.

Speaking on 4 September Mr Benn declared that if the Labour Party united round his policies it could win a landslide victory in a general election, whereas (he told the TUC at Blackpool four days later) if it was stuck with the policies in the 1979 manifesto it would be in the wilderness for a generation. That was the opposite of the opinion of moderate leaders like Mr Roy Hattersley, who told a meeting on the fringe of the party conference that a Benn victory in the deputy leadership election would 'cruelly impair' Labour's prospects of winning a general election. Mr Healey had offered, in June, his own updated version of the manifesto, as his personal platform: among other points it called for big increases in public investment, ceilings on imports of manufactures, liberation of British sovereignty from the toils of European Community law, and reduced defence spending, including cancellation of the Trident missile system. To outsiders this looked like Benn-and-soda. Mr Benn claimed to be fighting on policies, but personal recrimination prevailed; when the three candidates (Mr John Silkin having entered as a champion of reconciliation) appeared together on television on 10 September there were displays of bitter personal hostility, and at several meetings in the country Mr Healey was shouted down by hooligan Benn supporters.

The voting for the deputy leadership in the new electoral college took place on 27 September. On the first ballot Mr Healey received 45·627 per cent of the voting power, Mr Benn 36·627 per cent, and Mr Silkin 18·004 per cent. On the second ballot Mr Healey won by the tiny margin of 0·852 per cent. The closeness of the vote was unforeseen by the Healey camp, which had expected more support among the trade unions. Mr Benn's defeat, by a nice calculation, was due to the abstention of some twenty left-wing MPs of the Tribune group, who had deplored his identification of personalities with policies. Consequently the parliamentary vote was nearly two to one in favour of Healey on the second ballot; the union vote was 5 to 3 in his favour, the constituency vote 4 to 1 against him.

The reaction of different Labour figures to the election result was characteristic. The militant core of the left were furious. Mr Foot, whose hold over the party had been weakened by his failure to dissuade either right-wing MPs from defecting to the SDP or Mr Benn from challenging his own position by way of the deputy leadership, and by uninspiring opposition to Mrs Thatcher in Parliament, now again pleaded for party unity and tolerance. Mr Healey claimed a victory for 'the concept of a broad-based Labour Party'. 'We must see the divisions of the past two years behind us', he told the party conference. Mr Benn held the opposite view. 'It was an enormous victory for us', he claimed, 'because from the beginning . . . we have won the argument', and he promised to carry on the fight into the trade unions and the parliamentary party.

The delegates to the party conference, held at Brighton in the week beginning 27 September, showed by their cheers far greater favour for Mr Benn than for Mr Healey. Nevertheless on several points it voted in a contrary sense. Thus it decided by 5·3 million card votes to 1·3 million to refer back a proposal to nationalize the banks, insurance companies and other financial institutions, confining specific demands for future state ownership to the pharmaceutical and medical appliance industry. More important, in the short run, were its equivocal vote on the framing of the party's election manifesto and its elections to the policy-making National Executive Committee (NEC) and the party treasurership. The previous left-wing majority in the NEC was eliminated: Mr Foot was now reckoned to have 14 supporters in the committee against nine for Mr Benn and five of the 'soft left'. The moderate Mr Eric Varley replaced Mr Norman Atkinson of the hard left as party treasurer.

On the other hand, the tenor of the conference decisions on policy, nationalization apart, was distinctly in tune with left objectives. It voted by two to one for unconditional opposition to the presence of any nuclear weapons in Britain (though voting by over three to one against withdrawal from Nato). It demanded cuts in defence spending as part of a package, aimed at full employment, that included earlier retirement and a 35-hour week. It voted for repeal of all Conservative legislation on industrial relations, the strangulation and eventual abolition of private education, repeal of laws restricting local authority spending and of the new British Nationality Act (see pp. 32-33), expansion of the health service and elimination of private medical care, and mandatory sanctions against South Africa. It passed by a huge majority a detailed motion implicitly critical of the police forces; new authorities should be set up to control their policies, appoint their top officers and check their operations. It spurned any governmental policy on incomes that would limit free collective bargaining. The TUC, in congress three weeks earlier, had refused even to discuss pay restraint, but adopted a joint TUC-Labour document advocating 'a national economic assessment including analysis of the movement of pay and its impact on prices', which presumably implied some kind of indicative incomes policy.

The party split now widened further. In an attempt at reconciliation with the left, Mr Foot used his key position in the NEC to secure the re-election of Mr Benn and his left-wing ally Mr Eric Heffer as chairmen of the key home policy and organization sub-committees. But on the very next day, 10 November, Mr Benn, chosen to wind up for the Opposition in a Commons debate on the sale of shares in national oil and gas production, declared that a Labour Government would reacquire the alienated assets without compensation, contrary to a statement agreed by the Shadow Cabinet (of which Mr Benn was a member) and affirmed by Mr Merlyn Rees as first Labour spokesman in the debate that the assets would be restored to public ownership 'on terms which would ensure that no private speculative gains were made at the nation's expense'. A furious Mr Rees threatened to resign from the Shadow Cabinet. Mr Benn protested that he was only voicing party conference policy. Mr Foot called on him to undertake to respect the collective responsibility of the Shadow Cabinet. When he equivocated, Mr Foot gave him more rope in the shape of time to reconsider his position, but Mr Benn would still make no such promise, and on 13 November the party leader said he could not vote for him in the coming elections to the Shadow Cabinet. Despite this lead, on 19 November 66 MPs voted for Mr Benn, only 16 fewer than were needed for election. Mr Heffer scraped in, but the overall effect was a shift to the centre right, who now held 10 of the 15 places. Top of the poll was Mr Peter Shore, whose position as front-runner for succession to Mr Foot was thus confirmed. Of Mr Foot's Shadow Cabinet appointments on 24 November, the most significant was that of Mr John Silkin to defence; Mr Silkin had supported unilateral nuclear disarmament, though in a radio interview after his appointment he seemed to hedge on that opinion. Given charge of European affairs was Mr Heffer, a strong advocate of withdrawal from the EEC, which he declared had been a disaster for Britain.

Emerging from a meeting of the NEC on 16 December, Mr Benn said 'Speaking as deputy leader, because of course Denis Healey's entire majority has now defected to the SDP. . . .' Mr Foot's comment was, 'He is talking through his hat.' The party leader was now showing an unaccustomed militancy against the militant left. Intra-party strife broke out over two men, Mr Peter Tatchell, prospective Labour candidate for

Bermondsey, who had written an article calling for mass action outside Parliament to challenge the Government's right to rule, and Mr Tariq Ali, a well-known ex-communist firebrand, who had applied to join the Labour Party. Needled by a reference to Mr Tatchell at Commons question-time, Mr Foot exclaimed: 'The individual concerned is not an endorsed candidate for the Labour Party and as far as I am concerned never will be.' On 16 December the NEC voted by 15 to 14 to bar Mr Tatchell's candidature, and endorsed its organization sub-committee's vote to reject Mr Tariq Ali. Still more important, on Mr Foot's initiative, spurred by strong pressure from Labour moderates, it voted by 19 to 10 for an inquiry into infiltration into the party by Militant Tendency, a nationally organized marxist group.

Chapter 4

TORY DISSENT

THE palpable disarray of the Labour Party was matched though far from equalled by dissent among the Conservatives. Its primary cause was the state of the economy, especially the rise in unemployment. In January the gross number of registered unemployed was 2,419,452; from September to the end of the year the dread total of three million (representing 11 per cent of the work-force on a seasonally adjusted basis) was avoided only by a tiny shortfall. In December the figure was 2,941,000, but the underlying trend was upward. The Government's direct attack on unemployment was concentrated on training schemes and 'job opportunity' programmes for the benefit principally of school-leavers. The Prime Minister told the House of Commons on 27 July that Government spending on special employment and training schemes would rise by £150 million gross in 1981-82, creating 108,000 jobs, and by £700 million in 1982-83. On 15 December the Secretary for Employment, Mr Norman Tebbit, disclosed what he called 'the most far-reaching and ambitious set of proposals for training ever laid before Parliament'. A year's training would be offered to all school-leavers without jobs, with government allowances of £1,250 per annum for over-16s in training or in the Youth Opportunity Programme; 30,000 extra places would be provided in the Community Enterprise Programme in 1982-83. Typical of Labour criticism was Mr Len Murray's description of the proposal to withhold supplementary benefit to school-leavers refusing a training place at a mere £25 per week as 'industrial conscription'.

The basic theme of the Government's economic policy was defeat of inflation; until this was achieved, it contended, neither could monetary restraints be relaxed nor 'real jobs' created in industry and commerce.

Policy against inflation stood on three legs: control of public expenditure, control of the money supply (by interest rates and otherwise) and pressures to hold down wage increases. In the absence of an acknowledged incomes policy the Government operated on the wages front through its actions on public service pay, its cash limits on local authorities and nationalized industries, and the effect of its deflationary policy on the private sector, where (as in the public sector too) the threat of unemployment was the strongest sanction for moderate pay settlements.

Confrontation with the unions was inevitable. A severe example occurred in the civil service, a category which included not only personnel of Whitehall offices from top administrators to messengers but also civil employees of government agencies and the defence services all over the country. In November 1980 Ministers had declared a norm of 6 per cent for rises in public service pay in 1981-82 (see AR 1980, p. 23), and on 18 February 1981 it was confirmed that cash limits for local authorities would be based on that figure. In order to apply this policy in the civil service the government announced that the system of independent settlement of civil service pay was to be suspended, a stroke which angered the civil servants even more than the 6 per cent offered them. Their nine separate unions formed a united front, and in spite of a late enhancement of the offer to 7 per cent embarked from 9 March on a series of strikes in different branches of the public service, beginning with a one-day national stoppage on that day. The main selective targets were national computer centres dealing with inland revenue, passports, unemployment pay and vehicle and driving licences, ordnance factories and Admiralty dockyards, legal administration in Scotland and air traffic control; but other services were also attacked. In July the unions claimed to have stopped over £6,000 million in revenue payments, to have cost British Airways £40 million in lost traffic and to have nearly paralysed the Scottish legal system. The Government remained adamant, seeing the whole structure of its anti-inflationary policy to be at risk.

On 30 July the strikes were called off, a substantial majority of members of the nine unions (one of them dissenting) having voted to accept a Government offer of 7 per cent plus £30 per annum for all grades, an independent inquiry into civil service pay with wide terms of reference and arbitration on an award in 1982 if negotiations should fail, subject to a veto by the House of Commons on grounds of overriding national policy. Sir John Megaw, lately a judge of appeal, was appointed chairman of the inquiry team. The general secretary of the largest civil service union summed up the conflict thus: 'It was the best organized, most beautiful and disciplined strike action there has ever been in the post-war period.'; the acid test of whether the 'beautiful' action had been worthwhile would come when the unions took the 1982 claim to arbitration. Ministers refrained from claiming a victory, but it was evident that their two key objectives had been won—a modest pay rise in 1981 and the principle of parliamentary control over the pay of public servants. If one cause must be found for the failure of the strikes (as most people saw it), it lay in the lack of public support for a group of workers who were felt to be privileged in job security and indexated pensions at a time of high unemployment and inflation.

Meanwhile there had been other menacing industrial disputes. In some parts of the country water and sewerage workers came out on strike in February against the employers' 'final offer' of 10 per cent, until on 26 February their union leaders accepted a complex deal which would add 12·3 per cent to the water authorities' wages bill. A five-week strike by the National Union of Seamen which gravely affected British shipping and ports was called off when the employers agreed to arbitration on overtime pay, the main issue at stake. A one-day strike by bank employees on 22 April was ineffectual. Generally, however, in both the public and the private sectors settlements in single figures, or a little more, were being made, including acceptance of 7½ per cent by local authority manual workers and school teachers. On 5 June MPs voted themselves a rise of 18 per cent, but this was reckoned to add only 6 per cent to award increases that had been deferred in the past two years. In May it was announced that members of the armed forces would get a 10·3 per cent rise, while judges and high civil servants would be held to 7 per cent and National Health Service doctors and dentists to 6 per cent.

The hard side of Government policy was exposed in the Budget which the Chancellor of the Exchequer, Sir Geoffrey Howe, brought down on 10 March. Total government spending in 1981-82 would rise by 10·6 per cent over the previous year, in spite of severe economies, but borrowing would be cut by £3,290 million to a target figure of £10,500 million within a total public sector borrowing requirement (PSBR) of £14,000 million. The growth of money supply—which along with the PSBR was a touchstone of the Thatcher–Howe monetarist policy—would be held in the range 6 to 10 per cent. To make up for the spending increase taxes were raised on alcoholic drinks and tobacco (by 4p a pint on beer, 60p on a 70-cl bottle of spirits, 12p on a bottle of wine, 14p on 20 cigarettes), on petrol and derv (commercial vehicle fuel) by 20p a gallon and on car licences by £10 per annum; a 'windfall' tax on non-interest-bearing bank deposits was estimated to yield £400 million and a new tax on North Sea oil to yield £1,000 million. The scale of personal allowances against tax would be unaltered, and old age pensions would rise by only 9 per cent in November, thus squeezing the real incomes of pensioners by a percentage point or two. The increase of indirect taxes was estimated to raise the cost of living by about 2 per cent. Corporation tax was unchanged. The Chancellor announced that new business and risk-taking would be helped by a scheme of tax relief and government guarantees on loans.

Some Cabinet Ministers were reported to be angry at having this fiscal policy, with all its controversial elements, sprung on them in a Budget statement of which they had no prior knowledge or warning; but in face of considerable pressure Mrs Thatcher refused—for fear of leaks, she said with characteristic distrust—to change the traditional procedure whereby Budget secrets were shared by the Chancellor only with the Prime Minister until the last moment. For the Opposition, Mr Foot described the Budget as a catastrophe of the first order for the British people, 'a no-hope Budget introduced by a no-hope Chancellor'. On the Conservative side, criticism of the Budget's detail was strongest on the rise in petrol tax, especially among MPs for rural constituencies. On 16 March eight Tories voted against the increase and about 25 abstained,reducing the Government's majority to 14. Under this pressure the Chancellor agreed on 30 April to halve the increase of duty on derv; on a motion to do the same for petrol 13 Conservatives voted against the Government. Sir Geoffrey Howe warned the House that the loss of revenue would have to be made good, and on 2 July he heightened the tax on tobacco by the equivalent of 3p on a packet of 20 cigarettes.

Outside Parliament frenzied agitation was aroused by the planned economies in higher education, amounting to 15 per cent over three years. The chairman of the committee of vice-chancellors denounced them as 'a kind of madness'. The Government followed up by warning that universities whose intake of students from the United Kingdom exceeded in 1981 the number admitted in 1979 would suffer a loss of grant proportional to the income from the excess admissions. After the University Grants Committee (UGC) had failed to win any concessions on the cuts it warned the universities that structural economies would be necessary. On 1 July the UGC wrote to the vice-chancellors severally announcing cuts in grants and in authorized numbers of UK-based students. Some universities would lose 25 per cent of their grants. All were advised on the areas of teaching and research to be abandoned or reduced. An overall cut of 5 per cent in UK student numbers by 1984-85 was required. Resources would be increased for technical retraining courses and for extra-mural and adult education. The outcry was loud and strident. The National Union of Students described the cuts in student numbers as a devastating blow for aspiring pupils and their parents. The vice-chancellors claimed that compensation for redundancies would outweigh the financial savings. The UGC had told the Government that compulsory redundancies of 3,000 academics over three years would cost £200 million in compensation. The whole system of academic security of tenure continued to excite public controversy.

Besides cuts in public expenditure, business leaders had called for remedy of two adverse elements in the economic scene in the early months of the year, high interest rates and a high exchange rate for the pound, which cheapened imports and handicapped exports—although, thanks to North Sea Oil, intense competitive effort by exporters and depressed domestic consumption the balance of payments remained substantially positive. The Chancellor announced in his Budget statement that the Bank of England's minimum lending rate (MLR) would be cut from 14 to 12 per cent. In June, however, the high interest policy prevailing in the United States took charge, and the pound sterling, which had stood at over $2 in mid-June, fell by fits and starts to around $1·78 in mid-September. The Bank of England made little effort to stem the fall, but on 14 September it raised its overnight rate (replacing, as an index of short-term money market conditions, MLR, which had meanwhile been consigned to history by the Government in pursuit of its market-forces philosophy) by 1·5 per cent, and the clearing banks promptly raised their prime lending rates by 2 per cent. The era of high interest rates in Britain was resumed, with a slight easement later in the year. Yet the money supply continued to grow faster than planned.

It was against this background that, first, creaks and groans and later loud rumblings of dismay and dissent about the Government's economic policy were heard from some members of the Tory party. Before 1980 ended, Mr Edward Heath, the former Conservative Prime Minister, had already voiced these critical sentiments (see AR 1980, p. 29) and he continued vehemently to attack the Thatcher–Howe policies through 1981. But he was far from alone. One Conservative MP, Mr Robert Hicks, said on 28 January that if the Government continued with its present economic policies he, along with some 20 others on the back benches, might be prepared to join a centrist party. Speaking in the debate on the Budget on 11 March, Mr Edward du Cann, chairman of the 1922 Committee of Tory backbenchers, demanded a new programme for national recovery.

As to the Cabinet, the press in its simplistic search for short headlines had dubbed the economic hardliners 'dry' and the softliners 'wet'. One of the 'wettest' in the past was alleged to be Mr St John Stevas, who on 5 January was dismissed from the Cabinet by the Prime Minister, his post as Leader of the House being given to Mr Francis Pym. Mr Stevas, speaking on 16 February, expressed his fear that unemployment would get out of control and that 1982 would be too late for reflation; his hostility to Government policy became even sharper as the year wore on. Mr Pym, a suspected 'wet', was succeeded as Secretary of State for Defence by the 'dry' Mr John Nott, and the reshuffle required by the resignation of Mr Angus Maude and (outside the Cabinet) Mr Reg Prentice for personal reasons brought promotion for other supposed hardliners, including Mr John Biffen (to Trade) and Mr Leon Brittan (to the Treasury as Chief Secretary). Another drying exercise, carried out on 14 September, focused on the position of Mr James Prior, a recognized 'wet'.

He had publicly made known his wish to stay as Secretary for Employment and his implied intention to resign if he were offered, as had been forecast, Northern Ireland; but in the event, after long deliberation, he accepted that transfer, extracting the price of his continued membership of the inner Cabinet committee on economic and financial policy. An avowed 'wet', Sir Ian Gilmour, previously Foreign Office spokesman in the Commons, was sent to the back benches; he said of his dismissal: 'It does no harm to throw the occasional man overboard, but it does not do much good if you are steering full speed ahead for the rocks.' Lord Soames and Mr Mark Carlisle, whose degree of dampness was in neither case notorious, also resigned. Sir Keith Joseph moved from Industry to Education, Mr Patrick Jenkin to Industry, Mr Norman Fowler to Social Services, Mr Nigel Lawson to Energy, Mr David Howell to Transport (elevated to Cabinet ranking), Mr Humphrey Atkins from Northern Ireland to Sir Ian Gilmour's place as Lord Privy Seal. Mr Lawson and Mr Fowler were newcomers to the Cabinet, and Mrs Thatcher took the opportunity to bring into her Cabinet another woman, Lady Young, previously a junior Minister at Education, as Chancellor of the Duchy. While not all those promoted could be precisely categorized, the Cabinet changes undoubtedly wrung out much moisture. At the same time, Lord Thorneycroft, who had been audibly dripping, resigned on grounds of age from the chairmanship of the Conservative Party and was replaced by Mr Cecil Parkinson, MP, formerly a Minister of State at the Department of Trade and a Thatcher protégé, who unlike his predecessor was to attend Cabinet meetings.

Yet the 'wets' remained, some of them in high Cabinet places. Mr Pym, in a speech on 11 February, had defended government policy thus: 'Commonsense tells us that changed circumstances make adjustments necessary in both tactics and timing. . . . These adjustments in no way imply the abandonment of any of our main purposes nor any change in strategy.' But less than six months later he seemed to have moved towards a strategic reform. Speaking on 1 August he acknowledged that the recession was proving deeper and longer than anyone had expected, and added: 'The British people will not be prepared for very much longer to tolerate the worst effects of the recession if there is not a clear sign that the sacrifice will have been worthwhile.' Even the dry Mr John Biffen, Secretary for Trade, had said on 22 February, to the cue of the Government's relaxation of cash limits for the National Coal Board (see p. 35), that in the second half of their parliamentary term they would pursue a gradualist and practical policy rather than a hardline economic theory. But the Cabinet Minister who publicly gave himself the most critical rope without having it tightened round his neck was Mr Peter Walker, Minister of Agriculture and Fisheries. His pronouncement on 21 March that Britain's vast oil revenue was going to be used 'either as a unique source of capital to provide a British industrial base or as a tranquillizer to make the hardship of unemployment and inactivity a little less unpleasant' could have been delivered by an Opposition critic. So, too, could his remarks in New York on 22 June: 'This is not a decade for Western governments to become too fascinated by any economic theory. It is a decade for sane and pragmatic decision-taking.' High unemployment, he said, would bring high levels of crime, and perhaps a totally hostile approach by the young to the structure of our society.

Outside party politics, on 30 March the press published a memorial signed by 364 academic economists, including the president of the Royal Economic Society and several former chief economic advisers to governments, declaring that:

There is no basis in economic theory or supporting evidence for the Government's belief that by deflating demand they will bring inflation permanently under control and thereby induce an automatic recovery in output and employment. Present policies will deepen the depression, erode the industrial base of our economy and threaten its social and political stability.

There are alternative policies, and the time has come to reject monetarist policies and consider urgently which alternative offers the best hope of sustained economic recovery.

A chosen alternative was propounded by 14 of the most eminent of the critical economists on 13 October: a staged injection of £5,000 million (costing £3,000 million after savings on unemployment pay and social benefits) to boost the economy, mainly through capital investment, to be explicitly dependent on an agreement by the trade unions to moderate their wage demands; together with a fall by at least 10 per cent, possibly 20 to 30 per cent, in the international value of the pound in order to reconcile full employment with relative British wage and cost levels. The fight against inflation should continue, with monetary policy in reverse.

The Government were not without their own professional economic backing and could point to the failure of academic economists in the past to propagate doctrines and programmes to prevent the inflation that the Government saw as economic public enemy No. 1. Their constant and obdurate line of defence was that, until the money supply and public expenditure had been brought under anti-inflationary control, all proposed alternative policies amounted only to printing money and creating, for a short time, unreal jobs. Rounding on Tory critics of the Budget on 11 March Mrs Thatcher declared that to print money instead of raising taxes to pay for agreed expenditure was 'the most immoral path of all'. She had no wish, she told Conservative MPs on 23 July, to go the way of the Heath Government with a 'phoney boom'.

While resisting alternative policies the Government claimed with greater or less conviction the success of its own. In December 1980 the retail price index had been rising at an annual rate of 15·1 per cent; by September the rate had fallen to 11·4 per cent, despite the price increases

caused by the rise in indirect taxes. But the fall had come to an end, as
sharp rises in rates, fuel prices, mortgage interest and other elements in
the index had not yet been embraced. In December the annual rate of
increase was 12 per cent. Lower wage settlements and higher unemployment had brought a fall in the average standard of living. Official
figures published on 7 October showed that the total of real personal
incomes after tax had fallen by 3 per cent between the second quarter of
1980 and the second quarter of 1981, and the process was continuing.

A statement by the Chancellor on 30 July that 'we have come to the
end of the recession' provoked much outraged scepticism. He meant, he
explained a few days later, that output had stopped receding. Sir
Geoffrey Howe's analysis had some justification in terms of manufacturing output, which was slowly increasing after the first quarter and
showing a significant rise in labour productivity, but the inverse of the
latter factor was the alarming rise in unemployment.

Alarming it was to Conservatives not only as an economic and social
indicator but as a menace to their electoral security. Tory MPs approached the party conference, held at Blackpool from 13 to 16 October,
anxious both for their political survival and for the unity of the party. A
week earlier, in a speech at Manchester, Mr Edward Heath had asked: 'If
more than three million unemployed are necessary to get inflation down
to a level higher than it was two-and-a-half years ago, how many more
millions of unemployed will be required to bring it down to a level that
has never been revealed?' He had called for lower interest rates, British
adherence to the European Monetary System and exchange controls to
help build 'a ring-fence round European money and capital markets' (a
proposal greeted with some scorn in financial circles), a selective
programme of capital reinvestment, a massive labour retraining
programme, eventual abolition of the national insurance surcharge
(widely criticized as a burden on industry and a tax on employment), and
'a return to consensus politics'. To which Mrs Thatcher retorted:
'Consensus seems to be the process of abandoning all beliefs, principles,
values and policies.' Mr du Cann accused Mr Heath of disloyalty, proclaiming, 'We want no Teddy Benns in the Tory Party.' Mr Heath
addressed the party conference on 14 October in more restrained terms,
while advancing the same prescription. He, like Mrs Thatcher, he said,
wanted party unity but this could not be imposed by a single doctrine.
The economic situation was critical; young people would move further
into revolt, but the plight of people in their fifties who were made redun-
dant was even worse.

The Chancellor of the Exchequer's reply gave no hint of policy
changes. The first task must remain curbing inflation. The causes of high
unemployment went back many years, when people had persisted in
ignoring reality, in 'paying ourselves more than we earned'. Now clear

signs of progress were coming through; the rate of pay increases had been halved, productivity was 6 per cent up. The one thing that could set the country back was the Government's losing its nerve. When Mrs Thatcher addressed the conference two days later she received a standing ovation at the end of a characteristically adamant speech. 'I will not change just to court popularity. . . . If ever a Conservative Government starts to do what it knows is wrong because it is afraid to do what is right, that is the time for Tories to cry "Stop". But you will never need to do that while I am Prime Minister.'

The applause for Mrs Thatcher, compared with a cool reception for Mr Heath, showed clearly where the balance of party conference opinion lay. The delegates, traditionally hard-core Tory activists, showed their right-wing colour by rejecting a motion on law and order, supported by the Home Secretary, as being too weak. They cheered loudly when the new Employment Secretary, succeeding Mr Prior whom such stalwarts thought dilatory and damp over industrial relations reform, told them that his legislation would protect the weak against the strong and provide redress for those unjustly harmed. Among the public he scored less well with his remark that his unemployed father in the 1930s had not joined demonstrations but had 'got on his bike and looked for a job'. The idea of three million unemployed pedalling in search of non-existent jobs gave critics of the Government a propaganda bonanza.

In a debate on unemployment in the House of Commons on 28 October the appearance of Conservative solidarity was restored; Tory abstentions on an Opposition motion of no confidence were minimal or nil, and it was defeated by a Government majority of 63. Mr Foot's open-air style of rhetoric, tempered with detail both in criticism and in alternative proposals, was not effective. The economy, he said, had reached such a state of crisis that conventional reflation would hardly do more than relieve the increasing scale of unemployment. The Government had shown that it had not the competence, the will, the imagination or the humanity to deal with these problems. Mrs Thatcher's reply was comprehensive. Mr Foot's recipe, she said, was to spend more, borrow more, tax less and turn a blind eye to the consequences; the Opposition's proposals would cause a financial crisis and a sharp acceleration of inflation, which was a bonus for the rich and a heavy tax for the poorest. Within its essential financial strategy the Government had been flexible over public spending, for instance in advancing more money to British Leyland and the Belfast shipbuilders Harland and Wolff and in its measures to relieve youth unemployment. 'To accuse me of being inflexible is poppycock.' The Prime Minister received telling support from Mr Enoch Powell, Official Ulster Unionist, who observed that the question Mr Foot had to face was why increases in public spending year by year over the past eight years had been accompanied by a continued increase in the level of unemployment; yet Mr Foot thought a larger quantity of the same dose was going to produce the opposite effect. The problem lay much deeper, in a dramatic turn-round in Britain's international and domestic economic position.

On 2 December the Chancellor of the Exchequer announced a package of measures which the press but not he called a mini-budget. Employees' national insurance contribution was raised by 1 per cent. National Health Service charges for prescriptions, spectacles and false teeth were increased. Council house rents would rise by about 15 per cent, or £2.50 per week. Pensions and long-term social security benefits would fully keep pace with inflation, but not short-term benefits like initial unemployment pay, and no allowance for inflation would be made in rates of parental contribution to higher-education charges. Borrowing by nationalized industry would be held to £1,300 million. For defence £400 million more would be provided, and £800 million more for the employment programme, now running at £2,000 million a year. Net planned expenditure in 1982-83 would be £5,000 million higher than in the current year, at £115,000 million. In a debate on the package on 8 December Mr Heath made another powerful attack on Government policy; there had never been, he said, any practical or intellectual justification for monetarism. At the end of the debate 14 Conservatives abstained from the vote and the Government's majority fell to 42.

Nevertheless Mrs Thatcher and the Government stuck sternly to their guns. In end-of-year interviews the Prime Minister declared, 'We are through the worst.' The fruits of her policies, she proclaimed, were beginning to be reaped.

Chapter 5

GOVERNMENT ACTIONS AND REACTIONS

APART from the Finance Bill, the most important and controversial measure pressed through Parliament in its first session of 1981 was the British Nationality Bill, published on 14 January. This endeavoured to rationalize the law of nationality in the light of the huge immigration into Britain, mainly from overseas Commonwealth countries, that had taken place in the previous thirty years, though checked by successive measures of statutory control, and of the anachronisms and anomalies in the working of the British Nationality Act 1948 in radically altered times. That Act, based on the concept of separate nationalities for the Commonwealth's autonomous units, linked by a vague common 'citizenship of the Commonwealth', in place of the previous universal British subjecthood, had, *inter alia*, created a category of nationality known as 'citizenship of the United Kingdom and colonies' for inhabitants equally of the UK and of its non-sovereign dependencies. The scope of this curious category had been narrowed by the achievement of independence by one territory after another; but in many cases those departures had created fresh problems, the greatest being that of East African Asians who at independence had accepted the option of retaining their previous status. The 1981 Bill proposed to create three categories of British national status: British citizenship (not to be acquired automatically by birth in the United Kingdom, as had previously been the case, under the ancient *jus soli*, unless one parent was already a British citizen in the new sense or was permanently settled in the UK), citizenship of British dependent territories (amended in debate to 'British dependent territories' citizenship') and British overseas citizenship, covering all remaining present 'citizens of the UK and colonies'. Only the first category would have *per se* the right of abode in the UK.

The Bill aroused a storm of criticism from immigrant communities, from their former home countries, especially India, and from the churches and other defenders of their rights. When the Bill had its second reading on 28 January Mr Whitelaw promised to consider amendments where a case was made for changes in order to allay unnecessary fears. Both in the Commons and in the Lords, where the Bill had a strongly contested passage, a number of such amendments were made, but none to alter its main structure. The Bill had its third reading by a majority of 53 in the Commons on 4 June, and in the Lords on 20 October, when an Opposition motion declaring that it would cause injustice, greatly increase the number of stateless persons, create insecurity and exacerbate racial tensions was defeated by 149 votes to 92.

In that last Lords debate the Archbishop of Canterbury, branding the Bill as still bad despite such amendments as had been made, deplored particularly the defeat of one that would have perpetuated the *jus soli*. He wished to place on record, he said, 'our deep concern that on so fundamental a matter as nationality we seem to be about to pass into law a measure which in the view of the leaders of all our churches is questionable when judged by moral principles and the effects of which will be to sow doubts in an area where reassurance is desperately needed'. The Bill received the Royal Assent on 30 October, but it would probably not be implemented until 1983 because of the administrative upheavals required. Speaking for the Opposition, Mr Roy Hattersley had pledged its repeal by the next Labour Government. It was indeed regrettable that on so vital a constitutional measure political consensus had not been obtained. But the history of the subject since 1948 showed plainly that both Labour and Conservative Governments had been exercised by the nationality and immigration problem on the same grounds and on much the same lines.

Another aspect of Government policy that encountered much opposition beyond the party political arena was the financial nexus between central and local government. The cash limits imposed on local authorities had already caused a big increase in rates, the authorities' only recourse when the Treasury's support grant fell short of their budgeted needs. The average increase for domestic ratepayers for 1981-82 in England and Wales was 20 per cent, but this concealed wide variations, from 13 per cent in English shire counties to 40 per cent in Inner London, from 5·3 per cent in Bristol to 52·6 per cent in Kensington and Chelsea, a Conservative-controlled borough whose own economies were swamped by massive precepts from wider London authorities for police, education and the services of the Greater London Council. The latter having fallen into radical Labour hands in the May elections, in October it levied a supplementary rate of 20 per cent to pay for a policy of lower fares on buses and underground trains and for a consequent cut in its grant from central funds as a penalty for over-spending. One borough, Bromley, however, challenged the legality of the scheme and the consequent precept. On 17 December the House of Lords unanimously found against the GLC (see Pt. XIV, Ch. 2). The judgment caused total confusion. Mr Livingstone predicted a 200 per cent rise in fares and a dramatic contraction of the transport service. Mr David Howell, Secretary for Transport, said that the crisis was entirely the fault of the GLC and they must clear up the mess, though he had no intention of 'allowing the world's greatest urban transport system to collapse'. Negotiations for a solution, which had to be applied before 21 March 1982, were still afoot at the end of the year. Meanwhile other city councils which subsidized public transport were assailed by doubts as to the legality of doing so.

On 3 September Mr Heseltine, the Secretary of State for the Environment, declared himself deeply disappointed with the budgeting of local authorities in response to Government pressure. English authorities as a whole were spending over 5 per cent more than their target figures, but there were great contrasts between under-spenders and gross over-spenders. He was cutting a total of £300 million off the rate support grant for the worst offenders. On 22 March Mr Heseltine had warned that sizeable overspending might oblige him to seek more legislative powers and to ask the public to recognize that the traditional relationship between central and local government had changed. Six months later, in a public speech, he revealed his plan for remedying excess local spending. A first supplementary rate would be permissible, but no further supplementary rate could be levied without approval by a special poll of the electors. Mr Heseltine may well have been encouraged to frame this plan by the result of a poll voluntarily taken in the city of Coventry in August, when electors—of whom only 25 per cent voted—were asked to say whether they preferred cuts in local services or increases in rates, and chose the former by a majority of over seven to one. Many ratepayers indeed welcomed the prospect of being able to veto repeated rate increases. But local authority spokesmen of all parties rose as one man to protest that the cherished independence of elected local bodies was being eroded to the point of their becoming mere agents of central government policy. And a good many Tory MPs not only felt the same but were also highly suspicious of the use of the referendum as a regular instrument of British democracy.

Such was the backbench hostility that Mr Heseltine was obliged to withdraw the plan. On 16 December he scrapped his original Bill and substituted one which would confine local authorities in England and Wales to a single rate demand in any year. They could seek leave to borrow to meet unforeseen expenditure, but repayment of the loan had to be a prior charge on the next year's revenues. The Bill also confirmed retrospectively the penalties imposed on over-spending councils. Giving details of the 1982-83 rate support grant on 21 December, Mr Heseltine said that no authority would have to cut spending by more than 7 per cent in real terms, assuming that total wages bills would not rise by more than 4 per cent. The pill was sweetened by some relaxation on spending and borrowing for housing, the number of new houses started in 1981 having reached the lowest peacetime figure since World War I. The new Bill had been accompanied by a discussion document on the radical reform of the rating system that had been promised in the Conservative election manifesto. Various ideas for abolishing or greatly reducing rates were dismissed; left for consideration were a levy on income-earners who were not householders, tax relief for ratepayers, a local sales tax and a poll tax.

Rough water also attended the progress of the Government's policy towards nationalized industries. This could be summed up as (1) stiff limits on cash advances, to enforce economic viability, often at the expense of plant closures and loss of jobs, (2) no intervention in wage negotiations, (3) 'privatization'—the sale to the public of large sections of nationalized industry whose financial viability and prospects made them marketable. In none of those three respects was there smooth sailing in 1981. On 24 February the Government announced that it would inject a further £880 million into British Steel over 15 months to support its 'survival plan'. If the plan failed, powers would be taken to facilitate the virtual closure of the nationalized industry. A short time previously, the Government had been faced with the threat of a national strike of miners against a plan for pit closures which the National Coal Board (NCB) claimed was necessary in face of its cash limits. Thousands of miners were already out in various coalfields when on 18 February, after meeting the NCB and the miners' unions, the Government conceded further financial aid, the Board cancelled the projected closures and the strikers went back to work. 'The rest of the people will have to pay', observed Mrs Thatcher. Mr John Biffen, Secretary of State for Trade, admitted that the Cabinet had been scared by the threat of a miners' strike. The country had seen, he said, 'the capacity of certain sections of organized labour to exercise an extra-parliamentary authority which is, if you like, almost baronial': the Government, however, had been wise to conclude that this was not a case for putting its authority at risk.

At the end of January it was announced that British Leyland, the nationalized car firm, was to receive £990 million in additional state funding over two years, raising the total of government investment in it since 1975 to £2,065 million (see AR 1980, p. 28). The company was expected to return to profitability in 1983. Despite the extra money, British Leyland's cash position gave rise to a fierce confrontation with its workers' unions in the autumn. In reply to a demand for a 20 per cent wage increase the company offered 3·8 per cent, without the possibility of any improvement, describing this as an exact calculation of what could be afforded. The unions were incensed both by the scale of the offer and by the take-it-or-leave-it terms in which it had been made, and called on their members to strike from 1 November unless there were a substantial improvement. On 14 October Sir Michael Edwardes, chairman of BL, warned the unions that if the threatened strike went ahead he would dismiss all the strikers and seek government approval for closing the affected plants. 'This letter', said Mr Terence Duffy, general secretary of the engineers' union AUEW, 'and its implied threats could be counter-productive . . . we do not appreciate bullying'. On 16 October mass meetings of BL workers voted for the strike by large majorities. All the management offered in addition to the 3·8 per cent in abortive negotiations on 22 October was to guarantee a weekly minimum bonus of £3·75 under the productivity scheme—which had actually raised earnings by 13 per cent in a year.

The country was now within ten days of a strike which, if prolonged, was estimated to throw a quarter of a million people out of work, at BL, at its many suppliers and in business dependent on car workers' spending. Opposition and union leaders called frantically for Government intervention. The Government sternly refused. The Secretary of State for Industry, Mr Patrick Jenkin, said he was willing to talk with the union leaders but would have no part in the pay negotiation. At the last moment, on Saturday 31 October, at a meeting in which top officers of the Arbitration and Conciliation Advisory Service (ACAS) and the general secretary of the TUC, Mr Len Murray, participated, the company added £700,000 of 'new money' to its offer in the shape of an adjustment of the productivity bonus scheme, and the union general secretaries agreed to put the amended offer to their members. But it was too late to stop the strike. On the Sunday and Monday all major BL plants were at a standstill, very few workers passing strong picket lines, which incidentally defied the new law limiting the number of pickets. Although the company's shop stewards voted by 238 to 12 to reject the offer and continue the strike, at mass meetings on 3 November the workers themselves voted by substantial majorities at almost all BL plants to accept and go back to work.

The BL plants were soon in full operation again. A national disaster had been averted and another victory gained for Government policy of non-intervention on wages in nationalized industries after cash limits had been fixed. But the repercussions of the struggle, and the ill-will it had bred in the work force, continued to afflict the company's fortunes.

The policy of selling off parts of nationalized industry to private ownership was pressed forward against fierce Labour protests and pledges to reverse the process. In February £150 million was raised from the sale of shares in British Aerospace, which quickly commanded a market premium of 25p on the price of 150p. On 30 October half the share capital of Cable and Wireless was marketed at 168p per share and was five times oversubscribed, to yield the 'stags' a premium of around 30p. Socialists were not the only critics to observe the instant profits of speculators at the expense of the public purse. On 19 October the Secretary for Transport told the House of Commons that the capital of the National Freight Corporation would be sold to a consortium of its managers and employees for £53·5 million of which £47 million was a contribution to the NFC's pension fund. This interesting exercise in 'industrial co-partnership' was dubbed a confidence trick by one of the union leaders in the industry, but appeared to be well received by its alleged victims. At the same sitting the new Secretary for Energy announced a plan to sell the majority of shares in the production programme of the British National Oil Corporation (BNOC) and to bring the offshore operations of British Gas also into private ownership; BG's monopoly of the sale of gas to industry, but not to domestic consumers, was to be ended. Omitted from the plan was an earlier governmental proposal to deprive the gas boards of their monopolistic function of selling and installing domestic gas appliances, which had aroused a threat of a national gas strike by the intensely opposed unions. On 17 December Mr Nigel Lawson introduced his Bill to sell off the production interest of BNOC and British Gas. A new operating company, British Oil, would be formed and its shares marketed under governmental control. For Labour, Mr Merlyn Rees called the Bill a disgrace: 'it gives the Secretary of State extraordinary powers to do what he likes, how he likes, when he likes, with our vital energy assets.'

The converse of 'privatization' was refusal to invest Treasury money in capital enterprises which in the Government's view should, if they were viable, be financed from other sources. That was their attitude, for instance, towards the Channel Tunnel, a Commons select committee

having recommended in March that a single-tube rail tunnel be constructed, big enough to take road vehicles if later the rail traffic proved inadequate for economic viability. Far more elaborate was a plan promoted by
the chairman of British Steel and a powerful financial and industrial consortium for a combined bridge (at the extremities) and tunnel (in the
middle) carrying both road and rail traffic; it would cost £3,800 million
and was estimated to provide about 100,000 jobs for five years. A project
for a publicly-financed gathering system to bring waste gas from the
North Sea oil fields ashore, costing £2,700 million, was put to sleep by the
Government, although its champions reckoned it would pay for itself
several times over; the proof of that, Ministers implied, would be the
readiness of the oil companies and other interested parties to finance
whatever pipeline system they perceived as yielding a good return.

The domestic part of the Queen's Speech at the opening of Parliament on 4 November began with the words: 'My Government attach the
utmost importance to maintaining progress in reducing inflation by the
pursuit of firm monetary and fiscal policies, to further improving the
efficiency of the economy. . . . They hope to see this assisted by further
reductions in the level of wage settlements.' The Speech foreshadowed
only 15 Bills, against 39 introduced in the previous session; the most
important—and likely to be the most contentious—were Bills on employment and labour relations, local government finance and the partial denationalization of BNOC and British Gas. Other promised measures
would deal with Scottish local government, the coal industry (raising the
NCB's borrowing ceiling), criminal justice, mental health and transport.
All this was much as had been expected; the media noted the omission of
a freedom of information Bill, on which subject a measure had been
pigeonholed in the previous session after criticism that the rules that it
would substitute for the out-dated S.2 of the Official Secrets Act were
not nearly liberal enough.

In the debate on the Speech the Leader of the Opposition launched a
fierce and comprehensive attack on the Government's policies. His
hottest fire was directed against the disposal of BNOC interests to investors, who would include, he was sure, multinational oil companies grasp-
ing at the 'sell-out' of national assets, against the intended local government Bill as hostile to democratic principles, and against the labour relations Bill as a misuse of parliamentary time in debating legislation that
would only make matters worse. Mrs Thatcher, in reply, was assured almost to the point of exuberance as to the effect of the Government's policies: the country was displaying a new economic strength, big changes so
often shirked had now been made and a platform for future growth
established; 'in the coming year our confidence will be rewarded'.

On 23 November Mr Tebbit published a consultative document on industrial relations reform. Its main proposals were that trade unions

would be liable, to a maximum of £250,000, for illegal industrial action; action taken with political or personal motives would have no legal immunity; workers on strike could be fairly dismissed after a brief set period; closed shop agreements would be subject to periodic ballots; workers dismissed for non-membership of a union would receive increased compensation and could seek it from the union exerting pressure; union-only contracts would be unlawful; and state money would be provided for secret ballots on wage offers. The general secretary of the TUC exclaimed that the Government were going out of their way to pick a fight with the unions, and Mr Eric Varley promised that Labour would repeal any such Act.

Chapter 6

TRIALS AND TRIBULATIONS

THE *Annual Register* used to give considerable space to British murder trials, in long bygone days before mass warfare, genocide and international terrorism, not to mention television both live and fictional, made the violent deaths of individual persons seem too ordinary an occurrence. However, two trials, initially for murder, in the United Kingdom in 1981 deserve recording for the intense public interest and controversy they aroused.

On 20 February Mr Peter Sutcliffe was committed for trial on no fewer than 13 charges of murder. Upon his own admission he was proved to be the 'Yorkshire Ripper', so-called because his victims, all women, were, like those of the legendary Jack the Ripper, almost all prostitutes. The murders, committed over five years in the North of England, had been the object of a vast and much-publicized police exercise, without success until Sutcliffe, a lorry driver, was detained on the suspicion of an alert constable examining his vehicle on other grounds. When he appeared at the Central Criminal Court on 29 April, counsel on his behalf pleaded not guilty to murder but guilty of manslaughter of 13 women and of attempted murder of seven others. Although the Crown (the Attorney-General with the assent of the Director of Public Prosecutions) was ready to accept the pleas, the judge, after an adjournment, ruled that the issue must be left to the jury.

The trial turned on the question whether the defendant was legally insane. In the witness box Sutcliffe said he obeyed the voice of God; if he were freed he would kill prostitutes again. Counsel asked him: 'Do you think you are mad?' He answered: 'No.' On 22 May the jury, by a majority of 10 to 2, found Sutcliffe guilty of murder on all counts, and he was sentenced to life imprisonment. The verdict thus vindicated the judge's claim of the jury's right to decide the issue of insanity. The public were deeply concerned as to why Sutcliffe was not arrested sooner, especially when it was revealed that he had been interviewed four times, and that one officer's report of his belief that Sutcliffe was the man they wanted had apparently been buried in a mass of information and not followed up. Sutcliffe himself said in court: 'They had all the facts and they knew it was me for a long time.'

The other murder case, having long-term repercussions, involved a charge of murder against Dr Leonard Arthur, a respected paediatrician, who had prescribed 'nursing care only'—knowing, it was alleged, that this spelt death within a few days—for a newborn baby suffering from Down's syndrome (mongolism) whose parents had rejected responsibility for bringing up a child so handicapped. Before the trial, the murder charge was withdrawn, and attempted murder substituted. On 5 November Dr Arthur was found not guilty. While almost everyone was relieved that a distinguished and compassionate doctor had been cleared of a dreadful charge when after failing to persuade the parents he had followed established medical practice, widely different streams of thought on the moral issue gushed into the columns of the press and the broadcast studios. Was it ever right to take action, or inaction, that would knowingly forfeit life—a question directly touching on abortion and euthanasia? If a decision to do so was taken in the case of an infant whose mental or physical handicap would prevent its ever having a normal human life, who should decide? The parents, as the British Paediatric Association declared? Or the doctor after consulting the parents? Could it ever be a proper matter for judicial decision or legal rule? (In August a London borough council had obtained from the Court of Appeal a ruling that an operation to save the life of an infant with Down's syndrome should be performed, notwithstanding the objection of rejecting parents.)

Another extraordinary homicide case concerned the death of a Mr Barry Prosser in Winson Green prison after, it was alleged, he had been violently assaulted. In April an inquest jury brought in a verdict of un-lawful killing. On 30 September three prison officers accused of Prosser's murder were discharged by the magistrate on the grounds that no jury properly directed could convict on the evidence. There was an instant public outcry, in response to which, on 23 October, the Director of Public Prosecutions obtained from the High Court a voluntary Bill of Indictment charging the three officers with murder, thus bypassing the court of first instance.

An echo of a long-past trial was awakened when an effort by British authorities to secure the extradition of Mr Ronald Biggs, one of the es-caped convicts of the Great Train Robbery of 1963, who had found sanctuary in Brazil but had been shanghaied to Barbados, failed on appeal on 23 April. Biggs, no doubt regrettably, had become a British folk hero, whose enforced return to serve out a long gaol sentence would have been highly unpopular. In a report published in April the Press Council censured the *Sun* newspaper for 'inexcusably repeating an offence for which it was strongly condemned ten years ago', namely, buying and publishing Ronald Biggs's memoirs.

On 14 September a youth of 17, Marcus Serjeant, who had fired blanks from a toy pistol in the direction of the Queen at the Trooping the Colour parade in June, was sentenced to five years' imprisonment under the Treason Act. In evidence he was said to be obsessed with assassination.

Trials that did not happen left an odour of scandal. Following the case of the traitor Anthony Blunt (see AR 1979, pp. 23-24), allegations were made in the press and in books much publicized that a number of other senior officials in the intelligence and foreign services had in times past given information to the communist bloc. Those no longer alive and able to defend themselves it is well not to name, but two, Mr Leo Long and Mr Edward Scott, admitted to press investigators that they had passed information to potentially hostile powers, had been interrogated by MI5 security officers and had confessed, and without being promised that they would not be prosecuted had been allowed quietly to retire. The notion of a widespread cover-up in the interests of a Whitehall 'establishment', gained popular credence, but was vigorously repudiated by the Prime Minister.

Again in the field of crime and punishment, the IRA hunger strikes in the Maze prison in Northern Ireland (see p. 52) caused few hearts to bleed in Britain. Men convicted of murder, attempted murder or other terrorist crime aroused no more sympathy when they committed slow suicide than when they fouled their prison cells. No British political party opposed the Government's policy (as expressed by Secretary of State Humphrey Atkins on 30 June) of denying the convicts any token of political status and refusing to yield control of prisons by the lawful authorities, while seeking to maintain and improve prison regime for all their inmates—an aspiration daunted in Britain by shocking over-crowding, which led the Governor of Wormwood Scrubs to protest that he was in charge of a 'penal dustbin'. This view of the Maze trouble was not shaken by the April election of a hunger striker, who later died, as MP for Fermanagh and South Tyrone, but the subsequent passage of an Act to prevent long-term convicted felons from standing for Parliament, though not impeded, was not unanimous. The ending of the hunger strike endorsed in British eyes the policy of standing firm against such coercion. On 6 October the Secretary of State announced his decision on reforms in the Maze prison, the concessions applying to all prisoners.

If the hunger strike created Irish martyrs, British martyrs and heroes were created by the IRA terrorism. Such were a bomb disposal officer who perished by the explosion of a bomb in an Oxford Street store in London on 26 October, and his colleague who knowing his fate proceeded to defuse a similar bomb in a nearby shop. Another was Lieut. General Sir Steuart Pringle, commandant-general of the Royal Marines, whose courage when gravely injured by a car bomb on 17 October was exemplary. A horrible nail bomb was exploded by remote control outside Chelsea barracks on 10 October, injuring 40 people, including 22 Irish Guardsmen, and killing two passers-by, one of them a young Irish Roman Catholic. Mrs Thatcher echoed public feeling when she described this attack as 'callous, brutal and sub-human'.

Her policy of seeking closer relations with the Irish Republic, as the best way forward after the failure of successive attempts at a 'political solution' in Northern Ireland, was generally approved in Great Britain. On 6 November she talked at length with the Taoiseach, Dr Garret FitzGerald, at 10 Downing Street. The outstanding feature of their communique (see DOCUMENTS) was the decision to establish an Anglo-Irish Intergovernmental Council, involving regular meetings at ministerial and official levels to discuss matters of common concern. It would be for the two Parliaments to consider whether a similar Anglo-Irish parliamentary body should be formed. If British people had any doubts about the intractability of the Northern Ireland problem they were shattered by the reaction of the extremer Protestants in the province to these seemingly innocuous proposals. Mr Ian Paisley, MP, described them as 'a fresh attempt to hand us over to the enemy' and called the Prime Minister a 'traitor'. He and two other Ulster MPs were suspended from the service of the House after making a vulgar tumult and defying the Speaker. Mr Paisley declared: 'We have no other option but to call on the people of Northern Ireland to make it impossible for Mrs Thatcher's Ministers to govern the province.' The spectacle of so-called Unionists defying the Union Parliament and Government, of so-called loyalists displaying their crass disloyalty, and of a beefy gentleman in a clerical collar preaching hatred before the cross of the Prince of Peace offset the public revulsion at republican terrorism.

The notion of independence for Northern Ireland was promoted by Mr James Callaghan, the former Prime Minister, and received some press support. Mr Merlyn Rees, a former Secretary of State for Northern Ireland, said on 17 May that withdrawing the guarantee against any change in the constitutional position of the province without the assent of the majority of its population might well be a good step forward, though it would make little difference in practice. The practice remained as stagnant and hopeless as ever.

The Press

When 1980 ended, Times Newspapers Ltd, owners of *The Times*, its three supplements and the *Sunday Times*, had threatened closure by March 1981 unless meanwhile the papers were sold, preferably as a whole, to a suitable purchaser (see AR 1980, pp. 38-9). On 22 January the management announced that a bid by Mr Rupert Murdoch, chairman of News International, would be accepted provided that he reached agreement with the staff and their unions on production reforms. News International already owned two mass-circulation Fleet Street newspapers, the Sunday *News of the World* and the daily *Sun*, as well as others in Australia and the United States. Accordingly there was strong pressure for reference of the takeover to the Monopolies and Mergers Commission, which had been given a special oversight of newspaper mergers; Mr Murdoch said he had no objection to that course but it would take too much time, and the three printing unions concerned opposed a reference because they feared it might mean the end of the publications. In the emergency Commons debate on the issue on 27 January the Government issued a three-line whip, which produced a majority of 42 on mainly party lines. Mr John Biffen, Secretary for Trade, told the House he had agreed to the transfer without reference to the Commission but subject to a number of stringent conditions; among other things, guarantees of editorial independence would have to be incorporated in the company's articles of association and any change would require ministerial consent. Mr Murdoch, accepting the conditions, observed: 'The survival of *The Times* and the *Sunday Times* now depends on binding agreements being reached with the unions for economic manning levels and work practices.'

Such agreements were reached, after a struggle, on 12 February, and the deal was completed the next day. It was then revealed that News International had paid £12 million for Times Newspapers, plus a quarter of any profits above £5 million in any year after £20 million of profit had accumulated. The contingent payment seemed remote when the group had lost £15 million in the previous year. Sir William Rees-Mogg, who had resigned as editor of *The Times*, was succeeded by Mr Harold Evans, until then editor of the *Sunday Times*, who proceeded to make some radical changes in the make-up of the daily paper.

Another controversial press takeover was that of the Sunday *Observer* by a conglomerate known as Lonrho, headed by Mr 'Tiny' Rowland, whose operations had once been described by Mr Edward Heath as 'the unacceptable face of capitalism'. Mr Rowland, whose company already owned the Outram group of newspapers in Scotland (which launched a new Scottish Sunday newspaper in April), attempted various financial ploys in order to avoid reference to the Monopolies Commission, but eventually gave way. The Commission reported on 23

June that ownership of the *Observer* by Lonrho would not constitute a monopoly, but required safeguards for editorial independence. Eventually Mr Biffen gave his consent to the purchase subject to conditions similar to those imposed in the Times Newspapers case.

Mr Murdoch's pact with the unions did not save him from industrial troubles in the rest of the year. On 20 September production of the *Sunday Times* was stopped by a dispute over pay differentials launched by National Graphical Association machine operators. The management promptly suspended pay to all employees until the NGA gave a written undertaking to fulfil its promise not to disrupt production. In the following week publication of *The Times* was prevented by NGA picket lines. Mr Murdoch thereupon threatened to close both papers. The chairman of the TUC printing industry committee remarked that Fleet Street seemed to have a death wish. After mediation by Mr Len Murray a settlement was reached on 1 October and publication was resumed, but Mr Murdoch gave a further warning that any more disruption could cause the demise of both *The Times* and the *Sunday Times*.

Chapter 7

INTERNATIONAL AFFAIRS

ALTHOUGH the EEC budget and the Common Agricultural Policy (CAP) continued to dominate British relations with the Community, they were less prominent in public attention at home than in previous years. The budgetary settlement of May 1980 (see AR 1980, pp. 31 and 350) had given the UK a respite from excessive net contributions, and the 9 per cent rise in CAP farm prices, agreed on 1 April, was as nearly in line with British policy as could be expected. West Germany, having succeeded to the role of the Community's chief financier, appeared to have moved into concord with Britain over CAP reform, especially after Mrs Thatcher and Chancellor Schmidt had met at Chequers on 12 May. Herr Schmidt spoke for them both when he then said: 'We cannot have any solution by which some states get unlimited net transfers and some make unlimited payments.' In British eyes, France had now replaced Britain as the odd man out on those issues. But Britain was back in the pillory over fisheries policy. The obduracy of the Secretary for Agriculture and Fisheries in demanding a special regime for an island country so close to continental shores met little or no domestic criticism.

Speaking to the European Parliament on 8 July the Foreign Secretary, Lord Carrington, proposed three themes for development of the Community: renewal, enlargement and the search for collective identity.

Renewal, he said, must include reform of the budget and the channelling of resources into regional development, rehabilitation and training, energy, and perhaps new policies for industrial regeneration and urban renewal—'the problems of the 1980s'. In May Lord Carrington had told the President of the European Commission that the main thrust of Britain's presidency of the Community's councils, starting later in the year, would be long-term reform of the budgetary system. Great hopes were therefore laid upon the meeting of the European Council in London in November with Mrs Thatcher in the chair, and its failure to agree on the lines of budgetary reform was a corresponding disappointment. Reporting to the European Parliament at Strasbourg on 16 December, the Prime Minister quoted Edmund Burke, the famous first editor of the *Annual Register*: 'A state without the means of change is without the means of its conservation.'

The issue of international policy that aroused the greatest heat in public forums and the sharpest party-political division was nuclear defence. The Government was committed to the Trident missile system and the deployment of Cruise missiles in Europe; the Opposition was against both. The Labour and Liberal party conferences voted for uni-lateral nuclear disarmament; the SDP, as well as the Tory party, was against it. The leader of the Labour Party was a unilateralist; its deputy leader and chief spokesman on foreign policy was in the opposite camp. The campaign to convert Britain into a non-nuclear power gained some momentum during the year—150,000 people were estimated to have taken part in a demonstration for that cause in London on 24 October—and was much aided by imprudent statements by the American President and Secretary of State (see p. 69) which appeared to envisage a nuclear war confined to Europe and the possibility of Nato's being the first to use nuclear arms in a European war. Those statements may have been realistic, but realism was not the main inspiration of the unilateralist cause. Multilateral disarmament remained the hope of all.

Full cooperation with the United States was the keynote of the Prime Minister's foreign policy. The North Atlantic alliance, she told the Pilgrims on 29 January, must be made still more purposeful and resolute, extending its cooperation beyond Europe; its incoherence over Afghanistan must not be repeated. After an 'enormously successful' visit to President Reagan in February she declared British willingness to take part in a Western representative defence force which could be used any-where in the world, after consultation with the countries of the endangered region. Little more was heard, however, of this project. Mrs Thatcher's affirmation to the Pilgrims that setbacks for the United States were setbacks for Britain itself was out of tune with public opinion when the American Administration supported unsavoury regimes, in El Salvador and elsewhere, and picked quarrels with Colonel Qadafi of Libya, who was seen as no more than an international nuisance.

Nor did its aim of Anglo-American solidarity prevent the Government from pursuing its own 'European' policy in the Middle East. Lord Carrington said on 27 July that he was willing to meet the PLO leader Yassir Arafat if that would further the cause of Middle Eastern peace. In November, to the disgust of Secretary Haig, who called on him to 'cool it', he described the 8-point plan of Prince Fahd of Saudi Arabia—where Mrs Thatcher had been cordially received in April—as a 'positive and sound foundation for further steps'. Its rejection by the Arab summit conference (see Pt. V, Ch. 2) was thus a setback for British but presumably not for American foreign policy. Mrs Thatcher, billed to address the Board of Deputies of British Jews on 15 December, immediately after the Israeli annexation of the Golan Heights, courageously condemned it as unlawful and invalid and as hostile to the search for peace. If, she said, we demand the right to live in security and peace for one country, Israel, we must be prepared to accord it to others.

It was a common British view, contested by Mr Heath and other champions of Western development aid to the Third World, that the Brandt report (see AR 1980, pp. 492-9) was, like Camp David, if not dead, barely alive. Hopes of a major effect from the summit conference on the report at Cancún, Mexico, in October faded as the date approached. They were revived, as regards British policy, by Lord Carrington's statement on his arrival at Cancun that it was in Britain's interest to narrow the wealth gap between rich and poor countries; but that proposition was not visibly translated into action.

The Government was spared grave embarrassment by the reference of Canada's request for 'patriation' of its constitution to the Canadian Supreme Court (see p. 72-3) and by the latter's judgment that it was established convention for constitutional amendments required of Westminster to be backed by consensus among the national and provincial governments; for without such consensus there were clear signs that the measure would have a difficult, contested passage in Parliament.

In a major foreign policy speech on 8 April the Prime Minister warned Russia that intervention in Poland would be a disaster for the Russian as well as the Polish peoples; the Nato response, she said, would be far more effective than it had been over Afghanistan. Alarm and anxiety over Poland were sharply renewed when military government was imposed in December. British policy, however, was cautious and 'European'; President Reagan's imposition of sanctions against the USSR was sceptically viewed by the press. Lord Carrington told the House of Lords on 14 December that Britain would follow a policy of non-intervention in Poland and would expect all signatories of the Helsinki Final Act to do the same. He warned Moscow that any Soviet intervention would be regarded as a most serious violation of the Act and of European peace.

Chapter 8

SCOTLAND

IN 1981 Scotland saw the virtual collapse of the regional development policies developed in the 1960s, which had introduced large prestige projects aimed at providing basic industrial generators in key areas. The hoped-for build-up of subsidiary industries and component suppliers never materialized and none of the major projects ever became profitable, being remote from markets and suppliers. The final demise of the experiment was probably inevitable, given the depth of the current recession, but their going produced a disastrous job loss for Scotland.

By far the largest of the closures was that of the Linwood car plant in West Renfrewshire with the loss of 4,500 jobs, a figure already reduced by half from the previous year. The other major shutdowns were at the Ardeer nylon works of ICI (800 jobs) and British Leyland's Bathgate tractor plant (1,350 jobs)—ironically the original reason for the old British Motor Corporation coming to Scotland—and although not closed the Ravenscraig/Gartcosh strip mill was severely cut back (1,200 jobs).

While these redundancies were a serious blow to the industrial West Central belt of Scotland and were a major contributor to the Strathclyde Region's net job loss for the year of 32,600, the heaviest blows struck the Highlands of Scotland. At the beginning of the year Fort William and its surrounding area were reeling from the closure of the Corpach pulp mill of Wiggins Teape (450 direct jobs). The effect of this closure on forestry was minimized by the sale of surplus timber to Scandinavian paper producers. A second major setback came when the Government declined to support a £2,500 million gas-gathering pipeline to the Cromarty Firth for petrochemical production because of its potential effect on public sector borrowing. In the dying days of the year, British Aluminium closed its aluminium smelter at Invergordon (900 jobs) despite an offer of £100 million in additional energy subsidies. The Highlands and Islands Development Board was granted £10 million in special aid for the area to help replace the jobs by encouraging a more diversified industrial base, a task likely to occupy the full five year-term of the new chairman of the Board, Mr Robert Cowan, a Hong-Kong-based management consultant, whose appointment was announced in November.

Overall unemployment in Scotland reached 325,000 in December, an increase of 63,500, while the percentage rose from 11·6 to 14·4 per cent in the year. One young person in two was unable to find permanent work on leaving school. Traditional industries such as coal mining, textiles, engineering and shipbuilding showed continuing decline in their labour forces, but specialized capital goods manufacturers and those with high-value quality products were able to maintain their competitiveness, particularly in export markets. Even the whisky industry was adversely affected. Many distilleries were closed for extended periods during the summer and most bottling plants had periods of short-time working, but an eight-year battle with the EEC over grain pricing ended with a £45 million cash injection for the industry.

Takeover bids for Scottish companies raised strong passions over the level of indigenous control, and two major bids were referred to the Monopolies and Mergers Commission. The first, a bid by Lonrho for the House of Fraser, was refused by the MMC and the second, resulting from a takeover battle between the Hong Kong and Shanghai Banking Corporation and the Standard Chartered Bank for control of the Royal Bank of Scotland, was not resolved at the end of the year after a nine-month study. A third takeover battle for publishers William Collins of Glasgow by News International was repulsed, and Scottish control of the important Weir engineering group was retained through a rescue package in which the Scottish Development Agency played a leading role.

Two industries, electronics and oil, performed well, more than maintaining their respective labour forces of 40,000 and 100,000, and promising further expansion. Oil production rose with the addition of three new fields—Tartan, Buchan and Beatrice—taking output above seven million tonnes a month by the year-end and maintaining the UK's self-sufficiency with a healthy margin for export. Oil prices dropped slightly during the year to $32·25 a barrel and further development in the oil province was slowed by tax increases, but oil-related industries continued to expand and several major investment projects were announced to manufacture products developed for the North Sea and having world-wide marketing potential. Another notable energy event was the successful processing of fuel from the Dounreay prototype fast breeder reactor for re-use, although proponents of nuclear power suffered a setback with the Government's refusal to allow test drilling at Mullwachar in South Ayrshire to evaluate the site for burying nuclear waste in the future.

Scotland's position as the leading European centre for the manufacture of semi-conductor electronic components was confirmed in 1981 with the announcement of two further major manufacturing plants. The growing Scottish reputation for microchip design was enhanced at the first European conference devoted to very large-scale integration (of circuits on a microchip) organized by Edinburgh University. Application of electronic technology to other industries was given priority by the Government, who helped in the establishment of the UK's first micro-electronic application centre in Edinburgh; this will use the expertise of several Scottish universities and in particular Edinburgh University and Heriot-Watt University.

Medical research breakthroughs as important as the discovery of penicillin were announced in Glasgow and should give Scotland an important foothold in the bio-technology industry; development would take place on a new 'Science Park' run by Glasgow University.

The central role of Scotland's five New Towns in economic regeneration was confirmed by a Scottish Office review of their future. The decision was a rebuff for local authorities, but 1981 was a year of feuding between Government and the councils. The main battle-grounds were housing policies and the level of council spending. Many Labour-controlled councils fought a rearguard action against the Government's legislation allowing council tenants to buy their homes at preferential prices, and the Government were ultimately forced to take further legislative action to enforce their policies. Council overspending and the resultant rate rises, averaging over 30 per cent, resulted in similar confrontation, and the Government eventually had to cut off their rate support grant to Lothian Region to win the council's acceptance of spending cuts.

The strategic position of Scotland in the defence of the North Atlantic shipping lanes caused the Secretary of State for Scotland, Mr George Younger, to over-rule strong local opposition to the development of Stornoway airport as a major airbase for Nato. The decision to buy Trident nuclear missiles and base their submarine launchers on the Clyde also provoked strong opposition, in a year when pressure for nuclear disarmament gained in strength, and ensured a contentious public inquiry into the expansion of the chosen site on Loch Long in 1982.

General political activity, however, remained relatively quiescent in comparison with the political infighting raging in national political parties. There were no parliamentary by-election opportunities to test Scottish reaction to the SDP and Liberal alliance, although the SDP did gain two Scottish defectors—Mr Robert Maclellan, Labour MP for Caithness and Sutherland, and Dr J. Dickson Mabon, Labour and Cooperative member for Greenock and Port Glasgow. In the latter case, the defection resulted in the first serious rift in the Alliance because the Liberals were already well placed to make a challenge at a general election and the local constituency party was extremely reluctant to withdraw its candidate in favour of Dr Mabon.

In the Labour Party there were fewer signs of the left-right split, although the party leader, Mr Michael Foot, was given a rebuff by the Scottish Council of the Labour Party during a visit to Glasgow when a resolution strongly supporting Mr Tony Benn was passed. This resolution was masterminded by Scottish chairman Mr George Galloway, who was later rebuked for advocating communist membership of the Labour Party.

One Labour MP, Mr William Hamilton (Fife Central), well-known for his anti-monarchy views, was forced to subject himself to a second reselection conference by a left-wing challenge which had resulted in a tie in the constituency executive, but finally won.

The Scottish National Party failed to resolve its internal wrangle over the future direction of the party, and its electoral performance in the very few local authority by-elections was unremarkable.

Overall, 1981 was a difficult year economically, but, despite the problems, public perceptions of the future were more optimistic than elsewhere and Scotland's economy performed better in relative terms than other UK regions. Scotland escaped unscathed during the spate of street riots in English cities (see pp. 9-10) despite conditions of multiple deprivation in some urban areas at least as bad as those in Merseyside or parts of London.

Chapter 9

WALES

THE first wedding of a Prince of Wales since 1863 gave as much, if not more, pleasure to the people of the principality as to the rest of the kingdom. Wales took particular delight in the involvement of so many Welsh personalities in the festivities in London and in the wedding ceremony itself. Lady Diana Spencer was married in a dress created by a Welsh-born designer and her first official duty in October as Princess of Wales was to accompany her husband on a quite spectacular three-day tour of Wales. Huge crowds turned out to see the Prince and Princess and countless young children rushed forward to present her with flowers.

The Labour MP for Wrexham, Mr Tom Ellis, announced his support for the Council for Social Democracy (see p. 14) and then, following his constituency party's call for his resignation, he became the first of the dissident MPs to sever his connection with the Labour Party before joining the new SDP. The divisions characterizing the Parliamentary Labour Party were fully reflected amongst the Welsh group. Three Welsh MPs (including Mr Neil Kinnock) abstained on the final ballot for the deputy leadership, two supported Mr Benn and twelve voted for Mr Healey; but before the end of the year two of those, Mr Jeffrey Thomas (Abertillery) and Mr Ednyfed Davies (Caerphilly), made it known that they would not be seeking reselection and then that they would be joining the SDP. In the county council elections in May Labour gained 91 seats and won back control of Gwent and South Glamorgan.

Mr Gwynfor Evans relinquished the presidency of Plaid Cymru after leading the party for 36 years. Meeting at Carmarthen, the party's annual conference chose Mr Dafydd Wigley, MP for Caernarvon, as his successor. Mr Wigley, a moderate, defeated by 273 votes to 212 the other

Plaid Cymru MP, Mr Dafydd Ellis Thomas (Merioneth), who earlier in the year had helped set up a new organization called National Left to recruit socialists into the party, and who had also threatened in the House to move the writ for a by-election in Fermanagh and South Tyrone following the death of Bobby Sands (see p. 52).

There remained an undercurrent of violence in Welsh politics. Further attacks were made by arsonists on holiday homes and in October fire-bomb devices were found in an army careers office in Pontypridd on the planned route of the royal tour, and in the offices of the British Steel Corporation in Cardiff. The issue of second homes was given considerable publicity by the unauthorized publication of a letter written by Mr Denis Thatcher, husband of the Prime Minister, to Secretary of State Nicholas Edwards in which he drew attention to the delay in setting up a planning hearing for a proposed development at Harlech by a company for which he was a consultant.

Harlech Television (HTV) retained the independent television franchise for Wales but were asked to strengthen the Welsh representation on their board and to build more studios. Sir Goronwy Daniel was named as the head of the Welsh Fourth Channel Television Authority and Mr Owen Edwards was appointed as its director. The Commons Select Committee on Welsh Affairs, chaired by Mr Leo Abse, investigated broadcasting in Wales and questioned whether the £20 million being given to launch Sianel 4 Cymru was sufficient, as well as calling for BBC Wales and HTV to produce more English-language programmes to replace the Welsh programmes which would be moved to the new channel when it opened in 1982.

At the end of the year unemployment in Wales was running at 15·7 per cent, as compared to 12·2 per cent in the country as a whole. There were further redundancies in steel but the Welsh miners took successful industrial action to halt further pit closures. There was considerable disappointment at the failure of the Welsh soccer team to qualify for the World Cup finals, but there was some consolation in the promotion of Swansea City to the First Division. The Welsh Rugby Union somewhat reluctantly decided under pressure not to send a touring team to South Africa in 1982. The death occurred of Gwyn Thomas, the novelist and humourist *par excellence* of the Welsh valleys.

Chapter 10

NORTHERN IRELAND

THE best that can be said of 1981 in Northern Ireland is that it began and ended with blessed intervals of comparative peace. For the rest it was a year of anger, tragedy and gloomy portent. The so-called 'dirty protest' in the Maze prison ended on 11 January, but the IRA alleged that the Government had broken its promises, and 98 prisoners had to be removed to empty cells after smashing all their furniture. Terrorist killings were then resumed, one of the most horrific occurring on 22 January when Sir Norman Stronge, the last Speaker of the Northern Ireland House of Commons, and his son were shot dead in their home, which was then burned down.

Sensing that the hunger strike was a weapon of immense emotional potential, especially for winning sympathy abroad, the IRA now resumed it in pursuit of full political status for terrorist prisoners; but this aim was re-stated in 'five demands' which, if conceded, would have given the prisoners virtual internal control of the prisons. On 1 March Robert Sands began a fast which ended only with his death sixty-six days later. He was soon joined by other prisoners. The Government remained adamant. Chance played into the hands of the IRA, however, when Frank Maguire, the Independent MP for Fermanagh and South Tyrone, died on 5 March. Sands stood as a candidate, the Catholic SDLP dared not contest the seat, and on 9 April Sands was elected by 30,492 votes against 29,046 polled for the former Unionist Cabinet Minister Harry West.

The result had a shattering effect on Ulster politics, demolishing the premise of English policy that the IRA was not supported by the majority of Catholics. Moderate Protestant opinion virtually disappeared. Sands's election focused world attention on the hunger strike, and was a stunning propaganda victory for the IRA. They assumed that the Government would now give way, but Mrs Thatcher said that she would never submit to terrorist blackmail; 'the true martyrs', she declared, 'are the victims of terrorism'.

Various agencies, including the International Red Cross, tried to break the resulting stalemate, and on 29 April the Pope sent his private secretary, Newry-born Fr John Magee, to visit the Maze, but without success. The hunger strike had polarized the population as never before, and as Sands neared death both communities began to prepare for any contingency. After Sands died on 5 May severe disorders broke out in Catholic areas. In Belfast a Protestant milk roundsman and his young son were stoned to death, and many people were injured, but the security forces maintained control. Next day 600 extra troops were flown in from England.

Anti-British feeling in the United States, where almost the only voice heard was that of the terrorist, swelled the funds of the IRA, and enabled it to resume more active operations. On 14 May a Russian RPG rocket was used to destroy a police vehicle in Belfast, and on 19 May five soldiers were killed by a landmine in Co. Armagh. Two more hunger-striking prisoners, Raymond McCreesh and Patrick O'Hara, died on the same day, 21 May, and a fourth, Joseph McDonnell, died on 8 July. Further attempts to end the crisis by the Irish Commission for Justice and Peace (a group of Catholic priests and laymen) again failed. In all, ten prisoners died (the last on 20 August), each death being followed by serious outbreaks of violence; in all, 73 people were killed, most of them civilians. By the end of the summer, however, there were distinct signs that the relatives of hunger strikers, with the support of some of their clergy, were preparing to defy the IRA. When Patrick McGeown lapsed into unconsciousness on 20 August, his family at once authorized medical treatment, and the relatives of other strikers quickly followed suit. The IRA finally called off the protest on 3 October, bitterly blaming the Catholic Church.

Meanwhile the Ulster economy was rapidly disintegrating. Unemployment reached a staggering 20 per cent, and an average of 40 people a day joined the dole queue.

On 14 September Mr Atkins was succeeded as Secretary of State by Mr James Prior, and a new team of junior Ministers moved to the Northern Ireland Office. The change was at first welcomed. Atkins, though personally amiable, was politically a cipher, whereas Prior had the reputation of being a shrewd politician. His initial statements and actions, however, could scarcely have been more tactless. He had not attempted to conceal his displeaure at being sent to Northern Ireland, and initially he adopted a cold and hostile tone towards the Protestant majority. When the hunger strike ended he 'snatched defeat from the jaws of victory' (in the words of one of his critics) by conceding to all prisoners much of the substance of the IRA's five demands.

Ever since the Anglo-Irish summit of December 1980 (see AR 1980, pp. 35-7, 49 and 510-11) there had been growing unease among Protestants about the ultimate intentions of Westminster with regard to Northern Ireland. Many took comfort in Mrs Thatcher's reiterated assurances that the province would never cease to be part of the United Kingdom while a majority of the population so wished. But a groundswell of popular English opinion in support of ending the Union was evident, and there appeared to be a growing risk that Lord Carrington and the Foreign Office might succeed in urging a very different policy upon the Prime Minister. Such fears had been exploited by the Rev. Ian Paisley, MP, who early in the year launched a series of demonstrations which he called 'the Carson trail' in allusion to those organized by Sir Edward Carson in 1912 when Ulster Protestants had first banded together to resist Irish Home Rule. On 6 February 500 men brandishing firearms certificates paraded at midnight on a Co. Antrim hillside, and from time to time units of this shadowy force appeared briefly in loyalist rural areas.

The Official Unionist party was critical of these manoeuvres, fearing their adverse effect on English opinion and unwilling that the mantle of Carson should be assumed by Mr Paisley. But when, on 6 November, Mrs Thatcher met Dr Garret FitzGerald, Prime Minister of the Irish Republic, in London, and announced the setting-up of an inter-govern-mental council and agreement on wide areas of cooperation (see p. 42 and DOCUMENTS), the majority of Ulster Protestants realized that their anxieties had some foundation. England, they believed, no longer wished in her heart to have Northern Ireland united to her. An exultant IRA began a week of systematic killing of Protestants in the border areas.

On Saturday 14 November, the Rev. Robert Bradford, Official Unionist MP for South Belfast, was shot dead at a community centre in the city. He had planned to visit the United States in 1982 with Mr Paisley and other Unionist MPs to present the 'truth about Ulster' to the American people. The murder of a young Methodist minister who was also their public representative stirred the Protestant community to its very core. On the day of his funeral, services were held in almost every town and village in the Province, to mourn not him alone but all the victims of terror, and to show the Government that its security policy was found wanting. Mr Prior warned that there was no place for private armies, but even the moderate Official Unionists now declared their intention to form a defence force, though they later drew back. Mr Paisley organized a 'day of action' on 23 November, and upstaged other Unionist groups by bringing thousands of workers out on the streets to protest at security policy. That evening 5,000 men, many of them armed, marched under military discipline into the town square of Newtownards in Co. Down. Other units of the 'third force' paraded at points through-out the Province on succeeding days, their officers declaring that they would covertly protect Protestant farms on the Border and kill IRA men if apprehended on terror missions.

The last person to die by terrorism in 1981 was a young police con-stable killed by a bomb at Belfast's Unity Flats on 30 November. No murders occurred in December, the first month to be free of killing since June 1971. In all, 98 people died through political violence in 1981, 26 more than in the previous year. The total included 54 civilians, 13 police-men, 8 police reservists, 10 soldiers and 13 members of the Ulster Defence Regiment.

On 5 December Mr Enoch Powell, who had described Paisley as an 'inveterate and dangerous enemy of the Union', claimed that in 1979, after the murder of Lord Mountbatten and 18 British soldiers (see AR 1979, p. 49), a secret agreement had been reached between British and Irish officials to abandon Northern Ireland's constitutional status, and that there was a conspiracy involving American officials to create an all-Ireland state and close an obvious gap in America's Nato shield. Two days later, Mr William Clark, the US Deputy Secretary of State, after talks with the Republic's Ministers, said that it was the prayer of all Americans that Ireland should be united. (A Conservative MP asked Mrs Thatcher to assure President Reagan that she would not urge that Texas be handed over to Mexico.) The policy of the Reagan Administration on Ireland appeared to be moving away from an attitude of neutrality. On 20 December Mr Paisley's US visa was revoked by the State Department.

II THE AMERICAS AND THE CARIBBEAN

Chapter 1

THE UNITED STATES OF AMERICA

IN the early months of 1981 more than one experienced commentator on United States affairs reported that Americans seemed to be turning in upon themselves. It was not a retreat into isolationism—the pressure of events was for most of the year too great to permit such indulgence—but a more intense preoccupation with the internal state of the nation than had been customary for a good many years. The initiative for this concern came from Washington, but it no doubt accurately reflected the absorptions of most Americans. In his election campaign the previous year Mr Ronald Reagan had concentrated almost exclusively on the troubles of the economy and the need to strengthen the nation's defences, and he won handsomely. It was therefore hardly surprising that he should take up the same themes in his inaugural address as President, again almost to the exclusion of any reference to foreign affairs. His message was simple: Americans must first resolve their economic difficulties, and as they thus renewed themselves at home they would be seen as having greater strength throughout the world.

In attending to the nation's domestic problems the new President proved himself to be an adroit politician. He persuaded Congress to go along with a policy of tax cuts while increasing defence expenditure, accepting reductions in some of their most cherished social programmes, and planning for a balanced budget within three years. Unfortunately the economy remained recalcitrant. At the end of the year the nation was still in the grip of recession, with industrial production declining, interest rates staying high and unemployment rising above nine million, and the President's economic strategy under severe strain. Meanwhile events overseas did not wait on the resolution of America's domestic problems, but the evident lack of any clear foreign policy in Washington for much of the year caused a good deal of confusion in the rest of the world.

HOME AFFAIRS. Mr Ronald Reagan was sworn in as 39th President with traditional ceremony in Washington on 20 January. In his inaugural address he made clear that economic recovery would be the first priority of his Administration. 'These United States are confronted with an economic affliction of great proportions,' he said. 'We suffer from the longest and one of the worst-sustained inflations in our national history, which distorts our economic decisions, penalizes thrift and crushes the struggling young and the fixed-income elderly alike. It threatens to shatter the lives of millions of our people.' Prime among the burdens, the new President believed, was that of taxes, but great as it was it had not kept pace with public spending. 'For decades we have piled deficit upon deficit, mortgaging our future and our children's future for the temporary convenience of the present. To continue this long trend is to guarantee tremendous social, cultural, political and economic upheavals.' He said that in this crisis government was not the solution, it was the problem. 'It will be my intention to curb the size and influence of the federal establishment,' he said, 'and to demand recognition of the distinction between the powers granted to the federal government and those reserved to the states or to the people. All of us need to be reminded that the federal government did not create the states—the states created the federal government. So there will be no misunderstanding, it is not my intention to do away with government, it is rather to make it work— work with us, not over us—to stand by our side, not ride on our back. . . . It is time to reawaken this industrial giant, to get the government back within its means, and to lighten our punitive tax burden. These will be our first priorities, and on these principles there will be no compromise.'

During the next few weeks Mr Reagan completed his Cabinet and other senior appointments, and all his nominees, having been confirmed by the Senate, were sworn-in during January and early February. In addition to those announced in late 1980 (see AR 1980, pp. 55-6) they included Mr John Block as Secretary of Agriculture, Mr Terrel Bell as Secretary of Education, Mr William Brock as Special Trade Representative, Mr Richard Allen as Assistant to the President for National Security Affairs, Mr Murray Weidenbaum as chairman of the Council of Economic Advisers, and Mr William Clark as Deputy Secretary of State. Opposition from Congress forced the withdrawal, in June, of Mr Ernest Lefever from the post of Assistant Secretary of State for human rights. Later in the year the appointment of Mr Richard Allen also came into question when it was revealed that he had accepted $1,000 from a Japanese magazine for helping to arrange an interview with the President's wife, Mrs Nancy Reagan. Although the Justice Department, finding that Mr Allen, who had taken administrative leave of absence from 29 November, had not intended to keep the money for himself, cleared him of breaking the law, he had not resumed his post when the year ended. The President was able to make one further significant appointment during the year when he chose Judge Sandra Day O'Connor to fill the place on the Supreme Court vacated by Mr Justice Potter Stewart, who retired on 3 July after 23 years. Judge O'Connor was sworn-in on 25 September, becoming the first woman member of the Supreme Court in its 191-year history. Mr Reagan's choice was widely welcomed, particularly among liberal Americans who had not found much else to cheer about in the actions of his Administration.

The President began his attempt to fulfil his electoral promises on 18 February, when he introduced to Congress his programme of tax cuts and reductions in federal spending. Overall it was proposed that there should be a saving of $49,100 million in the expenditure planned by President Carter for fiscal 1982. Defence expenditure was to be increased by $7,200 million, and cuts in income and business taxes would reduce revenue by $53,900 million, resulting in a deficit for the year of $45,000 million. It was forecast that this deficit would be halved in 1983, and by 1984 a small favourable balance was expected. During this period it was planned that the tax burden on all Americans would be reduced by 30 per cent. Substantial reductions in the growth rate of public spending were proposed, increases being limited to 6 per cent a year compared with the 16 per cent of the previous two years, and the independent Federal Reserve Board was instructed to reduce the rate of growth in the money supply. Spending for what were described as the 'truly needy' (basic social services, unemployment benefits, old-age pensions) was to be financed as before, its proportion of the total federal budget increasing from 37 per cent in 1981 to 41 per cent by 1984, but substantial cuts were called for elsewhere. These included reductions in subsidies to industry and the better-off (including cheap lunches and student loans), the introduction of new user fees, cuts in some of the newer entitlement programmes, the delay, postponement or abandonment of some public investment programmes, the consolidation of federal aid into block grants to states, a cut in foreign aid, including funds provided for the United Nations, the World Bank and the International Monetary Fund, and a broad attack on waste in government.

The President's address was warmly received by the joint Houses of Congress, but it was generally recognized that it would be difficult to get the programme through intact. In the words of one Republican Congressman, Mr Mickey Edwards, 'Everyone whose ox has been gored, and that's going to include just about everybody, is going to be squealing.' Senator Edward Kennedy, a leading representative of the Democratic Party's liberal wing, observed that he was not prepared to see the social progress of a generation swept aside in a few short weeks.

However, before either House had formally voted on the programme the nation was plunged into a crisis such as had become sickeningly familiar in recent years. On the afternoon of 30 March, when walking from the Washington Hilton hotel after addressing a convention of trade unionists, Mr Reagan was shot by a gunman who opened fire with a .22 revolver at a range of about 10 feet. Six shots were fired, one of which hit the President in the side, the bullet lodging in his lung. Mr Jim Brady, the White House press secretary, was hit in the head and seriously injured, and a Secret Service agent and a policeman were also seriously hurt. The President was taken to the George Washington hospital where he successfully underwent an operation lasting more than two hours to remove the bullet and repair a collapsed lung. He made a quick recovery, being able to return to the White House within two weeks and to conduct a limited amount of official business from his hospital bed in the meantime, and the nation's affairs were not seriously impeded after some initial dithering. The Vice-President, Mr George Bush, was on a speaking engagement in Texas when the assassination attempt took place, and while he was flying back Mr Alexander Haig, the Secretary of State, announced on television with singular lack of conviction that he had assumed control at the White House pending the Vice-President's return. While it was later accepted that all Mr Haig was trying to do was to reassure the nation and the world that the American Government was carrying on, his statement added to the general confusion, since it was clearly laid down in the 1947 Presidential Succession Act that in the event of the incapacity of the President power devolved first upon the Vice-President and thereafter upon the Speaker of the House of Representatives, next upon the President *pro tem.* of the Senate, and only then upon the Secretary of State. The confusion did not last long, partly because it was quickly learnt that the President was not seriously incapacitated and partly because Mr Bush returned to carry on with commendable restraint and confidence.

The President's assailant, who was overpowered and arrested immediately after the shooting, was John Hinckley, the 25-year-old son of an oil company executive. Following his arrest he was detained for psychiatric investigation. An unposted letter found in his bedroom in Washington after the attack, and later published in the American press, suggested that an infatuation with a film actress, Miss Jodie Foster, might have been a motive for his action. The Federal Bureau of Investigation reported later in the year that it had found no evidence of a conspiracy behind the assassination attempt.

Four weeks after the shooting President Reagan was well enough to return to Congress to urge members again, in a nationally televised address, to enact his economic recovery programme. He noted that six months after the election there had so far been no results. Inflation, interest rates and unemployment were as high as ever, and the average worker's income was lower. 'Six months is long enough,' he said. 'The American people now want us to act, and not in half measures. They demand, and they have earned, a full and comprehensive effort to clean up our economic mess.'

On 7 May the budget resolution setting spending levels for the coming fiscal year was approved by the House of Representatives by 253 votes to 176, a significant victory for the President, for 84 Democrats voted with the Republicans. Five days later the resolution was also approved by the Senate by a vote of 78 to 20. As a result public spending in fiscal 1982 would be held to a total of $695,400 million, an increase of 5·2 per cent on the current year during which spending rose at the rate of 14 per cent. In June the President sent his detailed tax cut proposals to Congress, calling for a 5 per cent cut in October 1981, 10 per cent in July 1982 and a further 10 per cent in July 1983. The plan ran into immediate difficulties, as Democrats in Congress tried to persuade the President to drop his proposal for cuts in the third year and settle instead for 15 per cent during the next two years, but he would have none of it. All the weapons of presidential persuasion, including a direct television appeal to the people, were deployed during the last few weeks of July in support of his Bill, which he insisted should be ready for signing into law before the summer recess. The opposition in Congress capitulated, and on 29 July the House of Representatives voted by 238 to 195 to support his tax-cutting proposals, 48 Democrats voting with the Republicans. The Senate also voted for the Bill five days later, by 67 votes to eight.

Following the vote Mr Reagan, who had described his proposals as 'the most sweeping cutbacks in the history of the budget', said he believed that the first six months of 1981 would mark the beginning of a new renaissance in America. The *New York Times* commented that the tax and budget cuts represented the most striking change of direction in the balance between the public and private sectors of the American economy since President Roosevelt introduced the New Deal in the 1930s. But even amid the euphoria of victory the Administration was forced to recognize ominous signs that its planned programme of economic recovery was running into difficulties. Persistently high interest rates and continuing recession were two parts of the problem. The President responded aggressively: 'We did not sweat and bleed to get the economic package passed only to abandon it when the going gets tough,' he said to the National Federation of Republican Women on his return from holiday.

On 24 September he announced a further package of cuts in federal spending designed to save $16,000 million in 1982 and a total of $80,000 million over a three-year period. The saving would be achieved by cutting the 1982 appropriation for most government agencies by 12 per cent, abolishing the Departments of Education and Energy, reducing the federal non-defence payroll by 75,000 employees over the next three years, cutting an extra $27,000 million from welfare and entitlement programmes, and eliminating abuses in the tax code. The President defended his cuts by declaring that there was no choice but to continue down the road towards a balanced budget—'a budget that will keep us strong at home and secure overseas.'

In the last quarter of the year the road towards a balanced budget became more tortuous. By the end of October Mr David Stockman, the Budget Director, was admitting that the Administration's plans were already falling seriously behind schedule, and he told members of the National Press Club on 26 October that the aim was not now to get a 'zero deficit' by 1984 but 'a decisive trend towards a zero deficit'. Two weeks later Mr Stockman offered his resignation following the publication of an article in *Atlantic Monthly* which quoted him as saying that he had never had much faith in the Administration's economic theories and that the tax cuts were a 'Trojan horse' designed to help the rich. At a press conference in Washington on 12 November Mr Stockman did not deny the remarks but said they were a 'grievous error' and the fact that they had appeared under his name was a misunderstanding, as he believed he had been speaking off the record. His resignation was not accepted, but the incident clearly revealed the disarray within the Administration over its economic policies.

The *New York Times*, in a leading article, reminded its readers of a question that had been put to Mr John Anderson, one of the presidential contenders during the first Republican debate of the presidential campaign in 1980: 'How can any President curb inflation, cut taxes, increase defence spending and balance the budget all at the same time?' Mr Anderson's reply was: 'It's very simple. You do it with mirrors.' The newspaper commented that this answer was an acid summary of the political and economic history of the last two years. The metaphors had changed, from mirrors to Trojan horses, but the meaning was the same: 'The Administration has known for months that its economic policy cannot work—but has pretended to the public that it could. Now the public knows the truth too, and with any sort of luck Reagan will be forced to face his problem.'

The President showed no inclination to change course. Challenged by Congress on 23 November with an emergency spending Bill of $427,900 million, which he regarded as much too expensive and 'budget-busting', Mr Reagan exercised his veto, an act which brought government to a halt because it was without authority to spend more money. Mr Reagan said that faced with the choice of signing a Bill 'that would finance the entire government at levels well above my recommendations, and thus set back our efforts to halt the excessive government spending that has fuelled inflation and high interest rates and destroyed investment for new jobs', or holding the line on spending at the risk of interrupting government activities and services, he chose the latter. He again won the day, Congress voting an extension of the 1981 spending authority until 15 December. Further conflict at that time was averted by the agreement of both sides to a compromise spending resolution that would save an additional $4,000 million instead of the $16,000 million asked for by the President.

As the year ended the Administration was facing estimates from its advisers which put the deficit for the fiscal year 1982, assuming no further spending cuts or tax increases, at more than $100,000 million, which was more than twice the figure estimated earlier in the year. Thus further difficulties were heralded for the President's economic programme unless there was a quick end to the recession and some early indication that the policies were beginning to work.

Defence was the one major field of federal expenditure that the President was determined to increase. His original package of cuts allowed for a rise of $7,200 million in the defence appropriation for fiscal 1982, and for further substantial increases in 1983 and 1984, and although these increases were trimmed later in the year decisions were taken which indicated that Mr Reagan remained convinced that the nation had to improve its defensive capability. In August it was announced that the US was to proceed with the manufacture of the neutron bomb, or 'weapons with enhanced radiation effects', which meant weapons with warheads with minimal blast but lethal radiation impact on people. Production had been postponed by President Carter in 1978, but it was argued that as provision had been made for the neutron bomb in the 1981 budget it was logical to proceed with its assembly for stockpiling within the USA. It was also argued that its possession would provide the US with a stronger negotiating position when disarmament talks were resumed with the Soviet Union. On 2 October President Reagan initiated a further expansion of American strategic nuclear forces by ordering the construction of 100 MX intercontinental ballistic missiles and a new B1 bomber. It was announced that the first squadron of B1s, which were designed to replace the 30-year-old B52 bombers, would be operational by 1986, when the first MX missiles would also be deployed.

Mr Reagan said his new nuclear weapon programme had three objectives. These were to deter an attack by the Soviet Union, to ensure that the US remained capable of responding to future improvements in Soviet nuclear weapons, and to maintain a strategic balance with the Russians which was the keystone to future arms reduction.

The Government was plunged into a major conflict with a labour union in August when some 12,000 air traffic controllers went on strike in support of their demands for a 32-hour week and increased pay and pension benefits. The strike was illegal, for like all federal employees in the USA each of the controllers had taken an oath that he would not go on strike, and President Reagan was quick to respond with all the force of the law. Injunctions were taken out against the controllers and their union, the Professional Air Traffic Controllers Organization (PATCO), ordering them back to work, and the President warned that all those who did not return to work would be dismissed. A federal judge ruled the controllers in contempt of court, and imposed on the union a fine of

$100,000 an hour for as long as the strike continued, as well as ordering that its strike fund should be frozen. Military staff were brought in to help maintain civilian air services, and federal authorities began interviewing and training candidates for the strikers' jobs. On 6 August, when the controllers failed to meet the President's deadline for their return to work, they were dismissed from their jobs, and several of the union leaders were imprisoned.

Air services within the United States, and many transatlantic flights, were disrupted for some months as the dispute dragged on, and it was estimated that most of the major American airports were operating at less than 75 per cent of their normal level, while many internal flights suffered long delays. In October the federal Labour Relations Authority ruled that PATCO should be decertified, which effectively ended its existence as the recognized bargaining agent for the civilian air controllers and also brought to an end any hope that the controllers had of getting their jobs back. In December the President agreed that they might seek other government jobs, but made clear that they would not be allowed back in the control towers, not least because of the continuing animosity between the controllers who went on strike and the 2,000 others who had crossed the picket lines and continued to work. By this time it was reported that many of the dismissed controllers had in fact already found other employment of various kinds. Meanwhile Mr Drew Lewis, the Secretary of Transportation, warned that passengers and airlines would have to accept a long period of delays and other difficulties as it would take nearly two years to reconstruct the air traffic control system.

In space the Americans were able to make much more significant progress during 1981. On 12 April the first space shuttle, named *Columbia*, with two men on board was launched from Cape Canaveral, Florida, by three liquid-fuelled rockets and two booster solid-fuel rockets, the first to be used in manned spaceflight. Two days later, after 36 orbits of the earth, the shuttle re-entered the earth's atmosphere and glided down to a perfect landing on a sandy desert at Edwards air force base in California. Apart from the loss of a few heat-resistant tiles which were shaken loose during the blast-off *Columbia* was undamaged, and thus available for further space flights. The men on board were Commander John Young, a veteran astronaut who had made four previous flights in space, including a trip to the moon, and Robert Crippen, whose first space flight this was. On 12 November *Columbia* was sent up for a second mission, but because of a fault in a fuel cell the scheduled flight of five days was cut to 54 hours, when the vehicle was brought back for another perfect landing in the desert. The shortened flight was a disappointment for officials of the National Aeronautics and Space Administration (Nasa) who were out to prove that the shuttle was a reliable, cheap and easy way of putting scientific instruments in space, carrying out maintenance on them and bringing them back to earth when required. But the programme was already much delayed, more expensive than had been forecast, and Nasa was among the federal operations facing cuts in its budget. One effect of the cuts was the abandonment, as from 30 September, of a six-year project to seek, by means of giant radio detectors, signals from possible civilizations elsewhere in the universe.

Back on earth it was revealed during the year that the population of the United States had risen by more than 11 per cent in a decade to reach a total of 226,504,825. For many of them no doubt 1981 will be remembered as the year they were deprived of their national game for much of the summer. On 12 June baseball was brought to a halt by a strike of professional players in the major leagues, and the season was not resumed until 9 August, by which time much of its point had been lost. For the people of Washington the year also brought the demise of their evening newspaper, the *Washington Star*, which ceased publication on 7 August, leaving the nation's capital, having a population of some three million, with only one daily newspaper.

FOREIGN AFFAIRS. One of the most frustrating and discomforting episodes in the history of American foreign relations ended within half-an-hour of the inauguration of the new President on 20 January, when an Algerian aircraft left Teheran with 52 American hostages on board. The hostages had been seized when the American embassy in the Iranian capital was stormed by the mob on 4 November 1979 (see AR 1979, p. 59), and they were finally freed, 444 days later, when the US Government accepted a complex arrangement which included agreement to release more than $2,000 million of frozen Iranian assets, providing as guarantee more than half this sum in gold in London before the hostages were released. A document signed on behalf of the US Government by Mr Warren Christopher, the Deputy Secretary of State, declared that the US would, so far as was possible, restore the financial position of Iran to that which existed before 14 November 1979. In addition the US pledged that its policy was and would henceforth continue to be 'not to intervene, directly or indirectly, politically or militarily, in Iran's internal affairs', that it would revoke all trade sanctions, withdraw all claims currently placed before the International Court of Justice, preclude the prosecution against Iran of any pending or future claims relating to the seizure of the embassy or the hostages, and would freeze and prohibit any transfer of property and assets in the US within the control of the estate of the former Shah of Iran or any close relative being a defendant in litigation brought by Iran 'to recover such property and assets as belonging to Iran'.

The document was signed in Algiers on 19 January, but the negotiations leading to it had been long and tortuous, involving representatives of Algeria, who acted as mediators, of Switzerland, who represented the US in Teheran, of Britain, who handled the financial transactions in gold, and of West Germany who helped in a way which Mr Carter said he could never reveal publicly to the world. The impetus for the final resolution of the affair may well have come from the incoming Administration; for Mr Reagan had warned, on 12 January, that if the negotiations had not been satisfactorily completed by the time he took office the Iranian authorities would have to start again with a clean slate.

When the hostages were released they were flown first to Algiers and then to an American base in Wiesbaden in West Germany, where they were greeted by Mr Carter, acting as the new President's personal envoy. After greeting each of the hostages and talking to them for more than an hour Mr Carter said he had learnt that they had been much more seriously mistreated than had previously been revealed. Some of the hostages later reported that they had been manacled to chairs for weeks, had been forced to stand for long periods in the cold, had been kept in solitary confinement, and had on occasions been beaten, blindfolded and handcuffed, threatened with loaded pistols and rifles and with mock executions.

The reports of ill-treatment were received with anger in the US, and when the hostages arrived home on 27 January it was made clear that the Government would examine the Algerian agreement in every detail before deciding whether to honour it. Eventually, after nearly four weeks of close study, it was announced that the Administration would abide by the agreement, although it was also made known that President Reagan would not have negotiated with Iran for the release of the hostages had he been in office when they were taken. His policy when the rules of international behaviour were violated, he had warned, was to be one of swift and effective retribution.

The new Administration was equally forthright in its early statements on relations between the US and the Soviet Union. Mr Haig, the Secretary of State, told the Senate Foreign Relations Committee in January that he believed the major issue the US had to face was the 'transformation of Soviet military power from a continental and largely land army to a global offensive army, fully capable of supporting an imperial foreign policy'. He also accused the Soviet Union of fostering international terrorism. The President, speaking at his first press conference on 29 January, said that detente so far had been a one-way street used by the Soviet Union to pursue its own aims. He was opposed to ratification of the SALT II agreement, which Mr Carter had signed with Mr Brezhnev on 18 June 1979, but which had not been ratified by the Senate, because it permitted a continued build-up of strategic nuclear weapons on both sides and authorized the Soviet Union, in particular, to embark upon an immediate increase of warheads in large numbers. Although willing to begin 'discussions leading to negotiations' for a new strategic arms limitation agreement, the US, he said, was in no hurry to do so, believed that such negotiations must be linked to other issues, and must be concerned actually to reduce the numbers of nuclear weapons. In the meantime, as Mr Caspar Weinberger, the Secretary of Defense, announced, the US wanted to rectify the imbalance between Soviet and American strategic forces as quickly as possible.

The Russians responded by accusing the Reagan Administration of an orgy of military spending and by declaring that they would not allow the Americans to achieve military superiority; but if such verbal exchanges suggested a grave deterioration in relations there were actions to suggest otherwise. On 24 April the US lifted the embargo on the sale of grain to the Soviet Union, which had been imposed early in 1980 in response to the invasion of Afghanistan; in June it was revealed that talks were going on between American and Russian officials preparatory to the resumption of formal negotiations later in the year on limiting the deployment of medium-range missiles in Europe; and in August, following the announcement that the US was to go ahead with production of the neutron bomb, Mr Reagan disclosed that he had written to Mr Brezhnev offering to meet him to talk about ways of preserving peace (see DOCUMENTS). But, soon afterwards, he challenged the Russians to talk meaningfully about disarmament or become involved in an arms race they could not win, a statement that produced a predictably angry response from Moscow. Mr Reagan's challenge came at a time when further evidence was published in the West of the level of Soviet spending on arms, which was estimated to be running at more than $100,000 million a year, or between 12 and 14 per cent of the country's gross national product. It was reported that the Soviet Union had built some 250 intercontinental ballistic missiles in the past year, as well as more than 1,300 combat aircraft and 3,000 tanks, compared with the 275 aircraft and 650 tanks produced by the US.

In September Mr Haig met Mr Gromyko, the Soviet Foreign Minister, in New York for two long discussions which were described by both sides as frank, businesslike and serious. The outcome was an agreement that negotiations on limiting medium and short-range nuclear weapons in Europe would begin in Geneva on 30 November, and that Mr Haig and Mr Gromyko would meet again in the new year. On 18 November President Reagan offered to cancel plans to deploy 572 Pershing II and ground-based Cruise missiles in Europe if the Soviet Union dismantled its SS-20 and other medium-range missiles targeted against Western Europe, and it was stated that this would be the opening negotiating position of the US when the Geneva talks opened.

The American offer to eliminate intermediate-range nuclear missiles from Europe, which became generally known as the zero option, was part of a four-point plan put forward by Mr Reagan. The second point was that the scope of strategic arms talks should be broadened to embrace an overall reduction and not just the limitation of the number of nuclear weapons held by the two superpowers, with SALT (Strategic Arms Limitation Talks) being renamed START (Strategic Arms Reduction Talks). The third proposal called for the establishment of equality at lower levels of conventional forces in Europe, and the fourth called on the Soviet Union to accept Western plans for reducing the risks of surprise attack and the possibility of war starting as a result of misunderstanding or uncertainty.

President Reagan's initiative was warmly welcomed by America's allies, who had long been urging a more positive approach to negotiations with the Soviet Union, but the proposal was rejected by the Russians as being little more than a propaganda ploy. However, Mr Brezhnev adopted a more conciliatory attitude when he visited Bonn in late November, suggesting that the Soviet Union also wanted Europe to be free of nuclear weapons and that they would be ready for serious negotiations in Geneva. The talks began as scheduled, with Mr Paul Nitze leading for the American team and Mr Yuli Aleksandrovich for the Russian, and both sides agreeing that the negotiations should be conducted in private. But even as they began the US Administration became preoccupied with the crisis in Poland and its growing conviction that the Russians were intimately involved with the declaration of martial law in that country.

The first response was the suspension of American food shipments to Poland. President Reagan then warned that it would be impossible for the US to continue trying to help Poland resolve its economic problems if the people of that country were not left free of internal coercion and outside intervention, and said that the US was prepared to take punitive measures against Poland if the communist authorities continued their purge of trade union leaders and intellectuals. Americans in Poland were advised by the State Department to leave, and the Polish ambassador in Washington, Mr Romuald Spassowski, was granted political asylum which he sought after what he called the 'cruel night of darkness and silence' had descended on his country. On 23 December the US Government halted the Export-Import Bank's line of export credit insurance to the Polish Government, suspended Polish civil aviation privileges in the US and withdrew the right of Poland's fishing fleet to operate in American waters. On the same day the President announced that he had written to Mr Brezhnev warning him that the US would be forced to take 'concrete political and economic measures affecting our relationship' if martial law in Poland continued.

Six days later, on 29 December, President Reagan announced the introduction of economic sanctions against the Soviet Union for its 'heavy and direct' responsibility for the repression in Poland. The seven measures announced by the President were:

1. Suspension of the twice-weekly Aeroflot flights to the United States.
2. Closure of the Soviet purchasing commission office in New York.
3. Suspension of licences for the export of electronic equipment, computers and other high-technology materials to the USSR.
4. Postponement of talks on a new long-term grain agreement. (The current one-year extension of the 1975 grain agreement was due to expire in September 1982.)
5. Suspension of talks on a new US-Soviet maritime agreement, and the introduction of tighter restrictions on the entry of Soviet ships to American ports.
6. Introduction of a requirement for licences for the export to the Soviet Union of an expanded list of oil and gas equipment, and the suspension of issue of such licences, including pipe-laying equipment.
7. Agreements on energy and space and science and technology due for renewal would not be renewed.

The President indicated that the proposed second meeting of Mr Haig with Mr Gromyko was under review, and warned that further measures against the Soviet Union might be taken if the repression in Poland continued. The US wanted a constructive and mutually beneficial relationship with the Soviet Union, he said, 'but we are prepared to proceed in whatever direction the Soviet Union decides upon: towards greater mutual restraint and cooperation, or further down a harsh and less rewarding path'.

There was concern in Washington at the end of the year that the US had failed to win total accord among its European allies on the imposition of sanctions. There was considerable division of opinion both on the analysis of the nature of the Polish crisis and the Soviet Union's involvement in it, and on the effectiveness of any sanctions the West might introduce in altering the course of events in Poland. The strongest expression of disagreement with the US came from West Germany, which described the imposition of sanctions by America as a unilateral move made because the US believed that the Soviet Union inspired the imposition of martial law, a view which the West German Government did not share. In an attempt to avert further exacerbation among the allies it was agreed that the Foreign Ministers of the European Economic Community should meet early in the new year to review the situation in Poland and consider again the question of imposing sanctions.

The Polish crisis was not the first occasion in 1981 that America found itself at odds with its allies. Some public recognition of a growing opinion in the US that European members of the alliance should be ready to contribute more to the common defence not only of Europe but of its vital lifelines to oil and raw materials was made in February when Mr Frank Carlucci, Deputy Secretary of Defense, spoke at the annual Wehrkunde conference on defence in Munich. Noting that the total gross national product of Western Europe now exceeded that of the US he said that the US could not be expected to improve and strengthen its forces in Europe unless other allies increased their own contributions to the combined defence effort. 'Nor', he added, 'can the United States, unaided, bear the burden of promoting Western interests beyond Europe.' On the European side there was anxiety that the tough anti-Soviet line emanating from Washington in the early part of the year might have jeopardized the talks on limiting nuclear missiles in Europe, and there was continuing disquiet on the economic front at the persistently high interest rates in the US.

These differences were plainly visible when the leaders of the seven Western industrial countries—Canada, France, Italy, Japan, West Germany, the United Kingdom and the United States—met in Ottawa in July for their summit conference. After two-and-a-half days of talks the leaders emerged with evident satisfaction that the differences had not been allowed to get on top of them. They declared that the bonds of the West had been reinforced by their deliberations, which concentrated on the need to revitalize the economies of all the industrial democracies by continuing to fight to bring down inflation and reduce unemployment. As President Reagan had not responded to pressure for early action to reduce American interest rates the other leaders left Ottawa with the knowledge that they would have to take action at home to defend their currencies, but there seemed general satisfaction that many vague uncertainties had been resolved.

None the less some sensitive areas remained, particularly after the announcement that the US was to proceed with production of the neutron bomb had inspired large anti-nuclear rallies in many Western European capitals. A casual remark by Mr Reagan at this time in answer to a newspaper reporter's question, implying that there could be an exchange of tactical weapons against troops in Europe without the United States necessarily getting involved, caused a considerable furore in West Germany until it was explained that the President's remarks on limited nuclear war were entirely consistent with Nato policy. A bigger row erupted on 4 November when Mr Haig, the Secretary of State, revealed that Nato contingency plans included the explosion of a nuclear device as a warning to the Soviet Union against pressing a conventional attack on Western Europe. On the following day Mr Weinberger, the Secretary of Defense, denied that there was any such contingency plan. The confusion caused by such contradictory statements by senior men in Washington undoubtedly created some further uncertainty about the conduct of American foreign policy, and it was hardly surprising to read of the West German Chancellor, Herr Helmut Schmidt, pleading in a press interview for 'more harmony in the concert from Washington'.

During his election campaign Mr Reagan had spoken repeatedly of the need to reassert American power in the world, including the Middle

East, and shortly after assuming the presidency he referred to the need to 'refurbish our capability as a presence' in the area. What he meant by a presence, he explained, was that 'we're there enough to know, and enough for the Soviets to know, that if they made a reckless move they would be risking a confrontation with the United States'. The policy also included positive steps to help America's friends in the region defend themselves against what was seen as a growing Soviet threat, and on 7 March it was announced that the US was to sell additional military equipment to Saudi Arabia to improve the range of the F15 fighter aircraft they were already buying. In April it was revealed that the US had also decided to sell to Saudi Arabia five airborne warning and control system radar aircraft (known as AWACS), which would give the Saudis warning of all air movement at least 250 miles away, for delivery in 1985. The proposal was a controversial one, arousing intense opposition both from Israel and within the United States. For some months it seemed that the President would not be able to persuade Congress to support the deal, but he finally won a narrow majority of four votes in the Senate, on 28 October, in its favour.

The Israeli leaders took the opportunity to emphasize their opposition to the sale of AWACS when Mr Haig visited Jerusalem in March, but accepted with reluctance the need for the US to maintain relationships with some Arab nations hostile to Israel if it was to pursue a policy of creating an anti-Soviet alignment in the area, which Mr Haig had indicated was the US intention, both to prevent Soviet encroachment and to keep the peace. The US was quick to react when, in June, the Israeli air strike on the nuclear reactor at Tamuz, in Iraq, was seen as a grave threat to peace. The attack was condemned by President Reagan, who suspended delivery of four F16 aircraft to Israel and agreed that the US should support a resolution in the UN Security Council strongly condemning Israel for the attack 'in clear violation of the United Nations charter and the norms of international conduct', and calling on Israel to make appropriate redress to Iraq. The US found itself in further difficulty with its ally in July, when Israeli jets bombed Palestinian refugee camps near Beirut, in Lebanon, and more than a hundred people were killed. Mr Reagan sent his special envoy in the Middle East, Mr Philip Habib, to Israel to try to negotiate a ceasefire, and again deferred delivery of more F16 aircraft to Israel. Fighting continued on the borders of Lebanon and Israel for some days, but a truce was finally achieved with the cooperation of Saudi Arabia, exerting its influence on the PLO, and the US, doing the same on Israel.

Delivery of the F16 aircraft to Israel was resumed in August and relations between the two countries improved following a visit to Washington by Mr Begin, the Israeli Prime Minister, in September, during which it was made clear that Mr Begin agreed, as President Sadat of Egypt had on his visit to Washington a few weeks before, to resume talks on Palestinian autonomy. Progress in this direction was wrecked by the assassination of Mr Sadat on 6 October, which was seen in the United States as a severe blow to its policies in the Middle East, much of which were built on the alliance with Egypt and on American confidence in the Egyptian President's personal commitment to peace. Three former American Presidents attended Mr Sadat's funeral, and the US was at pains to emphasize its continuing commitment to Egypt to the Vice-President, Mr Husni Mubarak, who succeeded to the presidency and who had been visiting Washington a week before the assassination.

In an attempt to maintain its delicate diplomatic balancing act in the Middle East the US Government also sought to strengthen its accord with Israel, and in Washington on 30 November a 'memorandum of understanding on strategic cooperation' was signed between the two countries. The memorandum was designed, as it stated in its preamble, to build on the mutual security relationship that existed between the two nations, and to enhance strategic cooperation 'to deter all threats from the Soviet Union in the region'. Though the memorandum specifically declared that it was not directed at any state or group of states within the region, it did not go down well with the Arab countries, and in the event it failed also to establish any long-term improvement of relations with Israel. It was in fact suspended by the US Government eight days after its signing in protest at the Israeli Government's decision effectively to annex the Golan Heights, an act which, as a White House spokesman pointed out, was contrary to UN resolutions on which the Camp David peace accords and Middle East negotiations since 1967 had been based. It had also come as a total surprise to the American Administration, which had not resolved how to handle the problem when the year ended.

Elsewhere in the Middle East during 1981 the US found itself embroiled in a nagging conflict with Libya. In May the State Department expelled all remaining Libyan diplomats from the USA because of the Libyan Government's 'provocations and misconduct' around the world, including its support for international terrorism. In August there was an air battle between US and Libyan aircraft in the Gulf of Sirte. Two Libyan aircraft were shot down after they had, according to the American version, engaged in an unprovoked attack on American aircraft taking part in a naval exercise in what the US maintained were international waters, though Colonel Qadafi, the Libyan leader, claimed the Gulf as Libyan territorial water. Later in the year President Reagan said the US had convincing evidence that Libya had sent an assassination squad to America to kill him and other American leaders. He called on some 1,500 Americans living in Libya, most of whom worked in the oilfields, to leave the country as soon as possible, and authorized a measure invalidating American passports for travel to Libya because of the increased risks that Americans faced there.

Disorder in Central America was a continuing and frustrating pre-occupation for the US Government throughout the year. In February the State Department produced a collection of documents captured from guerrillas fighting in El Salvador which showed, officials of the Department believed, that communist powers were supporting attempts to over-throw the Government of President Duarte. Accordingly the US Government was persuaded to increase its support for the Duarte Government, despatching 50 American servicemen to act as advisers to the Salva-dorean army, though it was emphasized that they would not take part in combat operations, and providing more than $30,000 million in aid. At a press conference in Washington on 6 March President Reagan, in re-sponse to a question, said he thought there was no danger of El Salvador becoming 'another Vietnam'. His main concern, he said, was to stop guerrilla warfare and revolution spreading through the Americas.

The same concern tempered American relations with Nicaragua. Economic aid to that country was suspended in February while American officials tried to find out what was happening to it. The answer seemed to be that much of it was going to help the rebels in El Salvador, so the aid was not resumed. Later in the year Washington also became con-cerned at the expansion in the size of the Nicaraguan army and its acqui-sition of a large amount of Soviet-made arms, raising the suspicion that the country could become, like Cuba, a base for the spreading of sub-version through Central America. This the US was determined to pre-vent, not by unilateral action but in concert with other neighbouring countries with which it hoped to reach agreement in the coming year.

Chapter 2

CANADA

THE political life of Canada in 1981 was dominated by the continuing efforts of the federal Government to reach an agreement with the pro-vinces on constitutional reform. With only two exceptions, the ten pro-vincial premiers opposed various parts of Prime Minister Trudeau's constitutional proposals of October 1980, which required amendment by Westminster of the British North America Act, a British statute there-upon to be 'patriated', under the proposals, to the Canadian Parliament (see AR 1980, pp. 71-72). The governments of Quebec, Newfoundland and Manitoba all sought court rulings on the legality of the federal pro-posals, and received a wide range of opinions from their provincial courts. The key issues in contention were whether the federal Government could submit constitutional changes without the unanimous approval of all provinces and whether the proposals interfered with provincial rights in such areas as education, mobility of workers and ownership of natural resources.

Opposition to Mr Trudeau's plans in the British Parliament was revealed on 30 January when a Commons committee recommended that Westminster should reject any resolution received from Canada if it did not have the support of most of the provinces. Britain's high commissioner to Canada also let it be known that the UK Government might not recommend the motion to Parliament in the absence of provincial agreement. Prime Minister Trudeau indignantly observed that British MPs should recognize Canada's sovereignty and 'hold their noses' even if they did not like the contents of the Canadian legislation. The federal Government, and many of the dissenting provinces, began devoting considerable effort in London to influencing British officials and MPs (see p. 46).

Opposition leader Joe Clark and the majority of his Progressive Conservative caucus members proposed that, in the absence of provincial agreement, Parliament should pass a resolution to patriate the British North America Act as it stood and postpone further amendments. The Conservatives adopted a variety of techniques designed to delay progress of the Government's Bill through Parliament, and in February the Prime Minister conceded the opposition request that a final parliamentary vote on the constitutional proposals be delayed until after a ruling by the Supreme Court of Canada. Both federal and provincial government representatives appeared before the Court, whose hearings concluded on 4 May. The constitutional debate was removed from Parliament pending the Court's ruling. When this was finally delivered on 29 September, however, it did little to resolve the conflict. The Supreme Court ruled that the federal Government's proposals were legal within the strict limits of the law, but that they violated the convention which demanded a substantial degree of provincial consent.

This equivocal ruling obliged Prime Minister Trudeau to convene another federal-provincial conference, which took place in Ottawa during the first week of November. After extensive deliberations agreement was reached with all provinces except Quebec. The agreement maintained the extension of French language rights and the inclusion of a charter of fundamental rights as desired by the federal Government, but allowed provincial legislatures the right to override some of these provisions and also removed the previous veto held by both Ontario and Quebec over constitutional amendments. The substantial degree of consensus required by the Supreme Court of Canada having been achieved, Parliament proceeded rapidly to approve the new constitutional Act, which received royal assent on 8 December and was then forwarded to Westminster.

The isolation of Quebec on the constitutional agreement marked the conclusion of an eventful year for Premier René Lévesque. In April his Parti Québécois Government was returned to power with a huge majority over the provincial Liberal Party. Having been rebuffed by Quebec voters in a 1980 referendum on sovereignty association (see AR 1980, pp. 70-71) the PQ Government's electoral success reflected its efforts to downplay constitutional questions. Following the November federal-provincial accord, however, Premier Lévesque claimed to have been isolated by Ottawa and the other provinces. His party's convention later that month proceeded to adopt a resolution recommending that association with Canada as a precondition for the attainment of sovereignty be removed from the party platform, although Premier Lévesque argued that the convention had taken his complaints too far.

The other key federal-provincial dispute during the year involved energy price agreements between the producing provinces, chiefly Alberta, and Ottawa. In March the Alberta Government began reducing oil shipments to eastern Canada by 60,000 barrels a day in protest against the federal Government's National Energy Program, which had been introduced in 1980 in an attempt to increase Canadian ownership of the energy industry and provide greater revenue to the federal government. After protracted negotiations, Prime Minister Trudeau and Alberta Premier Peter Lougheed signed a memorandum of agreement on 1 September which provided for significantly increased domestic prices for oil and natural gas, as desired by Alberta, while still increasing Ottawa's share of production revenues.

In provincial elections, Progressive Conservative Governments were returned to power in Ontario and Nova Scotia. In Manitoba, however, the PC Government of Premier Sterling Lyon, after one term in office, was defeated on 17 November by the New Democratic Party headed by Mr Howard Pawley.

At the federal level, public opinion polls indicated that the Liberal Party had lost considerable popularity since its election victory in February 1980, and trailed the Progressive Conservative Party. Nevertheless, the leadership of opposition leader Joe Clark continued to be questioned throughout the year. At a party convention on 27 February, he received a vote of confidence but only by a two-to-one margin. At year-end a decision of his party's national executive to postpone the next national convention until 1983 was publicly criticized by a number of caucus members, who desired a leadership review in 1982.

A major reason for the Government's significant drop in popularity was the unsettled state of the economy. The issue of greatest public concern was interest rates, which rose during the first half of the year to record levels. By August the central bank rate reached an all-time record of 21·24 per cent and mortgage rates charged by lending institutions rose as high as 22 per cent. An internal study prepared by the Canada Mortgage and Housing Corporation warned that 100,000 Canadians faced loss of their homes by 1983. Bankruptcies, particularly of small businesses, increased by over 20 per cent. During the last half of the year the Bank of Canada allowed interest rates to decline gradually, and by December the bank rate was below 16 per cent.

Other economic indicators were similarly unsettled. The rate of inflation remained above 12 per cent throughout the year and reached a 30-year record of 13 per cent in July. The unemployment rate jumped from the 7 per cent range in September to 8·2 per cent, and by year-end almost one million Canadians were officially unemployed. While the country's GNP grew by 1·3 per cent during the second quarter, it fell by 1·6 per cent in the third quarter. In July the Canadian dollar plunged to a 48-year low of 81·34 cents against its US counterpart, although by year-end it had recovered to the 84·5 cent range.

Business leaders complained that the dispute over energy pricing between Ottawa and the producing provinces was a major cause of the country's economic uncertainty. The energy industry itself remained in the doldrums, even after the September accord, as a result of government policy which favoured Canadian-owned companies. The Government's efforts to increase Canadian control over this sector of the economy were aided by the purchase of Petrofina Incorporated by the public energy company Petro Canada.

Canada's National Energy Program was one of several items of contention in its relations with the United States. The American Administration also objected to Canadian attempts to limit US investment through the Foreign Investment Review Agency. These and other bilateral issues were discussed during a March visit to Ottawa by President Reagan. In November the Prime Minister announced the appointment of a new Canadian ambassador in Washington, Mr Allan Gotlieb, who as under-secretary of state for external affairs had attempted to establish new channels for dialogue between the two Governments.

In a budget speech delivered on 12 November, Finance Minister Allan MacEachen sought to reassure the United States by stating that the activities of the Foreign Investment Review Agency would not be expanded and that the Canadian Government's intervention in the energy industry would not be repeated in other sectors of the economy. The budget itself adopted a neutral fiscal and monetary stance, proposed the elimination of a number of tax-avoidance techniques used by businesses and higher income taxpayers, and reduced tax rates for the majority of Canadians. Protests from business leaders forced the Minister to introduce a series of amendments to his proposed tax changes before Parliament recessed in December.

and in October Prime Minister Trudeau was asked to serve as co-chairman for the North-South summit in Mexico. The Cancún meeting marked the culmination of a year-long series of visits by Prime Minister Trudeau to developed and developing countries and other meetings during which he had attempted to promote a more constructive North–South dialogue. In the November budget the federal Government reaffirmed its own commitment to double Canada's official development assistance by 1985.

Chapter 3

LATIN AMERICA

INTRODUCTION—ARGENTINA—BOLIVIA—BRAZIL—CHILE—COLOMBIA—
ECUADOR—PARAGUAY—PERU—URUGUAY—VENEZUELA—CUBA—
THE DOMINICAN REPUBLIC AND HAITI—CENTRAL AMERICA AND
PANAMA—MEXICO

ECONOMIC recession was the main theme of events in Latin America in 1981, but violence was still to the fore in public attention abroad. Interest in the rest of the world continued to be focused on the civil war in El Salvador, which the incoming Administration in the United States initially appeared to regard as the latest in the series of struggles by proxy between the superpowers. The Reagan Administration's apparent lack of interest in breaches of human rights was disheartening, but its diplomacy proved to be more sensitive to the nuances of such complex situations than had been at first feared. The guerrilla war in neighbouring Guatemala, ironically, continued virtually unnoticed, and contributed to the fact that, under Heads of Agreement worked out with the British Government, Belize (see p. 96) became independent at long last. On the other hand, the process of *abertura* ('opening' or liberalization) in Brazil continued, despite the illness of President Figueiredo, and the coup which overthrew President García Meza in Bolivia was followed by much more specific signs of return to civilian rule, being strongly backed both by fellow members of the Andean Pact and by the US Government. Aircraft accidents tragically claimed the lives of two national leaders, President Jaime Roldos Aguilera of Ecuador and General Omar Torrijos Herrera of Panama, but both countries confirmed a commitment to democratic processes. War between Argentina and Chile was stayed, and frontier hostilities between Peru and Ecuador were ended by established international machinery.

ARGENTINA

General Jorge Rafael Videla, who had held office as President since the military coup which overthrew the Government of President María Estela ('Isabel') Martínez de Perón in 1976 (see AR 1976, p. 80), spent the last three months of his term grappling with the economic crisis which the monetarist policies of his Minister of Finance, Dr José Martínez de Hoz, had proved unable to solve. On 2 February Dr Martínez devalued the peso by 10 per cent, a measure which he had consistently resisted. Three banks and several major companies had failed, and on 19 January the Banco Latinoamericano went into voluntary liquidation.

On 29 March, General Roberto Eduardo Viola, aged 55, who had been designated President by the military junta on 3 October 1980, was sworn in by its president, the commander-in-chief of the army, Lieut.-General Leopoldo Fortunato Galtieri, and in a broadcast to the nation the following day announced his intention of proceeding with a programme of political liberalization which would 'normalize' the position of political parties and trade unions, respect the freedom of a responsible press and revitalize the economy. Dr Lorenzo Sigunt, the new Minister of Treasury and Finance, immediately suspended dealings in foreign exchange for three days to carry out an effective devaluation of the peso by some 23 per cent. On 22 April, a new trade agreement with the Soviet Union was signed by which Argentina agreed to supply it with between 60,000 and 100,000 tonnes of beef annually in the years 1981 to 1984. The United States lifted the grain embargo two days later. The Reagan Administration had already asked Congress to lift its ban on arms sales to Argentina, despite the facts that the Videla Administration had on 12 March arrested 68 people at demonstrations organized by the 'Mothers of the Plaza de Mayo', and that at the end of March 989 prisoners were still admitted to be held on political charges, only 373 of whom had been tried and sentenced.

The Videla Administration had also formally rejected on 25 March the Vatican proposals for a solution to the Beagle Channel dispute (see AR 1978, p. 71, and 1979, p. 76), in connection with which there had been a series of incidents concerning individuals suspected of spying. On 25 April two Argentine officers were arrested in the Chilean town of Los Andes. Four days later the Administration of President Viola retaliated by closing all frontier posts and moving reinforcements to Mendoza; the posts were, however, reopened on 8 May after a personal appeal from the Pope to maintain a state of peace, which had been accepted the previous day by Chile. On 27 May President Figueiredo of Brazil met President Viola at the Argentine border town of Paso de los Libres, where the two Presidents issued a communique condemning all forms of 'interventionism' in Latin America, and firmly rejecting the proposals long supported in conservative and military circles in both countries for a 'Southern Cone' bloc.

Promises of liberalization met with some fulfilment. A number of political parties formed on 14 July a common front with the Unión Cívica Radical (UCR), with whose leadership the Government opened talks on 25 August. A few days later, on 9 September, its leader, Sr Ricardo Balbín, died in hospital aged 77. And when a general strike was staged on 22 July in defiance of the National Security Law by the General Workers Confederation (CGT), which had officially been disbanded in 1979, there were no reprisals. Ex-President Martínez de Perón was released from house arrest and went into exile in Spain on 11 July.

But it was his failure to cope with the economic crisis which finally led the junta to dismiss President Viola on 11 December, and in a last attempt to retain control by the military, still fearful as to what might happen to them in the event of a civilian inquiry into their past actions, General Galtieri assumed the Presidency himself on 22 December.

BOLIVIA

General Luis García Meza Tejada, who, following the coup that had brought him to power in July 1980, had proclaimed his intention to stay in power for 'twenty years if necessary' (see AR 1980, p. 78), was overthrown on 31 July. Shunned by its fellow members of the Andean Pact, his Government announced on 8 April its intention to resume its active role in that organization. Meanwhile the economy of the country worsened under the effect of repeated changes of government policy, the depletion of oil reserves and the exhaustion of the mines. At the beginning of June its foreign exchange reserves were exhausted, the United States meanwhile having withheld US $115 million in aid, and Venezuela a further US $40 million. In a move to arrest the decline, Law 18509 of 23 July reversed twenty-five years of government policy by reopening the mining sector to foreign investment. At this point a revolt broke out among the army, centred on the garrison of Santa Cruz and backed by the Bolivian Workers' Central (COB). Only the mediation of the Church averted a serious conflict. Upon the resignation of General Garciá Meza, power passed back into the hands of the military junta, who on 4 August appointed, to succeed him as President, General Celso Torrelio Villa, who had become chief of staff following the abortive revolt of General Humberto Cayoja on 27 June. In his inaugural address the new President promised to return the country to civilian rule within three years. As earnest of his good intentions he stated that the 1967 Constitution would stay in force until the elections.

In September a United States mission consisting of General Gordon Sumner and Mr Samuel Hart, both of the Department of State, visited La Paz to discuss the normalization of relations. The Government were seeking a stand-by credit of US $207 million from the IMF, and it was understood that US approval of this arrangement and of the resumption of aid would depend on such assurances as the new Government could give of its determination to proceed resolutely against the drug trade, whose unofficial profits were, it seemed, doing much to prop up its economy.

BRAZIL

The policy of liberalization, or *abertura*, pursued by the Government of President João Baptista Figueiredo since his inauguration in March 1979 (see AR 1979, p. 79), continued in the early part of the year, which saw the emergence of new political parties and strenuous efforts by the ruling Social Democratic Party (PDS) to maintain its position in the new multi-party system. The so-called Planalto Group's control over the administration, though challenged by signatories of a 'nationalist manifesto' released on 26 December 1980, was speedily reasserted by the house arrest of the two officers who had signed it, and it was the Group's candidate, Sr Nelson Marchezan, who emerged as the PDS nominee for the Presidency in 1982. But the growth of the Partido do Movimiento Democratico Brasiliero (PMDB, former MDB) into a major opposition force continued, while that of the newly-registered Partido dos Trabalhadores (PT) of Luís Inácio da Silva ('Lula'), occurring as it did in the countryside as well as the towns despite the re-arrest of the party leader, was also noteworthy. On 23 August a new trade union Central was formed at the Praia Grande Conference of the Working Class (CONCLAT).

In the economic field the main challenge confronting the Government was the unfavourable balance of payments, which since October 1980 it had been acting to rectify by a policy of strict import controls coupled with the effects of rising manufacturing output. Manufacturing, however, which had grown overall by some 35 per cent in 1980, fell off early in 1981 because of the world economic recession, leading to widespread unemployment in the big cities, especially in the vulnerable car industry, and real GDP was expected at the year's end to have risen by only one per cent in the year, the lowest rate of increase since 1963. Between May and October, however, the trade account improved with dramatic unexpectedness, following a steep decline in imports, and the balance of payments improved as hoped, only to be negated by the steep rise in United States interest rates. The rate of inflation dropped slightly, the national consumer price index rising by 95·6 per cent in 1981. Two other factors assisted this effort. Agricultural production was good, and frosts in July in the states of Paraná, São Paulo and Minas Gerais, though they reduced the production of wheat, sugar and groundnuts, did little significant damage to the coffee crop, which at 33·1 million bags was the largest for 16 years. And, against expectations, world oil prices remained stable, while the country's off-shore oil finds still waited to be brought into production. The programme of energy replacement continued to advance. In September the Angra dos Reis I nuclear power station was commissioned, and the Proálcohol programme for the distillation of anhydrous alcohol from sugar cane produced 4,600 million litres, as against 3,700 million in 1980, though the production and sale of alcohol-powered cars fell below expectations.

It was a sign of the great transformation President Figueiredo had achieved that, notwithstanding the resignation on 7 August of General Golbery do Couto e Silva as head of the presidential household, when on 18 September the President was incapacitated by a heart-attack there was no new military intervention (as there had been in 1968). The Vice-President, Sr Antonio Aureliano Chaves de Medonça, assumed the functions of the President *ad interim* on 23 September, despite the reported opposition of the powerful head of the Serviço Nacional de Informações (SNI), General Octávio Aguiar de Medeiros, though he, Professor Delfîm Netto and the Minister of Mines and Energy, César Cals, all showed themselves reluctant to be seen to be accepting Sr Chaves's leadership. On 12 November President Figueiredo reassumed his office, and the signs were that Brazil faced in 1982 another year of strict austerity.

CHILE

Chile, which since 1973 had served, under the direction of the so-called 'Chicago boys', as a textbook example of monetarist policies in action, found itself in 1981 in a state of severe economic crisis. In the early part of the year the annual rate of inflation had dropped to below 15 per cent, and, though less than in 1980, growth continued. But high interest rates acted to increase the short-term debt drastically, adding to a balance of payments deficit created by a steep rise in imports, mainly of consumer durables. And despite plans for further divestment of the public sector released in March, by which municipalities would have to dispose of virtually all assets which could be commercially operated, the private sector, which had benefited so much from the sale of public assets in recent years, was finding it harder to compete without state aid than its champions had suggested. In May the Viña del Mar Sugar Refining Company (CRAV) became insolvent, under the impact of the drop in world sugar prices on fixed-price forward contracts, bringing accusations of financial irregularities. Meanwhile concern at the stability of the banking system, under strong pressure to increase its loans to hard-pressed corporations, led to the government's assuming greater powers of regulation and control by the Banking Law of 19 August, and, under it, taking over control of the Banco Español and the Banco de Talca on 20 August, and of the Banco de Fomento de Valparaiso and the Banco Regional de Linares on 3 November. The Finance Minister, Sr Sergio de Castro, had reiterated, on 24 July, his intention to maintain the open economy, and the new Mining Code published at the end of the year called for private investment in all new major developments.

Unemployment in the Greater Santiago area continued to fall in the early part of the year. The labour movement still being divided, and the traditional May Day demonstration restrained by the continuing state of emergency, a major strike for higher wages at the El Teniente copper mine beginning on 22 April ended after 40 days without direct intervention by government when miners accepted a 2 per cent settlement and a bonus. The number of strikes, however, rose sharply. Subsequently, on 14 August, the Labour Law, the terms of which had played a major role in forcing the settlement, was modified to facilitate mass dismissals without compensation in the event of plant closures, and by relaxing the minimum wage provisions to allow the recruitment of apprentices up to the age of 50.

The position of President Augusto Pinochet, backed by the legislative junta of the armed forces, continued to be strengthened by his ability to maintain the balance between *'duros'* and *'blandos'* (hard- and soft-liners), the territorial dispute with Argentina (see p. 77) and the acceptance of his regime by the incoming Administration in the United States. The Foreign Minister, Sr René Rojas Galdames, visited Washington in June for talks with Vice-President Bush and Secretary of State Haig, and in the following month the Administration agreed to back a loan to Chile in the light of what it regarded as its improved record on human rights. Nevertheless the President still retained extensive powers of arrest, and by June a scandal involving the national security service (CNI), members of which were arrested on charges of being implicated in a bank robbery at Calama, suggested that improvement had still some way to go. Government hostility focused on the Coordinadora Nacional Sindical (CNS) for its public criticism of economic policy in a petition on 18 June, and two of its leaders, Manuel Bustos and Alamiro Guzmán, were arrested. But the Christian Democrats, though hitherto working within the existing institutional structure, declared their support for the

CNS on 11 August. Their President, Sr Andrés Zaldívar, had effectively been banished by prohibiting his re-entry to the country, and in a speech in September the President denounced the CNS as a 'communist front organization' and gave warning that political organization would be permitted only on local levels. An attack on a bank and police posts in Las Condes, a suburb of Santiago, at the end of June was used as evidence that the security situation still warranted extraordinary powers, after several years of claims to the contrary.

COLOMBIA

The security situation remained disturbed, and a further offer of an amnesty to the various guerrilla forces was rejected by local leaders. At the beginning of October the Government created a commission led by ex-President Dr Carlos Lleras Restrepo to study proposals for peace. By then, however, the country was already severely affected by strikes in protest over low pay and poor working conditions, though a national strike, scheduled for 21 October, was declared illegal by the Government and failed to mobilize the expected turnout.

Contributing to the unrest was the prevailing political uncertainty in the run-up to the presidential elections of May 1982. In September the Liberal Party, meeting at Medellín, nominated ex-President Dr Alfonso López Michelsen as its standard-bearer, his leading opponent within the party, Dr Virgilio Barco Vargas, having boycotted the convention together with his supporters. The Conservatives, in November, nominated Sr Belisario Betancur, their candidate in the 1978 elections. Since ex-President Carlos Lleras Restrepo was strongly opposed to Dr López as his own party's candidate, it appeared possible that for the first time for a decade a split in the Liberal Party could give the Conservatives a chance of success.

ECUADOR

At the end of January fighting broke out between the armed forces of Ecuador and Peru on the disputed section of their common frontier in the Condor mountain range adjoining the Peruvian department of Loreto. This territory was assigned to Peru by the Protocol of Rio de Janeiro of 1942—wrongfully so, in the eyes of many Ecuadoreans. Following mediation by the OAS (see Pt. XI, Ch. 6) a ceasefire was established on 2 February, troops of both nations were withdrawn on 17 March and the border was reopened on 2 April. Ecuador, however, refused to take part in the activities of the Andean Pact until May, when the political situation at home had been dramatically changed by the death of President Jaime Roldós Aguilera, aged 40, in an air crash near Guachamama, in the province of Loja. He and the Minister of Defence, General Marco Subía Martínez, together with their wives, the pilot and four others, were killed when their aircraft flew into a mountainside while on its way to Sapotillo for a military parade. An official spokesman stated on 8 June that the cause had been determined as pilot error.

The presidency was immediately assumed by the Vice-President, Sr Osvaldo Hurtado Larrea, aged 41, of the Popular Democracy-Christian Democratic Union (DP-UDC). A lawyer by training and former university professor of political science, the new President had been responsible as head of the National Development Council (CONADE) for drawing up the Government's five-year plan; while he vowed to continue the policies of his predecessor in principle he admitted in his inaugural speech on 15 June that economic conditions, and in particular the fall in world prices of coffee and cocoa, made it necessary for that plan to be modified. Though the transition of power had been generally peaceful, the election by a margin of only one vote of the late President's brother, Sr León Roldós Aguilera, as the new Vice-President had led on 2 June to fighting on the floor of Congress which required police intervention. (Ex-President Otto Arosemena Monroy, who had shot and wounded two Conservative deputies in a similar incident in September 1980, was ordered to be arrested by the Supreme Court in April and was sentenced to thirty days corrective detention in September). Having appointed Vice-Admiral Raúl Sorroza Encalada as Minister of Defence on 25 May, President Hurtado retained other members of his predecessor's Cabinet until a reshuffle in August was brought on by the resignation of Dr Carlos Feraud Blum as Minister of Government. He was replaced by Dr Galo García Feraud. In October normalization of relations with Peru was signalled by the reception in Quito of a visit by the Peruvian Minister of Industry, Sr Roberto Persivale, in order to re-establish bilateral trade relations. At the opening of Congress on 10 August, the President's new alliance, Convergencia Democrática, succeeded in gaining control and re-electing Ing. Raúl Baco Carbo as President of Congress.

PARAGUAY

The start of work on the joint Argentine-Paraguayan Yaciretá-Apipé hydroelectric project having heralded a future of abundant electrical energy, the Government of President Alfredo Stroessner announced in August an agreement with the Bureau Central d'Etudes d'Outre Mer to build a new cement plant which would triple Paraguay's annual production of cement and concrete products. Earlier in the year the Aracay generating plant had been linked to Asunción by a 220-kv transmission line at a cost of US $22·9 million. Inflation fell to 9·8 per cent for the year ending 30 November, and the export levy on meat was abolished in an effort to stimulate declining trade.

Politically, the Government continued to come under criticism for alleged violations of human rights by arbitrary arrest and the murder of Indian peasants; the Argentine Government officially protested when an Aerolineas Argentinas flight from Buenos Aires was refused permission to land on 6 August, on the grounds that one of its passengers was the Nobel Prize winner, Sr Adolfo Pérez Esquivel, who had planned to campaign against such abuses.

PERU

The Government of President Fernando Belaúnde Terry entered its second year confronted above all by the economic dilemma of countering inflation while reintroducing elements of a free market economy and maintaining the vast programme of public sector spending needed to achieve its objectives of reducing unemployment and malnutrition. Its chief instrument in this was the creation of a tripartite commission to administer its policy of *concertación*—collective agreement between management, labour and government on the control of wages and prices, to which both the major labour federations, the communist-led CGTP and the Aprista CTP, were committed. January opened with a 24-hour general strike called in protest at price increases averaging 48 per cent in basic foods and fuel. Strikes in the mining sector and a poor fish harvest in the early part of the year affected economic growth, which otherwise showed a substantial increase after several years of stagnation. The rise in agricultural production was particularly noticeable, aided by good weather conditions and the extension of rural credit.

At the same time, however, the rate of inflation continued to accelerate, reaching an annual rate of 81·6 per cent by May, and the worsening of the world trade position meant that the country did not benefit, as in the previous two years, from high prices for its mineral exports. Lower mineral prices, furthermore, decreased revenues, bringing the Government's budget deficit to a critical point by August. But when, after persuading the CGTP to call off a general strike projected for September, the President tried to end a six-week strike by the copper miners of SPCC and other state employees by rushing through a decree banning strikes which endangered 'the fulfilment of the budget', the policy of *concertación* was seriously endangered, and was saved only by a promise to review the legislation and an across-the-board 10 per cent wage increase for public sector employees with effect from 1 October.

Internal security, too, continued to give cause for concern. In January 130 people were arrested at Ayacucho on suspicion of complicity with the maoist terrorist organization Sendero Luminoso (Luminous Path). This organization, which was said to be led by a former professor of philosophy, Manuel Abimael Guzmán, and which had started operations on a small scale in 1980, was, however, only one of a number of such small groups. In October the Minister of the Interior, Dr José de la Jara y Urueta, was replaced by Air Force General (retd.) José Cagliardi Schiaffino.

URUGUAY

The year commenced with the military command still firmly in control of the Government of President Aparicio Méndez, who, however, had already stated his determination to retire. The appointment on 28 April of Rear-Admiral Rodrigo Invidio and on 14 May of General José Dario Cardozo as commanders-in-chief of the navy and air force respectively indicated a shift towards a more moderate stance, the former affirming on appointment his desire to see the restoration of republican, representative democracy.

Following the rejection by plebiscite of the armed forces' proposals for a new military constitution for the country in November 1980, talks with the traditional parties were resumed in July, and under a new compromise embodied in Institutional Act No 11 the armed forces conceded a progressive normalization of party activities and the appointment of a new President for a term of 3½ years to supervise the process. The sole candidate, designated on 1 August by a four-day meeting of the Joint Council of the Armed Forces, was a military officer, but one generally regarded as a political moderate.

The new President, Lieut.-General (retd.) Gregorio Conrado Alvarez Armelino, took office on 1 September, retaining the principal members of his predecessor's Cabinet, including General Yamandú Trinidad at Interior, Dr Estanislao Valdés Otero at Foreign Affairs and Sr Valentín Arismendi at Economy and Finance. On 29 September he met President Roberto Viola of Argentina for informal talks on the presidential ranch at Colonia. On 14 October trade unions were legalized for the first time since the so-called 'soft coup' of 1973; the effect of the law was to legalize only company unions and require the choice of union officials by secret ballot, to hold office only for limited terms. From the end of July the Government had already started to lift its proscriptions of some 300 politicians from political activity on an individual basis, though this affected only members of the traditional parties and President Alvarez reiterated that marxist-leninist parties would continue to be banned.

VENEZUELA

The Government of President Luis Herrera Campins continued to make use of its oil wealth to consolidate its diplomatic position in the Caribbean. On 2 and 3 April, President Forbes Burnham of Guyana paid an official visit to Caracas to discuss Venezuela's claim to some two-thirds of Guyana's national territory which had been 'frozen' for twelve years by the Protocol of Port of Spain of 18 June 1970. The Venezuelan Government, which had refused to supply Guyana with the concessionary oil which it had offered to other Caribbean countries in 1980 (see AR 1980, p. 89), indicated subsequently that neither would it do so nor did it envisage a renewal of the Protocol. In December, however, it indicated that it would look favourably on a request for aid from Mr Edward Seaga of Jamaica, after a similar request had been rejected by the United States.

The long struggle between ex-President Rómulo Betancourt and his former protégé, ex-President Carlos Andrés Pérez, for control of the Acción Democrática (AD), the country's leading party, currently in opposition, ended on 28 September with the death of the former in New York at the age of 73. Earlier, in mid-February, Sr Betancourt's candidate, Senator Jaime Lusinchi, had been elected secretary-general of the AD, which in the changed circumstances looked likely to win the elections of 1983.

CUBA

Having chosen for several years previously to disregard a series of opportunities to normalize relations with the United States, the Government of President Fidel Castro found itself confronted at the beginning of the year with a new US Administration determined to show that it was no longer prepared to accept the expansion of Cuban influence in the Caribbean. Indeed on 22 February Mr Edwin Meese, special adviser to President Reagan, stated that the United States had 'incontrovertible evidence' that arms from Cuba were reaching the guerrillas in El Salvador, a claim which was not widely regarded as significant. He added, however, that the United States might, if it felt it necessary, take direct action against Cuba to end the flow of arms.

The American change of attitude was accompanied by a general deterioration in relations between Cuba and other states in the region. On 13 February a group of refugees broke into the Ecuadorean embassy in Havana, took the ambassador and three others hostage, and demanded a safe-conduct out of the country. Three hostages were still held when on 20 February Cuban troops stormed the building, without the permission of the Ecuadorean Government, who withdrew their ambassador in protest. On 17 March Portugal withdrew its chargé d'affaires, Sr Francisco de Sales Mascarenhas, when the Cuban Deputy Foreign Minister, Sr Ricardo Alarcoń, accused him of complicity in the seizure before the assembled diplomatic corps. Six days later the Colombian Government broke off diplomatic relations with Cuba, alleging that Cuba had been giving aid and support to the Colombian terrorist organization M-19, a charge which was firmly denied. Costa Rica subsequently followed suit, on 11 May, after a Cuban attack on its Government at the United Nations. Cuba continued to maintain friendly relations with the Governments of Mexico and Nicaragua, however, and responded quickly to an invitation to establish closer links with Suriname.

THE DOMINICAN REPUBLIC AND HAITI

The Government of President Guzmán remained in power in the DOMINICAN REPUBLIC throughout the year. The Cabinet was reorganized in January, the President himself having been obliged to intervene to settle the teachers' strike of November 1980.

The economic position of HAITI, threatened at the end of 1980 by United States disapproval of the arrests of more than 400 in the biggest such operation since the succession of President Jean-Claude Duvalier in 1971, benefited from the support of the French Government, which agreed to triple its aid to Port au Prince. In January the President brought M Edouard Berrouet into his Cabinet as Minister of Interior and Defence in place of M Frantz Medard, and a fellow hardliner, M Edouard Francisque, as Minister of Foreign Affairs. Both M Sylvio Claude, who had been rearrested on 13 October 1980, and his daughter, Mlle Marie-France Claude, remained in detention.

CENTRAL AMERICA AND PANAMA

Dominating all other considerations in Central America during the year was the civil war in EL SALVADOR. It was estimated that on average through the year the conflict and its attendant violence by paramilitary groups and 'death squads' claimed the lives of some two thousand people a month. The civilian-military junta under the Presidency of Sr José Napoleón Duarte, reconstituted on 13 December 1980 (see AR 1980, p. 87), proved unable to assert its legitimacy and to gain control over the countryside, while a so-called 'final offensive' proclaimed in January by the Popular Liberation Forces (PLF) of the Farabundo Martí Liberation Front (FMLN) also failed to gain more than temporary tactical success. The Front, however, rejected a mediated settlement, as did the Foreign Minister, Fidel Chávez Mena, on 24 April, and offers of mediation by Mexico and Venezuela in April and by the Socialist International in May came to nothing.

Meanwhile the United States Administration had increased military aid to the Government of El Salvador to US $ 35 million for fiscal 1981, and economic aid in the same period to US $144 million, though on 24 September, after the visit to Washington of President Duarte, the US Senate was to make continuation of aid in 1982 conditional on improvement *inter alia* in the human rights position in the country. This followed a joint démarche on 28 August by the Foreign Ministers of France and Mexico, reiterated by their Presidents on 22 October, recognizing the guerrillas as a 'politically representative force', a view rejected on 8 December by the OAS (see Pt. XI, Ch. 6). Meanwhile the violence accelerated a decline in the economy, especially in the major export crops of coffee and cotton. Unemployment rose steeply and the rate of inflation was expected to exceed 50 per cent by the year's end. The FMLN offensive in July and August, aimed at destruction of electricity supplies and the disruption of communications, was climaxed by the destruction of the Golden Bridge, which effectively cut the country in two.

The belief in the United States that the Provisional Government of NICARAGUA, from which aid was withdrawn on 22 January, was supplying large quantities of arms to the FMLN in El Salvador seemed to outside observers to be at least exaggerated, and at worst dangerously to ignore the indigenous causes of the Salvadorean crisis. It aroused great indignation in Nicaragua, where the Provisional Government was still struggling to repair the economic damage caused in the course of its own struggle for power. A wide-ranging programme of nationalization was decreed on 20 July. But the Government was forced in September to declare a state of economic emergency and to prohibit strikes. Some sporadic activity by Somoçistas across the Honduran frontier continued, and was the subject in April of an official complaint to the United Nations. The Government continued to build up a strong militia force to defend it against these and similar attacks.

HONDURAS was affected by a heavy flow of refugees across its frontier with the Salvadorean province of Morazán, where Honduran troops were reported to have attacked and killed numbers of them in an effort to prevent the conflict from spreading to their own country. United States military aid was stepped up in March with the same objective. The Government of interim-President General Policarpo Paz Bonilla was embarrassed by political developments in advance of the elections, especially the dismissal of the Secretary of Finance, Sr Valentín Mendoza, for allegedly authorizing excessive payments for government land purchases. He was replaced by Sr Benjamin Villanueva. In the presidential election in November, held alongside congressional and municipal elections, Lic Roberto Suazo Córdova of the Partido Liberal (PL) defeated Lic Ricardo Zúñiga of the Partido Nacional (PN).

United States aid to GUATEMALA was also increased, and military aid was resumed in June, having been suspended since 1977 because of concern at the state of human rights in the country. The struggle between the Government of President Romeo Lucas García and a number of left-wing guerrilla groups continued, however, and together with activity by a number of 'death squads' cost the lives of some 600 people a month. The Defence Minister, General Angel Aníbal Guevara, resigned on 14 August to stand as candidate for the ruling Partido Revolucionario (PR) and the Partido Institucional Democrático (PID), in coalition with the Frente de Unidad Nacional (FUN) of Sr Roberto Alejos Arzú, in the presidential elections scheduled for March 1982.

The development of petroleum, export of which had begun in 1980, gave most promise in an economy which was generally sluggish, with rural unrest and lower world prices contributing to lower production of coffee and cotton. Petroleum strikes in Alta Verapaz in January, the Petén basin in April and the north in July combined to give promise of early self-sufficiency, but the rising cost of fuel in the meanwhile had ended production at the Exmibal nickel plant, a decision confirmed in November.

Despite the successful conclusion of Heads of Agreement with the British Government for the independence of Belize (see p. 96), internal political pressures did not allow the Guatemalan Government to proceed to a full-scale agreement before the granting of Belizan independence, and in consequence consular relations with the United Kingdom were broken off on 7 September.

COSTA RICA continued to enjoy domestic tranquility. Its Government's principal preoccupation during the year, however, was the economic situation, and the need to reschedule its national debt, currently running at US $2,600 million.

The death in an air crash on 31 July of the commander of the National Guard of PANAMA, General Omar Torrijos Herrera, the leader and guiding spirit of the Panamanian revolution since his seizure of power in 1968, and architect of the Canal Treaty with the United States, did not fundamentally affect the stability of the system which he had created (see OBITUARY). He was replaced by his chief of staff, Colonel Florencio Flores.

MEXICO

On 5 January President José López Portillo met President-elect Reagan on the frontier to discuss matters of common concern, a meeting which was pronounced 'an enormous success' by Mr Reagan's associates, and the meeting of the two Presidents in Washington in June resulted in the creation of two high-level committees on trade and political aspects of their relations. Despite this, President López Portillo continued to pursue his even-handed policy of friendship with Cuba and Nicaragua as well as with the United States. Diplomatically the year was dominated by the work leading up to the international summit at Cancún in October (see Pt. XI, Ch. 8), which the Administration had worked hard to secure, and the successful handling of which was regarded domestically as a triumph, whatever the value of the occasion internationally.

On 25 September, a month before the summit, Miguel de la Madrid, the 47-year-old Secretary of Hacienda (Finance) was nominated by the ruling Partido Revolucionaria Institucional (PRI) as its candidate for the 1982 elections, and, barring accidents, as President for the period 1982-88. Sr de la Madrid, who had held his current office only since 1979, had been responsible for the creation of the country's current development plan, and had visited both Cuba and Nicaragua earlier in the year to discuss international economic affairs. The leading opposition party, the right-wing Party of National Action (PAN), nominated as its candidate Pablo Emilio Madero, while a federation of five small parties on the left were also expected to field a unity candidate.

Local over-production of oil and the world oil glut had created problems for the rapidly-growing Mexican economy, and the growth itself had aroused criticism of persisting sharp disparities in wealth and income, and equally persistent charges of corruption in government. In September the majority of the ruling PRI in the Chamber of Deputies defeated an opposition motion to bring proceedings against Sr Oscar Flores Tapia, who had resigned as Governor of Coahuila after being accused of 'inexplicable enrichment' in that office.

Revenue from petroleum production continued to be used in particular to develop the production of basic foodstuffs, but anxiety about the rate of inflation grew with the decline in overseas demand for oil and the sharp 30 per cent fall in tourism in the first quarter of the year. When Sr Jorge Díaz Serrano, head of Pemex, tried in June to counter the fall in demand by cutting the price of benchmark crude by US $4 a barrel, he was forced to resign, and was replaced by Lic. Julio Rodolfo Moctezuma Cid. Increased sales to countries rather than the United States in the latter part of the year, and reintroduction of import licensing, were expected to counteract the losses to some extent, but the current account deficit was still expected to have risen during the year above the end-1980 figure of US $6,600 million.

Chapter 4

THE CARIBBEAN

JAMAICA—BARBADOS—GUYANA—TRINIDAD AND TOBAGO—BELIZE—
GRENADA—THE BAHAMAS—ST LUCIA—DOMINICA—ST VINCENT—TURKS
AND CAICOS ISLANDS—ANTIGUA—ANGUILLA—ST KITTS-NEVIS—
MONTSERRAT—CAYMAN ISLANDS—BERMUDA—SURINAME

JAMAICA

PRIME Minister Seaga of Jamaica lost little time in displaying his pro-US sympathies. In January he became the first head of government to visit the newly-installed President Reagan in Washington. It was announced, arising out of the meeting, that a high-level private-sector committee chaired by Mr David Rockefeller would be established to initiate capital investment and transfer of technology to Jamaica. The committee visited Jamaica during the year. Similar committees were established in the UK, West Germany, Venezuela, Puerto Rico and Canada, and a counterpart committee, the National Investment Promotion (JNIP), was established in Jamaica to facilitate local and foreign investment and joint ventures. Other pro-capitalist activities included the establishment of a committee to evaluate applications for divestment of state-owned corporations, the creation of a new national development bank to replace the virtually bankrupt Jamaica Development Bank, the transfer of the management of the Montego Bay Freeport to a US-based corporation in which 60 per cent of the shares would be held by foreigners, free licensing of imports and less protection for local industry, providing businessmen with a major portion of US$90 million outstanding in credit lines for raw materials and including a new import scheme under which various goods would require either no licence, informal licence, automatic licence or normally processed licence.

Prime Minister Seaga's unequivocal support for capitalism was evidenced also in the removal of the Cuban embassy from Jamaica, and in visits only to pro-capitalist countries such as Venezuela, Australia, the Philippines, South Korea, Japan, Puerto Rico, Canada and Antigua and repeated visits to the United States, which enabled him to secure sizeable loans which had eluded his predecessor. From the International

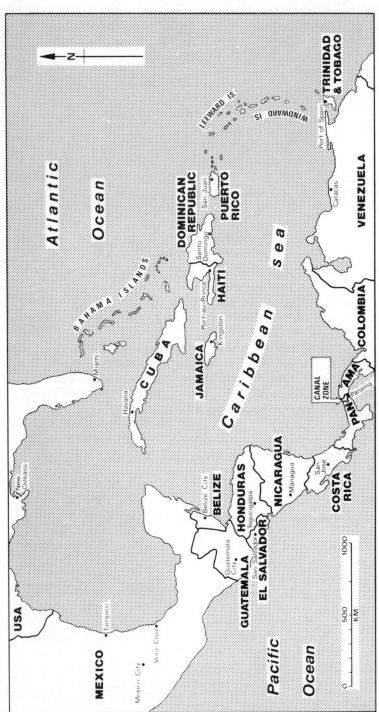

THE CARIBBEAN AND CENTRAL AMERICA

Several Central American countries featured prominently in international politics in 1981, notably El Salvador, Belize, Guatemala and Nicaragua. The map shows their strategic relationship with the USA, Cuba and the West Indies.

Monetary Fund Jamaica received a loan equivalent to US$650 million in various currencies under the Extended Fund Facility for the period 1981-84. The terms did not require devaluation of the Jamaican dollar, the laying-off of workers in the public sector or any adverse restrictions on the rights of workers. The Caribbean Group for Cooperation in Economic Development (CGCED) pledged US$350 million for specific economic recovery projects.

The Government also secured a loan of US$70 million from a syndicate of foreign banks, and refinancing arrangements were made with Jamaica's major creditors to a total of US$103 million; 311 new investment proposals involving nearly J$1,300 million had already been registered, and 16, worth J$64 million, were approved for commencement of activities. Additionally, sizeable loans and lines of credit were secured from the US, Venezuela, the UK, Sweden, Canada, US/AID and the US Export-Import Bank, among others.

Recalling for the country the legacy of economic and related woes after eight consecutive years of economic decline, Mr Seaga outlined a strategy for economic growth, based on the use of under-utilized production capacity, structural adjustments of the economy and private local and foreign new investments, designed to achieve a 3·7 per cent growth in the fiscal year 1981-82, 4 per cent in 1982-83 and 5 per cent in 1983-84. His Government managed to keep the inflation rate well below 10 per cent, significantly increased tax revenue collection and fixed limits on bank credit to the public sector and ceilings on domestic assets of the Bank of Jamaica (BOJ) and on its gross international holdings, on the contracting of new external debt by the public sector or the BOJ and on private-sector debts with government guarantees.

Nonetheless, at the end of the year there were no real signs of improvement in the economy. Up to September the trade deficit represented 41 per cent of the domestic export earnings, sugar production and banana exports declined by 17·4 per cent and 75·5 per cent respectively. The 1981 bauxite output was down to 11·5 million tonnes. Energy requirements accounted for nearly 40 per cent of the import bill. The high rate of crime was still causing concern.

Mr Robert Marley, internationally famous reggae music exponent, died of cancer. At the conference on the Law of the Sea in Geneva, Jamaica was confirmed as the site for the International Sea Bed Authority.

BARBADOS

The fourth Caribbean Festival of Creative Arts and Culture (Carifesta) was held in Barbados from 19 July to 3 August. Barbados was selected as the site for a regional office of the IMF. In the quinquennial elections held on 18 June the Barbados Labour Party, led by Mr J. M. G. Adams, the incumbent Prime Minister, won 17 of the 27 seats in an enlarged House of Assembly. The Great Train Robber Ronald Biggs, having been abducted from Brazil, was captured in Barbadian waters by the Barbadian police and was subsequently set free by the Barbados Supreme Court in denial of an extradition request from the UK.

The April Budget cut 1,800 taxpayers from the tax roll and increased personal allowances for 82,000 taxpayers. However, by September the Central Bank of Barbados was obliged to introduce measures to reduce bank credit for personal and consumer instalment purposes, and to increase the prime and lending rates of commercial banks to 13·5 and 14 per cent respectively. Also the Government was forced to increase bus fares by 33 per cent and to impose a transport levy, a health services levy and higher charges for various licences. The poor state of government finances which prompted these moves was in part due to the overrunning of estimates for a number of major government projects, and in part to the Carifesta hosting expenses. Additionally, unseasonal rains and labour difficulties led to a significant shortfall in the projected sugar harvest, and fewer visitors arrived although overall tourist earnings increased. The World Bank granted a US$12 million loan for building factory 'shells', and in December it was announced that the Inter-American Development Bank had voted US$60 million for various projects in Barbados. The Barbados Drug Plan officially began on 15 April.

GUYANA

For the Guyanese economy 1981 proved to be another disastrous year. There was negative growth for the sixth consecutive year. Sugar, bauxite, alumina and rice, major foreign-exchange-earning sectors, performed badly. By September the country's international reserves were *minus* G$487 million. Public debt was approximately G$3,100 million at the end of the year. In addition Venezuela intensified its claim for five-eighths of the territory of Guyana. This prompted a re-examination of the G$1,300 million national budget in order to find funds for the defence of the country. An austerity package was presented in which G$64 million was cut from overall public expenditure and the Guyanese dollar was devalued by approximately 18 per cent against the US dollar; on one estimate this would lead to a decline of nearly 34 per cent in workers' purchasing power. Additionally there were extensive government cutbacks and premature retirement of public workers.

The Government secured an interest-free loan of US$10 million from the Opec Fund for International Development, and a 15-year loan of

US$40 million from Trinidad and Tobago to help pay its oil bill. Its rela-
tions with Suriname cooled when it failed to give Suriname written
assurances that Guyana had no objections to the development of the
Kabalebo hydroelectric project, which would draw on a river used by
both Guyana and Suriname.

TRINIDAD AND TOBAGO

Dr Eric Williams, Prime Minister of Trinidad and Tobago, died in
office on 29 March (see OBITUARY) after celebrating 25 years of
unbroken rule by his party, the People's National Movement (PNM). He
was succeeded by Mr George Michael Chambers, who in the general elections on 9 November led the PNM to a resounding victory over all other
parties, winning 26 of 36 seats in the National Assembly. Eight of his
22-member Cabinet were newcomers, seven being appointed Senators
drawn from outside the party's rank-and-file organization.

The national Budget was seen as oriented towards the elections, containing as it did a generous package of tax relief costing TT$63·1 million
in an overall budget of TT$6,814·8 million for 1981-82. The country had
a strong foreign-exchange reserve position of TT$5,800 million. The cost
of living had risen at an annual rate of 18·7 per cent in 1980. The index
of domestic production showed no increase since 1977. Total gas reserves
in Trinidad and Tobago were estimated in a government White Paper to
be 14,100,000 million standard cubic feet.

The Government continued its divestment policy by offering shares in
government-owned enterprises to the public. It also enacted legislation
which enabled privately-owned local companies which agreed to offer
not less than 25 per cent of their shares to members of the local public,
when the stock exchange was established later in the year, to pay only 35
per cent corporation tax instead of 45 per cent for five years following
public incorporation and sale of shares.

The Appeal Court ruled that a 1978 Act that had declared the seat of
an elected representative to be vacant when he was expelled from the
party or left it voluntarily was null and void since it was not passed by the
requisite majority. The year was marked by large-scale industrial activity, especially by government-employed teachers over the recognition of
one union to negotiate on behalf of all teachers, by 52,000 monthly-paid
workers in the public service, and by workers in the sugar industry, who
signed a three-year wage agreement.

BELIZE

Belize, a British colony since 1862, became an independent state and 45th member nation of the Commonwealth on 22 September 1981, after 17 years of full internal self-government, the longest under British rule. Britain's independence gift was a paltry £12 million, half as a grant and half as a loan. The estimated 1980 costs to Britain for maintaining 16,000 British troops in Belize was £26 million. The security of Belize's independence in face of the Guatemalan threat was uncertain, since Guatemala had a population of over 7 million people compared with an estimated 150,000 in Belize. In March Guatemala and the UK reached an agreement about Belize, which led to more detailed negotiations and agreement later in the year by a joint commission in London. The 16-section agreement *inter alia* gave Guatemala permanent and unimpeded access to its nearly land-locked port of Puerto Barrios in the Bay of Honduras, the use and enjoyment of the cays offshore and rights in such areas of the sea adjacent to them as might be agreed. Section 12 of the agreement stated, however, that 'nothing in these provisions shall prejudice any rights or interests of Belize or of the Belizean people'.

Mexico and Venezuela agreed to incorporate Belize into the Mexico-Venezuela oil facility soon after it became independent. Belize would be the site of the Caribbean Community grain project as part of the regional food and nutrition plan. Belize had proven deposits of silver and asphalt in the Maya mountain range of southern Stann Creek and a high probability of oil, gold and nickel. The whole of the country's land and sea area had been leased to oil companies for hydrocarbon exploration.

The opposition United Democratic Party, which boycotted the entire independence celebrations, won 26 of 42 seats on six municipal councils in Belize, gaining majority control of most of them.

GRENADA

Grenada, beset by strong US obstructionist attitudes in international lending agencies, and by a campaign mounted by five Caribbean Community newspapers to discredit its human rights record, nevertheless managed to achieve a fairly productive year. Indonesia's over-supply and price-cutting tactics on the world market for nutmegs left Grenada with nearly one year's production on its hands, representing a loss of nearly EC$35 million, and put pressure on the island's 6,500 peasant proprietors.

The EC$160 million Budget for 1981 included EC$90 million for capital projects and EC$30 million for expansion of agricultural capacity. The money for the capital budget was obtained from Canada, Iraq, Algeria, Liberia, Syria, the European Development Fund, Opec, the World Bank, the Caribbean Development Bank, the USA and the USSR. Revenue was estimated at EC$69·4 million. The Government secured a EC$6 million grant from the EEC, secured export orders from Antigua and Dominica for salted fish, and began canning Grenada's own juices, jams and jellies. It further developed its parish-council-based democracy.

THE BAHAMAS

A US$300 million construction boom in the Bahamas created 1,500 new hotel rooms, with another 3,200 on the drawing board, together expected to produce 11,280 jobs. Nonetheless, the state experienced an unprecedented reversal in tourism: visitor spending declined by US$110 million from the 1980 level of US$595 million. The World Bank reported that real per-capita income of Bahamians declined by 6·4 per cent over a 9-year period and that there had been little redistribution of the national income. Tourism accounted for 60 per cent of the state's US$1,000 million-plus gross domestic product. The Bahamas Union of Teachers staged two major industrial disruptions, and a two-week strike by the Bahamas Electrical Workers Union led to a mass exodus of tourists. The year marked 15 years of rule by Prime Minister Pindling's Administration.

Given the troubled state of the economy, the presence of four parties and the restlessness of the country's young people—more than 65 per cent of the population being under 25—election year 1982 promised to be a hectic one. By the end of September 1981 the inflation rate was 11·9 per cent, the balance of payments came under pressure in the first half of the year, and foreign reserves were only US$102 million at the end of 1981.

ST LUCIA

The political squabble over the prime ministership was resolved when Mr Allan Louisy stepped down in favour of Mr Albert Cenac in May, after an EC$209·9 million Budget for 1981-82 had been defeated by a combination of the Odlum faction in the ruling party and the opposition United Workers Party. Mr George Odlum then broke from the ruling St Lucia Labour Party and formed the Progressive Labour Party. Prime Minister Cenac secured approval for a new EC$208·7 million Budget which included no new tax proposals. A second oil terminal was planned with Wynn Holdings of Saudi Arabia, and the agreement included the establishment of a development bank. Tourism and industrial development retrogressed and many workers were dismissed, temporarily laid off or rotated in employment. St Lucia's ambassador Dr Barry Auguste took office as chairman of the permanent council of the Organization of American States.

DOMINICA

Prime Minister Eugenia Charles had to deal with two attempted coups, a disloyal army (which was subsequently disbanded) and the aftermath of Hurricanes David and Allen. In the March plot former Prime Minister Patrick John and the head of the defence force, among others, were arrested and charged with conspiracy to overthrow the Government. Miss Charles announced in Washington that as far as aid was concerned the sky was the limit. She secured a loan of EC$37·5 million from the IMF for the period 1981-83.

ST VINCENT

The 1981 revival of St Vincent's sugar industry produced little sugar. A broad-based National Committee in Defence of Democracy was established to press for the withdrawal of two highly-controversial measures, the Essential Services and Public Order Bills. The Government of Prime Minister Cato apparently decided to let the Bills die a quiet death.

TURKS AND CAICOS ISLANDS

A 625-bed 'Club Meditérranné' project was expected to inject US$3 million annually into the local economy. Narcotic trafficking appeared to have come effectively under control. All six government airports were being upgraded with British capital.

ANTIGUA

Antigua and Barbuda attained independence from Great Britain and became the 157th member of the UN and a full member of the Organization of Eastern Caribbean States. Having achieved a 7·5 per cent average annual growth rate in GDP between 1977 and 1979, it received pledges of aid to the tune of EC$20 million from the Caribbean Group for Co-operation and Economic Development, and a loan of EC$10 million from Trinidad and Tobago to improve its water supply system. Its new EC$13 million airport was opened.

ANGUILLA

As a result of a revolt in the ruling party of Mr Ronald Webster his Government collapsed in June. Under the banner of a newly-formed party, the Anguilla Peoples' Party, Mr Webster's supporters won 5 of the 7 seats and he was reinstalled as Chief Minister.

ST KITTS-NEVIS

The legislature of St Kitts-Nevis formally agreed to remove Anguilla from the name of the state. This followed the decision of a High Court judge that eight Bills passed previously were unconstitutional. A concrete and steel pier costing EC$20 million was completed.

MONTSERRAT

Nearly 40 banks were issued with licences to set up business in the country. A loan of EC$117 million was secured from the Caribbean Development Bank to establish new spinning machinery and expand the production of cotton. CIDA donated 82 looms, and Dominion Textiles of Montreal donated a pre-shrinking and dyeing plant.

CAYMAN ISLANDS

Cayman continued to enjoy a high level of economic development based on off-shore banking, a construction and real estate boom, tourism and ship-to-ship oil transfer.

BERMUDA

The US$132 million 'balanced' budget included heavy taxes, levies and fees. Premier David Gibbons announced that the Cabinet undertook to increase company taxes only once during the life of the House.

SURINAME

The hybrid civilian-military Government of President Henck Chin-A-Sen and military commander Daysi Bouterse, in its second year in office, sought to establish proper economic planning, with strict control and pruning of government spending, and moved to obtain funds from international aid agencies and the Netherlands. The latter undertook to provide US$380 million in aid for 57 development projects as part of its independence gift to Suriname. The Surinamese Government allocated US$110 million to expand the rice industry by bringing another 30,500 hectares of land under cultivation and setting up storage, milling and drying facilities. It secured a US$16 million contract to supply Guadeloupe with 30,000 tonnes of rice over a two-year period. It declared its intention of introducing a land policy based on social justice and a plan for free medical care for all citizens, having already launched such a scheme for public employees; it had also implemented the 200-mile economic zone from the beginning of the year, and cracked down on Guyanese living illegally in Suriname.

It further announced that rule by decrees would continue until a new constitution was adopted. A major step towards institutionalizing the political structure was taken when a broad-based Revolutionary Front was established on 15 December, uniting all revolutionary and progressive forces in the country. The participating organizations were all the four federations of trade unions, the Federation of Poor Farmers (FAL), the People's Mobilization of the National Military Council, the Youth Council, the Association of Progressive Intellectuals (VOIS), the National Republic Party (PNR) and the Revolutionary People's Party (RVP). The presidium, the highest organ of the Revolutionary Front, would consist of six national leaders (the commander of the National Army, Daysi Bouterse, and five others). The draft of a new constitution was completed and sent to all 'functional groupings'.

III THE USSR AND EASTERN EUROPE

Chapter 1

THE USSR

IN 1981 the Soviet Union continued to compete with the West in seeing who could get into the worse political and economic mess. The Rake's Progress *à la russe* remained, however, readily distinguishable from the Western version. Economic difficulties stemmed from domestic sources, in an economy still largely self-sufficient and insulated from external fluctuations. The chief political problems, in contrast, were those of empire. The occupation of Afghanistan gave every appearance of being a long-term entanglement, though not—for the Kremlin—a matter of prime importance. The fluctuating military fortunes of the 80-90,000 Soviet troops in Afghanistan dropped, by and large, from the news; and there was no sign that the affair was having major consequences within the USSR. Events in Poland moved into the foreground. Soviet political control in Eastern Europe was at risk; the military crackdown by the Polish authorities in December was an attempt to stabilize the situation, but it brought a further deterioration of Moscow's relations with the West.

The Soviet response to these problems was characteristic of the Brezhnev era. Instead of a flurry of new ideas, new policies and new people, there was a stolidity bordering on petrification. No daring, or even modest, economic reforms were announced. A Party Congress passed by with no changes—for the first time in Soviet history—in the membership of the Politburo. *Pravda* gave more space to Brezhnev's 75th birthday than to any other item in the year's news. The authorities on several occasions showed signs, it is true, of being nervous about possible public disorder. But Russia's rulers had been afraid of popular unrest almost throughout recorded history. Of actual unrest there was little evidence. The number of active intellectual dissidents had been whittled down. Public demonstrations occurred only in out-of-the-way places like Georgia and Estonia. To the outside observer, the only hard evidence that became available during the year about the mood of the great Russian people was that they were drinking even more than before.

DOMESTIC AFFAIRS.—*Government and society.* There were no changes of personnel within the top leadership (the Politburo) during the year. In a formal sense, the major event of the domestic political calendar was the XXVI Party Congress, held in Moscow in late February. In recent times Party Congresses had been held every five years and provided a forum for major policy statements, both economic and political. They had also provided an occasion for changes to be made in top Party posts. The 1981 Congress was the first since the revolution at which the Politburo remained unchanged. In view of the high average age of the 14 full members of the Politburo (70 at the end of the year), this stability was widely held to result from a stalemate in the struggle for the eventual succession to Brezhnev as General Secretary and President.

The Congress approved a proposal to draw up a new long-term Party programme. The last such programme had been launched by Mr Khrushchev in 1961 and had been a source of embarrassment for most of the succeeding 20 years. It had proclaimed that the Soviet economy would be overtaking the developed West in per-capita output and living standards by about 1980, and entering the utopian condition of 'Full Communism'. The discrepancy between programme and outcome had been played down by the simple expedient of making no official reference to the programme. But, once the period to which it referred had elapsed, it was apparently felt to be necessary to put something—no doubt more discreetly worded—in its place.

The immobility in the top leadership was not reflected at lower levels. In the course of the year a number of the oldest Ministers in charge of industrial branch ministries retired and there were also changes among the regional Party secretaries. The top industrial administrators had in many cases been in post since the re-establishment (in 1965) of branch ministries soon after Krushchev's fall. The remarkable fact was not that such changes occurred but that many of them had not occurred sooner.

Mr Brezhnev continued to receive awards, decorations and tributes by the cartload. His 75th birthday, on 19 December, was the epicentre of a positive explosion of such awards. With a straight face, Mr Babrak Karmal presented him with Afghanistan's highest award, the Sun of Freedom. The home team chipped in with another Order of Lenin and a Gold Star. *Pravda*, whose total length is usually six or eight pages, devoted 6¼ pages to birthday tributes.

Outside the economic sphere there were a few decrees and pieces of legislation that were of more than minor interest. The crime of 'hooliganism' was given an even wider definition than it already had, and anyone caught 'violating social order' could now be imprisoned for 15 days without trial or the right of appeal.

On 24 September the press published an unusual and somewhat unexpected decree on sports facilities. This said that too much emphasis had hitherto been placed on the provision of facilities for selected specialist sportsmen, and not enough had been done for the general public. This imbalance was to be rectified. In addition, the daily exercise period at work was to be taken more seriously and the youth fitness test was to be made more demanding and more widely used. Concern about the overall health of the Soviet population probably lay behind this decree. Some age-specific mortality rates had recently begun to increase —a most unusual development for an industrial country.

At the session of the Supreme Soviet on 23-24 June a new law was passed on the status of resident foreigners in the USSR. Much of it was routine, but it also contained the first legal formalization of Soviet practice in detaining or expelling foreign citizens. According to Article 25, not only the interests of preserving state security, but also 'other reasons laid down in the legislation' could be grounds for either prohibiting or enforcing departure from the USSR. And Article 4 required foreigners in the Soviet Union not merely to observe Soviet laws but also 'to behave with respect' towards the 'traditions and customs' of the Soviet people.

Optimists interpreted Article 4 as an instruction to get very drunk very often. That this was indeed a Soviet custom, and one that was being more scrupulously observed with each passing year, was demonstrated in a remarkable study by the American economist Professor Vladimir Treml, published by the Center of Alcohol Studies. By a number of ingenious devices Professor Treml was able to make reasonable estimates for a number of key items on which Soviet official statisticians are reticent. He concluded that in 1979 the average Soviet citizen over the age of 15 consumed the equivalent of 15·24 litres of pure alcohol. This was more than twice as much as in 1955 and accounted for 7·6 per cent of average earnings in state employment.

The Economy. Final data on national economic performance in 1981 were not available at the time of writing, but it was clear that it had been one of the poorest years for growth since World War II. Unusually, no official figure had been given by the year's end for grain production. The grain harvest was known to have been poor and was estimated at about 175 million tons—about 60 million tons less than the planners had hoped. The output of livestock products being approximately static, the farm sector as a whole could have experienced little or no increase in output.

The official Soviet expectation, towards the end of the year, was that national income utilized would be about 3 per cent up on 1980 (against a plan target of 3·4 per cent) and gross industrial output 3·4 per cent up (against a 4·1 target). Recalculated to fit Western definitions and valuation procedures, the growth rates of total output and of industrial sector output would come out somewhat lower than this.

During the year a final version of the 11th five-year plan (for 1981-85) was published. The main targets, set against the long-run slowdown of growth in the USSR, were generally considered to be over-ambitious, despite the fact that they were the lowest ever set in a Soviet five-year plan.

SOVIET ECONOMIC GROWTH, 1966-1985
(official data; per cent per annum growth rates)

	1966-70	1971-75	1976-80	1981-85 plan
National income utilized	7·1	5·1	3·8	3·4
Gross industrial output	8·5	7·4	4·5	4·7
Gross agricultural output[a]	3·9	2·4	1·7	2·5
Investment[a]	7·4	7·2	5·0	2·0
Output of main fuels[b]	5·2	5·4	4·2	3·1

(a) growth rate between five-year averages. (b) oil + gas + coal in coal fuel equivalent.
Sources: Narodnoe khozyaistvo SSSR v 1979 g.; Pravda 24 January and 20 November 1981.

Growth in 1981 was below the average rates aimed at for 1981-85. In particular, the output of primary fuels grew by less than 2 per cent. The final revisions to the 11th five-year plan accordingly trimmed planned investment spending to an exceptionally modest increase. President Brezhnev, speaking in November about the plan, described the 'food programme' as the central problem of the five-year plan, 'both in an economic and in a political sense'.

The leaders' worries about food supplies were reflected in a decree published in January which allowed more scope for private enterprise in Soviet agriculture. The tiny smallholdings allowed to Soviet households had been producing about a quarter of the total food production of the country. The decree removed the severe limitations on the numbers of livestock kept on such holdings for households which made contractual arrangements with state and collective farms to cooperate in livestock raising. This was described by an eminent Western specialist on Soviet agriculture as the most important concession to the private sector since 1935.

Shortages of manufactured consumer goods, as well as of food, remained a major irritant. The scope and nature of the shortages, especially in the less important cities, were illustrated in an article in the literary weekly, Literaturnaya gazeta. The paper conducted the experiment of sending a correspondent to Krasnodar (a city of over half a million people) without toothbrush, soap, razor blades, shaving cream, underclothes, socks or writing materials, and with instructions to attempt to buy these items on arrival. He reported that a full day's search in the shops of Krasnodar yielded none of these things.

In its trade with both West and East the Soviet Union experienced severe problems. For all the gaps in the West's 'post-Afghanistan' economic sanctions against Moscow, Soviet acquisition of grain and technology imports continued to be made more difficult and expensive than it would otherwise have been (see AR 1980, pp. 105-6). In April President Reagan lifted the partial embargo on US grain sales to the USSR, but by that time the Soviet hard-currency balance of payments was deteriorating. After the small surplus in trade with the West in 1980, the Soviet Union seemed to be heading in 1981 for a renewal of its long-running deficit. This had been comfortably covered in recent years by gold and arms sales for hard currency, but the gold market was down from its 1980 peak levels in most of 1981. It was estimated that some 150-200 tons of Soviet gold were sold during the year—a relatively large outflow. Ordering of Western equipment remained low until the autumn, when a huge and complex deal was made with a number of West German and other West European firms, in which some $10,000 million worth of pipe and pipeline equipment would be exchanged for deliveries of Soviet gas to Western Europe at a rate of about 3 million cubic feet a day in the late 1980s. US opposition to this deal failed to deflect West Germany from going ahead with it.

Meanwhile Poland's economic collapse put a strain on intra-Comecon trade while also facing Soviet policymakers with the possibility that Moscow might have to assist Poland with hard currency finance. During 1981 the USSR in effect extended credit to Poland in its bilateral trade. After the introduction of martial law in Poland in December President Reagan announced limited US economic sanctions against the USSR, which were to be extended if there was no return to liberalization in Poland. The extent of West European support for such measures was unclear, but at the end of the year there was some uncertainty about the future of the natural gas deal, and about East-West trade generally. Meanwhile it had been reported that the Soviet Union was planning to reduce its oil deliveries to Eastern Europe in 1982 in order to divert oil to hard-currency-earning exports to the West. Given the economic disarray of much of Eastern Europe, this looked a desperate expedient.

Dissent and emigration. Throughout the year the Soviet authorities showed signs of nervousness about possible unrest among the population. The fear seemed to be that the 'Polish disease' might spread. In April a Central Committee decree called for Party officials at all levels to take more account of complaints and other communications from the populace. At some time during 1980 or 1981 a practice known as 'open letter days' was initiated at Soviet workplaces. On these occasions local Party officials would respond to questions and complaints at a public meeting. As though such meetings were not enough of an innovation in themselves, some Soviet papers went so far as to describe turbulent meetings at which evasive replies provoked an outcry from the audience. The topics, according to the Soviet press, were bread-and-butter issues: bus services, gas supplies and the like. The message was clear: we, the Party, despite past evidence to the contrary, are always willing to listen to any problems you may have, and perhaps even to do something about them. The intention was apparently to forestall any development of the more disturbing complaints procedure represented by Solidarity.

The outside observer could see little indication that the Soviet people were in fact about to rise up and denounce their leaders. Consumer supplies might have improved very little if at all, but they had certainly undergone no sharp deterioration. There were unofficial reports in the summer of two strikes at a factory in Kiev, but such events had not been unknown in past years (see AR 1980, p. 99). The appearance was also reported of some clandestinely printed leaflets and *samizdat* articles expressing support for Solidarity. But such expressions appeared to be confined to the milieu of students and the intelligentsia.

Perhaps more worrying to the Soviet authorities was the continuation of demonstrations and disturbances arising out of nationalist sentiment in some of the republics. In late March there were two separate demonstrations in Tbilisi over the alleged russification of Georgian culture; demands were made that more Georgian history should be taught at Georgian educational institutions. In October there was an outburst of anti-Russian sentiment on the part of several hundred young Estonians after a basketball match.

The fortunes of the dissident groups concerned with human rights appeared to be at a low ebb. A number of arrests early in the year virtually wiped out the group which had been monitoring Soviet official abuses of psychiatry in repressing political dissent. The last well-known member of the group, Feliks Serebrov, was sentenced on 21 July to four years' hard labour, to be followed by five years of 'internal exile' for 'anti-Soviet agitation'. In September Anatoly Marchenko, well-known as the author of a horrifying account of an earlier spell in the labour camps (*My Testimony*), was arrested again and sentenced to ten years in the camps. The only conspicuous victory for the dissidents came at the end of the year. Andrei Sakharov, the most widely known and respected of the active dissidents remaining in the USSR, went on a hunger strike together with his wife Elena Bonner, in an attempt to force the Soviet authorities to issue an exit visa to Liza Alekseeva, the wife of Mrs Bonner's son. (The son was already in the US.) The hunger strike began in late November, and the Soviet authorities capitulated quickly, permitting Alekseeva to leave in mid-December.

Other would-be emigrants fared less well. The issuing of exit visas to Soviet Jews was sharply reduced as relations between Moscow and

Washington continued to cool. From a peak of 51,000 in 1979, the number allowed to leave had fallen to 21,000 in 1980. It was little over 8,000 in the first nine months of 1981.

Arts and sciences. The limits set by the censor in the arts continued to shift slightly back and forth, with no clear overall change. The international music festival held in Moscow in May aroused considerable local interest because it featured twentieth-century music. Avant-garde music, however, was not represented; the Soviet composer Tikhon Khrennikov continued to denounce it as an ideological device of anti-communists—a curious claim, presumably intended to show that anti-communism had run out of live ammunition. Another international festival, the Moscow film festival, in July, was used for a further hint (to foreigners) of liberalization. *Agony*, a new Soviet film about Rasputin, was shown uncut. It conveyed the daring idea that there were some decent people in the pre-revolutionary parliament, and scarcely mentioned the Bolsheviks. Huge crowds tried to get in to see it. The expectation was that it would be generally exhibited later on in the USSR, but in a heavily censored version.

Two well-known and very different Soviet novelists died in the course of the year. The more orthodox of the two was Boris Polevoi, who died on 12 July at the age of 73. He was best known for an extremely popular war novel, *The Story of a Real Man*, published in 1946. The other was Yuri Trifonov, who died on 28 March at the age of 55. Though not considered an 'underground' or 'dissident' writer, Trifonov had in his later works drawn a harsh and unflattering picture of a Moscow intelligentsia whose cynicism and self-seeking careerism were its most prominent characteristics.

The prolonged and extensive Soviet programme of manned space flight came to a halt on 26 May when a mission returned to earth from Salyut-6 after 75 days in space. Soviet spokesmen said there was to be a pause in the programme while the results of the past five years were assessed.

There were hints of a renewal of ideological controversy in genetics. In June speeches given earlier by the scientists A. D. Aleksandrov and N. P. Dubinin were published. The latter argued that it was un-marxist to stress nature rather than nurture in human development, and that genetic engineering was dangerous. Aleksandrov replied that these views were unscientific and (of course) un-marxist.

On 20 November a match for the world chess championship, held in Merano, Italy, ended in victory for the reigning Soviet champion, Anatoly Karpov, over the challenger, Soviet expatriate Viktor Korchnoi, by 6 games to 2.

FOREIGN POLICY.—*Relations with other socialist countries.* Soviet troops in Afghanistan settled to a long war of attrition against guerrilla forces which were divided but not easily conquered. A proposal from the European Community for talks about Afghanistan, without the participation of the official regime in Kabul, was rejected by the Soviet Union in early July.

By the end of the year Soviet official actions and statements on events in Poland seemed, in retrospect, to have followed a consistent line. For most of the year, while the contest between Solidarity and the Polish Party swayed back and forth, the Soviet authorities constantly urged the Polish leadership to act more firmly, and denounced at least part of Solidarity for aiming to dismantle 'socialism' in Poland.

Top-level consultations were frequent. On 13 January the Soviet First Deputy Minister of Defence, Marshal Kulikov, visited Warsaw. In late April, when preparations for the Polish Party Congress looked dangerously democratic in Moscow, the Politburo's senior ideologue, Mikhail Suslov, went to Warsaw. In August there was a Soviet home fixture when Kania and Jaruzelski had talks with President Brezhnev in the Crimea (see DOCUMENTS). It was reported that in December, just before the Polish authorities introduced martial law and arrested Solidarity's leaders, two Soviet Politburo members made what was intended to be a secret visit to Warsaw. They were Andrei Kirilenko and Yurii Andropov—the latter being the head of State Security.

Exactly what was said on these occasions was not revealed. The general line was probably indicated, however, by a letter from the Soviet Party Central Committee to its Polish counterpart in early June. It was probably not intended that the text of this letter should see the light of day, but it was leaked in Warsaw and then published on 12 June in *Pravda.* The language was sharp and masterful, and the message plain. The Polish leadership was accused of making 'endless concessions to anti-socialist forces'. The Polish press, radio and TV were described as being in the hands of 'the enemy'. Kania and Jaruzelski were criticized by name. They were said always to express agreement with the Soviet Party but then to do nothing. Poland could still be saved, the letter concluded, if healthy forces in the Polish Party mobilized.

To illustrate the meaning of the word 'mobilize', the Soviet leaders had arranged a Warsaw Pact land exercise close to Polish borders from 17 March to 7 April, and in September they set up the biggest Soviet naval exercise since World War II. The latter was held in the Baltic and involved some 25,000 troops carrying out landings on the Lithuanian and Latvian coast, which is not far from that of Poland.

When the 'healthy' forces in the Polish Party did mobilize in December, the official Soviet view was that the USSR was a mere bystander in what was a purely domestic Polish affair; if anybody was interfering in

Polish internal affairs it was the USA. This view was not popular in Washington. It was quite well received, however, in Bonn; the ink, after all, was scarcely dry on the biggest deal in the history of East-West trade, and it was primarily a Soviet-West German deal (see p. 105 above).

Relations with the non-communist world. During the year relations between the Soviet Union and the United States went from very bad to even worse. Relations with the West in general, epitomized by an apparent stalemate in the 'Helsinki review' talks in Madrid, were only a little better.

Moscow began the year with a useful card in its hand: the strong opposition in Western Europe to the deployment of additional Nato nuclear weapons there, and the associated strains and stresses within the Western alliance. By saying that the Soviet Union was willing to negotiate over armaments, while a hawkish and suspicious Administration in Washington held back from the idea, Mr Brezhnev stood to make friends and influence people. This, accordingly, was what he said, both in his speech at the Party Congress in February and in letters to Western governments in early March.

In mid-September, at a meeting with leaders of the British Labour Party, Mr Brezhnev specifically offered some reduction in the deployment of Soviet medium-range nuclear missiles in exchange for a Nato decision not to deploy Pershing and Cruise weapons in Europe. A similar message was also conveyed by the Soviet leader in an interview with *Der Spiegel*, published on 2 November.

By that time, however, the run of play had shifted somewhat against the USSR. A propaganda point was handed to the West when a rather aged Soviet 'Whiskey'-class submarine managed to beach itself on the Swedish coast near a Swedish naval base, on the night of 28 October. To Moscow's embarrassment, the Swedish authorities detained the vessel for nine days, interrogated the captain and claimed that the submarine was carrying nuclear weapons. Then, on 18 November, President Reagan announced that he, too, was prepared to do a deal over the reduction of nuclear weapons in Europe. It was almost certainly a different deal from the one that President Brezhnev was prepared to do, but the statement was nonetheless interpreted either as a victory for West European moderation over American belligerence or as a cunning blow to the official Soviet solar plexus, or both.*

After a long delay, therefore, Soviet–US talks on nuclear weapons were again on the agenda. This was still the case when the year ended, but the military crackdown in Poland had led to a further sharpening of

* The texts of an exchange of personal letters between President Brezhnev and President Reagan, and of President Brezhnev's speech in Bonn on 23 November about nuclear disarmament, are printed in the DOCUMENTS section below.

exchanges between Moscow and Washington, with the American President threatening that such talks would be suspended unless Poland returned to the more liberal state of chaos prevailing before the imposition of martial law.

Chapter 2

THE GERMAN DEMOCRATIC REPUBLIC—POLAND—
CZECHOSLOVAKIA—HUNGARY—ROMANIA—BULGARIA—
YUGOSLAVIA—ALBANIA—MONGOLIA

THE GERMAN DEMOCRATIC REPUBLIC

THE first intra-German summit for 11 years took place in December when the West German Chancellor, Herr Helmut Schmidt, paid a three-day visit to the East German communist leader, Herr Erich Honecker. On the third day came the news of the imposition of martial law in Poland. Herr Schmidt completed his visit according to plan and was warm in his praise of the good-neighbourly atmosphere of the meeting. 'It was clear to me,' he told an interviewer, 'that the events in Poland would have no consequences for our talks here.' Both sides calculated that reasonably good international relations could survive a dangerous international climate. The two leaders found some common ground in their assessment of the Polish problem since both were becoming increasingly reluctant to pay the cost of aiding Poland.

The arrangement known as the 'swing', under which the East Germans were getting an annual interest-free overdraft of up to DM 850 million on their trading account with West Germany, was extended by six months to the middle of 1982 until a new agreement had been reached. Herr Honecker was told that the deal would have to be seen in a general political context. In other words, the East Germans would have to make some concessions on issues of interest to West Germany. These included lowering the currency charge for West German visitors to East Germany, making family reunification easier and allowing younger East Germans to visit the West (hitherto, only pensioners had been allowed out).

During the year the citizens of East Germany were assured by their leaders that despite the international economic recession their living standards would continue to rise. At the conference of the Socialist Unity (Communist) Party in April a relatively rosy picture of the East German economy was painted, rosier indeed than was justified. The Prime Minister, Herr Willi Stoph, promised that more and better consumer goods would be available and that basic food prices and rents would remain low. In fact East Germany was facing big problems. State subsidies to hold down consumer prices were growing fast, and were expected to reach an annual rate of DM 300,000 million by 1986. Imports were costing more—in precious foreign currency. East Germany was called upon to step up financial aid to Poland, and the Soviet Union demanded that the East Germans make a still bigger contribution to the Warsaw Pact's defence.

East Germany's planners decreed that trade with Western countries must be increased, to earn the money to pay for the import of new technologies. But Western experts considered the chances of a major East German trade expansion to be limited. The country's present volume of trade could be maintained only by lowering prices. By looking on the bright side, the Party leadership was implying to the public that Poland's economic ills would not be allowed to spread to East Germany. The Party conference was a demonstration that the East German leaders had the situation well under control. Nonetheless they were plainly afraid that the desire for freedom might be catching, so they expressed themselves to be much in favour of a tough line against Polish dissidence.

East Germany weighed in heavily on the side of the Soviet Union in the debate about medium-range nuclear missiles. The East German case was that the United States had been forced by the pressure of world opinion to come to the negotiating table. The Government in East Berlin argued that Nato's concept of a 'zero option' was quite different from most people's understanding of the term. The aim of the United States was to cause the Soviet Union to dismantle its SS-20 missiles without replacing them, while America dispensed solely with the planned deployment of Pershing II and Cruise missiles in Western Europe. This, said the East Germans, left Western Europe with some 700 US forward-based systems—weapons excluded from America's idea of a zero option.

Among East German citizens there was considerable sympathy for the West German peace movement, and in particular for suggestions that Europe should be declared a nuclear-free zone. In an open letter to the Soviet leader, Mr Leonid Brezhnev, during his visit to Bonn in November, the East German dissident, Herr Robert Havemann, wrote that 36 years after the war it was urgently necessary to conclude peace treaties and to withdraw 'occupying troops' from both parts of Germany. The position of West Berlin must be secured, he added, and the superpowers would have to guarantee that an aggressive military potential would never again be created in Germany. 'How we Germans then solve our own national problem would be a matter for us. The solution would certainly not be more frightening than the risk of nuclear war.'

Herr Honecker paid a state visit to Japan in May. He had been fishing a long time for an invitation, and it proved to be worth waiting for. There was business to be done. Herr Honecker took with him an impressive shopping-list, and agreements required signature. But, more important for Herr Honecker, the visit was a political event, East Germany's coming out into the capitalist world, a demonstration of acceptance over and above mere diplomatic recognition. He had set a foot gingerly in that world before, but his reception in Tokyo was a unique experience. Herr Honecker spent a lot of money in Japan, mostly on heavy industrial plant and technological equipment. The East Germans also bought 10,000 Japanese cars to help fill a gap in the delivery of Russian models.

Trade between East Germany and Japan was flourishing, and the East Germans were probably happy to reduce their dependence on their West German neighbours a little. With memories of the Soviet invasion of Afghanistan fading rapidly, Japan was trying to build up trade with the Comecon countries, and hoped that Herr Honecker would put in a good word with the Russians on their behalf. The West Germans were somewhat jealous about Herr Honecker's reception, the trumpet fanfares, the guards of honour, the meeting with Emperor Hirohito. And an eyebrow or two was raised at the award to Herr Honecker of an honorary doctorate of law for his work 'in the cause of peace'. But the West Germans comforted themselves by saying that these were expressions of Japanese regard for the Germans generally, in East and West.

The East German Government continued to demand that West Germany should recognize a separate East German nationality. In addition it insisted that the respective missions in the two German states should be upgraded to the rank of embassies. Herr Honecker said it was only a question of time before a solution to this problem was found, and he was encouraged in this view by the statements of some Social Democrat politicians in West Germany. However, the official West German position remained unchanged: that German citizenship was indivisible.

POLAND

What had begun as Poland's year of liberty ended dramatically in bloodshed and repression. The first-ever military coup in a communist-ruled country saw martial law imposed. The ferocity, scale and precision of the crackdown produced a traumatic shock.

The country's politics were characterized by repeated waves of dangerous tensions, broken by short periods of peace and negotiations between the Government and the independent union Solidarity. The union was increasingly forced into contentious political activism by the regime's paralysis, its procrastination in implementing the August 1980 agreements (see AR 1980, pp. 111 and 505-10) and its failure over the collapsing economy. The Communist Party—disintegrating and bitterly divided on how to deal with Solidarity—played into the hands of the union's radicals by retreating under pressure before attempting to regain lost ground.

Strikes proliferated in January and February, demanding implementation of the agreements with Solidarity. Millions refused to work on Saturday 24 January. Wildcat strikes involving 700,000 workers and students spread in nine southern provinces in protest against unlawful dismissal of workers and against Party members' privileges, demanding dismissal of corrupt and inefficient officials and punishment of those responsible.

Party leader Kania accused Solidarity of becoming a 'political opposition'. Mr Lech Walesa, back from Rome where the Pope embraced him and counselled 'courage and moderation' (15 January), toured the provincial trouble-spots defusing tensions. An episcopal letter, while condemning the use of force, insisted on strict implementation of the August 1980 agreements. For the first time bishops helped directly in settling local disputes between social groups and the authorities.

In an unprecedented move at the Party plenum (9 February) Defence Minister General Jaruzelski became Prime Minister, replacing Mr Pinkowski. Two Deputy Premiers were dropped and a well-known journalist, Mr Rakowski, was appointed Deputy Premier in charge of relations with trade unions. Jaruzelski promised to consult Solidarity on new laws, warned that counter-revolution would be stopped, and called for a three-month moratorium on strikes. This was agreed by Solidarity. In Moscow Kania and Jaruzelski assured President Brezhnev that they would act quickly to overcome 'anarchy and disarray'.

The Government's draft labour code accepted the right to strike, the principle of organizational pluralism and partnership with the workers in managing the economy. After long sit-ins by students, an Independent Association of Polish Students was accepted by the Government, together with increased university autonomy.

In March the strike truce was broken when 500,000 workers protested against a massive militia raid in Bydgoszcz, where Solidarity members participating in a borough council meeting were beaten up and ejected. The Pope appealed for 'patience and perseverance'. Cardinal Wyszynski met General Jaruzelski. The use of force—believed to be organized by Party hardliners—was condemned in the Walesa-Rakowski negotiations, which set up six working groups to discuss jointly the main points of conflict. A general strike was averted. The press and Walesa accused the Government of being dilatory and acting only under coercion.

Kania warned that the system would not be changed in a 'social-democratic direction'. Solidarity prevented workers' redundancies until the Government produced a plan for economic stabilization. After several sit-ins the authorities recognized the private peasants' independent trade union Rural Solidarity. After further warning strikes Solidarity won the right to have its own radio and TV studios and air-time on the state network. The first issue of *Solidarity Weekly* appeared on 3 April. In Warsaw, Soviet Party theoretician Suslov accused Poles of revisionism, and hardline Politburo member Olszowski talked about 'anarchy'. The Grunwald Patriotic Association, supported by Party activists, blamed Jews for Poland's ills. In 40 provinces grassroots Party members organized networks of 'forums' or 'horizontal structures' demanding internal Party democracy and changes in the leadership. They attacked hardliners and the distortion of information policy. Only the Katowice forum in Silesia produced a neo-Stalinist, harsh resolution against 'creeping counter-revolution'. This was condemned by Kania but praised by Moscow.

On 28 May Cardinal Wyszynski, the venerated spiritual leader of Poland, died (see OBITUARY). Funeral services were relayed by all the media. Bishop Glemp, Wyzsynski's private secretary, succeeded him as Primate of Poland on 7 July.

In April meat and butter rationing was introduced. Most foods and many industrial consumer goods quickly followed. Shops were empty, yet eye-witness evidence confirmed that food stocks were deliberately withheld in state warehouses.

Between February and October extensive intermittent Warsaw Pact land and sea manoeuvres along Poland's borders involved up to 200,000 troops and 100 Soviet ships. Harsh Soviet press warnings multiplied. The Polish Party plenum (9 June) discussed a Soviet Central Committee letter indicating the need for a change of leadership, and condemning the Polish Party for withdrawing in the face of Solidarity-led counter-revolution. Kania endorsed the Soviet criticisms but stated that 'renewal' could not be safely reversed. Rakowski warned: 'The Party had shed blood at Poznan in 1956, on the Baltic coast in 1970 and it would not survive a third tragedy.' Soviet efforts to unseat Kania only strengthened his position despite strong attacks by hardliners Olszowski and Grabski. Meanwhile Walesa openly attacked Solidarity radicals, toured the country appealing for moderation and protested against anti-Soviet slogans spread by 'provocateurs'.

The emergency Party Congress on 14 July failed to produce a comprehensive programme. It stressed 'socialist renewal' and struggle in defence of socialism. For the first time 200 Central Committee members were elected secretly; 183 newcomers included Solidarity members. Seven out of 11 outgoing Politburo members were dropped: hardliners Grabski, Zabinski, Moczar and reformists Fiszbach, Jagielski, Klasa, Jablonski. The new Politburo of 15 included Kania, Jaruzelski, Olszowski, Barcikowski, Czyrek and unknown people—a rough balance between reformers and hardliners. Kania was elected leader by a two-thirds majority over Barcikowski in a secret ballot. Jaruzelski promised cooperation with Solidarity but stressed his 'trust in the army' to 'save the nation from catastrophe'. The Party lost over half its members: a million joined Solidarity, 70,000 were purged for corruption and 200,000 simply left.

Throughout July and August 'hunger marches' occurred in several cities in protest against food shortages. Solidarity insisted, without success, on supervising the production and distribution of food. The economy was disintegrating. Although on average only one hour per worker was lost through strikes, factories were operating at 60 per cent capacity for lack of components, spare parts and vital materials. National income decreased by 15 per cent, industrial production by 18 per cent, coal extraction by 28 per cent; $25,000 million were blocked in unfinished investments and Poland's debt to the West rose to $27,000 million. Repayment of $2,400 million due in 1981 was rescheduled provided that $500 million interest was paid by 28 December.

In July the Government's draft economic reform restricted central planning to outlining strategic goals. The independent, self-governing and self-financing enterprise became the basic economic unit. Laws on workers' self-government and enterprises, on censorship and on education were later passed by the Sejm but without some important Solidarity proposals.

Walesa warned that confrontation was unavoidable in the absence of political solutions, i.e. institutional recognition of the organizational pluralism already achieved. Harmful local strikes, he said, could break Solidarity. In the Crimea Brezhnev instructed Kania to change the course of events in Poland (see DOCUMENTS).

The first Solidarity Congress met twice in Gdansk on 5 and 26 September. Ten million members and 30,000 activists in 44 branches were represented. Solidarity described itself as a 'social movement' pledged to save the country from ruin by 'restructuring the state and the economy on a democratic basis, an all-round social initiative but without violating international alliances'. The programme provided for free parliamentary and local elections; separation of political authority from economic administration by creating a Social Council for National Economy; philosophical, political, social and cultural pluralism and 'honest and loyal dialogue' with the authorities. Walesa was elected chairman of Solidarity's national commission of twenty by 55 per cent of votes over his radical opponents Jurczyk, Gwiazda, Rulewski. He warned the radicals against trying to replace the authorities, saying that the ensuing totalitarianism would be worse than the present one. The basic disagreement was between those like Walesa seeking agreements to stabilize the situation, and others who advocated continuous pressurizing of the regime lest Solidarity were destroyed by being sucked into the power structure.

The Soviet ambassador in Warsaw violently protested to Kania against the anti-socialist and anti-Soviet 'orgy' at the Congress. Economic sanctions were threatened and the Party was accused of weakness and indecision. The Politburo condemned Solidarity for threatening bloodshed and counter-revolution. Jaruzelski warned that troops would stamp out anarchy and anti-Sovietism.

At the Party plenum on 18 October Kania resigned. Jaruzelski, elected First Secretary, spoke in favour of dialogue but demanded renegotiation of the August 1980 agreements with Solidarity and suspension of the right to strike. Solidarity rejected any renegotiation but agreed to review some thousand local agreements.

The military factor had been creeping in for some time. Military operational teams were sent to parishes and towns to 'help local apparatus' and to 'monitor' observance of law and order. Since February nine generals had been appointed in high Party and government positions. Jaruzelski repeatedly warned that the army might be used. Military service was extended for some conscripts.

On 4 November Walesa met Jaruzelski and Archbishop Glemp. Negotiations between Solidarity and the Government on the formation of a Front of National Accord were vitiated by mutual mistrust. After repeated appeals from Walesa and the Primate strikes began dying down. Nonetheless peasants continued sit-ins and 100,000 students protested against the Education Bill.

On 2 December the militia stormed the Warsaw fire brigade academy and ejected occupying students. The mass media, supervised by Olszowski, accused Solidarity of adventurism, counter-revolution and striving for power. Harassment of union members increased. In Radom, the Solidarity national commission threatened a 24-hour general strike if Parliament passed the emergency powers sought by Jaruzelski. Walesa accused the regime of bad faith and cheating. Polish radio played taped extracts from Solidarity's Radom discussions as evidence that the union wanted confrontation. In letters to the Sejm, Archbishop Glemp opposed any government emergency powers. He invited Jaruzelski and Walesa to another meeting. The Prime Minister declined. The Sejm threatened to reject Jaruzelski's emergency laws.

On 11 December Marshal Kulikov, commander of the Warsaw Pact forces, arrived in Warsaw for the fifth time in 1981. On 12 December in Gdansk Solidarity's national commission called for an immediate general strike if emergency powers were introduced; it demanded a new national power-sharing agreement with the Party, a referendum on confidence in the Government, free elections and the guaranteeing of Soviet military interests. At the end of the session, by which time communications with the outside world had been cut, a despairing Walesa told radicals: 'Now you've got what you've been looking for.'

On 13 December at midnight martial law was imposed by Jaruzelski as chairman of a Military Council of National Salvation consisting of 20 high-ranking officers. In a comprehensive crackdown the country was sealed off within and without. A curfew was imposed from 10 pm to 6 am. All organizations and institutions, including Solidarity, were suspended. The Party vanished and the power vacuum was filled by the army. All major cities were cordoned off with armour and artillery, and key plants militarized. In a broadcast on 13 December Jaruzelski spoke of a country on 'the brink of an abyss of civil war'. He promised there would be no return to the pre-August 1980 days and that the economic and democratic renewal would continue once Poland had been 'normalized' (see DOCUMENTS).

Militia and internal security forces—not the army—applied draconian regulations. Solidarity's premises were occupied and files confiscated. In the first 18 days of military rule, according to official information, 5,069 were interned, including 70 per cent of Solidarity leaders and 99 members of the former Party leadership, including Gierek and Jaroszewicz. Over 300 workers were sentenced by military courts to imprisonment of up to seven years for organizing strikes, and 33,000 others faced 'minor' charges. The Party and local government were massively purged. Independent sources reported 40,000 workers, academics, journalists, intellectuals and clergy interned in 49 detention centres, to which eventually priests and food parcels were admitted. Walesa, under house arrest in a government villa outside Warsaw, refused to talk to the military without his advisers and Archbishop Glemp. He was visited by Bishop Dabrowski, who went to Rome to brief the Pope. The Pope's envoy, Archbishop Poggi, arrived in Warsaw to assess the situation with Glemp and Jaruzelski.

In an appeal smuggled out by Walesa he called on 15 December for strikes or passive resistance but avoidance of bloodshed. The Church, supported by the Pope, spoke of a 'nation terrorized by military force' and appealed for peace to avoid a 'fratricidal war'. It also demanded freedom for internees, for Solidarity and Walesa as an essential element in any return to a balanced social existence.

For two weeks occupational strikes in 500 plants and mines, and street demonstrations, spread in the country, particularly in Silesia, Lodz, Lublin, Warsaw, the Baltic coast, Cracow and Wroclaw. They were broken by massive security forces using armour and tear gas. The militia opened fire. Official sources gave the number of killed as nine, with 400 injured. Independent sources spoke of over 200 killed and over 1,000 injured.

Towards the end of the year Solidarity reorganized itself as an underground network, circulating information sheets, calling for passive resistance and go-slow at work—in most cases successfully applied. Officially the situation was described as calm. Pledges of loyalty were demanded from workers. Food suddenly appeared in the shops and the curfew was lifted for Christmas and New Year's eve. Schools and universities remained closed.

In his New Year message the Pope fully supported Solidarity as a worldwide workers' heritage. Solidarity in Poland reminded soldiers that they were Poles who should put conscience before orders.

Thus Jaruzelski crushed active resistance by massive force but did not propose any alternative. The Military Council was divided as to what to do next.

CZECHOSLOVAKIA

The country's own economy and the crisis in Poland were the main preoccupations of the Czechoslovak authorities in 1981.

It soon transpired that the sixth five-year plan (1976-80) had fared badly, the growth rates being under-fulfilled by a quarter or more. Most experts accepted that an about-turn from massive investment in new productive capacity to intensive modernization became imperative. A 'Set of Measures' to restructure priorities and improve cumbersome planning came into effect from 1 January, but soon proved inadequate to reform the inert economic mechanisms and attitudes. Plan compliance in 1981 actually lagged behind the paltry performance of the previous year. Despite obfuscation of statistics it had to be admitted that the year's economic growth barely touched the half-point mark. Since the population increased by around 0·6 per cent, the per capita growth was zero. Some branches of industry, such as the building trade, chalked up negative rates, and others, particularly the exporting industries, scored bad failures in key programmes. Agriculture slumped by over 3 per cent, the grain-for-fodder sector falling short of plan by the gigantic figure of 1·6 million tonnes.

Poland failed to deliver the contracted amounts of coal as well as other merchandise, including components for cooperative ventures, and Romania interrupted the agreed supplies of electric power in the second half of the year after its economic situation had gravely deteriorated. The 18·8 million tonnes of Soviet oil bought in 1981 probably cost the Czechoslovaks $20 a barrel, over five times the price they paid in 1970. It became clear that in 1982 Soviet oil deliveries would be 10 per cent below the expected level, not only because Moscow wanted to sell its oil in the West for worthier currency but also because the Czechoslovaks could no longer afford to pay. For ideological reasons and with an eye to Poland, the Government rejected the option of borrowing in the West, and its total indebtedness stayed under $4,000 million. Instead a programme of severe austerity, public expenditure cuts and tightly controlled savings was ushered in.

The targets for the seventh five-year plan (1981-5) were twice scaled down during the year. Even so, the quinquennial economic directive remained in the form of a guideline which was to be further adjusted in 1982. Five-year planning had in fact lost its practical significance, because even the goals now cited were obviously beyond reach, the economy being governed by emergency decrees and a sequence of downward adjustments to what remained of plan quotas. The year saw the beginning of the end of the unwritten social contract accepted after the defeat of the reformist Prague Spring in 1968, whereby the population abdicated political aspiration in exchange for material well-being. The Government found it increasingly hard to keep its side of a bargain which had earlier suited it so well.

On the internal market the lists of goods in short supply were getting longer and price rises accelerating. Petrol, diesel and heating oil jumped by 25-30 per cent. Unpublicized increases continued, while prices of staple foods were kept down for political reasons, again through fear that the public might react to a rapid decline in living standards as the Poles had done. On the whole, however, the Czechoslovak consumer remained immeasurably better off than his Polish counterpart. The crisis had bitten industry and farming, but the direct impact on the consumer was as yet cushioned by the throttling-down of heavy industry growth. Regime spokesmen warned, nevertheless, that things could not go on in the same way much longer: if 1981 was 'a complicated year', they said, 1982 would be still worse. Federal Prime Minister Lubomír Štrougal predicted a period of 'great trial'.

The Communist Party's answer consisted of the imposition of tighter criteria of performance, coupled with a saturation campaign designed to mobilize the public for greater exertion. A fully-fledged market-orientated reform remained beyond the ideological pale. At its 16th Congress in April, the Party doggedly insisted that its policies had been right all through the 1970s and would be pursued further without any basic change. It was the economic managers who were charged with failing the leadership's expectations; not a word was said about the inadequacy of the command system itself.

Of developments in Poland, the Czechoslovak authorities and media were even harsher critics than Moscow itself. According to Prague, the counter-revolutionary cabals in Poland ought to have been severely censured and combated long before the military took action in December. The reformist threat to Czechoslovak communism in 1968 was often cited as a lesson for Polish communists. The Polish workers' militancy did not spill over into public or trade union attitudes in Czechoslovakia. Observers noted popular disapproval of what was represented as the Poles' attempt to have a good time without actually working for it. Prague rendered support to Polish hardliners not only in criticizing their opponents and by giving them publicity in the media but also, so rumours had it, more tangibly in offering them printing facilities in Czechoslovakia when Solidarity controlled Polish printing shops and when the state of emergency was being secretly prepared. Czechoslovak-Polish trade declined by 7 per cent in volume—10 per cent in Czechoslovak imports and 4·3 per cent in exports. Tourist traffic between the two countries was twice restricted during the year, first by limiting currency allocations and then by making tourism dependent on written invitations endorsed by Czechoslovak police. Prague radio began to beam three hours of viscerally orthodox broadcasts to Poland in April. General Jaruzelski's 'state of war' was greeted with acclaim and relief as a means whereby the Party was restoring its leading role.

The surviving human rights movement expressed solidarity with Polish endeavours to change the system of communist governance. The dissidents suffered, however, another blow when in April the police made the discovery of a French van bringing in prohibited political litera-ture the excuse for a new crackdown. A number of activists were de-tained, of whom seven were still in gaol at the end of the year, awaiting trial. Several vicious sentences were meted out, including 7½ years (reduced on appeal by two years) to Rudolf Battěk, whose one offence was writing to socialist statesmen in Western Europe.

The authorities had to acknowledge the existence of a religious up-surge, especially among the younger generation. They led campaigns against the so-called 'secret church' of believers, priests and even unoffi-cially ordained bishops who transgressed the narrow channels tolerated by the state. A number of such persons were sent to gaol, for example two priests and four laymen who had operated a clandestine printing press for religious *samizdat*. The issuing of uncensored texts through self-help continued in the non-religious field as well. Novels, poems, essays and even scholarly treatises on philosophical, historical and economic subjects circulated widely without the government's imprima-tur.

The two ritual events that marked internal politics were the 16th Communist Party Congress in April, to which Leonid Brezhnev's pre-sence added some lustre, and the central and local government elections in June in which nearly 100 per cent of votes were cast for single-list can-didates. The real significance of the year, however, lay in the economic tensions and the orthodox criticism of Poland, rather than in these mani-festations of stale convention.

In the only personal changes at the top of the establishment, in June, Miloš Jakeš was advanced to the position of highest economic overseer in the Praesidium and two of his colleagues were demoted. Persistence of tenure was still the name of the personnel game.

President and Party leader Gustav Husák travelled to Libya,

Ethiopia and South Yemen in September, but his planned visit to Austria was put off because relations between the two countries worsened once again. The Prague regime boasted of having sent (and reclaimed) a secret service agent to collect information in Austria, mainly about Czechoslovak emigrés. The Austrians did not receive this kindly. High-level visitors in Prague included, besides Brezhnev, the Romanian leader Nicolae Ceauşescu (in May), Babrak Karmal from Afghanistan (in June), and Erich Honecker (in November-December). Czechoslovakia participated in the developing tourist and trade war in Eastern Europe with new restrictions on travel to Poland, Hungary and Yugoslavia and prohibitions on its own citizens from taking many items with them on a foreign holiday, including all food, beverages and cigarettes.

HUNGARY

The two main concerns of Hungarian policy-makers and people in 1981 were no different from those of the previous year—fear of possible negative effects of the crisis in Poland and anxiety about Hungary's economy. Those two themes ran through virtually every major issue to arise and prompted two sometimes contradictory responses. On the one hand, the authorities took care to ensure that the Polish 'virus' of demands for independent trade unions did not infect the Hungarian working class. To this effect, they argued that independent unions were superfluous in Hungary, that they did nothing to improve the economic situation in Poland (and thus by analogy would not help in Hungary either) and that, in any event, the root cause of the Polish crisis was that Poles were idle and workshy. There is some evidence that the last argument was not uninfluential, in as much as many Hungarians were afraid that their standard of living would be impaired by the repercussions of the Polish crisis. At the same time, there were signs of tightening up.

At the 24th Congress of the National Council of Trade Unions (held in December 1980), the secretary-general, Sándor Gáspár, asserted that in Hungary unions were 'independent organizationally and functionally' of the Party, that they enjoyed an equal status *vis-à-vis* the state administration and that the state accepted that workers did need protection. He also dropped a hint that the appointment of enterprise directors from the shop floor was under consideration, although this did not materialize. In general, Gáspár's was a sophisticated restatement of the standard policy of the Hungarian Party.

A concrete measure which probably had the Polish events as its background was the decision to speed up the introduction of the five-day working week. This was initially very popular, but when it emerged that enterprises were expected to maintain the same level of output and the same plan targets, and that in actual practice workers would still be expected to work for 44 hours a week (over five days instead of six), there was considerable resentment. In effect, this measure was used to increase productivity, while being sold to the population as a liberalizing step.

What was possibly most striking about Hungary's policy-makers was their determination not to be deflected from their adopted strategy of making the country's economy more efficient. To this end, several price increases were introduced, regardless of the fall in the standard of living. Indeed, in 1981, for the third year running, real wages either fell or stagnated. The plan for 1982 projected only a small increase. This was an indication of the party's political courage, in that higher prices had been responsible for the destabilization of Poland and the Hungarian consumer's dissatisfaction with austerity had no genuine legitimate political channels of expression. A price rise in January and February 1981 affected some foodstuffs, newspapers, petrol, postal service and telephones. A further increase, in meat prices, was decreed in June. The deterioration in the standard of living was indicated by the fact that, whereas in 1975 a kilogram of pork had been earned in 2·75 hours (average), by 1981 this cost had risen to 4 hours.

Foreign trade, on which Hungary was heavily dependent, continued to pose serious problems, especially trade with the dollar area (i.e. the West). Western bankers began to feel that Hungary was close to its credit limit, especially in the light of the Polish debacle and Romania's failure to meet its obligations on time. Hungarian leaders were very concerned to keep up debt service payments and achieved this largely at the cost of consumption growth. At the same time, Hungarian spokesmen stressed the calm and orderly nature of the country's development, in order, presumably, to reassure Western creditors. The decision to make the currency, the forint, 'convertible' had the same function. Since convertibility applied exclusively to certain commercial transactions and the authorities retained their power of administrative regulation of international exchanges, it was no more than a nominal or façade move.

The reform of economic management in the direction of diminished central control proceeded slowly. It took two forms. The Hungarians accepted that the private sector would have a greater role to play and encouraged entrepreneurs to undertake a wider range of activities. That would have the added benefit of bringing some of the unregistered or secondary economy under state supervision. Secondly, planners recognized that the growing concentration of the size of manufacturing enterprises—these had halved in number between 1960 and 1980 through mergers—had not brought the hoped-for results. Hence the virtues of smallness were rediscovered and numerous forms of small-scale enterprises were made legal with the aim of deconcentration.

Tightening-up was restricted to the political sphere and was more a matter of mood than of concrete measures. The party leader, János Kádár, made two rather militant speeches in order to warn 'the enemies of communism' that 'no one would be permitted to fool around with the fate of the people and the nation'. This was backed up by a strikingly hardline article in the party journal *Pártélet*, which called for greater vigilance against non-marxist ideas, especially among intellectuals.

The particular target of these warnings was the small opposition, which remained active. The contributors to a large-scale *samizdat* volume dedicated to the deceased opposition political thinker István Bibó were warned that there were limits to the party's patience. The attempt to establish a bookshop selling *samizdat* works was foiled by the security police. Dismissals of opposition activists and restrictions on their travel abroad continued. But there were no arrests or trials in 1981, albeit there was fear in opposition circles that a major clamp-down might follow the military coup in Poland.

ROMANIA

Romania suffered a second consecutive year of food shortages, even more severe than the previous one. All basic foodstuffs were affected, including meat, sugar, edible oil, rice and flour and finally bread. By September an atmosphere of panic had gripped the population, with people buying any food in sight in any amounts. The Government retaliated with a decree punishing by up to five years' imprisonment the hoarding of food, vaguely defined as having amounts in excess of the needs of a family for one month. Rationing was introduced throughout the country, mostly by setting limits to the amounts purchased at one time. A patchy situation resulted, some regions being badly affected, others less. In the capital Bucharest a degree of order was re-established by mid-November, all inhabitants receiving a fixed monthly amount of sugar and oil from a shop where they registered for this purpose; and there was some increase in supplies, with many items at significantly higher prices. Queuing for food remained a dominant feature of everyday life.

The mood of the country turned to open discontent and several violent incidents were reported. In one of them, miners in the Motru valley were reported to have attacked with stones a visiting high government official, possibly President Nicolae Ceauşescu himself. Another in the town of Giurgiu on the Danube apparently resulted in injury to several policemen and the death of a local Communist Party secretary. It was suspected that many more incidents had taken place, particularly involving peasants trying to buy food in the towns. A decree issued in the autumn restricted these purchases. In particular, the authorities were trying to put an end to the widespread use of cheap bread as animal feed, which had led to a bread shortage.

A moderate increase in acquisition prices for agricultural produce was announced in December. But the main approach of the government to the food problem, embodied in a law on regional self-supply which was passed in November, was to provide that all counties as well as smaller communities should cater for most of their needs from locally available resources, and should receive missing items from central reserves only in exchange for items they produced in excess.

Industry did not fare much better. In November the country's four main industries, coal, oil, metallurgy and petrochemicals, were officially reported to have shown grave shortcomings in 1981. At a meeting of the Central Committee of the Communist Party, President Ceauşescu criticized all the state economic departments for very severe deficiencies and maintained that the plans drawn up by the leadership could have been implemented but that the determination to do so was not there. This and other signs indicated that the administration and the workforce were alike suffering from apathy and disappointment, and that the practice of falsifying production figures to cover up for failures had reached a peak. In a case which was given much publicity, three top mining officials were dismissed for having reported the delivery by one mining centre of over one million tons of coal which had not in fact been produced.

In a move towards more realistic planning, the overall growth target of the Romanian economy was reduced to about five per cent for 1982 and coal production targets were also brought nearer to the real possibilities.

These domestic economic difficulties were reflected in the country's foreign trade problems. Romanian industry continued to depend heavily on energy and raw materials imported from the convertible currency area, and because the world market for industrial products was in recession this expenditure had to be balanced with exports of food and agricultural produce to a degree higher than the country could afford. In a statement in November, Ceauşescu made it clear that all negotiations with the Soviet Union, the other Soviet bloc countries and Comecon, aimed at securing supplies of energy and raw materials from that area, had failed and that in 1982 Romania would have to import more of these items than before for hard currency. The country's hard-currency reserves were earmarked strictly for the minimum necessary imports to keep industry going. But many delays of payments due in 1981 alerted the Western banking community to the danger that a major problem in Romania's foreign debt might be in the making. Faced with alarming reports in the Western press on this subject Romania settled in the autumn most of its current debts, but not without leaving an uneasy sense of more trouble to come. Anxiety over Polish debt weighed heavily in Western bankers' assessment of Romania's credit.

The crisis in Poland was probably the Romanian leaders' chief foreign policy concern. It was feared on the one hand that the Polish events, rooted in the same kind of economic inefficiency and mismanagement as Romania suffered from, might spark off some form of discontent in the country; and the other that a Soviet invasion of Poland, being incompatible with Romania's own foreign policy, would worsen its relations with the rest of the Soviet bloc, while damaging its links with the West within a general worsening of East-West relations. Reporting on Polish events was kept to a minimum, while official pronouncements indicated that Romania expected the Polish Government to put a halt to the rise of Solidarity. General Jaruzelski's military takeover was greeted in Bucharest with satisfaction.

Few foreign policy initiatives were taken by Romania in 1981. One was a peace campaign in November-December whereby President Ceauşescu tried to define a Romanian position on the issue of medium-range nuclear missiles in Europe and suggested that smaller European states should become involved in the US-Soviet talks on this issue in Geneva. Mr Ceauşescu's initial attitude was one of approximately equal sympathy towards the Soviet and American positions and of cautious approval for the proposals made by President Reagan. Subsequently, however, the formulation of the Romanian position was subtly changed, so as to match almost entirely the Soviet negotiating stand. This coincided with a visit to Bucharest by Soviet Foreign Minister Gromyko and suggested that Romania had become more vulnerable to Soviet pressure than before.

BULGARIA

For Bulgaria 1981 was more than anything else 'the Jubilee Year'; the 1300th anniversary of the Bulgarian state was marked by events throughout the year, the main celebrations taking place in October. The 90th anniversary of the Bulgarian Communist Party (BCP) was celebrated in August and the 70th birthday of Todor Zhivkov, the BCP's leader since 1954, on 7 September.

In contrast to these festivities, 1981 also witnessed the unexpected death, on 21 July, of Zhivkov's daughter Lyudmila, aged 39, Politburo member and chairwoman of the Committee on Culture. A controversial and fascinating personality, she was both hated as an embodiment of nepotism and admired for her unorthodox ideas and relatively liberal management of the cultural scene.

The BCP's 12th Congress, followed by general elections and the forming of a new Government, in April and June respectively, brought few but significant personnel changes. The most important was the appointment of a new Prime Minister, Grisha Filipov (aged 62), to replace Stanko Todorov (61) who had headed the Government since 1971. Todorov became Chairman of the National Assembly. Filipov was believed to be more closely connected with Moscow than his predecessor.

The BCP Congress gave Zhivkov, until then First Secretary, the title of Secretary-General. It reduced the number of Politburo members from 14 to 12, eliminating 84-year-old General Ivan Mihailov and the ailing Tano Tsolov, but re-electing once again 83-year-old Tsola Dragoycheva. Politburo candidate members were reduced from five to three and CC secretaries increased from eight to ten.

Other personnel changes in 1981 included the election, in March, of a new trade union chairman, Petar Dyulgerov (52), until then a BCP CC secretary, and, in December, of a new first secretary of the Komsomol, Stanka Shopova (27). The Bulgarian Agrarian Union held its congress in May without any major changes in its ruling bodies.

The Party Congress approved 'theses' on the socio-economic development in 1981-85 and until 1990, on the basis of which the eighth five-year plan (1981-85) was approved by the National Assembly in December. The main growth targets were somewhat higher than in most other East European countries, but lower than those of the previous five-year plan and also slightly lower than those outlined by the 'theses'.

The predominant feature in economic policy in 1981 was the effort to improve the supply of goods and services to the population, in order both to avert developments like those in Poland and to present a picture of prosperity in the anniversary year. Indeed, provisions improved, especially of fruit and vegetables, but various items remained in short or irregular supply.

To support these efforts, the promotion of the 'self-sufficiency' system in staple foods continued, with increased emphasis on the role of personal plots of the population and auxiliary plots of enterprises. Industrial enterprises were obliged to produce consumer goods out of surplus and waste materials. Bigger enterprises were encouraged to open trade and service facilities for their workers. Despite all efforts the standard of living hardly improved, and even a risk of an adverse development was indirectly admitted when Zhivkov pledged (in October) 'not to let the standard of living of our people deteriorate'.

The application of the new economic mechanism initiated in 1978, and in particular the organization and remuneration of labour by brigades, continued. In December a new decree on 'improvement of the economic mechanism' was announced, to come into force early in 1982.

Cultural life was very much affected by the 1300th state anniversary, with increased interest in historic heritage, restoration of old monuments, a campaign for people to donate to the state documents of national significance, etc. Historical and patriotic subjects in literature and the arts were encouraged. Cultural propaganda abroad reached new heights and the courting of Bulgarians living abroad intensified.

Bulgaria's foreign policy turned from the 1980 emphasis on worldwide peace propaganda to sharper focus on the Balkans. The initiatives of Zhivkov were at the centre of attention: a 'package' of proposals aimed at good neighbourly relations in the Balkans, presented at the Party Congress, and a suggestion for turning the Balkans into a nuclear-free zone and convoking a multilateral top-level conference on the subject, voiced in October.

Relations with Yugoslavia remained frosty, marred additionally by a border incident, but with some small examples of intensified contacts on a lower level.

The only non-communist country visited by Zhivkov was Greece (May). He went to Moscow three times: for the Soviet Party Congress in February, for the traditional Crimean meeting in August and for Brezhnev's birthday in December. Official visits were paid to Bulgaria by Austrian Chancellor Kreisky in May, West German Foreign Minister Genscher in July and several state and government heads of developing countries, including Mrs Indira Gandhi in November. Many communist leaders from all over the world spent their vacations in Bulgaria.

YUGOSLAVIA

Serious civil disorders in the Albanian-speaking Autonomous Province of Kosovo broke out in the spring (see map, p. 129). Trouble started with a student demonstration on 11 and 12 March, against overcrowding and poor food in the student hostels at the University of Priština. They soon escalated into a more general protest about conditions in Kosovo. The chief ingredients in the explosive mixture were Albanian nationalism, memories of past injustices at the hands of the Serbs who dominated Kosovo before the fall of Aleksander Ranković in 1966 (see AR 1966, p. 283) and a protest against the failure of the regime to satisfy the economic aspirations of Yugoslavia's poorest region. Police and troops were involved in violent clashes with demonstrators and there were several deaths. The province was sealed off for a time and a state of emergency declared on 3 April. Rumours flourished concerning the numbers of casualties. The official total was 9 dead and 202 wounded, but unofficial estimates, encouraged by Radio Tirana, spoke of hundreds of dead, including many children. (See also pp. 130-1).

A purge of members of the provincial government and the League of Communists (LCY), the dismissal of university staff and students, and trials of those alleged to have initiated the demonstrations, were the first reactions of the authorities. Mahmut Bakali (aged 45), a relatively young intellectual, was replaced as president of the LCY in Kosovo by the ex-partisan leader Veli Deva (aged 59). A reshuffle of provincial govern-ment posts elevated another wartime veteran, Ali Šukrija (aged 62), who became provincial president whilst retaining his position on the Kosovo LCY praesidium. Hundreds who were accused of participating in the demonstrations were summarily tried and sentenced to periods of up to 60 days imprisonment. Throughout the summer and autumn scores of alleged ringleaders amongst the Albanians of Kosovo and Macedonia received longer sentences, including terms of 15 years.

Allegations that the unrest was inspired by the Hoxha regime in Albania were not conclusively proved, although Radio Tirana was not slow to criticize the Yugoslavs for their handling of the affair, and to express Enver Hoxha's sympathy for the plight of his separated brethren in Kosovo. An official Yugoslav note of protest, accusing the authorities in the Peoples' Republic of encouraging irredentist elements who were plotting to form a Kosovo republic detached from Yugoslavia, was re-jected by the Albanian envoy in Belgrade. Tirana's counter-accusations included the charge that Albanian radio broadcasts were being jammed, in contravention of international law. Despite these polemics a new Albanian-Yugoslav trade agreement was signed in December, which en-visaged the exchange of goods worth $130 million in 1982.

The causes of the Kosovo riots were debated throughout Yugoslavia in an attempt to discover what had gone wrong. From this it emerged that much of the economic assistance given to the province during the post-war period had been used inefficiently; that the LCY in Kosovo was in need of a severe shake-up; that corruption and nepotism were rife; and that the federal authorities had ignored signs of impending trouble.

Tito's successors had other problems to test their mettle. In the first half of the year inflation rose to almost 50 per cent, and yet another stabilization programme was launched. Unemployment grew to over 850,000 (14 per cent of the work force) by the end of the year; foreign in-debtedness soared to almost $20,000 million (about $900 per capita); and the current balance of payments deficit was $1,700 million. Talks were held with Efta and the EEC concerning the growing trade imbalance between Yugoslavia and the members of those two groups. Yugoslavia's exports to each covered less than 40 per cent of the cost of imports. Trade with Comecon and the Third World was more nearly in balance, but the deficit with the developed industrial countries reached $3,000 million.

The stabilization drive, which involved measures of retail price control and attempts to stimulate exports, had a limited success. In December strict currency controls were imposed and personal imports were drastically reduced. Hopes expressed by federal Ministers, that 1982 would see inflation reduced to under 30 per cent and a rise of 12 per cent in export earnings, appeared to be wildly optimistic.

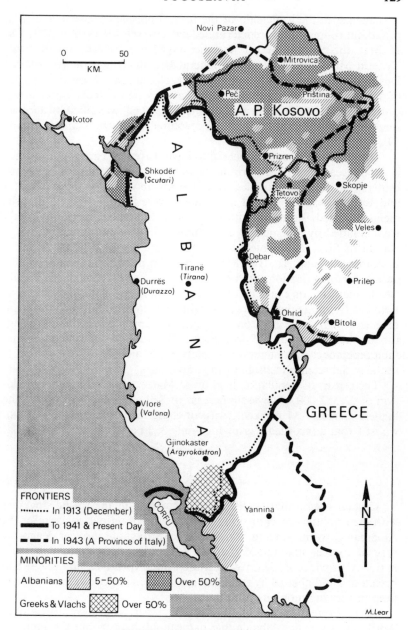

ALBANIA AND ITS NEIGHBOURS
This map shows the historical frontiers of Albania from the start of World War I, and in particular the Albanian ethnic majority in the Kosovo province of Yugoslavia (formerly Serbia) where disturbances took place in 1981.

Changes in the leadership of the federal presidency and of the LCY presidium followed the predetermined pattern (see AR 1980, p. 123). On 15 May the Slovene Sergej Kraigher (aged 67) replaced the Bosnian Cvijetin Mijatović (aged 68) as federal President, and on 20 October Dušan Dragosavac (aged 62) of Croatia replaced Lazar Mojsov (aged 61) of Macedonia as LCY president. The vacancy on the federal presidency caused by the death of Stevan Doronjski (aged 62) was filled by another representative of the province of Vojvodina, Radovan Vlajković (aged 59).

The events in Kosovo appeared to have stirred up nationalist feelings in other areas, and stern warnings were issued by government and party leaders that divisive activities would be severely dealt with. In Croatia and Bosnia trials of alleged nationalists were held and severe punishments awarded. Relations with the Roman Catholic Church in Croatia were clouded by a dispute over the unveiling of a mosaic in the parish church of Straževan which depicted the late Cardinal Stepinac and a prominent layman, Dr Ivan Merc, who died in 1929 and whose candidature for beatification was being promoted by the Church. In Bosnia two Franciscans on the staff of a religious newspaper were sentenced to terms of five and a half years and eight years imprisonment for political offences. Whilst pressure on the Catholics appeared to be increasing, that on the *Praxis* group of professors in Belgrade was relaxed, following their acceptance, 'as a temporary solution', of an offer of research posts in the social science institute of the university.

The census of population held on 31 March recorded a total population of 22,352,000, an overall increase of 8·9 per cent in ten years. The highest increase, 34 per cent, was amongst the Albanians of Kosovo, whilst Croatia recorded a growth of only 3·3 per cent.

ALBANIA

Certain events that occurred in Yugoslavia in the spring, together with their political repercussions, were a cause of serious concern for the Albanian Government and its news media throughout the year. Yugoslav official sources maintained that the grave disorders in the Albanian-majority province of Kosovo in March and April (see pp. 127-9) had been aided and abetted by the Albanian regime. The two sides were soon deep in very acrimonious press polemics.

Zëri i Popullit, the Albanian official paper, said in an article on 8 April that it was not Albania that had caused the riots but the wretched economic and political conditions of the Albanian inhabitants of Kosovo: their poverty and general backwardness and their lack of any political rights or democratic freedoms. For instance, the average personal incomes of the province were the lowest in the country, its unemployment figures the highest. The paper criticized the use of large security forces against the demonstrators. It also stated that, whilst Albania had never interfered in Yugoslavia's internal affairs, it could not refrain from protesting whenever it thought the legitimate rights of the Albanians living in that country were being violated. In a second article on 23 April, the Albanian paper supported the demonstrators' demand that Kosovo should become a separate republic within the Yugoslav federation. However, it expressed the hope that the controversy would not harm the trade and cultural exchanges between the two countries.

The issue of Kosovo was taken up by Enver Hoxha, the Communist Party leader, when he addressed the Eighth Congress of the Albanian Workers' Party in November. After reiterating some of the points made in the official party paper in April, he said that his country had not made any territorial claims on Yugoslavia nor asked for any frontier changes. Hoxha devoted as much time to Kosovo as he did to a highly critical review of Yugoslavia's allegedly revisionist domestic policies, its system of self-management, its acute economic problems. Several other Albanian officials spoke along similar lines. On 4 December Yugoslavia sent a note to Albania in which it protested about 'crude interference' in Yugoslavia's internal affairs by the Albanian Congress. But Albania rejected the protest.

The main domestic topic discussed at the Eighth Party Congress, held between 1 and 8 November, was the country's economic plan for 1981-85. It forecast that industrial production would grow by between 38 and 40 per cent, and the production of consumer goods by between 33 and 35 per cent. In the industrial sector, which would absorb 46 per cent of all investments, priority would be given to the production of oil, coal, gas and hydroelectric power. It was planned that by 1985 about 43 per cent of the country's exports would consist of products of the energy industry. The Prime Minister, Mehmet Shehu, admitted that a number of unspecified industrial targets had not been fulfilled in the previous five-year plan. In agriculture, too, there had been some shortfalls in manufacturing plants, dairy products and fruit. He said these shortcomings were due to the cessation of Chinese economic aid in 1978 and to poor economic planning and management.

An official statement issued on 18 December announced that Mehmet Shehu, the Prime Minister, had killed himself 'in a moment of nervous crisis'. He had been head of the government since 1954 and had shared absolute power with Enver Hoxha since the end of World War II. The low-key publicity about the death of such a leading political figure suggested that Shehu's suicide had caused the Albanian regime a good deal of embarrassment (see OBITUARY).

MONGOLIA

The 18th Congress of the Mongolian People's Revolutionary Party (MPRP) at the end of May produced a minor reshuffle of the top leaders. The Party Central Committee elected by the Congress had 91 full members (the same number as that elected at the 17th Congress five years before), including 21 new ones who were mostly recently appointed Ministers and officials; there were 71 candidate members (61 in 1976), of whom 45 were new.

The first plenary meeting of the new Central Committee dropped Namsrayn Luvsanravdan from membership of the Politburo and chairmanship of the Party Control Committee (posts he had held for many years), and made Col.-General Bugyn Dejid, Mongolia's Minister of Public Security, chairman in his place, with candidate membership of the Politburo. The Minister of Agriculture, Mangaljavyn Dash, was elected to the Party secretariat. Nyamyn Jagvaral, thought to be responsible for Party policy on agriculture, slipped from full to candidate membership of the Politburo. Two candidate members were promoted to full membership of the Politburo, Ulan Bator's Party First Secretary, Batochiryn Altangerel, and the chairman of the Mongol-Soviet Friendship Society, Damdiny Gombojav. President Yumjaagiyn Tsedenbal, First Secretary of the MPRP, was re-elected Party leader, but with the title of General Secretary, which he had used from 1940 to 1954.

The Institute of Party History received a new director, Badamyn Lhamsuren, who had been a candidate member of the Politburo and Secretary of the MPRP Central Committee until 1972, when he went abroad to study. Soon after the Party congress, the institute was redesignated the Institute of Social Sciences and given social planning tasks. At the beginning of December 1981, the MPRP Central Committee reappointed Lhamsuren a candidate member of the Politburo.

A month after the Party congress, general elections were held to the People's Great Hural or national assembly, whose first session on 29 June elected a new Government for the next five years. The session approved the appointment of a new Minister of Agriculture, Surenhoryn Sodnomdorj, a Soviet-trained veterinarian, and elected Jagvaral a deputy chairman of the Hural's presidium (MPR Vice-President). Of the 370 deputies to the Hural (354 in 1977), 68 per cent were elected for the first time. Later in the year, Gombojavyn Naydan replaced Jamsrangiyn Dulmaa as Minister of Light and Food Industries, and Luvsanravdan was appointed ambassador to Romania. At Gandantegchinlen, Mongolia's only active monastery, a new abbot—Hamba Gaadan—was also elected

Mongolia's first spaceman, pilot-cosmonaut Jugderdemidiyn

Gurragchaa, was launched into space at the end of March aboard the Soviet spaceship Soyuz-39, commanded by Vladimir Dzhanibekov. A day after lift-off, Gurragchaa and Dzhanibekov docked with the Salyut-6 space station. Gurragchaa, a 34-year-old captain in the Mongolian air force, was the world's 101st spaceman. The research programme for his seven-day space flight included 20 or more experiments, including an earth resources study of parts of the MPR's territory to help in the search for mineral deposits and fresh water supplies, methods of eliminating atmospheric pollution, and preparation of maps showing land usage and condition.

Gurragchaa and Dzanibekov were made 'Heroes of the Soviet Union' and 'Heroes of the MPR', and were awarded the Orders of Lenin and Suhbaatar; the Mongolian order was also presented to Gurragchaa's 'understudy', Maydarjavyn Gandzorig. A hero's welcome was laid on for Gurragchaa when he returned to Ulan Bator in May. At the MPRP Congress, he was elected to the Party Central Committee, and soon afterwards appointed deputy head of a department of the Central Committee.

President Tsedenbal, 65 on 17 September 1981, was again awarded the Order of Suhbaatar by the Hural, 'for outstanding services to the MPRP and the Mongolian people in implementing the Party's general line', and another Order of Lenin by the USSR Supreme Soviet. Delivering the Central Committee's report to the 18th Party Congress, Tsedenbal declared that the building of communism in Mongolia was guaranteed by 'alliance, friendship and brotherhood' with the Soviet Union. He pledged that the Mongolian Party would continue to 'expose resolutely' what he called the 'anti-popular and anti-socialist policy of Chinese ruling circles', and to 'wage uncompromising struggle against their great-power hegemonism and expansionism'. China was preparing for war against Mongolia, Tsedenbal said, and trying to justify its 'expansionist plans' by the 'falsification of history and actual reality'.

In June, the USSR Defence Minister, Marshal of the Soviet Union Dmitri Ustinov, paid a five-day visit to Mongolia, during which he inspected units of the Soviet army's three divisions stationed in eastern Mongolia at the MPR Government's request. Shortly after Ustinov's visit, the Mongolian Party and Government newspaper *Unen* published an account of an interview Tsedenbal had given to BBC correspondent John Osman. 'In the vicinity of our border,' Tsedenbal told him, 'the Chinese are concentrating forces and building strategic military installations. . . . The Chinese are systematically sending agents into Mongolia to carry out subversion.' He also said that Peking was trying to 'use for these purposes the Chinese immigrants resident in Mongolia'.

In both his Congress speech and BBC interview, President Tsedenbal talked about a Mongolian proposal that the states of Asia and the Pacific should sign a convention of mutual non-aggression and non-use of force. In August, details of the formal proposal were circulated with messages to the leaders of 50 Asian and Pacific countries and permanent members of the UN Security Council, including China.

The guidelines for the Mongolian seventh five-year plan (1981-85), adopted by the 18th MPRP Congress, noted the country's inability to achieve a substantial increase in agricultural production. At the beginning of 1981, its total livestock stood at 23,771,400 head, 513,200 fewer than a year before. The number of privately-owned animals (4,161,300) continued its gradual decline since 1975.

The cereal crop in 1980 (258,500 tonnes) had been over 72 per cent down on the previous year because of drought, the yield being one of the poorest ever. In 1981, at 325,800 tonnes, it was still considerably down on the planned minimum of 580,000 tonnes.

It was reported that capital investment and gross industrial production over the sixth plan period (1976-80) had risen by 120 per cent and 58 per cent respectively, against targets of 80-100 per cent and 60-65 per cent. The 1981-85 target for capital investment was more modest than the preceding one, at 23-26 per cent. Meanwhile, the seventh plan target for gross industrial production was revised upwards, from a 52-58 per cent to a 60 per cent increase.

IV WESTERN, CENTRAL AND SOUTHERN EUROPE

Chapter 1

FRANCE—FEDERAL REPUBLIC OF GERMANY—ITALY—BELGIUM—
THE NETHERLANDS—LUXEMBOURG—REPUBLIC OF IRELAND

FRANCE

A YEAR which opened with what appeared to be the final formalities before President Giscard d'Estaing's re-election closed amid signs that the 'state of grace' in which M François Mitterrand had ruled since his unexpected victory in May was drawing to a close. For over two years the return of the incumbent President over a warring and demoralized left had seemed as near a certainty as anything in politics. Only at the end of 1980 did a set of bad by-election results give any firm signs of *le grand tournant* that was to give France her first directly-elected Socialist President.

In the early weeks of the year the legion of would-be contenders thinned rapidly in face of the difficulties of obtaining finance as well as the 500 signatures from mayors, departmental councillors and parliamentarians in thirty departments needed for nomination. Eventually there were ten candidates. M Georges Marchais, the Communist, had been campaigning for several months. M Mitterrand was endorsed by a special Socialist congress in January. M Jacques Chirac, the Gaullist former Prime Minister and mayor of Paris, won the backing of his party in February, but failed to head off challenges from Mme Marie-France Garaud and the veteran Michel Debré. Finally, M Giscard d'Estaing threw his hat in the ring in early March. The remaining candidates were a Radical from the Centre-Left, a Trotskyist, an Ecologist, and a representative of the Unified Socialist Party. None could hope to survive the first ballot, but the election offered a platform and a hope of influencing support for the four leaders.

After seven years in office M Giscard d'Estaing could warn of the perils of socialism but had little new to offer. Though he pictured France as the world's third-ranking military power, and as an advanced industrial state weathering recession better than many of its neighbours, with inflation around 14 per cent and unemployment at 1·6 million, he was inevitably on the defensive. In April he unveiled proposals to create a million jobs by 1985, largely by more widespread early retirement and squeezing out immigrant labour. No young person who wanted a job would go without one, he promised. M Chirac's alternative, aiming at renewed high growth, was characteristically bold, but unconvincing. However, he could mount an impeccably conservative onslaught on the President's record. M Mitterrand's plan involved raising low wages, a shorter work-week, large-scale public and private investment, the creation of 210,000 public sector jobs, improved training facilities and social security relief for small firms.

It was a largely domestic election. While M Chirac struck a strongly nationalistic note, and Mme Garaud campaigned for a tougher line with the Russians, foreign issues made little headway. M Giscard d'Estaing was further hampered by the patrician aloofness of his later years and an unsavoury residue of unresolved political *affaires* (see AR 1979, p. 129; and 1980, p. 133). His chief challenger, François Mitterrand, on the other hand, seemed fatally weakened by the remorseless hostility of the Communists, whose support would ultimately be essential. However, in his third attempt at the presidency he found an effective campaigning style, projecting an image of 'quiet strength'—a reassuring promise of reform rather than revolution.

Nevertheless, on 26 April, when 81·08 per cent of the voters went to the polls, M Giscard d'Estaing headed the poll with a lead of 670,000 votes over M Mitterrand. Though his margin was uncomfortably small, in previous elections the right had tended to rally in the second ballot. But M Chirac refused to give the President his blessing, and his earlier attacks had left their mark. M Marchais' score of 15·54 per cent was a notably poor one. Putting a brave face on ill fortune, the Communists swung unconditionally behind M Mitterrand. In the second ballot on 10 May, with a turnout of 85·85 per cent, he swept to victory by 15,708,000 votes (51·75 per cent) to 14,642,000 (48·24 per cent).

TABLE I

THE PRESIDENTIAL ELECTION: FIRST BALLOT

	Votes '000	%		Votes '000	%
Giscard d'Estaing	8,155	28·21	Lagmiller (Ext. Left)	667	2·30
Mitterrand (Socialist)	7,486	25·90	Crepeau (Centre Left)	641	2·21
Chirac (Gaullist)	5,188	17·95	Debré (Gaullist)	481	1·66
Marchais (Communist)	4,457	15·42	Garaud (Gaullist)	384	1·32
Lalonde (Ecologist)	1,133	3·88	Bouchardeau (PSU)	320	1·10

On taking office on 21 May M Mitterrand appointed a caretaker Government under M Pierre Mauroy, dissolving the predominantly right-wing Assembly with a view to securing a Parliament that would back his programme. The new Government was rapidly obliged to support the franc and pledge itself to remain in the European Monetary System, as speculators and the Bourse took fright at the unexpected

Socialist victory. However, its main initial activity was to introduce some of the more popular increases in welfare payments and the minimum wage, which did not require legislation, paying for them with a special tax on the banks and oil companies and higher petrol prices.

Meanwhile, as M Giscard d'Estaing bitterly accused M Chirac of 'premeditated treason', a Gaullist commented: 'Giscard wants Chirac's hide, and Chirac wants Giscard's. All *we* want is to survive the election'. Within 48 hours of the presidential result the two main parties of the right, the Giscardian UDF and the Gaullist RPR, had unsentimentally agreed an electoral pact. But this was not enough to halt the Socialist advance. In the first round of the parliamentary elections on 14 June, on a turnout of 70·36 per cent, the Socialists gained at the expense of all the other parties. The Communists, who had suffered yet another reverse,

TABLE II

THE PARLIAMENTARY ELECTION: FIRST BALLOT
(*Metropolitan France*)

	Votes '000		%	
	1978	1981	1978	1981
Socialists + Left Radicals	7,019	9,377	24·98	37·77
RPR (Gaullists)	6,304	5,193	22·43	20·91
UDF (Giscardians)	5,739	4,767	20·42	19·16
Communists	5,792	4,003	20·61	16·12
Extreme Left	910	330	3·27	1·33
Other Right	906	751	3·22	3·02
Other Left	809	142	2·88	0·57
Ecologists	611	271	2·18	1·09

reached a second-ballot agreement 'for a coherent and durable majority' with the Socialists, though M Mitterrand refused to negotiate a governmental programme with them before the final result, which consolidated the Socialist victory. Of the 491 seats, the Socialists held 285 (compared with 117 in the previous Parliament), the Communists 44 (86), the RPR 88 (155) and the UDF 63 (119). Not only had the Socialists routed the right, but they had decisively reversed the balance on the left, so long dominated by the Communists.

M Mauroy's Government of 44 included five women and new ministries of Free Time and National Solidarity. It also had four Communist Ministers—the first since 1947. M Mitterrand had required from the Communist Party a pledge of unfailing loyalty to his programme in government, local administration and the factories. No friend of Communism, he saw the value of securing his left flank and seeing that the

Communists shared in some of the inevitable unpopular decisions ahead. Powerful voices inside the Communist Party urged abstention to avoid being a captive minority. But it was in some degree prisoner of its unitary rhetoric, and entry into government might quieten some critics of its debacles at the polls.

The new Government's ascendancy was confirmed in July when the Assembly approved M Mauroy by 302 votes to 147. He promised Bills to extend nationalization, decentralize government, abolish the State Security Court, repeal the previous Government's law and order legislation (see AR 1980, p. 132), increase worker participation and reform the tax system. Measures to pay for higher social benefits raised death duties, higher rates of income tax, VAT on luxury hotels and taxes on company expenses. The Government also halted expulsion of illegal immigrants, offering work permits to all who could prove they had been in France since the beginning of the year and held a job; but controls on new immigrants were reinforced. The Cabinet also cut back the programme of nuclear power construction, thus annoying both supporters of the previous Government and environmentalists, who had backed Mitterrand in the hope that all new plant would be stopped.

The local government Bill, which came before Parliament in July, set out to 'overthrow Napoleon', changing the departmental prefects into 'Commissioners of the Republic' and ending local authority tutelage. Mayors and chairmen of departmental councils were to have more power and responsibility—a prospect not all of them relished. Local taxation was to be reformed. And there were to be directly-elected regional councils. Troubled Corsica was to have special arrangements. The Opposition, declaring the integrity of the Republic in danger, battled furiously but were swamped by the Government forces. In the autumn the Bill received a more protracted mauling in the Senate, still dominated by the centre and right. Parliament also voted abolition of the death penalty.

The nationalization Bill likewise had a controversial passage after initial rejection by the Senate. Though encompassing only eight major groups it represented a major extension of public ownership: almost one-third of manufacturing industry would now be held by the state, whose influence would be further extended by the takeover of the remaining private banks. The Budget was officially summarized as embodying one aim, employment; one method, stimulating the economy; and one means, solidarity. Expenditure would rise by 27·6 per cent to 788,000 million francs (£84,000 million). Receipts would rise by only 19·0 per cent. Consequently the projected deficit would be 95,000 million francs (some £9,200 million). Family allowances and pensions would increase; there would be 71,000 new public sector jobs, and support for employment would increase by 45 per cent. This would be paid for by higher tobacco and petrol taxes, dearer car licences, an 'unemployment tax' on high incomes, and a wealth tax on some 200,000 better-off families.

In November, frustrated at the parliamentary log-jam, the Government pushed through a Bill authorizing it to legislate much of its social programme by ordinances—reduction of the work-week, longer paid holidays and a lower retirement age. Such law-making by decree had previously been assailed by the Socialists, but the desire to bring speedier benefits to working-class supporters prevailed over their pledge to give Parliament a more influential role.

Parliament was the least of the Government's worries. The attitude of employers, on whom the Government was relying for much of its recovery programme, was a different matter. The *patronat* was angry over nationalization and increased personal and company taxation and suspicious of Socialist *dirigisme*. Professional groups in general resented tighter tax controls and the Government's plan to halt private medicine in public hospitals. Despite a campaign of reassurance by M Mauroy, their mood remained sullen. The farmers were also uneasy over relations with the new Government, and dissatisfied by the outcome of their annual review in the autumn. By November, moderates like M Jacques Delors, Minister for Planning, were urging a 'pause' in the reform programme, but M Mauroy and M Mitterrand insisted on pressing forward.

Not the least of their difficulties was the economic situation. The Socialists inherited rising prices and unemployment and a foreign trade deficit, none of which could rapidly be reversed. Industrial production fell by 1·3 per cent over the year, with GDP marking time. Retail prices rose by 13·6 per cent (compared with 13·5 per cent in 1980). Since earnings rose by 14·1 per cent on average, the living standards of those in jobs were holding up well—but unemployment went over two million in October (8·5 per cent of the work-force). The trade deficit for 1981 was estimated at £3,500 million, and the franc had to be devalued by 8·5 per cent in the course of the summer. The Bourse, which collapsed in the wake of the Socialist victory, recovered slightly but remained nervous.

Foreign Affairs and Defence
Although there was considerable continuity in foreign policy, there were substantial changes in tone and emphasis, most pronounced in East-West relations and the North-South dialogue. In some ways a firmer attitude towards the Russians preceded the change in leadership. Disillusioned with his failure to budge Mr Brezhnev on Afghanistan, M Giscard d'Estaing had already been more prepared to stand up to the Russians. But the assurance of the new Minister for External Relations, M Claude Cheysson, that 'we are the best allies of the United States' was nevertheless a new note.

However, although M Mitterrand endorsed the Atlantic alliance and backed the Americans over Afghanistan and the installation of new missiles in Europe, he would not be an easy ally. American criticism of the appointment of Communist Ministers was brusquely rejected, and his joint declaration with the Mexican President on El Salvador in October was also unpalatable to the Americans. The appointment of M Cheysson, formerly EEC Commissioner for the developing countries, signalled a desire for better relations with the Third World. Opening the UN conference on the future of the world's poorest countries M Mitterrand promised that by 1988 France would devote 0·7 per cent of GNP to overseas aid. The new policy rested on strengthening ties with three 'relay' countries, Mexico, Algeria and India. The President visited Mexico in October, and Algeria in November, healing many old scars there. Mrs Gandhi visited Paris in November.

Meanwhile, the Government sought to put relations with black Africa on a fresh basis, while maintaining a military presence there. The most notable achievement was the promotion of an OAU force, largely paid for by France, to replace the Libyans in Chad. There was also an attempt to redefine France's position on the Middle East. Despite M Mitterrand's Israeli sympathies, Israel's raid on an Iraqi nuclear reactor, in which a French technician was killed, was firmly rebuked, and France pledged help in rebuilding the reactor. The Israelis were also nettled by M Cheysson's flattering remarks about the Arabs and a well-publicized meeting with Mr Yassir Arafat in August. However, though Mr Begin termed him 'no friend of Israel' on the eve of his visit to Jerusalem in December, M Cheysson delighted his hosts by dismissing the European Community's Venice declaration on the Middle East as 'an error and an absurdity'. Relations between the two countries became warmer than at any time since the break with de Gaulle following the 1967 Arab-Israeli war.

Not so relations with Iran, which deteriorated after France delivered 36 Mirage F-1 interceptors to Iraq, and worsened when it granted political asylum to Mr Bani-Sadr and then allowed monarchists who seized an Iranian patrol boat to stay in France. Nor did the new Government find relations with its European neighbours running entirely smoothly. During the summer winegrowers of the Midi spoiled shipments of Italian wine, while farmers in the south-west destroyed lorries of Spanish fruit and vegetables. The Spaniards were further annoyed by the French refusal to extradite suspected Basque terrorists, especially when the Interior Minister, M Gaston Defferre, drew an inept parallel between them and the wartime Resistance. However, though the Franco-German link lost some cordiality after M Giscard d'Estaing's departure, M Mitterrand, while recognizing that it had at times verged on an unhealthy exclusivity within the Community, was quick to praise and endorse an 'exemplary relationship'.

France reacted sharply to the military takeover in Poland, though it was reluctant to tread the sanctions path advocated by President Reagan. Indeed, the most direct effects were internal. The Communist refusal to condemn the military takeover subjected the Government to its first serious internal stresses. However, neither side was prepared to provoke a complete break.

The anxiety with which many military men viewed the Socialist triumph was soon dispelled. The suspension of nuclear weapons tests at Mururoa Atoll was no sooner announced than reversed. An initial inclination to curb overseas arms sales showed signs of easing. And it soon became clear that a commitment to cut military service to six months would be a dead letter—ostensibly to avoid aggravating youth unemployment. In general the new Government identified itself with de Gaulle's stance of military independence. It was sceptical of Nato's doctrine of graduated deterrence. Its emphasis would be more on strategic than on tactical nuclear development. During the budget debate in October the Defence Minister, M Charles Hernu, announced the construction of a seventh missile-bearing submarine, though this would not actually enter service until 1994. There were hints, too, that work was to begin on neutron weapons.

THE FEDERAL REPUBLIC OF GERMANY

INTERNAL AFFAIRS. Though it had ridden the economic storms of recent years better than most countries, West Germany was hit hard by the world recession. By the end of the year unemployment had risen to 1·7 million, the highest level for 26 years, and was expected to peak at two million in the winter months. A tight monetary policy was hampering investment, domestic demand for goods continued to fall and a sharp drop in growth was prevented only by a rise in exports—a consequence of the de-facto devaluation of the mark. Federal expenditure in 1982 was fixed at DM 240,800 million, a modest increase of 4·2 per cent over 1981. New borrowing was pegged at DM 26,500 million, which was DM 15,000 million less than in 1981. The Germans had to tighten their belts, though not to the point of acute discomfort. Children's allowances were cut, social insurance contributions increased and public sector pay was decreased by 1 per cent. Additional economies had to be made when it became clear that revenue would still fall far short of expenditure: unemployment benefit cost much more than had been envisaged, and the recession greatly reduced the income from taxation.

From the beginning of the year deep dissension within the Social Democratic Party (SPD) raised doubts about the stability of Chancellor Helmut Schmidt's Government and its chances—in the longer term—

of survival. Disagreements which had been smouldering for years, but were kept under control by the party's traditional sense of discipline, suddenly burst into the open.

Herr Schmidt was at odds with considerable factions on a range of vital issues, among them the deployment of Nato medium-range nuclear missiles, defence spending generally and the development of atomic energy. One of the SPD's deputy chairmen, Herr Hans-Jürgen Wisch-newski, said in February that the party was in worse shape than at any time since 1945, and the Social Democrats' parliamentary floor leader, Herr Herbert Wehner, warned that the SPD could suffer the fate of the British Labour Party. At the federal election only five months previously the coalition had won a greatly increased majority. Paradoxically, it was partly this victory which brought the discontent to the surface. In October 1980 the electorate voted emphatically for the return of Herr Schmidt, but showed itself to be far less keen about his party.

The increase in the coalition's majority from 10 to 45 seats was almost entirely due to the impressive performance of the junior partner, the Free Democratic Party (FDP). Consequently, the Free Democrats began the new term by seeking to exercise greater influence on Government policy. Some left-wing Social Democrats saw the Government as knuckling under to the United States on the missiles question. Herr Schmidt, hand in glove with the Free Democrat leader, Herr Hans-Dietrich Genscher, the Foreign Minister, was charged with abandoning party principles. There was a feeling on the left that it was high time for the SPD to undergo a period of regeneration in opposition.

The Social Democrats fared disastrously in the West Berlin election on 10 May. Their share of the poll fell from 42·7 per cent to 38·4 per cent, the FDP's from 8·1 per cent to 5·6 per cent. The Christian Democrats increased their vote from 44·4 per cent to 47·9 per cent—in a city where the SPD had dominated since the war. The Berliners were, above all, repudiating a political party whose reputation had been besmirched by a series of scandals and affairs. It was in the wake of one of the most serious of these that the former mayor, Herr Dietrich Stobbe, himself innocent, resigned in January. He was replaced by the federal Minister of Justice, Herr Hans-Jochen Vogel. The affair which brought down Herr Stobbe and his Senate involved an architect, Herr Dietrich Garski, who borrowed large sums of money to finance building contracts from a bank owned by the city of West Berlin. Almost all the loans were underwritten by the city government. After his firm ran into difficulties, Herr Garski left the country, and the Berliners had to pick up his bills.

Herr Vogel decided to call a mid-term election, and tried hard to make up lost ground. But the malaise of the SPD had gone too deep, and anyway he was too late on the scene. Moreover, he was challenged by a heavyweight candidate, Herr Richard von Weizsäcker, who had been nursing West Berlin for the Christian Democrats for several years and had contested the mayoralty at the previous election. The Free Democrats, previously the SPD's allies in the city government, declined the invitation to form a coalition with the CDU. So Herr von Weizsäcker set up a minority CDU Government, 'tolerated' by the Free Democrats.

A feature of the Berlin election which gave all the established parties cause for concern was the progress made by a group of candidates calling themselves the Alternatives. Their supporters were a motley collection of ecologists, squatters, anti-materialists, commune dwellers and people sometimes described as positive drop-outs. The Alternatives captured 7·2 per cent of the votes and were represented by nine seats in the new parliament. They did not intend to form an alliance with any other party and intended to rotate their deputies after two years.

In June the former Minister of State in the Foreign Ministry, Herr Klaus von Dohnanyi, was elected mayor of Hamburg in succession to Herr Hans-Ulrich Klose, who resigned after a dispute in the ruling SPD over nuclear power. Traditionally, the SPD in Hamburg was right of centre, but under Herr Klose it developed a strong list to the left. In February a special conference of the Hamburg party voted against the city's collaboration with the neighbouring state of Schleswig-Holstein in building a nuclear power station at Brokdorf on the lower Elbe. The opposition to the plant was led by Herr Klose, who was not infrequently out of step with federal party policy. He resigned when the city's proposed withdrawal from the Brokdorf project ran into political and legal difficulties.

Although the Chancellor remained the most popular politician in the country, opinion polls in October showed that his party could now expect only 33 per cent of the total vote, compared with 42·9 per cent in the 1980 election. The public standing of the Government had not been so low since the closing months of Herr Willy Brandt's Administration in 1974. The opposition, composed of the Christian Democratic Union (CDU) and the Bavarian Christian Social Union (CSU), was supported by just over half the electorate.

The campaign against nuclear rearmament, which challenged the Nato decision to deploy American medium-range nuclear missiles in Western Europe, gathered momentum during the year. In Germany the campaign, dubbed by its organizers the peace movement, fell into three, not always distinct groups: the ecologists, *alias* the greens; the political left, including communists of various shades; and church followers. But a demonstration by about 300,000 people in Bonn on 10 October proved convincingly that the movement was capable of concerted action. According to a poll by the Emnid Institute, taken a few weeks after President Reagan's inauguration, 57 per cent of Germans were against the deployment of nuclear missiles on their territory. A poll by the

Allensbach Institute a few months later found that 53 per cent supported the Nato decision on deployment—coupled with the plan to negotiate an arms limitation agreement with the Soviet Union.

Some observers considered that the anti-nuclear movement was a symptom of a growing German patriotism (or nationalism), which had a strong flavour of anti-Americanism. All the established parties were worried about losing supporters to the peace campaign, the Social Democrats in particular, and there was much talk of the need for a 'dialogue' with the young. Several times Herr Schmidt threatened to resign should the party reverse its backing for nuclear arms deployment. But it was clear that the party conference due to take place in April 1982 would postpone a decision, to allow time for progress to be made in the arms control negotiations between the superpowers.

West Germany's most famous spy, Günter Guillaume, whose arrest in 1974 brought about the resignation of Chancellor Willy Brandt (see AR 1974, p. 156), was released from prison in September, and sent home. Guillaume, who was sentenced to 13 years' imprisonment for treason in 1975, was the centre-piece of a spy swap. Also released by the West Germans was Renate Lutze, a former secretary in the Defence Ministry, who had been sentenced to six years' imprisonment for spying in 1979.

West Germany's neo-nazis could no longer be dismissed as harmless cranks. They were increasingly militant and well armed, and had made so many unpleasant friends abroad that the authorities were beginning to refer to a neo-nazi international. In the first half of 1981 they committed 43 acts of violence. The Interior Ministry estimated that nearly 20,000 Germans belonged to extreme right-wing organizations, mainly the National Democratic Party (NPD), which blossomed in the late 1960s, or to a group headed by a Munich newspaper publisher, Herr Gerhard Frey, whose weekly *National Zeitung* had a circulation of well over 100,000. The National Democrats formed the core of the largely non-militant old right. Their party was a haven for old nazis with fond memories of the Third Reich. The genuine neo-nazis numbered about 1,400, of whom 800 were organized in 22 'action groups' and 600 were lone wolves. The authorities reckoned that about 150 neo-nazis either engaged in violence or might do so in the future.

Terrorists who tried to kill the commander of the US army in Europe, General Frederick Kroesen, on 15 September were probably banking on winning sympathizers in a climate of opinion which was increasingly hostile to American defence and foreign policies. An anti-tank grenade, fired from a hillside at a range of about 200 metres, hit the General's car as he was being driven to his headquarters in Heidelberg. General Kroessen and his wife were slightly hurt. This was the tenth attack on American military personnel or property in West Germany during the year. On 31 August a bomb explosion at the US air base at Ramstein injured 20 people. The terrorist organization known as the Red Army Fraktion (RAF) admitted planting the Ramstein bomb, and the authorities believed it was the RAF which shot at the General.

FOREIGN AFFAIRS. After the Soviet invasion of Afghanistan and the imposition of martial law in Poland, detente seemed to be on its last legs, but the West German Government still cherished the belief that it could be brought back to life. West Germany, regarded by the Russians as their main contact in Western Europe and by the Americans as their most important Nato ally, found itself performing a key function in the relationship between the superpowers. But Herr Schmidt preferred to describe the German role as that of interpreter rather than mediator. He was called upon to play this role during the visit to Bonn of the Soviet leader, Mr Leonid Brezhnev, from 22 to 25 November. Four days before Mr Brezhnev's arrival in the German capital, President Reagan had made this offer to the Russians: scrap your SS-20 missiles and we will abandon plans to deploy Pershing IIs and Cruise missiles in Western Europe. This so-called zero solution had always been close to Germany's heart, and Herr Schmidt warmly welcomed the Reagan speech as a positive approach to the US-Soviet arms limitation negotiations which opened in Geneva on 30 November.

The Russians, however, condemned the offer as a propaganda ploy. Mr Brezhnev insisted during his Bonn visit that the Soviet Union did not possess superiority in the medium-range nuclear field. On the contrary, he said, Nato had one-and-a-half times more nuclear warheads for use in the European theatre than the Russians had. He urged the West to consider the Soviet proposal for a moratorium on the deployment of nuclear missiles, at least for the period of the Geneva negotiations. Herr Schmidt countered that unless the Russians started to scrap their SS-20s the deployment of American missiles from the end of 1983 was inevitable. (For President Brezhnev's speech in Bonn, see DOCUMENTS.)

Herr Schmidt pressed for a summit meeting between President Reagan and Mr Brezhnev, and he continued to do so after the crackdown in Poland. The Chancellor was on a visit to East Germany for talks with the Communist leader, Herr Erich Honecker, when military law was enforced. The visit was completed on schedule, and in an interview Herr Schmidt caused surprise by commenting that both he and Herr Honecker were shocked that the military action 'was necessary'. West Germany's response to the Polish crisis was attacked in Western media as tame and cringeing, and relations between Washington and Bonn became strained. On 18 December the Bundestag passed a resolution to suspend official aid to Poland until the repressive measures against the Polish people were stopped, and subsequently Herr Schmidt's Government called for an end to martial law, for the release of prisoners and for a resumption of talks between the Polish Government, the free trade union Solidarity and the Catholic Church. But West Germany would not agree to join in economic sanctions against the Soviet Union and/or Poland.

Martial law, the Germans were convinced, was imposed by General Jaruzelski—albeit yielding to Soviet pressure—to pre-empt a Soviet invasion. In the German view that tragedy was closer to 13 December than some Western Governments had imagined. And, because the danger remained, the Germans considered it was madness for the West to provoke the Russians by interfering too blatantly. The German assessment was based largely on a first-hand account of events in Poland by its deputy Prime Minister Mr Mieczyslaw Rakowski, who paid a brief visit to Bonn after Christmas, and on the evidence of the Church in Poland.

Germany's policy of non-interference was designed principally to safeguard the Ostpolitik. Herr Schmidt's Government was also anxious not to endanger the Geneva arms control talks. As the year ended Germany was desperately waiting for a sign from Poland that the reform course had not been irretrievably abandoned.

The Chancellor's visit to Saudi Arabia in April was one of the most difficult missions he had undertaken. In Riyadh he had to explain why his Government did not find it possible for the time being to supply Saudi Arabia with the Leopard 11 tank and other weapons. Quite apart from the blow to the German arms industry, this non-decision, taken after many months of dithering, could spoil Germany's chances of getting a lion's share in Saudi Arabia's industrial development. Although Herr Schmidt had pretended not to believe in the connection between arms sales and economic cooperation, the German industrial lobby had been given to understand that German tanks and German civil engineering were inseparable parts of a deal. Herr Schmidt's Government was in the process of reviewing its policy on arms exports. For many years Germany had stuck more or less to the principle that German arms should not be delivered to areas of tension. The Chancellor felt that the term 'area of tension' was restrictive, and should be replaced by guidelines which took more account of the national interest and the need to establish, not least in areas of tension, a military balance.

ITALY

When the year opened, the Government, a coalition of Christian Democrats, Socialists, Social Democrats and Republicans formed in October 1980 under the Christian Democrat Prime Minister Arnaldo Forlani, was in difficulties owing to the aftermath of the November 1980 earthquake in southern Italy and to a resurgence of left-wing terrorism. Red Brigaders, fomenting revolts in prisons in which their comrades were held, were seeking to undermine the prison system and hence the state. In December 1980 they had kidnapped Judge Giovanni D'Urso, head of a department in the Ministry of Justice dealing with the placing of prisoners in gaols, and early in January they proclaimed that he had been condemned to death but that he might be reprieved if their comrades in prison in Trani and Palmi were allowed to publish their political views in the press and on television. The Government firmly rejected this demand, but on 11 January the Socialist daily *Avanti!* published a Red Brigade communique, as did also two other papers, followed by two more (including the Rome *Messaggero*). The Red Brigades then issued a further communique which, while repeating their slogan 'Destruction of all prisons and liberation of all proletarian prisoners', said they had attained their objective and would therefore liberate D'Urso—which they did on 15 January.

Next day the Government secured a vote of confidence in the Chamber by 353 votes to 243 on its handling of this episode, though the Communists claimed it had made 'inadmissible concessions'. Continued support from its coalition partners was important for the Government's credibility in its efforts to secure international loans for reconstruction in the south. Tactical support was reaffirmed by the Socialists at their congress in Palermo in April.

Political campaigning now concentrated on the voting, due on 17 May, on five Radical-promoted referendums, the most important of which concerned changes, contested between Catholics and Radicals, in the law of 1977 permitting abortion. Pope John Paul II, while confining himself to general principles, made no secret of his own views against abortion, thereby provoking Communist and Socialist protest at 'Vatican influence'. Into the midst of this controversy came the attempt, on 13 May, on the Pope's life by a Turkish terrorist (see p. 150). This episode caused deep concern throughout Italy, but had little effect on the voting in the referendums; for less than a third of the votes favoured the anti-abortion movement, and the electorate overwhelmingly rejected the other issues.

The referendums soon paled into insignificance, however, when on 21 May Prime Minister Forlani released the names of 963 people, including leading figures in public life, the army and intelligence, said to have had links with a secret masonic lodge known as P2—Propaganda 2, Oriental Rite—then under judicial investigation following discoveries made by the Milan public prosecutor's office. This affair, described as the biggest scandal to strike the post-war republic, resulted in numerous arrests and suspensions from office; the P2's organizer, Licio Gelli, a fugitive from charges including political subversion, was already in hiding in South America. But it also brought down the head of government. Forlani, who had set up a commission of three leading jurists to decide whether P2 came under the constitutional ban on secret societies, on 25 May summoned the coalition party leaders to discuss the situation with him, but the Socialist leader Bettino Craxi boycotted the meeting. The Socialists had been the first to raise a hue and cry about P2, and Craxi now plainly hoped to bring down the Government and perhaps lead its successor. Faced with this disaffection, Forlani resigned on 26 May. The Socialists called for a basic change in the political system, while the Communist leader Enrico Berlinguer, demanding a 'government of alternative democracy', criticized Forlani for having held the P2 membership lists for two months without taking action. Allegations about P2 links affected members of all the leading parties except the Communists.

President Pertini (himself a Socialist), who had remained completely aloof from the scandal, wanted above all to avoid a general election in these unpropitious circumstances. He first asked Forlani to form a new Government, but when this proved impossible he called on Senator Giovanni Spadolini, leader of the small Republican Party, on 10 June. In making this courageous choice President Pertini, while bypassing the controversial and ambitious Socialist Craxi, was proposing, for the first time in three and a half decades, to break the Christian Democrat monopoly on the premiership—the only other head of government not a Christian Democrat was the first post-war Prime Minister, the Action Party leader Ferruccio Parri (see OBITUARY). Senator Spadolini (56), a historian and past editor of the *Corriere della Sera* who had led the Republican Party since 1979, secured the support of the Socialists and the benevolent neutrality of the Communists. On 15 June he presented a four-point draft plan to the President, involving measures to combat inflation, reform public life, tighten up law and order and clarify foreign policy. He also stated that P2 should be suppressed—as too did the three jurists appointed by Forlani, whose report, published that day, found it to be a secret association violating article 18 of the Constitution. Local elections, held on 21 June, helped Spadolini's negotiations, since the centre lay parties, and especially the Socialists, all did well while both Communists and Christian Democrats sustained some losses. On 28 June he announced his Government—a five-party coalition including the Liberals in addition to the previous partners. Its structure remained basically the same, with 15 Christian Democrat Ministers, seven Socialists, three Social Democrats and one each for the Republicans and Liberals. Prominent Ministers whose posts remained unchanged were the Christian Democrats Virginio Rognoni (Interior), Emilio Colombo (Foreign Affairs) and Beniamino Andreatta (Treasury), and Giorgio La Malfa (the only Republican) as Budget Minister. The Government secured votes of confidence in the Senate on 9 July (by 182 to 124) and in the Chamber two days later (by 369 to 247).

A lull in left-wing terrorism had ensued since January, and some even thought the worst might be over. The Front Line organization had been virtually liquidated, some 180 Front Liners—and 340 Red Brigaders—being in prison, though relics of them were being recruited by the Red Brigades. Far-left terrorists had been badly hit in Turin and Genoa but still had a viable organization in Rome and Milan and in the Veneto. On 14 April the anti-terrorist squads achieved an important coup with the arrest of the long-sought Red Brigade leader Mario Moretti, believed to be the last but one still out of prison of the 15 involved in the abduction and murder of Aldo Moro in 1978. Three days later a warden at the Rebibbia prison in Rome was shot dead in revenge—again demonstrating the vital part played by prisons in the Red Brigades' thinking.

That the Red Brigades were by no means done for was shown by four kidnappings in the next six weeks. One of the victims, Ciro Cirillo, was a prominent Christian Democrat politician in the Naples region; two others, Giuseppe Taliercio and Renzo Sandrucci, were high-up executives in Venice and Milan; and the fourth was Roberto Peci, brother of Patrizio Peci (now in prison) whose confessions had led to the arrest of several Red Brigaders. They suffered different fates. Taliercio was found murdered in Mestre on 6 July; but Sandrucci and Cirillo were released on 23-24 July after adherence to conditions laid down by their captors. Peci, who was not a member of the political or industrial establishment but an object of pure vendetta, was found shot dead on 3 August, his body dumped in a derelict house near Rome.

There was a further lull in the autumn, though five policemen were killed in October/November. On 17 December, however, came the dramatic abduction of the Red Brigades' first international victim, General James Lee Dozier, a senior commander at Nato's base in Verona. The Government firmly refused to negotiate with the terrorists, who, President Pertini maintained, were being manipulated from abroad. At the year's end Dozier was still being held, put on trial by a 'people's court' according to anonymous telephone calls. Friends were said to have offered a £1 million reward for information leading to his release. Some 40 kidnaps for ransom took place during the year, including one case of a millionaire tycoon whose body was kept hidden for three months in a freezer while his captors continued to negotiate. A Christmas amnesty affecting some 12,000 prisoners (a third of the total) aimed to reduce the shocking overcrowding in prisons.

The economic situation remained serious, with industrial performance declining, and unemployment and inflation at around 20 per cent. In February the Government introduced measures designed to curb inflation and overcome the soaring deficit in the balance of payments, due in part to sharp rises in oil prices. On 22 March the lira was devalued by 6 per cent against other EMS currencies, and bank rate was raised to a record 19 per cent, while on 16 April the public sector borrowing requirement (PSBR) was cut by 5,000,000 million lire. After the fall of the Forlani Government, a 30 per cent deposit on imports was imposed on 27 May. Five weeks of panic selling on the stock exchange led to the closure of the bourses (unprecedented, except after Caporetto in 1917) for five days on 8 July. On 26 September the Government introduced an austerity Budget for 1982 aiming to cut expenditure by 9,700,000 million lire (£4,600 million), hold down the PSBR, and bring inflation down to 16 per cent.

The Foreign Minister, Emilio Colombo, on a visit to the USA in February assured President Reagan of Italian support for US policies, in the Middle East and elsewhere, and in December Italy supported the USA's stiff stand over the Polish crisis—about which the Communist leader Enrico Berlinguer said events in Poland showed that the cycle of history beginning with the Russian revolution was coming to an end. The Communist Party's relations with Moscow worsened, largely because of its support for Solidarity, whose leader visited Italy in January at trade union invitation. At the Soviet Communist Party Congress in March, which Berlinguer did not attend, his substitute, Giancarlo Pajetta, was not allowed to speak in a full session. The Chamber voted on 2 October by 244 to 225 in favour of deploying 110 US-built Cruise missiles at Comiso, in south-east Sicily, and rejected by 261 to 192 a Communist proposal to scrap these plans. But big demonstrations in favour of European nuclear disarmament took place in Rome on 24 October. On 19 November at Strasbourg the Italian and German Foreign Ministers published a joint declaration on European aims covering increased and broader-ranging political cooperation within the EEC.

The Turkish terrorist Mehmet Ali Agca, accused of shooting the Pope in St Peter's Square on 13 May, was sentenced in the Rome Court of Assizes to life imprisonment on 22 July. There was no question of his extradition, nor was there any legal conflict between Italy and the Holy See over his trial in an Italian court.

BELGIUM

When the year began, Belgium faced the highest level of unemployment in the European Community, industrial output was at the bottom of a recession, business investment was flagging, as was personal consumption, and the steel industry—a major employer and a fundamental part of Belgium's industrial base—was close to bankruptcy. The public financial deficit, virtually out of control, was a national crisis in its own right. Prospects of resolving these very serious problems were much reduced by the fact that average hourly wages were close to the highest in the world, creating serious difficulties for the export-dependent economy (exports being equivalent to over 50 per cent of GDP) and leaving the home market very vulnerable to imports.

The Government's very mild package of austerity measures, introduced at the beginning of the year, was wholly inadequate to the situation; as confidence ebbed, the franc came under massive speculative pressure and it was plain that the international exchange markets were looking for a devaluation of at least 10 per cent. Acutely aware that in Belgium's open economy (imports, too, being equivalent to over 50 per cent of GDP) any devaluation would knock on directly into prices through the system under which wages were fully linked to the cost-of-living index, the Prime Minister attempted to bring in tougher policies. In trying to suspend wage-indexation, he lost the support of the Socialist partners in the coalition and his Government fell at the end of March, though Mr Martens's resignation was not finally accepted by the King until 2 April.

A new coalition Government, virtually identical with its predecessor but under the premiership of Mr Eyskens, took office. In quick succession, the new Government survived several crises, any one of which could easily have led to the Prime Minister's resignation. Nevertheless, the coalition held together because of an acute awareness on the part of its Social Christian and Socialist members that failure to compromise would lead to a general election in which they might well lose ground. But by midsummer the Government was looking very fragile, the Prime Minister being unable to get through Parliament any of his plans to transfer incomes away from households and the state sector towards productive industry. Soon the crisis came: the Socialists, whose main support lay in Wallonia, insisted that financial aid be given to the region's virtually bankrupt steel industry before they were prepared to transact any other government business, however pressing. This dispute within the coalition, though ostensibly economic, had an essentially regional, and therefore intercommunal, basis. The outcome was a refusal by the other parties to give what they saw as a potentially permanent subsidy to Wallonia. Amid bitter recriminations the Government resigned.

After an unsuccessful attempt to form a Government by Mr Claes, who had been Minister of Economic Affairs in the Eyskens Administration, the King called a general election for 8 November. Fought mainly on a single issue—how to save the economy—the campaign was nevertheless overlaid by nuances of political ideology and regional identity, as well as mirroring popular dissatisfaction with the conduct of recent Governments. This complexity showed itself in an extreme form in the Brussels area, where the two cultural groups overlapped and where voters had to choose among no fewer than 816 candidates, making up 24 lists, in order to elect 34 members.

The election results gave the Social Christians 61 seats (a heavy net loss of 21), the Socialists 61 (a gain of three) and the Liberals 52 (a gain of 15). Among minor parties, the Volksunie (Flemish nationalists) made gains in Flanders at the expense of the Social Christians while in Wallonia the French-speaking nationalists lost ground to the regional wing of the Socialist Party. As a result of the advance by the right-wing Liberals, enabling them to negotiate on equal terms with the Social Christians and the Socialists, it became practicable for any two of the three major parties to muster sufficient seats to form a coalition Government. Accordingly, Mr de Clercq, the Liberal leader, was asked to form a Government; he failed because the Social Christians were not prepared to be junior partners, in the sense that Liberals would hold the premiership and key ministries. Mr Nothomb, a Social Christian, then attempted to put together a broad coalition of all three main parties, but without success. At this point a Social Christian-led coalition with the Liberals was attempted by Mr Martens, who ultimately obtained the necessary pledges of support, confirmed in Parliament on 20 December. The new Government, the fifth led by Mr Martens since 1979, had a reliable majority of only six in the National Assembly. Largely because of this fragile margin, the Prime Minister asked to be voted special powers enabling him to by-pass Parliament in order to implement his economic policies, which included contentious proposals to modify the indexation of wage increases, cut company tax and reduce the public deficit as the recession continued.

THE NETHERLANDS

In the general election held on 26 May, the Christian Democrat-Liberal coalition Government forfeited its small majority in the Lower House. The Christian Democrats lost one seat, leaving them with 49, and the Liberals lost two, fewer than expected, allowing their representation to fall to 26. Nevertheless, a major defeat for the Labour Party, which suffered a net loss of 9 seats, leaving it with only 44, meant that the Christian Democrats became the largest single party in Parliament. The most important development was the emergence of D'66, the social democratic party, which more than doubled its representation from 8 to 17. At the extreme ends of the political spectrum, three of the ultra-left parties increased their seats from six to nine, while the three right-wing parties gained two, raising their total to six.

Formation of a Government proved a long and arduous task, a new dimension being added by the large gains of D'66, which meant that it could hardly be excluded from any coalition. The Labour Party stood by its resolve not to participate in an Administration containing the Liberals. Although to many people a Christian Democrat-Labour-D'66 coalition seemed the only real solution, major differences separated the three parties on economic policy, nuclear arms deployment and nuclear power stations, and the question which party should have the premiership. Three and a half months later, in early September, agreement was reached, barely in time for the Queen's Speech from the throne on 15 September. The new Government included six Christian Democrats, six Labour and three members of D'66. Mr Van Agt of the Christian Democrats continued as Prime Minister. Overall, the Government enjoyed a 34-seat majority in the Lower House.

However, there were very serious doubts as to whether it could remain sufficiently united to survive for long, given the number of issues on which the parties differed. Among these, in view of the end-year deadline set by Nato, was the decision whether to station Cruise and Pershing nuclear missiles in the Netherlands. The Labour Party had a commitment not to let in the missiles on any conditions; D'66 was reluctant but not totally against; while the Christian Democrats wished to base their decision on the results of the US-Soviet nuclear disarmament negotiations. Similar, but less severe, differences existed about continuation of the nuclear energy programme.

Equally, policies to deal with the economy were a source of serious dissension within the new Government; unemployment was the most important single issue. The Labour Party was looking for the creation of additional jobs, to be funded by natural-gas revenues. The Christian Democrats were thinking more in terms of curbing official spending and easing the burden of tax and social security charges for employers as a means of encouraging expansion.

Within little more than a month, the refusal of the Christian Democrats and D'66 to accept a deficit-financed job-creation programme proposed by Mr Den Uyl, the Labour Minister of Social Affairs, led to the Government's resignation. However, the three parties soon patched up their differences, enabling the coalition to be reconstituted on 4 November. In effect the Labour group secured the consent of the other two parties to implementing a programme to create 60,000 new jobs at a cost of £600 million. In December, the number of jobless stood at nearly 450,000.

During the year, the Bill to legalize abortion previously passed by the Lower House was approved by the Upper House by a vote of 38 to 37.

LUXEMBOURG

The Treaty of Economic Union with Belgium was renewed for a further ten years in March. The revised text of the agreement clearly put both partners into a relationship of equality, moving away from the previous concept which implied Luxembourg's quasi-dependence on Belgium. The treaty opened the opportunity for Luxembourg to take over some of the central bank functions exercised on its behalf by Belgium.

A massive drop in steel output, on which the economy depended, created a crisis in mid-year, raising the question of large cuts in productive capacity. Inevitably, the severe recession in the steel industry had a depressing effect on the rest of the economy. Industrial output was 9 per cent lower than in 1980 and growth in GDP was negligible. However, unemployment at the end of the year was fewer than 2,000, amounting to a mere 1·1 per cent of the economically-active population.

THE REPUBLIC OF IRELAND

An early general election was expected after the success of the ruling Fianna Fail party in the Donegal by-election in the previous autumn and the apparent improvement in Anglo-Irish relations which followed Mrs Thatcher's visit to Dublin (see AR 1980, p. 151). The Taoiseach, Mr Charles Haughey, chose instead to prepare the ground slowly. The January budget nudged drink and petrol prices a little higher while providing marginal relief for income-tax payers. It was calculated to calm the growing concern over unemployment and a record deficit in the public accounts. This hint of normality, if not of optimism, looked like pre-electoral strategy. So did the Government's delay in launching the procedure for filling the parliamentary vacancy created by the appointment of the Foreign Minister, Mr Michael O'Kennedy, as Ireland's member of the EEC Commission. Events, however, now began to turn against Mr Haughey.

In the country's worst civic disaster for many years, 48 young people died when fire swept through a discotheque in the Taoiseach's North Dublin constituency on St Valentine's Day. The Fianna Fail annual conference, due to start the following evening, had to be postponed until April. Its value as an election springboard was severely eroded in the interval by the deteriorating economy, by the emerging crisis of the H-block hunger strikes and by a testiness between Dublin and London over Mrs Thatcher's assurances to Unionists disturbed by the earlier rapport between the two Governments. A temporary freeze of electricity and transport charges, combined with subsidies on basic food items, struck a last dogged note of confidence before the long-awaited dissolution of the Dail in mid-May. The partial brake on inflation was welcomed even if few saw justification for confidence.

As in the general elections of 1973 and 1977, Northern Ireland featured little in the confrontation between the major parties, although supporters of the hunger strike nominated candidates in a number of constituencies. The colourful and expensive campaign, involving helicopters, a whistle-stop train, special coaches and newspaper advertising on an unprecedented scale, concentrated on economic issues and on the personalities of the principal contenders, Mr Haughey and the Leader of the Opposition, Dr Garret FitzGerald. Dr FitzGerald's Fine Gael party had been the major partner in the 1973-77 coalition Government but now sought a mandate to rule on its own. Fianna Fail stood on its record; the Labour Party put forward a package of mildly socialist measures; Fine Gael offered tax reforms, including a reduction of the basic income tax rate from 35 to 25 per cent and a novel proposal to transfer £9.60 per week from various tax allowances as a direct payment to all non-wage-earning housewives.

Fianna Fail clearly lost the election, for its previous substantial majority was converted into a minority of 78 seats in the new 166-seat Dail (which had been expanded in size to reflect the population increase of the 1970s). It was less easy to say who had won. Labour also lost seats, among them that of its leader, Mr Frank Cluskey. Fine Gael, comparatively speaking, did best, but if its 65 seats were the greatest number it had ever held it was still far short of a majority. The Labour Party now approved a pact drawn up between its new leader, Mr Michael O'Leary, and Dr FitzGerald to create a fresh coalition which, with the votes of four independent deputies, displaced the Fianna Fail Government on 30 June. The incoming Taoiseach, Dr FitzGerald, brought to the premiership a reputation for integrity, exceptional competence as one of the country's leading economists and an untarnished record from his term as Foreign Minister in the previous coalition. None of this seemed to guarantee long life to his minority Administration.

What followed was at least dramatic. The new Taoiseach took a number of steps which might have been considered daring for a leader with a secure majority. He omitted from his Government some senior members of his own party who represented its not uninfluential conservative wing, notably the former Finance Minister, Mr Richie Ryan, and the former EEC Commissioner, Mr Richard Burke. He also ignored the geographical distribution of portfolios, traditional in Irish politics, by failing to appoint more than one Minister from the province of Connacht. The animosities generated by Dr FitzGerald's insistence on shaping the team he wanted were to continue to the end of the year. His Government certainly did not lack new blood. The Ministers for the key departments of

Finance and Agriculture, Mr John Bruton and Mr Alan Dukes, were newcomers to Cabinet; the Foreign Minister, Professor James Dooge, was a veteran party mentor whom Dr FitzGerald appointed, under the Taoiseach's prerogative, to be a member of the Senate. Mr O'Leary became Tanaiste or Deputy Taoiseach and three other Labour deputies became Cabinet Ministers: they included the only woman on the Government front bench, Mrs Eileen Desmond, Minister for Health and Social Welfare.

The country had scarcely begun to analyse the significance of the appointments when the Taoiseach announced that the national finances were in a much weaker state than he had appreciated in opposition. A supplementary budget on July 21 increased VAT as well as the taxes on a wide range of consumer items. Whether sufficient Independent deputies would accept these austerity measures was quite unsure; but in the event the Budget passed, and the likelihood grew that the coalition would not only survive in office but would govern with a firmness out of proportion to its apparent parliamentary instability.

The hunger strikes in Northern Ireland continued to present serious political and security problems for the Republic. Both Mr Haughey and Dr FitzGerald tried reasoning with the relatives of the hunger strikers, encouraging recourse to the European Commission on Human Rights and commending the intervention of the Irish Roman Catholic bishops' Commission on Justice and Peace. The efforts of both outgoing and incoming Taoiseach met with rebuff and insult. An *ad hoc* group of Dail deputies who went to Belfast before the election were no more successful. Two champions of the hunger strike, one of them himself on hunger strike, were elected to the Dail in border constituencies: this caused a momentary sensation but was of little immediate consequence since they neither could nor wished to take their seats. Widespread popular support for the strikers was scarcely noticeable outside the border area, but a concentration of demonstrators in Dublin, many of them brought in for the occasion, led to serious riots in July during a march on the British embassy.

By now Dr FitzGerald was making no secret of his frustration at what he considered to be the simplistic rigidity of the British Prime Minister. Mrs Thatcher, in his view, had elevated the minor matters of prison work and clothing to grand issues of principle to be resisted in the name of law and order. In reality, he argued, they were only 'a crisis within a crisis'. Without concession of political status, he felt that they could be dealt with flexibly, thereby depriving the IRA of the most effective propaganda weapon with which it had yet been presented and which worked to the benefit of subversion as death followed death. That effect followed especially in America, where funds for Irish extremists were handsomely augmented by the well-intentioned but ill-informed community of Irish origin, and also in Europe, where what was seen as patriotic self-sacrifice struck a chord of sympathy.

The end of the hunger strikes, brought about by the strikers' families rather than through any political agency, freed the Government's hand to deal with wider questions. On Northern Ireland, the Taoiseach introduced an unexpected theme in October when he announced a 'crusade' for constitutional reform in the Republic. Its purpose would be to eliminate those elements of the Republic's constitution which distressed and alienated Northern Protestants. These factors encompassed aspects of family law—especially the prohibition of divorce—and nationalist aspirations such as the claim to jurisdiction over 'the whole island of Ireland'. The demand for reform had come in the past from a minority of cross-bench opinion in the Dail, from progressive Roman Catholics in the aftermath of the second Vatican Council and from media commentators. Dr FitzGerald, in his time, had belonged to all these categories, but it remained remarkable to find the head of government committing himself to so forward a position. Mr Haughey, on behalf of Fianna Fail, denied that the Republic had been in any degree a sectarian state and declared his party opposed to relinquishing the claim to jurisdiction over Northern Ireland. Others objected that reform should be promoted for the sake of human rights and fair administration in the Republic itself without reference to Northern Ireland. The Taoiseach chose to continue along the lines he had set out, and an Attorney-General's committee was established to examine and report on desirable constitutional change.

Dr FitzGerald's initiative appeared to restore a better climate between Dublin and London after the tension surrounding the hunger strike. The news that an Anglo-Irish intergovernmental council would be inaugurated as a permanent institution to advise on matters of common concern, even before it could be given its proposed parliamentary tier, was the main outcome of the Taoiseach's visit to Downing Street in November (see p. 42 and DOCUMENTS), and neither Mr Haughey's disappointment nor Dr Paisley's denunciation deprived the proposal of the sliver of hope which it represented.

The economy posed seemingly insoluble difficulties. The projected deficit of £900 million for the year, which the July budget sought to staunch by some £150 million, had come down merely to £850 million at the year's end. Inflation explained the unsatisfactory result without pointing to an answer, since the 22 per cent inflation rate for the year had been partly caused by the July taxes—a situation little better than the lower rate of 17 per cent left by Fianna Fail at the expense of high interest liability on excess borrowing. Borrowing and austerity alike pushed unemployment towards the unprecedented figure of 130,000. Fine Gael Ministers, including the Taoiseach, pointed not only to income restraint but indeed to a cut in living standards as the inevitable road to recovery.

However realistic, this harsh analysis, sustained throughout the autumn and winter, put pressure on the coalition partnership. The Labour Party, with its trade union affinities and special concern for social welfare, would have preferred a greater emphasis on spending as the way out of recession. Ironically, the one element in the Government's programme which would have augmented spending power, the Fine Gael promise to cut direct taxation, troubled many Labour supporters on ideological grounds. Fianna Fail intelligently exploited these weaknesses, accusing the Government of illogicality and confusion.

The National Understanding on wages and salaries (see AR 1980, p. 150) being due to end in the autumn, the Government appointed an advisory committee which recommended a 9½ per cent rise for the coming year, and in the same breath cut it to 6½ per cent because of the upward move of EMS currencies (including the Irish pound) against sterling. Union-management-government talks failed several times to reach agreement on a new understanding, and 1981 ended with the prospect of 'free-for-all' bargaining. Government action itself implied that settlements of the order of 12 per cent spread over 15 months might be acceptable. Farmers also ended the year with the first upward turn in their incomes for many months, the result of much judicious lobbying by successive Ministers in Brussels.

Pre-Christmas opinion polls showed considerable popular approval for the Government, and for the Taoiseach in particular, notwithstanding the politically dangerous decisions forced by circumstances on the coalition Cabinet: the indefinite deferral of an international airport for the pilgrimage centre of Knock in County Mayo, a no more than tentative reprieve for a state-owned sugar factory threatened with closure in County Galway, a relentless edging-up of mortgage rates. Against the background of recession it was perhaps also an act of courage to proceed with the opening of the long-promised and aesthetically superb National Concert Hall in Dublin.

Chapter 2

DENMARK—ICELAND—NORWAY—SWEDEN—FINLAND—AUSTRIA—
SWITZERLAND

DENMARK

THE year was again dominated by severe economic problems, exacerbated by a deadlocked parliamentary situation unable to produce a strong majority Government. Mr Anker Jørgensen's minority Social Democratic Government, in office since October 1979, had some success in slowing down the growth of public spending, and shifting spending priorities from social services to economic measures. But unemployment reached 9 per cent, while 20 per cent interest rates severely hit industry and agriculture and a foreign debt totalling 25 per cent of GDP was a serious burden on the external account. Average wage rises in the two-year decentralized wage agreements reached in January and February were held at 7·8 per cent for 1981 and 9·1 per cent for 1982, but a strike by abattoir workers (22 April-6 May) hit exports. In March, high-cost energy imports being a major factor in Denmark's balance of payments difficulties, the Government forced through an agreement ending the A. P. Moeller consortium's 50-year concession (1962-2012) on all Danish North Sea oil and gas. The Government also succeeded in concluding with the main opposition parties—Conservatives, Liberals, Centre Democrats and Christian People's Party—a new three-year defence agreement (1982-4) providing for a total 2 per cent real growth in defence spending.

It was on economic policy that the Government foundered. In May Mr Jørgensen reached an agreement on this with the three small centrist parties, the Radicals, Centre Democrats and Christian People's Party. But when, in November, he introduced a plan to force pension funds and insurance companies to invest part of their assets in equity capital in industry and in cheap loans to industry and agriculture, these parties, led by the Centre Democrats, refused to support him and the Government fell on 12 November. In the subsequent election campaign the two largest non-socialist parties presented a joint programme of sharply cutting public expenditure and business taxes. The election, held on 8 December, produced the following result (1979 result in brackets):

	Seats	% of Votes
Social Democrats	59 (68)	32·9 (38·2)
Socialist People's	20 (11)	11·3 (6·0)
Radical	9 (10)	5·1 (5·4)
Centre Democrats	15 (6)	8·3 (3·2)
Liberal	21 (22)	11·3 (12·5)
Conservative	26 (22)	14·4 (12·5)
Christian People's	4 (5)	2·3 (2·6)
Progress	16 (20)	8·9 (11·0)
Left Socialists	5 (6)	2·3 (3·6)
Single Tax	0 (5)	1·2 (3·6)
Greenland	2 (2)	
Faroes	2 (2)	

The main losers were the Social Democrats (−9 seats), with disappointing results for the Liberals (−1) and Progress Party (−4), whose leader, Mogens Glistrup, had been sentenced to four years' imprisonment for tax fraud on 23 November. The main gains went to the Conservatives (+ 4), the Socialist People's Party (+ 9), and the Centre Democrats (+ 9). The number of parties in the Folketing went down from 10 to 9, but there was still no majority support for either a socialist or a nonsocialist Government. As a consequence, on 30 December, after unsuccessful negotiations between the Social Democrats, Socialist People's Party and Radical Liberals, Anker Jørgensen once again formed a minority Social Democratic Government.

ICELAND

The overriding priority of Mr Gunnar Thoroddsen's Centre-Left Government remained to reduce Iceland's high inflation rate, running at about 58 per cent in 1980. On 1 January, as part of this policy, a currency reform substituted one new Krona for 100 old Kroner. This reform was accompanied by a price freeze from 1 January to 1 May, followed until the end of 1981 by rigorous price controls which in effect continued the freeze but with greater flexibility. The Government also attempted to hold stable the international value of the new Krona, but was forced to undertake three devaluations during the year (of 3·85 per cent on 29 May, 4·76 per cent on 25 August and 6·5 per cent on 10 November) to compensate partly for falls in the value of Western European currencies against the US dollar, partly for the erosion of export competitiveness by Iceland's higher domestic inflation rate. Finally, the Government legislated for quarterly indexed wage rises lower than the full amount due, as part of its efforts to reduce inflationary pressures. A moderate wage settlement was reached on 14 November, though this was to last only six months and widespread dissatisfaction among union members raised the prospect of higher wage demands in spring 1982. By the year's end all these various anti-inflationary measures had reduced the inflation rate to an estimated 50 per cent. This, however, still left a long way to go to the target of a rate approximating that of Iceland's main trading partners.

NORWAY

This eventful year saw the appearance of Norway's first woman Prime Minister, the end of eight years of Labour government, and the first Conservative Administration since 1928. It started dramatically in January when police reinforcements were flown into Finnmark from all over Norway to clear large demonstrations as work began on the access road to the highly controversial Alta-Kautakeino hydroelectricity project. This show of government determination was followed, however, by the anti-climax of seven months' delay (23 February to 28 September) when it was discovered that legislation requiring the registration of Lapp monuments along the route had not been complied with. On the party-political front, the period from February to April was dominated by rivalries and splits in the Labour Party. On 30 January the Prime Minister, Mr Odvar Nordli, announced his resignation, ostensibly on health grounds. He was succeeded on 4 February by the party's vice-chairman, Mrs Gro Harlem Brundtland. On 4 April, at the Labour Party congress, she also succeeded in ousting as Labour's chairman Mr Reuilf Steen, who along with two other Ministers had already resigned his government post as Trade Minister on Mrs Brundtland's appointment as Prime Minister. Mrs Brundtland thus reunited the offices of Prime Minister and party chairman which had been divided since 1975.

Thereafter politics were dominated by the campaign for the election on 14-15 September. Among the main issues were taxation policy and the Government's handling of the economy (the imposition of another four-month price freeze on 15 August highlighting its failure to control inflation), abortion law reform (the Christian People's Party's demand for the repeal of abortion on demand casting serious doubts on the three main non-socialist parties' ability to form a coalition), and the proposal for a treaty-based Nordic nuclear-free zone (officially supported by the Labour Party but regarded by many non-socialists as a danger to Norway's security).

The election result (as amended following a second election in two constituencies on 7 December) was as follows (1977 result in brackets):

	Seats	% of Votes
Labour	66 (76)	37·3 (42·2)
Socialist Left	4 (2)	4·9 (4·1)
Conservative	53 (41)	31·6 (24·7)
Christian People's Party	15 (22)	9·3 (12·4)
Centre	11 (12)	6·7 (8·6)
Liberals	2 (2)	3·9 (3·2)
Progress Party	4 (0)	4·5 (1·9)

The election's main loser was the Labour Party. Labour remained the largest single party, but as its own losses outweighed the Socialist Left's gains there was no longer a socialist Storting majority to keep it in office as a minority Government. The 'middle parties' were also losers, notably the Christian People's Party with its unclear position on participation in a non-socialist coalition. The election's victors were the Conservative Party and the two extreme parties, on the right the anti-tax, anti-welfare state Progress Party, on the left the anti-Nato Socialist Left party.

Coalition negotiations between the Conservative, Centre and Christian People's Parties broke down over the abortion issue, and on 14 October the Conservatives formed a minority Government with Mr Kåre Willoch as Prime Minister. The new Government, dependent on the other two parties' parliamentary support for those policies on which they had previously reached agreement, took office with a programme of cutting direct taxes and generally reducing the state's regulating role in economic and social life.

SWEDEN

For the second time since the non-socialist parties came to power in 1976, a three-party coalition under Mr Thorbjörn Fälldin collapsed through internal dissension, which seriously damaged the voters' confidence in their ability to govern and improved the chances of a Social Democratic victory in the 1982 election.

The non-socialists' disagreements arose over implementing the Government's proposal to cut marginal income tax rates by an average of 10-15 per cent over the period 1982-5. This proposal was part of a two-year 5,200 million Kroner package of public spending cuts and incentives for industry, announced on 3 February to coincide with the conclusion of a private sector wage agreement giving an average 7 per cent rise over two years with inflation guarantees. The tax-cutting proposal was initially rejected by the Social Democrats and trade unions as favouring higher income groups. However, in view of the Government's slender one-seat Riksdag majority, the Centre and Liberal parties were anxious to reach a compromise with the opposition in order to secure broad support for this important measure of tax reform. They therefore sought negotiations with the Social Democrats and on 24 April obtained their agreement in principle to support the cuts in marginal tax rates, in return for their postponement until 1983 (after the election), a weakening of inflation-indexation of tax rates, and cuts in tax relief to home buyers. The Moderates, not represented in these negotiations, rejected the result as an 'historic capitulation'.

On 4 May Mr Gösta Bohman, Moderate leader and Economy Minister, took his party out of the coalition and on 8 May Mr Fälldin resigned. However, the Moderates were unwilling to force an election which would return a socialist Government. On 19 May they therefore supported the continuation in office of a two-party Centre-Liberal Government with only 102 of the Riksdag's 349 members, and (under their new chairman, Mr Ulf Adlesohn, after late October) continued to support the main lines of Government economic policy while opposing the 'tax agreement'. The non-socialists' main hope for winning the 1982 election lay in the adoption by the Social Democrats at their autumn congress of the widely unpopular proposal for 'wage-earner' funds, under which union-controlled funds financed by taxes on firms' profits and wages would be invested in industry, eventually leading to the unions' achieving a dominant position in the economy.

On 14 September the Government devalued the Krona by 10 per cent in an attempt to increase Swedish industry's export competitiveness. This was accompanied by a price freeze until the end of 1981, more public spending cuts, measures to encourage investment and labour flexibility, and a cut in VAT from 23·46 per cent to 20 per cent. The economic situation remained serious, with no growth, inflation about 10 per cent, unemployment rising sharply to some 4 per cent of the labour force, and the budget deficit estimated at 70,000 million Kroner, over 12 per cent of GDP.

On 27 October a Soviet submarine, alleged by Sweden to be carrying nuclear weapons, was discovered deep in Swedish territorial waters outside the Karlskrona naval base. By the time the submarine was released on 6 November Sweden's relations with the Soviet Union had been severely strained and the proposal for negotiations about a Nordic nuclear-free zone had received a serious setback.

FINLAND

On 27 October 81-year-old President Urho Kekkonen resigned because of rapidly failing health after 25 years in office. Although the timing was unexpected—his latest six-year term did not expire until 1984—the event was not, because of the President's increasing frailty. The succession question thus dominated Finnish politics throughout the year, implicitly until 7 September when he went sick, openly thereafter.

A spring Government crisis over the national two-year wage agreement signed on 9 March had already demonstrated that Kekkonen's domination of political life was ending. From January to April Mr Mauno Koivisto's four-party centre-left coalition was split over the agreement, particularly the indexation clauses and the necessary accompanying social security legislation. The People's Democrats voted against the indexation clauses in the Eduskunta on 24 February. When, in March, they dissented over the social security legislation, the Social Democrats insisted on Government unity and the coalition's fall seemed certain.

Then on 2 April Kekkonen intervened to tell Koivisto to restore Government unity by 10 April or resign. On 6 April Koivisto publicly rejected the ultimatum, saying he would not make his Government's survival dependent on the People's Democrats' position on this legislation, although he did hope for as much agreement as possible; his coalition's fall, followed by elections, was too high a price to pay for unanimity. Koivisto's stand forced his own party to support him, the Centrists could not risk incurring sole responsibility for the Government's collapse, and the People's Democrats compromised by confining their dissent to the Government protocol. Koivisto had challenged Kekkonen's power to break Governments, and had won. His personal authority and presidential chances were both enhanced while constitutionally the outcome was seen as having strengthened the Premier's position *vis-à-vis* the President.

A second coalition crisis in the autumn over financing the 1982 budget deficit—the Centre Party wanted to raise the sales tax, the two left-wing parties to raise the charges on employers—was speedily resolved after Kekkonen fell ill. Thereafter the parties' main attention was directed to the forthcoming presidential election which, following Kekkonen's resignation, was fixed for 17-18 January 1982. During November the parties chose their candidates, the main ones being: for the Social Democrats, the very popular Mauno Koivisto; for the Centre Party, Johannes Virolainen (after the rank and file had rejected the leadership's choice, Ahti Karjalainen); for the People's Democratic League, its Socialist chairman, Kalevi Kivistö (against the votes of the Communist Party's hardline minority group); for the National Coalition, its former chairman Harri Holkeri; and for the Swedish People's Party, Professor Jans-Magnus Jansson, editor of *Hufvudstadsbladet*.

AUSTRIA

The year began with a minor ministerial reshuffle after the departure for the Creditanstalt-Bankverein of the controversial Finance Minister and Vice-Chancellor, Dr Hannes Androsch (see AR 1980, p. 159). He was succeeded by Herr Herbert Salcher, previously Minister of Health, and Herr Salcher by Dr Kurt Steyrer. Herr Fred Sinowatz, the Minister of Education, became Vice-Chancellor, and the new Ministers were sworn in on 20 January.

Dr Androsch's resignation from government, if not from politics, allowed the ruling Socialist Party (SPÖ) again to present a united front. The political temperature dropped accordingly, although investigations continued into the scandal over the financing of Vienna's new general hospital, further arrests being made in July and heavy sentences passed in November on defendants in the first trial arising from it. Although the SPÖ held a successful party conference in May, at which it adopted its long-awaited 'Economic Programme for the Eighties', it was evident that party confidence had been shaken. Opinion polls now indicated that the

SPÖ could expect to lose its absolute majority at the general election due in 1983, and to perform still worse if the Federal Chancellor, Dr Bruno Kreisky, did not stand for re-election. Despite these uncertainties, the SPÖ gained an additional seat at the expense of the Freedom Party (FPÖ) in October elections for the provincial assembly in Styria, although the People's Party (ÖVP) retained its absolute majority.

The Government's main domestic achievement was enactment of the new Media Law, passed on 12 June, which modernized or abolished a mass of obsolete legislation. Their main domestic preoccupation remained the economy. Although Austrian prosperity remained outwardly unimpaired, real growth in GDP fell to zero during 1981 and, after the record foreign trade deficit of 1980, rising energy costs and severe industrial recession produced a record number of bankruptcies. The Government continued to give priority to full employment and to their social and economic development programmes, but in April announced a programme of retrenchment in expenditure planned for 1982, and in November postponed the purchase of fifty fighter aircraft for the Austrian air force. They also continued to lobby the EEC for a financial contribution to the cost of building a new motorway, arguing that Community transit traffic would benefit substantially from it. The 1982 budget, laid before Parliament on 14 October, was presented as a 'saving budget' with a stabilizing effect; nonetheless the gross deficit envisaged for 1982 was almost AS 60,000 million, or 10,000 million more than 1981, mostly due to increased levels of debt servicing. Against this, annual rates of unemployment and inflation, at 2·4 and 6·8 per cent respectively, were only marginally higher than those for 1980, and exports also picked up slightly. By December Austrian economic forecasters were once more expressing 'reserved optimism'.

Internationally Austria took an active part in the 'North-South Dialogue' and presented its own proposals for Third World development at the Cancún summit in October. Most bilateral exchanges were with Eastern Europe and the Middle East. In January the Minister of Trade, Herr Josef Staribacher, visited Moscow to sign a long-term agreement on economic cooperation. This was followed on 6-10 April by a visit from the Soviet Prime Minister, Mr Tikhonov, his first to a Western country, during which an important contract was signed for delivery of 800,000 tons of seamless oil pipes. President Ceauçescu of Romania paid a successful state visit in June, but in September the Czech Government postponed indefinitely the state visit by President Husak planned for October after the discovery that a Czech agent had been active among refugee dissidents in Vienna (see p. 121). Meanwhile a steady stream of Polish refugees was arriving in Austria and on 8 December, when nearly 30,000 had applied for asylum, the Government was forced to reintroduce the visa requirement for Polish visitors. The imposition of martial law in

Poland prompted a joint statement of concern from the three main Austrian political parties on 15 December.

No such unanimity existed over Dr Kreisky's Middle East policy, after the murder on 1 May of the president of the Austro-Israel Association, Herr Heinz Nittel, an arms-smuggling incident at Vienna airport on 1 August in which the official PLO representative was involved, and an attack by Arab terrorists on a Vienna synagogue during the Sabbath service on 29 August in which two worshippers died. One of the killers later acknowledged responsibility for the Nittel murder, and the synagogue attack caused a further deterioration in relations between Austria and Israel. Although the Austrian authorities concluded that those incidents were the work of a hardline Palestinian splinter group, the PLO representive had already left Vienna after the airport incident and, in the wake of President Sadat's assassination in October, the Government unanimously decided that the post should remain unoccupied for the time being.

SWITZERLAND

In comparison with its neighbours, Switzerland was undoubtedly in an enviable situation in 1981: full employment (with 700,000 foreign workers), practically no strikes bar a certain unrest in the printing industry, a record year in tourism with an increase of the formerly traditional British guests, a real boom in the building industry and in four referendums full agreement of the electorate with Parliament and Government.

But shadows were not lacking in this pleasant scene. After a period of relative stability, prices—particularly house-rents, due to higher mortgage interest—began rising, the deficit-spending of the Federal State could not be stopped, and the more or less permanent struggle between the left and right wings of the Socialist Party exerted an unhappy influence upon the collaboration of the four-party Federal Council, although the two Socialists among the seven members tried to maintain trustful relations with their colleagues.

On 5 April the left-wing initiative for a new policy towards foreign workers—no temporary restrictions for the typical seasonal workers, more rights and privileges unkown to Swiss citizens working abroad—was rejected by the overwhelming majority of 1,300,000 to 250,000, but less than 40 per cent of the electorate went to the polls. Meanwhile the Government and Parliament had framed a new law for foreigners which would be submitted to another referendum in 1982, offering more opportunities for foreign workers and their families to stay permanently in Switzerland. The main object of Swiss policy remained stability of the number of foreign residents, nearly one million out of the country's 6¼ million inhabitants.

Ten years after the introduction of women's right to vote, on 14 June, by 800,000 votes to 526,000 the people affirmed the equal rights of both sexes as a constitutional principle, later to be embodied in various laws applying equality in civil law and in education and labour affairs, and enforcing equal pay for men and women in the same jobs. This time just over 30 per cent went to the polls, notably including a great many women. On the same day a new constitutional clause was approved to protect consumers by giving consumer organizations the same right as the main professional unions to participate in pre-parliamentary drafting of consumer legislation.

Year after year the annual deficit of the Swiss Confederation had lain between 1,000 and 1,500 million Swiss francs, and within half a dozen years the public debt had grown to 20,000 million francs, the budget being charged with 1,000 million francs of interest. All political parties were agreed in seeking to overcome this deficit spending, but a deep rift had opened between the Socialists and the three other partners in the Federal Council on how to establish the budgetary balance. Nearly half the revenues of the federal state depended upon income tax and indirect taxes. This system being restricted in point of time up to the end of 1982, a common agreement for prolongation until 1994 was finally reached between the four Government parties. On 29 November, in a referendum, the people approved the prolongation by 818,000 votes to 367,000. Indirect taxes would be increased by 600 million francs, direct taxation reduced by 310 million francs. Only 29·8 per cent of the electorate, however, went to the polls. These measures would not by any means produce the equilibrium urgently needed. The main task of the coming years would still be to find a way to cure the ailing budget.

Nuclear power stations remained the subject of deep public controversy. After nearly 20 years of debate the Federal Council finally agreed at the end of September to the construction of a big nuclear plant at Kaiseraugst on the Rhine border with Germany, but the Opposition, supported by the left-wing parties, at once launched an initiative for a referendum. Despite the traditional reluctance of a neutral state, Switzerland received two state visits, welcoming the popular President of Italy, Sandro Pertini, and the President of Austria, Rudolf Kirschläger, thus demonstrating its particularly friendly relations with these two neighbouring nations. At the end of the year the Federal Council, in an unequivocal statement, uttered its misgivings about the military regime in Poland.

In the last session of the year the Swiss Parliament elected the Socialist Mrs Hedi Lang President (Speaker) of the National Council, thus honouring both the equal rights of women and an efficient social worker from the small Zürich town of Wetzikon. At the same time Vice-President Dr Fritz Honegger, the Liberal-Radical head of the Department of Economics, was unanimously elected State President for 1982, and Federal Councillor Pierre Aubert, a former Socialist MP, Vice-President of the Federal Council. Federal Chancellor Dr Karl Huber, of the Christian Democratic Party, having resigned in the middle of the year at the age of 68, Parliament elected Dr Walter Buser, the Socialist candidate, to this highest office of the administration. Buser became the first Chancellor from the Socialist Party. These elections were regarded as a step towards bridging the gap between the governmental parties.

Chapter 3

SPAIN—PORTUGAL—MALTA—GIBRALTAR—GREECE—CYPRUS—TURKEY

SPAIN

ON 5 January the Minister of Defence announced a Bill to reduce slightly the high age of retirement of officers in the armed services. Under it a number of right-wing officers would unwillingly pass into the reserve. On 9 January the Cabinet approved arrangements for the return to the Basques of their ancient right to levy and collect taxes for both their own and the national administration, and confirmed the first timid steps towards the establishment of a Basque police force. The central police forces were to remain in Euzkadi, but under a measure of control by a council under the co-presidency of the Basque and central Governments. On 10 January General Alfonso Armada Comyn, shortly to be appointed deputy chief of staff of the army, and the notoriously ultra-right GOC of the Valencia military district, General Jaime Milans del Bosch, met to discuss what should be done to stem 'the disintegration of the sacred unity of Spain' and the publication of news and opinions on the armed services and paramilitary police offensive to their concept of themselves as upholders of values on which Spain's greatness and freedom depended. Little was to be expected, they maintained, from a Government drawn from a party (the UCD) whose divisions were eroding respect for all authority and order.

The Cabinet reshuffle of the previous September (see AR 1980, pp. 165-6) had not reconciled the factions within the UCD. The differences between them over the extent to which devolution was politically expedient, and over economic and social priorities, remained unresolved. The Christian Democrats and Liberals, increasingly dissatisfied with Adolfo Suárez's personal style as Premier and party leader, were demanding the democratization of the party's structures, confident that internal elections on the basis of proportional representation would give them a greater say in the executive. The Social Democrats were threatening a defection if a Divorce Bill, drafted by their leader Francisco Fernández Ordóñez, Minister of Justice, were not rapidly enacted. Both within and outside the party there was widespread opposition to its provision for divorce almost on demand.

In mid-January the Christian Democrats and Liberals became explicitly critical of the leadership. On 29 January Suárez resigned both as Prime Minister and as party chairman. The party executive proposed as UCD candidate for the premiership Leopoldo Calvo Sotelo, then Second Deputy Prime Minister and economic overlord. The party's annual congress, held on 6-9 February, endorsed the candidature by acclamation, and a majority of delegates chose Suárez's brother-in-law Augusto Rodríguez Sahagún, Minister of Defence, as leader of the party. Calvo Sotelo was duly nominated Prime Minister by the King on 10 February, and now had to seek in the Lower House a vote of confidence on his programme.

The King and Queen had recently returned from a visit to Euzkadi, undertaken against the advice of Suárez and the security forces. Coolly received in Vitoria, the capital of the new autonomous region, they had been warmly welcomed in Bilbao on 3 February. On the following day the King, with the Queen at his side, addressed the Basque Parliament gathered in the historic assembly hall in Guernica. Soon after he had begun to speak the members of Herri Batasuna, effectively the political wing of ETA-militar, broke into a civil war hymn. They were shouted down and forcibly expelled by the other members of the Parliament. The King, who had remained impassive throughout the disturbance, renewed his speech. He spoke of his belief in democracy and of his confidence that the Basque people, with their ancient liberties restored to them, would recover their faith in themselves and their future.

By going to Euzkadi, by his serenity when confronted by violence and by his speech the King had won over to himself many a Basque. The discovery on 6 February of the body of the young engineer in charge of the construction of a nuclear power station near Bilbao, kidnapped by ETA-militar eight days earlier, further deprived that revolutionary and separatist organization of popular support. Hopes rose of peace in Euzkadi. They received a severe shock a week later when an ETA detainee died in Madrid as a result of his treatment while under interrogation by the police. When, in the face of public disgust, the Minister of Justice ordered an investigation, some 200 senior police officers resigned in protest. Senior military officers persuaded the police to withdraw their resignations.

Calvo Sotelo presented his programme to the Cortes on 18 February. For his immediate confirmation as Prime Minister he required an overall majority, that is, the vote of 11 members above the UCD's 165. In order to gain the support of the nine-strong right-wing Democratic Coalition (CD) he declared his intention to take Spain into Nato, to intensify the fight against terrorism and to cut public spending. Only three of the nine voted for him, however, while a vague undertaking to continue the process of devolution failed to win him the support of the nine Catalan nationalist moderates (CIU). The Left and the Basques voted against him. Under the constitution there would have to be a second vote, when a simple majority would suffice. It was scheduled for 23 February.

On that day, as the members began voting, Civil Guards burst into the Chamber. They fired some shots, and their leader, Lieut.-Colonel José Antonio Tejero (see AR 1980, p. 166), advanced to hold at gunpoint the President of the Cortes. General Manuel Gutiérrez Mellado, the First Deputy Prime Minister, was manhandled as he tried to challenge Tejero. The members were told to await the arrival of 'the competent military authority', later identified as General Armada. A detachment of the armoured division quartered near Madrid appeared outside the King's residence, and another ordered the state radio and television to stop broadcasting. In Valencia General Milans del Bosch declared a state of emergency in his extensive military district, and ordered a tank regiment to patrol the streets of that city. By telephone he urged other district commanders to follow his lead: a 'power vacuum' existed in Madrid; the country was in danger; he was carrying out, he alleged, the King's orders.

In fact, King Juan Carlos, informed of the rebellion, immediately convened the joint chiefs of staff committee (JCSC), and commanded it to maintain the constitutional order. By telephone he disabused all the district commanders and instructed them to obey orders only from the JCSC. As the whole Cabinet was held captive in the Cortes, he told the under-secretaries of state to take over civil affairs. This 'acting' Government assured the public that the democratic order would prevail. The JCSC ordered all service and police units to barracks, except those with specific duties. The Madrid armoured units obeyed. The state radio and television resumed and at 1 am on 24 February the King broadcast through television a brief message. Dressed in the uniform of commander-in-chief of the armed services, he gave a summary of what he had done, then said solemnly: 'The Crown cannot tolerate actions whose object is to disrupt by force the democratic process.'

The King's declaration undermined the rebels' position: they could hardly justify their actions as a defence of authority while disobeying their commander-in-chief. Nevertheless, Milans del Bosch did not withdraw his tanks until 5 am and Tejero did not release his captives and surrender until shortly before noon. Immediately afterwards the King received the leaders of the four main political parties. He warned them of the dangers of openly antagonizing the armed forces at that juncture, and of leaving it to the Crown to confront them and bear direct responsibility in such events.

Over the next month 32 officers and one civilian were indicted for their overt participation in the event. It was common knowledge that many more servicemen and civilians were implicated. Action against them was judged inexpedient. The summary court-martial procedures of the previous regime had been abolished; the new process of law was complicated. The defence was to make full use of its complexity to delay into 1982 the trial of the 33.

Calvo Sotelo's premiership was duly endorsed by the Cortes on 25 February. He rejected advice to form a coalition Government. Nevertheless the Socialist and Communist parties promised their support in 'measures to strengthen democracy'. Two laws were rapidly enacted in April. One defined in greater detail than earlier legislation 'acts of rebellion' and increased the penalties for them; the other stipulated the duties of the Government of the day in exceptional circumstances ranging from natural disasters to insurrection. The process of devolution was slowed down by agreement between the UCD and Socialists. The labour organizations, equally anxious not to embarrass the Government, signed a tripartite agreement with the Government and the employers' federation (CEOE) on employment policy, and throughout the year kept their word somewhat more faithfully than the CEOE.

The armed services were given a new role in the fight against terrorism: combat troops and naval units were deployed to patrol the Pyrenees and the north coast, to intercept ETA incursions from French bases. The French refused to hand over suspected terrorists but removed them to the island of Yeu. One of the two branches of ETA, the *político-militar*, declared an armistice. The police forces were thus able to concentrate on fighting the activities of the other branch, the *militar*, but appeared as indifferent as before to democratic methods. In May an ETA-militar group killed a general and three other persons in Madrid: a Civil Guard unit in Almería thereupon detained, interrogated and shot three youths. Its commander, an army officer, alleged that the youths had attempted to escape, but their bodies showed signs of having been mutilated before death, and they were innocent. The official investigation into the affair remained unfinished at the end of the year.

The Divorce Bill was approved in August, amended to require one year's separation where both parties sought it, and five years if either objected. In October the Government forced the director-general of the state radio and television to resign. He had allowed programmes offensive to many Spaniards; the Government was anxious to deprive the extremists of their claim to be the sole upholders of traditional Christian values. Throughout the summer the Government gave much publicity to its intention to seek Spain's admission into Nato, hoping thereby to divert military interest from internal affairs. The left campaigned against the entry. Public opinion polls gave lower percentages to those in favour of entry than to those against, but when the Government sought parliamentary authority for it on 29 October it obtained, with the help of the CD, the Catalan and unexpectedly the Basque nationalists, 186 votes against the left's 146. The formal request for admission was despatched on 2 December.

Between those dates there was a fresh political crisis. Dissatisfied with a rightward trend in the Government on social and economic issues, the Social Democrats formally seceded from the UCD. Calvo Sotelo, to the chagrin of some UCD founder members, among them Adolfo Suárez and Rodríguez Sahagún, seemed attracted by a call from the leader of the Democratic Alliance, Manuel Fraga, for the formation of a 'greater right' instead of a centre union. Calvo Sotelo forced Rodríguez Sahagún to resign the party leadership, and prevailed upon a majority of its executive to give it to himself. Adolfo Suárez left the party. On 2 December Calvo Sotelo reshuffled his Cabinet, making only one concession to his critics by dismissing his Minister of Health, Jesús Sancho Rof. In May several hundred people had been affected, some fatally, by a pulmonary disease; by November the affected numbered thousands, and over 200 had died. The Minister had made light of the affair at first, and had still not acted with alacrity after its cause had been established—the consumption of denaturized rape-seed oil fraudulently sold as olive oil.

The rightward trend did not placate the military extremists. In October a court martial awarded Captain Milans del Bosch, the rebellious General's son, a derisory sentence for grossly insulting the King. In November the extreme right gathered 100,000 adherents at a rally in Madrid; many, in defiance of the law, wore military-style uniforms; some were members of the security forces off-duty. On 5 December a statement was published in support of the 23 February rebels, signed by 100 captains, lieutenants and sergeants, and inspired by officers of higher rank.

PORTUGAL

The programme which the new Prime Minister, Francisco Pinto Balsemão, put before the Assembly in January was identical with that of his predecessor. Balsemão promised to press for Portugal's admittance to the EEC, to encourage private enterprise, to curb unemployment and inflation, and above all to amend the constitution. As the Democratic Alliance held 134 of the Assembly's 250 seats, approval of the programme was a formality. Its fulfilment was foreseeably difficult.

The scheduled date of entry into the EEC had to be postponed to 1984 in the light of Portugal's backward administrative and economic state. The pruning of the country's 400,000-strong bureaucracy proceeded but slowly. In the immediate results, expectations of the continuing reorganization of the collective farms in the Alentejo into less extensive cooperatives were disappointed. Agriculture suffered severely from a drought which afflicted almost the whole of the Iberian peninsula: Portugal had again to import some 60 per cent of its food requirements.

Balsemão decided in the spring on a five-year development plan, which, he hoped, would result in an average growth rate of 5 per cent per annum. An improvement in agricultural output could not be other than long-term. Industrial expansion offered the possibility of a more rapid rise in the low general standard of living, but would undoubtedly increase the oil bill. Provided that the income from upmarket tourism and the remittances of the 1,500,000 Portuguese working elsewhere in Western Europe was maintained, the balance would come from the country's gold reserves.

Balsemão's plan met with the full approval of the Democratic Alliance; not so his personal approach to the problem of constitutional reform (see AR 1980, p. 168). The two-thirds majority in the Assembly required by the constitution for its reform was out of reach of the Alliance by itself. The late Dr Sá Carneiro's abrasive relations with President Eanes had hardened the latter's resolve not to authorize a referendum, the alternative way to reform. On being sworn in for his second five-year term as President, Eanes had promised to cooperate with the new Premier. Balsemão hoped to succeed by cajolement where Sá Carneiro had failed. He hoped also to soften the socialist opposition to reform.

Balsemão insisted that the marxist-socialist commonplaces in the constitutional text were immaterial. What really mattered was the authority vested in the Council of the Revolution to override the Assembly: Portugal could not be deemed a democracy while the elected civil power was subordinated thus to the military. The semi-presidential, semi-parliamentary system established in the constitution had been a major factor in Portugal's years of the political instability from which the Socialist Party no less than the Alliance had suffered. The preponderant role given the state in the management and development of the economy had no parallel in the EEC. Balsemão preferred to talk of expansion of the private sector and free enterprise rather than of denationalization.

He had to face strong criticism of his conciliatory attitude at the annual congress of his own Social Democratic Party (PSD), held on 20-22 February. He emerged the stronger, after the election of a greater number of supporters than of opponents to the party's national council. Nevertheless, his critics remained dissatisfied. Members of the other parties in the Alliance, the Centre Democrats (CDS) and the Monarchists (PMM), also attacked the 'weakness' of his dealings with the President and Council of the Revolution.

On 18 July the Council, chaired by the President, rejected for the fourth time the Bill to reopen banking, insurance and certain industries to private enterprise (see AR 1980, p. 168). Balsemão's critics in the Alliance demanded that the Government resign in protest. The Cabinet refused, but accused the Council of breaking the most elementary rules of democracy. It announced also that it would divert monies earmarked for the state industries to social services.

The critics were not satisfied. On 9 August Balsemão threatened to resign from both the leadership of the party and the premiership unless the party council gave him a near-unanimous vote of confidence and his critics promised to desist from attacking him. He failed to get that near-unanimity and therefore resigned. The critics could find no one to take his place. The council was reconvened and in a new vote a greater number than before did as Balsemão wished. He withdrew his resignation from the leadership and Eanes asked him to form a new Government. This time he prevailed upon the CDS leader Diogo Freitas do Amaral to accept the deputy premiership and the Ministry of Defence.

In presenting this Government's programme to the Assembly on 14 September Balsemão gave top priority to Portugal's economic problems: the balance of payments deficit was going out of control. Over the next month he worked on a draft of a Constitutional Reform Bill, consulting the President and the Socialist leader, Mario Soares, in the hope of producing a text acceptable to some at least of the Socialists. All seemed to be going well when on 26 October the Council of the Revolution issued an apologia of itself as the 'guardian of the revolution' and of the President's powers under the existing constitution. The political parties and not the Council, it said, were to blame for their own difficulties. The defence of the President's position was backed by the Socialist Party in a statement issued on the next day.

In December abnormally heavy rains brought the drought to an end, causing further damage to agriculture, and the Government expressed its fear that in consequence Portugal would have to import as much as 75 per cent of its food during 1982.

MALTA

The election on 12 December for all 65 seats in the National Assembly under a complicated form of proportional representation was fiercely

The Prince of Wales and Lady Diana Spencer on the day their engagement was announced; they were married in St Paul's Cathedral amid great public rejoicing on 29 July 1981.

On 30 March 1981 an attempt was made on the life of President Reagan on a Washington Street. Above, the President immediately after he had been shot and wounded; a secret service agent hustles him into his motor car. Below, the scene as the would-be assassin is overpowered; encircled is the colonel carrying the black box with the code that could launch nuclear war.

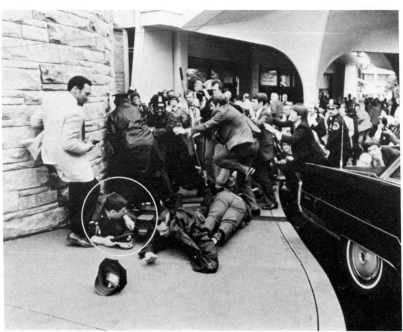

Gamma

The extraordinary scene immediately after the assassination of President Sadat at a military parade in Cairo on 6 October 1981. All but one or two flee the saluting base as gunmen pour bullets into their victim.

Pope John Paul II, seriously wounded by a Turkish gunman in St Peter's Square, Rome, on 15 May 1981, sinks into the arms of his aides.

Colonel Antonio Tejero Molina, gun in hand and supported by armed civil guards, declaims from the rostrum of the Spanish Cortes which they had seized in an abortive coup attempt on 23 February 1981.

conducted. The result was close. Mr Dom Mintoff's Labour Government was returned to office with 34 seats; Mr Eddie Fenech Adami's Nationalist opposition won 31 seats but the party increased its share of the poll from 48·5 per cent in 1976 to 50·9 per cent. After the election, Mintoff stressed the sovereignty of parliament, Adami talked of the sovereignty of the people. It was a reversal of their roles since Mintoff was always the populist hero whereas his opponents had stressed the rule of law.

It was the Labour Party's third successive election victory under Mintoff, who could properly claim to be its chief architect. The Nationalists condemned the creeping authoritarianism that many people had resented under Labour Party rule. State power, which touched everyone in Malta, was used by the Government both to reward its friends and to curb its opponents. Yet Mintoff could successfully appeal to his record as the Great Benefactor—old age pensions, child benefits, maternity allowances, housing schemes and similar appurtenances of the welfare state. Other issues in the election were probably of less effect, but they included the proposal by Fenech Adami that Malta should apply for membership of the EEC, in opposition to Mintoff's stand for Mediterranean neutrality.

On 22 June Mintoff had met the Council of Ministers of the Ten at Luxembourg, seeking increased financial aid, better trading access to the European market and help for Malta's agriculture. He suggested that Malta might be given some form of special associate status *vis-à-vis* the Community, but he also believed that a neutral Malta could become 'a bridge of friendship between her northern European neighbours and her southern Arab-African friends'. When his request was rejected, he turned on the Foreign Ministers: 'Even the old gods of Olympus had not behaved with such condescension towards poor mortals.'

Relations with Malta's 'southern Arab friends' were soured by the continuing quarrel with Libya. On 26 January Mintoff accused Qadafi of breaking a promise under the 1976 agreement to refer disputes affecting off-shore oil drilling rights to the World Court. The dispute over the median line dragged on without being resolved.

The expulsion of the Blue Sisters—the nursing sisters of the Little Company of Mary (see AR 1980, p. 170)—was postponed *sine die* on 3 January, when a government statement announced the resignation of Professor Cremona, the Chief Justice, three days before his due date of retirement. Professor Cremona had been Chief Justice since 1971 and was a judge of the European Court of Human Rights at Strasbourg. The Opposition protested vigorously to the President, Mr Anton Buttigieg: 'This is not the first time that the Government has abused its powers in a way which nullifies the constitutional guarantees by not allowing the Superior Court to carry out its duties.'

Such disputes, common enough in these small islands, flare up, cause great excitement and then subside. In 1981 they included allegations (31 July) that British nationals had been recruited to stage a coup d'état against Mintoff. During the weeks preceding the December election, a further quarrel arose between Mintoff and Britain when journalists of the BBC and *The Times* were refused permission to cover the contest.

GIBRALTAR

On 7-8 January Sir Ian Gilmour, Minister of State at the Foreign Office, visited Sr Perez-Llorca, the Spanish Foreign Minister, and Sr Ponset, the Minister in charge of Common Market negotiations, in Madrid: there followed an announcement that, within the North Atlantic alliance, there might be a joint use of the naval base at Gibraltar by Spain and Britain. Related matters of EEC and Nato membership, and Spain's delay in opening the frontier at La Linea, were taken up by a delegation of MPs to Madrid in April, when it became clear that the Spanish Government—shaken by the recent attempted coup (see p. 169)—was genuinely concerned to try and minimize Anglo-Spanish differences, if only to enlist London as an ally on the road to Brussels.

EEC membership also troubled the British Government over Gibraltarian demands for full citizenship status under the new legislation on British nationality (see pp. 32-33). It was proposed to grant only 'citizenship of British dependent territories', on the same basis as Hong Kong or the Falkland Islands. The Gibraltarians, however, were members of the European Community and they resented being second-class citizens. In the House of Commons Mr Albert McQuarrie, chairman of the all-party British-Gibraltar group, and twenty other Conservative MPs voted with the Opposition on the report stage of the British Nationality Bill, reducing the Government's majority to only 25. In the House of Lords the Government was defeated by 150 votes to 112 on an all-party amendment (moved by Lord Bethell) granting Gibraltarians full British citizenship.

On 21 July it was announced that King Juan Carlos had decided to boycott the royal wedding because the Prince and Princess of Wales were to board the royal yacht in Gibraltar on their honeymoon. The royal couple were accorded a tumultuous welcome on the Rock on 1 August.

Indeed the Gibraltarians had good cause to welcome the visit and the support they were given in Parliament, since they also suffered as much ill-fortune as good. On 23 November, the Ministry of Defence announced that the naval dockyards at Chatham, Portsmouth and Gibraltar were to be closed from 1983. It meant the loss of about 800 jobs unless the yard could be converted to commercial use, although a further 1,000 would continue to be employed on facilities—refuelling, communications and accommodation—to be retained by the Royal Navy. Mr Alex Kitson of the Transport and General Workers' Union (which had 5,000 members on the Rock) visited Gibraltar (1-3 December) to pledge his support for a campaign against the closure.

Most of the year's diplomatic activity was concerned with the vexed question of the Spanish frontier. The free movement of goods and people between Gibraltar and Spain had been agreed (it was thought) between London and Madrid under the Lisbon Agreement of April 1980 (see AR 1980, p. 171), as from June 1981. That date came and went; the frontier remained closed. Then, following a visit to London on 4 October by the Spanish Prime Minister Sr Sotelo, final impetus was given to an old dialogue. Sir Joshua Hassan, Gibraltar's Chief Minister, remained sceptical; many Gibraltarians now wondered whether, after so long a time, it would be in their interests to have the frontier opened if it meant giving access to Spanish workers for longer than a day's work and return. It was left to the new year, however, for agreement on a May 1982 date for lifting the 1969 blockade.

GREECE

For Greece 1981 was a year of particular significance. For not only did it enter the EEC as the tenth full member on 1 January but on 18 October a radical Socialist Government, which was basically opposed to Greek membership of the Community, was elected to office by a convincing margin. Although it had been widely predicted that Andreas Papandreou's Panhellenic Socialist Movement (Pasok) would win the elections, the size of its victory appeared to surprise even its own supporters. This gave the party a clear overall majority of 172 seats in the 300-member Parliament, in which for the first time in many years only three parties were represented. Pasok's share of the vote (48 per cent) was almost double that of 1977 (25 per cent), while the ruling New Democracy Party led by George Rallis saw its share decline from 42 per cent (172 seats) to 36 per cent (115 seats). The Communist Party of Greece (KKE) marginally increased its share from 9 to 11 per cent and its seats from 11 to 13.

Even before the campaign officially got under way in August, Pasok had been able to seize the initiative and force the ruling New Democracy Party on the defensive. In his effort to win over the crucial 12 per cent share of the vote achieved by the Union of the Democratic Centre (EDIK) in 1977, Papandreou significantly tempered the radical socialist rhetoric that had characterized the party in the early years after its foundation in 1974. He no longer insisted that Pasok was a class-based, marxist party and emphasized that his programme of radical domestic renewal, coupled with a vigorous assertion of Greek sovereignty in foreign affairs, constituted no threat to the existing social order.

He significantly modified his previous intransigent hostility towards the Nato alliance and towards the EEC. In determining the country's relationship with the former, consideration was now to be given to the international balance of power and to the re-equipment needs of the armed forces, and efforts were to be made to negotiate special terms with the EEC, to be put to the people in a referendum. Pasok also qualified its threat to close the US bases in Greece, negotiations over the future status of which had been broken off by the Rallis Government in June. No modification of Pasok's uncompromising attitude towards Turkey could, however, be detected.

Mr Papandreou promised to 'socialize' large sectors of the economy and stressed that Pasok was a movement rather than a mere party. Proclaiming himself the champion of the non-privileged against the privileged, he argued that only Pasok offered a realistic chance of ending the virtually unbroken monopoly of power enjoyed by the right since the end of World War II. He made much of New Democracy's failure to curb an inflation rate of approximately 25 per cent which opinion polls had consistently indicated to be the principal concern of the electorate.

Unable to match Mr Papandreou's promise of *Allagi*, or Change with a Capital C, New Democracy chose instead to emphasize its pro-Western orientation and the economic achievements of post-war right-wing Governments. It pointed to the part it had played in restoring democratic institutions after the collapse of the Colonels' dictatorship and to its role in bringing about Greece's accelerated accession to the EEC. It challenged the sincerity of Pasok's commitment to parliamentary government and claimed that a Socialist victory would prove the first step towards one-party rule. Like Pasok, New Democracy sought to attract those who had supported the traditional centre in 1977, while at the same time trying to win back the allegiance of the ultra-conservatives who had given the National Camp a 7 per cent share of the vote in 1977. During the campaign the National Camp withdrew from the contest and urged its supporters to support New Democracy to avoid splitting the right-wing vote.

But New Democracy met with little success in winning over disaffected centre voters; for the results indicated that Pasok had been able to attract virtually all the votes cast for the traditional centre in 1977, the three centre parties achieving only a 1·5 per cent share of the vote. Although the Communist Party of Greece fell well short of its stated target of 17 per cent, a breakthrough figure in the complex system of 'reinforced' proportional representation under which the elections were held, it was able to derive comfort from the poor showing of its arch-rival, the 'Eurocommunist' Communist Party of the Interior (KKEes) which received only a 1·4 per cent share of the vote. The ultra-right-wing Party of the Progressives registered a 1·7 per cent share.

The results of the simultaneous elections for the 24-strong delegation to the European Parliament produced some significant changes in the pattern established in the national elections. The share of the vote achieved by both main parties declined significantly, Pasok's from 48 to 40 per cent, New Democracy's from 36 to 32 per cent. At the same time the Social Democratic KODISO-KAE increased its share six-fold from 0·7 to 4·2 per cent and the Communist Party of the Interior almost four-fold from 1·4 to 5·2 per cent.

The new Government, the first Socialist Government in the country's history, was sworn in on 21 October. It was remarkable for the fact that Mr Papandreou himself retained the defence portfolio, a clear indication of the significance he attached to defence matters and to maintaining good relations with an officer corps that had recently held power for seven years, and for the lack of previous ministerial experience of Cabinet members. One of the few Ministers known outside the country was the film actress Melina Mercouri, who became Minister of Culture. The poor showing of New Democracy led to the replacement of George Rallis as leader of the official Opposition by Evangelos Averoff, formerly Minister of Defence and Deputy Prime Minister.

The new Government moved rapidly to establish its credentials as a radical and reforming Administration by calling for changes in the EEC's Common Agricultural Policy and unsuccessfully seeking to obtain a guarantee of Greece's eastern frontiers by its Nato allies, a move clearly aimed at Turkey. Mr Papandreou also moved quickly to grant full diplomatic status to the PLO office in Athens. Innovations on the domestic front included recognition of the communist-controlled wartime resistance against the Axis, an end to official celebrations of the defeat of the communists in the 1946-9 civil war, the abolition of political censorship and the introduction of a simplified system of accents in writing the language.

Queen Frederika, the widow of King Paul and the mother of ex-King Constantine, died in Madrid on 6 February. The decision of the Rallis Government to allow her to be buried alongside her husband at the family estate at Tatoi outside Athens was criticized in opposition circles, as was the decision to allow the ex-King to visit Greece for six hours to attend his mother's funeral, his first visit since he went into exile in December 1967. Further controversy involving the royal family occurred in connection with the wedding of the Prince of Wales to Lady Diana Spencer. The Greek Government objected to Constantine's being invited as 'King of the Hellenes' and President Constantine Karamanlis declined to attend the wedding, his place being taken by Mr Rallis.

A series of earthquakes in the Athens region towards the end of February (the largest, on 24 February, registering 6·6 on the Richter scale) killed 20 people, destroyed thousands of houses and left 75,000 temporarily homeless. In Loutraki on the Gulf of Corinth a number of hotels, empty in the off-season, collapsed. The tremors also caused damage to the Parthenon and other antiquities. In late July and early August there were numerous forest fires, the most serious of which caused extensive damage to the northern suburbs of Athens. On 24 May the first barrels of crude oil from a Greek deposit were pumped from the Prinos oilfield, off the island of Thasos.

CYPRUS

The year began on an unusually optimistic note when a new round of talks took place in the first week of January between the negotiating teams of the Greek and Turkish communities in a bid to reunify the island since its division in 1974. These were organized by United Nations special representative Hugo Gobbi, a newcomer to the Cyprus scene whose energy and enthusiasm brought a much-needed boost to the long-drawn-out negotiating process. At the same time in the previous year discussions on the territorial and constitutional future of the island had come to a halt and had been resumed only in September, after months of delicate diplomacy. Hopes of a breakthrough were still high in February 1981 but fell a month later when the Turkish Cypriot side announced that it was not going to present its own long-awaited proposals for a settlement.

In May, President Kyprianou made it clear that unless some progress was made at the talks the case would be taken to the UN General Assembly. Then in August the Turkish Cypriots suddenly announced their intention to put forward proposals after all. However, when the Greek Cypriot side studied them, President Kyprianou's reaction was that they did not even form a basis for negotiations, let alone a recipe for an eventual solution. A short time later, the weekly sessions of the inter-communal talks became deadlocked and ceased.

The results of the parliamentary elections, the first since the death of Archbishop Makarios in 1977, caused dramatic changes in the House of Representatives. In an unexpected comeback, Mr Glafkos Clerides's right-wing Democratic Rally party secured 12 of the 35 seats at stake. The communist Akel Party gained the most votes—one per cent more than the Democratic Rally—but under the newly-introduced proportional representation system the two parties' allocation of seats was 12 each. This left President Kyprianou's Democratic Party, which won eight, still controlling the balance of power, while the socialist party Edek won the remaining three. Mr George Ladas of the ruling Democratic Party was elected Chairman (Speaker) of the new House.

Despite predictions of a greater defeat for the President's party, his personal standing and political strength increased, leaving little danger of any serious challange to his leadership until the presidential elections due in 1983.

Economically, the country did better than expected despite an inflation rate of 13·5 per cent and an increase in unemployment, which ran at about 2·8 per cent, low by European standards but high for Cyprus. The Cyprus Chamber of Commerce declared 1981 to be the 'Year of Exports', and following numerous trade missions and exchange visits, mainly with its Arab neighbours, Cyprus succeeded in increasing its volume of exports by 13 per cent. Another big boost to the economy came from tourism, which earned the country a record CY£102 million compared with CY£70 million in 1980. The number of tourists visiting the island increased by 20 per cent and work began on the construction of a new international airport at Paphos, an increasingly-popular resort in the south-west of Cyprus.

In November, a major scandal involving the management of Cyprus Airways was uncovered, and the newly-appointed chairman, Stavros Glatariotis, revealed numerous examples of mismanagement under the previous board of directors. Mr Glatariotis said that the company had lost CY£2 million last year and that a top-level inquiry had begun into the airline's affairs. During the same month the airline also announced that it had decided in principle to buy two Airbus 310s at an estimated cost of CY£54 million. A letter of intent was filed with Airbus Industries leaving options open until March 1982, but there was considerable opposition to the idea from local businessmen and politicians, who maintained that the airline could not afford the price and that the Government was in no financial position to guarantee the deal.

There were scandals in other areas of government as well: the Council of Ministers dismissed 'in the public interest' the director-general of communication and works, Mr P. Kazamias, and the director-general of the Ministry of Education, Mr P. Adamides. In June, the director and spokesman of the Public Information Office, Mr Miltiades Christodolou, resigned after 16 years in office amid reports of irregularities in his department. The Government decided to separate the responsibilities of the post, appointing Mr Kypros Psyllides as acting director-general and Mr Panos Ioannou as government spokesman.

The year also saw police investigations into seven separate bombing incidents, the discovery of the biggest-ever drugs cache in the country (five and a half tons of cannibis resin) and a hijack drama involving a Libyan plane which passed twice through Cyprus airspace before finally landing at Beirut. The law also dealt with the commissioner of cooperatives, Andreas Azinas, who had been under investigation for over a year on charges of violating Central Bank regulations. He was gaoled for eighteen months for misappropriating CY£168,000.

Despite its ups and downs, the year which began on an optimistic note also ended on one, if the optimism was somewhat guarded. December saw the resumption of the intercommunal talks, following the tabling of an evaluation of the Cyprus situation by UN Secretary-General Dr Kurt Waldheim and his local representative Hugo Gobbi. The document, which met with an angry reception from the Greek Cypriots, was eventually acknowledged as a means of resuming the talks, although both sides made their objections known. The appointment of the new UN Secretary-General, Mr Javier Perez de Cuellar, was also acknowledged as an advantage for the talks. He had formerly been UN representative in Cyprus, and was very familiar with the intercommunal problem.

At the end of the year, President Kyprianou refuted charges by mainland Turkey's Premier Admiral Ulusu that the National Guard was increasing its fighting power 'beyond its defence requirements'. The President repeated his offer of demilitarization for Cyprus as evidence of the peaceful intentions of the Government and the Greek Cypriot people towards the Turkish Cypriots.

TURKEY

On 30 December the head of state, General Kenan Evren, announced a time-table for the restoration of civilian parliamentary rule. A new constitution was to be drawn up and submitted to a referendum in autumn 1982. Laws on political parties and on elections would then be enacted to allow parliamentary elections in autumn 1983 or spring 1984, at the latest. The constitution was to be drawn up jointly by the Consultative Assembly and the ruling National Security Council. The 160 members of the former were selected by the latter from among 11,000 applicants and the Assembly held its first meeting in Ankara on 15 October. Members of political parties at the time of the military takeover on 12 September 1980 were barred from the Assembly, and General Evren made it clear that at least the old party leaders would not be able to stand in the first parliamentary elections. The inauguration of the Consultative Assembly was followed by the formal abolition of political parties and the seizure of their assets. All political activities by the former politicians had earlier been banned, and when the former leader of the Republican People's Party, Mr Bulent Ecevit, circulated a reply to a denunciation of his record and that of his party by General Evren he was sentenced to four months' imprisonment. This occasioned many protests in the West, the EEC Commission proposing that a loan of $600 million, agreed earlier, should be withheld from Turkey.

While Mr Ecevit's former rival, Mr Süleyman Demirel, leader of the dissolved right-of-centre Justice Party, kept a prudent silence, and enjoyed a full social life, other politicians were in trouble. Retired Colonel Alpaslan Türkes, leader of the extreme right Nationalist Action Party, was put on trial with many of his followers, accused of organizing the murder of opponents and attempting to subvert the constitution by force. Mr Necmettin Erbakan and his main followers in the religious National Salvation Party faced the lesser charge of violating the secularist legislation of the republic. After two periods of detention, Mr Erbakan was released pending a verdict. Professor Behice Boran, leader of the small Turkish Workers Party, of marxist inspiration, who had fled to West Germany, was deprived of her Turkish nationality when she disobeyed a summons to return.

The total number of political prisoners changed little during the year. The Prime Minister, retired Admiral Bülent Ulusu, announced on 21 December that military courts had convicted some 4,000 persons, that some 25,000 had been charged and were under arrest, and that some 2,000 were detained but had not yet been charged. Fourteen death sentences passed on terrorists had been approved, and ten of them executed; 56 other death sentences were awaiting review or confirmation, and many more had been demanded both for alleged terrorist and for broader political offences. Capital charges were thus prepared against the leaders of the banned Confederation of Revolutionary Unions (DISK), the marxist rival of the Turkish Labour Confederation (TÜRKIŞ), which was allowed to continue functioning after the coup. There were reports in the West, denied by the Turkish authorities, that some of the accused, including the former mayor of Istanbul, Mr Ahmet Isvan, had been maltreated. The Prime Minister stated on 21 December that 370 cases of alleged torture had been passed to the courts, and had led to 28 arrests, while 69 more faced trial on torture charges.

There was little doubt, however, that the tough law-enforcement measures taken by the military authorities had largely re-established internal security. Political murders dropped from some 2,000 during the nine-months' tenure of the last civilian Government to 282 during the first year of military rule, most of the casualties occurring soon after the takeover. Huge quantities of illegally held arms, including 40,000 rifles, half a million hand guns and 23 rocket launchers, were seized.

Many measures were taken to strengthen the authority of the state, and, in particular of its military rulers. While there was no formal censorship of newspapers, extremist publications were closed down, journalists were detained and in some cases sentenced, national papers were banned for brief periods and news occasionally controlled. The military appointed their own men to manage the official media—broadcasting, the main news agency and state information services—and purged opponents from them. Key personnel in the administration, including state economic enterprises, were replaced, and university autonomy was severely curtailed. Four years' compulsory service was decreed for medical graduates, while academics were asked to work for two years in universities in deprived areas.

Discipline brought its rewards in the economy, which continued to be managed by Deputy Prime Minister Turgut Özal, who had been Mr Demirel's chief economic adviser before the coup. With strikes banned, compulsory wage arbitration, a tax reform leading to increased revenues, higher prices for state-produced goods and the freeing of interest rates, inflation was brought down from almost 100 to under 40 per cent, and exports increased by an estimated 50 per cent. As remittances from emigrant workers also increased, while foreign aid was available in reasonable quantities, shortages of fuel and of industrial inputs were eliminated, and after two years' of stagnation GNP registered a growth of some 4 per cent, in spite of a disappointing harvest.

The management of the economy generally found favour in the West; the International Monetary Fund released credits at regular intervals, while in May the OECD pledged $940 million in aid to Turkey. However, the tough internal measures taken by the military regime threatened both aid already pledged and prospects of obtaining a further $1,000 million from the OECD in 1982. Political criticism was expressed mainly in West Germany and in north-west Europe, but US support for the Turkish generals was spelt out when Defence Secretary Mr Caspar Weinberger visited Ankara on 5 December. The visit followed the election of Mr Papandreou to power in Greece. While friendly messages were at first exchanged between the Turkish and the new Greek Governments, relations were strained after Mr Papandreou tried unsuccessfully to obtain a Nato guarantee against Turkey. The year thus ended in recriminations between Ankara and Athens both on the Aegean (where the two countries were in conflict over the continental shelf, territorial waters and air space) and on Cyprus. Turkey had earlier attempted to improve relations with Greece, first by agreeing to the latter's return to the military structure of Nato, under modified command arrangements for the Aegean air space, and then by inducing Turkish Cypriots to table constitutional and territorial proposals at the intercommunal talks in Nicosia in August.

Turkey remained strictly neutral in the Iran-Iraq war, which brought it indirect benefits as trade with both countries had to switch to the overland route, while their stricken economies sought supplies from Turkish sources. Some aid was obtained from and trade increased with oil-producing Arab countries, and Pakistan was the first country officially visited by General Evren.

The centenary of the birth of Mustafa Kemal Atatürk, founder of the Turkish Republic, was marked with great solemnity both in Turkey and abroad and allowed the military regime to establish its credentials as the guardian of Atatürk's heritage.

V THE MIDDLE EAST AND NORTH AFRICA

Chapter 1

ISRAEL

ALTHOUGH there were national elections in 1981, the year was dominated by the broad issue of war and peace. In particular, Israel undertook two major military operations, against the Iraqi nuclear reactor and PLO terrorist bases in Beirut.

The attack on the nuclear reactor near Baghdad took place on 7 June, in the belief that Iraq was about to start manufacturing an atom bomb. Israel argued that Iraq was receiving materials which were not needed for peaceful nuclear purposes, had no nuclear research programme and no need for nuclear energy, and had sworn to destroy Israel. The attack was condemned by the UN and by Britain and other powers, although President Reagan suggested it was defensive in purpose. But the USA joined in the UN Security Council condemnation, after demands for punitive action against Israel had been dropped. The US held up delivery of four F-16 fighter planes; this action drew a sharp protest, and the embargo on deliveries was lifted on 18 August. The Iraqi reactor was effectively destroyed.

The attack on bases in Beirut on 17 July followed a series of PLO raids into Israel and the installation of Syrian SAM missiles in central Lebanon. There were wildly conflicting reports of casualties—according to the PLO, 134 were killed and 587 wounded, whereas 'neutral' reports spoke of 50 to 60 dead. In spite of UN condemnation and a rebuke from Washington, Israel continued to mount air attacks, although concentrating on PLO targets outside the Lebanese capital. The Beirut raid was a culmination of four months of increasing tension on the Israeli-Lebanese border, which was in no way slackened by the peace mission of President Reagan's special envoy, Mr Philip Habib. Syrian forces were drawn into the conflict; at least one Syrian fighter aircraft was shot down as well as two Israeli unmanned 'drone' aircraft. The main attack on Beirut was provoked by PLO shelling of the Israeli seaside resort of Nahariya on 15 July, when three civilians were killed and 25 wounded. A novelty in the PLO attacks was the use of hang-gliders, which, however, met with no success.

Another source of discord with the USA was the American intention of selling five AWACS radar planes to Saudi Arabia; once again, Israel protested when the Reagan Administration succeeded in securing the approval of the Senate on 28 October, after the House of Representatives had disapproved the sale. On the credit side, talks in Washington between President Reagan and Israel's Prime Minister, Mr Menachem Begin, led in September to broad agreement on future US-Israel joint military planning. Mr Begin claimed that this heralded a 'new era' in US-Israeli relations. On 31 November the two Governments announced a 'strategic cooperation agreement', designed to meet possible threats in the Middle East from the Soviet Union or from Soviet-controlled forces. There would be joint naval and air exercises, and cooperation in weapons research and development. Israel, however, suffered a serious setback when, on 18 December, the US suspended the agreement, because of Israel's action, four days earlier, in formally extending Israeli law to the area of the Golan Heights won from Syria in 1967. On 20 December Mr Begin unilaterally abrogated the agreement, in a speech which accused the US of diplomatic blackmail and antisemitism. Although this step stopped short of outright annexation, it was condemned by the European Community as well as the USA, and attacked with great bitterness by Arab countries. A minor strike by Druse Arabs living in the area took place, and at the end of the year Israel faced the threat of UN-imposed economic sanctions.

Israel also suffered some uncertainty over the modalities for the withdrawal of its armed forces in April 1982 from the last section of the Sinai peninsula to be handed back to Egypt. Israel, Egypt and the US agreed on 14 May to set up a multinational peacekeeping force for Sinai, after the completion of the Israeli withdrawal, and signed the agreement on 4 August. But European powers, which had been asked to participate, suggested totally misconceived conditions, such as linking participation with the 1980 EEC Venice declaration on Palestinian rights, and implying that the peacekeeping force would 'supervise' the Israeli withdrawal. Israel's Government repeatedly pointed out that the force's task would begin only after Israeli withdrawal was completed and that it had no connection with the Venice declaration. The appropriate formula was agreed on 30 November.

Israel's withdrawal was not prejudiced by the murder of President Sadat of Egypt, which occasioned deep and sincere regret. Prime Minister Begin attended the funeral. In addition, Israel and Egypt reached agreement on practical arrangements on the ground in Sinai following the withdrawal, establishing permanent crossing-points and providing the movement of traffic.

Considerable concern was caused in Israel by the 'peace-plan' presented by Prince Fahd of Saudi Arabia at the Arab Summit in Fez in November, after it had been aired for several months and welcomed by the British and other European Governments. In Israel's view, its eight points offered neither explicit recognition nor hope of real security. The total and immediate breakdown of the Fez summit (see p. 189) was, therefore, a matter for some relief. The apparent inability of a majority of Arab states to contemplate any kind of peace with Israel, however, triggered the Government's decision about the Golan Heights.

Among other foreign policy events, at the beginning of 1981 the Islamic summit in Taif declared a 'jihad' or holy war against Israel. During the year Mr Begin made a number of personalized attacks on Western leaders, in particular the West German Chancellor, Herr Helmut Schmidt, and the British Foreign Secretary, Lord Carrington. But towards the end of 1981 it seemed that Israel was making some diplomatic progress. The new French Government under M Mitterrand pledged friendship on 7 December. Several African countries hinted at resuming diplomatic relations, and an unexpected approach was made to the Soviet Union, when Foreign Minister Moshe Shamir met his Soviet opposite number Mr Gromyko in New York in late September. It was a matter of satisfaction to the Begin Government that the European peace initiative appeared by the end of the year to have collapsed, after being denounced by France's Foreign Minister M Cheysson.

Mr Begin faced many problems on the domestic front. He had to contest elections held on 30 June, after a campaign marked by vilification and some violence. His Likud Party emerged only fractionally stronger than the main Labour opposition, but was better placed to form a coalition Government, with the help of the two religious parties and a small extreme right-wing group. This gave Mr Begin a bare majority, with 61 out of 120 seats in the Knesset, of which the two main parties held no less than 95. Mr Begin's new Government was approved by the Knesset on 6 August after a heated debate. The Likud took all key posts, and, along with its Liberal partners, 14 out of 17 Cabinet seats.

Mr Begin's success was surprising, in the light of the many problems faced by his previous Administration. The least of them was the trial, for corruption, of his Minister for Religious Affairs, Mr Abuhazeira. He was acquitted, but indirectly censured by two of his three judges; one result of the trial was that automatic immunity of Cabinet Ministers on charges of fraud could not in future be invoked. More serious seemed Mr Begin's loss of the support of Mr Moshe Dayan, who remained a folk-hero until his death in October (see OBITUARY). The Prime Minister suffered from periodic ill-health, and in November fractured his thigh in a fall in his home.

A serious quandary arose out of Israel's inability to affect the drastic cut-down on Jews leaving the USSR (see p. 106). It had been hoped that Jewish emigration would run at an annual rate of upwards of 30,000; instead, monthly figures dropped to under 400 in the last quarter of the year. There was concern about Israel's almost stagnant population, which increased by only about 70,000 during 1981, to a figure of 3·7 million.

There were economic difficulties, too, chief among them inflation; relief was shown when the inflation rate dropped during the year from well over 80 per cent to 'only' 66 per cent. The Minister of Economics, Mr Aridor, worsened the trade balance by considerable hand-outs during the election campaign, increasing subsidies and lowering the prices of many imported goods. In this spending spree in May and June, £160 million was pumped into the economy, a policy condemned as short-sighted by the governor of the Bank of Israel, Mr Arnon Gafny. There was a crippling strike of the El Al national airline in the autumn, and the economy kept its head above water only through the successful effort to foster science-based, export-intensive industries. High hopes were held out of benefits from the proposed Mediterranean–Dead Sea canal, on which all planning was completed and which aroused the protests of Jordan and other Arab states.

Troubles in the occupied territories of the West Bank and Gaza included bombings, strikes, student demonstrations and the clandestine activities of the PLO, involving even the murder of Palestinian moderates who dared to support the Camp David peace process. In November Bir Zeit University was closed for a two-month period. The worst incidents were on the West Bank, referred to by the Begin Government as Judaea and Samaria. The main cause was the presence and constant reinforcement of Israeli settlements, numbering over 80 by the end of the year, with another 70 planned. Particular Arab objections were to the acquisition of land for these settlements and the increased Israeli use of water resources. The principal executor of settlement policies was the Minister of Defence, General Sharon. Israeli actions included the speeding-up of talks with Egypt on Palestinian autonomy—within the framework of Camp David—the transfer of administrative authority from military to civilian bodies, the formation of a league of 60 villages which showed signs of wishing to cooperate, the planning of a self-governing Arab Council and the arming of some moderates for their own self-defence.

The situation was only a little less tense in the Gaza Strip, where a number of Israelis and Arabs were killed, including Colonel Shahaf, the governor of the town of Rafah, in July. In December this town was sealed off, and the whole Strip was proclaimed a closed military area. A number of terrorist cells were broken up. Towards the end of the year there were disturbing reports that the PLO was in process of establishing bases in Jordan, from which they had been excluded by King Husain for the past decade.

Fewer significant troubles afflicted the city of Jerusalem. The most prominent Arab member of parliament, the Bedouin chieftain, Sheikh Abu Rabia, was murdered in Jerusalem on 12 January and there were several minor bomb explosions. Several Arab newspapers were temporarily shut down for publishing information classified as secret and there was renewed bickering over the rights of the Arab-owned East Jerusalem electricity company. Battles took place, too, between religious zealots and others over the use of certain roads on the Sabbath and over excavations in the ancient City of David, adjoining the southern wall of the Old City.

All in all, 1981 was an extremely difficult year for the state of Israel.

Chapter 2

THE ARAB WORLD—EGYPT—JORDAN—SYRIA—LEBANON—IRAQ

THE ARAB WORLD

NO progress was made towards complementing the Israeli-Egyptian peace with a comprehensive settlement. President Reagan's Administration was initially less firm with Israel than Mr Carter's but then reacted strongly to high-handed Israeli behaviour which also united the otherwise divided Arabs (see p. 186).

The murder of President Sadat in October, by removing Camp David's principal architect, reinforced the need to consider alternatives. One hopeful sign in this direction had been the ceasefire in southern Lebanon between Israel and the PLO, negotiated in July by the US Government with Saudi help, and on 9 August the Saudi Prime Minister, Prince Fahd, advanced a plan for restoring the *status quo ante bellum* of 1967 while implicitly recognizing Israel's right to exist. This was cautiously welcomed by President Reagan but immediately dismissed by Mr Begin, and although Mr Yassir Arafat, chairman of the PLO, was in its favour—perhaps the Saudis had consulted him in drafting it—his colleagues were not.

Already in April the Palestine National Council's meeting at Damascus had, as usual, jibbed at dropping from the Palestine Charter the formal commitment to abolish the state of Israel. Neither this Palestinian opposition nor the inevitable Libyan denunciations might have been enough to defeat the Saudi project had not Syria also taken violently against it; this appeared to be a shift from Syria's previous support for some form of negotiated peace based on UN resolutions. It was enough to frustrate the Saudi plan; when at Fez in November it was submitted to the Arab summit, President Asad's refusal to attend broke up the meeting and prevented its discussion.

This debacle symbolized the rift between the Steadfastness Front (Syria, Libya, Algeria, South Yemen and the PLO), all in varying

degrees pro-Soviet and anti-American, and the conservative and potentially pro-American Gulf states, since May linked in the Gulf Cooperation Council (see p. 207). Nor was the parallel rift narrowed between
Iraq, with its Saudi and Jordanian partisans, and the Syrian and Libyan
supporters of Iran in the Gulf war, though Iraq left the Saudi camp to
oppose the Saudi peace plan. To these divisions the isolation of Egypt,
Sudan and Oman, and the Moroccan-Algerian tension in the Sahara,
must be added to compose the familiar picture of Arab disunity.

However, on 14 December another Israeli *coup de théâtre* reunited
the Arabs and gave them hope of greater sympathy from the Reagan Administration. Israel's virtual annexation of the Golan Heights was, like
the earlier air-raids on Lebanon and Iraq, a defiance of the US Government, and it ended the US-Israeli strategic cooperation agreement after
only fourteen days of existence and stimulated Arab reconciliation.

The PLO could at year's end record several gains. It had secured
varying degrees of recognition from, among others, the USSR, Japan,
Greece and Spain. Its cooperation in the ceasefire of July had somewhat
mended its terrorist image. To the European support gained at Venice in
1980 (France's new Socialist Foreign Minister soon turned away from a
little flirtation with Israel) had been added vague but significant pro-
Palestinian expressions by ex-Presidents Nixon and Carter. Above all,
Israel's behaviour had reduced US goodwill to a degree unknown since
1956 and thus given the Palestinians a chance, if they had the courage
and sagacity to exploit it, of US support. But the PLO had again shown
itself divided, and, although Arafat had in April gained an extra
representative on the executive, so too had his extremist opponents.

The year brought increasing US involvement in the Middle East. The
Reagan Administration insisted that the greatest danger to the area was
Soviet military power and that this danger could best be met by
committing US military power against it. This attitude was manifested in
striking military demonstrations in Egypt and elsewhere, particularly
after Sadat's death, by selling, despite Israeli protests, sophisticated aircraft to Saudi Arabia, by shooting down two Libyan aircraft in disputed
air space and by acceding to Israeli wishes for a strategic cooperation
agreement (see p. 186).

No similar new Soviet drive could be seen, though Jordan did enter
the Soviet arms market by buying anti-aircraft missiles there. Iraq, once
the largest recipient of Soviet arms, no longer got them in quantity. But
Soviet political influence encouraged convergence between the pro-
Soviet states (e.g. the treaty concluded in August between Libya, South
Yemen and Ethiopia) and exploited every ounce of the anti-American
feeling aroused by Israeli behaviour, flamboyant US military movements
and the violent American reactions to alleged Libyan plots.

EGYPT

Before his assassination on 6 October President Anwar Sadat seemed near failure. Israel would not complete the Camp David process by allowing genuinely full autonomy to the Palestinians, and President Reagan's Administration seemed less likely than Mr Carter's to press Israel to do so. The vultures of Muslim fundamentalism, once tolerated as safer than communism, darkened the sky, making Sadat their most illustrious victim and feeding on his failures—neglected infrastructure, imbalance between rich and poor and suspected corruption. His successor gave promise of greater attention to these problems without abandoning Sadat's foreign policies.

Egypt's bilateral relations with Israel bumped along, upset by Israel's intervention in Lebanon, its attack on Iraq and proposal for a Gaza-Dead Sea canal. Egypt therefore shrank from Israel's coveted 'normalization' but had to avoid giving Mr Begin any excuse to delay evacuation of Sinai. The treaty required a force to patrol it; the USSR would veto UN involvement, so a new international force was needed. A US-Egyptian-Israeli agreement was signed in Washington on 3 August. Egypt and the US wanted some European participation, which Israel seemed ready to accept under protest (see p. 186). The future of Israeli military installations in Sinai was settled by President Sadat and Mr Begin in June; they would pass to Egypt intact.

Sadat was publicly confident that the Palestinian autonomy talks, suspended in 1980 and resumed in September 1981, would soon reach agreement, but considered Palestinian participation essential to the peace process. In January his Foreign Minister urged peaceful methods on the PLO and advocated mutual Israeli-PLO recognition. While in Washington in August Sadat advised the Americans to deal with the PLO, being impressed by the recent Israeli-PLO ceasefire (see LEBANON) and the Saudi peace plan (see ARAB WORLD).

The Washington visit also symbolized Egypt's commitment to strategic cooperation with the US and its readiness to give the 'rapid deployment force' facilities (not, Sadat stressed, bases) and to hold joint exercises. The glaring US presence in Cairo, where the US embassy was the largest outside London, caused headshaking by thoughtful Americans.

For Sadat, relations with the Arabs were secondary, but Libya's Chad adventure raised his blood-pressure as threatening Sudan, which had resumed diplomatic relations with Egypt in March, followed in May and July by the exchange of presidential visits. Sadat abounded in warnings to Libya and conciliated Saudi Arabia; he acknowledged its importance in any Middle East settlement, supported its acquisition of

AWACS aircraft and welcomed its peace plan. Egypt also supplied Iraq with surplus Soviet weapons.

General Badawi, the Defence Minister, was killed in a helicopter accident on 2 March and replaced by General Abu Ghazala. The millionaire contractor and intimate of Sadat, Othman Ahmad Othman, appointed a Deputy Prime Minister in January, had to resign in May after accusing, in published memoirs, Nasser and others of corruption. Also in May the authorities released Ali Sabri and others arrested in 1971 for conspiring against Sadat (ses AR 1971, p. 200).

Internal affairs were soon causing concern. After arrests of 'communists' and terror squads from Syria and Libya came signs, especially in the universities, of growing Muslim fanaticism, culminating in mid-June when Muslim-Coptic rioting killed 14 people. On 3 September the Government acted against 'fomentors of sectarian hatred', including the fiery Coptic leader, Pope Shenouda, as well as politicians of the left and the old right, academics and journalists, especially Muhammad Haikal, favourite guru of Western pressmen. By 6 September arrests had risen to 1,500. Emergency security measures were approved in a referendum on 10 September; a few days later the press revealed a 'Soviet plot' and the arrest of prominent Egyptians including a former Deputy Prime Minister, Abdul Salam Zayyat; the Soviet ambassador and other diplomats were expelled.

On 6 October, while Sadat took a military parade, soldiers dismounted from a lorry, ran to the saluting base and opened fire, killing him (see OBITUARY) and others, including a Coptic bishop. The assassins, all immediately arrested, had been led by Lieut. Khalid al Islambuli and were said to belong to the extremist group *Takfir wa hijra* (see AR 1977, p. 182). Though security had been incredibly lax, widespread army disaffection was not suspected. Sadat was buried on 10 October amid Western mourning, apparent Egyptian indifference and odious rejoicing in Libya. Serious but separate attacks followed in Assiut and Cairo, but there was no immediate attempt to overthrow the Government, despite alleged plans for a Khomeini-style revolution.

Sadat was immediately and smoothly replaced by Vice-President Husni Mubarak, who was confirmed as President by referendum on 14 October. A Soviet-trained fighter pilot and air force commander, he was reputed to be an efficient and honest administrator, if slow-witted. His succession had long been foreseen—Sadat had already hinted at retirement. Apart from appointing Fuad Muhiuddin as Vice-President, Mubarak made no Cabinet changes and promised to continue Sadat's policies, which he had always supported. But he ended Sadat's frequent polemics against the Arabs, and the Saudis responded by suggesting that the new President be given a chance. His style differed from Sadat's—no more interminable speeches, autocratic decisions without consultation, or personality cult—and he would probably attend to those humdrum internal matters which Sadat had neglected for the 'great game' of diplomacy. On 8 November, in a speech to Parliament, Mubarak spoke of 'dissolving economic disparities', and without renouncing Sadat's opendoor policy he suggested that it be directed to increasing productive capacity and employment and supplying necessities, not luxuries. His popularity was reported to be increasing, and on 28 December the Muslim Brotherhood leader Telemsani promised him support for a programme of reform and advocated national unity. On 30 December the Government won two by-elections from the main opposition party without the usual charges of vote-rigging.

Security naturally preoccupied the new regime. Many fundamentalists were arrested and officers with such sympathies transferred to civilian employment. Some of those arrested in September and unconnected with fundamentalism, including Haikal, were released on 25 November and received personally by the President. On 13 December charges were dropped against Zayyat and by year's end Mubarak claimed that 86 of those arrested in September had been freed.

The trial of Sadat's assassins began on 21 November. The defence pleaded tyrannicide as justifiable by Islamic law, but the court refused to hear witnesses to this plea and discharged the defence lawyers.

Externally the alleged Libyan danger was emphasized, after Sadat's murder, by sending 50,000 men to the frontier and two American AWACS aircraft arrived on 15 October to patrol it. In November came the joint US-Egyptian exercise Bright Star. The Defence Minister said that Egypt could now dispose of four of the latest American F16 fighters and would receive US aircraft and armoured vehicles worth $3,500 million over five years.

Oil production was high. It had ended 1980 at 700,000 barrels per day and in 1981 new wells were discovered in the Red Sea. Oil exports were earning $3,000 million annually. The other foreign exchange earners were prospering (emigrants' remittances $2,800 million, Suez Canal dues and tourism $700 million each) but increasing more slowly, while food imports were costing $4,400 million, up 25 per cent on the year, and imports on private account had now risen to $2,000 million. A balance of payments deficit of $500 million might appear in 1981. Egypt's foreign debts had risen in a year by $2,000 million to $14,000 million. In August the Egyptian pound was devalued by 20 per cent.

Inflation was reported to be higher at 25 to 30 per cent. Subsidies were 11 per cent of GNP; those for food cost almost $3,000 million and for energy nearly $2,000 million. These high levels impeded agreement with the IMF. The price of fuels was raised by 20 per cent in December.

On 26 February Egypt ratified the nuclear non-proliferation treaty and there followed a series of deals for a nuclear energy programme—

eight reactors to produce about 1,000 megawatts each. Agreements were signed for two reactors each from France, the USA and West Germany.

In March it was announced that Egypt's population had risen by a million in a year to 43 million.

JORDAN

Under King Husain's wise leadership Jordan remained the only stable country in the Arab heartland. Yet he faced a paranoiac neighbour in Syria, Israeli encroachment in territories still his by international law and the insensitivity of a US Administration which was nevertheless economically important to Jordan. The slight improvement in relations with the USSR seemed based on objective calculations of advantage, rather than anti-American pique.

Syria's hostility, due to suspicions of Jordanian collusion with the Muslim Brothers' terrorist operations in Syria, soon revived after a temporary lull (see AR 1980, p. 192). On 3 February Jordanian police caught a commando of Rifa'at Asad's militia from Syria infiltrating Jordan, allegedly to assassinate Muslim Brothers in exile there. On 6 February the Jordanian chargé d'affaires in Beirut was kidnapped and held until April by Lebanese with suspected Syrian connections. Accusations were exchanged; Syria charged Husain with surrendering the West Bank in 1967 and claiming illegally to speak for the Palestinians. Elements of the PLO under paramount Syrian influence taunted Jordan with not allowing the PLO to operate there. These exchanges slackened, but did not end, with the diplomat's release. It appeared that despite political friction some of the joint enterprises set up with Syria in happier days were still functioning.

In May Husain visited Moscow, for the first time since 1976. That he should support President Brezhnev's call for an international conference to settle the Middle East problem was understandable, given the King's constant opposition to Camp David; so, too, was Jordan's purchase of Soviet anti-aircraft missiles, finalized in November, since they cost less than half the equivalent US missiles.

In April Secretary of State Haig visited Jordan. The King urged on him the need to stop Israeli encroachments in the West Bank, to recognize the PLO as representing the Palestinians and to return the peace negotiations to the UN. Husain's visit to President Reagan in the US on 2 November was described as a success, though he could not meet US wishes for Jordan's participation in the Camp David process and disregarded the President's warning against buying Soviet arms. He urged the US to support Prince Fahd's peace plan.

Jordan remained Iraq's most loyal Arab supporter not only in expressions of sympathy but also by facilitating Iraqi imports through Aqaba, and this loyalty was rewarded by financial help, including, it was reported, payment for Jordan's purchase of anti-aircraft missiles. The two Governments acted to improve communications between Aqaba and Iraq, and Iraqi funds were allocated for joint projects in Jordan. The largest under study was one for piping Euphrates water to Jordan. Another, though far from certain, was for a pipeline from Iraqi oil-fields to Aqaba.

Jordan protested against Jewish settlement on the West Bank and the proposed Mediterranean-Dead Sea hydroelectric canal through Gaza, and remained the channel for the oil states' contributions to resisting Israeli penetration of the West Bank economy. Jordan was vigilant against attempts to explore the 'Jordanian option' under which Jordan would form the nucleus of a Palestinian state. This idea was the more unwelcome in that some Israelis advocated making Jordan responsible for the Palestinians without a return of the West Bank, thus turning the King and his Transjordanian subjects into a minority in a state overcrowded with discontented refugees.

While, indeed because, the King had to combat such designs he still opposed any Palestinian attempt to resume guerrilla warfare from Jordan and this exposed him to abuse by the PLO's left wing. The strong Syrian influence on the PLO was also used against Jordan, though Yassir Arafat himself seemed to understand the King's position.

Husain's foreign preoccupations did not impair the consistent and realistic economic policy which distinguished Jordan from other Arab states. Inflation did not exceed 12 per cent, income tax and customs yields improved and gross domestic product was growing by 8·5 per cent a year. The 305,000 Jordanians abroad were remitting over $600 million annually and there was some reversal of the drain of brain and muscle to the Gulf states. Jordan's finances depended unduly on foreign aid, now nearly 40 per cent of total expenditure, and the visible trade gap was widening, one important factor being the increased cost of oil. The growing concentration of population in Amman (more than half Jordan's total) and the consequent water shortage there remained worrying.

There was a small cholera outbreak in July which impaired fruit exports and tourism; the latter suffered also from Israeli action to increase El Al's share of the Levant tourist business.

SYRIA

Syria's expensive involvement in Lebanon brought dangerous confrontation with Israel. Relations with Iraq and Jordan continued bitter and those with Saudi Arabia uneasy; though needing Saudi money, President Hafiz al Asad sabotaged Prince Fahd's peace plan. The resulting ill-feeling was outweighed by the unifying effect of Israel's virtual annexation of the Golan Heights. At home, terrorists, presumably Muslim Brothers, continued killing scores or even hundreds of people. Nevertheless, efforts to apply commonsense and market forces to the floundering economy had some success.

Syria's Lebanese role was not diminished. The anarchy in Beirut was more than Lebanon's forces could tackle alone and the Syrian-manned Arab Deterrent Force had constantly to intervene. Dangerous hostilities in the Beqa'a (see p. 198) confronted Syria with Israel and threatened an international crisis until the US negotiated a ceasefire.

The Saudi-arranged detente with Jordan (see AR 1980, p. 182) broke in January when Jordan caught a Syrian murder commando on Jordanian soil and its radio alleged mass killings in Aleppo by Ba'ath forces. Syria accused Jordan of protecting the Muslim Brothers. In February the Jordanian chargé d'affaires was kidnapped in Beirut, Syrian agents being held responsible, and kept prisoner till April.

There was little respite in the war of words with Iraq; Syria still supported Iran, perhaps even channelling arms to it. However, the transit of goods through Syria to Iraq continued; the Kirkuk-Banias pipeline was functioning and the other line to Lebanon was reopened in December.

Syria had previously not rejected a negotiated, rather than military, solution to the Palestinian question. But now, in April, during the Palestine National Congress in Damascus, Syrian propaganda opposed excision from the Palestine Charter of the call to abolish the Jewish state, and then Asad rejected Prince Fahd's peace plan of 8 August with its implicit recognition of Israel's right to exist. In November he boycotted the Arab summit in Fez where it was to be discussed. However, Israel's annexation of the Golan Heights on 14 December rallied all the Arab Governments to Syria, and Asad set off to tour Arab capitals.

Relations with the USSR were strengthened. Soviet naval exercises in July were reported to include a practice landing on the Syrian coast, and a five-year trade agreement signed in June was designed to increase trade with the USSR by 150 per cent. Military visits to Moscow in January and September apparently gave less satisfaction, the Russians being readier to supply tanks than advanced aircraft. Asad's attitude to the US seemed often paranoiac but this did not prevent Syria's cooperating with the American envoy over the Lebanon ceasefire and welcoming the shift in US policy which followed the Golan annexation.

Presumably Libya was financing arms purchases from Russia, Syria being unable, and the Saudis unwilling, to do so. Perhaps the Libyan connection explained Syria's sudden declaration on 8 September extending its territorial waters from 12 to 35 miles offshore following the Libyan-US hostilities on 19 August (see p. 215), the effect of a similar claim. Nevertheless bilateral relations with Libya seemed somewhat awry. By year's end no constitutional advances towards Libyan-Syrian unity had been made, though Colonel Qadafi visited Damascus in August.

At home the Minister of Information claimed on 28 February that the Muslim Brothers had killed 300 government and party officials but were now in retreat. Nevertheless outrages continued, with reports of disorders in Hama, Raqqa and Aleppo, and culminated in an explosion in Damascus on 29 November, killing 90 people.

Abdul Ra'uf Qasim's Government, largely technocrats, studied the economy and how to improve it. Foreign exchange reserves covered at most one month's civilian imports. Oil earnings fell; existing fields were nearing exhaustion and increasing consumption was leaving less to export. Production of other export commodities had also fallen, thanks partly to low producer prices. Imports had risen and invisible earnings fallen, partly because of Beirut's black market in Syrian currency. Defence cost over 30 per cent of the budget and the Gulf states were sometimes unpunctual or obstructive in paying their promised contributions to the Lebanese operation. Subsidies, mainly on diesel oil, flour and sugar, were costing $1,500 million annually and much expense came from ill-planned development, such as a paper mill to process non-existent straw and sugar refineries whose capacity exceeded Syria's beet crop.

The technocrats delayed and revised the new five-year plan, cutting over-ambitious projects and doing more for agriculture, whose producer prices were raised. The Government increased prices of subsidized goods and instituted, alongside the official exchange rate, a parallel floating rate to encourage emigrants' remittances and restrict non-essential imports. These measures had some success. Government revenue in January-May was 80 per cent higher than in 1980 and expenditure only 23 per cent higher, and the parallel rate fell nearly 30 per cent. The black market, however, did not vanish, imports stayed unacceptably high and inflation was probably at least 30 per cent per annum. Other economic shortcomings remained, especially those inseparable from extensive state trading and the traditional bureaucracy, which prevented Syria's overland transit trade from profiting fully from the closure of Iraq's Gulf ports.

The revised five-year plan was eventually approved on 16 August by the National Assembly, which was then dissolved. A new Assembly was elected on 10 November, all 295 seats being won by the Government coalition.

LEBANON

Security in Lebanon deteriorated through the year: Palestinian forces provoked Israeli reprisals, Maronite militias engaged Syrian troops of the Arab Deterrent Force (ADF) and Major Sa'ad Haddad's Israeli-supported enclave resisted the UN Interim Force (Unifil) and the Lebanese army. Israel extended its pro-Maronite intervention into the Beqa'a, and its air-raids killed hundreds of Lebanese and damaged essential facilities. In July American mediation produced an imperfect ceasefire. Insecurity, virtual partition and war damage threatened Lebanon's economy as never before.

There were repeated attacks by Haddad's militia, and some by Palestinians, on Unifil. The Lebanese army, trying to assert the Government's control, was refused entry into Haddad's enclave and was sniped at by the Palestinians.

More trouble started on 2 April with fighting between the ADF and Maronite forces in Beirut and Zahle, a Greek Orthodox town in the Beqa'a vacated in January by the ADF and then infiltrated by Falange (Maronite) militias. The ADF besieged Zahle and on 16 April landed troops by helicopter on a nearby mountain. Israel's high command intervened to support the Falange and on 28 April the Israelis downed two Syrian helicopters. Syria riposted by moving anti-aircraft missiles into the Beqa'a. The US urged restraint on Israel and asked for similar Soviet influence on Syria. Israel protested that the missiles threatened its security by impairing its ability to overfly Lebanon at will. On 6 May the US despatched Mr Philip Habib, a senior diplomat of Arab descent, to the Middle East while the USSR sent a deputy Foreign Minister to Damascus. Weeks of meetings and journeys produced no public agreement but averted a Syrian-Israeli war. Mr Habib returned home on 27 May.

The Arab League was meanwhile seeking a ceasefire between the ADF and the Falange. Arab Foreign Ministers were meeting in Beirut in June when Israel's attack on Iraq diverted Arab attention (see p. 185) but on 30 June the ADF lifted the siege of Zahle and the Falange garrison withdrew. Despite all Mr Habib's efforts, the missiles were still in the Beqa'a, and although the Israelis kept vowing to 'take them out' they were still there in December. In mid-July rocket and artillery exchanges were resumed across the frontier and on 16 July Israeli aircraft heavily attacked Lebanon, killing hundreds in Beirut and destroying important installations. This complicated Habib's task (he had returned on 8 July) and angered the US Government. On 24 July a ceasefire followed his arduous negotiations, essentially by agreement between Israel, Syria and the PLO. The ceasefire broadly held and there were no further major hostilities, though Lebanon contained so many warring factions, especially partisans of Iraq and Iran, that bloody skirmishes and bombings were frequent. During the year the French ambassador was murdered, the Iraqi embassy blown up and the Jordanian chargé d'affaires kidnapped.

Now undisputed Falange and Maronite leader, Bashir Gemayel negotiated a ceasefire with the Syrians and promised to break with the Israelis. Presumably therefore the Falange were innocent of a series of outrages against Palestinian and left-wing targets from September on by a mysterious 'Front for Liberating Lebanon from Foreigners'. Violent disorder stemmed from partisans of Imam Musa Sadr, an Iranian-born leader of Lebanese Shias who vanished in Libya in 1978; they blew up one Libyan aircraft and in December hijacked another to proclaim their indignation.

In the south the Falange could not control Haddad, still clashing with Unifil, which he besieged in November, and with the Lebanese army from which, though cashiered in February, he was demanding, with menaces, huge arrears of pay. On 6 November he announced, but soon withdrew, his resignation.

Meanwhile the US was reported to want Unifil strengthened to enable it to take over the frontier area from Haddad, while placating Israel by withdrawing Palestinian forces northwards and the ADF into the Beqa'a. A senior State Department official visited Beirut and Damascus in October. Given Israeli pugnacity and Syrian suspicions of the US the plan seemed optimistic, but a more modest scheme advanced in November promised at least peaceful coexistence in Beirut; all the varied unofficial gunmen were to be disarmed and removed from west (Muslim) Beirut and replaced by Lebanese government forces, while east (Christian) Beirut would be left to the Falange. The city would thus remain divided and there seemed little hope of ending the *de facto* Maronite UDI regime elsewhere.

In 1981 Lebanon's economy seemed less capable than before of riding out the storm. Insecurity hampered tax collection; customs revenue fell amid widespread smuggling through unofficial ports and war damage to Beirut harbour; the drive for an effective Lebanese army had doubled defence expenditure; and subsidizing petroleum products, until prices were raised by 36 per cent in October, was costing annually nearly $500 million. Compensation payments for war damage and casualties (2,000 people killed in 1981, over 500 of them in Israeli air-raids) were another heavy burden. The substantial budget deficit was filled by bank borrowing, which encouraged inflation, and by aid from abroad. The Arab governments did not pay all the annual $400 million they had promised, though Saudi Arabia contributed generously. In discussions with the EEC, starting in October, Lebanon sought grants and loans of $200 million.

Unpaid oil company bills frequently interrupted supplies until met by the Saudis. The Israeli raids in July caused further interruptions by damaging the Sidon refinery. In November agreement was reached with Iraq and Syria for resumed pumping to the Tripoli refinery, closed since 1976.

The 1981 budget had no allocations for development. Business growth and investment fell and Lebanon's most successful company, Middle East Airlines, turned a profit of $2.2 million in 1980 into a loss of $17 million in 1981. Exports seemed about as high as in 1980, though Iraq and Syria were replacing Saudi Arabia as principal markets.

IRAQ

A largely static war continued as Iran refused any compromise peace; though indecisive, the fighting went badly for Iraq. Israel's raid on Iraq's nuclear reactor rallied Arab and other sympathies. Development projects multiplied, absorbing foreign technology and labour.

Would-be mediators attempted to negotiate peace—the UN, the Islamic Conference organization and the Non-Aligned movement—but all foundered. Iran insisted that Iraq evacuate all Iranian territory in any ceasefire—a politically impossible humiliation. Iraq appeared to drop its demand for the evacuation of the Gulf islands but still insisted on sovereignty in the Shatt al Arab, the recovery of certain areas promised under the 1975 agreement and non-interference in Iraq's internal affairs.

Iraq's military failure to penetrate further into Iran doubtless reinforced Khomeini's doctrinaire rigidity. Iran's early spring offensive failed but in September Iraq had to withdraw across the Karun and lift the siege of Abadan. Otherwise there seemed to be little movement. Both sides published unreliable communiques and by discouraging foreign journalists prevented objective reporting. Though both were probably avoiding major engagements to conserve manpower, Iraqi casualties must have been worryingly high; one estimate gave losses of 10,000 in the war's first seven months. Both sides were accused by the Red Cross of breaking the Geneva Convention on prisoners of war, and Iraq by Amnesty International of torture. The war damaged Iraq's economy by closing the Shatt, thus drastically reducing oil exports and forcing the use of expensive land routes for imports; hence the gravity of Iraq's failure to take Abadan and thus put the Shatt outside artillery range.

Military supplies would normally have come mainly from the USSR but on 15 March the Defence Minister said that that they had not had 'a single cartridge' from Russia since the war began; later another senior figure charged the USSR with dishonouring its commitments. On 31 May President Saddam Husain accused it of arming Iran via Syria and Libya.

In March *Pravda* reported an attack at the Soviet Communist Party Congress by the Iraqi communist leader Aziz Muhammad on the Ba'ath's 'destructive military adventure' and repression of communists. Clandestine radio stations under Soviet influence were anti-Iraqi. Various minor agreements were nevertheless concluded with the USSR.

Iraq's policy had long been to diversify sources of arms supply. Four of a consignment of 60 Mirage aircraft arrived from France on 31 January, Egypt sold Iraq surplus Soviet equipment and Italy contracted for twelve naval ships.

The year's most sensational event was an Israeli air-raid on 7 June which destroyed Iraq's nuclear reactor. No objective evidence for Israeli claims that the reactor had military potential came from its French builders or IAEA personnel who had inspected it. Unlike Israel, Iraq had ratified the nuclear non-proliferation treaty.

The raid was condemned by Europe and the US, whose UN delegation actually consulted their Iraqi colleagues on the wording of the Security Council's censure motion on 19 June. The raid rallied Arab sympathies behind Iraq; Saudi Arabia offered to pay for a new reactor and France agreed to build it. However, Gulf generosity to Iraq did not prevent its joining its Libyan and Syrian enemies against Prince Fahd's peace plan (see ARAB WORLD).

Less was heard of Kurdistan, though Kurds kidnapped foreigners employed on development projects and attacked lorry convoys from Turkey.

Little internal political news emerged from Baghdad's habitual secretiveness, Syrian and Iranian reports of disaffection being untrustworthy. In November a London newspaper reported that forty people had been executed for planning a coup. President Saddam Husain's personality cult continued; he was interviewed on American television, gave his name to Baghdad airport and had a new presidential yacht costing $15 million called the *Qadisiya Saddam*, linking his name to a celebrated Arab victory over Iran.

Oil exports remained below one million barrels per day, even with the Turkish and Syrian pipelines reopened. Government revenues were cut and foreign exchange reserves fell from $35,000 million to $20,000 million. But loans and grants of at least $16,000 million from Saudi Arabia, Kuwait, the UAE and Qatar were reported. Economic development proceeded apace and new contracts worth $20,000 million were awarded, though the 1981-85 plan allocated only half the previous plan's funds to investment. The new plan stressed social as well as economic investment; it excluded foreign capital. Social policy included a campaign to increase population by giving financial advantages to those marrying under 22 and a lump sum for each extra child, and another campaign to reduce smoking. The budget approved in April showed expenditure and revenue up 40 per cent on 1980 but in approximate balance at $65,000 million.

Contracts were signed for *inter alia* road and rail expansion, designing a Baghdad underground, sewerage, irrigation and vehicle factories. Japan was a prominent supplier of technology, though dislocations caused by the war and the flight of Japanese experts when it began led to claims for compensation. There were sizeable contracts with Indian and US firms, and Britain, which on 24 June signed a technical and economic cooperation agreement, secured contracts for consultancies for the underground, water and sewerage developments and for equipment for railways and cold storage. The emphasis on overland communication was natural, for the war prevented sea-borne trade—war-damaged Basra was reportedly silting up.

Much skilled and even unskilled labour was imported—an ominous trend familiar in other Gulf oil states. Besides technicians already recruited from OECD countries, agreements were made or planned for immigration from the Philippines, Bangladesh, Pakistan, China, Tunisia and Egypt.

Chapter 3

SAUDI ARABIA—YEMEN ARAB REPUBLIC—PEOPLE'S DEMOCRATIC
REPUBLIC OF YEMEN—THE ARAB STATES OF THE GULF

SAUDI ARABIA

ONCE again domestic events were overshadowed by external affairs, as Saudi Arabia continued with the difficult, and often frustrating, task of attempting to convert its undoubted financial power into sustained and successful diplomatic influence. A summit conference of Islamic countries held in Taif from 25 to 28 January was attended by 28 heads of state and by ten other political leaders. Noteworthy absentees were Iran, Egypt, Afghanistan and Libya. The most important issues discussed were the question of Palestine and the future of Jerusalem, the Soviet occupation of Afghanistan and the continuation of the Iraq-Iran war. Much rhetoric was in evidence, particularly in the publication of the 'Meccan Declaration' which called for a new *jihad*, or struggle, against Israel; but little agreement emerged on how to transform words into actions. There were some critical comments, particularly from the delegations of the poorer states, about the lavish ostentation of the surroundings in which the conference was held.

In its relations with the littoral states of the Persian Gulf Saudi Arabia was able to make some slow and cautious progress. The Foreign

Ministers of the six states—Saudi Arabia, Kuwait, Bahrein, Qatar, the United Arab Emirates and Oman—met in Riyadh in February to discuss cooperation against both internal and external threats to their security; and in May a Gulf Cooperation Council (GCC) was established with its headquarters in the Saudi capital. Although there were many differences of opinion, most strikingly over Oman's willingness to cooperate closely with US military forces, the council began also to discuss methods of economic cooperation and ways in which the duplication of expensive development projects might be avoided. Defence matters were, however, the prime concern of the GCC, and in December Saudi Arabia signed a security agreement with Bahrein. At the same time the Saudi Interior Minister, Prince Naif, accused Iran of sinister and aggressive intentions in the Gulf. At the end of the year there were indications that Riyadh's support for Iraq, in its war with Iran, was increasing.

The Israeli attack on the Iraqi nuclear reactor at Tammuz near Baghdad on 7 June caused much anger and consternation in Riyadh. The fact that the Israeli planes were believed to have flown through Saudi airspace gave added urgency to the Government's desire to secure Advance Warning and Control System aircraft (AWACS) from Washington. Riyadh was greatly irritated by the intensity of opposition within the USA to this sale, by the very slow progress of the debate in the Capitol, and by Washington's attempt to impose restrictions on the use of the aircraft. When approval for the sale was finally given on 28 October the Government expressed its gratitude to President Reagan, but the narrowness of the final vote in the US Senate (52 votes to 48) failed to eradicate doubts about the reliability of Washington as an ally.

As in previous years Riyadh was a city much visited by Western political leaders. During her Gulf tour in mid-April Mrs Thatcher tried to assure the Saudi Government that the Rapid Deployment Force proposed by the US was in no way a threat to the stability of the Gulf, nor would it prompt the Kremlin to seek a more active role in the region. Herr Schmidt's visit later in April was even more difficult; for he had to inform the Saudi Government that West Germany could not supply the Leopard tanks and other weapons that were being sought. King Khalid's state visit to Britain in June set the seal of friendship on Anglo-Saudi relations which had been damaged by the showing of the television film *Death of a Princess* in April 1980 (see AR 1980, pp. 34 and 199). In October Prince Fahd attended the Cancún economic summit meeting.

The most serious setback for Saudi diplomacy occurred in late November when the Arab summit conference at Fez collapsed so suddenly (see p. 189). The meeting had been called to discuss the so-called Fahd plan—a set of eight proposals by the Saudi Crown Prince, designed to form the basis for possible negotiations with Israel as an alternative to the much-criticized Camp David agreements. The proposals had been roundly condemned by Israel, but they had received close attention in both Arab and Western capitals, and political leaders and diplomats alike had spoken of the document in optimistic terms. Many regarded its most important point as that which stated that 'all states in the region should be able to live in peace', this being seen by many observers as an implicit recognition by Saudi Arabia of Israel's right to exist, at least behind its pre-1967 frontiers. Saudi confidence about the plan was rudely and abruptly shattered when Syria refused to attend the conference, which broke up in confusion after less than five hours' discussion. King Hassan of Morocco announced that the summit had been 'suspended', but there was no way in which Arab disunity, or Saudi dismay and embarrassment, could be disguised.

The obvious rift between Damascus and Riyadh was, however, quickly overshadowed by the announcement on 14 December of the Israeli Government's virtual annexation of the occupied Golan Heights (see p. 186). This action aroused great hostility and resentment throughout the Arab world, and when President Asad visited Riyadh on 22 December Prince Fahd promised full support for Syria in its efforts to get Israel to rescind that decision. At the same time the Crown Prince announced the postponement of a visit to Washington which he was due to make in mid-January, and the year ended with renewed uncertainty about the future of US-Saudi relations.

Saudi oil policy remained in favour of price moderation, and of a unified approach by the producing countries. Petroleum production remained at relatively high levels. Industrial development went ahead, and on 12 April King Khalid opened one of the showpiece projects, the King Abd al Aziz airport in Jeddah. This airport, covering an area of over 40 square miles, cost more than £2,300 million to construct.

Internal affairs appeared to be relatively tranquil but there were reports of sporadic disturbances among the Shia population of the eastern province and in September Iranian pilgrims clashed violently with Saudi soldiers in the holy city of Medina. No appreciable progress appeared to have been made towards creating the promised consultative council.

YEMEN ARAB REPUBLIC

For the Yemen Arab Republic 1981 was a relatively tranquil year compared with some in the recent past. It began, however, with the assassination of the Minister of Local Government, formerly Minister of the Interior, Lieut.-Col. Muhammad Khamis, on 15 January as he was travelling by road from Hodeida to Sanaa. In the ambush one of the attackers was also killed and another gunman was arrested by the

Minister's guards. Although no obvious motives for the attack were established the killing was widely believed to have been the work of members of the National Democratic Front (NDF), a rebel group which continued to receive support from the People's Democratic Republic of Yemen (see AR 1979, p. 198). There were reports throughout the spring and summer of sporadic clashes between NDF guerrillas and government troops, particularly in the area around Jebel Raymah, south-east of Hodeida. On 20 April Lieut.-Col. Lutfi al Kilabi was named as the new Minister of Local Government.

In April there were authoritative reports that the veteran politician Mr Abdullah al Asnag had been tried in secret and executed, but official sources would confirm only his arrest. Mr al Asnag had been appointed a presidential adviser in March 1979 after serving as Foreign Minister from 1975. According to the reports he was found guilty of acts of treachery against President Saleh, of dealings with the US Central Intelligence Agency, and of 'suspect relations' with an un-named Arab country. The latter was widely believed to be Saudi Arabia, for Mr al Asnag had been a prominent supporter of closer ties with that state.

Relations between Sanaa and Riyadh were not always harmonious. In March it was announced that the YAR would in future purchase the bulk of its oil supplies from its northern neighbour and no longer from Kuwait, but the Government remained suspicious of Riyadh's assumed desire to exercise greater control over the affairs of the YAR. The continued presence of Soviet military advisers in Sanaa again gave rise to disquiet in Saudi circles, as did the visit to Moscow of the YAR President in late October.

The economy remained weak and foreign exchange reserves again declined; in September they were believed to be less than $700 million. Remittances from Yemenis working in Saudi Arabia fell steeply as the latter country sought to replace them with workers from south and south-eastern Asia. The need for foreign aid therefore remained very great.

PEOPLE'S DEMOCRATIC REPUBLIC OF YEMEN

News of events in the People's Democratic Republic of Yemen remained scanty throughout 1981 and such political changes as did occur were both obscure in their origin and subject to conflicting interpretations. On 19 January a meeting of the People's Supreme Assembly (PSA) dismissed Mr Salim al Bid from his post as Deputy Prime Minister; Mr al Bid had previously been a prominent member of the political bureau of the ruling Yemeni Socialist Party (YSP). In early March it was reported in Beirut that Mr Muhammad Saleh Mutea, who had been Foreign Minister of the PDRY from 1975 to 1979, had been tried and executed after conviction of spying for Saudi Arabia; but other sources stated that the former Minister had been shot while trying to escape from prison. The PDRY authorities refused to confirm news of his death.

On 4 May Colonel Ali Ahmad Nasser Antar was relieved of the post of Minister of Defence, which he had held since 1977, and was appointed Minister of Local Government. This change was widely regarded as a demotion and it was seen also as a sign of the growing power of the President, Ali Nasser Muhammad, a political rival of Colonel Antar. Some reports also suggested that the Colonel had been removed from the Ministry of Defence because of his refusal to take orders from Soviet military advisers.

A series of by-elections to the PSA, and local council elections, were held in June, and the President announced that the YSP had achieved an unsurprising 94·6 per cent support.

The PDRY's relations with the USSR, Ethiopia and Libya remained close. On 19 August, in Aden, Libya, Ethiopia and the PDRY signed a treaty of friendship and cooperation which claimed to have as its purpose the limitation of US influence in the Middle East (see p. 215). In mid-November representatives of the three states met again in Addis Ababa and there condemned Washington for holding the prolonged military exercise known as Operation Bright Star in the Middle East.

In early December the President of the Yemen Arab Republic visited Aden and the two Governments agreed to cooperate on economic and political matters. The PDRY also promised to halt its support for the National Democratic Front guerrillas in the YAR (see p. 205). Local observers, however, remained highly sceptical about the extent of any possible cooperation in view of the deep distrust which continued to prevail between Sanaa and Aden.

THE ARAB STATES OF THE GULF

KUWAIT—BAHREIN—QATAR—UNITED ARAB EMIRATES—OMAN

FOR some years after the British withdrawal in 1971 the Shah had posed as the policeman of the Gulf. This was never popular amongst the Arabs but it took his fall and the subsequent war between Iran and Iraq to force the states of the western coast to realize that they had to work more closely together. They had already set up many forms of technical co-operation—their Health, Education and Agricultural Ministers, for example, met regularly—and there were joint services such as the Gulf Postal Union, but there was surprisingly little coordination in the fields of foreign affairs, defence, economics and development policies. The Shaikh of Qatar's call for a Common Market in 1975 had attracted no response and there continued immense and wasteful duplication of effort.

In February 1981, the Saudis, as the leading Arab state, called for a conference to establish a Gulf Cooperation Council (GCC). They were worried by the possible effects of the Islamic revolution upon the Shia population which formed a sizeable minority in most Gulf states and an actual majority in Bahrein, and by the fact that the Russians were showing no signs of leaving Afghanistan and might move nearer still to the Gulf if Iran collapsed. In April Shaikh Zaid of Abu Dhabi went to Riyadh and in the following month he acted as host to a summit meeting of the rulers of five other states, Saudi Arabia, Kuwait, Bahrein, Qatar and Oman. A meeting of Foreign Ministers in Muscat had already shown the possibility of agreement.

The outcome was to set up what the Kuwaiti Foreign Minister was to call a 'political, economic and social grouping to face external threats'. A secretary-general, Abdullah Bishara, the former Kuwaiti ambassador to the UN, was appointed to head a strong secretariat, and five specialist committees were established. These were to formulate a unified oil policy, to coordinate economic and social planning, and to arrange co-operation in matters of industry, commerce and culture. It was stressed that there was no attempt to replace the Arab League and that the framework was very loose; for, as Bishara said, 'the baby is just born—don't ask if it has any teeth'. The heads of state were to meet twice a year and specialist Ministers more frequently.

The Finance Ministers met, discussed a common currency and recommended the removal of tariffs between members. The Foreign Ministers for their part agreed to increase cooperation in political and security affairs, but no concrete measures were announced, apart from a vague scheme to abolish embassies in favour of liaison offices. The Foreign Ministers met again in November, endorsed the Fahd plan (see p. 203-4) and 'rejected all attempts by foreign powers to find a foothold'. The subsequent meeting of the heads of state proved less successful still, and practically the only decision was to postpone the summit scheduled for six months ahead. It was clear from the beginning that there were fundamental differences between the members on two matters of major importance.

One was a failure to agree on an oil-pricing policy. KUWAIT firmly refused to follow the Saudi line of holding prices down, which was adopted half-heartedly by most of the others. Kuwait preferred to cut production, particularly when major companies refused to pay premium prices during the glut. Some of the other states also cut production.

The second disagreement was over what was 'the external threat' mentioned by the Kuwaitis. The only member of the group to have diplomatic relations with Russia, they claimed to be convinced that the Soviets posed no menace to the area. The Foreign Minister went to Moscow before the establishment of the GCC, perhaps to persuade the Kremlin that the proposed organization was not an alliance directed against it. In the autumn the Shaikh visited Bulgaria, Romania and Hungary, to which Kuwait had already made a loan. Kuwait continued to buy Russian arms and in October joined with the USSR in setting up a joint exhibition on space exploration. The Kuwaitis tried to persuade their sceptical colleagues to admit Soviet diplomats. Publicly they stated that the Americans, with their proposal of having a rapid deployment force (RDF) available for use in the area and probably requiring bases there, constituted a bigger bogey than the Russians.

OMAN, on the other hand, was still involved in sporadic hostilities with the Russian-dominated PDRY (five of whose regular soldiers were captured on Dhofari territory in the summer) and regarded South Yemen's alliance, under Russian patronage, with Libya and Ethiopia as a major threat to the stability of the area. It declared its willingness to admit Western troops in case of emergency and allowed the Americans to have everything short of a permanent base. US engineers developed the airfields at Masirah and Thamrait near Salala, which had the third longest landing-strip in the world, and set up dumps of weapons and supplies for the RDF. Oman, with Egypt and Somalia, took part in the American-directed operation Bright Star in December, and US marines practised landings on its beaches. Oman continued to rely on the West for arms, buying 35 Chieftain tanks from Britain for £40 million. The other states opposed any formal dependence upon the West and, to avoid dissension, Omani proposals for the coordination of defence were shelved with the minimum of discussion. It was also significant that, whereas Oman alloted 40 per cent of its budget for defence, the Kuwaitis spent less than 10 per cent.

The difference in approach was seen after Mrs Thatcher's first visit to the Gulf in March, where her stalwart sentiments that the Russians could be stopped only by force and her readiness to provide troops were warmly welcomed in Muscat, received tepidly in the United Arab Emirates (where she was reported to have concluded an arms deal), and attacked in Kuwait. The following month the British Defence Minister John Nott had to stress that no forces would be deployed unless they were specifically requested. Mrs Thatcher's second visit in the autumn, when she went to Kuwait, also caused controversy, exception being taken to some of her remarks about the Palestinians.

The Kuwaitis continued to be vociferous supporters of the Palestinian cause, which attracted less interest in the southern Gulf. The southern states, also, did not share the Kuwaiti dread of Iraq, which from time to time gave ominous hints that it had territorial claims against its neighbour: following its usual policy Kuwait paid Danegeld, making interest-free loans of $2,000 million in April and $7,000 million in December. The Iraqis were believed to be behind the explosion of five bombs in Kuwait in June and certainly they refused to hand back the suspected culprits. The Kuwaitis felt themselves threatened, too, by Iran, which they held responsible for bombing oil installations in October, an action seen as a warning not to give too much support to Iraq.

The importance of the Gulf on the world stage was shown by the number of foreign statesmen visiting the area. In addition to Mrs Thatcher, King Juan Carlos, Mrs Gandhi, Chancellors Schmidt and Kreisky, King Husain, Colonel Qadafi, President Asad, the Portuguese Prime Minister and the Dutch Foreign Minister (on behalf of the EEC) were amongst those received in some of the states.

In domestic affairs two states made moves in the direction of widening political participation. In March KUWAIT held elections to replace the National Assembly dissolved in 1976. There were 520 candidates for the 50 seats but the electorate was only 43,000 in a population estimated at 1,300,000. The franchise was restricted to men of long Kuwaiti descent, and votes for women proved an important issue. The result was an Assembly consisting of youngish, well-educated, middle-class men of moderate opinions, extremists of both left and right being defeated. The Assembly pledged itself to work with the Shaikh and his slightly modified Cabinet, and in early sessions confined itself to reviewing legislation promulgated since 1976. It was felt, however, that in due course the Assembly would assert the considerable powers given it by the constitution. The architect of Sydney opera house was commissioned to design a new building for the Assembly.

In OMAN, the Sultan, reacting perhaps to the criticism that he had become rather remote from his people, created by decree a State Advisory Council in October. The Government nominated its 45 members, 17 of whom represented the state, 11 the private sector and 17 the regions. It received financial independence and a secretariat and chose its own executive, through which it could advance criticism and suggestions to the Sultan. It was hoped that it would promote better coordination of the state and private sectors in planning development.

Another new feature was the first use of the strike weapon, which was illegal both in Kuwait, where about 3,000 men working for the oil company walked out, and in the UAE, where junior government employees complained that the budget had frozen their wages. In both cases the authorities had to make concessions.

More serious was the discovery of a plot in BAHREIN, timed apparently to coincide with the National Day in mid-December. Organized by a Shia imam who had been expelled in 1979, it had aimed at kidnapping Ministers and at taking over the radio station. Those arrested consisted of 45 Bahreinis, 13 Saudis, a Kuwaiti and an Omani, and weapons, false police uniforms and faked documents were found. It was stated that Teheran radio was due to announce that the conspiracy had succeeded and to call for a simultaneous Islamic uprising throughout the Gulf. The Iranian chargé was expelled and the Bahreini Minister of the Interior suggested that the Gulf Cooperation Council (GCC) should set up its own rapid deployment force for such emergencies.

In the UAE there was a realization that important political changes were bound to follow the serious illness of Shaikh Rashid of Dubai, Prime Minister and Vice-President of the Federation. Since they had commanded their state forces in war against each other in the 1940s, relations between him and Shaikh Zaid, President of the Federation, had never been easy. DUBAI had never been willing to accept any primacy on the part of its neighbour and had refused to play its full part, particularly in financial matters, in the new state. No successor could match the authority and shrewdness of Shaikh Rashid but in the meanwhile both he and Shaikh Zaid were re-elected for another five years.

On a happier note one may record the wedding of Shaikh Muhammad, the son of Shaikh Zaid. The local press reported that 10 million fairy lights were erected at a cost of $35 million and that the father of the bride handed over a dowry which included a shopping centre with 55 boutiques, an hotel and three high-rise buildings.

In RAS AL-KHAIMAH a rapist was executed by firing squad after receiving 130 lashes. Loudspeaker invitations to witness the event attracted 10,000 spectators. There were also executions for adultery in ABU DHABI. This reversion to strict Muslim law was symptomatic of a general trend throughout the Gulf in reaction to the Islamic revolution: life for expatriates also became more difficult.

In QATAR few events caused bigger headlines than the victory of its football youth team over England.

OMAN continued its efforts to preserve and appreciate its ancient culture. The dhow *Sohar*, funded by the Ministry of the National Heritage and built and sailed by the explorer Tim Severin, successfully reached Canton in what became known as the 'Sindbad Voyage'.

When most of the Gulf states announced their development plans, it became evident that the GCC would have much to do to prevent overlapping, since no state wished to be seen lagging behind the others in any field of endeavour. Bahrein announced that it would set up a new Gulf University which would aim at 10,000 students by the year 2000. Oman planned to build a university which would have 1,000 places and cost £500 million, much of that going to British firms. The British were also to play a role in expanding the existing university at al-Ain so that it could accommodate 12,000 students. Since, in addition to five in Saudi

Arabia, there were already universities in Kuwait and Qatar, it was by no means clear how so many students would be found.

Al-Ain had long been specially favoured by Shaikh Zaid, who had served as Amir there before coming to the throne. It was decided that an international airport should be built there at the cost of £120 million as soon as the extensions to Abu Dhabi airport, less than 100 miles away, had been completed at a cost of £200 million. Al-Ain is a similar distance from the contiguous airports at Dubai and Sharjah.

The UAE announced its first federal five-year plan, which, in addition to much expenditure on social projects, envisaged an increase in oil-prospecting and refining. It was anxious to have capital-intensive industries in order that it might shed some 300,000 immigrant workers, of whom at least 60,000 had arrived illegally. Kuwait had a similar problem and also aimed at increasing its refining and petrol-based industries. There were, however, plans for a model industrial town stretching for 24 miles along the coast near Ahmadi. The Kuwaiti budget foresaw expenditure of $6,000 million on development, and an interesting idea was that an almost equal sum should be set aside for future generations. Omani schemes were less ambitious and its five-year plan concentrated on agriculture, fishery and natural gas. A plan was made to revive the copper mines that had once supplied ancient Babylon, and another, perhaps purely visionary, was to build an oil pipeline from the Gulf coast to the shore of the Indian Ocean, thus bypassing the Straits of Hormuz.

Statistics showed that Kuwait, Qatar and the UAE took the first three places as the countries with the largest GDP per capita in the world. Other matters of financial interest were the development of the Gulf insurance scheme, ARIG, which was hailed as an eventual rival for Lloyds of London, and the increasing control that the newly-created Central Bank of the UAE managed to exert. Foreign banks were forbidden to have more than eight branches and this meant that some 90 offices, many of them British, would have to close. Many, however, welcomed this measure as providing a measure of banking discipline.

Chapter 4

SUDAN—LIBYA—TUNISIA—WESTERN SAHARA—ALGERIA—MOROCCO

SUDAN

THE country celebrated its 25th anniversary of independence but not without political and economic difficulties. In March an unsuccessful attempted coup, in which Syria and Russia were implicated, was organized by a retired brigadier and resulted in the arrest of eleven people including army officers. As a precaution against political unrest, the Government put into custody nearly 10,000 people who were described as vagrants, squatters, refugees and unemployed. Railway workers, transport and catering workers, textile workers and judges went on strike and protested against their low salaries, employment conditions and inflation. Three Cabinet reshuffles resulted from seriously deteriorating economic conditions and reflected political instability. President Nimairi dissolved the National Assembly and ordered elections to a new Assembly with fewer than half the former number of members (366). The purpose was to reduce the Assembly's powers and devolve them to the newly-created regional assemblies. The President also dissolved the Southern regional assembly and the Southern high executive council, and a transitional council was formed for a period of six months.

In accordance with the policy of decentralization and regionalism, the northern part of the country was divided into five regions, each with a governor (*ḥākim*), a deputy governor, regional ministers and a regional assembly. Though this regional system was intended to facilitate administration, critics envisaged the emergence of regional nationalism detrimental to the interests of national unity.

Libyan intervention in Chad dominated the political scene. Sudan condemned this intervention and called for the withdrawal of Libyan troops. It was reported that about 10,000 Chadian refugees crossed the border into Sudan. As a precautionary measure Sudanese troops were re-grouped along the Chad border and the Government accused the Libyans of bombing Sudanese villages there. In facing this threat President Nimairi asked for military assistance from the USA and Egypt. Libya was implicated in the explosion at the Chad embassy in Khartoum in which one man was killed. In consequence of these events, the Government ordered all Libyan diplomats out of the country and recalled its envoys from Tripoli. Eventually tension between Sudan and Libya was lessened after the withdrawal of Libyan troops from Chad.

In view of the Libyan threat and the aftermath of President Sadat's assassination in October, the USA agreed to develop air, naval and ground forces by supplying military equipment, including tanks and jet fighters. Training teams were sent to Sudan to teach the use of American equipment. Sudanese and American troops conducted joint manoeuvres, Operation Bright Star (see p. 208). After a visit by the Vice-President, China agreed to supply arms to Sudan.

President Nimairi continued to support Egyptian foreign policy in relation to Camp David. In this context Saudi Arabia was reluctant to render financial help and warned Sudan to discontinue any idea of reconciling Egypt with other Arab countries. Sudan's close ties with Egypt prompted Libya and the PLO to ask Arab countries to cut off diplomatic relations with Sudan. This was rejected by an urgent meeting of Arab

Foreign Ministers held in Tunisia. In consequence PLO officials in Khartoum were asked to leave the country.

On the African front, the Presidents of Uganda, Djibouti and Somalia visited the Sudan and discussed mutual cooperation. At the meeting of the Organization of African Unity held in Nairobi President Nimairi, with the Presidents of Tanzania, Nigeria, Kenya, Guinea and the Foreign Ministers of Sierra Leone and Mali, agreed on a programme for a ceasefire and a referendum in the Western Sahara. President Nimairi also attended the Islamic summit in Saudi Arabia and the funeral of President Sadat, and on a private visit to the USA he discussed with President Reagan and leading American politicians mutual relations and American assistance to Sudan.

The country continued to be in deep economic recession and financial difficulties. The Government succeeded in rescheduling $600 million out of a $3,000 million international debt acknowledged by government sources. The annual trade deficit of nearly $500 million and the IMF demand for stringent economic measures to rectify the deficit prompted the Government to devalue the Sudanese pound by 12½ per cent and to increase taxes on oil by 40 per cent and on imports by 10 per cent. Its decision to phase out subsidies on sugar, petrol and wheat prompted demonstrations by Khartoum University students and in other places. The much-debated scheme, Kenana sugar factory, was opened in March with a cost increased from $113 million to $620 million.

Despite the gloomy financial prospects, the Government continued to borrow and invest in development projects. Balance of payments support included loans totalling $137 million from Opec, Saudi Arabia, Switzerland and the Netherlands. The IMF lent $79 million to cover export shortfalls. The agricultural sector received $250 million for modernization and for new agricultural projects from European countries, the World Bank and Arab oil-producing countries. Spain agreed to lend $32 million for supplying tractors and buses; the USA approved $100 million for military equipment and $50 million for essential imports; West Germany approved $123 million for development aid for 1981-82. Also the EEC agreed to lend $110 million over four years for agricultural development and communications. Saudi Arabia approved a loan of $29 million to enlarge the storage facilities for refined oil products at Port Sudan. The European Development Fund lent nearly $11 million for the second phase of Juba University construction. The Southern Region also received $7·4 million from Kuwait for a housing scheme in Juba.

The Government gave its approval for ten industrial, agricultural and communication projects at a cost of Sud.£43 million. Oil explorations continued, the Chevron Oil Company budgeting $70 million for this purpose. Mineral exploration concessions in the Red Sea province were granted to France Total Exploration. Protocols of economic cooperation to the amount of $276 million were signed with the Netherlands, China, France and Egypt. Sudan and Egypt agreed to set up a Commerce and Investment Bank to finance development projects with a capital of $20 million shared by both countries.

LIBYA

Domestically 1981 was a quiet year. In January the annual meeting of the General People's Congress (GPC) called for intensive military instruction for the young in the 'revolutionary training centres'—a new name for schools. Projects for nuclear energy and railways were announced and more land was brought under cultivation, producing corn at five times the world market price. In the towns, huge subsidized state supermarkets drove most privately-owned shops out of business. Libya had to cut the price of its oil three times, and during some months production was reported to be as low as 500,000 barrels a day—less than a third of what once it had been. The state was able to shrug off the corresponding loss of revenue.

One of the GPC's decisions was to abolish the Foreign Ministry, international relations through official channels having been declared an anachronism. Ambassadors abroad were replaced by spokesmen who had in theory been elected by the local Libyan community. Some countries seized the opportunity to expel them but most regarded the change as purely verbal.

In foreign affairs the first half of the year saw Qadafi at his most rumbustious. In January, after a visit from President Oueddeye, the Colonel declared that Libya and Chad were indissolubly united 'by history and blood'. This alarmed other countries bordering the Sahara and, led by Nigeria, twelve of them met at Lomé and condemned the merger. France saw it as a 'threat to the security of Africa' and suspended an oil agreement. A further consequence was a quarrel with the Sudan, which sheltered the dissident forces of Hissène Habre: relations were broken and Khartoum complained of bombings and attempted coups. Sadat and the Saudis were denounced as inventively as ever; the Saudi desire for AWACS aircraft was seen as 'blasphemous', violating the integrity of the holy cities. The old rivalries with Morocco over the Sahara and with Malta and Tunisia over territorial limits showed no sign of diminishing, while in March there was a new quarrel with Greece, which refused to hand back a Libyan defector. In the same month, while deploring terrorism, Qadafi gave his blessing to the aims of the Basque separatists and the IRA. President Obote complained that Libya was trying to destabilize his country, and the hand of Qadafi was seen behind unrest in other African states. In April, when the Mauritanian Premier visited Tripoli, Qadafi suggested a union of the two countries which would also embrace Algeria and the Western Sahara, but no one else showed the slightest enthusiasm for the idea.

The Israeli bombing of the Baghdad nuclear installation and the meeting of the OAU summit, at which Qadafi succeeded in obtaining the presidency for next year, seemed to have induced him to shed some superfluous quarrels. Relations were restored with Morocco, Jordan and Iraq and a wide-ranging agreement was made with Tunisia. Having received a request from Oueddeye, Qadafi withdrew his troops from Chad without demur. This retreat, coupled with the election of M Mitterrand, led to improved relations with France. Qadafi made approaches to the Saudis and did not savage the Fahd plan (see pp. 203-4) although he declined to attend the Fez summit on the pretext that he held no official position. Only Egypt and the Sudan were excluded from this new benevolence: a public holiday was called to celebrate the murder of Sadat and shortly afterwards President Nimairi declared that he expected a Libyan invasion at any moment.

The US was also not forgiven. On 6 May Washington expelled all Libyan diplomats for 'provocations and misconduct' and urged all its own 2,000 citizens in Libya to leave. A month later the Americans let it be known that they would help any country threatened by Qadafi's interventionism, but the Administration resisted calls for a boycott of Libyan oil, continuing to take a third of that country's production for $9,000 million. In July the American press reported that the CIA was plotting to murder the Colonel, but even if Washington's plans were not so drastic it clearly wished to humiliate him. On 19 August the Sixth Fleet entered waters in the Gulf of Sirte known to be claimed by Libya and when two aircraft came to investigate they were shot down. Qadafi could only react verbally, threatening to launch a world war and to attack US bases in Crete, Turkey and Sicily and make the Gulf of Sirte 'redder than the Red Sea' with Americans' blood if they dared to return. Washington pressed the oil companies to withdraw from Libya and in November Exxon decided to cease operations. This was followed by an official claim that Qadafi had sent a squad of assassins to murder the President and a call for sanctions against Tripoli. Qadafi riposted that the Libyans did not take Reagan so seriously—they were unable to do so because they kept repeating his old films on television.

Naturally Qadafi had to maintain his links with Moscow, which he visited in May. He was not an easy ally, calling publicly for independence for Afghanistan and berating his hosts for not doing enough for the Arabs. In August he formed a close alliance with Russia's two Red Sea friends, Ethiopia and South Yemen. Neighbouring countries reacted with alarm, seeing this as a Kremlin-inspired move to destabilize the

Arabian peninsula and East Africa, particularly as Libya admitted supplying arms to Omani and Somali dissidents.

The union with Syria announced in 1980 with such eclat (see AR 1980, p. 211) was allowed to drift. President Asad said in March that they were 'searching for a formula that achieves unity with real popular content' but apparently they could not find one, even during a visit by Qadafi to Damascus in August.

'The Supreme Thinker and Guide' spent considerable sums on publicizing his 'universal theory' and financing congresses to discuss it. A seminar in Caracas was attended by 774 people from 54 countries. A new idea was that women should be 'revolutionary nuns'.

TUNISIA

The year opened with a series of strikes. In February all secondary schools were closed and bus and railway workers paralysed communications. The Government had to award pay rises of 20 per cent and to promise to hold down prices.

Undeterred, the Prime Minister, Mohammed Mzali, continued his plans for widening political participation beyond the narrow clique of officials of the sole party, the PSD. In April the party relaxed its grip upon the trade union organization, the UGTT. Since the riots of 1978 the UGTT had been ruled by government nominees but now many leaders arrested then were restored to office. The UGTT's new secretary-general, Taieb Baccouche, a 38-year-old professor of linguistics, had never been a party member.

Also in April the Government announced that other parties would be recognized provided that they accepted the constitution, rejected violence and had no foreign ties. The Communist Party resumed official existence after 18 years and two Social Democrat parties, the MDS and the MUP, differing more in personalities than in policies, also received recognition.

The *Mouvement de la tendence islamique* stood apart in glowering fanaticism. Its members were said to have assaulted tourists drinking wine and threatened to throw vitriol at women swimming in Ramadan. In August over 100 members were brought to trial on vague charges such as insulting the head of state, spreading false news and setting up an illegal organization. Prison sentences ranging from 6 months to 11 years were imposed upon 84 of them (27 *in absentia*). Demonstrations on the streets of Tunis and complaints of torture followed.

In October campaigning started for the first multi-party elections in Tunisian history. Opposition leaders stated their case on the state television network, while Mzali stressed the Government's economic achievements. After sharp debate the UGTT decided to participate, in alliance with the PSD, although Baccouche declined to be nominated.

The results of the voting on 1 November proved an anti-climax: the Government won all the seats with nearly 95 per cent of the poll. At local level there was clearly intimidation and fraud, and Mzali was evidently embarrassed by an outcome that could only induce scepticism. Ahmed Mestiri, leader of the MDS, which had received 3·3 per cent, formally said that the results had been faked, but some of his associates felt that the mere fact that multi-party elections had taken place constituted a real advance. Certainly the return of 22 Deputies of an independent UGTT would have been unthinkable a year earlier.

In February the Government set out a new five-year plan calling for investment of about $20,000 million, of which it was hoped a quarter would be raised abroad. The main emphasis would be upon reviving the phosphate industry, increasing agriculture and fishing and improving the infrastructure. There were plans to quadruple the refinery at Bizerta and to develop solar energy. Tunisia also inaugurated an 85,000-acre national park—the first in North Africa.

In foreign affairs Tunisia concentrated on doing nothing that would upset anyone. Relations with its neighbours, edgy since the Gafsa raid (see AR 1980, p. 213), became more cordial, and agreements for various forms of cooperation were signed both with Libya and with Algeria. Tunisia continued to rely upon France and the US for weapons, receiving a loan from Washington for $95 million-worth of aircraft.

WESTERN SAHARA

Throughout the year there were constant rumours of secret negotiations between Morocco and Algeria which would deprive the Polisario of its original main supporter. King Hassan and President Chadli shook hands at the Taif summit in January and in November each head of state received the other's Foreign Minister in the highest-level official contacts since diplomatic relations had been broken off five years before. Even if Algerian help were reduced, however, Polisario was able to make use of bases in Mauritania, particularly after that country broke off relations with Morocco in March.

During the winter the Moroccans almost completed a 'Berlin Wall', 200 miles long, of rocks and minefields sealing off the agricultural areas and those producing phosphates from the desert sands, which they proposed to abandon to the enemy. Within that area the Moroccans held elections for the Assembly in Rabat and went ahead with work on a railway linking Marrakesh with El Ayoun and perhaps eventually with Dakar.

In February King Hassan boasted that the war was over, but the two following months saw particularly heavy fighting. In August Polisario claimed to have killed 135 Moroccan soldiers and in October the biggest battles of the entire war took place at Guelta Zemmour near the Mauritanian frontier. The Moroccans admitted that a garrison of 200 men had been overwhelmed by a force of 3,000 equipped with tanks. Three Moroccan aircraft attempting to intervene were destroyed and Rabat claimed that the enemy were using weapons too sophisticated to have been used by Saharans alone.

Diplomatically Polisario lost much of the ground that it seemed to have won at the 1980 OAU summit in Freetown (see AR 1980, p. 215) when its case was supported by 26 votes to 24. This year at Nairobi its backers had dwindled to 8, and although its representatives apparently got the better of an unseemly bout of fisticuffs with their Moroccan opposite numbers they proved no match in diplomacy for the King in person. Hassan refused to negotiate directly with them but won general support by offering a referendum with 'controlled procedure' which would ensure that he could not lose. It seemed impossible that the contending parties would ever agree upon such fundamental problems as who was qualified to vote, what question should be put and whether the Moroccan army and administration should remain in the area during any campaign. In August a committee of African statesmen including Presidents Moi, Nyerere and Shagari made little progress in drawing up the rules. Hassan contrived to appear the more reasonable of the contenders and so gained another opportunity to win the war either by arms or by diplomacy.

ALGERIA

In February President Chadli made a speech on the state of the nation without once mentioning the name of his predecessor, Houari Boumédienne. Thus after two years he turned his back on the myth that 'the revolution was continuing'. Pragmatism had now formally replaced ideology, and later Chadli was to differentiate between 'those who work and those who wave slogans'. The country was ruled by a handful of officers, owing all to the President, many of whom had been in disfavour under the previous regime. The annual congress of the sole party, the FLN, in July resulted in purges; and the two men once mentioned as the main contenders to succeed Boumédienne, Abdel Aziz Bouteflika and Mohammed Yahyawi, were replaced on the Politburo by Ministers chosen by the President. In December Bouteflika and Belaid Abdessalem, who as chief of the state corporation Sonatrach had once been practically the second man in the country, were banned from political activity.

Plans were made to decentralize banking and other state enterprises, smallholders and private business were encouraged and luxury goods appeared in the shops. Visiting in June, Lord Carrington recognized that Algeria was now the biggest Arab market after Saudi Arabia. British firms won a contract for £200 million-worth of housing as part of the drive to improve living standards.

There were two other breaks with the ethos of the sternly Muslim Boumédienne. Although many women had achieved distinction in the war of independence, the late President had firmly set his face against any extension of their rights: Chadli prepared plans for their greater participation in national life. He also took vigorous action against Muslim extremists.

In foreign affairs Chadli had already abandoned Boumédienne's vision of Algeria as leader of the Third World, and he did nothing spectacular in 1981. In February he toured sub-Saharan Africa and in June he went to Moscow for the first time. Algeria was disappointed that its services in negotiating the return of the American hostages from Iran did not apparently attract much gratitude, but it continued on friendly terms with the West. Relations with France became much warmer after the election of President Mitterrand, who visited Algiers in November. They had never been cordial with Giscard, during whose last years Algeria seemed to regard Italy as its best European friend: now ties with Rome were loosened.

In Arab affairs Algeria continued to be a member of the Steadfastness Front, although its adherence seemed less enthusiastic as its distrust of Colonel Qadafi's ambitions increased. Various agreements were made with Tunisia, and the possibility of war with Morocco over the Sahara receded.

However, Algeria's main overseas preoccupation was to try to obtain long-term contracts to sell its natural gas before the projected Russian pipeline from the Urals could compete—particularly as it was estimated that proven oil reserves would not last beyond the year 2000. A 20-year agreement was made with Belgium, but the high price demanded prolonged negotiations with France and the USA.

MOROCCO

By the summer of 1981 the Moroccan economy was in complete disarray. The World Bank reported that a third of the population of 20 million were below the poverty line. The world-wide recession and the increasing difficulty of finding work in EEC countries added to the problems, but the final blow came with the almost complete failure of the winter and spring rains. Nearly a third of the cattle and sheep died, while cereal and sugar crops were halved. The deficit absorbed an estimated half of the country's reserves.

The Government, claiming that rationing was the only alternative, raised the prices of essential commodities, some by as much as 85 per cent. The CDT, the more leftist of the two trade union federations, called for a strike. On 21 June there were scenes of the utmost violence in Casablanca in which it was said that soldiers were stoned to death and police dogs set on fire. Official figures recorded that 67 people had been killed and 500 injured but some observers put the first figure in hundreds and the second in thousands. The Government blamed the CDT and their Social Democratic allies, the USFP, and arrested several thousand people, but it hastened to reduce prices. The King, whose portraits (to be seen everywhere in Casablanca) were untouched in the rioting, promised a complete review of domestic problems and announced a major programme to create almost a million new jobs during the next five years.

Even earlier there had been some cracks in the astonishing front of national unity which had persisted for over six years since the beginning of the Saharan problem. In the spring some 60 Deputies split away from the ruling RNI, a loose grouping of independents whose main bond was support for the King. Led by Abderrahim Kasimi, they complained that rural interests were being systematically sacrificed to those of the urban and business communities. In May the USFP, led by Abderrahim Bouabid, decided on a partial boycott of communal elections, which they claimed would not be fairly conducted. In August the party, proving itself more nationalist than the King, attacked Hassan's agreement for a referendum in the Sahara as throwing away the fruits of many years of sacrifice. Stung, the King retaliated by ordering the arrest of Bouabid, seven of his colleagues on the USFP executive and 30 officials of the CDT and closing down their newspapers.

For two decades Bouabid had been implicitly recognized as the leader of 'the loyal opposition' and while some of his colleagues had been imprisoned or even murdered his person had always seemed sacrosanct. This time, however, he was brought to trial, although potentially grave charges were dropped. He and most of those arrested were gaoled for a year on a minor charge.

In 1980 a referendum (see AR 1980, p. 217) had extended the life of Parliament for two years beyond its original mandate, due to end in the autumn of 1981. The USFP deputies refused to recognize this and boycotted the Assembly, whereupon the Government declared that they had forfeited their immunity and placed them all under house arrest. After a month, following the reverse at Guelta Zemmour in mid-October (see p. 218), in the interests of national unity they returned to their seats, but as individuals rather than as a party. The final political event of the year was a major riot on the campus of Rabat University which led to 100 arrests.

In foreign affairs, the threat of a hostile majority in the OAU was removed (see p. 218) and relations were restored with the two powers whose enmity was potentially dangerous—formally with Libya and tacitly with Algeria. Relations continued close with Saudi Arabia, yielding a reported $1,000 million in aid and setting up joint projects, while Kuwait helped to prospect for oil. It was hoped that prestige would accrue from Morocco's chairmanship of the Arab summit in Fez in November, but some diplomats blamed its precipitate collapse on over-hasty action by the King. Morocco benefited from the tendency of the Reagan Administration to see countries as either 'good' or 'bad'. Morocco was definitely 'good' and received much attention, including considerable arms supplies.

VI EQUATORIAL AFRICA

Chapter 1

ETHIOPIA—SOMALIA—DJIBOUTI—KENYA—TANZANIA—UGANDA

ETHIOPIA

COLONEL Mengistu Haile-Maryam retained his position of unchallenged supremacy, to the extent that he came to be described as 'the socialist emperor'. After two years work by the commission for establishing a marxist-leninist party (COPWE), the party itself had still not materialized by the end of the year, but COPWE continued to be active and extended its organization down to regional and provincial level, in the process recruiting activists from several of the disbanded civilian marxist organizations. The delay in establishing the party was ascribed to Mengistu's desire to assert his independence of the Soviet Union, which pressed for its formation in the shortest possible time, but may equally have reflected internal problems, especially the role to be given to civilians and the question of regional autonomy. In his Revolution Day speech in September, Mengistu stated that 'the negative role of people who amass personal wealth has reached a serious stage', and instituted a campaign against corruption; only one member of the ruling military council was charged, however, and he embarrassed the regime by claiming at his trial that many of his former colleagues should have been in the dock beside him.

The various internal insurgency movements appeared less threatening than in previous years. The situation in the Ogaden was well under control, as increasing numbers of its Somali inhabitants returned from refugee camps in Somalia. The Government achieved uncontested control over much of southern and central Eritrea, for the first time in many years permitting unconvoyed traffic on major roads and allowing foreigners to visit the capital, Asmara. The Eritrean People's Liberation Front (EPLF) retained its northern stronghold at Nacfa, where, after an unsuccessful Ethiopian assault in late 1980 and early 1981, the war appeared to have reached a stalemate. Following a meeting at Tunis in April, at which the Eritreans' principal Arab backers threatened to withdraw support unless the various guerrilla movements united, the EPLF established itself as the sole effective force in the province by occupying the territory of its rival the Eritrean Liberation Front (ELF) in western Eritrea in August, forcing some 4,000 ELF guerrillas to take refuge in the Sudan. Much of the most serious fighting of the year was in Tigré province, just south of Eritrea, where the EPLF's ally, the Tigré People's Liberation Front (TPLF), attacked the provincial capital and other centres in September.

Emphasizing its increased capacity to control provincial life, the Government launched an attack on the churches, especially on the Ethiopian Lutheran Church in its centre in Wallega province. It announced the success of its literacy campaign in reducing illiteracy from 93 per cent under the old regime to 65 per cent. The campaign was conducted in ten major languages, by contrast with the imperial Government's emphasis on Amharic. Economic progress was mixed. A bumper coffee harvest of some 4½ million bags was achieved, allowing a surplus for barter deals with socialist countries after meeting Ethiopia's international quota, though the value of the crop was reduced by a decline in export prices. Tea and sugar production was also expanded. On the other hand, the FAO reported a decline in food grain production, and at various times during the year the Government claimed that between 3·9 and 5 million people were in need of emergency relief.

The search for external economic assistance was the most prominent feature in Ethiopia's foreign policy, especially in view of Soviet pressure for the repayment of loans of some $2,000 million for military assistance during the 1977-78 war. European Community aid of $250 million over five years under the Lomé Convention was announced in July, and in August the Government indicated its willingness to discuss compensation terms for Western companies nationalized since 1974. In April, Signor Colombo became the first Western Foreign Minister to visit Ethiopia since the revolution, and Italy later became Ethiopia's largest single Western aid donor. Steps were taken to revive the tourist industry, and the chief of tourism in Haile-Selassie's Government was released from prison and immediately appointed to a high advisory position.

In August, Ethiopia signed a tripartite mutual defence and cooperation treaty with Libya and South Yemen in Aden, which was also expected to attract substantial Libyan aid, especially for mining developments in Eritrea. However, good relations were maintained with Sudan, and a senior official was immediately despatched to Khartoum to reassure President Nimairi that the treaty carried no hostile implications. The Government continued to rely on Cuba and the Soviet Union in the military sphere. The number of Cuban troops in the country was reported to have fallen to about 8,000 by the end of the year. The Soviet Deputy Defence Minister, Marshal Solokov, paid a week's visit to Eritrea in June and July.

SOMALIA

The increasingly embattled regime of President Siyad Barre remained in power despite indications of a slump in its domestic popularity. Two of the most important members of the Government, the Defence Minister and the chief of security, were dismissed in April. The main organized opposition group, the Somali Salvation Front (Sosaf), claimed responsibility for bomb explosions in Mogadishu in January and again in August, and combined with Somali dissidents in Aden in September to form the Somali Workers Party. Libya admitted providing military assistance to Sosaf, and this, combined with the tripartite treaty between Libya, Ethiopia and South Yemen (see p. 215), prompted the Somali Government to break off diplomatic relations with Libya in August. Though public expression of dissent remained strictly prohibited within Somalia, journalists reported a sharp increase in private criticism of the regime, especially in the northern part of the country.

Relations with Ethiopia remained extremely poor. The Somali-backed Western Somalia Liberation Front (WSLF) suffered leadership upheavals in February, but claimed to have killed nearly 300 Ethiopian troops in Ogaden between January and early August; its effectiveness appeared to be declining. Somalia's traditionally strained relations with Kenya improved, however, following President Siyad's renunciation of Somali claims on Kenyan territory at the OAU summit in Nairobi in June. The $40 million American military aid package to Somalia was cleared in January, as one of the last acts of the Carter Administration, and a small party of American troops took over the former Soviet air and naval base at Berbera, but the United States delayed the major works needed to make the base operational.

Heavy rains between March and May ended the two-year drought, and although they caused immediate problems in overcrowded refugee camps the rural economy had substantially improved by the end of the year. The United Nations estimated refugee numbers in the middle of the year to be 650,000, about half those claimed by the Somali Government, and to be falling towards the end of the year as a result of the rains and of reduced fighting in the Ogaden. The IMF provided a $50 million credit in July, to support a 50 per cent devaluation of the Somali shilling, but there was no sign of any substantial economic improvement, and banana exports declined sharply. Development and relief aid was received from a large range of mostly Western sources.

DJIBOUTI

President Hassan Gouled was re-elected unopposed in June and carried out a Cabinet reshuffle in early July, Barkat Gourat Hamadou remaining as Prime Minister. In August, a new opposition party was formed, the Djibouti People's Party, led by two Afar former Prime Ministers, Ahmed Dini and Abdallah Kamil; it was immediately banned, and its leading members were arrested, most of them being released later in the year. President Hassan paid his now customary round of visits to his principal neighbours and international backers, including Ethiopia in January, Somalia and Sudan in April, and France and Saudi Arabia in September. Some 4,000 French troops continued to be stationed in the country and the port of Djibouti increased in importance as a refuelling station for US warships, visits by which outnumbered those by French vessels for the first time in 1980. Work started on a container terminal, and, helped by a convertible currency and good air and sea communications, the economy improved its position as the principal regional entrepot. Djibouti continued to act as host to about 50,000 refugees, principally from the Ogaden.

KENYA

Kenya, though politically stable in 1981, was beset by mounting economic difficulties and glaring social inequalities. Dr Zachary Onyonka, the Minister for Economic Planning and Development, admitted in February that 'we are facing a much more difficult year; the era of soft options is over.' He expected inflation to rise above 13 per cent, employment to stagnate, and the balance of payments deficit to reach £400 million sterling. Agriculture continued to be the mainstay of the economy, accounting for a third of GDP, but food, particularly maize and milk, had to be imported on a substantial scale. The growth of manufacturing output slowed down as emphasis shifted from import substitution to export promotion. The border with Tanzania remained closed, thus cutting off the Zambian as well as the Tanzanian market, while the chaotic situation in Uganda restricted trade not only with that country but also with Burundi, Rwanda and Zaïre. On the other hand, foreign investors were still attracted and the Government was assisted by a two-year IMF standby credit of US $308 million and by a $200 million Eurocurrency loan. The Kenyan currency was devalued by nearly five per cent in February.

Mr James Osogo, the Livestock Development Minister, lost his parliamentary seat in April because of malpractices during the 1980 general election campaign. The Kenya African National Union (KANU), the ruling party, barred the veteran politician Mr Oginga Odinga, who resigned as chairman of the Cotton Lint and Seed Marketing Board in mid-April, from standing for Parliament. The independent *Nation* press group, owned by the Aga Khan, fell into official disfavour for supporting Mr Odinga (who had criticized ex-President Kenyatta), and its popular daily, *The Daily Nation*, was threatened by President Daniel Arap Moi with closure for 'deliberately misleading the public' over the Government's dispute with the doctors in May; the bulk of government advertising was transferred to *The Standard*, its Lonrho-owned rival. The latter criticized the management of the country's economy—the responsibility of Mr Mwai Kibaki, the Vice-President and Minister for Finance, who was said to be locked in a power struggle with Mr Charles Njonjo, the Minister for Home and Constitutional Affairs, with the party vice-presidency (held by Mr Kibaki) as the immediate prize. However, in November President Moi announced that no KANU elections would be held during his year of office as chairman of the OAU. His term began in June, when the OAU summit was held in Nairobi.

In May the High Court acquitted Mr Alfred Muthemba, a Nairobi businessman, of plotting to overthrow President Moi and another Kenyan of misprision of treason. Mr James Karugu, who had instituted the prosecution, resigned as Attorney-General. In May several hundred government doctors, who had been debarred from private practice in 1980, staged a nation-wide strike; the Government granted their salary demands, but rejected their claim to other allowances. After two weeks' restraint, it cracked down on the strikers, arresting some 20 of them. University of Nairobi students sympathized with the doctors, but also had grievances of their own. The university was closed on 18 May following disturbances, and the passports of some 10 members of staff were withdrawn. Third-year students were readmitted in mid-July and other students early in August after signing pledges of good behaviour.

The three East African Presidents attended summit meetings at Kampala in January and Nairobi in July and claimed to have reached 'complete understanding on bilateral and sub-regional issues'. They decided to revive the Inter-State Security Committee and (with Zambia) to look into the affairs of the recently-collapsed East African Shipping Line. Kenya and Tanzania agreed in February to stamp out cattle-rustling, poaching and smuggling along their common border. President Moi stated that Kenya would not be used as the base for guerrilla attacks against Uganda, but relations between the two states were strained in September when a number of Kenyan lorry-drivers were killed, allegedly by Ugandan soldiers. President Siyad Barre of Somalia renounced all claims to Kenyan territory; in August Kenya and Somalia agreed to establish regular joint patrols on both sides of the border to counter the activities of armed Somali groups (known as *shifta*) and the next month signed an agreement to promote cooperation between their respective news agencies. In April Kenya, Ethiopia and Sudan reactivated the Tripartite Commission, set up in 1973 to deal with border demarcation and security and joint development projects. Djibouti was to be invited to attend the next meeting.

TANZANIA

President Julius Nyerere blamed external factors rather than his own socialist policies for Tanzania's grave economic situation, but faced growing domestic and international criticism. By June, when Mr Amir Jamal, the Minister of Finance, presented his 1981-82 Budget, foreign reserves were depleted, payments to foreign suppliers were in arrears, industry (starved of machinery and spare parts) was operating well below capacity, thus creating widespread shortages, and inflation was over 36 per cent. Mr Jamal announced measures, including petrol rationing and a massive tax on luxury imports, to reduce foreign exchange expenditure, as well as steps to improve the performance of inefficient state-owned companies and above all to raise crop production—independent observers predicted in October that maize stocks would be exhausted by December and that 170,000 tons of imported food would be needed to avert famine. The minimum wage of government workers was raised from shs.480 to shs.600 per month, while the price of maize, the staple food, was doubled, though still subsidized. A two-year, special-drawing-rights agreement of £195 million sterling with the IMF, concluded in September 1980, was suspended after only one drawing because Tanzania was unable to honour the terms imposed. Talks were resumed in June (when anti-IMF demonstrations were staged in Dar es Salaam, the capital) aiming at a £250 million three-year extended fund facility, but no agreement was reached by the end of the year. Both the IMF and the World Bank, whose president visited Tanzania in November, urged the Government to devalue the currency.

The high cost of maintaining 10,000 troops and 1,000 policemen in Uganda—estimates ranged from £500,000 to over £2 million a month—was one reason for the withdrawal of the bulk of the troops by the end of June. However, under a new defence agreement signed in August, the Government undertook to provide Uganda with a training mission, said to comprise 1,000 soldiers and 1,000 policemen. Tanzanian troops were flown to the Seychelles in November following an unsuccessful attempted coup by mercenaries, reinforcing the Tanzanian military and police personnel permanently stationed there. President Nyerere was active in African affairs, especially in his capacity as chairman of the six front-line states. In October he attended the Commonwealth conference in Melbourne.

In January President Nyerere dismissed the chairman and general manager of the Air Tanzania Corporation for mishandling an international business contract; the chairman also lost his ministerial portfolio, while another Minister was unseated in December as a result of an election petition. A 13-man National Education Commission, appointed early in the year, was to report by mid-1982 on the progress in education since 1962 and on the educational programme recommended for the next 20 years: the goal of self-sufficiency in trained manpower by 1980 had not been achieved, while that of eradicating illiteracy by the end of 1985 was not attainable. In April Mr Aboud Jumbe, the President of Zanzibar, released ten people detained in 1980 for conspiring to overthrow his Government; in June he appointed Mr Hamisi Amiri Nsumi, senior deputy registrar of the Court of Appeal of Tanzania, a judge of the Zanzibar High Court. Because of the grim economic situation, the celebrations to mark the twentieth anniversary of Tanganyika's independence on 9 December were cancelled.

UGANDA

As a result of the hotly disputed 1980 general election (see AR 1980, p. 227), the legitimacy of President Milton Obote's Government was weak. Elements of the opposition adopted the tactics of guerrilla warfare and a grim security situation was compounded by the lawless behaviour of the Uganda National Liberation Army (UNLA); economic recovery was painfully slow. President Obote, however, was determined that Uganda should 'regain and play her rightful role in Africa'.

In June the President, as Minister of Finance, introduced an austerity Budget designed to revive production, check inflation, and attract foreign loans and investment. His Government negotiated with the IMF an aid package of US $180 million, spread over 13 months, subject to conditions which included a massive devaluation of the Ugandan currency, spending cuts, higher coffee producer prices and general fiscal reform; assistance was also given by the World Bank, the International Finance Corporation, the EEC and bilateral donors—in November Britain made a gift of £25·5 million, of which £22 million was to wipe out old debts. India, which was visited by the President in November, provided commercial credits. Private investment was also encouraged and Asians expelled in 1972 were given back title to their expropriated properties.

Whether the country had the capacity to absorb this outside aid was questionable. With few exceptions the Cabinet, which was ethnically well-balanced, lacked technical competence. Moreover, like the Uganda People's Congress (UPC) from which it was drawn, it was subject to internal division. One faction was grouped round Mr Paulo Muwanga, the Vice-President and Minister of Defence, and another round Mr Christopher Rwakasisi, a Minister of State in charge of security. Mr Muwanga was said to have resisted Dr Obote's proposal to appoint Mr Nathan Akena Adoko, the President's cousin and previously head of the

General Service Unit, as chairman of the Public Service Commission. The tension within the UPC hierarchy had a tribal component; the Langi group, to which President Obote and Brigadier David Oyite-Ojok, his army chief of staff, belonged, were alleged to be trying to prise Acholi from key political and army positions—many leading soldiers were Acholi, including Major-General Tito Okello, the overall army commander, as was also Mr Otema Alimadi, the Prime Minister. The powerful Brigadier Oyite-Ojok combined his army duties with the chairmanship of the Coffee Marketing Board, five of whose top executives were arrested in July on charges of fraud; he drove a Mercedes car with the registration number D001!

Though 27 per cent of the national budget was allocated to the security services, President Obote lacked firm control over the army, which comprised an undisciplined regular force of some 10,000 men and an even less disciplined militia of perhaps 8,000. That the soldiers were predominantly northerners exacerbated the country's north-south division, while their misbehaviour—amounting, in the words of one reporter, to a 'reign of terror, torture and murder'—confirmed many southerners, and the Baganda especially, in their implacable hatred of the Obote regime. But parts of the north also suffered, as Acholi and Langi soldiers combined to wreak havoc in the West Nile region following the departure of the Tanzanian troops early in June. Thousands of civilians fled to Zaïre, where they joined an estimated 150,000 Ugandan refugees from the 1979 war—another 80,000 or so were in Sudan, which was visited by President Obote in April. Military training was provided by some 30 North Koreans, and Tanzania agreed in August to provide army instructors. Arrangements were made for officer training in Kenya, Sudan and Egypt. The British Government undertook to provide a small contingent as part of a Commonwealth training mission. The police, numbering about 8,000, were better trained and disciplined than the army, but, as a more dispersed force with lighter weapons, could not counterweigh the army; in September they were promised heavier weapons. There was an upsurge of violence in Kampala, the capital, in November, when diplomats and aid officials demanded greater security for themselves and their vehicles, which were subject to a rash of hijackings.

The international press was accused of distorted reporting of unrest; a Canadian freelance journalist was expelled in September and two British journalists the next month. The local press suffered too: in March the pro-Democratic Party (DP) twice-weekly publication *The Citizen* and several weeklies were banned for 'irresponsible' reporting. The editor of the pro-Government *Uganda Times* was temporarily detained in June for the same offence.

The final state of the parliamentary parties after the 1980 general election was: UPC, 74; DP, 51; Uganda Patriotic Movement (UPM), 1. In April Parliament, sitting as an electoral college, elected 10 special members; these, together with 10 presidential nominees and 10 officers representing the army, gave the UPC the two-thirds majority in the 156-member Parliament required to amend the constitution. Mr Paul Semogerere, the DP leader, continued to head the official parliamentary opposition, but as DP members and supporters were constantly harassed and (it was alleged) beaten physically the party's secretary-general—Mr Francis Bwengye—allied himself with the extra-parliamentary opposition. The latter claimed that, after the Government had been overthrown by force, fresh elections would be held.

By May three main underground movements had emerged (there were also lesser groups): the Uganda Freedom Movement (UFM), in which Mr Andrew Kayiira, a Minister in ex-President Lule's Government, was prominent; the People's Revolutionary Army (PRA), the military arm of the Movement for the Struggle for Political Rights, headed by Mr Yoweri Museveni, vice-chairman of the military commission in 1980 and leader of the UPM; and the Uganda National Rescue Front (UNRF), also known as the Northern Regiment. The last was predominantly a grouping of ex-Amin soldiers (and perhaps UNLA deserters) advised by Mr Felix Onama, a former UPC secretary-general, and led by Brigadier Moses Ali, Amin's Finance Minister, who however denied any continuing connection with, or sympathy for, the former dictator. Shortage of funds and equipment lessened the effectiveness of these groups, as did the lack of unity. However, in July several of the leaders met to plan a joint strategy. The PRA and UFF (Uganda Freedom Fighters), led by ex-President Lule, merged to form the National Resistance Movement, which drew its support from southern and western Uganda. The Movement's combined army was controlled by Mr Museveni, but operated under a council headed by Mr Lule. A coordinating committee was established to link with the UFM, which was active in the Kampala area, and the UNRF, whose area of strength was in the north-west. Local resistance committees supplied food, information and recruits to the insurgents encamped within eighty miles of Kampala. Ex-President Godfrey Binaisa also gave his support to the anti-Obote movement: he was deported from Kenya and took up residence in Britain in October.

Four DP parliamentarians were detained in June, allegedly for terrorist activities; in the next month the number of DP detainees was put at 500 out of a total in detention of over 7,000, of whom some 3,000 had belonged to Amin's army: 1,420 of the latter were released in July and over a thousand in October. In January a High Court judge sentenced former President Amin's commissioner of police to death, but the British-born Mr Bob Astles, who was head of the former dictator's anti-smuggling unit and a Ugandan citizen since 1975, was acquitted in

October of the murder of a Ugandan fisherman; however, he remained in detention, possibly to face other charges. In February the Rev. Howell Davies was appointed Bishop of famine-stricken Karamoja, becoming the only white bishop in Uganda.

Chapter 2

GHANA—NIGERIA—SIERRA LEONE—THE GAMBIA—LIBERIA

GHANA

A DISMAL year ended dramatically on New Year's eve when Flight Lieut. Jerry Rawlings, with the help of the 5th army battalion and the reconnaissance unit from Burma camp, ousted President Hilla Limann and his People's National Party. It had been by Rawlings' good offices that Limann had been elected to the presidency two years earlier (see AR 1979, p. 226). Now, after a similarly brief term of government, he had been removed by the same armed forces, which resumed control. Yet there was a difference. Earlier coups were carried out by relatively senior officers of the regular army and police. Rawlings insisted that his second seizure of power was not a coup but a revolution, and both his background and temperament were populist rather than military. There was a flavour of Fidel Castro, an element perhaps of Qadafi, in his purpose, and it may be significant that he visited both Cuba and Libya during the year.

The revolutionary coup picked up the reins of power held by Rawlings from June to September 1979 (see AR 1979, p. 225). His renewed intervention was not altogether unexpected. On 4 June he had staged a massively attended, hugely popular rally in Accra on the anniversary of his earlier seizure of control. He was seen as a heroic figure, coming from outside the ranks of the established political elite. If there was to be a programme for his new Government it would probably be the simple (and difficult) campaign against corrupt practices. In a national broadcast the day after the coup the 35-year-old former air force officer declared a 'holy war against all forms of corruption'. In 1979 he had promised a 'limited form of house-cleaning'. In September 1981 he was quoted very differently: 'What I regret most is not having had a clearer understanding of the system. I thought it was just a question of cleaning it up, getting rid of the rottenness. I did not realise that the return of democracy would permit those same corrupt forces to retain their hold on Ghanaian life. We have not transferred power through the ballot box, we have just transferred administration around members of the same elite. The people know this. They don't even register to vote. They know that democracy is just a veneer to impress the outside. I will admit to naiveté when the ARFC was in power. I am less naive now.'

The preceding months had been full of doubt. Throughout the year inflation was running in excess of 120 per cent. Oil prices were high, petrol was scarce; doctors, engineers, teachers continued to emigrate to Nigeria. The cost of even basic foodstuffs was prohibitively expensive on the black market and they were in desperately short supply in the shops. As cocoa prices fell on the world market, smuggling increased across the border to take advantage of the higher French price. The local currency (cedi) was now valueless. Meanwhile Dr Limann reshuffled his Government from time to time, sacking nine of his Ministers on 2 October, but those appointed were not essentially different from those he dismissed.

Inland, in the Northern region, there were ugly riots between the rival local communities, the Konkomba and Nanumba. Over six hundred died in tribal warfare during late April and early May near the market town of Bimbilla. Rioting flared up again on 26 June, when a further eighty or more were killed. The army was brought in to restore order.

Against massive discontent, Limann struggled on as best he could. He paid a successful visit to Britain (12-15 May), when he dined with the Queen and lunched with the Prime Minister. He was able to secure the £10 million worth of emergency aid he asked for, but all to no avail. At the end of the year he was seeking (unsuccessfully) to evade arrest, Parliament had been dissolved, political parties abolished, the constitution abrogated and the franchise suspended, under the threat of military executions to come. A melancholy end to a dismal year.

NIGERIA

In 1981 the institutions of civilian rule functioned with heightened self-confidence and overcame several obstacles. The personal prestige of President Shehu Shagari increased, as did his ability to transcend party loyalties and to establish good relations with state governors of other parties than his own. The speed and efficacy of government decision-making was still, however, not fully adequate for Nigeria's needs.

The Nigerian People's Party (NPP) broke its accord with the ruling National Party of Nigeria (NPN), but this surprisingly failed to hinder government actions. All but two of the NPP federal Ministers resigned their offices and nomination of their replacements had not yet been approved by the end of the year. Two highly-trusted Ministers, however, Dr Ishaya Audu (External Affairs and NPP's vice-presidential candidate in 1979) and Mr Ademola Thomas (Finance) were asked by the President to withdraw their resignations and did so, while withdrawing at the same time from NPP. In the legislature, voting did not generally follow party lines and the federal Government was able to gain majorities for key legislation by lobbying and appeal to the national interest. The legislative output, however, remained low, only eleven federal Bills being passed from 1 October 1979 to July 1981, and most state legislatures being equally unproductive. Relations between state governors and state legislatures were often strained.

The vital Bill for revenue allocation, giving 58 per cent to the federal government, 32 per cent to the state governments and 10 per cent to local government councils, was disallowed by the Federal Supreme Court, having been passed only by a joint committee and not by the two houses of the federal legislature. The resulting stoppage in the flow of federal funds to states made all parties anxious to speed the passage of a new Bill, which passed with ease in December. The federal share was reduced to 55 per cent while the state share rose to 35 per cent, but, since Abuja, the capital territory, previously financed by the federal government, was to be treated as a state and draw a share of state revenue along with the other nineteen states, there was little overall change.

The 1983 elections were beginning to cast their shadow before them, producing a frenzied but so far unsuccessful effort by the four parties, NPP, UPN, GNPP and PRP (Rimi faction), to form an alliance to fight NPN. Largely because of the unwillingness of Chief Awolowo to re-nounce his claim and other personal rivalries they failed to agree on any likely presidential candidate. Meanwhile the NPN consolidated its position and drew closer to Alhaji Aminu Kano's faction of the PRP. The NPN conference at Port Harcourt seemed to have tacitly agreed that Shehu Shagari would obtain the party's presidential nomination in 1983 (the constitution allows him two four-year terms), but there was great rivalry for the gubernatorial nominations, federal Ministers and state governors from the same states having often been close rivals. Neverthe-less, the NPN was able to achieve public reconciliations between a number of rivals, including Governor Aper Aku and Federal Minister Isaac Shaahu, both of Benue state.

The radical governor of Kaduna state, Balarabe Musa of PRP, who continued to confront the NPN-dominated state legislature, was success-fully impeached and replaced by Abba Rimi, the deputy governor, who, though of the same party faction, was able to establish better relations with the legislature. In Kano state, where the Maitatsine Mohammed Marwa religious riots of December 1980 (see AR 1980, p. 231) were found by a court of inquiry to have caused over 4,000 deaths, further riots broke out in July 1981 when a mob, irate at a letter from Abubaker Rimi, the radical PRP governor, threatening the Emir of Kano, Ado Bayero, with dismissal, burned down the governor's house and murdered his brother and his political adviser. Violence also arose in Oyo state from a quarrel over local government areas between Ife and Modakeke, resulting in some 50 deaths, while in Bendel state deaths were caused by a fight between rival villages. Despite these events law and order was generally maintained, and relations between political parties remained far less violent than they had been in the First Republic (1960-66).

Nigeria was experiencing a most vociferous demand for subdivision of units at state and local government level. Few state governors were prepared to resist the demand for new local government areas, and the original 302 approved in the 1979 constitution had increased to over 500, though local government elections had yet to be held. The demand for creation of more states had not yet been met because of the difficulties of the constitutional process of state creation. The President, aware of the dangers of too much subdivision, sought to keep the process within bounds. In Plateau state the support by the deputy governor, Danladi Yakubu, for a breakaway 'Middle Belt' state to be carved out of Plateau embittered relations between him and the state governor, Solomon Lar.

In foreign affairs President Shagari scored a great success in his state visit to Britain in March and in his successful reconciliation of the border quarrel with the Cameroon Republic, which seemed to be very dangerous when five Nigerian soldiers were killed by a Cameroon border patrol. In December a Nigerian unit was sent to join the OAU peacekeeping force in Chad (see p. 243), and Nigeria also supplied the overall UN commander, General Ojiga.

The Nigerian economy suffered a severe slump in the middle of the year owing to decreased demand for oil. Sales fell from 2,000,000 barrels per day to 700,000, and Nigeria was forced to reduce its price from $40 to $36 per barrel; this, together with a Saudi Arabian cutback in production, restored oil sales to 1,500,000 barrels per day by the end of the year. The basic minimum wage was raised by the legislature, following a general strike in May, from 100 to 125 naira (c.£100) per month. Work on development projects and on the creation of the new capital at Abuja proceeded apace, and the steel complex at Ajaokuta, with a capacity of a million tons per year, was completed at the high capital cost of 1,000 million naira. Complaints of corruption at all levels continued. The President himself remained above corruption but though well aware of its dangers found it difficult to take effective action.

Nigerians were delighted by President Shagari's announcement, in his 1 October speech celebrating the 21st anniversary of independence, that Yakubu Gowon (head of state 1966-75) was no longer a wanted person and was free to return to Nigeria. The army remained quiet; General Akinrinade retired as chief of staff and was replaced by General Jalo. The replacement of Adamu Suleiman, acting inspector-general of police, by Sunday Adewusi as substantive inspector-general was followed by vigorous police action against armed robbers and those accused of sedition.

The entire academic staff of all Nigerian universities went on strike for the first two months of the 1981-82 session over their pay review and the government's financial allocation to universities, but the expansion of all sectors of education continued.

1981 saw the death of several distinguished Nigerians, including Usman Nagogo, Emir of Katsina, and Shehu Kangiwa, Governor of Sokoto State.

SIERRA LEONE

General elections promised for October were postponed until early 1982. Instead, in that month the ruling All People's Congress held a convention at Sucktarr. The ailing state of the party led to attempts to revitalize it through territorial reorganization and the adoption of a socialist self-reliant ideology. However, chronic dependence on external economic assistance and the exposure of major financial scandals in the spring (the 'Vouchergate' affair) and autumn revealed an enormous gulf between the Government's aspirations and reality.

Undoubtedly, corrupt and inefficient administration contributed to the desperate state of the economy but adverse international circumstances were mainly to blame. Diamond and agricultural exports remained low, import costs spiralled (fuel costs alone increased by 150 per cent in eighteen months), and government revenues and foreign exchange reserves tumbled in consequence. Government inability to control the economy, particularly the cost of basic foodstuffs, had much to do with the industrial unrest in August-September. Faced with a general strike organized by the Sierra Leone Labour Congress, the Government declared a state of emergency and detained briefly some 200 people. Another state of emergency was declared in December following the disclosure of the theft of an estimated Le 40 million by civil servants. While President Siaka Stevens struggled to implement a recovery programme based on government cut-backs and food self-sufficiency, he faced sporadic denunciation from opposition groups in exile—the Sierra Leone Alliance Movement in Britain and a revived Sierra Leone People's Party in the USA.

THE GAMBIA

Hopes of a return to normality after the political unrest of October 1980 were dashed when, on 30 July, a group of self-styled marxist dissidents, whose organizations had been proscribed the previous autumn (see AR 1980, pp. 233-4), joined forces with mutinous elements from the paramilitary Field Force to launch a coup d'état during President Sir Dawda Jawara's absence at the royal wedding in London. The rebels hoped to capitalize on public discontent with corruption in official circles and the Government's failure to overcome the severe economic problems resulting from world inflation and the cumulative effect of drought. In 1980-81 the groundnut crop had shrunk to 40,000 tonnes (against 140,000 tonnes in a good year) and tourism was down by 20 per cent. The result was a balance of payments crisis, a fall in national and personal earnings, and the necessity of a tough budget a few weeks before the coup. In the event, support for the coup was largely confined to youthful elements in the Banjul urban area, and even here rebel popularity suffered as a result of the violence and pillage accompanying their action. Perhaps 1,000 people died in the insurrection and damage to property and goods was estimated at £10 million.

President Jawara returned to Dakar where he invoked once more The Gambia's 1965 defence agreement with Senegal. Within a week 2,800 Senegalese troops had put down the rebellion and restored him to power. A state of emergency was declared and about 1,000 persons detained, including two opposition leaders—Sheriff Dibba (National Convention Party) and Pap Cheyassin Secka (of the defunct National Liberation Party). Their exact part in the rebellion remained to be established, as did that of foreign powers initially claimed to have been behind the rebels. The rebel leader, Kukoi Samba Sanyang, an unemployed political activist and one-time failed candidate of the NCP, fled to Guinea-Bissau with several companions. Despite repeated attempts to extradite them they remained there at the end of the year. Seven other rebels were condemned to death in December by an international panel of judges appointed by the Gambian Government to avoid charges of political bias on the part of the local judiciary.

One momentous consequence of the coup was the hastening of political union with Senegal. Close relations existed between the countries but in the past The Gambia had stopped short of political union. In December its Parliament agreed to a confederation with Senegal which, while apparently retaining Gambian sovereignty, allowed for the creation of a confederal Executive and Parliament, immediate joint security arrangements (the Field Force was disbanded), common foreign policies and the eventual creation of a customs and monetary union. The Senegambian Confederation was to be inaugurated in February 1982.

LIBERIA

Nine months after the overthrow of the Tolbert Government (see AR 1980, p. 234) Liberia seemed little nearer economic recovery or political normality. The economy limped along while the soldiers fought among themselves. In June, 13 rank-and-file soldiers were executed for plotting the death of the head of state, Master Sergeant Samuel Doe, apparently in order to share the benefits of power so visibly enjoyed by their superiors. Two months later a growing rift within the ruling People's Redemption Council between a radical faction, increasingly disturbed by backsliding over domestic reforms and a Western bias in foreign policy, and a pragmatic pro-American group led by Doe and two senior colleagues, Generals Qwiwonkpa and Podier, erupted into bloody confrontation. General Thomas Weh Syen and four other PRC members were shot, allegedly for seeking to overthrow the Government. Civilian Ministers were subjected to military discipline and radicals among them were ousted. Togba Nah Tipoteh (Economic Planning) prudently left Liberia; Chea Cheapoo (Justice) was arrested; and Gabriel Matthews (Foreign Affairs) was replaced by one of the many former Tolbert officials now serving the military Government.

The trend towards conservative economic policies and closer ties with the USA, already apparent in mid-1980 (see AR 1980, p. 235), accelerated. American economic and military assistance was stepped up; in April commando troops exercised with Liberian forces. The IMF, in return for financial restraint and investment in productive agricultural projects, provided a further $65 million. However, with external debts standing at $700 million, iron ore exports continuing to stagnate, and 57 per cent of revenues going on debt servicing and oil imports, the outlook remained grave and uncertain. Ties with radical states weakened—the Libyan mission was closed and the Soviet embassy reduced—and educational links with the socialist states terminated. One glimmer of hope was the creation of a commission to draft a new constitution, eventually to pave the way for a return to civilian rule.

Chapter 3

SENEGAL—MAURITANIA—MALI—GUINEA—IVORY COAST—
UPPER VOLTA—NIGER—TOGO—BENIN—CAMEROON—GABON—CHAD—
CONGO—CENTRAL AFRICAN REPUBLIC—EQUATORIAL GUINEA

SENEGAL

THE year began with the voluntary departure from power, almost unheard of in Africa, of President Leopold Sédar Senghor, to be succeeded, under the constitution, by the Prime Minister, Abdou Diouf. Dr Abdoulaye Wade, leader of Senegal's second largest legal party, the Parti Démocratique Sénégalais (PDS), called for immediate elections under the supervision of the armed forces. This move was personally denounced by their commander-in-chief, General Idrissa Fall. The transition took place smoothly, and 1981 saw the emergence of Diouf as an astute politician and surprisingly decisive figure. His choice of his old friend Habib Thiam as Prime Minister showed he was very much his own master, and although the Government contained a number of Senghor loyalists the ex-President showed no sign of wanting to engage in back-seat driving. Two of his most loyal supporters, Adrien Senghor, his nephew, and Louis Alexandrenne, were dropped from the Government in a reshuffle in July.

One of President Diouf's most significant political actions was the further liberalization of Senegal's multi-party democracy. This process had been started in the Senghor era, but the number of constitutional parties had been limited to four. In April, a change in the constitution removing the limit on the permissible number of parties brought in a range of different groups, from marxist mini-parties to the more broadly-based Rassemblement Nationale Démocratique led by the noted historian, Cheikh Anta Diop. The appearance by the end of the year of eleven political parties tended to reinforce the position of the ruling Parti Socialiste (PS), while the PDS suffered a loss of prestige. In September it was involved in an obscure affair in which party members were accused of threatening state security, allegedly with Libyan support.

The success of Diouf ultimately depended, however, on his handling of Senegal's notoriously fragile economic situation. Economics had never been his predecessor's strong point, but Diouf's reputation had always been that of a technocrat who did his homework. Senegal was suffering from the classic developing-country syndrome of high bills for oil imports, top-heavy urban bureaucracy, stifling budget deficits and monoculture (groundnuts). At least in the last respect Diouf was lucky in 1981; plentiful mid-year rains gave promise of a good groundnut harvest.

Senegal felt encouragement at the French electoral victory of the Socialists, with whom the Senegalese leadership felt they had special relations as members of the Socialist International. Diouf showed his firmness of purpose at the end of July, when, faced with the attempted putsch in The Gambia, he sent a contingent of Senegalese troops to help restore President Jawara to power (see p. 236). By the end of the year Senegal and the Gambia had joined to form the Senegambian confederation. There were some in Senegal who had misgivings about this development, because The Gambia could be a possible source of unrest, but the general view in Dakar was that there had been no alternative to intervention in July, and once the troops were there Senegal had no alternative but to insist on confederation, so that it could continue to control the security situation in its unstable neighbour.

MAURITANIA

Mauritanian politics remained overshadowed by the continuing war in the Western Sahara, now a struggle between the Polisario movement and Morocco (see p. 217). Although Mauritania had been on the sidelines of the war since 1979, the pressures from Morocco, Algeria and from Polisario itself remained considerable. In March there was an attempted coup in Nouakchott, which the head of state, Lieut.-Colonel Mohamed Khounia Ould Haidalla, attributed to pro-Moroccan influences. After the coup was put down (and at least four of its leaders executed), Mauritania broke diplomatic relations with Morocco. Although for reasons of survival Mauritania stopped short of open support for the Sahraoui, no regime in Nouakchott could control the country's long borders. In consequence Polisario frequently used Mauritanian territory for transit and to launch attacks, with the result that tension between Morocco and Mauritania continued through the year, and was not helped by the collapse of the OAU peace-making effort in November (see Pt. XI. Ch. 6).

At the end of April, President Haidalla dismissed the four-and-a-half month old Government of Prime Minister Sidi Ahmed Ould B'Neijara, and replaced it with a Cabinet composed entirely of military men. This abandonment of an experiment aimed at a progressive return to civil rule was attributed to the insecurity created by the March coup attempt.

MALI

Despite the continuing disastrous state of the economy, and the pronounced political malaise, the widely predicted demise of the shaky regime of President Moussa Traore did not materialize. Uncertainty about insecurity emanating from Arab states to the north (Western Sahara war, Libyan subversion) led to new attempts to move closer to black African neighbours, but the bid to re-enter the Union Monétaire Ouest Africain (UMOA) foundered.

GUINEA

The left-wing regime of President Sekou Touré was, paradoxically, one of the least enthusiastic in Africa about the election of President Mitterrand in France, partly because of a quarrel some two years previously over Mitterrand's criticism of Touré's dictatorship. Nevertheless, Guinea's coolness towards the communist bloc continued, along with a progressive influx of Western capital, especially into mining industries, reinforced considerably by petrodollars. Not surprisingly, emphasis on Islam increased in the country's educational and cultural life.

IVORY COAST

Faced with serious falls in world cocoa and coffee prices, the Ivory Coast economy continued in a budgetary straitjacket, in spite of growing optimism over offshore oil. Until the country should achieve self-sufficiency in oil, expected in 1983, it waged a lonely war against the injustice of the international commodity markets. Withholding the cocoa crop from the market at the end of 1980, which was estimated to cost over £100 million in revenue, did not influence the price decline. Despite considerable Western pressure, Ivory Coast refused to sign the new International Cocoa Agreement.

Politically, President Houphouet-Boigny continued to show his total domination of the domestic scene by keeping all potential successors on tenterhooks as to when he was going to name a Vice-President, who would be his constitutional successor. Medical reasons obliged him to restrict his activities shortly after his 76th birthday in October, but at the end of the year there was still no Vice-President. Houphouet-Boigny was the first African leader to be received at the Elysée by President Mitterrand, who clearly valued the advice of '*le vieux*'.

UPPER VOLTA

The military Government of President Saye Zerbo, which came to power late in 1980, and put an end to Upper Volta's second experiment in multi-party democracy since independence in 1960, found itself faced with the same problems of intolerable poverty and lack of resources as its predecessors. The military very soon came up against the trade union opposition which had helped sabotage the preceding Government. In November a general ban on strikes was announced and the Government dissolved the principal trade union organization. Meanwhile, the inquiry continued into the assets of leaders of the previous regime, many of whom were in detention.

NIGER

Though able to keep its head above water economically, thanks to uranium revenues, 1981 was a worrying year for Niger. The Libyan invasion of neighbouring Chad exposed the whole eastern border to possible penetration, and there were a number of incidents. In January all the staff of the Libyan embassy were expelled for activities 'incompatible with their diplomatic status'. The Libyan withdrawal from Chad at the end of October led to a slight thaw in relations with Tripoli, and in fact Libya had continued to buy Niger's uranium. President Kountché returned from the Franco-African summit in November with the news that the French, the main customer for Niger's uranium, had agreed to a 20 per cent increase in the floor price.

TOGO

For Togo, 1981 was another quiet year with no political upsets, and a concentration on the economy, by way of the fourth National Development Plan (1981-85), which was launched during the year.

BENIN

As the regime of President Mathieu Kérékou moved towards its tenth anniversary, there was increasing wonderment in Africa that a country which had once been synonymous with chronic instability should now be enjoying so prolonged a period of internal peace and relative prosperity. The secret seemed to be, first, that Kérékou had finally succeeded in shaking down the army, and, secondly, that by officially maintaining marxism-leninism as the regime's ideology while in practice retaining solid links with the West, the People's Republic of Benin was succeeding in having its cake and eating it. The arrival in power of the French Socialists suited Benin very well, bearing in mind its continued membership of the franc zone and other economic ties with France, and President Kérékou was one of President Mitterrand's first visitors, preaching reconciliation. Symbolic of Benin's new stability was the release in May of three detained former Presidents.

CAMEROON

The continuing dramas in Chad brought a renewed focus on Cameroon in 1981, drawing attention both to its remarkable economic success story under President Ahmadou Ahidjo and to the tight authoritarian nature of the regime. Oil production had risen from 700,000 tons in 1977 to 4 million tons in 1981, with the prospect of a possible 10 million tons in 1985, and there were plans to build a liquefied natural gas complex. The impact of all this on revenues were hard to gauge, since oil revenues did not enter the state budget. At the same time some of the social problems which accompany oil booms (corruption, over-rapid urbanization) were beginning to manifest themselves. There were reports of student discontent in February, and of border incidents with Nigeria in June, drawing attention to Cameroon's cool relations with all its neighbours.

GABON

Although in 1981, a year of oil glut and declining prices, some of Gabon's expectations for the year were not realized, the prudence with which its financial affairs had been conducted of late meant that serious dislocation was avoided. Nonetheless the price of earlier post-1973 extravagance was still being paid, in the form of heavy debts and sundry white elephants.

President Bongo's concerns in 1981, however, were more political. Like President Mobutu to the south, he was very apprehensive at the defeat of President Giscard d'Estaing in the French elections, because the Socialists had been among his critics. In September, after visiting President Mitterrand, he denounced French media criticism of him, and hinted that he could seek other friends, having already paid an urgent visit to President Reagan in Washington. On a number of occasions he stressed that Gabon was not an exclusive French preserve, and seemed to be going out of his way to diversify his contacts. In August M Maurice Robert, a former intelligence agent, whom President Giscard had appointed ambassador in Gabon at Bongo's request, was replaced by a career diplomat.

Gabonese opposition elements had taken heart from the change in France. In December their expectations led to serious trouble at the university in Libreville, which resulted in the dismissal of the rector and the arrest of a number of students; the demonstrations were accompanied by a wider wave of discontent, with calls for the establishment of a second political party.

CHAD

The year was another turbulent one for this sprawling war-torn country. Having experienced in December 1980 a Libyan military intervention which had helped Goukouny Oueddeye, the President of the GUNT (Gouvernement de l'Unité Nationale Tchadienne) and his supporters to eliminate the FAN (Forces Armées Nationales) of the former Defence Minister Hissène Habre from the capital Ndjamena, at the beginning of January Libya proclaimed the union of the two countries (see p. 215). Although President Oueddeye was reported to have consented to this during a visit to Tripoli, he met with considerable criticism within the GUNT. Although there was a substantial Libyan military presence, extending to the Salamat region on the border with the Central African Republic, the fief of the pro-Libyan Foreign Minister Ahmat Acyl, the union rapidly proved to be fictitious. This was partly due to strong opposition from the GUNT Vice-President, Lieut.-Colonel Wadel Abdelkader Kamougué, who resisted the presence of Libyan troops in his own area in southern Chad. International criticism, as well as Western reluctance to assist with reconstruction while the Libyan presence was being maintained, also contributed to a progressive loss of enthusiasm for the Libyan connection, especially when the massive financial aid expected did not materialize.

There was some surprise and even misgiving in Africa and in the West at the neutral role, attributed to French oil dealings with Libya, played by President Giscard d'Estaing; the helplessness of Chad's African neighbours was also highly evident. The Libyans could claim that by their boldness they had helped bring peace to Chad; and only the Americans were enthusiastic in pushing the Egyptians and Sudanese to help reconstitute and arm the defeated forces of Hissène Habre. After the change of government in France, however, President Mitterrand indicated that France was willing to aid Chad even before a Libyan withdrawal.

President Oueddeye visited Paris in September to consolidate the new relationship, and when French diplomacy managed to secure the establishment of an OAU force (see Pt. XI, Ch. 7) the world was once again surprised by Colonel Qadafi's sudden decision at the end of October to withdraw his troops. By the end of the year the OAU force was tenuously in place, but already under criticism from President Oueddeye for the limits of its mandate, barring it from acting against the army of Hissène Habre, which had taken the opportunity of the Libyan withdrawal to consolidate its position in the east of the country.

Meanwhile there was a concerted effort, spearheaded by the French, with support from international agencies, to begin the rehabilitation of the much damaged country and its capital, and to repatriate the thousands of refugees from neighbouring countries.

CONGO

The year saw a continuing consolidation of power by the Government of President Denis Sassou N'guesso, which had come to power in a bloodless change in 1979 after fifteen years of revolution, coup, plot, assassination and other forms of political storm. New prospects of oil wealth, after the early disappointments of the 1970s, helped create an atmosphere of optimism. The signing of a friendship treaty with the

USSR in May, which disturbed some observers, in fact did not brake a progressive political and economic liberalization, certainly assisted by the arrival in power of the Socialists in Paris.

CENTRAL AFRICAN REPUBLIC

In March the troubled Government of President David Dacko finally held the promised presidential elections, but the result scarcely solved his political problems. Dacko obtained just over half of the votes cast (50·23 per cent) against 38·11 per cent for his nearest rival, Ange Patassé. Three other candidates scored single figures. The result led to violent demonstrations, particularly from the supporters of Patassé, and the declaration of a state of siege, which was lifted in July. The 1,500 French troops in the country, on alert after the Libyan move into Chad, were not directly used in the maintenance of law and order.

The election of President Mitterrand was greeted with scenes of jubilation in Bangui, the capital, and in view of continued tension and outrage, and of reports that Dacko was increasingly ill, as well as tired of power, it came as no surprise when the head of the army, General André Kolingba, seized power in a bloodless coup on 2 September. There were even reports that Dacko had asked him to take power, and that the French President had been in the know beforehand. Patassé, who had initially welcomed the coup, had moved, by the end of the year, to denouncing the new dictatorship.

EQUATORIAL GUINEA

In April nearly 200 people were arrested following the discovery of an alleged plot to overthrow the Government of President Teodoro Obiang Nguema. The accused, including a number of army officers and senior civil servants, were said to be partly ethnically inspired (coming mainly from areas of Ebebiyin and Mikomeseng), but also protesting against the presence of a 400-man contingent of Moroccan troops serving as a kind of Praetorian guard to the President. The subsequent trial failed to clear up the mysteries around the reasons for the plot; one soldier was executed and a number of others sentenced to long prison terms.

In September, following the visit to Malabo of a Spanish military mission, Spain agreed to reinforce its military links with its former colony in the field of training and provision of arms. Observers in Madrid believed that the agreements gave Spain a central role in the defence of Equatorial Guinea, and linked it to the oil exploration being carried out there by Spanish oil companies.

VII CENTRAL AND SOUTHERN AFRICA

Chapter 1

THE REPUBLIC OF ZAÏRE—RWANDA AND BURUNDI—GUINEA-BISSAU AND
CAPE VERDE—SÃO TOME AND PRINCIPE—MOZAMBIQUE—ANGOLA

THE REPUBLIC OF ZAÏRE

'AS a political survivor', wrote a British journalist who visited Zaïre in
May 1981, 'President Mobutu is in a class of his own.' Certainly the
President's sixteenth year in power saw no evidence of any decline in his
adroitness at containing his enemies or manipulating his backers. The
most vocal threat to his position came from Mr Nguza Karl I Bond, who
resigned his post as Prime Minister while on a visit to Brussels in April
(see AR 1980, p. 244). Mr Nguza aligned himself with other politicians in
exile opposed to President Mobutu, and published a withering
indictment of the regime, *Appel du 30 Juin*, in which he called on the
people of Zaïre to overthrow Mobutu. In September Mr Nguza carried
his anti-Mobutu campaign to the United States, where he provided a
Congressional committee with details of the regime's corrupt practices.
President Mobutu countered by threatening to break off diplomatic
relations with Belgium, whereupon the Belgian Government issued a
statement condemning declarations by exiled Zaïrean politicians which
could be interpreted as calls to violence. The US Administration
pointedly refrained from giving Mr Nguza any official recognition and
affirmed support for 'the recognized and legitimate Government of
Zaïre'.

To Mobutu the Reagan Administration was clearly more congenial
than that of President Carter with its embarrassing interest in human
rights, but the defeat of M Giscard d'Estaing in the French presidential
election deprived him of his closest ally in Western Europe. The French
Socialists had long been highly critical of the regime in Zaïre, and one of
President Mitterrand's first moves was to have the venue of the annual
Franco-African summit transferred from Kinshasa to Paris. But in September the French President's special envoy, Guy Panne, spoke in
Kinshasa of 'reinforcing the cooperation between France and Zaïre' and
in October President Mobutu, in Paris for the Franco-African summit,
was cordially received by President Mitterrand, before going to
Washington where he was offered further US military and economic aid.

Zaïre's creditors were no less obliging. Its external debt stood at over
$4,000 million, while debt servicing for 1981 was put at $800 million. The

IMF agreed to provide special drawing rights of $1,600 million, the largest credit ever given by the Fund to an African country, and the Club of Paris, representing the country's major official creditors, again agreed to reschedule Zaïre's debts. Foreign creditors held that the Zaïrean Government had made strenuous efforts to set its finances in order, and, distasteful as many aspects of Mobutu's regime might seem, they saw him as a rampart against chaos: if they hoped to get their money back, they had to continue their support.

The Party of the Popular Revolution (PRP), founded in 1967 and drawing much of its support from the Simba rebels of the mid-1960s, was reported still to be operating as a guerrilla force in the mountainous areas of northern Shaba and southern Kivu, but there was no evidence that the movement's influence spread beyond this remote area. The Front pour la Libération Nationale du Congo (FNLC), which had been responsible for the two invasions of Shaba in 1977 and 1978, gave no sign of any activity.

Since 1977 a form of legalized opposition had developed in the Zaïrean Parliament, where deputies made use of the right to question Ministers to bring up criticisms of the regime. At the end of 1980 a group of thirteen deputies had drawn up a highly critical address to the President, implying that he himself was responsible for the injustices from which the country was suffering. Copies of this address eventually reached Europe: it was never published in Zaïre. Instead the thirteen deputies were arrested and stripped of their civic rights. The President devised an effective means of reducing the influence of Parliament by giving more power to the Central Committee of the ruling party, all of whose 120 members were chosen by himself and rewarded with an annual salary of $60,000, twenty times the average salary of a medical doctor.

In June the Roman Catholic bishops of Zaïre issued a statement that painted a sombre picture of conditions. In many parts of Zaïre the Church, with its network of schools, hospitals and clinics, appeared to be a force making for stability. Still profoundly influenced by its colonial past, it seemed as yet unaffected by the revolutionary ideas that were inspiring the Roman Catholics of Latin America. Nevertheless the President urged the youth movement of the Popular Revolutionary Movement to monitor sermons in order to 'unmask reactionary clergy'.

By keeping a tight control on all sources of information the regime made it impossible both for Zaïreans and for outsiders to gain a balanced picture of the state of the country. According to Mr Nguza Karl I Bond, 'national cohesion, which was at one time the regime's only achievement, is steadily breaking down.' But the commanding position occupied by President Mobutu faced no really formidable challenger.

RWANDA AND BURUNDI

Both countries enjoyed a peaceful year politically. Both were ruled by men who had come to power through military coups, President Juvenal Habyalimana of Rwanda in 1973, President Jean-Baptiste Bagaza of Burundi in 1976; and by 1981 both felt firmly enough established to allow their people to exercise the vote. In Burundi a referendum was held in November to approve the country's new constitution. Strongly influenced by the Tanzanian model, it provided for a President elected by universal suffrage and asserted the 'dominant role' of the 'single mass party', the Union pour le Progrès National (UPRONA).

At the end of December elections were held in Rwanda for the country's Parliament, the National Development Council. All Rwanda citizens were required to be members of the only party, the National Revolutionary Development Party. The list of candidates, who were required to have had at least four years' secondary education, was winnowed to leave no more than two in each of the 64 constituencies.

GUINEA-BISSAU AND CAPE VERDE

The new Government of Guinea-Bissau, established after the November 1980 military coup which overthrew President Luis Cabral (see AR 1980, p. 247), consolidated its position. The only reported dissent came from high-school students who staged a demonstration in the capital in February, allegedly protesting against the Cuban methods of academic assessment introduced in 1974.

For Guinea-Bissau the most serious development of the year was a devastating crop failure, leading to the loss of 70 per cent of the harvest and leaving the country with a 70,000-tonne food deficit. Adverse weather conditions were the immediate cause, but the situation was made worse by the lowering of the country's water level, a long-term consequence of the Sahelian drought. The Government laid special stress on the need to improve peasant agriculture and to develop the country's mineral resources. There were reports of the discovery of substantial phosphate deposits and hopes of finding bauxite. A World Bank credit enabled the Government to engage a British company to continue the work of exploration for off-shore oil.

The Governments both of Guinea-Bissau and of Cape Verde were reported to have rejected a Soviet request to be allowed to establish naval bases in their territories. But the extraordinary congress of the PAIGC (African Party for the Independence of Guinea-Bissau and Cape Verde) in Bissau in November passed a resolution calling for closer relations with the socialist bloc, and President Vieire spoke of the Soviet Union and other socialist countries as Guinea-Bissau's natural allies.

The strained relations between Guinea-Bissau and Cape Verde resulting from the overthrow of President Cabral led the Government of Cape Verde reluctantly to accept the dissolution of the proposed union between the two countries.

The Cape Verde Government continued to make impressive progress with its development schemes, designed to encourage agriculture, industry and fisheries. One indication of their success was the decline of emigration from the islands, 15-20,000 a year before independence, to a third of that figure. But remittances from overseas emigrants remained vital to the islands' economy.

SÃO TOME AND PRINCIPE

Mr Miguel Trovoada, Prime Minister from 1975 to 1979, who was arrested and detained without trial in 1980 (see AR 1980, p. 248), was released on 12 July, the sixth anniversary of the islands' independence. In September the President, Manuel Pinto da Costa, paid his first official visit to Mozambique.

MOZAMBIQUE

On 29 January a force of South African commandos drove into a suburb of the capital, Maputo, and attacked houses occupied by members of the African National Congress. At least twelve ANC men were killed. Some days later President Machel paraded eight army officers in disgrace before a mass meeting in Maputo for failure to prevent the attack. The President spoke of the country being 'ready for war' with South Africa, while the ANC was regarded as 'the legitimate representative of the South African people'. In accordance with the terms of the 1977 Soviet-Mozambique treaty of friendship the USSR sent Soviet warships to the country's two main ports.

In March the Government expelled four US diplomats whom it accused, together with two high Mozambican officials, of being in a 'spy ring' organized by the CIA. The US did not deny this accusation but asserted that the move had been instigated by Cuban counter-intelligence officers then visiting Maputo. At the same time President Reagan announced that food aid would be cut. President Machel gave vent to his resentment in a speech to the Popular Assembly in October, denouncing the US for its 'aggressive actions' and accusing the Reagan Administration of encouraging South Africa in its attacks on Angola.

The Mozambique Government's intense suspicion of South Africa was compounded by the activities of the Mozambique Resistance Movement. Belief that the MRM was receiving logistical aid from South Africa was strengthened by the discovery of documents relating to meetings between South African officers and MRM leaders, obtained after Frelimo captured a major MRM base in December. The insurgents' main area of operations was in Manica province, where regular attacks were made on roads and villages. Frelimo counter-measures followed the well-established anti-guerrilla strategy of grouping the rural population into protected villages, a strategy that coincided with the Government's proclaimed policy of 'socializing the countryside' by establishing 'communal villages' where the population could be more effectively provided with the basic amenities of health and education.

The most successful feat for which the MRM claimed responsibility was the attack in October on roads and rail bridges across the river Pungwe, thirty miles north-west of Beira. In the attack the oil pipeline between Beira and Zimbabwe, not used since 1965 but due to be restored to service in December, was damaged. Since the route was even more important to Zimbabwe than it was to Mozambique, the attack on the Pungwe bridge was interpreted in Mozambique as having been planned by South Africa as part of its efforts to 'destabilize' its recently independent black neighbours and to counter the regional cooperation plans of the Southern African Development Coordination Conference.

Strained relations with South Africa and the United States made it all the more important for Mozambique to cultivate better relations with other countries. The most significant development was the 'burying of the hatchet' with Portugal, the former metropolitan power, with which relations had been strained ever since independence. In March the Mozambique Foreign Minister, Sr Joaquin Alberto Chiassano, visited Lisbon. In May a cooperation agreement was signed between the two countries, and in December President Eanes of Portugal became the first head of state from a Western country to visit independent Mozambique; reports spoke of a 'rapturous welcome'.

Other Western countries with which ties were strengthened were Sweden and the United Kingdom. Sweden provided $100 million of aid over a two-year period, and in August the Swedish Prime Minister, Mr Fälldin, visited Maputo. Sr Chiassano visited London in January and was given a notably cordial official welcome. At the same time Mozambique maintained its close ties with the communist world; 1,300 Soviet citizens and 1,200 Cubans were reported to be aiding Mozambique in 1981, at least a third being military advisers. During the year negotiations for entry into Comecon were continued.

The President delivered a series of speeches in which he spoke of purging the police and the armed forces of those members responsible for 'arbitrary arrests, beatings and torture'. This move, clearly inspired by public complaints, was seen as the second stage in the attack which the President had begun in 1980 on inefficiency and corruption in the bureaucracy (see AR 1980, p. 249).

ANGOLA

Throughout 1981 the MPLA Government continued to be faced with the three dominant problems that had preoccupied it since independence in 1975: the struggle to revive an economy still grievously suffering from the consequences of the Portuguese exodus, the civil war with Unita and the involvement, through the hospitality accorded to Swapo guerrillas, with a hostile and aggressive South Africa.

South African military incursions across the Namibian border into southern Angola continued to occur regularly. The South Africans alleged that their only concern was the pursuit of Swapo guerrillas or the destruction of Swapo bases, but increasingly the incursions led to confrontation with the Angolan armed forces. In January the Angolans claimed to have shot down three South African helicopters and in July they reported incursions by a South African infantry brigade and three battalions. In August the Angolan Government accused South Africa of launching an 'invasion' on a scale larger than anything attempted since the initial incursion in October 1975, when about 2,000 South African troops were involved; in September 1981 Angolan reports put the number at 45,000, a figure which South African military spokesmen dismissed as 'laughable'.

Western journalists were allowed to visit the war zone in southern Angola in September. They reported that the South Africans enjoyed unchallenged supremacy over the air space of a belt extending at least 100 miles north of the Namibian border. They found evidence of South African air raids on towns and villages where there was no trace of Swapo activity.

The South African authorities continued to affirm that their activities were directed only against Swapo. To the Angolan Government and to many Western observers it seemed more likely that the escalation in military operations arose from a determination to create a buffer zone in southern Angola which could be handed over to Unita, making it increasingly difficult for Swapo to send its guerrillas into Namibia.

This suspicion was confirmed when US newspapers published confidential reports of a conversation between the South African Minister of Defence, General Magnus Malan, and the US Assistant Secretary of State, Mr Chester Crocker, in Pretoria in April. General Malan admitted that the South Africans wanted to see Dr Jonas Savimbi in control of southern Angola.

Western correspondents who visited Dr Savimbi's headquarters in May reported that Unita appeared to control most of Angola's extreme south-eastern province, Cuando Cubango. Unita guerrillas continued to make regular attacks on the Benguela railway and the movement claimed responsibility for an attack on the country's only oil refinery near Luanda on 30 November, though the Angolan Government attributed it to South African saboteurs. Dr Savimbi admitted receiving assistance from Saudi Arabia and some African states, probably Senegal and the Ivory Coast. He also enjoyed the backing of influential lobbyists in London, Washington and Paris. But the greatest change in his fortunes came from the encouragement extended by President Reagan. In December Dr Savimbi visited Washington, where he had 'high-level discussions', including an interview with the Secretary of State. An official US statement referred to Unita as 'a legitimate political force in Angola'. The Reagan Administration was anxious to secure the repeal of the 'Clark amendment', passed in 1976, forbidding the sending of military aid to any faction in Angola. But Congressional opposition left the amendment still in force.

The United States remained the only major country that refused to recognize the MPLA Government, a refusal directly linked with the presence of Cuban troops in Angola. The Angolan Government bitterly resented the US veto on a Security Council resolution condemning South Africa for its 'invasion' in September and accused the US Government of 'shameful connivance' with South Africa. Yet American oil companies, especially Gulf Oil, continued to enjoy cordial relations with the Angolan authorities, and a US Congressional delegation which visited Angola in August was given a friendly reception. In December there were reports that President dos Santos was anxious to open talks with the US Government with the aim of normalizing relations.

The Cubans continued to maintain up to 20,000 troops in Angola, but in December there was talk of attempting to synchronize the withdrawal of Cuban troops with the movement of South African forces out of Namibia. The possibility of Brazil's sending troops to Angola was mooted. The Soviet presence in Angola was stressed by the South Africans after they had captured a Russian sergeant-major and killed four other Russians, two of them women, during their operations in September. But the Soviet approach to Angola appeared to be one of caution and there was no evidence of a substantial reinforcement of the established Soviet military presence. The main source of additional military aid to Angola seemed more likely to come from other African states—Libya and Algeria were mentioned.

Cordial relations with other Western countries were maintained. In January the French Foreign Minister, M Jean François-Poncet, became the first senior Minister from a Western country to visit Luanda.

Relations with France became even warmer after the presidential election, and in October President dos Santos met President Mitterrand in Paris.

With its ample deposits of oil and diamonds and its massive agricultural potential Angola could become one of the richest countries in Africa, but it was beset by huge economic problems, most of them related to the catastrophic effects of the Portuguese withdrawal. Reports spoke of widespread absenteeism and inefficiency in industry and an appalling shortage of basic mechanical skills—few black Angolans had the opportunity of learning to drive in colonial times. Large quantities of food had still to be imported to feed the towns, yet with a population of less than 7 million the country should easily have been self-sufficient in basic foodstuffs. Peasant farmers were reluctant to grow cash food crops, since there was nothing on which to spend their money in local markets.

Outside observers were impressed by the fact that there was little evidence of corruption in Angola. Ideologically the Government maintained its marxist orientation, but economic ties were much closer with the West than with the Communist bloc. Western countries accounted for 92 per cent of Angola's foreign trade and provided an increasing range of technical assistance. But when half the country's budget was set aside for defence expenditure it was clear that the Government would not be able effectively to tackle the economic problems until the civil war with Unita and the undeclared war with South Africa had been ended. Over half a million people had been forced to leave their homes as a result of the fighting.

Chapter 2

ZAMBIA—MALAWI—ZIMBABWE—NAMIBIA—BOTSWANA—LESOTHO—
SWAZILAND

ZAMBIA

FOR most Zambians 1981 was a depressing year. In sharp contrast to neighbouring Zimbabwe, Zambia continued to suffer from declining living standards and deteriorating social services. In a population of 5·8 million no less than 1 million young people were said to be unemployed. The price of copper remained low and production declined. (Duties on the export of copper and cobalt dropped from 54 per cent of revenue in 1974 to 6 per cent in 1980). The only bright spots were provided by reports of an excellent maize harvest, sufficient to meet the country's needs, and agreements made with commercial banks for a $150 million loan to pay for essential oil imports and with the IMF for a £109 million credit. But so long as the price of copper remained depressed there seemed no way of rescuing the country from its economic malaise.

President Kaunda was clearly still much preoccupied with the implications of the abortive coup of October 1980 (see AR 1980, p. 254). In January he accused South Africa of sending commandos into Zambia to rescue people detained after the coup. In June the Zambian authorities expelled two US diplomats and declared four other US citizens, none still resident in Zambia, prohibited immigrants, alleging them to have been involved in CIA activities designed to explore the possibilities of replacing Kaunda as national leader. There were further reports of plots involving mercenaries, and those accused after the 1980 coup were put on trial, but no verdict had been reached by the end of the year, possibly because the prosecution was finding it difficult to obtain incriminating evidence. Deep discontent among some Zambian businessmen and civil servants was a fact long evident, but how far individual Zambians were prepared to go in plotting to overthrow the President remained as obscure as ever.

Much more clearly visible was the opposition to the regime among trade unionists. Their discontent began to emerge in late 1980 when the Government introduced a local government law clearly designed to strengthen the hold of the party (UNIP) on local administration. Under the new legislation, which came into force on 1 January, the right to participate in local government elections, either as candidate or as voter, was restricted to party members—yet no more than 8 per cent of the population held party cards. To trade unionists this looked like a plan to create a costly new bureaucracy for the benefit of the party faithful. In January sixteen shop stewards who had taken part in elections were expelled from their unions. The Government retaliated by suspending the party membership of seventeen leading trade unionists. Since all leading trade unionists were required to be party members, this was tantamount to expelling the leaders from their own unions. At the same time the Government incurred further odium by reducing the subsidy on local corn, forcing the price to rise by between 30 and 50 per cent. Miners on the copperbelt responded to the attack on their leaders by launching a series of wildcat strikes which lasted for eight days. Bank employees expressed their support by joining in the strike. There were violent clashes between miners and police, and in Kitwe the party headquarters building was set on fire by a crowd of unemployed youths. Order was restored when it became apparent that the Government was prepared to withdraw the expulsion order on the union leaders.

The chairman of the Zambian Congress of Trades Unions (ZCTU), Mr Frederick Chiluba, a 36-year old Bemba, was reported to see himself either as a Zambian Lech Walesa or as a successor to the late Simon Kapwepwe, who died in 1980. When strikes among skilled mineworkers broke out again in July, Mr Chiluba declared: 'We are demanding that the Government puts an end to socialization and spends its revenue on improving the lives of ordinary people.' Mr Chiluba and three other union leaders were arrested and kept in detention for three months. ZCTU made threatening noises but was clearly not prepared to push the issue to the point of confrontation.

In February President Kaunda reshuffled his Government, removing the two senior members of the party hierarchy: Mr Mainza Chona, the secretary-general, was replaced by a veteran politician, Mr Humphrey Mulemba, while Mr Nalumino Mundia took over from Mr Daniel Lusilo as Prime Minister. These changes were interpreted as a face-lift for the party, intended to give it a more respectable image. They were clearly also the latest in that succession of moves of which President Kaunda had shown himself such a master designed to prevent any one individual accumulating too much power. Although the President's reputation had been tarnished by his inability to devise means of countering economic decline and his tolerance of inefficiency and corruption among the party faithful, his commanding position had not been seriously challenged, and was strengthened by the absence of any obvious successor.

In foreign relations there was a decline in American and a growth in Russian influence, following the military agreement with the Soviet Union concluded in 1980 (see AR 1980, p. 253). Territorial disputes continued with Zaïre and Malawi, both countries laying claim to border territory that Zambia claimed as its own. In September South Africa was accused of attacking Zambian territory from bases in the Caprivi Strip. Relations with Zimbabwe, strained in 1980 because of Zambia's close association with Zapu, were much improved in July when President Kaunda paid his first visit to Salisbury and was greeted with a hero's welcome in recognition of the part he and his country had played in Zimbabwe's war of liberation.

MALAWI

The personal ascendency of the Life President, Ngwazi ('conqueror') Dr H. Kamuzu Banda, remained as firmly established as ever. The annual convention of the Malawi Congress Party, to which all Malawi citizens were obliged to belong, held at Zomba in September, passed ten resolutions fulsomely adulatory of his work. Nevertheless some signs of internal dissent could be detected: a flood of anti-Banda leaflets included some emanating from the Malawi Democratic Union, a group said to draw its support from local intellectuals, businessmen and civil servants and to have connections with the Socialist League of Malawi (Lespma).

The most vocal opposition to the regime continued to be expressed by groups of exiled politicians. Three groups, Lesoma, the Malawi Freedom Movement and the Congress for the Second Republic, came together at a conference held at Mbeya in south-west Tanzania in June, but personal rivalries prevented the establishment of a united front.

The most significant political event was the third summit meeting of the nine member states of SADCC, the Southern African Development Coordination Conference, held at Blantyre in November. Throughout the 1970s Dr Banda had been abused by many African nationalists as the 'Uncle Tom of Black Africa' on account of his Government's unwillingness to support the liberation struggle in Mozambique and Zimbabwe and its close diplomatic and economic relations with South Africa. By participating in an organization designed to lessen its members' economic dependence on South Africa, Dr Banda brought his country out of its isolated position.

Significantly, Malawi did not abstain from the conference's resolution condemning South Africa for recent 'aggressive actions', yet there was no renunciation of Malawi's existing ties with South Africa. As Dr Banda told members of the New Zealand Parliament during his visit in September, 'I prefer to deal openly with South Africa and not secretly, not denounce them in public and deal with them in secret. To kill apartheid is to go there'.

South African aid was particularly important in the construction of the new, centrally-placed capital, Lilongwe. By 1981 Lilongwe, with a population of over 120,000, could be described as an 'imposing garden city' and its construction had clearly boosted the development of the previously neglected Northern and Central provinces. During 1981 work was completed on the rail-link between the new capital and the Zambian border and on the Kamuzu international airport.

For Malawi's economy 1979 and 1980 had been particularly depressing years. The growth rate fell from 7·9 per cent in 1977 to 0·8 per cent in 1980, while the external debt rose from K399 million in 1979 to K540 million in 1980. In 1981 the economy showed signs of an upturn with reports of a bumper maize harvest and an extremely good tobacco crop. Nevertheless, Malawi's economy remained almost entirely dependent on agricultural exports (tobacco, tea and sugar) whose prices were liable to wide fluctuations. Malawi turned to the World Bank for a structural adjustment loan, whose first tranche of $25 million was received in 1981.

ZIMBABWE

Zimbabwe entered its second year of internationally recognized independence, the officially-designated 'year of consolidating the people's power', amid unwelcome political disruption. Despite a pact between the two parties making up the Patriotic Front (PF) Government—the Zimbabwe African National Union, or Zanu-PF, led by the Prime Minister, Mr Robert Mugabe, and the Zimbabwe African People's Union, or PF (Zapu), led by Mr Joshua Nkomo, the Minister of Home Affairs—violence had broken out among their supporters in November 1980 (see AR 1980, pp. 258-9). Further clashes occurred during February at Entumbane, near Bulawayo, raising the death toll to around a hundred.

The cause of the unrest was the continuing presence of former nationalist guerrillas at assembly points established after the ceasefire of December 1979, and the activities of armed gangs still at large in the countryside. On 21 January the Government renewed the Emergency Powers Act to help control the persisting unrest and accelerated the process of disarming the former combatants and integrating them into the new Zimbabwe national army. The process was completed in mid-May with the disarming of the last two major groups of guerrillas, those of Mr Mugabe's former military wing, the Zimbabwe African National Liberation Army (Zanla) at Middle Sabi, and Mr Nkomo's Zimbabwe People's Revolutionary Army (Zipra) at Gwaai River. With the help of British instructors under General Sir Edwin Bramhall, most were absorbed into the new army. Others were demobilized with a guaranteed pension for two years. On 7 August Lieut.-General Andrew (Sandy) Maclean was appointed supreme military commander of the Zimbabwean armed forces, numbering about 45,000 men. The former Zanla leader, Lieut.-General Rex Nhongo, was appointed army commander with Lieut.-General Lookout Masuku, of Zipra, as his deputy.

Contrasting regional support for the two factions within the PF was highlighted by the results of local elections held during the year. In November 1980 Mr Mugabe's Zanu-PF gained control of all municipal councils except that at Victoria Falls, in the north-east of the country, which was won by Mr Nkomo's PF (Zapu). Dr Tizirai Gwata became Salisbury's first black mayor. Zapu's predominance within Matabeleland was confirmed by its success in the Bulawayo elections, twice postponed through political violence but held finally on 6-7 June. At Government level a dispute arose in January following Mr Nkomo's transfer from the Home Affairs Ministry to that of the Public Service. Mr Nkomo claimed that the reshuffle violated his agreement with the Prime Minister, but eventually accepted the post of Minister without Portfolio, with special responsibilities for security, defence and the public service. Other Cabinet changes saw Mr Witness Mangwenda becoming Foreign Affairs Minister and Mr Richard Hove taking over Home Affairs. In March Mr David Smith, the white Minister of Trade and Commerce, resigned on medical advice and in April Mr George Silundika, Minister of Posts and Telecommunications and a veteran Zapu leader, died.

White politics, too, showed signs of fragmentation. In April Mr

André Holland, for 11 years an MP and member of Mr Ian Smith's Rhodesian Front party (RF), resigned from Parliament to form the Democratic Party. He declared the party's aim was to form a constructive opposition, in contrast to the antagonistic stance of the RF, and to extend 'the hand of genuine friendship' to the Government. At a by-election for his old seat, however, Mr Holland was defeated by the RF candidate, and in two further contests during the year Mr Smith's party, renamed in June the Republican Front, retained its hold over all 20 white seats in the House of Assembly.

The direction of Zimbabwe's economic policy became clearer during 1981. A three-year Z$4,000 million reconstruction and development programme, announced in November 1980 by the Minister of Economic Planning and Development, Dr Bernard Chizero (see AR 1980, p. 257), was launched at an international donors' conference in Salisbury in March. The conference, 'Zimcord', was attended by representatives from 45 countries and 25 international agencies. By the close of the conference Zimbabwe's aid target of £838 million had in fact been exceeded, pledges made since independence in April 1980 having reached over £889 million, the highest amount of aid given to any developing country. The principal donors were the World Bank (£205 million), the United Kingdom (£122 million), the United States (£119 million), the EEC (£83 million), France (£49 million) and West Germany (£43 million), while smaller commitments were made by Sweden, Canada, Italy, China, the Kuwait Fund for Arab Economic Development and other sources. The aid, 38 per cent of which was pledged as grants, the remainder as 'soft' loans, was earmarked for rural development, post-war reconstruction, education and technical training.

On all fronts conspicuous progress was made during the year. Schools, clinics and hospitals were built in rural centres. An estimated half-a-million refugees were resettled. Enrolment in secondary schools rose by 94 per cent and in September primary education was made free.

On 24 June the report of an influential commission of inquiry, dubbed the 'poor people's charter', was tabled in Parliament. The commission, chaired by an economist, Mr Roger Riddell, investigated prices and the pay and conditions of workers. The report recommended an increase in minimum wages, the provision of housing for industrial workers and land for agricultural workers and the introduction of social security, pension and job-creation schemes, to be partly met by taxes on wealth and capital gains. Although not binding on the Government the proposals of the commission were broadly endorsed by the 1981-82 Budget in July and by the Prime Minister in December when he announced new minimum wage-rates in both the private and public sectors, a ceiling on upper-level salary increases and a ban on dismissals.

Continued economic growth at a high level brought its own problems and exposed weaknesses in Zimbabwe's commercial infrastructure. High consumer demand put pressure on domestic manufacturing, and both public and private borrowing requirements quickly outstripped the money supply. The Budget, introduced by Senator Enos Nkala, provided for a 37 per cent increase in government expenditure, principally on social services, and helped push the inflation rate to 19 per cent. A 3 per cent increase in the bank rate in September restored stability in the money market and was a factor behind the inflation figure of about 16 per cent for the year. The major success of the year came in the agricultural sector, where output was up by 40 per cent. The value of mineral production, however, dropped by 9 per cent, largely as a result of deflated world prices, transport difficulties and a shortage of skilled manpower. Tobacco was again the country's leading export and fuel the major import.

The single most significant obstacle to progress was Zimbabwe's economic dependence on South Africa. Paradoxically, the country's greatest ideological foe was also its biggest trading partner, supplying 35 per cent of Zimbabwe's imports and taking 19 per cent of its exports. Moreover, pending the reopening of the Beira (Mozambique) to Umtali oil pipeline, closed since UDI in 1965, the country was wholly dependent on South Africa for fuel and petroleum products. Equally important was the railway through South Africa as a link between Zimbabwe and its external markets. The link became even more vital in November after guerrillas of the Mozambique Resistance Movement, allegedly backed by South Africa, sabotaged road and rail bridges connecting Zimbabwe with the port at Beira (see p. 249). Not surprisingly Mr Mugabe declared that while Zimbabwe supported the aims of black liberation in southern Africa it was in no position to provide operational bases for African National Congress (ANC) guerrillas or participate in economic sanctions against South Africa.

When, however, by mid-year, an acute shortage of locomotives and of engineers to maintain them created a major transport crisis, Zimbabwe declined a loan of rolling-stock from South Africa, preferring to suffer reduced exports. The principal casualty of the policy was the record 1981 maize crop, of which only half the surplus could be exported. At the same time Zimbabwe continued to promote the efforts of the Southern African Development Coordinating Conference to reduce through regional cooperation the member countries' economic dependence on South Africa.

In February Zimbabwe established formal diplomatic relations at ambassadorial level with the Soviet Union and with Poland, and relations with other states were consolidated by visits made by the Prime Minister during the year to Nigeria, the United States, North Korea,

China, Japan, India, Pakistan and Australia. Within the country the policy of africanization was continued, blacks replacing whites where possible in the civil service, local government and the police. Professor Telford Georges, a West Indian, became the first black Supreme Court judge and Professor Walter Kamba the first black vice-chancellor of the University of Zimbabwe. In January the Government bought a majority shareholding in Rhobank, one of the country's major commercial banks, and acquired control of Zimbabwe Newspapers Ltd and hence of the country's five largest newspapers.

The second half of the year brought a noticeable change in the political atmosphere and a souring of the policy of racial reconciliation. Legislation to counter espionage and sabotage was promulgated following an upsurge of violence attributed to the activities of South African agents operating to disrupt political order and overturn the Government. Agents were blamed for the assassination in Salisbury of a senior ANC executive on 31 July, for explosions at Inkomo barracks on 16 August which destroyed Z$36 million worth of arms and ammunition and for the bombing on 18 December of the Zanu-PF headquarters in the heart of the capital.

New regulations in October to control political meetings appeared to be directed against the opposition and minority parties. White morale in particular was shaken during November by a 'meet the people' tour of the country by the Prime Minister. At a series of rallies in rural areas Mr Mugabe forcefully attacked white 'disloyalty'. He alleged a plot by senior white politicians to engineer a coup and referred to the arrest of an RF MP, Mr Wally Stuttaford, by the security police. His repeated declarations in favour of a one-party state caused concern that safeguards for white representation endorsed by the Lancaster House agreement (see AR 1979, pp. 253-4) were at risk. Fears of what they termed 'creeping communism' caused a record number of whites, almost 22,000, to emigrate, most to South Africa. At the end of the year the white population was estimated at 180,000, compared to a peak of 277,000 in 1976. The Government introduced measures to discourage the emigration flow while actively recruiting expatriates from India, the United Kingdom and Australia to replace the departing skilled personnel. Zimbabwe remained attractive to tourists: over 300,000 visited the country, the highest annual figure since 1972.

NAMIBIA

Western attempts to resolve the dispute between the world community and South Africa over Namibia entered a new phase after the outright failure of the Geneva conference in January. Namibia, also known as South-West Africa, had been administered by South Africa since the peace treaty of Versailles, initially as a League of Nations mandate. At Geneva in January an unsuccessful attempt was made to secure agreement on procedures to implement resolution 435 of the UN Security Council, which required a ceasefire and free elections as a prelude to independence. Both South Africa and Swapo (the South West Africa Peoples' Organization), which was conducting an Angola-based guerrilla campaign in Namibia, had accepted resolution 435. At the Geneva talks, the South African negotiators appeared to play for time, believing that the pending change of Administration in Washington would create a more favourable climate for negotiations. South Africa was anxious that the moderate Democratic Turnhalle Alliance should do well in the pre-independence elections and feared that a Swapo victory would promote Soviet ambitions in the sub-continent.

Once established in office the Reagan Administration set out to achieve a Namibian settlement as a major foreign policy objective, aiming to secure the departure of Cuban forces from Angola. An intense diplomatic offensive was launched, involving visits by American officials to the frontline states and Pretoria and eventually a visit to Washington by the South African Foreign Minister, Mr R. F. Botha. At the end of the year it appeared that conditional acceptance of a set of constitutional principles had been secured from the contending parties in the first phase of the new American-sponsored plan. Full freedom of speech and assembly were to be guaranteed and elements of proportional representation were to be introduced in the Assembly to be elected to frame a constitution. The next phase of this negotiation, it appeared, would concern the establishment of a time-table and detailed arrangements for the election and independence.

During the year South African security forces mounted a series of pre-emptive strikes aimed against Swapo bases in Angola. The largest of these was 'Operation Protea', in August, which was denounced at the United Nations as a 'grave violation'. Angolan accounts described widespread devastation of towns and villages in southern Angola. In London the Foreign Office described the incursion as 'highly dangerous' for the stability of Southern Africa.

During operations in Angola the South African forces captured a Russian army non-commissioned officer, also Soviet tanks and equipment, and said that there was irrefutable proof of Cuban and Russian military involvement. In operations in 1981 the South African army claimed to have killed 2,500 Swapo insurgents while 56 South African servicemen lost their lives. As the year ended the negotiations were still on track but no agreed time-table for elections and independence had emerged.

BOTSWANA

Dr Quett Masire, interviewed in July twelve months after becoming President of Botswana on the death of Sir Seretse Khama, said that his country's relations with South Africa were purely on an economic basis. There could be no question of diplomatic relations until the situation had changed in South Africa. Botswana's policy was not to allow its territory to be used as a launching pad for activities against its neighbours.

In January Botswana complained that South African troops had fired on Botswana Defence Force positions on the Namibia border and at Kazangula on the Zambesi river. These were unprovoked attacks, according to Dr Masire. South Africa undertook to investigate the complaint.

In November Dr Masire, speaking at the opening of Parliament, said Botswana was planning an aggressive industrial policy, geared to promoting both local and foreign investment. To meet the increased need for power it was planned to commission the Morupule power station in 1985-86. The project was to be based on Botswana's own coal resources.

LESOTHO

In 1981 relations between South Africa and the landlocked kingdom of Lesotho deteriorated sharply. In October a mortar attack on an army barracks near Maseru appeared to have come from South African soil. The Prime Minister of Lesotho, Chief Jonathan, accused South Africa of allowing the so-called Lesotho Liberation Army (guerrillas of the exiled Mokhehle faction of the Basutoland Congress Party), to operate from South African territory. In a letter to the UN Secretary-General in November the South African Foreign Minister, Mr R. F. Botha, rejected any inference that South Africa was implicated in the attack on the army barracks.

Lesotho had been governed under a suspended constitution since 1970, when Chief Jonathan declared a state of emergency in order, it was reported, to forestall a probable BCP victory at the polls. The LLA was held responsible for bombs which exploded at the Hilton hotel, the airport and elsewhere during the year. At the same time there were a series of political murders and abductions of critics of the regime.

In November Chief Jonathan said that he intended to call a general election in the new year.

SWAZILAND

In April some Southern African leaders, including delegations from Swaziland, Lesotho, Botswana and Mozambique, held an unscheduled meeting in Mbabane. The talks concerned the possibility of South African military moves against neighbouring countries that harboured exiles of the African National Congress (ANC), which was mounting an urban and rural guerrilla campaign in South Africa. In November two South African refugees, members of the banned ANC, were imprisoned for terms of 2½ years and six months for importing arms into Swaziland. In December it was reported that the ANC position in Swaziland was becoming precarious. Two ANC men had been killed in a shoot-out with unknown men near the South African border control post at Oshoek.

It was announced that the planned rail link between Swaziland and the Transvaal would be built at a cost of between R50 million and R60 million and would be completed, it was hoped, by the end of 1984. The line would assist the export of coal and agricultural produce from Swaziland.

The diamond jubilee celebrations of King Sobhuza were held in September and were attended by the Princess Margaret, Countess of Snowdon.

Chapter 3

THE REPUBLIC OF SOUTH AFRICA

IN 1981 hopes of significant constitutional reform by the Botha Administration were greatly weakened. There was a rightward swing among the Government's white Afrikaner supporters, and the Prime Minister, Mr P. W. Botha, drew in his horns. At the same time the incidence of sabotage and urban guerrilla activity by the banned African National Congress was considerably stepped up. The South African authorities struck back at the start of the year by mounting an Israeli-type commando raid over the border into Maputo, Mozambique, attacking ANC headquarters (see p. 248).

The Prime Minister seemed shaken by the result of the general election held on 29 April. His ruling National Party did not lose any seats to the extreme right-wing HNP (Herstigte Nasionale Party), which was seeking to capture the conservative Afrikaner vote: but the NP did lose a surprising number of *votes* to HNP candidates, and Mr Botha, although still firmly in the saddle, appeared to take fright. The National Party won a massive majority of 110 seats in Parliament, though losing six seats to the PFP (Progressive Federal Party), the principal opposition party in Parliament, and two to the NRP (the new Republic Party), a party chiefly of Natal province. The NP gained one seat from the NRP. The PFP gained nine seats, six from the NP and three from the NRP. The PFP total was 26 seats and the NRP could muster only eight seats.

Mr Botha was less concerned by the modest inroads made on his left flank by the PFP than by the electoral potential of the HNP, which had picked up Afrikaner votes across a broad front. On a small further swing, it appeared, the HNP would win numbers of seats from NP. For Mr Botha the most important consideration was the unity of Afrikaner-dom. The National Party, which was becoming polarized into reformist and reactionary factions, was potentially vulnerable to HNP propa-ganda. Poised between two options—to speed up reform and risk an all-out Nationalist split, or to batten down the hatches and face increasing displays of black anger—Mr Botha opted for the latter course. The re-formist rhetoric which had aroused great hopes at home and sympathetic interest abroad faded into the background.

The spectacular economic boom of 1981, which had been primed by a buoyant international gold price, began to run out of steam as the year ended. By mid-November the price of gold had dropped below $400 an ounce from a peak of about $700. The rand dived in consequence, losing 23 per cent of its value against the US dollar over the year. On the balance of payments the current account swung from a R3,000 million surplus to an expected R4,000 million deficit, a considerable shift for an economy the size of South Africa's. Inflation, running at 15 per cent, was at its worst since the 1920s, but the economy was inherently strong and a full-blown recession was not in sight.

The Botha Administration continued to enjoy good relations with the English-speaking business establishment. Yet there were some signs of disenchantment. Businessmen had expected substantial reforms to be introduced. The Prime Minister, sensing their disquiet, called a con-ference with business leaders, the second since he became Premier (see AR 1979, p. 264), but said little to convince the businessmen that pur-poseful change was on the way. Mr Harry Oppenheimer of the Anglo-American Corporation said the private sector felt it had reason for dis-appointment. The high hopes of two years previously had been followed by a general sense of disillusion.

The rising incidence of sabotage, with attacks on police stations and other so-called 'hard' targets, was the most ominous trend of 1981. The incidence of sabotage increased 200 per cent in the first six months of the year, costing the country millions of rands. Bomb blasts shook central Durban on two occasions, injuring shoppers, and there were similar inci-dents in East London and Port Elizabeth, though casualties remained light. Guerrilla attacks were for the most part directed at army and police posts and strategic targets such as power stations and railway lines.

The most audacious of such ANC operations during the year included a rocket attack on the headquarters of the South African army at Voortrekkerhoogte, Pretoria, and a rocket and grenade attack on a police station at Wonderboom, a suburb of Pretoria, in which a policeman died and a number were injured. In Cape Town some damage was caused to a government building housing pass-law records which was set alight with incendiary explosives. There was also some political violence on the right, including suspected arson at the home of the leader of the opposition, Dr F. Van Zyl Slabbert, in which Dr Slabbert's sleeping wife and children narrowly escaped death or serious injury.

As the year began it was plain that Mr Botha had no intention of repealing the major apartheid statutes such as the Group Areas Act, enforcing residential segregation, or the laws prohibiting marriage or sexual intercourse across the colour line. But there were still some hopes for alleviation of the worst aspects of the apartheid system and the achievement of constitutional reform through the agency of the nominated President's Council, a multiracial advisory body. There was surprise and some dismay when the Botha Government turned down recommendations by the President's Council which would have restored District Six, Cape Town, and Pageview to the coloured (mixed race) and Indian communities respectively. These areas had been zoned for whites some years earlier and the inhabitants had been removed elsewhere. The forced removals had caused intense resentment. It had been generally expected that the proposed concessions would be granted as symbolic gestures of reconciliation.

The central grievance of black and coloured South Africans, as always, concerned the franchise. These communities still had no representation in the South African Parliament. It had been expected that in 1981 the President's Council would put forward proposals to restore the parliamentary franchise to the coloured community, which had been taken away in the 1950s. By the year's end no such proposal was forthcoming. The Transvaal leader of the National Party, Dr Andries Treurnicht, commanding the biggest single block of supporters in the Nationalist parliamentary caucus, had let it be known publicly that he would oppose any move to restore the coloured vote, even on a separate roll. The Botha Administration faced determined ideological opposition from the powerful Treurnicht faction, which insisted that whites only should preside over the political destinies of so-called 'white South Africa'.

If there was disagreement over coloured policy, there was unanimity among Afrikaner Nationalists about the political rights of black Africans. Both the Botha and Treurnicht factions agreed that the black majority should have no citizenship in South Africa but should exercise such rights in the separate tribal territories which were scheduled to be given 'independence' or had already accepted that status, like Transkei, Venda, Bophuthatswana and Ciskei. The implications of this policy became clear during 1981 when hundreds of African squatters from the Transkei and the Ciskei were deemed to be 'aliens' in the Cape peninsula and were summarily deported. The citizenship question, affecting the rights of Africans to live and work in the urbanized and industrialized areas of South Africa, became a major source of black anger and resentment during the year. Reports from the Ciskei in particular emphasized an alarming incidence of economic hardship and hunger among people desperate for employment in the urban areas.

During 1981 the black trade union movement, beneficiaries of reforms already put through by the Botha Administration, began to grow rapidly and to flex its muscles. The labour field had proved to be the one area in which reform went beyond rhetoric and was to some extent translated into practice. Reform of labour legislation had made it legal for Africans to organize themselves in recognized trade unions. There were more than 115 strikes by black workers in the first ten months of 1981. More and more union leaders were talking of the need to become involved in broader community issues. Labour consultants warned that, in the absence of political rights for black Africans, political pressures would continue to build up in the union movement. The Government sought to counteract this trend by laying down restrictive conditions for the registration of black trade unions and denying benefits to unions that declined to register. Nevertheless the non-registered union movement grew steadily and many managements chose to recognize unregistered unions, as they appeared to be representative of workers and were effective channels of communication. An interesting trend was the use by the new black unions of consumer boycotts as a lever in disputes with employers. The consumer boycott proved to be a potent weapon against companies manufacturing foodstuffs, sweets and similar products.

The South African security police and the security authorities of the Ciskei, an Eastern Cape tribal area which became politically independent during the year, cracked down on black trade unions, so much so that some observers felt that the spate of detentions of trade unionists cancelled out the benefits of the reforms. In September the Ciskeian authorities swooped on the General Workers Union, the Allied Workers Union and the Food and Canning Workers Union and detained 205 black trade unionists and union officials. In December Mr Thozamile Gqweta and Mr Sisa Njikelana, president and vice-president respectively of the Allied Workers Union, were taken into custody by the security police and their offices were raided. They were placed in detention without trial under the security laws.

In the Transvaal 17 young blacks and whites, many of them university students interested in labour affairs, were also detained. In December the security police announced that some of the 27 would be charged in court and others would give evidence at the trials. The charges, it was stated, would concern aiding and abetting the banned African National Congress. On Christmas Eve two of the 27 detainees were brought to court and charged with assisting the ANC in plans to sabotage the Johannesburg TV broadcasting tower.

During the year a number of trials were held in various parts of the country under the security laws. In September four members of the ANC were gaoled in Pretoria for a total of 48 years after conviction under the Terrorist Act. They were found guilty of various offences connected with the activities of the ANC. In the same month two members of the white extremist organization the 'Wit Kommando' were sentenced to terms of ten and five years for sabotage. The case arose out of bomb attacks during 1979 on the offices of leading Afrikaner intellectuals who were known to favour reform. In August three members of the ANC were convicted in Pretoria of offences involving the sabotage of the Sasol oil-from-coal plant at Secunda, which caused R3 million damage, and other offences. There were demonstrations by blacks and the singing of freedom songs in the public gallery and outside the court as the three men—Johannes Shabangu, 26, David Moise, 25, and Anthony Tsobobe, 25—were sentenced to death.

Some observers took the view that reform was merely in abeyance while Mr Botha mended his political fences. Others held that the reactionary Treurnicht wing of the National Party was now in a position to impose a permanent veto on reform. As the year ended Mr Botha was resolved to maintain Afrikaner nationalist unity and to ensure that Afrikaner hegemony in South Africa was not endangered. The extremists on both sides of the colour line were making the running. The English-language newspapers were again under intense pressure and press freedom was in jeopardy. Moderates in all groups were on the defensive and losing ground. The stage was set for a protracted struggle.

VIII SOUTH ASIA AND INDIAN OCEAN

Chapter 1

IRAN—AFGHANISTAN

IRAN

THE self-confidence of the Iranian revolution ebbed away during 1981. Bitter feuding erupted between the President, Abol Hassan Bani-Sadr, and the Islamic Republic Party (IRP) during the early months of the year. By March open and bloody fighting had taken place in the streets of Teheran between supporters of the religious hierarchy and those mobilizing behind Bani-Sadr. The IRP leaders were accused of sanctioning torture and political oppression no less than that experienced under the Shah. More importantly, the Mujaheddin-i Khalq organization of Muslim-oriented left-wing guerrillas increasingly put their backing behind Bani-Sadr, and a campaign of minor bombings began throughout the country to unsettle the IRP.

Bani-Sadr's position was systematically undermined from March onwards. A Majlis commission was set up to review his activities during the riots in that month. Most of the President's personal advisers were arrested. His newspaper was closed. Ayatollah Khomeini made direct public attacks against Bani-Sadr and opened the way for his dismissal as commander of the armed forces on 10 June. The Majlis voted for Bani-Sadr's impeachment on 21 June, when formal warrants for his arrest were issued. Retreat into hiding gave Bani-Sadr an opportunity to reach a political accommodation with the Mujaheddin-i Khalq and to lead the opposition against the clerics from inside the country, though he still failed to draw together a coherent party under a clear political banner. On 29 July Bani-Sadr staged a spectacular escape from Iran to arrive in France, where he was granted political asylum.

The growing grip on power by the IRP and in particular by its leader, Ayatollah Beheshti, was abruptly challenged by the Mujaheddin, whose bombing campaign came to a head in an explosion on 28 June at the headquarters of the IRP. Detonated during the course of a major IRP meeting, the bomb killed 72 persons. Among the victims were Ayatollah Beheshti himself, the Chief Justice, four Ministers of State and six deputy Ministers. Assassinations continued of leading clerics and their supporters, culminating in a second multiple assassination on 30 August in the office of the Prime Minister. In this incident 31 persons were killed, including the new President, Mr Rajai, and the Prime Minister,

Mr Bahonar. In reprisal, the IRP mounted a bloody attack on all known offices of the Mujaheddin and began mass arrests of all denounced as being its members. By December it was estimated that as many as 2,271 Mujaheddin or their sympathizers had been summarily executed in a mere six-month period following the fall of Bani-Sadr.

Mujaheddin assassinations were not entirely halted by the terror instituted by the Government. The revolutionary prosecutor-general, Ali Qoddusi, was murdered on 5 September and Assadollah Madani, a leading pro-Khomeini cleric of Azarbaijan, assassinated on 11 September. Mujaheddin-promoted unrest struck schools, where many arrests of their supporters were made. Massoud Rajavi, the Mujaheddin leader, set up a government in exile in Paris on 1 October, but by the end of the year the punishing blood-letting by the regime was having an effect on the strength of the Mujaheddin, whose political influence appeared to be diminishing.

As a result of the frictions between Bani-Sadr and the IRP in the first quarter of the year and the assassinations later, there was considerable shuffling of official positions. Mr Rajai was elected as the second President of the Republic on 24 July with 10·89 million votes from a possible 12·12 million. Mr Mohammad Javad Bahonar was appointed Prime Minister on 4 August after several other of the President's nominees had been rejected by the Majlis. A third President was elected on 2 October, when the new head of the IRP, Hajatoleslam Ali Khamenei, won 96 per cent of the national vote. The interim Prime Minister, Hajatoleslam Mahdavi Kani, was replaced in October after some difficulty in the Majlis. Hussain Moussavi became the new Prime Minister though most of the previous Cabinet was retained.

Unrest continued in most of the tribal areas of Iran throughout the year. Kurdestan remained the most antagonistic to the regime in Teheran, and running battles between the army and the irregulars supporting the movement for Kurdish autonomy went on with only minor gains for the central government, including the fall of the town of Bukhan in October. Guerrillas still commanded the countryside over wide areas even by the end of the year and the Kurdish revolt continued as a running sore. Activities by other dissident regional groups flared from time to time but were mostly on a lesser level than in 1980.

Outside the narrow but important political cockpit of Teheran the regime's principal preoccupation was with the war against Iraq. Gradually, and with enormous losses in men and equipment, the Iranians pushed back the Iraqis over small but important areas of the war front. A first drive came in January around Ahwaz, which was repulsed but which established the pattern of action and inaction in which the Iraqis sought to hold their lines against limited but determined Iranian counter-attacks. In June the Iranians pushed forward around Susangerd, and in

September a significant victory was gained as the Iraqis gave up their bridgehead to the east of the Karun River near Abadan. In the closing days of 1981 a new Iranian offensive was launched in the Qasr Shirin sector, when both sides claimed victory. In the air, activity was sporadic and rarely decisive. Iranian raids on the northern Iraqi oilfields in May and July had only temporary impact on levels of oil output there. In September Iranian aircraft bombed Iraqi power stations in the south and caused extensive damage in an area where previous attacks had put all oil-exporting terminals out of action. In retaliation, on 30 September Iraqi aircraft struck at the oil pumping station of Gurreh, which fed crude oil from the major oilfields to Kharg Island terminal, considerably hindering Iranian oil exports. Meanwhile, Abadan refinery and city were reduced to ruins and the expensive petrochemical works at Bandar Khomeini were also hit in Iraqi air raids.

The war of attrition between the two sides continued despite pleas by the Muslim world for an early peace. The Islamic Conference sent peace missions to Iran in March and October but these were rejected. The Government consistently held to the view that no negotiations could take place until Iraqi soldiers were entirely withdrawn from Iranian territory, and by the end of 1981 they were convinced that Iranian arms would prevail in any case.

The hostages from the US embassy in Teheran were released in January 1981 after prolonged negotiations. Financial considerations dominated the settlement, with $11,100 million of assets exchanged, much handled through the Bank of England. Iranian terms for the agreement were, in the final analysis, moderate, and it appeared that the Ayatollah Khomeini had determined to be rid of the hostages regardless of cost. The good offices of the Algerian Government were vital in securing the agreement. Final settlement of claims was left to a special claims court set up at The Hague, the work of which was expected to go on for up to three years. Settlement of the hostages dispute did nothing to improve relations between Iran and the USA.

Great difficulties were experienced by the Iranian authorities in maintaining regular flows of oil for export. Exports were estimated at approximately one million barrels a day during the second and third quarters of the year, after a first quarter in which production was barely enough to cover domestic demand. After the Iraqi destruction of the Gurreh pumping station production fell again, with exports fluctuating around 400,000 to 500,000 barrels a day.

Combination of the poor levels of oil exports and the financial drain of the war with Iraq depleted the country's foreign exchange position. By year-end official reserves were put at some $2,000 million, at a time that import costs were running at $900 million per month. Oil revenues were then thought to be not more than $500 million per month. Austerity measures were introduced in September and the annual budget of $37,000 million ceased to be relevant in a deteriorating situation. Inflation rose rapidly and was officially acknowledged to be more than 25 per cent. Efforts to reinvigorate domestic agriculture and industry were only partially successful and Iran remained heavily import-dependent at a time that unemployment was worsening. State efforts to subsidize lower-budget families were effective in the main towns and cities but a degree of economic distress was reported from provincial areas.

AFGHANISTAN

This was the second full year of the Soviet armed occupation of Afghanistan. In several respects the main events were uncannily similar in kind to those of the previous year (see AR 1980, pp. 270-1).

Internationally the Soviet-imposed Babrak Karmal regime continued to receive much censure and criticism, notably from the Islamic Conference summit in Saudi Arabia in late January, from the Non-Aligned Foreign Ministers' meeting in New Delhi, 9-13 February, and from various other international organizations and meetings, particularly the UN General Assembly. During the year several much publicized attempts were made (by the United Nations, the European Community and some individual Governments, including—rather tentatively—that of Babrak Karmal) to reach a political settlement, though without making any apparent progress.

Internally, armed resistance to the regime continued sporadically in various localities throughout the year. The armed forces of the Afghan Government were repeatedly weakened by defections and by casualties. They suffered losses at the hands of mujaheddin (literally, holy warriors) guerrillas, and increasingly were obliged to rely on Soviet troops for support. It was reported on 1 April 1981, for instance, that the four Afghan army units which had been stationed in the capital had been replaced by Soviet forces and sent to the provinces to fight the mujaheddin, and there was apparently a considerable increase in Soviet forces inducted into Afghanistan towards the end of the year. There was some evidence at various times throughout the year of continuing bitter rivalry between the two main factions within the ruling communist party, the People's Democratic Party of Afghanistan (PDPA), which occasionally erupted into armed violence and political murder.

President Karmal announced his resignation from the post of Prime Minister on 11 June, though he retained his offices as President of the Republic and as General Secretary of the PDPA. A number of Cabinet changes and PDPA appointments announced on the same day seemed overall to strengthen the position of President Karmal's Parcham (Flag) faction over the rival Khalq (People) faction, to which his murdered predecessor, President Hafizullah, had belonged. A special congress was convened in Kabul on 15 June to launch a 'National Fatherland Front', a mass organization first publicly mooted by Karmal in December 1980 and intended—though without any conspicuous initial success—to promote national unity.

Publicly intermittent controversy arose during the year, and especially in June and July, between the Soviet Union and China regarding control of the Wakhan salient, that mountainous, sparsely populated but strategically sensitive tongue of Afghan territory stretching from the north-east corner of the country to the Chinese border, which is a thin sliver of land between the Soviet Union and Pakistan.

Chapter 2

INDIA—PAKISTAN—BANGLADESH—SRI LANKA—NEPAL

INDIA

PROVISIONAL results in the 1981 census, held in February and March, showed the population of India as 683,810,051—an increase of 24·8 per cent over the 547,949,809 figure for 1971. The national figure incorporated estimates for Jammu and Kashmir, where the census was postponed until April and May, and for Assam, where it had not been held because of the local unrest.

In an address to the joint session of both Houses of Parliament on 16 January the President, Mr Sanjiva Reddy, said that both the national economy and the law and order situation in the country were improving overall after the damage caused by the present Government's predecessors until their conclusive electoral defeat in January 1980 (see AR 1980, p. 272). Inflation, the President claimed, was down from 23 to 15 per cent, and recent food grain production was up to record levels. (In July, however, India ended four years of self-sufficiency in grains when it purchased 1·5 million tons of wheat from the United States, and by September the erratic impact of the monsoon caused some experts to predict that the Government would be forced back into the international market as a result of a poor harvest caused by widespread flooding in July followed by an early end to the monsoon). Nevertheless, the country's balance of payments position, the President admitted, continued to cause concern and the trade deficit in 1980-81 was expected to increase considerably, despite the Government's efforts to increase exports and to encourage import substitution. Mr Reddy also admitted that the agitation in Assam, which had so disrupted the flow of oil in 1979-80, had 'not been called off'. (Assam suffered severely from flooding when the Brahmaputra burst its banks at several places in July.)

On 7 May the Lok Sabha (House of the People), the Lower House of the Indian Parliament, annulled the resolution adopted by the previous House on 19 December 1978 expelling Mrs Gandhi for breach of privilege.

By-elections were held for seven Lok Sabha seats on 14 June. Congress (I) held four seats in Uttar Pradesh. One of these was won by Mr Rajiv Gandhi, the Prime Minister's elder son, who by a 237,000 majority won the seat formerly held by his brother Sanjay.

On 23 July the Election Commission decreed that the Congress (I), led by Mrs Indira Gandhi, was the main Indian National Congress and withdrew recognition from the Congress (U) led by Mr Devaraj Urs. The Commission's decision stemmed from the fact that by this time a majority of those members of the All-India Congress Committee, the Lok Sabha, the Rajya Sabha (Upper House) and the state legislatures who had belonged to the Congress at the time of its split and reformation in January 1978 now professed allegiance to the Congress (I). From July onwards the Urs group was further split by dissension and defections. In late August its rump was redesignated the Indian National Congress (Socialist), and rather inconclusive efforts were made during the rest of the year to forge a common front against Congress (I).

On 27 July the Essential Services Maintenance Ordinance was promulgated by the President, empowering the Government to ban strikes in a wide range of specified 'essential' public services and to imprison strikers for six months after a summary trial. A Bill incorporating all the provisions of the ordinance, and making lock-outs in essential services subject to the same penalties as strikes, was passed by the Lok Sabha on 16 September after a 17-hour sitting. All opposition amendments were rejected by the Government. The Rajya Sabha passed the Bill on 18 September after a 16-hour sitting.

Major outbursts of communal rioting between Hindus and Moslems broke out in the notoriously turbulent and corruption-ridden state of Bihar in May and in Hyderabad, the capital of Andhra Pradesh, in July. Caste conflicts, particularly concerning the reservation of government jobs and university places for Harijans ('Untouchables'), erupted into a series of violent riots in Gujarat, especially between January and April. The militancy of some Harijans had increased under the influence of the Dalit Panthers, a movement originating in Maharashtra which had spread to Gujarat. In April and again in August there were reports that large numbers of Harijans in particular villages of Tamil Nadu were converting to Islam. In Madras in October it was reported that about 1,000 Harijans had converted to Buddhism. After a secret conference of leaders of thirteen Naxalite (extreme left-wing peasant-based) groups held at the end of January and February, it was announced that they had agreed to abandon terrorist methods and insurgency and to concentrate on public political agitation. Terrorism, whether Naxalite- or non-Naxalite-activated, nonetheless continued in several states, and increased markedly in Kerala and West Bengal. In December Mrs Gandhi met formally with opposition leaders, for the first time, to assess the security issues involved in the agitation in Assam and in the Punjab.

The non-communist opposition to Mrs Gandhi's Congress (I) fared badly in the seven parliamentary and 23 state legislature constituencies contested during the second quarter of the year, failing to win a single seat. Electoral turn-out was low, being about 36 per cent overall and 25 per cent in some constituencies. The erstwhile Janata party split into at least five factions, each too busily criticizing the others to mount any effective opposition to Congress (I). By contrast the Communists had some successes.

An eight-party coalition led by Mrs Indira Gandhi's Congress (I) party was sworn in on 28 December as the Government of the southern Indian state of Kerala. It replaced a marxist-led coalition which had collapsed in the previous October, and in consequence Mrs Gandhi's party had control of 16 of India's 22 states.

Throughout much of the year critics accused Mr A. R. Antulay, chief minister of Maharashtra and a close supporter of Mrs Gandhi, of political corruption. The matter attracted much press comment and at one point Antulay submitted his resignation—not to the state governor as required by the Constitution but to party leaders in New Delhi, where it was refused. Eventually the opposition took the matter to court, but no judgment was made before the end of the year.

The inception of the Reagan Administration soon led to heightened negotiations between the American and Pakistani Governments regarding American arms supplies (particularly F-16 fighter-bombers) to Pakistan in the wake of the Soviet occupation of Afghanistan. These negotiations also heightened Indian apprehensions about both American and Pakistani policies, apprehensions which were manifest, though with markedly different intensities, throughout the year. In August India disclosed that it had acquired from the Soviet Union MiG25 interceptor reconnaissance aircraft, capable of flying at 2,400 mph, and known to Nato as 'Foxbat'. Throughout the year there were a number of unconfirmed press reports that India was about to sign a contract to purchase nearly 200 advanced French Mirage-2000 war planes, whose acquisition was advocated by one Indian defence expert on the grounds that they would be a good delivery system for nuclear weapons in the interim period before India perfects a missile capability.

On 15 September Pakistan made a proposal to the Indian Government for immediate consultation 'for the purpose of exchanging mutual guarantees of non-aggression and non-use of force' in the spirit of the Indo-Pakistani agreement signed at Simla in 1972. Some weeks of uncertainty elapsed before the Indian Government confirmed that it had received such a proposal both orally and in writing, and there was much press comment and speculation in both countries as to whether such a proposal was genuinely practical and whether it would have relevance to the future of Kashmir.

Both India and Pakistan participated in the first two meetings of seven South Asian countries held at foreign secretary (i.e. senior official) level to promote South Asian regional cooperation. Stemming from initiatives taken by President Ziaur Rahman of Bangladesh and further promoted by the Sri Lankans, a first meeting was held in Colombo in late April and a second in Kathmandu in early November.

In a move which was widely construed as a major step in the gradual but mutually wary improvement in Sino-Indian relations, which had been tentatively improving since 1976, China's Foreign Minister, Mr Huang Hua, visited New Delhi from 26 to 29 June, the first such visit by a Chinese Minister since that of the late Mr Zhou En-lai in 1960. It was agreed to begin discussions on the long-standing border dispute between the two countries, and talks began at senior official level in Peking in December.

In early December the Soviet Union offered to buy 500 million square metres of cloth, worth $500 million, from India each year for the next two decades, an agreement described by *The Economist* of London as 'perhaps the most ambitious deal ever dreamed up in the textile trade'.

The annual report of the Reserve Bank for the period July 1980 to June 1981, released in early October, estimated that the economy as a whole had expanded by 7 per cent of GNP in real terms and that there had been a sharp increase in agricultural production. But the report also predicted that the trend of deterioration in the balance of payments was unlikely to be reversed during the next two years. After very protracted negotiations and much public and private controversy the IMF gave its final approval in November to India's application for a three-year loan of 5,000 million Special Drawing Rights (about US$5,700 million) to finance balance of payments needs.

Even more emphatically than in the previous year Mrs Gandhi was an indefatigable traveller in India and abroad, and official hostess to many foreign visitors, most notably at the Non-Aligned conference of Foreign Ministers in New Delhi (see Pt. XI, Ch. 7). Her own extensive travels took her, *inter alia*, to the Commonwealth conference in Melbourne and to Cancún in October, to Geneva in May and on a ten-day visit to Bulgaria, Italy and France in November. The Presidents of Kenya, West Germany and Botswana respectively made state visits to India during the year. Mr John Biffen, the UK Secretary of State for Trade, attended the fourth meeting of the Indo-British Economic Committee in New Delhi towards the end of January. Mrs Margaret Thatcher, the British Prime Minister, paid an official visit to India from 15 to 19 April, at a time when there had recently been a further increase in Indo-British trade, which reached over Rs 1,450 crores (£845 million) in 1980, and when the UK continued to be India's largest bilateral aid donor. Mrs Thatcher was questioned very sharply and repeatedly at her press conferences about the treatment of Indians in Britain and the implications of the British Nationality Act (see pp. 32-33).

PAKISTAN

The presence in Afghanistan of Soviet troops, estimated to number more than 100,000, continued to influence Pakistan's policies both at home and abroad. By the end of the year the number of Afghan refugees seeking security in Pakistan was estimated by the UN authorities at 2·4 million, the largest concentration of refugees in any country.

The violation of Pakistan's air space and territory by Afghan military aircraft and ground forces continued to increase in frequency. In a letter to Dr Kurt Waldheim, UN Secretary-General, the Pakistan ambassador informed him on 24 October that since April 1979 such violations had numbered 379. Early in December Afghan helicopter gunships strafed two civilian buses, killing five persons, including one woman. President General Mohammad Zia-ul-Haq informed the Pakistani people that 'there was a pattern in recent border violations by Afghanistan, and the Government was fully alive to the situation'.

On the diplomatic front Pakistan adopted a flexible approach towards negotiations with Kabul without sacrificing basic principles on the main issues, namely withdrawal of Soviet troops from Afghanistan and a political settlement ensuring full respect for the independence, sovereignty, territorial integrity and non-aligned status of Afghanistan. Towards the end of August the Soviet Deputy Foreign Minister, Mr Nikolai Firyubin, visited Pakistan for an 'exchange of views' on bilateral matters and the international situation. On 22 September the President said: 'Pakistan could not wage war against the Soviet Union. But in international forums and through mutual dialogue Pakistan has told the Soviet Union that their action in Afghanistan would never be accepted.' The Soviet conditions that talks with Kabul should be preceded by a recognition of the Karmal regime, and that Soviet troops would be withdrawn only after negotiations based on the Karmal Government's proposals had succeeded, were equally unacceptable to Pakistan.

The US decision to sell arms to Pakistan, including some F-16 aircraft, triggered off allegations from New Delhi of preparations for war by Pakistan. Islamabad maintained that its efforts to modernize its defences were motivated solely by its wish to preserve its freedom and independence and that it should not be a cause of concern to India.

The British Prime Minister, Mrs Margaret Thatcher, who visited New Delhi in April and Islamabad in October, was reported in the Pakistan press as having said at a press conference in New Delhi that 'one cannot ask for the right to defend oneself and deny that right to other sovereign nations'. The Pakistan Foreign Minister, Mr Agha Shahi, described Indian fears over the sale of arms to Pakistan by the US as 'unfounded' and called for an armaments dialogue between the two countries. Subsequently, he reiterated his earlier offer to India of a mutual non-aggression pact as a means of allaying fears expressed by India with regard to the American package of economic assistance and military sales to Pakistan. 'If they (the Indians) still think it is a threat to their security,' he said, 'we are ready to enter into a non-aggression pact with them.'

Islamabad repeatedly denied allegations by India, and by some other quarters, that Pakistan was engaged in making a military nuclear device. In an interview published in the *Sydney Morning Herald* on 29 October, President Zia-ul-Haq was quoted as saying : 'We have neither the intention nor the capability of making a nuclear bomb. Pakistan had no option but to acquire nuclear technology for peaceful purposes.' On 19 November Pakistan introduced in the UN General Assembly's main committee two draft resolutions proposing a nuclear-free zone in South Asia, with security guarantees to non-nuclear-weapon states. President Zia-ul-Haq expressed on 4 December the hope that the hand of friendship extended by Pakistan towards India would yield positive results.

In a televised address to the nation on 24 December, the President announced the setting-up of Majlis-i-Shoora (Federal Council) which would perform the functions of an interim parliament. It would consist of about 350 members, nominated by the President. 'The objective underlying the creation of the Federal Council,' General Zia explained, 'is to associate the people in the affairs of the state. These selected leaders of the country are entrusted with the responsibilities of participation, association and advice in the affairs of state. We cannot have elections under the prevailing situation, for Pakistan's internal and external conditions are not ideal in many respects.' The 1973 constitution not having been abrogated, but only suspended, the door was left open for the restoration of parliamentary government at a future date.

On 2 March a Boeing 720 aircraft of Pakistan International Airlines (PIA), with more than 100 passengers on board, was hijacked on an internal flight between Karachi and Peshawar and forced to land at Kabul in Afghanistan. One passenger, Mr Tariq Rahim, an official in the diplomatic service of Pakistan, was shot dead by the hijackers, and his body was thrown out of the aircraft at Kabul airport. Subsequently, the aircraft was flown to Damascus where the hijackers demanded the release of 55 persons who had been gaoled in Pakistan. Pakistan met the hijackers' demands and on 15 March obtained the release of the hostages, whose ordeal had lasted for 13 days, the longest hijack drama in the history of world civil aviation. President Zia-ul-Haq said at Islamabad that the hijacking 'was the result of a deep-rooted conspiracy against Pakistan and was not the doing of just a few misguided youths. . . . This conspiracy was helped by certain anti-Pakistan elements abroad.'

On 29 September an Indian airliner was hijacked from India to Lahore. Pakistani commandos released the hostages in a 45-second operation, and returned them to India.

For the fourth year in succession, the economy attained significant gains in both physical and financial terms. Output and productivity continued to increase at a creditable pace. The budget and balance of payments deficits were kept within manageable limits. The Government's policy of encouraging the private sector provided impetus to investment. The Government let it be known that there would be no more nationalization.

The rate of monetary expansion decelerated from 18·5 per cent in 1979-80 to 14·7 per cent in 1980-81. However, the price pressures increased during the year. This was attributed to the steep rise in the prices of imports, particularly oil and industrial raw materials. The terms of trade showed a severe worsening which neutralized the favourable effect of the export performance on the balance of trade.

The State Bank of Pakistan, in its annual report for 1980-81 on the state of the national economy, concluded with the remark that 'the price situation continues to remain a cause for serious concern', and recommended to the Government that 'it was necessary to curb the rising tendency of prices not only through appropriate demand management policies but by further improving measures on the supply side'.

Growing at the rate of three per cent annually, Pakistan's population in the 1981 census stood at 83,782,000 as against 65,309,000 in 1972 and 32,500,000 in 1947, the year Pakistan won its independence.

BANGLADESH

The continuing political and personal ascendancy of President Ziaur Rahman (see OBITUARY) during the first five months of 1981, his assassination in Chittagong on 30 May in an alleged coup attempt, the declaration of emergency and the smooth assumption of power by the Vice-President,

Mr Justice Abdus Sattar (born 1906), and then Sattar's decisive victory in the presidential election—these were the principal events in another internally turbulent year for Bangladesh. The newspaper *Ittefaq* reported in July that 185 political murders had taken place in the first half of 1981.

Until his assassination the political system of Bangladesh undoubtedly revolved around President Ziaur, who was the chief decision-maker, the founder and head of the Bangladesh Nationalist Party (BNP) and the apparent instigator of virtually all Bangladesh's main policy moves—appointing and dismissing Ministers, for instance, in April, and implementing purges against the army and corruption generally. Repeatedly he had insisted that he had become President Ziaur and was no longer General Ziaur. In the last five months of his life he was characteristically energetic and visible in busying himself with national affairs at home and abroad, travelling indefatigably and promoting causes—notably Islamic cooperation, food aid and South Asian regional cooperation—in which he enthusiastically believed.

Provisional results of the national census held in March 1981 estimated that the population of Bangladesh was 89,940,000, with an average annual growth rate of 2·36 per cent. The country's principal economic problems remained, first, the failure of domestic food production to keep pace with the growth of population, and secondly the heavy dependence on jute for foreign exchange earnings in the prevailing adverse world trading conditions.

Sheikh Hasina Wazed, the daughter of Sheikh Mujibur Rahman, who had lived in exile, mostly in India, since her father's assassination in 1975, was elected president of the Awami League on 17 February. She returned to Dacca on 17 May to mass acclamation from her supporters.

Broadcasts by Chittagong radio, immediately following Ziaur's assassination on 30 May, claimed that a revolutionary council of seven, headed by Major-General M. Abdul Manzur, had taken power, suspending the Constitution, proclaiming martial law, abrogating the treaty of friendship with India signed in 1972 and affirming Bangladesh's claim to South Talpatty (New Moore island). The coup collapsed on 1 June, and General Manzur was said to have been arrested and then shot dead while trying to escape.

According to a government White Paper released publicly in August the abortive mutiny at Chittagong and the assassination of the President were the result of elaborate preparations carefully planned by General Manzur with the help of six of his senior officers. The White Paper described the background to the plot and its planning, preparation, collapse and immediate aftermath. It gave details of the trial of the accused, explaining that, as all the mutineers were army personnel subject to the Army Act, it was decided to try them by court martial and not by open trial in a civilian court. Major-General Manzur was accused of seeking to instal himself as head of a martial-law Government after killing the President.

On 4 June Vice-President Sattar announced that the presidential election would be held within 180 days as required by the constitution, and that he would not himself be a candidate, and on 16 June that the election would take place on 21 September. This was criticized by the opposition groups, who maintained that there would be insufficient time for them to campaign and that the country would still be flooded by the monsoon in September. The Election Commission declared on 27 July that the election had been postponed until 15 October, and it was later deferred until 15 November. A Constitutional Amendment Bill adopted on 8 July enabled Mr Justice Sattar to accept the nomination of the ruling BNP as its presidential candidate.

In the presidential election the Acting President defeated his nearest rival, Dr Kamal Hussain of the Awami League, by a margin of 8,522,717 votes. The 31 candidates together polled 21,607,253 votes, 55·47 per cent of the electorate. Justice Sattar secured 65·8 per cent of the votes cast and Dr Hussain 26·35 per cent.

'Business as usual', consistent with the spirit of Zia's policies, was the motif of those responsible for Government policies from early June onwards. Bangladesh's representatives accordingly played such roles at the UN, in international organizations generally (most notably in the Islamic Conference system, the Non-Aligned Movement and the Commonwealth) and at Cancún. Bangladesh was at pains to maintain cordial relations with all its neighbouring countries, with Nepal and Burma but most notably with China and India. Given the almost circumvallating power of India the last was the most difficult. In August the Ministry of Foreign Affairs issued a White Paper setting out Bangladesh's claim against India on South Talpatty island. In December the foreign secretaries of Bangladesh and India reviewed the question of demarcating the remaining undetermined sectors of their common boundary.

The Aid to Bangladesh Consortium approved aid to Bangladesh totalling $1,350 million for 1980-81 and $1,625 million for 1981-82.

SRI LANKA

The year was marked by communal violence between Sinhalese and Tamils but saw continuing economic growth and the strengthening of links with Britain, the Commonwealth and the Arab world.

Serious disturbances took place in June and August. Police rioted in Jaffna, causing the burning of the public library and market and an attack on supporters of the Tamil United Liberation Front (TULF). This happened during elections for the new district development councils, but did not prevent the TULF from winning all those in Tamil areas. An emergency was declared for one week on 4 June. Further rioting broke out in Sinhalese areas of southern Sri Lanka and a state of emergency declared on 17 August was extended for four months. In protest against these events the TULF, which formed the official opposition, withdrew from Parliament from 8 June until 3 November.

The electoral decimation of the Sri Lanka Freedom Party (SLFP) in 1977 (see AR 1977, p. 271) and the loss of civic rights by its leader Mrs Sirimavo Bandaranaike (see AR 1980, p. 282) strained the party organization. In August the parliamentary leader Maithripala Senanayake and Mrs Bandaranaike's son Anura took over the party's offices after their suspension from party membership. Legal proceedings began between the two factions to determine the ownership of party property and the standing of members suspended and later expelled on the authority of Mrs Bandaranaike. This assumed great importance because of the possibility of losing parliamentary status. By December there were three parliamentarians in the 'Sirimavo' group and four in the 'Maithri-Anura' group and the issue was referred to the Commissioner of Elections on 20 December. On 22 December the SLFP(M), as the press named the Maithripala Senanayake group, had talks with the Lanka Samasamaja Party (LSSP) about forming a united left alliance.

A lesser crisis arose in the ruling United National Party (UNP) over critical remarks made by several politicians during the communal rioting in Ratnapura, strongly suggesting that Tamils were to blame. President J. R. Jayawardene supported the expulsion from the UNP of Neville Fernando, MP for Panadura, on 17 September. Under the constitution this laid Fernando open to exclusion from Parliament and his seat became vacant on 23 December.

The economy was marked by continuing inflation and a balance of payments deficit, and the exchange rate for the rupee dropped sharply in September. Oil drilling was begun in the Gulf of Mannar on 27 September but without result. A new daily English newspaper The Islander was published from November by the politically ambitious businessman Upali Wijewardene.

The Minister of Finance, Ronnie de Mel, presented his fifth budget on 12 November. Estimated expenditure was Rs.38,991 million and income Rs.17,809 million, a gap to be covered largely by foreign aid receipts of Rs.14,190 million. Proposals for new revenue included a 10 per cent surcharge on wealth tax and a business turnover tax for imports and manufacturing industry. Excise on tobacco and liquor and motor car fees were increased. Main expenditure changes included salary and allowance increases for public servants and incentives for the tea, rubber and coconut industries.

President Jayawardene visited Saudi Arabia from 6 to 8 September and Prime Minister Ranasinghe Premadasa went to the Commonwealth heads of government meeting in Melbourne and then to Singapore in October. In Melbourne Premadasa criticized protective tariffs which created serious problems for poorer countries seeking to diversify into manufactures. Premadasa, on a visit to four Asean members in April, had suggested that Sri Lanka might join the Association and after his return from Singapore on 15 October he expressed confidence that this would eventually happen.

Queen Elizabeth and the Duke of Edinburgh visited Sri Lanka between 21 and 25 October for the first time since 1954, and nine years after Sri Lanka became a republic, to attend the celebrations of the fiftieth anniversary of universal suffrage, and were rapturously welcomed.

President Jayawardene celebrated his 75th birthday on 17 September. The president of the Communist Party, Dr S. A. Wickremasinghe, died in Moscow on 29 August aged 80; he had been first elected to the colonial legislature in 1931. Hema Basnayake, the former chief justice, died at 79 in December, while Sir Bennet Soysa, a former senator and mayor of Kandy, died at 93 in October. William Gopallawa, the last Governor-General of Ceylon and first President of Sri Lanka, died on 30 January (see OBITUARY).

NEPAL

Nepal's first direct parliamentary elections since 1959 were held in May 1981, following the amendment of the constitution in December 1980. All 112 elective seats were contested in the 140-member Rashtriya Panchayat (Parliament). The other 28 members were appointed by King Birendra. About 1,100 candidates contested the elective seats, even though explicit party identities were prohibited, the reintroduction of a multi-party system having been rejected in a referendum in May 1980. On 14 June Mr Surya Bahadur Thapa, the outgoing Prime Minister, was re-elected under the new constitutional arrangements by 121 votes as the sole candidate. Two days later he announced his new Cabinet.

On 19 September the exchange rate for the Nepalese rupee was standardized at 13·20 per US dollar. From March 1978 the official rate had been 12 per $ and there had also been a 'second' official rate applied to most merchandise trade except with India, which had been introduced at 16 per $ in March 1978 and had been appreciated to 14 per $ in February 1980.

Throughout the year Nepal's leaders actively sought to extend international recognition for King Birendra's scheme, first mooted in 1975 (the year Sikkim was absorbed in India), that the country be recognized and respected as 'a zone of peace' between India and China. The peace-zone proposal was accepted by China and many other countries, but not by India. Mrs Gandhi's Government continued to be markedly reluctant to endorse anything which would in their view dilute their 'special relations' with Nepal.

India's Foreign Minister, Mr P. V. Narasimha Rao, visited Nepal in late November, and was followed by the President of India, Mr Sanjiva Reddy, who began a four-day state visit on 7 December. In November Kathmandu was the scene of a second meeting of foreign secretaries of seven South Asian countries to promote regional cooperation.

Chapter 3

SEYCHELLES—MAURITIUS—BRITISH INDIAN OCEAN TERRITORY—
MALAGASY—COMORO STATE

SEYCHELLES

ON 25 November a group of mercenaries seized control of Pointe Larue international airport, ten miles from Victoria, capital of the Seychelles, apparently as a first step in an attempt to overthrow the socialist regime of M Albert René and install his ousted rival, Mr James Mancham. According to the Seychelles Defence Ministry, the attackers, who had arrived as tourists on a scheduled flight from Swaziland, were armed with rocket-propelled grenades, rocket launchers, hand grenades and submachine guns. The Ministry's communique continued: 'After very heavy fighting at the cost of very few casualties, the defence forces, which included the police force and the people's militia, succeeded in dislodging the mercenaries and regaining full control of the airport.' Most of the mercenaries escaped, taking the dead body of one of their number, by hijacking an Air India plane which had landed for refuelling in the midst of the battle, and forcing it to proceed to Durban.

There 44 men were detained by South African police, but 39 of them were released on 2 December. The remaining five, who were allowed out on bail, would be charged, provisionally, with kidnapping. The Seychelles Government claimed to have captured five of the assailants, who would be charged with murder or conspiracy to murder. Those charged in South Africa included the probable leader, Colonel 'Mad Mike' Hoare, aged 62, a notorious Irish soldier of fortune.

South African complicity was strongly suspected by the Seychellois, but the Pretoria Government denied it vigorously. It was no secret, said South Africa's Foreign Minister, that there were at least two militant dissident Seychelles groups, which had several times approached his Government for help in their plans to overthrow the René regime, but 'on each and every occasion their representatives had been told that it was not the policy of the South African Government to concern itself with adventures of this nature'.

The South African decision to release most of the mercenaries brought an outcry in the Seychelles, in black Africa and elsewhere round the world. Mr Kurt Waldheim, the UN Secretary-General, said the decision 'cannot but encourage those who contemplate such grossly illegal actions as hijacking and the reprehensible use of mercenaries'. The Seychelles Government called for a UN inquiry into the whole affair, to which the Security Council agreed. In Washington a State Department spokesman said that the United States was in contact with six other countries that had signed a 1978 agreement to cease all flights to a country refusing to extradite or prosecute hijackers, but no such penalty was in fact imposed on South Africa, which indicated that the released men could still be charged with hijacking. To the Pretoria Government's embarrassment, it was revealed that several of the mercenaries were South African army reservists, and one of them claimed that he was a senior serving officer in South Africa's intelligence service. In London, Seychelles exiles claimed that they had backed the attempted coup, financially and otherwise. A fuller account and explanation of the mismanaged affair awaited the trials of the mercenaries in South Africa and the Seychelles in the new year.

The adverse effect on tourist traffic, a major source of foreign exchange worth £33 million a year, was immediate but apparently short-lived, despite the imposition of a 10 pm to 5 am curfew. In March the Seychelles rupee was revalued by 15 per cent, a move which made the country more expensive for visitors but had the desired effect of cutting inflation from double figures to 4 per cent. President René's 1982 budget was orthodox and he continued his gradualist and pragmatic policy.

The Seychelles remained strictly non-aligned, denying any sort of military commitment to either global power group and receiving economic aid from both East and West and from the Arab world. A new lease of the American satellite station was negotiated at an annual rental of £1¼ million until 1990.

MAURITIUS

The year was very much a pre-election period, as the Labour Government under Sir Seewoosagur Ramgoolam held on to its power largely by avoiding major confrontation issues and by not calling Parliament. The prospects for a return of the Labour Government, which had been in office since independence in 1967, had been much lessened by a split in the right-wing party, the PMSD, which under the flamboyant leadership of Mr Gaston Duval had given support to Labour over the past four years. The split threatened to put two right-wing candidates into many constituencies at the next election, often against the Labour candidates, and could thus benefit the marxist-based MMM opposition led by the dynamic and effective Mr Paul Bérenger, who very nearly brought electoral victory to his party in the 1976-77 election.

In spite of continuing economic difficulties—and a running battle for aid from the IMF and World Bank, which had provided bridging loans to reduce the balance of payments deficit, but on onerous terms and with forthright criticisms of the country's ability to manage itself—Mauritius continued to be a rare example of a politically stable, small (one million people), independent, multiracial country maintaining a free press, a free judiciary and an independent unarmed police force. So far, the marxist-based opposition had pursued its aims within the island's constitutional framework, and even its stirring-up of the trade unions—in which it was strong, and through which it had, in the past, closed Port Louis docks and done great harm to the economy—had slackened more recently. These facts may explain why international agencies, and governments of a wide range of developed countries, continued to try to help Mauritius through its problems.

Although, strategically, Mauritius continued to attract the attention of the great powers interested in the Indian Ocean, its economy was dominated more by sugar and world prices. The London *Economist* suggested during 1981 that technological innovation was bringing nearer the day when sugar could be turned economically into petrol, but this good long-term news for Mauritius could not be much comfort in the shorter-term period, with oil in glut.

At least one of the many delightful tourist hotels on the island had installed solar systems to provide hot water. The tourist industry's continued growth confirmed the broadening attraction of Mauritius.

BRITISH INDIAN OCEAN TERRITORY

The controversy over the status of Diego Garcia and the future of its erstwhile inhabitants re-emerged midway through the year. On 29 June talks opened in London between the British Government and an all-party delegation from Mauritius. The discussions focused on additional compensation for the former inhabitants of the Chagos Archipelago resettled in Mauritius. The Foreign and Commonwealth Office announced that a further £300,000 would be added to the £1,250,000 offered as a final settlement of Britain's obligation to the evacuees. This was rejected as inadequate by the Mauritian delegation, which sought an additional £8 million. When the negotiations adjourned without agreement on 2 July it was understood that a solution would be pursued through diplomatic channels.

Diego Garcia, which is claimed by Mauritius, remained a sensitive political-strategic issue. On 13 August the British Government disclosed its previous agreement to US plans to expand the island's military facilities in order to accommodate B52 bombers on a regular basis. This heightened military profile ensured that the Chagos archipelago would remain the focus of the littoral states' attention in their increasingly polarized debate over the superpower naval presence and the possible transformation of the Indian Ocean into a 'zone of peace'.

MALAGASY

The dislocation of the Malagasy economy (seen in shortages not only of imported goods, such as spare parts, but also of food, notably rice) continued to have side-effects throughout 1981, some direct, some indirect. The Government of President Didier Ratsiraka, avowedly socialist and non-aligned, sought ways of improving relations with the West, a task made easier by the arrival in power of the Socialists in France.

In February violent clashes between police and university students, which led to deaths, were the culmination of a long educational malaise which had been progressively politicized. In March the elderly Monja Joana, leading opponent of the regime, detained in December 1980, joined the National Front for the Defence of the Revolution, the ruling coalition which had been in power for four years, and was subsequently released. He also denounced those who used his name to destabilize the regime. In November there were further disturbances in the capital Antananarivo, instigated more by unemployed youths than by students.

COMORO STATE

The regime of President Ahmed Abdallah was one of those which was apprehensive about the change of Government in France, because the traditionalist Abdallah had been installed in power in 1978 after a mercenary-conducted operation led by the notorious Colonel Bob Denard, and the French left had been highly critical of the continued presence of mercenary officers training the 300-man presidential guard. Even before May there had been rumours of an attempted coup, and illegal tracts were distributed.

286

SOUTH ASIA AND INDIAN OCEAN

In October President Abdallah visited the Elysée and found common ground with the French President on the question of Mayotte, which was claimed as one of the Comoro islands but which had voted in 1975 to remain French. The French Socialists favoured in principle the reintegration of Mayotte with the independent Comoro state. No calendar for such a development was revealed. The Comorian President did publicly declare, however, that there was nothing to stop France maintaining its base on Mayotte in the event of reintegration.

IX SOUTH-EAST AND EAST ASIA

Chapter 1

MALAYSIA AND BRUNEI—SINGAPORE—HONG KONG—BURMA—
THAILAND—INDONESIA—PHILIPPINES—VIETNAM—KAMPUCHEA—LAOS

MALAYSIA AND BRUNEI

DATUK Sri Dr Mahathir Mohamad Iskandar became the fourth Prime Minister of Malaysia on 19 July. His predecessor, Datuk Hussein Onn, had announced in May his intention to resign, on grounds of ill health, as president of the dominant party within the ruling National Front coalition—the United Malays National Organization (UMNO)—and as Prime Minister. Dr Mahathir was elected president of UMNO in June in an uncontested poll which settled the succession to highest national office. Datuk Musa Hitam, who was elected deputy-president of UMNO, became Deputy Prime Minister and also Minister for Home Affairs in place of Tan Sri Ghazalie Shafie, who assumed the portfolio of Foreign Affairs.

Dr Mahathir set the tone of his new Administration by extolling virtues embodied in the Malay slogan: *bersah* (clean), *cekap* (efficient) and *licin* (smooth). To serve these ends, he introduced a clocking-in system for civil servants and enlarged the category of people obliged to declare their financial assets. He indicated his international priorities by according, in September, full diplomatic status to the office of the Palestine Liberation Organization in Kuala Lumpur and by his refusal, in the same month, to attend the meeting of Commonwealth heads of government in Melbourne.

In October, an underlying tension in Anglo-Malaysian relations came to a head when Dr Mahathir announced that all future government purchases of British goods and services had to be cleared first by his office. He stated subsequently: 'We will buy British when it is absolutely necessary, when your prices and services are way ahead, but otherwise I think we will show a definite preference for non-British sources.' This policy of open discrimination was precipitated by a decision by the London stock exchange to adjust its rules in order to make surprise take-over bids more difficult to execute. In September, Malaysia's National Investment Corporation, acting through British agents, had secured control of Guthrie Corporation, which owned large plantations in the Federation, by means of a 'dawn raid'. Dr Mahathir construed the decision by the stock exchange as a deliberate attempt to frustrate Malaysia's policy of securing national control of national assets.

In June, Datuk Harun Idris, former Chief Minister of the state of Selangor, then serving a prison sentence for corruption and criminal breach of trust, stood successfully for one of the posts of vice-president of UMNO. In August, he was granted remission of sentence and released. Although he was permitted to assume his party office through ministerial dispensation, he was refused a royal pardon which would permit him to stand in a parliamentary election and hold an office of state. The 1966 Societies Act was amended in April to require any club, society or association to register either as a political or as a non-political body. Any comment on government policy made by a society in the latter category would incur the risk of deregistration. The passage of an amendment to Article 150 of the constitution empowered the King to declare a state of emergency in any circumstances should he believe that a threat was posed to public security.

In January, the Government announced the defection and return to Malaysia from China of Musa Ahmad, the chairman of the proscribed Malayan Communist Party. In July, the Government expelled three Soviet diplomats allegedly involved in espionage. They also detained, in this connection, Siddiq Muhamad Ghouse who had served as political secretary for seven years to Dr Mahathir, then Prime Minister designate.

In March, Tan Sri Abdul Rahman Yakub resigned as Chief Minister of the state of Sarawak in favour of his nephew and former federal Minister for Federal Affairs, Datuk Abdul Taib Mahmud. In the same month, elections for the state assembly in Sabah were won overwhelmingly by Berjaya, the ruling party, which secured 43 out of 47 seats contested.

A sustained improvement in relations between Brunei and Malaysia was indicated in March when the Chief Minister of Sarawak, Tan Sri Yakub, paid his first official visit to the sultanate a week before he retired from office. He was accompanied by his successor, Datuk Taib. In April, Sultan Sri Hassanal Bolkiah travelled to Indonesia, where he was received by President Suharto. Acting Foreign Minister General Maraden Panggabean announced that the Association of South-East Asian Nations (Asean) would welcome the membership of the sultanate after it had attained full independence. In June, a representative from Brunei attended, as an observer, for the first time ever, the annual meeting of Asean Foreign Ministers.

SINGAPORE

Mr J. B. Jeyaratnam of the Workers Party won a by-election in the Anson constituency held on 31 October. He became the first opposition politician to gain election to the Legislative Assembly in over thirteen years. The by-election followed the death of President Benjamin Sheares in May (see OBITUARY) and the appointment of Devan Nair, the sitting People's Action Party (PAP) member, to succeed him as head of state. Mr Jeyaratnam polled 7,012 votes against 6,359 votes secured by Pang Kim-hin of the PAP in his sixth attempt to challenge the political monopoly of the ruling party. In December, when Mr Jeyaratnam took his seat in Parliament, a fierce clash ensued between him and Prime Minister Lee Kuan Yew over the introduction of amendments to the anti-corruption law.

Cabinet reshuffles in January and April indicated the continuation of a process of political self-renewal initiated by Lee Kuan Yew in order to provide for effective political succession. Four senior Ministers relinquished office, including two founder members of the PAP: Dr Toh Chin-chye, Minister of Health and one-time Deputy Prime Minister, and Jek Yeun-thong, Minister of Culture and, concurrently, high commissioner in London.

China's Premier, Zhao Ziyang, visited Singapore in August. Prime Minister Lee Kuan Yew informed him that his Government would have to make up its mind about political priorities in South-East Asia. It could not expect to enjoy friendly relations with the majority of countries of the region and, at the same time, reserve the right to intervene in their internal affairs through support for insurgent movements. Premier Zhao's failure to respond to this admonition did not obstruct the conclusion of an agreement to exchange trade representatives.

In September, Singapore served as the venue for a meeting between three Kampuchean resistance leaders, who issued a joint declaration committing them, in principle, to the formation of a coalition Government in opposition to that established in Phnom Penh by Vietnamese force of arms. In November, when negotiations in Bangkok between the respective factions had reached an impasse, Deputy Prime Minister Sinnathamby Rajaratnam and Foreign Minister Suppiah Dhanabalan intervened personally to promote an alternative loose coalition. In Bangkok, Mr Rajaratnam held out the prospect of his Government's supplying arms to such a coalition, which proved a matter of contention at a meeting of Foreign Ministers from Asean in December. Differences between Singapore and Malaysia on this issue persisted with the first visit by Dr Mahathir to the island state in his capacity as Prime Minister in December.

In February, the Singapore Airline Pilots Association was fined for taking illegal industrial action. It was subsequently deregistered and a new union formed in which foreigners could only be associate members and could not hold office. In July, the new Changi airport was officially opened. It had been constructed at a cost of £250 million and was designed to handle ten million passengers a year.

HONG KONG

Export growth was less buoyant than import growth in the early months of the year, but from May onwards the balance improved and for the last three months exports were almost a quarter ahead of those a year earlier, while the trade deficit was a fifth below the comparable 1980 level. Real economic growth was about 8 per cent. The main weaknesses were a 17 per cent increase in consumer prices, an excessive growth in bank credit, for both consumption and property development, and a lack of real growth in industrial wages since March 1979.

Sluggish wage levels were caused by the large influx of labour from China in 1979 and 1980 and a consequent increase in unemployment, which however remained well below European and North American levels. Measures to stop illegal immigration introduced in 1980 appeared effective in reducing the influx from China. In the second half of the year manufacturing activity and the visible trade balance improved and prices of shops, offices, flats and land for development dropped as supply increased. In October the Governor announced a large increase in the government flat-building programme and exclusion of the cost of land in fixing the sale price of cheap government flats. The Government authorized the extension of the underground Mass Transit Railway along the north side of Hong Kong Island and of a waterfront highway parallel with it, and commissioned an engineering study for a new airport on an island off central Lantau. Modernization of the Kowloon-Canton railway continued and the very rapid growth of traffic made it clear that much greater space was required in the Kwaichung container terminal.

Sir Murray MacLehose made clear his wish to retire, after several extensions of term, and the appointment of Sir Edward Youde to succeed him as Governor was announced in December. Proposals were made for the setting-up in 1982 of district management committees and partly-elected district advisory boards to secure local advice and participation. The relationship with neighbouring areas of China developed further, and in order to facilitate access for people and goods between Hong Kong and the adjoining Shenzhen Special Economic Zone the Chinese authorities decided to move their customs and immigration controls to the further side of the zone. There were again statements by senior Chinese leaders indicating their wish to maintain the mutual benefits resulting from the prosperity of Hong Kong.

BURMA

President Ne Win informed the fourth Congress of the Burma Socialist Programme Party (BSPP) on 8 August that he would cease to be head of state in November, when a new Government was formed following the quadrennial elections in October for the National Congress and for People's Councils at state and lower levels. He proposed to remain as Chairman of the BSPP for a further four years, so retaining control of affairs while avoiding the day-to-day burdens of government and preparing for an orderly succession when he relinquished power. On 9 November the new National Congress elected the Council of State and the Council of Ministers. Brigadier-General San Yu, who had until August been Secretary-General of the BSPP, was elected Chairman of the Council of State, and so President of Burma. The Prime Minister and other senior Ministers were re-elected, but serving officers holding civilian posts, including Ministers, were required to resign their commissions.

U Ne Win's steps to achieve reconciliation with his opponents, including amnesty, honours and pensions, persuaded a large number of Burmese politicians to return home, but were less successful in bringing the minority races back into the fold. The Karen National Union rejected the gesture and there was fighting between the army and Karen, Shan and Naga groups. The Burmese Communist Party (BCP) guerrillas were less aggressive and engaged more in drug smuggling to make up for reduced Chinese support, while trying to revive their activities in the central (Burmese) areas. The new Chinese Prime Minister paid his first overseas visit to Rangoon in January. The Chinese, however, while promoting discussions between the Government and the BCP, still gave the BCP guerrillas essential support.

The change towards greater use of market forces and private initiative produced further encouraging results. Economic growth in 1980-81 was 8·3 per cent, and 5·7 per cent was forecast for 1981-82. The use of incentives and new crop strains produced a 1980-81 rice harvest of over 13 million tons, nearly half as much again as in 1975, and increased output of wheat, maize, jute and cotton. Output of mineral oil began to recover after declining in 1980, and three new onshore oil fields, which were expected to double known reserves, were discovered. New farming methods resulted in greater domestic demand for oil products, and construction of a third nitrogenous fertilizer plant was begun. Larger crops also strained storage capacity and the transport system. The official rate of inflation fell below 5 per cent per annum from over 30 per cent in 1975, but reliance on foreign loans had by 1980-81 raised the ratio of debt service to export earnings to 28 per cent. There was, however, no sign that U Ne Win would permit use of foreign or domestic equity in place of government borrowing.

THAILAND

There was a minor further incursion by Vietnamese troops into Thai territory in January, and in June the Vietnamese Deputy Foreign Minister threatened to repeat the larger June 1980 attack if Thailand should repatriate large numbers of Khmer refugees without the permission of the Heng Samrin regime in Kampuchea. There were also reports of new Vietnamese formations being moved up to the border. The threat of invasion created less alarm than in 1980. Nevertheless the authorities continued to improve the equipment of the forces and to increase their numbers. Four new army reserve divisions were founded, to be built up to full strength over several years, as were ranger units composed of local armed civilians who could relieve the regular army of routine internal security tasks.

The security forces claimed to have eliminated all Communist Party of Thailand (CPT) major bases except some in the south. Loss of support from China and of sanctuaries in Laos and Kampuchea, combined with internal dissension over strategy, weakened the CPT guerrillas. There were also defections by radical intellectuals, although it was feared that some of those returning to Bangkok might be doing so in order to engage in urban terrorism.

Differences between the Social Action Party (SAP) and the Chart Thai, the two main political parties represented in the Government, and the customary opposition in Bangkok to efforts by Ministers to rectify distortions in the economy led to the resignation of the Commerce Minister in January and in March to a bitter dispute between Chart Thai and SAP Ministers over oil supply arrangements; the SAP, including the Deputy Prime Minister in charge of the economy, Boonchu Rojanasathien, left the coalition. In March General Prem Tinsulanonda reshuffled his Cabinet, giving military and police officers more posts than civilian politicians. There was disillusionment with the disputes and indecision in the Cabinet and on 1 April a coup was attempted by a group which included the deputy commander of the army, the commander of the first military region around Bangkok and a group of colonels known as the Young Turks, a combination which would formerly have proved irresistible. General Prem, however, had support from the King and in the navy, the air force and military regions outside Bangkok, and the coup rapidly collapsed. Its leaders were retired from the army and pardoned; there were subsequently rumours of further coup attempts.

In the autumn round of retirements and promotions General Prem retired as commander of the army and Major-General Arthit Kamlang-ek, who had played a leading part in resisting the coup, was promoted to command the first military region. In August General Kriangsak, who was a former supreme commander of the armed forces and Prime Minister, won a by-election in the north-east handsomely and attracted substantial support in the Lower House as a possible alternative Prime Minister. In order to strengthen his own support in the Lower House General Prem persuaded the SAP, but without Boonchu, to rejoin his Cabinet.

The economy suffered from a low level of domestic savings for investment, due partly to artificially restricted interest rates, a large trade deficit and rising foreign debts, an inefficient bureaucracy and the vested interests of bureaucrats, businessmen, students and workers in Bangkok. The 1980 trade deficit amounted to some US$ 2,500 million. It continued to rise in the first half of 1981. On 12 May, however, the baht was devalued by about 1 per cent against the US dollar and again by 8·7 per cent on 15 July. This action, together with higher interest rate ceilings and good crops, helped to check the outflow of capital, to stimulate exports and to raise the return in baht terms to farmers and other primary producers. Little improvement was visible in the performance of the bureaucracy. Bangkok, however, seemed to react less violently than in the past to sharp increases in retail prices for food, petroleum products, electricity and transport. Despite these increases consumer price growth was a third less than in 1980.

The fifth five-year plan beginning in October was designed to improve the opportunities, output and incomes of the poorer sections of society, especially in the rural areas, to rectify structural distortions and to decentralize and improve the efficiency of public administration, while policy for industry was to be designed to produce exports, greater efficiency and more jobs. With this in mind the budget for 1981-82 concentrated heavily on productivity and services in the rural areas. The first flow of natural gas was brought ashore in August through the newly-completed pipeline from the Gulf of Thailand, giving prospect of large reductions in energy imports. There were further gas strikes and, onshore, a commercial oil strike.

INDONESIA

The approach of general elections, due in May 1982, increased government sensitivity to criticism, both at home and abroad. Although political campaigning was supposed to be limited to a short period before the elections, the government party, Golkar, became increasingly active in the rural areas. President Suharto devoted much of his National Day speech in August to stressing the role of the armed forces in upholding the constitution and the state ideology and in ensuring stability. There were renewed public campaigns against corruption, especially in state

corporations and in the judiciary; over 50 judges and 15 public prose-
cutors were dismissed, transferred or reprimanded. Bans were
announced on gambling and on television advertising, partly to please
devout Muslim voters, but in the latter case perhaps for fear of creating
excessive economic expectations in rural areas.

A criminal procedures law was passed in a more liberal form than originally proposed, following sharp criticism by lawyers in Parliament. A
presidential decree provided that former Communist Party members and
political detainees might vote in the elections, while in December it was
announced that the death sentences on two leading figures connected
with the Gestapu coup of September 1965 (see AR 1965, p. 354) had been
commuted to life imprisonment. The Government was caused some
embarrassment in December by the leaking of a report to the President
by members of the appointed East Timor provincial assembly which
described corrupt and brutal behaviour by the forces in the territory. In
the UN General Assembly, however, the majority for a resolution critical
of Indonesia was virtually halved as compared with 1980.

The budget presented in January included large increases in subsidies. The cost of those on fuel and on rice, wheat and sugar rose by
over four-fifths and that on fertilizers by almost half. Including
recurrent and development expenditure, domestic revenue and foreign
aid, the budget was again balanced. Over two-thirds of domestic
revenues, however, came from oil corporation taxes arising mostly
from sales abroad and production with little connection with the main
domestic economy. Revenues from economic activity other than oil
were well short of recurrent expenditure, so tending to exert
inflationary pressure. Nevertheless, the official price index, which
covered a limited range of basic commodities and services, the most
important of which were heavily subsidized, rose by under 10 per cent,
a distinct improvement on 1980.

The rice harvest was over 22 million tons, three-fifths above the 1971
level. Crude oil production began to rise again, but was still below the
1977 level, while oil prices declined in real terms. Liquid natural gas
output levelled off, pending the construction of new liquefying plants,
and earnings from other export commodities fell by a third. There was in
consequence a prospect of a sharp fall in government revenues, and the
budget prepared at the end of the year provided for reduced recurrent
expenditure, including reductions of over one-third in food and fuel
subsidies and no increase in civil service pay. Development expenditures,
however, were to increase by over one-third to 55 per cent of the total
budget, including a two-thirds increase for education and large allocations for agriculture and communications.

PHILIPPINES

With an eye to the new American Administration and to the Pope, who paid a pastoral visit in February, President Marcos took further steps to make his regime look more liberal, without weakening his control. On 17 January he formally ended martial law, which he had introduced in September 1972. In preparation for this change he signed a number of new decrees providing him with wide powers in the field of security and public order to replace permanently those provided temporarily under martial law, including powers of preventive arrest and immunity for himself and his officials for acts performed in office. In theory he ceased to issue decrees after 17 January, but in practice further decrees followed during the rest of the year, all dated just before 17 January, while decrees issued under martial law remained in force. Nevertheless demonstrations and strikes occurred which would have been suppressed under martial law and there was some lessening of authoritarian pressure, although Mr Marcos took powers in August to appoint judges for new trial and appeal courts to replace all the existing lower courts.

Having lifted martial law, Mr Marcos announced that a presidential election would be held in May. He then had the constitution, introduced under martial law in 1973, amended in 1976 and of doubtful validity, changed again to replace the proposed transition to a parliamentary form of government led by a Prime Minister by a system providing for a dominant presidency. Under this version the President was to be directly elected for a six-year term, to be eligible for further terms of office and to have powers to issue decrees and to nominate and dismiss the Prime Minister, who could also be dismissed by the Assembly. Ministers were to be controlled by the President and merely supervised by the Prime Minister. The President could also dissolve the Assembly. On 7 April these changes were put to a referendum which, according to the Government, supported them. The opposition, which nevertheless did better than expected, described the referendum as a 'complete farce', with widespread cheating and vote-buying.

The presidential election was held on 16 June. The main opposition grouping decided to boycott the election, having failed to get the permitted campaigning period lengthened to 60 days or themselves represented on the Election Commission. In an attempt to force voters to turn out the Election Commission was reported to have issued summonses to 6·5 million people who had not voted in the April referendum. The official claim for votes cast for Mr Marcos equalled about 70 per cent of eligible voters. Mr Marcos was sworn in on 30 June and subsequently appointed the Finance Minister, Cesar Virata, as his first Prime Minister.

Mr Virata also became Chairman of an Executive Committee set up to act as head of state should the President be incapacitated.

Economic growth in 1980 was down to 4·7 per cent, below earlier forecasts, and there was little improvement in 1981. Rice output failed to reach expected levels because of bad weather and the rising price of fertilizer, and the Agriculture Minister suggested in the autumn that a shortage might develop. Domestic oil production fell to half the levels forecast in 1979, and demand for and prices of leading export commodities were depressed. As a result export earnings fell, import costs rose sharply and the trade and payments balances deteriorated, the international reserves declined and external debt and the debt service ratio rose. The inflation rate was also higher than in other Asean countries and, as returns on capital fell and several of the larger business groups encountered difficulties, the financial system came under some pressure.

VIETNAM

The growing drain on manpower and resources created by the occupation of Laos and Kampuchea, the pressure exerted by China along the northern frontiers, internal resistance (notably in the Central Highlands), the need to make some return for military and economic aid received from the USSR and inept policies and management continued greatly to depress the economy, which still suffered from acute shortages of food and essential consumer goods. Better weather, higher prices for farm products and the beneficial effects on productivity of greater reliance on incentives and individual enterprise resulted in some improvement in food supplies, although the failure to organize an efficient transport system made it difficult to move surpluses produced by the individualist southern farmers to deficit areas.

By the winter the product contract system, which had produced a distinct improvement in output where it had been tried, had spread to four-fifths of collectivized farms in the north. Under this system plots of land were allocated for several years to individual peasants, families or groups who agreed to supply set amounts of produce from these plots. They still received work points for collective work done, but were also entitled to some or all of the surplus over quota from their own plots on which they had carried out operations such as transplanting, cultivating and harvesting.

In industry and other urban occupations state concerns began to make use of piece rates, and small private enterprises employing up to 20 people were allowed to undertake production or services. In parts of the south the authorities also began, it was said with excellent results, to allow private middlemen to undertake the purchase of produce such as pigs from farmers for sale to state agencies. Larger-scale manufacturing, however, continued to suffer acutely from the managerial incapacity of the cadres and from shortages of energy, raw materials, components and spare parts. Inadequate light industrial production and the siphoning-off of food products, including rice, for export to the Soviet bloc led to major shortages of incentive goods, with the result that higher payments to the peasants for produce, piece-work wages and—for administrative and government workers—cost-of-living allowances induced rapid inflation.

Throughout 1980 and 1981 an effort was made to weed out the more incompetent and conservative cadres, at senior ministerial as well as lower levels, and to bring in younger men with some technical and managerial competence, whatever their class origins. Nevertheless these economic policies, although successful in improving output, were ideologically heterodox and strongly disapproved of by the many rigidly orthodox leaders and rank and file of the Communist Party of Vietnam (CPV). In the summer the election to the chairmanship of the State Council of a former Secretary-General of the CPV, Truong Chinh, whose ruthless efforts to impose collectivization had in 1956 provoked northern peasants to revolt, and the advance of another hardliner, To Huu, within the party made it appear for a time that the 1979 changes would be abandoned. Popular discontent with the existing system, however, even in the north, and the favourable results reported from experiments with more liberal methods, persuaded the tenth plenum of the CPV in November to agree to support incentives and extend the product contract system to all agricultural cooperatives. It seemed that, for a time at least, pragmatic economic policies would be followed.

KAMPUCHEA

The greater part of the country was reported to be troubled by increasing guerrilla activity by the Khmer Rouge and other opponents of the Vietnamese occupation and more Vietnamese troops had to be brought in to try to stem the deterioration. Nevertheless the area under crops in 1980 had almost doubled. This resulted in a winter harvest of some 700,000 tons as against 400,000 in 1979 and a considerable reduction in the food aid required, so that many refugees returned from the Thai border areas. The weather in 1981 was less favourable. There were both floods and drought, as well as mismanagement by officials, and a reduced winter crop was expected.

The chief political assets of the Heng Samrin regime in Phnom Penh were still fear of the return to power of the Khmer Rouge and appreciation of the less restrictive economic and social conditions now permitted.

This interest in greater freedom was recognized by the inclusion in a draft constitution of protection for small industries and of the right of peasants to buy and inherit land. The regime's principal source of weakness was popular distrust of the Vietnamese. Vietnamese-style elections for the regime's National Assembly were held on 1 May. Heng Samrin as President and Pen Sovan as Vice-President and Defence Minister were both accorded votes of over 99 per cent. The existence of a People's Revolutionary Party of Kampuchea was revealed in May when it held what was described as its fourth congress. Pen Sovan, who had lived in Vietnam from 1954 to 1978, was elected Secretary-General of the Party. He was, however, replaced as Secretary-General by Heng Samrin on 4 December, possibly because he had shown signs of becoming too independent of Hanoi and of leaning instead towards Moscow.

LAOS

There were reports that members of resistance groups operating in Laos had received training in China and from the Khmer Rouge in Kampuchea, and in May China and Vietnam each accused the other of incursions across the China-Laos border. Shots were exchanged across the Mekong between Lao and Thai troops on 7 February and the Thais closed the two main river crossings for a fortnight. In the autumn, however, a new ten-year agreement was signed for the sale of electricity from the Nam Ngum dam to Thailand and the Thais also undertook to consider the opening of a third border crossing opposite Savannakhet; this would greatly assist the shipment of goods between northern and southern Laos. As part of its efforts to revive the economy by using market forces and private enterprise, the Lao Government had itself earlier issued instructions to abrogate all regulations which hindered the free movements of people and most goods within Laos in order to try to assist the development of free markets and to 'encourage private citizens to act as agents in selling and buying goods'.

Chapter 2

CHINA—TAIWAN—JAPAN—SOUTH KOREA—NORTH KOREA

CHINA

Politics. At last, nearly five years after his death, the Communist Party of China published on 29 July its official verdict on Mao Zedong. This was part of a long 'Resolution on Certain Questions in the History of our

Party . . .'. A distinction was drawn between the man and his 'thought'. The man was regarded as having made vital contributions in building the Party and army, winning nationwide victory, establishing the People's Republic and 'in advancing our socialist cause'. But for the last twenty years of his life he became tyrannical and pushed an economically and socially disastrous leftist line, culminating in the Cultural Revolution which, 'initiated by a leader labouring under a misapprehension and capitalized on by counter-revolutionary cliques, led to domestic turmoil and brought catastrophe to the Party, the state and the whole people'.

However, the true intents of the Resolution were revealed by the attempt to produce a balanced view of Mao which would not be too divisive in its implications. Thus Mao's mistakes were those of a 'great proletarian revolutionary' and he was stated to have been alive to threats posed first by Lin Biao and then by Jiang Qing and the rest of the Gang of Four. His foreign policy of safeguarding China's unity and national security was also praised. Mao Zedong 'thought', however, was defined as the 'synthesis' of China's experience in applying marxism-leninism, to which many outstanding leaders made contributions as well as Mao.

The sixth plenary session of the Central Committee (26-28 July), which passed the Resolution, also made important changes in the leading personnel of the Party. Hua Guofeng, who was criticized in the Resolution for leftist errors after Mao's death, was demoted from the post of Chairman to Vice-Chairman, ranking seventh and last. The following new appointments resulted from what were officially described as elections by secret ballot by the members of the Central Committee: Hu Yaobang, Chairman of the Central Committee; Zhao Ziyang, Vice-Chairman (ranking fourth); Deng Xiaoping, Chairman of the Military Commission; and Xi Zhongxun, member of the secretariat. The Standing Committee of the Political Bureau was to comprise the Chairman and the six Vice-Chairmen, Ye Jianying, Deng Xiaoping, Zhao Ziyang, Li Xiannian, Chen Yun and Hua Guofeng.

The personnel changes and the Resolution on Party history may be regarded as the culmination of Deng's ascendancy, which had been built up stage by stage since his return to high office in 1977. But his appointment as Chairman of the Military Commission, which had hitherto been the concurrent post of the Party Chairman, suggested that his personal political weight was required to deal with the armed forces and that his ascendancy was by no means unchallenged.

In China's 'new historical period'—the official description—both the Communist Party and the People's Liberation Army, which had lost much popular prestige, continued to undergo painful readjustments. The Resolution on Party history also set forth what it described as ten 'key pointers' for the future, of which economic construction was identified as the central task to which all other work 'must be subordinated'. The significance of this for the Party and the army was already apparent from the economic reforms already undertaken. Both were being required to be reformed and to give up many of their dominant positions in Chinese society. Thus the call of the fifth Central Committee Plenum of February 1980 to establish a proper division of work between the Party and Government administrations led to many uncertainties and bureaucratic resistance. By the end of 1981 a major effort was launched to rectify the Party's style of work and to tackle various common malpractices of bureaucratism and corruption. The effort was spearheaded by a long series of excerpts from Deng Xiaoping's speeches and reports (many hitherto unpublished) in issue No. 21 of *Red Flag*, the Party's theoretical journal.

The army, which was no longer attracting China's best and brightest and was receiving a progressively smaller share of the national cake, appeared to become the main centre of opposition to the new reforms. The army newspaper became the leading source for accusations of 'bourgeois liberalism' against various writers. In effect the journal was presenting itself as the centre of Maoist orthodoxy against the trend towards giving greater licence to intellectuals and—by implication—to professional experts. In particular a film script by the army writer Bai Hua became a *cause célèbre*. Protected by high political leaders, he continued writing after making a mild self-criticism. By the end of the year the simmering controversy about the extent of tolerable cultural freedom was brought to a head by an attack by Hu Qiaomu (the influential head of the Chinese Academy of Social Sciences) on the orthodox guidelines for relating literature to politics set out in Mao's 'Yenan Talks' of 1942.

Earlier in the year the trial of Jiang Qing and her associates, known as the Gang of Four, together with the six old generals of the Lin Biao confederacy, ended in Peking on 25 January. Jiang Qing and Zhang Chunqiao, who alone had defied the court, were sentenced to death with a two-year reprieve. The others were to be imprisoned for periods ranging from sixteen years to life.

Government: The fourth Session of the National People's Congress, attended by 3,154 deputies, was held in Peking between 30 November and 13 December. Major reports were delivered by Premier Zhao Ziyang on the work of the Government and by Finance Minister Wang Bingqian focusing mainly on economic affairs. Laws were passed on income taxes for foreign enterprises and on economic contracts. A draft law on civil procedures was accepted in principle. Premier Zhao's report was notable not only for its analysis of economic affairs but also for its attack on the 'intolerably low efficiency resulting from overlapping and overstaffed administrations with their multi-tiered departments, crammed full of superfluous personnel and deputy and nominal chiefs who engage in endless haggling and shifts of responsibility'. The Premier said that the State Council had formally decided to restructure its own departments and to prune its staff rigorously with the aim of improving its efficiency and giving a lead to other levels of government. At the same time the State Council would seek to define by statute the specific duties and limits to the powers of officials and their departments.

Sun Yat-sen's widow, the internationally well-known Soong Ch'ing-ling, died in Peking on 29 May at the age of ninety (see OBITUARY). Shortly before her death she had been made honorary Chairman of the People's Republic.

The Economy: In his report to the NPC, Premier Zhao stated that the total output value of industry and agriculture in 1981 increased by only 3 per cent over 1980. This was less than the 5 per cent which had been planned originally, but it reflected the decisions taken late in 1980 and in February 1981 to revise the plan in order to reduce the yawning budget deficits which fuelled inflation. As a result the budget deficit was expected to be 2,700 million Yuan (down from 12,700 million Yuan and 17,000 million Yuan deficits of 1980 and 1979 respectively). However it was felt that the basic balance between state revenue and expenditure was still unstable. Financial outlays could not be reduced indefinitely. Part of the problem was that China's new economic policies had the effect of reducing governmental revenue. The Premier also predicted that the sixth five-year plan due to begin in 1982 would continue for its duration the policy of readjustment (originally scheduled to end in 1982), so that more rapid rates of economic growth would not be possible until the following five-year plan.

The policy of economic readjustment, however, was judged to be successful even though the reforms were painful and often led to new problems and uncertainty. Peasant income continued to rise. According to the Premier's report, 'with increased purchasing prices for farm and sideline products and the reduction of tax burdens in some rural areas, state revenue fell by 52,000 million Yuan from 1979 to 1981 while peasant income increased accordingly'. At the same time, in the urban sector jobs were found for more than 20 million people, and this together with wage rises and the reduction in state revenues meant that the urban employed benefited by 40,500 million Yuan in total increased income. Concurrently, an important shift took place in the proportion between consumption and accumulation in state revenues: the former rose in 1981 to 70 per cent from 63·5 per cent in 1978, while the latter correspondingly fell.

Agriculture witnessed a profound change in organization and patterns of output. The established commune structure was progressively dismantled, especially in the poorer areas, in favour of a variety of 'responsibility systems' whereby households contracted to produce a certain quota with the right to market independently any surplus. This yielded a large growth in cash crops, and grain production rose to over 320 million tons to register the second most successful harvest on record. This was all the more remarkable in view of the terrible droughts in north China in the spring and the flooding in the south-west in the summer. Nearly 1,000 million Yuan was spent on disaster relief, and for the first time China called on UN relief funds for assistance. The value of heavy industrial output continued to register a decline, estimated in 1981 at 5 per cent. Light industry registered a 12 per cent growth in output value on top of the 18 per cent registered the previous year. The majority of enterprises were allowed measures of independent decision-making on resource procurement and marketing.

Nevertheless massive weaknesses remained. Use of energy remained highly inefficient. Forty per cent of China's 100-million-ton oil production was burnt in almost crude conditions for electricity generation. The intention to switch more to coal still remained to be realized. Industry was especially uneconomic in its use of energy, though some progress was achieved. The inefficiency in the Chinese urban economy was remarkable not only in comparison with capitalist countries, but even in Chinese terms. Every 100 Yuan invested in capital construction now yielded 11 Yuan as opposed to 22 Yuan during the first five-year plan (1953-57). Transport posed yet further problems.

But perhaps the most deep-set problem concerned China's population growth. Despite great success in limiting it in urban areas and moderate success in the countryside, the continual population pressure on the scarce arable land and the limited urban areas was increasingly evident even to the casual Western visitor. This was reflected in the growth of American exports to China, comprising grain and other agricultural primary products. Indeed a World Bank report predicted that by 1985 the value of US exports to China (currently over $8,000 million) would exceed that of Japan (currently $13,500 million). The value of China's overall trade reached about 10 per cent of its GDP. A positive trend was the growing proportion of manufactured goods in China's exports. The export of machinery increased by about 50 per cent in 1981, and industrial products made up well over half of China's exports. Generally China's total foreign trade was estimated as 10 per cent up on the previous year and it was also thought to be broadly in balance.

Foreign Relations. Late in 1980 Peking's dominant leader, Deng Xiaoping, was supposed to have listed three long-term tasks for China: continuation of the struggle against alleged Soviet hegemonists, reunification of Taiwan and economic construction. Perhaps it was consciousness of the Soviet occupation of Afghanistan which caused China's leaders to emphasize in South Asia the need to ameliorate local disputes. For its part China sought to improve relations with India. Following a visit there by Huang Hua, the Foreign Minister, an Indian delegation came to Peking to resume negotiations on the disputed border after an interval of nearly twenty years. Meanwhile, impressed with the difficulties faced by the Soviet Union and by China's need for international tranquility in which to concentrate on its domestic economy, China's leaders began to aver that a world war was no longer inevitable, and some even speculated that the Soviet Union might have begun to decline as a world power.

The reunification of Taiwan posed particular problems with the United States. On the eve of the 70th anniversary of the 1911 Revolution, whose leader Sun Yat-sen is revered on both sides of the Taiwan straits, Peking's most senior leaders made great concessions towards peaceful unification. Taiwan would be allowed to retain its economic system and its own armed forces and its leaders would be offered a share in the government of China as a whole. The Reagan Administration continued to insist on America's right to sell arms to Taiwan. As a result Sino-American relations grew tense. Chinese official commentaries denounced US advocates of such arms sales in increasingly virulent terms. As the year ended the senior State Department official responsible for Asian affairs was due to visit Peking to try and mollify the Chinese Government. But the omens were far from positive, as each side's room for manoeuvre was strictly limited.

TAIWAN

As the People's Republic of China (PRC) made its most serious concerted attempts so far to prepare the way for political reunification of Taiwan with the mainland, and as Kuomintang (KMT) leaders sought to thwart such attempts by referring to the province's social, political and economic well-being, based on the principles of the party's founder Sun Yat-sen, the economy of Taiwan appeared to falter. For the first time in 18 years Taiwan was reported to have a budget deficit, and another was expected in 1981-82, confirming the cumulative effects of high energy costs, the world recession, increased protectionism, competition from similar economies such as South Korea and Hong Kong, and domestic wage inflation.

Petrochemicals and construction encountered particular difficulties, the brunt being borne mainly by small labour-intensive companies. Raw materials for the petrochemical industry, which provided a third of Taiwan's exports and a third of its manufacturing jobs, cost more than in the United States or in oil-producing countries. The construction industry suffered a recession as the Government, worried by inflation and property speculation, adopted restrictive monetary policies. Weaker companies had to resort to black-market credit at annual interest rates reported to be 35-40 per cent; meanwhile demand was depressed and some over-extended companies collapsed.

To help restore competitiveness the Government devalued the currency by 4·86 per cent against the US dollar on 12 August, fixing the new rate at NT $38 to the US $. Among Taiwan's competitors, South Korea had devalued in 1980 and the Hong Kong currency had been allowed to depreciate in 1981. Other decisions raised the number of overseas banks permitted to operate in Taiwan, and included plans to give foreigners access to the Taiwan stock market, subject to rules encouraging long-term investors. Another sign of Taiwan's attempt to conform to international practices was the announcement of regulations to prevent trade-mark counterfeiting and false marking of place of origin, to take effect on 1 August. Foreign companies had complained of lost sales and damaged reputations resulting from Taiwan firms' counterfeiting products such as vehicle parts, sporting goods, clothing design and cosmetics. Under the regulations, manufacturers and exporters applying to export goods bearing trademarks must prove their authority to use them.

The search for a fresh approach to economic problems was evident in a major Cabinet reshuffle on 23 November, which included a new Minister of Finance, Hsu Li-teh, formerly finance commissioner of the Taiwan provincial government, and a new Minister of Economic Affairs, Chao Yau-tung, formerly chairman of the China Steel Corporation. Both appointments were ascribed to the need to reinvigorate the rather conservative financial establishment and to promote the transformation of Taiwan into a technology-intensive industrial area. Chiu Chuang-huan was appointed Vice-Premier, Lin Yang-kang Minister of the Interior, Soong Chang-chih Minister of National Defence, Lien Chan Minister of Communications, Lee Teng-hui governor of Taiwan and Shao En-hsin major of Taipei: all except Soong Chang-chih were native Taiwanese. Another important change was the appointment of Chen Shou-shan, also a native Taiwanese, as head of the Taiwan garrison command, the province's highest security force. The command had received adverse publicity in the United States after the death in Taiwan of Chen Wen-cheng, an assistant professor at Carnegie-Mellon University, Pittsburgh, after questioning on 2 July about alleged activities in the US in support of the Taiwan independence movement.

In local government elections on 14 November, the first since those of November 1977 when rioting followed allegations of ballot-tampering, there was a turn-out of nearly 77 per cent in the poll for the Taipei city council and 72 per cent in those for the provincial assembly and for mayors and magistrates. Of successful candidates for the assembly and councils 129 were members of the KMT and 41 were classified as independents; of the mayors and magistrates 15 were KMT members and four were independents. More of the elections were contested than ever before and they appeared to have been conducted without incident.

In international affairs, the PRC's initiative on reunification brought increased efforts to commit the new American Administration to an even more overtly supportive policy towards Taiwan, translating into action earlier Republican statements of support, which had angered the PRC. Taiwan wanted the US to supply the F-16 fighter as a replacement for the obsolescent F5E. Had the US agreed, the sale would have been more valuable politically than militarily, since the People's Liberation Army was still equipped with obsolescent MIG 19s and MIG 21s. In refusing, but extending the agreement for manufacture of the F5E under licence in Taiwan, the US pleased neither Taiwan nor the PRC. While Taiwan's relations with the US had become an issue in the US-PRC strategic relationship, the development and diversification of international relations through trade offices continued. Taiwan ranked 20th in the world trading and 16th in the world exporting league-tables: foreign trade in the January-November period was US $40,300 million, an increase of 11·9 per cent compared to the same period in 1980; exports were up 15·4 per cent at US $20,707 million, and imports up 8·4 per cent at US $19,593 million. International relations were also promoted through technical cooperation: of the 81 agricultural demonstration teams and technical missions sent to developing countries in the past 20 years, 40 remained in 22 countries.

JAPAN

Viewed from Tokyo, 1981 was a year when everybody was out of step except Japan. No other nation seemed as anxious as Japan to get on with the job of earning a living. Nobody else sought to come to terms so quickly and effectively with the second oil crisis—the one about prices, following the one about prices *and* supplies. The OECD said of its only Asian member: 'Japan's economic performance outclassed that of every other Western industrial country in dealing with the oil shocks.'

Only Japan appeared to be able to keep unemployment within acceptable limits; it even worried when the percentage 'surged up' to 2·39 per cent in May, the highest level since the 2·45 per cent of February 1959. Trading partners with workless percentages in double figures were hardly likely to be carried away with admiration.

Somehow, in a world in deep recession, Japan's real growth of GNP

continued fastest among OECD members, though few Japanese considered the targeted 4·7 per cent for 1981 to be proper growth compared
with the heady years of the late 1960s and early 1970s. Productivity, too,
remained buoyant.

Perhaps more important than transient figures was the fact that Japan
was taking the industrial problems of the age much more seriously than its
competitors. Every advanced nation found itself lumbered with basic industries that had outlived their time, their usefulness or their facilities, yet
faraway Japan seemed to be the only one learning to live with the present.
Far older industrial powers demanded time to put their factories and plants
in a state to offer 'fair competition' to their Japanese counterparts; they
called it 'restructuring'. Japanese industrialists were probably too busy
planning developments for the next decade to ponder what sort of time-
scale the West had in mind. Ten years was one European forecast, possibly
deduced from a keyless calculator. But was Japanese industry supposed to
mark time for another ten years (car exports to the UK alone had been
under restraint since 1975) until the West caught up, and then go hand-in-
hand into the 21st century? Didn't Japan's wartime adversaries have a
phrase 'The speed of the convoy is the speed of the slowest ship'?

It was progressive and innovative industries like automobiles and
electronics (and even restructured shipbuilding) that were enabling Japan
to ride out the economic storm, even though half of its vehicle exports
were under foreign curbs. Western consumers' spending might be cut by
the recession, but they still wanted all the cars and television sets and
videotape recorders Japan could supply because they apparently liked
the quality, the price and the after-sales service, plus the fact that the
goods were there. Was it wrong to have anticipated buying trends for
years ahead in countries 5,000 or 10,000 miles away, simply by
employing marketing skills long familiar in the West?

On the other hand, Japan was growing used to foreign exporters
calling its system of distributing domestic and imported products a non-
tariff barrier that resembled the Rubik Cube in its complexities. Yet the
system had served Japan well for 300 years and still did (and incidentally
employed a lot of labour). When Japan's turn had come to penetrate
world markets over the past 12 or 15 years, had there been any *cri de
coeur* from Japanese exporters about the distribution system of 140
countries now taking Japanese products? Not that anybody could recall,
including Japan's trading rivals, who were now becoming decidedly
vocal because that nation's performance as a seller far exceeded its pro-
pensity as a buyer, especially of manufactured goods. Like oil, trade was
now politics. Japan was bombarded with threatening protectionist
phrases from Washington and Brussels (the former adding strong hints
that Japan should increase its defence spending and take over some of
America's Pacific burdens).

Japan's accent on exports instead of increased domestic consumption as the solution of economic problems made its US and EEC trade surpluses snowball spectacularly, because those partners either could not or would not return the compliment. The partners said 'could not', because the Japanese market was closed (a slight exaggeration, seeing that the country bought $140,000 million worth of goods overseas in 1981); Japan said 'would not', meaning that its market was most definitely open but foreigners were not trying hard enough to sell. The truth was that Japan was no market for slouches; only if foreign manufactures were as good as or better than the domestic equivalents could they hope to succeed in such a highly competitive environment.

Trade surpluses became the stuff of friction, and America was growing ever more conscious of feeding Japan raw materials and getting back superlative manufactured products in return. The new Reagan Administration went to the aid of its ailing automobile industry —already second to Japan in 1980 and 1981—by stemming the rising tide of Japanese car imports. Too late in the day America realized that Japan had merely been teaching it a lesson of substituting small vehicles with low petrol consumption for the traditional gas-guzzlers. But the forced concession to the US alerted the EEC, which saw itself as the recipient of additional Japanese export largesse.

At the eye of the trade storm was Mr Zenko Suzuki, the Japanese Prime Minister, who, when sworn into office a year before, might have defined economics as the art of being economical. Now, having learned something about economics, he had to be a trade expert as well. He bustled round the capitals of six of the Ten and EEC headquarters at Brussels; possibly surprised and delighted their leaders by assuring them that the countries of Western Europe and Japan 'are all blessed with hard-working citizens'; and became 'acutely aware of the necessity further to promote mutual understanding between Japan and Europe . . . on the foundation of consistent and continued exchange and dialogue between our peoples'.

Exchange and dialogue certainly continued throughout the year. The European media, the Eurocrats and the EuroMPs saw to that. The media had Mr Suzuki badly word-mangled on his 'peace mission' and promised further ructions at the Ottawa summit in July. In actuality the various leaders 'said it with flowers' (or flowery phrases) as was their wont; even Britain's Prime Minister Mrs Thatcher merely wagged a finger while talking to Mr Suzuki at the summit about Japan's trade surplus with her country. Come to think of it, what Prime Minister could order his people (especially 117 million Japanese) to buy foreign if they preferred home products?

However, Mr Suzuki persuaded Keidanren (Japan Federation of Economic Organizations) to send a fact-finding delegation of leading industrialists, bankers and businessmen to Europe in October and they got the rough side of their counterparts' tongues in the various capitals. They returned to Japan somewhat bruised and professing surprise at the seriousness of the European economic and unemployment situation. With Japan in possession of the world's finest information-gathering facilities through its giant trading companies, Keidanren should not really have been surprised. Still, as there had been no let-up in the European demand for Japanese consumer products, they probably thought the reports of the Continent's early economic demise had been slightly exaggerated. The analogy of a dying man hastily spending his fortune did not occur to them.

Anyway, Mr Suzuki, still playing the boy on the burning deck, pressed Cabinet colleagues, businessmen and bureaucrats to come up with something positive to solve the recurring trade frictions. He ended up with a 'Task Force' and a package bringing forward by two years the complete programme of import tariff reductions scheduled under GATT, together with some modifications of Japan's more irritating non-tariff barriers. In fact, 1,600 import duty cuts due up to 1984 were to be effected by April 1982. After years of prodding, Britain managed to get a slice off Japanese duties on whisky, confectionery and biscuits and the Japanese were thus able to extract one small thorn from their own flesh.

So Mr Suzuki set the scene for a merrier Christmas and a happier new year (he hoped) in foreign parts, but at home he took an axe to his Cabinet. Fifteen out of 20 heads fell—an old Japanese custom, nothing personal. Expectation of life for a Japanese Cabinet Minister over the past 20 years had been nine months, because there had been 26 new or re-shuffled Cabinets in those two decades. 'Hardly enough time to make a serious mistake,' remarked one political pundit. Therefore no Minister sacked (or, rather, temporarily suspended, because his number could come up again in a year or two) was too downcast, except perhaps Mr Sunao Sonoda, who had succeeded Mr Masayoshi Ito as Foreign Minister only in May and now gave way to Mr Yoshio Sakurauchi, making three different Foreign Office heads in seven months.

Mr Ito had found himself the centre of controversy because the Washington joint communique commemorating Suzuki-Reagan talks mentioned 'the alliance between Japan and US'. An *alliance*—that was something new. Or was it? No new military implication there, Mr Suzuki assured his Diet. But Mr Ito felt obliged to resign and the Prime Minister doubtless resolved always to glance through communiques before publication in future, even those running into hundreds of words.

During his short reign at the Foreign Ministry, outspoken Mr Sonoda perpetrated what politicos called 'slips of the tongue'. For instance, it was alleged, 'joint communiques are not binding'. They may or may not be, but was there any need to say it? The man chosen as one of Japan's best-dressed in 1978 became a sartorial target, too: a weekly periodical reported that one parliamentarian had taken exception to Mr Sonoda's wearing tinted glasses, a gold bracelet, a diamond tie-pin and a ruby ring ('It's not ruby, it's coral sent by a relative in the coral business,' said his wife). 'These show the taste of a *nouveau riche*—foreigners get the impression that Japan is a *parvenu* nation', declared the parliamentarian. Obviously, whatever Mr Sonoda's political achievements, looking like Diamond Jim Brady while performing them was strictly *de trop*. So it was curtains again—until the next time. And the call could come from Mr Suzuki himself, only 18 months ago an unknown pressed into the premiership, now impressive enough to be described as possibly a second Eisaku Sato, who was Japan's Prime Minister for a record 7 years 8 months. No two-year Premier he!

SOUTH KOREA

Chun Doo Hwan was formally inaugurated as President for a seven-year term on 3 March 1981, but anxiety about economic difficulties and continuing student protests persisted. Those authoritarian institutions largely destroyed after President Park Chung Hee's death in October 1979 were reinstated: a pliable parliament, a pervasive surveillance, indirect presidential elections and a controlled press. In the course of the year emergency measures were relaxed somewhat but daily restrictions remained.

Elections to a new electoral college on 11 February produced a massive victory for the President's Democratic Justice Party, which won 3,676 of the 5,278 seats, making Chun's election a formality. His victory was further strengthened by elections to the National Assembly, on 25 March, in which his party won elected seats in all the electoral districts except one in South Cholla province and one in Cheju island. However, the victory was flawed by the absence of a credible opposition, following the dissolution of the main political parties and the banning of over 800 politicians in 1980.

Three major amnesties in the course of the year freed some 7,000 prisoners. On 25 September, responding to international pressure, the authorities admitted to holding 3,000 people under a security law permitting imprisonment without trial. Most detainees, however, were common criminals and the number of political prisoners was probably not more than 500. The amnesties did not affect two leading opposition figures: Kim Dae Jung and Kim Jong Pil remained in prison, though the former had his death sentence for sedition commuted in January to life imprisonment following international appeals for leniency. At the end of May Kim Young Sam, the former leader of the banned New Democratic Party, was released from house arrest.

Beneath the appearance of calm, political life became increasingly polarized. Authoritarian military figures were firmly in control, while the liberal element comprising moderate politicians, clergymen and intellectuals was largely eliminated. Students, long recognized as the staunchest advocates of democracy, continued to engage in anti-government protests despite stern disciplinary measures. Their demonstrations fluttered briefly in the spring but were even more marked when the colleges reopened in October. The university authorities responded by expelling or suspending scores of students. Although these protests constituted no serious threat to government, their persistence in the face of considerable repression testified continuing unease. The tenor of student protests changed, becoming explicitly anti-US and anti-Japanese.

Chun received an important gesture of support when on 2 February he became the first head of state to visit President Reagan. At the meeting the USA agreed to sell South Korea 36 F-16 jet fighters. Previously President Carter had refused South Korea's request for F-16s because of the country's alleged violation of human rights. Washington also appealed to Tokyo to grant economic aid to South Korea to help it over its economic problems. Japanese aid in 1981 was $80 million but in the autumn Chun asked Japan for a further $6 million in credits and $4,000 million in private investments and bank loans. The funds were needed to fuel South Korea's five-year economic plan due to begin in 1982. Foreign debts were high at $30,000 million at the end of the year, while unemployment rose, although reliable unemployment statistics were not available.

Despite continuing economic difficulties and protests President Chun felt strong enough to lift the thirty-year-old curfew with effect from 6 January 1982, except in sensitive border areas, a measure calculated to boost the Government's standing as one that had successfully overcome the turbulence of 1980.

NORTH KOREA

Kim Chong Il was named as the 'sole successor' to his father Kim Il Sung at a press conference on 8 October, held to celebrate the thirty-sixth anniversary of the founding of the Korean Communist Party.

Internationally the North Koreans retained their somewhat bellicose image by firing on a US SR-71 Blackbird reconnaissance aircraft on 26 August. The aircraft was on a routine flight of the sort made regularly over many years. North Korean soldiers also fired across the border on five occasions in 1981 but such incidents appeared unlikely to escalate.

North Korea maintained a policy of equidistance in the Sino-Soviet

dispute, both praising the USSR and alternately denouncing 'domina-
tionism'—the North Korean code-phrase meaning Soviet expansionism.
Most striking was its continuing tacit support for Prince Sihanouk of
Kampuchea in clear violation of Soviet wishes. Overseas the North
Korean presence in Zimbabwe grew appreciably in the year.

X AUSTRALASIA AND SOUTH PACIFIC

Chapter 1

AUSTRALIA—PAPUA NEW GUINEA

AUSTRALIA

IN Australia's politics, no major changes occurred, but many elements of instability in detail became apparent, affecting both state and federal levels. At the sole general election, for the legislative assembly and a third of the legislative council of New South Wales on 19 September, the Australian Labor Party (ALP) Government of Mr N. Wran increased its majority in both Houses. This was also the first Australian election in which political parties received grants towards their campaign expenses from government funds. The Liberal and National Country Parties opposed this in principle and did not participate in the scheme, but the result of the election left them in disarray, with disputes over leadership and over the terms of their coalition in opposition.

In Victoria, the Liberal Government was also unsettled by leadership disputes, which culminated in the resignation from the premiership and from parliament of Mr Rupert Hamer in May after nine years in office. At year's end his successor, Mr Lindsay Thompson, had restored a fair degree of stability to the state's Liberal regime, though faced with more vigorous opposition from the ALP. In Western Australia, the Premier, Sir Charles Court, resigned in December after eight years in office and 29 in the state parliament, solely because of age, and was succeeded in Government and Liberal Party leadership by a successor trained and chosen by himself, Mr Ray O'Connor.

The most unstable situation developed in Tasmania, as a direct outcome of confrontation between developmental and environment-protection groups (see AR 1980, p. 315). This dispute related to the building of dams for hydroelectric power development in the hitherto relatively unspoiled mountain and river reserves of south-west Tasmania. Tasmania's industrial strategy had hitherto depended largely on the exploitation of its water resources, and in this process the state hydroelectric commission had acquired great prestige and the support of all major parties, until the environmentalists, with strong support from similar mainland groups, challenged the commission's plans. The ALP Premier, Mr D. Lowe, had some sympathy with the environmental case, and proposed a compromise scheme involving less flooding of 'the wild', but this was rejected by the legislative council's anti-Labor majority, and then by

Mr Lowe's ALP colleagues, who voted him out of office. He resigned from the party, with two colleagues, leaving the new ALP Premier, Mr H. Holgate, without a clear majority. Mr Holgate's Government then held a referendum, offering only a choice between the two dams, but the conservationists advised those preferring no dams to mark their ballots accordingly. The result showed a majority favouring the commission dam, a substantial minority favouring no dams, and a small minority favouring the alternative dam. To escape a possible no-confidence vote, the Government procured the prorogation of parliament and entered on negotiations for a settlement.

In Queensland, the litigation following a split in the ALP opposition (see AR 1980, p. 317) ended in a victory for the 'New Guard'. The Bjelke-Petersen National Country-Liberal Government remained in firm control, but engaged in frequent disputes with the federal Government over land rights for Aboriginals (opposed by Queensland) and over the declaration of a marine park covering the northern part of the Great Barrier Reef, barring mining and drilling; Mr Malcolm Fraser's federal (Commonwealth) Government finally proclaimed the park in November.

In the Commonwealth Parliament, the position of Mr Fraser's Liberal-Country coalition was weakened by internal disputes, by loss of control of the Senate, and by signs of declining public support. In April, the Minister for Industrial Relations, Mr A. Peacock, a senior Liberal leader in Victoria and an obvious candidate for future federal leadership, resigned from Cabinet because of policy differences with Mr Fraser and complaints that the latter was dictatorial in style and had endeavoured to undermine Mr Peacock's position. The rest of Cabinet rallied behind Mr Fraser, and Mr Peacock played little part in parliamentary affairs thereafter.

When Parliament resumed on 18 August after the winter break, as a result of the 1980 general election (see AR 1980, p. 318) the balance of power in the Senate had passed to the five Australian Democrats and an Independent. They and the ALP opposition were pledged not to use their position to force a dissolution, as a Liberal-Country Senate opposition majority had done in 1975, and the ALP introduced an amendment to the Constitution making a repetition of those events legally impossible, debate on which was adjourned until 1982. However, varied interpretation of the pledge caused disputes among the different groups which lessened their effectiveness as a brake on Fraser Government policy.

The first main issue arose over the 1981-82 Budget, opened on 18 August. This was deflationary in emphasis, providing for a small domestic surplus and an overall deficit of only A$146 million. The most contentious item was a considerable extension of indirect taxation, which came as a surprise since earlier in the year the Treasurer, Mr J. Howard, had announced that after studying a possible new indirect tax such as

VAT he had abandoned the proposal because of its likely inflationary effect. He now introduced Bills providing for an immediate increase in the rate of exising sales taxes and the imposition of sales tax as from January 1982 on a wide range of goods hitherto exempt. The ALP Senators wished to reject all the new taxes, on the ground that its pledge applied only to Appropriation Bills and existing taxes, but the Australian Democrats regarded themselves as precluded from interfering beyond a certain point with any important components of the Budget.

Accordingly, when the Bills reached the Senate, the increases in existing taxes were passed, but the new sales taxes were referred back to the House of Representatives, as allowed by the Constitution (which does not permit Senate amendment of such money Bills), with a request that certain of them (in particular those on clothing, books and news-papers) be omitted. The Representatives refused; the Senate majority then 'pressed' the request, thus reviving a long-standing dispute between the Houses as to whether the Constitution permitted such repetition of requests. The Representatives resolved (with ALP support) that it did not, and Mr Fraser announced that the Government would revive the relevant Bill after three months in accordance with the constitutional provisions concerning deadlocks between the Houses. However, the Democrats had meanwhile announced that, if the disputed Bills were brought in again, they would pass them, so this issue ceased to provide a possible basis for an early double dissolution and appeal to the electors.

Subsequently the ALP, Democrats and Independent in the Senate joined to reject outright a Bill dealing with university fees for second degrees which the Constitution did not protect from Senate veto, where-upon Mr Fraser said the Government would keep in mind the option of a double dissolution, and pointed out the disciplinary effect of this on the Senators—including perhaps his own 'wet' followers who had expressed some agreement with the opposition on these issues. But he also said frankly that he was unlikely to seek an early dissolution, the obvious reason being a succession of opinion polls suggesting that if a general election were held during the last quarter of 1981 the ALP would probably be returned to power.

In economic affairs, the record was fair by OECD comparisons. In-flation remained at about 10 per cent, unemployment a little less than 6 per cent of the full-time work-force, and the exchange rate was firm, the foreign trade deficit being more than offset by continued high inflow of private capital. The drought which began in 1980 ended with good winter rains, and the declining world prices for meat and wheat were offset by good harvests; the wool market was firm and stocks were down to 200,000 bales.

Stock exchange prices, however, were sluggish and suffered two con-siderable periods of decline. Industrial disputes increased, many being concerned with a trade union campaign to achieve a 35-hour standard working week; many individual employers and some major groups negotiated settlements which conceded shorter hours, and the economy began to adjust to a probable 38-hour week. The Commonwealth Conciliation and Arbitration Commission finally abandoned its five-year effort at linking industrial peace with regular cost-of-living adjustments and approved agreements depending on 'productivity' deals, because in its judgment the unions had failed to observe the rules of the system; hence the interrelation between collective bargaining and industrial awards became even less predictable.

The 'minerals boom' continued to attract substantial investments, and promising oil flows were achieved in the Cooper Basin of central Australia, but the important coal and iron ore components had to operate at lower prices and profits because of the worldwide downturn in the steel industry. The economic development most damaging to the Fraser Government was a sharp increase in interest rates, including mortgage rates for home buyers. Standard finance company debenture rates reached 16 per cent, and rates for many business and second mortgage purposes were over 20 per cent. Such rates, unknown since the 1930 depression, were particularly resented by the four out of five Australians who were or were becoming home-owners. This caught the Fraser Government in a dilemma, because its general policy favoured non-interference with market developments, while there was much public and parliamentary pressure for intervention.

The polarization of political thought became accentuated by Government policies and by changes in the organization and platform of the ALP. Although long committed to 'small' government and encouragement of private enterprise, the Fraser Government had been cautious about dismantling inherited examples of collectivism, and had been strongly criticized for this by Liberal Party branches. Accordingly, in April a committee of senior Ministers, commonly dubbed 'the Razor Gang', was appointed to recommend reductions in the public service and the winding-up or sale of various government activities. Substantial reductions in the public service were made, chiefly by leaving vacancies unfilled; some unions resisted by rolling strikes and overtime bans, particularly in social security services. The Prices Justification Tribunal was abolished, and many regulatory committees merged or scrapped. The government-owned TAA airline was converted to a public company, but proposals for selling shares to the public were successfully resisted by the Country Party component of the coalition, because of the threat to country air services. Other 'privatizing' proposals, such as selling off government bookshops, were under consideration. The ALP opposition strongly opposed all such measures.

A federal conference of the ALP in July adopted a new national organization, increasing the membership of its governing body to 100, a quarter of whom must be women, and abandoning the 'federal' basis of equal state representation which Labor (like the other major parties) had hitherto used; representation was now to be in scale with regional population. An attempt to strengthen the party's commitment to socialism was narrowly defeated, but narrowly carried was a commitment to introduce a republican constitution, converting the Queen's position in Australia to that of 'Head of the Commonwealth' only.

Greater differences between ALP and Lib-Country foreign policies also became evident. In particular, the US alliance, strongly supported by the Fraser Government, was increasingly criticized by the ALP, and although Mr Tom Hayden, the ALP leader, did not advocate its abandonment, as did some state branches, he pledged a future Labor Government to requiring Australia's full participation in the use of American bases such as the North-West Cape signals transmitter, and a written treaty governing the use of Darwin airport by B52 bombers. The ALP (and much press) attitude to the (British) Commonwealth, shown by derisory comments about the Commonwealth conference at Melbourne in September, was one of indifference rather than dislike, but there was outright opposition to Australian participation in the Sinai peace force favoured by the Liberals, and substantial opposition to many aspects of Fraser Government defence planning.

PAPUA NEW GUINEA

The coalition Government comprising Prime Minister Sir Julius Chan's People's Progress Party, Deputy Prime Minister Iambakey Okuk's National Party, Mr Roy Evara's United Party, Father John Momis's Melanesian Alliance and Mr Galeva Kwarara's Papua Besena continued in office through 1981, despite persistent friction. Mr Kwarara was forced by his own colleagues to resign party leadership in favour of Mr Gerege Pepena; Mr Evara, conversely, was forced out of his Primary Industry portfolio by the Prime Minister, but retained his party leadership. The Prime Minister sacked or forced out of office four other Ministers during the year. These events indicated both a high rate of misbehaviour among national leaders and the powerful cohesive force of high office.

For PNG 1981 was another difficult year. The major export industries—copper, coffee and cocoa—were hit by falling prices; Australian aid continued to fall at the planned rate of 5 per cent in real terms and the 1982 Budget brought down in November was traumatic. Dozens of social, environmental and development projects were swept away, and the public service of 50,000 was cut by 4 per cent, with a 6 per cent cut to come in 1982. In this situation the extravagance of the Chan Government in its first year (1980), when it bought an expensive but obsolete executive jet and prematurely ordered replacement passenger aircraft for Air Niugini, was brought into high relief.

As politics warmed up in anticipation of the May/June 1982 national elections (the second since independence in 1975), government extravagance was a potent issue for the Pangu Party opposition of Michael Somare, and so too was the increasing influence of foreign companies seeking easy pickings in resource industries, especially timber and fish, by dubious methods.

Provincial government, in its third year of full-scale operation, was also an election issue. Mr Okuk (Transport), and Mr Evara initiated cold war against provincial government in late 1980 and early 1981 by persuading a rump Cabinet to let them allocate so-called sectoral funds directly to national MPs instead of the provinces. But by year's end this form of *de facto* recentralization was being widely condemned as irrational and corrupting. Provincial government was proving expensive but still had the benefit of the doubt.

In November the Foreign Affairs and Trade Minister, Mr Noel Levi, at last tabled the White Paper on foreign policy which was commissioned in 1979 under the Somare Government. Most changes had been anticipated in ministerial speeches and the final definitive turn from the Somare policy of 'universalism' ('friends to all and enemies to none') to 'selective engagement' was largely uncontroversial. In the event the White Paper did not identify enemies clearly, and indeed it foreshadowed an exchange of diplomatic missions with the USSR, resources permitting. Nevertheless the Government did move closer to China and Asean during the year. Mr Okuk visited China in May and Mr Levi attended the Asean Foreign Ministers' meeting in Manila in June as a special observer.

Relations with Indonesia, however, remained clouded by the West Papua issue, and full membership of Asean seemed out of the question, while relations with China also suffered from the Mr Okuk's politically opportunistic vist to Taipei later in the year.

It was PNG's burgeoning relationship with the Philippines which loomed largest by December. Not only questionable timber deals involving a threat to the integrity of provincial as well as national government, but also illegal and semi-legal migration and business activities by the 4,000 strong Filipino community, became an election issue as the Government's pacemaker, Mr Okuk, called for a return to traditional (i.e. white) sources of expert recruitment.

Chapter 2

NEW ZEALAND

THE year was dominated by two events: the highly controversial South African Springbok rugby tour, which, in turn, helped Mr Robert Muldoon's National Government get itself re-elected by a narrow margin in December.

The Springbok tour saw New Zealanders more remorselessly pitted against each other than at any time in recent decades, cutting a swathe across class, ethnic, religious and family affiliations, although opposition was generally less pronounced in rural and provincial centres than in the cities. Throughout, the Government steadfastly refused to budge from a policy of discouragement without interference. Against a rising tide of protest from activist bodies such as the Halt All Racist Tours organization (HART) and church, civic, student and women's groups, the Government continued to maintain that it had fulfilled its obligations under the 1977 Gleneagles Declaration which had urged Commonwealth Governments to take active steps to discourage sporting contacts with South Africa. Nevertheless, doubts as to whether Mr Muldoon had in fact done all he could to stop the tour intensified when Mr Ces Blazey, chairman of the New Zealand Rugby Football Union, denied that the Prime Minister had ever specifically asked him to do so.

In the event, the tour's eight weeks between July and September led to over a thousand arrests, disruption of transport and communications, arson against public facilities, extensive, often violent, set-piece confrontations between specially-armed police squads and major demonstrations, the use of the armed forces to support logistically a costly policing operation, the cancellation and obstruction of arranged fixtures, and the country's almost total preoccupation with the issue for much of the year.

Reverberations of the tour echoed at the Commonwealth heads of government meeting in Melbourne. There, Mr Muldoon deliberately went out on a limb to attack the tour's critics and personally denigrate black African leaders, including Mr Mugabe and President Nyerere. Already strained over the tour issue, Mr Muldoon's relations with Prime Minister Fraser of Australia were further upset by the former's castigation of the conference's declaration of principles for relations between rich and poor countries (see DOCUMENTS). There was little doubt among Commonwealth leaders in Melbourne—or New Zealand observers—that Mr Muldoon's behaviour was primarily designed for direct appeal in the forthcoming general election.

In that contest, National was returned to office with 47 seats and 38·9 per cent of the vote; the Labour Party gained 43 seats, but for the second election running actually polled more votes than its rival, while the Social Credit Political League regained the remaining two seats while polling some 21 per cent of the total vote.

The Government based its election campaign on a programme of future economic growth emphasizing major capital investments in steel, aluminium, oil refinery expansion, synthetic fuel from natural gas, forestry and processing. This central plank was maintained notwithstanding the October withdrawal of a key Swiss partner in a planned aluminium smelter and official reservations regarding the employment and foreign exchange advantages of these projects, as well as the Government's lacklustre record in promoting economic growth during its six years in office.

The Labour Party emphasized employment creation, curbs on interest rates, utilization of local skills and resources to promote a diversity of small-scale enterprises, tax reform, the overhaul of existing government programmes and services, and more open, accountable procedures of government. Labour's campaign was handicapped in marginal provincial constituencies by its uncompromising opposition to the Springbok tour, by a drift of its traditional support to Social Credit, and by the general problem of credibility after having spent so much of the contemporary era in opposition. Those seats Labour did win from the Government were in city constituencies.

Although the campaign was a quiet affair, turnout was high, despite obvious disillusionment with both the prime alternatives, six voters in every ten being unwilling to support either major party. A heavy concentration by the news media on the three party leaders probably worked most to Mr Muldoon's advantage.

A younger, more professionally qualified body of new representatives was elected to Parliament, the number of women MPs doubling to a record eight. In the new Government itself, Mr Muldoon settled for continuity and experience; the major surprise was his appointment of the previously inexperienced Mr Warren Cooper as Minister of Foreign Affairs and Overseas Trade.

The economic problems that faced the new Government were daunting. In the year to October 1981, New Zealand had a current account deficit of $950 million in its balance of payments. Although exports increased by 14 per cent, imports grew even faster, by 19 per cent. Because it was an election year, the Government loosened monetary conditions, a policy which pumped up spending and sustained an annual inflation rate of 16 per cent; budgeted a massive internal deficit exceeding $2,000 million; and ran an overvalued exchange rate. Foreign debt reached a record level of $5,000 million—approximately one-fifth of the country's gross domestic product. Exporters remained heavily subsidized, and personal levels of taxation went unrelieved, distorting local investment, worsening costs for essential services, and driving up wage demands. According to official figures, unemployment rose in 1981 to 5·5 per cent, although the real figure was probably higher.

In foreign trade, serious problems were encountered through the failure of Iran to pay for large export orders of lamb. In return for allowing imports of the same product, the US Administration insisted that New Zealand sign the GATT code on subsidies—a potential weapon against numerous New Zealand exports. The New Zealand Dairy Board moved to stabilize the international market through its massive purchase of 100,000 tonnes of surplus butter from the US and a long-term trade agreement, valued at NZ$350 million, to supply the USSR. Progress towards closer economic relations with Australia moved slowly, the main issues that awaited resolution being the phasing-out of export incentives and the dismantling of an import licensing system that had long kept sectors of New Zealand industry over-protected, inefficient and uncompetitive.

In June, the Anzus Council met in Wellington, where New Zealand voiced concern at the Reagan Administration's policy towards the Law of the Sea negotiations. At this meeting US Secretary of State Haig urged Australian and New Zealand participation in the Sinai international monitoring force, and eventually New Zealand agreed to participate with a minor air-service support contribution, subject to joint West European and Australian involvement.

In Parliament, an Official Information Bill was introduced which closely followed the report of the Danks committee (see AR 1979, p. 323). The Bill included a presumption that official information should be disclosed unless there was 'good reason' for withholding it; review of refusal to disclose could be sought through the Ombudsman; an Information Authority would be established to regulate information access; and the Official Secrets Act would be repealed. The Bill drew fire, however, for its inclusion of a clause providing severe penalties for anyone transmitting abroad information deemed likely to harm New Zealand's international interests.

An important social innovation was embodied in Family Courts and Family Proceedings Acts, providing for the establishment of separate family courts less formal, less adversarial and with more specialized judges than the ordinary courts. Fault as a factor relevant to the dissolution of marriage was eliminated. The Government also further amended the controversial 1979 National Development Act (see AR 1979, p. 321) allowing the relevant planning tribunal flexibility in determining review procedures.

In its 1981 annual report, Air New Zealand described 'the most traumatic year in the airline's experience'. Reasons cited for the company's $30 million loss included fuel prices, deterioration of the New Zealand dollar, inflation and a decline in traffic. In April, Justice Mahon produced his report on the 1979 Air New Zealand DC-10 crash on Mount Erebus, Antarctica, indicting the company itself for failure, for that flight, to check accurately its computer navigational system. Air New Zealand was also accused of 'orchestrating a litany of lies' throughout the inquiry. The report and its aftermath helped precipitate the resignation of the airline's chief executive, Mr Morrie Davis.

The year also saw visits to New Zealand by the Queen and the Prince of Wales, the abolition of the Commission for the Future, and a world record for the women's marathon set by local Alison Roe.

Chapter 3

THE SOUTH PACIFIC

THE year was most significant for developments occurring throughout the French South Pacific. On 19 September, Pierre Declercq, independence leader and secretary-general of Union Calédonienne, was assassinated near Noumea. This event was immediately followed by civil and industrial unrest and, in early November, by further rioting and destruction of property owned by whites. The response was indicative of an increasingly strong independence movement in NEW CALEDONIA, campaigning for immediate French withdrawal and condemnation of France as a colonial power. Clearly this movement was unimpressed by the new French Council of Ministers' call for a radical change of policy in New Caledonia and for recognition that the indigenous Melanesians were living in a state of unacceptable inequality—especially over land distribution.

In December, French civil engineers released disturbing news about the physical damage sustained to the nuclear weapons test site at Mururoa atoll in FRENCH POLYNESIA and the consequent leak of radio-active material. This brought renewed protests from Australia, New Zealand and their South Pacific Forum partners about the unabated pro-gramme of underground testing that continued on the atoll during 1981.

At the twelfth South Pacific Forum meeting, held in Vanuatu during August, it was decided that the Prime Minister of Fiji, Ratu Sir Kamisese Mara, would lead a deputation to Paris to discuss with President Mitterrand decolonization of the French Pacific territories. (In July, however, Mr Francis Sanford, Vice-President of French Polynesia's Council of Government, had visited Paris in an abortive attempt to per-suade the authorities to grant the territory full internal self-govern-ment—something supported by all major political groupings in French

Polynesia). The August Forum meeting also condemned the dumping or storage of nuclear wastes in the Pacific, rejected Soviet plans to conduct a marine survey in Melanesian waters, and welcomed a proposal to establish a Pacific Islands Fund to assist smaller island countries.

Also during August Mr Peter Kenilorea, who had led the SOLOMON ISLANDS since independence in 1978, was defeated as Prime Minister by his long-standing personal rival Mr Solomon Mamaloni. This change occurred constitutionally under a system in which Parliament itself can change a Government or a national leader without a general election. The new Government stated as a priority its plans to strengthen provincial administration.

In VANUATU, provincial elections saw a return to public life of some figures previously discredited by the failed secession attempt of 1980. A related quarrel between Vanuatu and France, aggravated in 1981 by the decolonization issue in New Caledonia, and causing the ambassador from Paris to be declared *persona non grata*, was sufficiently resolved by Vanuatu's allowing a resumption of French aid.

In FIJI the Governor-General, Ratu Sir George Cakobau, warned against disruptive political forces within the country. These remarks were aimed at the Fijian National Party and the newly-formed Western United Front, groupings that urged policies clearly favouring Fijian ahead of other communal interests. These developments indicated dissent within the long-ruling Alliance and added a new measure of fragmentation to Fiji's politics. The likelihood that no single party would be strong enough to govern on its own after the 1982 general election was increased.

In WESTERN SAMOA there was a serious, prolonged and socially divisive strike by public servants. Regarded by local observers as easily the most traumatic event of recent times, and involving more than 6,000 employees, this three-month dispute involved union refusal to accept the Government's 8 per cent pay offer. The strike not only damaged Western Samoa's already parlous economy, but was regarded as a direct assault on the country's traditional methods of dispute settlement. Resentment was incurred by the way in which the Government attempted to enlist the social standing of the matais (land title-holders) as a means of influencing strikers to return to work. The Government eventually conceded a settlement in July that was well in excess of what it originally offered.

The final stage in a lengthy, often tortuous legal dispute was reached in London when the Rev. Mr Kaburoro, leader of the Banaban Islanders resident on Rabi Island, Fiji, accepted in April a $14·5 million compensation payment in respect of the British Phosphate Commission's 50-year exploitation of the original home of Banaba (OCEAN ISLAND) in the Central Pacific. Acceptance of compensation indemnified British, Australian and New Zealand governments—original operators of the British Phosphate Commission—against further legal action.

For the South Pacific 1981 also saw the visit of Indian Prime Minister Mrs Indira Gandhi to Fiji; the death of Mr Albert Henry, former Premier of the Cook Islands; a May election defeat for four of the seven sitting People's Representatives in the Kingdom of Tonga; and ratification of the second Lomé Convention with the European Community by Fiji, Papua New Guinea, the Solomon Islands, Tuvalu, Kiribati, Western Samoa and Tonga.

XI INTERNATIONAL ORGANIZATIONS

Chapter 1

THE UNITED NATIONS AND ITS AGENCIES

THE UN suffered another year of frustrations. The decision of President Reagan to conduct lengthy reviews of American policy delayed or complicated negotiations, particularly on disarmament, the Law of the Sea, and global economic and monetary issues. This, together with the intransigence of parties in disputes, encouraged regional bodies or other alignments, such as the Islamic Conference, the Organization of African Unity and the Non-Aligned Movement, to tackle problems themselves and to gravitate towards South-South economic negotiations, as North-South ones made little progress despite the summit meetings at Ottawa and Cancún. The Secretary-General decried the erosion of the system of multinational cooperation

The President of the 36th General Assembly—Ismat Kittani of Iraq—voiced a growing concern that the Assembly needed not new resolutions (despite the 137 items on the agenda) but the political will to implement past decisions. The value of UN expenditures was also questioned, although more than 85 per cent of its resources were for economic and social activities.

In the election of a Secretary-General for five years from 1 January 1982 Dr Kurt Waldheim was prepared to stand for a third term, but Salim A. Salim of Tanzania was favoured by the African and other Third World countries. After 16 Security Council ballots, in which China vetoed Dr Waldheim and the US vetoed Mr Salim, both candidates removed their names and the Peruvian diplomat Sr Javier Perez de Cuellar was recommended unanimously and confirmed by the General Assembly. Sr Perez had been at the UN representing his country and as an under-secretary-general for special political affairs, and had been a special representative for Dr Waldheim in Cyprus and to Afghanistan.

Three new members joined the UN—Antigua and Barbuda, Belize and Vanuatu (New Hebrides), bringing membership to 157. The five states elected for two years to the Security Council from 1 January 1982 were Guyana, Jordan, Poland, Togo and Zaïre, which joined the five permanent members and Ireland, Japan, Panama, Spain and Uganda.

The Assembly was suspended on 18 December, to resume in 1982. Its President decried the absence of evidence of any increasing political will to solve issues and urged members to re-examine their obligations. He deplored the world's nuclear explosive power, which was equivalent to no less than three tons of TNT per person.

The International Year of Disabled Persons, as 1981 had been designated by the UN, aimed at 'full participation and equality' for the world's 450 million disabled. Its efforts were directed towards increasing public awareness of their abilities and needs on national, regional and local levels, and then towards launching practical plans for the first year of a continuing era of understanding and action. More than 120 national committees and liaison offices were formed to carry out plans in prevention, health, education, training and traffic safety; most established long-term programmes.

Disability was especially prevalent in developing countries, because of malnutrition and disease-related insanitary conditions. In the mid-1970s there were an estimated 140 million disabled children under 15 in the world, of whom 120 million lived in developing countries with no access to rehabilitation services. In October a world symposium discussed the problems of developing regions, and focused on their priority needs in the context of their environment.

POLITICAL

MIDDLE EAST. The hesitant disclosure of America's foreign policy and the run-up to Israeli elections on 30 June delayed tackling the Middle East problems, which were further complicated by the fighting in Lebanon and Israel's part in it.

On 7 June Israel attacked the Iraq nuclear plant near Baghdad, claiming it was designed to produce bombs; but in January inspectors from the UN International Atomic Energy Agency (IAEA) had found nothing to suggest the plant did not accord with the Non-Proliferation Treaty which Iraq had signed and Israel had not (see pp. 185 and 201).

The Security Council unanimously adopted a resolution which condemned Israel's bombing, judged Iraq entitled to compensation and urged Israel to adopt IAEA safeguards. The Assembly also condemned the attack, called for redress and later asked the Security Council to prohibit all forms of cooperation with Israel in the nuclear field. When the Baghdad plant had been declared safe IAEA inspectors confirmed the findings of January.

Although the Knesset rejected annexation of the Golan Heights in March, it rushed through legislation on 14 December to impose its laws and administration over the Heights occupied in 1967. The Assembly declared the action 'null and void' and requested the Council to invoke Chapter VII (sanctions) if Israel failed to comply with its resolution. The Security Council unanimously condemned Israel's action and called for it to be rescinded not later than 5 January 1982 or the Council would take 'appropriate measures' (see p. 186).

The UN Disengagement Observer Force (UNDOF) on the Golan Heights was regularly renewed for two six-monthly periods, and the mandate of the UN Relief and Works Agency (UNRWA) for Palestinian refugees was extended from June 1981 for three years, although an $80 million deficit threatened its educational programme.

The precarious position of the UN Interim Force in Lebanon (Unifil), as a buffer between Israel and the PLO and left-wing Lebanese, was further complicated by fighting between the (Syrian) Arab Deterrent Force and the right-wing Falangist militia. The latter, like Major Sa'ad Haddad's Christian force in the south, was supported by Israel. Unifil suffered attacks and abuse from both sides.

In March Major Haddad's forces killed two Unifil Nigerian soldiers and wounded 20 others, of whom one died. Acting for the Security Council its President condemned the action. Under-secretary-general Brian Urquhart visited Beirut, Damascus, Jerusalem and Unifil during April, while Dr Waldheim repeatedly urged a ceasefire in the Zahle area and southern Lebanon.

Clashes and bombing continued, escalating to a crisis over the Syrian siting of surface-to-air missiles. The President of the Security Council, in its name, appealed urgently for an immediate end to all armed attacks. Dr Waldheim sought a ceasefire, through Unifil and the UN Truce Supervision Organization, with Yassir Arafat, who was prepared to accept an informal cessation of hostilities if Israel did; on 24 July the Israelis told a US envoy that Israel accepted a temporary arrangement. Thus both sides agreed to a ceasefire without recognizing each other. The mandate of Unifil was renewed for six months in June and December. As in the November vote on UNDOF, China voted for Unifil, whereas previously it would not take part.

NAMIBIA. Negotiations for Namibian independence stalled as South Africa questioned whether the UN would implement impartially the Security Council's 1978 plan, submitted by the contact group of Canada, France, the UK, US and West Germany. The 'pre-implementation' meeting for a ceasefire was held from 7 to 14 January under the auspices of the UN. It made no headway because of the intransigence of the South African-backed Windhoek Alliance, although the South-West Africa People's Organization (Swapo) leader pledged that, after agreement on the date of the ceasefire, it would surrender 'its title as the sole and authentic representative' of the Namibian people, designated by a UN General Assembly resolution of 1973. Although the contact group insisted that 'only a settlement under the aegis of the UN would be acceptable to the international community', South Africa was relying on the change in US Administration to extract advantages.

In March the General Assembly, by 125 votes to 0, called on the

Council to impose comprehensive sanctions on South Africa. South Africa's credentials were rejected; it had been barred from General Assembly sessions since 1974 by reason of apartheid. On 30 April a Council resolution for comprehensive mandatory sanctions, including an oil embargo, was vetoed by France, the UK and US. A special international conference on sanctions against South Africa from 20 to 27 May adopted a declaration demanding measures to cripple South Africa economically, and another called on the contact group to pressurize South Africa into granting Namibian independence.

In August South Africa attacked inside Angola. A Council resolution condemning it and calling for an immediate withdrawal of troops and compensation was vetoed by the US; whereupon the Assembly met in special session (again South Africa was debarred), called on the Council to adopt mandatory sanctions, and urged the prompt implementation of the Council's independence plan.

The contact group continued to seek a formula for a set of constitutional principles acceptable to all parties. But South Africa launched an attack 150 miles inside Angola, allegedly against a Swapo headquarters. On 10 December the General Assembly recommended that the Council approve a full range of mandatory sanctions; the contact group abstained but no country voted against. A week later the group handed modified constitutional proposals to South Africa and the Windhoek parties.

KAMPUCHEA. The Secretary-General continued his efforts for a settlement of the Kampuchean problem, sending his special representative in March for talks in Thailand, Vietnam, Philippines, Singapore, Indonesia and Japan. Following a General Assembly instruction Dr Waldheim convened an international conference on Kampuchea from 13 to 17 July. The USSR did not attend, nor did Vietnam, Laos and the Phnom Penh regime, which advocated a regional conference between themselves and the Asean countries, with Dr Waldheim as an observer in his personal capacity, followed by a broader conference to guarantee the regional agreements. Some 80 countries were represented at the July conference. It called for negotiations on a ceasefire, withdrawal of all foreign (Vietnamese) forces under supervision of a UN peacekeeping or observer group, elections supervised by the UN, the establishment of a neutral and non-aligned state and a commitment by the five permanent members of the Security Council, together with all states in South-East Asia, to respect the sovereignty of Kampuchea. Delegates proposed a committee for the economic assistance of Kampuchea and development of the states in the region, and established one to follow up the work of the conference. Vietnam and Laos denounced the proposals.

The General Assembly credentials committee again accepted those of the erstwhile Khmer Rouge. On 21 October it called for a ceasefire, withdrawal of foreign troops and elections under UN supervision. A UN team to investigate whether Soviet chemical weapons had been used in Kampuchea, Laos and Afghanistan reported that, as the members were not allowed to visit the sites, they could neither confirm nor deny the American allegations.

AFGHANISTAN. In January the time seemed propitious for a dialogue between Iran, Pakistan and the People's Democratic Party of Afghanistan; accordingly Dr Waldheim appointed Sr Perez as his personal representative to promote a political solution. But Iran would not take part, whereas the Kabul Foreign Minister, at the Non-Aligned meeting in February, appeared ready for such talks.

Sr Perez visited Pakistan and Kabul in April and again in July and August. On 24 August President Babrak Karmal proposed bilateral, trilateral or even multilateral talks with UN participation, but Pakistan insisted that Kabul should be designated only as a party and not as an autonomous regime. On 18 November the General Assembly called for withdrawal of foreign troops and respect for the political independence and non-aligned character of the country, and asked Dr Waldheim to continue his efforts and to explore the possibility of appropriate guarantees for all neighbouring states. Meanwhile the plight of over two million Afghan refugees in Pakistan taxed its resources and those of the UN High Commissioner for Refugees (UNHCR), which was helping to care for 1·7 million of them.

IRAN-IRAQ. The war that started in September 1980 continued spasmodically. Dr Waldheim's representative—Olof Palme—visited the area periodically, attempting to reach a settlement in January, February and June. He then presented both Governments with proposals for the elements of a settlement. Parallel peace efforts were made by the Islamic Conference organization and the Non-Aligned nations, all in vain.

The outstanding issue of the American hostages was resolved. On 19 January President Carter asked Dr Waldheim to inform UN members, the Security Council and the International Court of Justice that Iran had agreed to free the American hostages and had complied with the Council's resolutions and the decisions of the Court. He expressed appreciation of Dr Waldheim's untiring efforts and those of other members of the UN to achieve the hostages' release.

OTHER DISPUTES. The intercommunal talks between Greek and Turkish Cypriots continued, described by Dr Waldheim as 'generally constructive, although, regrettably, with limited practical results'. Hence the renewal of the mandate of the UN force in Cyprus. On 22 April the

Secretary-General's special representative, Hugo Gobbi, announced agreement to establish a committee for tracing persons missing since the Turkish army marched in (1974). As both parties had submitted their constitutional and territorial aspirations, in November the Secretary-General offered his 'evaluation' to identify major points of 'coincidence' between the plans, and suggestions for productive negotiations. The parties agreed to use these as a basis of negotiation.

Following the 1980 General Assembly resolution that Belize should become independent by the end of 1981, the UK negotiated with representatives of Belize and Guatemala, which claimed Belize as its territory. They agreed an outline pact in March, but in July the parties failed to embody it in a treaty. Guatemala asked the Security Council to consider the dispute, but the Council decided independence could not be postponed. It was celebrated on 21 September and four days later Belize became a UN member (see pp. 335-6).

The eight-year-old dispute over the delimitation of the continental shelf between Malta and Libya simmered on, as Malta sought oil. In January Malta claimed that Libya had 'laid down a new condition' for submission of their dispute to the International Court of Justice. Libya told Dr Waldheim that it would ratify the agreement of 1976 provided drilling for oil was stopped pending a decision. Malta insisted that the agreement had been unconditional and pressed for quick action by the Security Council. It met on 30 July, when its President appealed for moderation and Dr Waldheim said he would continue to follow the situation and try to persuade the parties to ratify and exchange their 1976 agreement.

The attempted coup by mercenaries in the Seychelles on 25 November and subsequent hijacking of an Indian plane aroused indignation, particularly when 39 of the mercenaries were released by South Africa. The Security Council condemned the aggression and hijacking and decided that three of its members should investigate the origins and financing of the coup and evaluate economic damages (see pp. 282-3).

DISARMAMENT. Little progress was made on disarmament, although the world's arms bill was estimated at $550,000 million. Concern centered on initiating talks between the US and USSR outside the UN.

In anticipation of the UN second special session on disarmament in 1982 the UN Committee on Disarmament created four *ad-hoc* working groups. They dealt with comprehensive disarmament, banning the development and use of chemical weapons, also of radiological weapons, and an international agreement by nuclear-weapon states not to attack non-nuclear-weapon states. Among the 53 resolutions on disarmament and international security adopted by the General Assembly, it asked the Committee on Disarmament to initiate negotiations on a comprehensive nuclear test ban treaty, a matter previously exclusively dealt with by the UK, US and USSR.

A convention and three protocols restricting the use of booby-traps, anti-personnel mines, fragmentation and napalm bombs was opened for signature on 10 April, when 35 states including the UK signed it, but not the US as it was reviewing policy.

The conference on the Indian Ocean as a zone of peace, planned for 1981, did not materialize because of the sensitive situation there. Again the Assembly adopted resolutions on nuclear-free zones from Africa to South Asia, and Egypt ratified the non-proliferation of nuclear weapons treaty.

ECONOMIC

DEVELOPMENT. Pressures for global economic negotiations continued at the UN, but were deadlocked. At the Ottawa summit there was a slight thaw, and at Cancún in October both the UK and the US agreed to participate in global negotiations, but 'on a basis to be mutually agreed' (see pp. 373-4).

The disadvantaged position of the Least Developed Countries (LDCs) became a major concern of the UN, which organized a conference of more than 140 countries in Paris from 1 to 14 September to transform the economies of the LDCs. They comprised 31 countries, 21 of which were in Africa. In the past they had received less aid per person than the middle-income developing states, and only 18 per cent of the aid given. The conference made no breakthrough, but provided some promissory notes. Aid donor countries tentatively agreed to try to double their aid to the LDCs or provide them with 0·15 per cent of their GNP in aid, but without a time-schedule. The programme also provided for individual aid consortia for as many of the LDCs as requested them.

Commodity agreements were negotiated for cocoa and tin under the auspices of UNCTAD, and for textiles assisted by GATT. After a lively battle UNCTAD adopted a resolution for the gradual conversion of flags of convenience into conventional ship registers, as the developing countries believed this would help them to develop a fairer share of world shipping.

ECONOMIC AND SOCIAL COUNCIL. At its first session the overall UN economic and social body ECOSOC rubber-stamped many resolutions of the Human Rights Commission, and debated issues of population, drug control, the status of women, agrarian reform, problems of youth and of the aged. Again it was concerned with refugees and displaced persons in the Horn of Africa.

ECOSOC gave high priority to conditions in South Africa, condemned apartheid, racism and collaboration with Pretoria by Western states and

Israel. It invited the Security Council to consider mandatory sanctions against South Africa, and endorsed support for national liberation movements and freedom of association for black unions.

The July session focused on the deteriorating world economy and the dilatory global economic negotiations. Dr Waldheim warned that unless there was a change of policies people living in absolute poverty could exceed 800 million in ten years. He cautioned against the dangers of uni-lateral financial measures and trade barriers, and called for a global food security network, cooperation on energy, increased aid for the poorest countries and the maintenance of open world trading.

The Council considered the social aspects of UN development activities, consumer protection, environment and human settlements. It endorsed the implementation of 'health for all by the year 2000' for its international development strategy and requested the Secretary-General to establish a committee, representing agencies for emergency aid, to coordinate action, collaborate with the International Red Cross and consider preventive plans for disaster-prone places. The Council also called for efforts to rehabilitate the Sudano-Sahelian region and to assist the people of Namibia.

ENERGY. The much-anticipated conference on new and renewable sources of energy met in Nairobi in August to consider national energy plans, the energy crisis, its effect on poor countries and the role of the UN. In preparation for the meeting experts had examined the feasibility of eight technologies—solar energy, biomass, hydropower, wind and ocean power, geothermal energy, tar sands and oil shale, fuelwood and charcoal—and studies were made of the use of peat and draught animal power.

The conference called for an orderly transition from a world economy based chiefly on hydrocarbons to one based increasingly on new and renewable sources, in a way 'socially equitable, economically and technically viable and environmentally suitable'. It agreed that a UN inter-governmental body should guide the implementation of its pro-gramme and that the General Assembly of 1982 should decide on future institutional arrangements, since the US and EEC opposed a UN energy agency favoured by the developing countries.

The International Atomic Energy Agency (IAEA) smarted over Israel's claim that Iraq's nuclear plant was designed to produce an atomic bomb, despite findings of IAEA inspectors to the contrary. Its conference in September condemned the bombing of the Iraqi plant and ordered a halt to technical assistance to Israel. The director-general, Sigvard Eklund, retired after 20 years to be succeeded by Hans Bliz.

MONETARY. High interest rates superseded oil prices as the year's economic bugbear, as developing countries incurred drastically accumu-lating debt repayments. The International Monetary Fund (IMF) was called on to expand loans to developing countries despite its stringent conditions, and was facilitated by a large loan from the Saudi Arabian Monetary Agency. In reviewing its policy towards multinational loans the US delayed payments, and in December Congress cut back on the funding of the World Bank's soft-loan affiliate, the International Development Agency (IDA).

China received its first loans from the World Bank, IMF and IDA, and both Poland and Hungary applied for membership in IMF. Although Mr A. W. Clausen of the US, who succeeded Mr Robert McNamara as president of the World Bank, considered an enlarged energy programme worthwhile, at the Cancún summit President Reagan alone opposed an energy affiliate to the World Bank and also a fresh allocation of Special Drawing Rights.

SOCIAL

HUMANITARIAN. Half of the world's ten million refugees were in Africa and 80 per cent of these were in the poorest countries. A UN conference on African refugees was held on 9-10 April, attended by delegates from 99 states, but not by the Soviet Union, which held that it was not responsible for the aftermath of colonialism. Conference delegates pledged $560 million. The other large concentration of refugees was that of Afghans who had fled to Pakistan.

A number of UN agencies were involved in relief—Unicef, the World Food Programme, the UN Disaster Relief Organization, but especially the office of the UN High Commissioner for Refugees (UNHCR), which received the 1981 Nobel peace prize for the second time. The former High Commissioner Sadruddin Aga Khan was asked to make recommendations to the Human Rights Commission on the problem of mass exoduses, and UN members were requested by the General Assembly to suggest ways of averting large flows of refugees and to facilitate their return.

The World Health Organization (WHO) continued to battle with the giant corporations against the promotion of their baby foods and cigarettes in developing countries. It drafted a voluntary code banning advertising of substitutes for breast milk, because of dangers from dilution and inadequate sterilization, which was adopted in May with only the US opposed. WHO also fought the increase in smoking in developing countries, the large sums deployed in advertising and the sale of higher-tar cigarettes there than in the West.

HUMAN RIGHTS. The UN Human Rights Commission considered violations in an ever-lengthening list of states, South Africa, Namibia, Israeli-occupied territory, Kampuchea, Afghanistan, Chile, El Salvador, Bolivia, Guatemala and Western Sahara. In a new departure it agreed to provide help towards the restoration of human rights in three African states—Equatorial Guinea, the Central African Republic and Uganda. Its sub-commission on minorities asked the Secretary-General for information on persecution of the Bahai sect in Iran to present to the Human Rights Commission in 1982.

The Commission completed a draft declaration to eliminate religious intolerance, later adopted by the General Assembly, but did not finish the drafts on torture or the rights of the child. It declared hostage-taking a grave violation of human rights and called for a study on conscientious objection to military service.

OTHER ISSUES

THE SEA. Despite the shock given by the US Administration's intention to review the whole informal text of the proposed Law of the Sea the 10th session of the Conference made headway.

It met in March and April, when Mr Tommy Koh of Singapore was elected President in place of the late H. Shirley Amerasinghe, and then resumed throughout August. It resolved several substantive matters, including a formula for the delimitation of overlapping maritime boundaries, and agreed that Jamaica should be the seat of the International Seabed Authority, and West Germany the seat of the law tribunal. Most significantly, the conference decided that the informal text of some 300 articles should be revised and issued as an 'official' draft, subject to further negotiations, and that the conference should complete its work in 1982.

New rules for safety of life at sea (1978 Protocol to the SOLAS Convention) entered into force on 1 May. The *Amoco Cadiz* spillage of 230,000 tons of oil in 1978 enabled the Inter-Governmental Maritime Consultative Organization to stiffen measures on tanker safety and the prevention of pollution.

LABOUR. The 67th session of the International Labour Organization (ILO) adopted new labour standards for free collective bargaining, equal opportunity for men and women with family responsibilities, and safer, healthier work-places, and updated a declaration on apartheid. The Polish trade union leader Lech Walesa addressed the conference, an act which appeared to vindicate the ILO's recommendations to Poland on modifying its labour laws to conform to ILO conventions. The ILO director-general's offer to lead a team to Poland when martial law was imposed was not accepted.

In March ILO's governing body decided it was pointless to pursue any further the charges against the USSR of suppressing freedom of association in the case of two unions, since Russia refused any cooperation.

ENVIRONMENT. Regional agreements on environmental protection progressed with the help of the UN Environment Programme. In March West African states approved a treaty to protect their coastal waters from pollution. In April Caribbean states initiated a wide-reaching plan of 66 projects, from oil spills and watersheds to mitigating natural disasters. Also in April the five Asean states adopted a plan for environmental protection of their coastal area from industrial pollution and against over-fishing. Then in October eight East African and Indian Ocean states launched a programme on conservation and development of marine resources and control of oil and other pollution. Previous programmes were already functioning for the Mediterranean and the Gulf area.

Chapter 2

THE COMMONWEALTH

THE major event in a busy Commonwealth calendar was the heads of government meeting held in Melbourne in October. It provided a valuable stage in the process of consolidating the Commonwealth techniques of consultation. The final declaration bore strong overtones of the Brandt Report; this was inevitable, as the conference represented a blend of North and South interests in the largest gathering of its kind since the Lusaka conference of 1979 (see AR 1979, p. 336). As Mr Malcolm Fraser, Australia's Prime Minister and host to the conference, put it, 'economic inter-dependence is not just a slogan but a reality; a world divided into rich and desperately poor countries can be neither a stable, harmonious nor morally acceptable world'.

Following this theme, the unanimous Melbourne declaration, a somewhat prolix manifesto (see DOCUMENTS), stressed that it was imperative to revitalize the dialogue between the developed and developing countries, with a willingness to accept real and significant changes. While urgent humanitarian considerations demanded action, self-interest warranted a constructive approach to the great human problems; certain national inhibitions and habits must be abandoned.

The Melbourne meeting was, as is customary, preceded by a conference of Finance Ministers; originally planned to be held in New Zealand, its venue was shifted to Nassau in the Bahamas as part of the protest against the Springboks' rugby tour of New Zealand (see p. 318). This event was prevented from escalating into a grave Commonwealth crisis by the statesmanlike response of Commonwealth leaders, notably Africans who had the most reason to feel affronted at what many felt to be New Zealand's less than wholehearted resistance to apartheid.

The Finance Ministers had an auspicious opening to their discussions when it was learnt that the recent decline in the fortunes of the Commonwealth Fund for Technical Cooperation (CFTC) was to be reversed. A stable financial basis covering the next three years was guaranteed by major donors to the Fund. Nevertheless, the world economic outlook was profoundly gloomy, and delegates were left to derive what satisfaction they could from the fact that many of the initiatives to remedy world recession arose from the Commonwealth. The Ministers had somewhat anxious discussions about the future and proper roles of the World Bank and IMF.

The British Nationality Act 1981 (see pp. 32-33) passed after almost a year's debating in both Houses of Parliament, was bound to have vital consequences for the Commonwealth. It introduced three categories of citizenship in legislation of great complexity:
(1) British citizenship, covering those who already have the right to live in Britain.
(2) British Dependent Territories' Citizenship, covering the estimated 3 million people living in Britain's remaining colonies and associated states, which originally included Hong Kong with its 2·6 million people and Bermuda, Gibraltar, the Falkland Islands and minor outposts: they would have the inherent right to enter and live in their own territories but not Britain or other Commonwealth territories.
(3) British Overseas Citizenship, designed to cover 1·5 million people, mostly of Chinese origin, living in Malaysia, and 200,000 East African Asians, mostly now in India awaiting admission to Britain. These people would be left virtually stateless, and although no rights conferred by the United Kingdom were being taken from them they felt that they had enjoyed a certain degree of protection. This third category of citizenship cannot be passed on to the second generation, so it will eventually die out.

The Bill met with a great deal of opposition from the Labour and Liberal parties and a few Conservatives, and a number of liberalizing changes were accepted. The Government strenuously defended the Bill throughout long debates, insisting that it had no racial motivation. Gibraltar, as a result of a revolt against the Government in the House of Lords, gained full British citizenship for its inhabitants if they so wished. An attempt to secure the same status for the residents of the Falkland Islands failed, but it was reported that the islanders had been given an assurance that they would be able to return to the United Kingdom if they were deprived of their right of entry by the Act.

Belize joined the Commonwealth as its 45th member state when it became independent on 21 September. Belize, on the Caribbean coast of Central America (see map p. 92), had a population of 150,000. It became a constitutional monarchy with Queen Elizabeth II as head of state. Mr

George Price, Premier since 1964, had played a major part in resisting the efforts of Guatemala to take over the country and with British help had succeeded in mobilizing Commonwealth and international support for its independence and integrity.

The following month Antigua-Barbuda became the Commonwealth's 46th member. The new state, with a population of 74,000, consists of the islands of Antigua, Barbuda and Redonda in the eastern Caribbean. Mr V. C. Bird, Premier of Antigua, became Prime Minister of Antigua and Barbuda, a constitutional monarchy with a two-chamber Parliament.

The Commonwealth Secretary-General, Mr Shridath Ramphal, in response to a question on Pakistan's readmission to Commonwealth membership at a meeting of international journalists on 10 September, said:

'No approach of any kind has been made to the Secretariat; but I am aware that it has been the subject of some bilateral contacts. It is the kind of matter that most appropriately evolves in quiet conversation. You know, of course, that the process of consultation does not imply automaticity. The concurrence of all member countries is involved; and there is the important convention that the request for membership should be broadly reflective of the wish of the body-politic. Since this is the first time such a matter will be arising, I expect Commonwealth leaders would want to consider the wider questions of policy and procedure before dealing with any particular case.'

The operations of the Commonwealth media exchange scheme, financed by Australia and Britain, were reviewed at the Melbourne conference, which approved Secretariat proposals to widen its scope. An additional contribution from Australia was welcomed, as were offers by Cyprus, Papua New Guinea and India. The meeting looked for support from other governments as well. A report by a Commonwealth committee on communications and media issues agreed on further action to advance Commonwealth cooperation in this field. On the initiative of Australia, a seminar bringing together members of the committee with representatives of governments and the media—editors and working journalists—was planned, to use the report as a basis for detailed recommendations on measures to assist the media in developing Commonwealth countries.

A feature of the Commonwealth year was as always the wide range of activities catered for. One at first glance seemed an unlikely subject: how to borrow money from the banks and other sources of external finance. A seminar on Third World borrowing in international capital markets was held in Uppsala and Stockholm, Sweden, organized by the Commonwealth Secretariat and the Dag Hammarskjöld Foundation. The capacity to deal with international banks and financial institutions was of growing importance to oil-importing Third World countries, which had a current account deficit of $70 million in 1980. A large part of these deficits must often be covered by commercial borrowing.

Low-cost equipment appropriate for agriculture and rural development in the South Pacific was assembled in a Commonwealth workshop in Fiji, organized by the Commonwealth Secretariat's food production and rural development division. Technicians from thirteen Commonwealth countries completed a three-week course on the construction and operation of biogas systems, part of the Commonwealth Science Council's Asia/Pacific rural technology programme. Developments in the programme concerned *inter alia* rural light engineering industries, the economic use of by-products from paddy fields, and the management and use of the water hyacinth.

Chapter 3

DEFENCE ORGANIZATIONS AND DEVELOPMENTS

THE GLOBAL SCENE

DURING 1981 the military-strategic scene witnessed a series of crises which provoked confrontation, strained power alignments and accelerated militarization programmes. Towards the end of the year the prospect of superpower intervention increased as the crises in Poland and Central America challenged the regional hegemony of the Soviet Union and the United States respectively.

Washington's assertive foreign policy had immediate repercussions. In February President Reagan halted planned troop withdrawals from South Korea and pledged continuing US military presence in the Pacific. Japan remained a focus of US concern in countering the Soviet military build-up in the Far East. But despite Japanese apprehension over Soviet military expansion and consolidated presence in the Kurile Islands, Washington failed to persuade Tokyo to increase its military spending and assume responsibility for the defence of the north-west Pacific.

Uncertainty predominated in the Sino-American relationship. In June the United States offered to sell 'lethal' weapons to China. The strategic implications of this were minimized by Peking amid reports of a jointly-operated US-Chinese intelligence installation in western China monitoring Soviet missile tests. Closer Sino-American relations remained dependent on US arms policy towards Taiwan (see p. 305).

Security links between the South-East Asian nations and their Antipodean neighbours strengthened with the agreement among the Five-Power Defence Arrangement members to enhance their military profile.

The Anzus alliance continued to strengthen its contribution to the defence of Western security interests in the Pacific and Indian Oceans, as US Secretary of State Haig acknowledged at the 30th annual Anzus council meeting in June. He emphasized the need for strategic consensus between Washington and its Asian-Pacific allies. Antipodean apprehension over the possible extension of Anzus responsibilities did not preclude increased Australian patrolling capabilities in the Indian Ocean or Australia's offer of additional base and surveillance facilities to the United States.

Washington's bid to counter Soviet military advances in Africa and Asia accelerated the militarization of the Indian Ocean, previously triggered by the invasion of Afghanistan. Its elaborate base facilities confirmed Diego Garcia as the hub of a US strategy which included an extensive programme of naval deployment and substantial arms shipments to vulnerable allies, notably Saudi Arabia and Pakistan. The US gained access to base facilities at Berbera and Mogadishu and established a communications centre in Oman. In November the beginning of Operation Bright Star, involving the participation of US troops in a series of coordinated military exercises in Egypt, Sudan, Somalia and Oman, confirmed the existence of the US Rapid Deployment Force.

A spate of crises in Africa and the Middle East overshadowed developments in the Indian Ocean. Pretoria's renewed military intervention in Angola aggravated the confrontation in southern Africa. In November the regional conflict gained a new dimension with reports that a Soviet South Atlantic fleet, operating from Angola, was monitoring the Cape oil route.

The crisis over Syria's deployment of SAM missiles in Lebanon midway through the year raised the level of superpower diplomatic and military activity and revived Moscow's political fortunes in the region. The display of Soviet Mediterranean naval strength, including joint military exercises with Syria in July, presaged a consolidation of military-security links between Moscow and its regional clients. Soviet arms supplies to Baghdad were resumed in August. In addition Moscow reiterated its support for the Palestinians, vied with Washington for influence in Jordan and sanctioned the proposed anti-Western Indian Ocean front between Libya, Ethiopia and South Yemen.

Washington remained committed to countering destabilizing trends such as Libyan adventurism in North Africa. As a consequence the US found itself challenged by vigorous opponents, notably Libya in the Gulf of Sirte crisis (see pp. 71 and 215); excluded by discriminating clients from regional security arrangements such as the Gulf Cooperation Council; and compromised by a recalcitrant ally, Israel, with its raid on the Iraqi nuclear reactor and its virtual annexation of the Golan Heights.

The assassination of President Sadat threatened to undermine the entire Camp David peace process and improve Moscow's position in the Middle East balance of forces at Washington's expense. The United States responded with defence aid to bolster Egypt and Sudan and redoubled its efforts to ensure the sale of AWACS surveillance planes to Saudi Arabia.

American attempts to redress the global balance so as to curtail the widening range of political and military options available to the Soviet Union rehabilitated the concept of containment and raised the spectre of a new 'cold war'.

Both Washington and Moscow experienced uncertainty and frustration in their relationships with smaller powers, which suggested that the superpower ability to control events in the Third World had diminished.

THE NORTH ATLANTIC TREATY ORGANIZATION

The political cohesion, collective resolve and strategic relevance of the Atlantic alliance were seriously tested during 1981. The threat of disarray haunted the Allies in their response to arms control, the global military-strategic balance, regional crises in the Third World and the threatened East-West confrontation over Poland.

The Reagan Administration's policy of peace through strength sharpened ongoing debates over defence expenditure and burden-sharing within the alliance. In May Nato Defence Ministers reaffirmed their commitment to increase annual defence spending by three per cent up to 1986. However, optimism had waned by July, when West Germany announced its inability to achieve the three per cent target for 1982. US pressure on its European allies to increase their military contributions to the alliance coincided with Anglo-American moves to expand Nato's role and sphere of influence beyond Europe. But this met resistance from European members who were primarily concerned not to deflect Western attention and resources from the European theatre.

Defence Ministers attending the nuclear planning group (NPG) meeting in Bonn on 7-8 April emphasized the need to counter the destabilizing effect of Soviet SS20 missile deployment. They confirmed the 'dual track' decision adopted in December 1979 to pursue a policy of deployment together with negotiated limitation of theatre nuclear forces (TNF) in Europe. The NPG's communique noted that actual or threatened Soviet intervention in Poland would undermine the prospects for effective arms control negotiations. Simultaneous reports from Brussels indicated that Nato had drawn up a list of retaliatory measures which would form the basis of a Western response to Soviet military intervention in Poland. The NPG's deliberations were endorsed by the Nato Council meeting in Rome on 4-5 May.

Friction within the alliance over the lack of consistency in Washington's policy pronouncements, the prospects for the proposed TNF talks and the growing nuclear disarmament movement was exacerbated in July by talk of a Nordic nuclear-free zone (see p. 361). The ill-timed announcement of US plans to move its West German bases further to the east caused additional controversy. In August, the Reagan Administration's unilateral decision to manufacture and stockpile the neutron bomb further impaired the fragile cohesion of the alliance.

Nato's military activities were not immune from intra-alliance tensions. The participation of South American navies in 'Ocean Venture 81' (August-October), one of the largest naval exercises ever held in the Atlantic, provoked Norwegian resistance to the attempted expansion of Nato's responsibilities. The exercises coincided with Nato's ten-day naval exercise, 'Atlantic Ocean Safari', and three other allied maritime manoeuvres in the Norwegian, North and Mediterranean Seas.

In September Nato opened its 'Autumn Forge' series of manoeuvres, involving an estimated 300,000 allied troops in coordinated operations from Norway to Turkey, against a background of heightened East-West tension over Poland and an unprecedented display of Soviet military force in the Baltic. On 5 September 22,000 troops from eight Nato countries participated in exercise 'Amber Express'. A subsequent exercise, 'Certain Encounter', tested US reinforcement capability.

During the two-day NPG meeting in October the Defence Ministers sought US assurances that Washington's confusing statements over the possibility of limited nuclear war in Europe did not signal a departure from agreed alliance deterrent strategy. Having debated the so-called 'zero option' the allies reaffirmed Nato's 'dual track' policy and unanimously supported Washington's arms reduction policy. Even this superficial unanimity was later undermined by the continuing reluctance of the Netherlands and Belgium to support Nato's nuclear modernization programme.

The December sessions of alliance assemblies witnessed the resurgence of a long-standing threat to Nato's political coherence and strategic credibility. Disquiet on the northern flank was superseded by the threatened disintegration of the southern flank. This overshadowed the Eurogroup's deliberations on the problem of transatlantic communication on 7 December. The subsequent two-day meeting of the defence planning committee in Brussels, which was dominated by the Aegean dispute and the future of the southern flank, ended on 9 December without a final communique because of Greek demands that Nato collectively guarantee its security against Turkey. The conditions for continued Greek membership of Nato's integrated military command structure preoccupied the Nato Council meeting on 10-11 December. The Council also witnessed Spain's formal application to become the sixteenth Nato member state.

The military takeover in Poland left the alliance bereft of a coherent, coordinated response and in danger of disarray. On 23 December the allies failed to agree on a common programme of action because of differences between the United States and Europe over the nature of the threat posed by the Polish situation. The division was sharpened on 29 December when President Reagan announced unilateral sanctions against Moscow and warned Nato of the dangers if the allies failed to make a similar response.

THE WARSAW TREATY ORGANIZATION

The Warsaw Pact's growing military power was much in evidence in 1981. Western defence analysts estimated that technological improvements to the already numerically superior Warsaw Pact ground forces, coupled with the Pact's acknowledged superiority in theatre nuclear weapons, had created a dangerous imbalance on the central front.

In February Western reports indicated that Soviet deployment of triple-warhead SS20 missiles was nearing completion. Existing medium-range SS4 and SS5 missiles were subsequently reported as being replaced by the mobile SS20s. The introduction of new shorter-range missile systems and tactical nuclear aircraft consolidated the Warsaw Pact's theatre nuclear force capability. This deployment was complemented by the development of more sophisticated missiles and fighter aircraft, and by the anticipated introduction of the T-80 main battle tank.

Soviet military expenditure levels continued to alarm the West. On 17 November the Soviet Finance Minister announced that projected defence expenditure for 1982 would be 5·3 per cent of the state budget expenditure. President Ceauşescu reversed the trend of previous years by calling for cuts in Romania's defence spending.

Throughout the year the Warsaw Treaty member states were preoccupied with the turmoil in Poland and its implications for the defence structure of the alliance. At the 26th Congress of the CPSU held in Moscow, 23 February to 4 March, President Brezhnev confirmed the line adopted by the Warsaw Pact summit in December 1980, which had agreed to support Polish attempts to deal with the crisis. In April the Czechoslovak Party leader reaffirmed the Brezhnev Doctrine and warned that the Soviet bloc would not remain passive while the communist system in Poland was threatened.

Mr Brezhnev also called for renewed detente and a summit meeting with President Reagan; urged new arms control talks which should include a ban on neutron weapons and limits on US and Soviet submarine deployments; confirmed his previous conditional offer to withdraw troops from Afghanistan; called on Nato to halt its nuclear modernization programme and proposed a freeze on TNF levels.

The threat of military intervention in Poland conferred exceptional significance on the intensive military activity sustained by Warsaw Pact forces during 1981. This began in January when Soviet troops were engaged in joint manoeuvres with Polish army units. These were followed by similar exercises with Hungary and the GDR. Poland was the operational focus of Soyuz 81, a joint Warsaw Pact exercise held from 17 March to 7 April. The manoeuvres involved token units of Soviet, Polish, East German and Czechoslovak forces in joint operations designed to test cooperation between the ground, naval and air forces of the participating states. The Warsaw Pact's military focus on the Baltic area continued during joint training exercises between Soviet, Polish and East German naval units in July. On 7 August a Soviet naval force of approximately fifty vessels was reported to have carried out a landing exercise on the Soviet Baltic coast.

On 13 August TASS reported that joint exercises of Soviet military and naval units (West 81) would be held in the Baltic and Byelorussian military districts between 4 and 12 September. The subsequent naval build-up in the Baltic involved over sixty Soviet ships from the Pacific, Atlantic, Northern and Black Sea fleets and presaged the most extensive manoeuvres staged by the Soviet Union since World War II.

The military council of the Warsaw Treaty Organization met in Budapest on 29 October as Poland moved closer to total military control. Eastern Europe's preoccupation with the Polish problem was temporarily alleviated during the two-day meeting of the seven Foreign Ministers in Bucharest, 1-2 December. The annual meeting was reportedly concerned with the Geneva TNF talks (see pp. 344-5), the Madrid review conference and President Ceauşescu's continued independent line on foreign and defence policy. His most recent deviations included his call for a Balkan nuclear-free zone. The Foreign Ministers proceeded to endorse President Brezhnev's disarmament initiative and supported the idea of a European disarmament conference, but omitted any mention of the Polish crisis.

The declaration of martial law in Poland on 13 December evoked a cautious and low-key response from its Warsaw Treaty allies. The absence of a Polish representative from the gathering of Warsaw Pact leaders in Moscow on 19-20 December underlined the gravity of the situation and fuelled Western speculation over the possibility of Soviet military intervention.

MUTUAL FORCE REDUCTIONS

The Vienna negotiations between the Western alliance and the Warsaw Pact on conventional force reductions in central Europe entered their eighth year in 1981. Set to resume in January, the talks faced the prospect of continuing deadlock over the key issues of accurate data on troop strengths and acceptable measures to verify compliance with a future reduction and limitation agreement. This stumbling-block was worsened by the continued impasse on SALT and the protracted debate at the Madrid review conference.

The nineteen nations in Vienna had previously accepted the principle of reducing ground force manpower to a common collective ceiling of 700,000 and combined ground and air force personnel to 900,000 on each side. When the talks resumed the West renewed its claim that the Eastern bloc had misrepresented its troop strength by 150,000 (see AR 1980, p. 343). The Warsaw Treaty negotiators merely reiterated their refusal to change their position and the perennial deadlock continued.

In May the Nato Ministerial Council attributed the lack of 'substantial progress' at Vienna to the Warsaw Pact's refusal to provide the necessary clarification on troop strength data. In response, TASS complained that Moscow's previous unilateral initiative on troop and tank withdrawals from East Germany (see AR 1980, p. 344) had been ignored by Nato. Moreover, the lack of progress at the 24th round of talks was cited as evidence of Washington's aversion to arms control procedures. The Soviet Defence Minister, Marshal Ustinov, signalled the intractability of the problem in July when he claimed that the opposing forces in central Europe were 'already roughly equal'.

This consistently unproductive disarmament forum, overshadowed by the TNF debate during 1981, received a potential fillip in November from President Reagan's arms reduction initiative (see p. 66). Washington argued that a gesture towards equality in the conventional theatre would alleviate tension by reducing the potential for aggression. Subsequent hopes of progress at Vienna, however, proved to be premature.

ARMS CONTROL NEGOTIATIONS

A turbulent political-strategic environment provided an inauspicious beginning for arms control processes in 1981. Throughout the year recurring political confrontation between the superpowers lent itself more readily to talk of arms races than of arms control.

The Reagan Administration's concern to restore nuclear equivalence with the Soviet Union and renegotiate the SALT II Treaty provoked Moscow's instant defence of the concept of strategic parity between the two superpowers. The SALT agreement concluded between Presidents Carter and Brezhnev in Vienna 1979 remained suspended. But speculation over Washington's acquiescence in a renewed strategic dialogue with Moscow gained substance in October, when US plans for arms reduction talks (START), as opposed to talks limiting the growth of strategic arsenals (SALT), raised expectation of a resumption of superpower negotiations 'early in 1982'. These were confirmed by President Reagan in his November arms reduction package (see DOCUMENTS).

In contrast, West European pressures for a resumption of the SALT-related superpower talks on limiting theatre nuclear forces (TNF) in Europe gained momentum early in the year as a consequence of the growing anti-nuclear movement in Nato countries and a vigorous Soviet 'peace campaign'. President Reagan subsequently made improvements in East-West relations contingent on Soviet willingness to discuss a 'genuine' reduction in nuclear arms.

US arms control policy was developed a stage further by Secretary of State Haig's assurance to the Nato Council meeting in May that Washington would resume negotiation with Moscow on LRTNF in Europe within the SALT framework.

In June President Brezhnev renewed his peace offensive. He appealed to the West to prevent a further spiral in the arms race, to accelerate the arms control process, and hinted that a proposed Nordic nuclear-free zone could be extended to Soviet territory. However, the conditional nature of President Reagan's counter-offer of a superpower summit did little either to mitigate Moscow's strong adverse reaction to the US decision to manufacture and stockpile neutron weapons, or to dispel West European disquiet over Washington's plans to restore US strategic nuclear superiority. President Reagan's ultimatum to Moscow to negotiate disarmament or lose the ensuing arms race provoked a vehement Soviet response implying acceptance of the challenge.

The Haig–Gromyko talks began in New York on 23 September. This first high-level contact between Washington and Moscow since the advent of the Reagan Administration produced agreement to resume negotiation on the reduction of European TNF levels in Geneva on 30 November, and to continue the new US-Soviet dialogue in 1982, but failed to resolve the differences over which weapons constituted TNF.

Superpower arms control diplomacy intensified as the Geneva talks approached. On 18 November President Reagan announced a major peace programme calling for dramatic reductions in theatre and strategic nuclear weapons, and proposing the so-called 'zero option', which was subsequently tabled at the formal opening of the Geneva talks. This proposal entailed an offer to abandon the deployment of 572 Cruise and Pershing II missiles in Western Europe in exchange for the USSR's agreement to dismantle its SS missiles targeted against Western Europe. Moscow rejected the plan as a basis for negotiation at Geneva and countered with its own 'zero option' initiative, which similarly formed the basis of the Soviet initial proposal at Geneva. During the Bonn summit later in November, President Brezhnev indicated Soviet willingness to go beyond the moratorium on the deployment of new SS20 missiles, offering to withdraw, unilaterally, some medium-range missiles provided the moratorium was observed (see DOCUMENTS).

The Geneva negotiations on theatre nuclear forces in Europe opened on 30 November amid unusual secrecy. Hopes that a constructive dialogue would permit real progress received a major setback in mid-December when the future of the talks was jeopardized by the military takeover in Poland. The suspension of the Geneva negotiations became one of the diplomatic options open to Washington as it sought to effect a vigorous response to the imposition of military rule in Poland.

There were few signs of progress in other areas of arms control. The political climate hampered progress in the Geneva comprehensive nuclear test ban negotiations and disrupted talks on chemical and biological warfare disarmament. However, on 10 April 35 nations, excluding the United States, signed the Conventional Weapons Convention. In August a Soviet draft proposal for a treaty on a space weapon ban was communicated to the UN Secretary-General.

THE CONFERENCE ON SECURITY AND COOPERATION IN EUROPE

The second phase of the 35-nation European security review conference, designed to revive detente in Europe, opened in Madrid on 27 January in an atmosphere charged with uncertainty. The new session was dominated by disagreement over rival proposals for a European disarmament conference previously tabled by Poland and France, and by the threat to the continued existence of the Helsinki process.

The Soviet-backed Polish proposal called for a conference on military detente and disarmament but it lacked adequate guarantees for verification of security measures required by the West. The French initiative proposed new confidence-building measures (CBMs) in Europe, extending from the Atlantic to the Urals, which would be 'militarily significant, binding and verifiable'. Initially this met with opposition from the Soviet bloc, which demanded the inclusion of US territory in any security zone.

The gulf between East and West widened with Moscow's attempt to make acceptance of its proposal a precondition for continuing the Helsinki process, and with Washington's insistence on a balance of progress on security, human rights and economic cooperation.

The deadlock appeared resolved on 18 February when the Reagan Administration announced its Helsinki strategy and publicly supported the French proposal. This opened the way for possible compromise over an eventual disarmament conference. Similar hopes were raised by President Brezhnev's suggestion that the Soviet Union might accept the geographical extension of confidence-building measures provided counter-concessions were made by the West.

Optimism quickly faded however, as the closing date, 5 March, approached with no progress on the final draft proposal. Western failure to stimulate the proceedings by limited extensions of the conference deadline led Nato states to accuse Moscow of stalling and to threaten a

Western withdrawal from the conference. On 31 March the neutral states presented a compromise draft concluding document in an attempt to retrieve the European security process. This was accepted, although with reservations. The conference adjourned on 7 April in an atmosphere of recrimination, as the West clearly linked Poland's fate to the survival of detente.

When the conference reconvened on 5 May, Soviet complaints of Western interference in Russia's internal affairs, and Washington's accusations of Soviet rearmament and political and military intimidation in Poland, intensified the East-West diplomatic confrontation. This ensured continued deadlock and prompted pressures for a further adjournment. Four months behind schedule and with the key issues of military security and human rights unresolved, the participants agreed to a three-month recess on 24 July.

The second review meeting resumed on 27 October with Western criticisms of Soviet violations of the Helsinki Final Act. The Soviet Union continued its attempts to transfer the responsibility for security arrangements to an East-West disarmament conference. Likewise the United States persisted in its demand for a precise definition of a European security framework at Madrid as a precondition for its participation in such a conference. In December an Austrian compromise formula on the scope of a possible future disarmament agreement, coupled with hopes for an early breakthrough in the Geneva negotiations on TNF, temporarily encouraged a more optimistic outlook at Madrid. This was shattered by the declaration of martial law in Poland, which called the entire Helsinki process into question.

Chapter 4

THE EUROPEAN COMMUNITY

FOR the European Community 1981 was a rather disappointing year. Buffeted by political events both internal and external, and confronted by an apparently unrelenting economic recession, the Community's institutions found themselves unable to exert any significant influence on decision-makers in any of the EEC's member states, and progress towards genuine common policies was once again hesitant.

On 1 January Greece joined the Community as its tenth full member. On 6 January the former Luxembourg Prime Minister Gaston Thorn presided over the first meeting of his new 14-member Commission. It was an unhappy first meeting: the initial task of sharing out portfolios generated considerable bitterness. The new Irish Commissioner, Mr Michael O'Kennedy, was dissatisfied with the subordinate role he was assigned as

Special Delegate for the President, and a British Commissioner, Mr Christopher Tugendhat, eventually called on Mrs Thatcher to intervene with M Thorn personally to prevent him from taking away his Budget portfolio. The death of the Danish Agriculture and Fisheries Commissioner, Mr Finn Olav Gundelach, a week later threatened to unravel M Thorn's elaborate political compromise; in the event Mr Gundelach's post was taken over by the Danish Agriculture Minister, Mr Poul Dalsager.

International tension was only slightly relieved by the release in January of the 52 American hostages held in Iran. The continued Soviet presence in Afghanistan, Israel's embittered relations with Syria and Iraq, the assassination of President Sadat of Egypt and, most of all, the declaration of martial law in Poland on 13 December all added up to an ominous international picture which the Community found itself illequipped to influence.

Meanwhile, the continuing economic difficulties brought in train political upheavals. The most notable of these were the election of M François Mitterrand as President of the French Republic on 10 May, and the victory of the strongly anti-EEC Pasok party of Mr Andreas Papandreou in the Greek general election of 18 October. There were also elections in Belgium, Denmark, Ireland and the Netherlands, and a change of Government in Italy.

The incoming Commission also had to contend with a prolonged and at times bitter row over the salaries of European public servants. An effort to bring them into line with those of national officials caused a series of disruptive strikes in the first half of the year.

A symbolic obstacle was crossed with agreement in principle on the format of a European passport, an idea first suggested at the Paris summit of 1974. The Foreign Ministers of the Ten made considerable progress on the details at their meeting of 16 March, and expressed the hope that the common passport would be introduced by 1985.

In June *Eurobarometer*, in its regular survey of attitudes towards the Community among its 270 million inhabitants, revealed that it was far less popular than ever before: only half of those polled thought the Community 'a good thing'. In response to what they saw as dwindling enthusiasm for the European idea, the West German and Italian Foreign Ministers, Herr Hans-Dietrich Genscher and Signor Emilio Colombo, presented their colleagues on 17 November with what they termed a 'Draft European Act'. This proposed not only a common foreign policy, close cultural cooperation and more joint action to combat international crime and terrorism but also a degree of coordination of security policy, an area hitherto scrupulously avoided. The Draft Act was politely received both by the Ministers and by heads of government at their summit in London on 26-27 November, but appeared to have little prospect of being treated as a matter of priority.

The Presidency of the Council of Ministers was held by the Netherlands from 1 January to 30 June, and by the United Kingdom from 1 July to 31 December.

External Relations. Events in the Middle East, together with the imposition of martial law in Poland on 13 December, dominated the Ten's efforts to work towards a common foreign policy. External relations were granted more prominence than ever before at the regular meetings of Foreign Ministers, and several special informal sessions of the 'Schloss Gymnich' type were held. Europe showed a growing reluctance to follow the American line on foreign policy.

On 10 February President Sadat of Egypt paid the European Parliament the calculated compliment of choosing its Luxembourg session as the occasion for a major speech calling on the Ten to help him bring about a 'mutual and simultaneous recognition between Israel and the Palestinians'. Despite American disapproval, the European Community attempted to keep alive its Middle East peace initiative by sending the Dutch President of the Council, Christoph van der Klaauw, on several fact-finding missions to the region between February and June. But by the time he reported back to the Luxembourg summit on 29 June Israel had launched its dramatic attack on the Iraqi nuclear research centre, effectively forcing the Ten to mark time. The assassination of President Sadat in October added to European uncertainties over the Middle East. On 3 November Lord Carrington, now President of the Council as well as British Foreign Secretary, flew to Riyadh to explore further the possibility of EEC backing for Prince Fahd's eight-point peace plan, which, however, went into limbo when the Arab League meeting at Fez collapsed. On 7 and 8 December the French Foreign Minister, M Claude Cheysson, said on a visit to Israel that he did not think 'the French, the Europeans, the Americans or the Russians should try to tell the countries in the region what to do'.

On 12-13 October the Ten's Foreign Ministers met in Luxembourg to decide on a concerted response to an American invitation to the United Kingdom, France, Italy and the Netherlands to send troops to join the peacekeeping force due to supervise the Israeli withdrawal from the Sinai desert in April 1982 under the terms of the Camp David accords. Despite initial misgivings about the consistency of European participation with the terms of the Venice Declaration of June 1980 (see AR 1980, pp. 347-8), it was announced on 23 November that the four countries would indeed be willing to send troops to Sinai.

Another European initiative, on Afghanistan, also met with little success. At their Luxembourg summit of 29-30 June the ten heads of government endorsed a British proposal for a two-stage conference to try to establish Afghanistan as an independent non-aligned state. On 5 July

Lord Carrington opened his presidency with a trip to Moscow to sound out the Soviet view. He was courteously received, but commentaries in the Soviet offical media soon made it clear that such a plan could not form the basis of Afghan independence.

On Poland, the EEC proved its willingness to foster the process of reform there by granting food aid at 15 per cent below world prices, at a total cost to the Community budget of about £55 million. General Jaruzelski's imposition of martial law on 13 December caught the Ten by surprise; on 15 December the Foreign Ministers warned Moscow against a direct military intervention in Poland, but as the year ended it seemed highly unlikely that the EEC would follow President Reagan in imposing economic sanctions against the Soviet Union.

On 11 December a top-level American team headed by Secretary of State Haig arrived in Brussels for talks at the EEC Commission on trade. Two familiar grievances were aired: EEC export subsidies on farm produce and allegedly unfair steel export pricing policies. The talks proved unexpectedly positive, with an agreement on a formal review of the trigger price mechanism for steel imports into the US.

On one issue Washington and Brussels remained firmly united throughout the year: concern about their growing trade deficits with Japan. On 19 May the EEC Council issued a stern warning to Tokyo, demanding restraint on imports into the Community of 'sensitive' commodities such as motor cars, and better access to Japanese markets for European exporters. This met with a postive response: in June West Germany and the Benelux countries (albeit to the disappointment of those who had called for a common Community approach to the problem) reached agreement with the Japanese on reduced car import levels; on 14 June the Japanese Minister for International Trade and Industry, Mr Rokusuke Tanaka, urged his country's traders to import more manufactured goods from the EEC; and on 17 June, while on a visit to Brussels, he said Japanese car exports would be maintained 'at 1980 levels'.

Continued military rule in Turkey disturbed EEC Governments, and on 3 December the Commission warned that it might suspend preparations for the granting of aid worth a total of $650 million.

Budget Reform and the European Parliament. The single most important and most demanding task M Thorn and his thirteen fellow Commissioners faced as they took office was that of reviewing the Community's finances. The Foreign Ministers had agreed in May 1980 that the Commission would bring forward proposals to prevent the surging cost of the Common Agricultural Policy (CAP) from exhausting too rapidly the Community's hard-pressed financial resources, and to solve the problem of the UK's heavy net contributions to the EEC budget. The intention had been that any new budgetary arrangements would come into force in 1982.

The Commission's reform proposals were outlined to the Foreign Ministers at the end of June and were further elaborated on 26 October. There were four main points: EEC cereal prices were to be more closely aligned with world prices; support levels for each agricultural commodity were to be geared to production targets set for a five-year period; there was to be special help for small farmers; and other common policies, such as energy research, the Regional Fund, intra-Community trade, industrial strategy and job retraining were to be developed.

The member states' reactions to these proposals were largely predictable. The UK Government's main concern was for a long-term settlement of its net contribution problem, possibly gearing contributions to each member state's *per capita* GDP. West Germany, having now reluctantly inherited the mantle of biggest net contributor to the budget, was anxious to see a fixed ceiling put on its payments. These two were joined by the Netherlands in arguing that growth in the cost of the CAP should not be allowed to outstrip the Community's ability to pay for it out of its existing 'own resources'. This idea was firmly opposed by France and Ireland, who were joined by Italy, Denmark and Greece in maintaining that there should be no permanent ceiling on agricultural spending. The Greeks and Italians wanted more money from the CAP for Mediterranean agriculture. Another bitterly-contested issue was that of the milk sector, still accounting for a third of all farm spending.

Negotiations at both ambassador and Foreign Minister level throughout the autumn aimed at reaching final agreement at the London summit on 26-27 November. This proved impossible, and a special informal meeting of Foreign Ministers in London on 14-15 December failed to break the deadlock.

The controversial circumstances under which the Community's budget had been adopted at the end of 1980 presented the new Commission with another immediate problem. Three member states, West Germany, France and Belgium, were refusing to pay their share of about £200 million of social spending insisted on by the European Parliament. Only after the Commission had threatened a European Court action was a settlement arrived at on the basis of a political compromise.

A 26·5 MEUA* draft budget for 1982 was announced by the Commission on 26 May and formally presented to the Parliament on 15 September. MEPs called for more regional, social and research spending, and savings on the CAP. Despite the failure of the Finance Ministers to agree on a final draft, the budget was accepted by Mme Simone Veil, the President of the Parliament, and passed into law.

Agriculture and Fisheries. Agreement was reached on new agricultural price levels for the 1981-82 marketing year on 1 April, the earliest

* One MEUA (million European units of account) equalled approximately £560,000.

date for completion of the annual farm price review since 1974. The farm lobby had argued that a 15·3 per cent rise would be needed to maintain agricultural incomes, and the Parliament had voted for a 12 per cent rise. The Commission's formal proposals were for an average rise of 7·8 per cent. In the event, the Agriculture Ministers settled on a figure of 9·5 per cent, with an increase of 0·5 per cent to 2·5 per cent on the milk producer levy. This decision, Agriculture Commissioner Poul Dalsager told the Parliament on 8 April, would add roughly 1,096 MEUA or 8·5 per cent to the Community's agriculture budget in a full year. The British Minister, Mr Peter Walker, came under pressure to revalue the green pound (the rate at which Community food prices are translated into sterling) but resisted on the grounds that any revaluation would reduce the benefits of the price rises to British producers.

The principle of free and fair trade was compromised by two ostensibly unrelated events in August. Large-scale exports of cheap Italian wine to France provoked angry incidents, followed by a French Government decision to hold up several large consignments of imported Italian wine on the grounds that its documentation was not in order. On 27 August the British Ministry of Agriculture announced a policy of slaughter in dealing with a poultry sickness, Newcastle disease, involving a ban on all imports of poultry products from countries which did not operate a similar slaughter policy. The move was viewed by France as a thinly-disguised pretext for banning its export of turkeys, then at a price advantage over British birds. On 9 September the Commission reviewed the 'wine war' and the 'turkey war', and decided to give France and the United Kingdom respectively ten and fourteen days to account for their unilateral actions. In the event, it was not until 14 October that the French and Italian Agriculture Ministers agreed that the wine consignments held up at French customs posts, by now amounting to a million hectolitres, would be released over a two-month period. As for the 'turkey war', on 19 November, after France had announced that it, too, would adopt a slaughter policy for Newcastle disease, Mr Walker offered to look at proposals to settle the problem on a Community basis.

The British presidency also saw repeated efforts to settle the question of differing rates of duty on wine, beer and other alcoholic beverages. They were abortive, and a temporarily suspended European Court action against the UK over its comparatively high duty rates on wine was therefore due to be reopened in January 1982.

As 1981 opened, there were high hopes of an agreement on the ever-elusive ideal of a Common Fisheries Policy. In an attempt to break down French resistance to existing proposals on catch quotas and access to British waters, Mr Walker blocked an agreement with Canada which would mainly have benefited West German long-distance trawlermen. At the Maastricht summit of 23-24 March Mrs Thatcher enraged Herr

Schmidt by refusing to give way on this point until the entire CFP package was agreed, and the issue was shelved for the duration of the French presidential election campaign. M Mitterrand's victory further put back the prospects of progress towards an agreement, and on 27 July the Commission was forced to go ahead on its own and reopen two North Sea herring fisheries in the absence of any Council decision on the matter. By autumn it looked as if a settlement might be reached: on 29 September the United Kingdom gave its blessing to agreements with Sweden and the Faroe Islands as well as to that with Canada, in return for a reform of fish marketing arrangements and a £14·75 million allocation of restructuring aid for the fishing industry. This appeared to clear the way for a final agreement at the Fisheries Ministers' November meeting, but the Danish elections intervened, preventing that country from negotiating effectively.

Enlargement. With Greece safely incorporated into the Community, the way seemed clear in 1981 for the EEC's third enlargement: the accession of Spain and Portugal to the Treaties of Rome, Paris and Euratom. In fact, Greek EEC membership only served to add to the misgivings in certain national capitals about the advisability of admitting two less prosperous countries at a time when the Community's future course seemed so uncertain and the process of internal reform remained incomplete. Commission forecasts of an olive oil surplus of 200,000 tons once Spain joined the Community did much to heighten worries that further enlargement was out of the question until a well-constructed policy for Mediterranean agriculture had been put into effect. Nevertheless, 1984 remained the target date for Spanish and Portuguese entry.

When the Spanish Foreign Minister, Señor José Pedro Perez Llorca, met his EEC counterparts in Brussels on 16 March he was given assurances of the Community's determination to admit his country to full membership in due course. Significant progress was made in negotiations between Madrid and Brussels on the exact terms of Spanish entry, although the crucial question of agriculture was left unresolved.

The Portuguese Prime Minister, Mr Francisco Pinto Balsemão, was worried by EEC reluctance to settle the central problem of his country's negotiations for membership, that of textiles. On 13 April he warned in Paris that his country would not join the EEC 'at any price', and at a ministerial meeting with the Ten on 27 October Portugal rejected efforts to restrict its textile exports to the Community. However, on 16 December the first financing convention on pre-accession aid was signed, the Community agreeing to put up 10 MEUA out of 35 MEUA needed for a two-year investment programme.

Economics and Industry. On 11 June Ministers of Industry, Finance and social affairs from all Ten member states gathered in Luxembourg for an unprecedented exchange of views on means of tackling what had become the main focus of economic thinking in the Community in 1981: unemployment. On 23 November the EEC's statistical office, Eurostat, reported that by the end of the year some ten million people would be out of work in the Community. The trend of industrial output, however, was reported to be steady in the autumn, and in December the Community's leading businessmen reported that they felt a general upturn had begun to occur. The latest available figures for 1981 showed an EEC average inflation rate of 12·5 per cent, the highest rates being experienced in Greece, Ireland and Italy.

On 22 July, presenting the Draft Medium-Term Economic Policy Programme (1981-85), Commissioner François-Xavier Ortoli called for an active consensus in tackling unemployment and the reduction of dependence on imported energy. The Commission's views differed from those of several member states with more orthodox economic views, and there was a vigorous debate on the emphasis to be given to economic growth in formulating long-term policies.

The European Monetary System, in its second full year, weathered the impact of exchange rate stresses with more resilience than its critics had expected. On 22 March Italy announced that it was devaluing the lira, and on 4 October, after an entire weekend of intensive bargaining, the EMS underwent the largest realignment it had experienced since its establishment in March 1979. The Deutschmark and the Dutch guilder were revalued by 5¼ per cent, and the French franc and the Italian lira were devalued by 3·0 per cent.

The difficulties of the steel industry once again dominated EEC policy in the field of industry. The system of mandatory production cuts introduced in October 1980 under Article 58 of the Treaty of Paris (see AR 1980, pp. 353-4) was due to expire on 30 June, and attempts were made to replace it with a series of voluntary quotas. However, representatives of the EEC steel industry having failed to reach a satisfactory agreement, at an all-night session on 24-25 June the ten Industry Ministers agreed on a three-point plan to deal with the steel crisis. Mandatory quotas were to be continued on certain products corresponding to about 70 per cent of all steel output, while voluntary quotas would be allowed on the rest; national aids to steel industries were to be phased out by 1985, and until then would be subject to strict guidelines administered by the Commission; and between 1981 and 1984 some 212 MEUA was to be spent in Community aid for early retirement and short-time working schemes. These measures were backed up by a series of large price rises and stringent production cuts announced shortly afterwards.

Chapter 5

COUNCIL OF EUROPE—WESTERN EUROPEAN UNION—NORTH ATLANTIC
ASSEMBLY—EUROPEAN FREE TRADE ASSOCIATION—ORGANIZATION
FOR ECONOMIC COOPERATION AND DEVELOPMENT—NORDIC COUNCIL—
COMECON

COUNCIL OF EUROPE

DURING its 69th session on 19 November 1981, the Committee of
Ministers of the Council of Europe agreed on the lines of the Council's
contribution to European revival in the political, cultural and social
fields, so necessary, in harmony with other pluralist democracies, in face
of world-wide interdependence. The Ministers reaffirmed the importance
of increasing the depth and scope of political discussion amongst the
'Twenty-one'.

The Madrid meeting following up the Conference on Security and
Cooperation in Europe (CSCE) was a main item on the agenda of both
the Committee of Ministers and the Parliamentary Assembly. Both
organs renewed their call for agreement on a substantial and balanced
concluding document in order to keep the CSCE process alive. The two
bodies reiterated their profound anxiety about the situation in Afghanistan, and the Committee of Ministers supported, on 2 July, the proposal
for an international conference on Afghanistan put forward by the ten
members of the European Community on 30 June.

By its debates on 'Europe and mounting world tension', on 'relations
between Europe and the USA and Canada', and on the activities of
OECD, the Parliamentary Assembly underlined its role as the world's
largest forum of parliamentary democracies. The newly-elected Spanish
president of the Assembly, Mr de Areilza, stressing this role, suggested to
the parliamentary delegations from Finland, Canada, the US, Australia,
New Zealand and Japan that they join their European colleagues—apart
from the debate on the OECD report—in discussions on major political
problems which all of them had to face. The Parliamentary Assembly
emphasized democratic Europe's political and moral responsibility in a
major debate on 'Global prospects—human needs and Earth's
resources', a problem vital for the future of mankind. A colloquy
organized by the Assembly in October in Madrid examined Europe's role
in the promotion of human rights in Latin America.

The situation in Turkey remained a question of major concern
through 1981. At its sessions on 14 May and 19 November, the committee of Ministers discussed, in the presence of the Turkish Minister of
Foreign Affairs, developments in this member state with a view to an

early restoration of a sound and stable parliamentary democracy. The Parliamentary Assembly debated the situation in Turkey during its sessions in January, May and October, and regretfully concluded that, in the light of its rules of procedure, it would be out of order to envisage the continuance of a Turkish parliamentary delegation to the Council of Europe. Seeing the existing state of affairs in Turkey to be incompatible with the provisions of the Council's Statute, the Assembly decided to take up a position on this question at its January 1982 session, after taking into account the progress made in Turkey towards the establishment of democratic institutions and observance of the provisions of the European Convention on Human Rights.

The defence of democracy against acts of intolerance and terrorism continued to preoccupy the Council of Europe. The Assembly submitted detailed recommendations to the Committee of Ministers on the Council's contribution to the solution of problems concerning terrorism. The Ministers adopted a 'Declaration regarding intolerance—a threat to democracy' on 14 May and committed itself to reinforcing efforts to prevent, at national and international levels, the spread of totalitarian and racist ideologies, and to acting effectively against all forms of intolerance.

Challenges to modern society by scientific and technical development had always been of concern to the Council of Europe. Its fifth parliamentary and scientific conference met in June 1981 in Helsinki, seeking an answer to the question, 'Can parliamentary democracy meet the challenge of modern technology?' With its various intergovernmental activities in the field of mass media, the Council continued to set forth with vigour the fundamental values common to its members in the vital sphere of freedom of information and expression. The Committee of Ministers welcomed the decisions taken by Spain in June and France in October to recognize the right of individual petition provided for in the European Convention on Human Rights, and reaffirmed the importance they attached to strengthening the protection of human rights in Europe and their effective defence under the Convention.

Following the judgments of the European Court of Human Rights in the London *Sunday Times* case, the Committee of Ministers satisfied itself that under Article 54 of the Convention the Government of the United Kingdom had taken the necessary steps to amend its legislation on contempt of court and that it had granted the just satisfaction required by the European Court's judgment; and declared in April 1981 that it had completed its task in this case.

The year saw the 25th anniversary of the creation of the Council of Europe Resettlement Fund. Since 1956 this operational body had increased the total of outstanding loans to more than $1,000 million. The Fund had proved a particularly suitable instrument to reduce imbalances between the countries and regions of northern and southern Europe, and had given priority to problems posed by labour migration.

Another celebratory date was the 20th anniversary of the signature of the European Social Charter. Considered as second in importance only to the European Convention on Human Rights, the Charter represented a guarantee that European Governments would seek the highest social standards for their citizens: in October 1980, the Council of Europe had launched a campaign for urban renaissance, the first seminar being organized by the Swansea city council in the UK.

Suggestions by some people in high positions that the European Community should widen its interests from economic affairs and establish itself as the mouthpiece of Europe on political matters, and on defence and even social, educational and technical issues, were ill-received by various institutions. In the present climate, it was argued, it would be folly to weaken such established bodies as the Council of Europe (of 21 nations), Nato and OECD, and for Europe to put all its eggs in one basket.

WESTERN EUROPEAN UNION

The Assembly of WEU was concerned to protect and strengthen its role as the only intra-European parliamentary institution empowered to debate defence questions—in the words of Mr Fred Mulley (UK), who was re-elected its president at its June session in Paris. It sought closer and more realistic relations with its own ministerial council and a dialogue with the European Parliament in the light of the European Community's advance into the political field. It called on the WEU Council to take steps towards the establishment of a European Union, based on harmonization of the Brussels and Rome treaties and linking the responsibilities of the two parliamentary bodies and the two secretariats.

Urged by Mr Douglas Hurd, MP, British Minister of State, and General Rogers, supreme Nato commander, who were guest speakers in June, it passed resolutions calling for increased defence provision in the light both of the heightened menace of Soviet arms and of the need to negotiate from strength for the limitation of armaments, the second leg of its stance on this subject. It rejected by majority vote an amendment opposing the modernization of nuclear weapons in Europe. At its December session it expressed general approval of the 'zero option'. Despite a plea by M Baumel (France) on behalf of its general affairs committee to take a decision about enhanced radiation nuclear warheads, *alias* the neutron bomb, it shelved the issue by adopting a 'previous question' motion tabled by a Dutch Liberal member. It heard a remarkably tough speech by M Lemoine, Secretary of State to the Minister of Defence in the French Socialist Government, who urged the Assembly to reinforce its action and increase its influence, particularly by diversifying the subjects it examined. France's deterrent potential, said M Lemoine, formed a whole and was meaningful only in the context of independence; there was no way France could negotiate on even part of the armaments involved.

WEU's interests were already fairly diversified. Subjects debated by the Assembly included Poland, towards which, meeting before the military takeover, it urged moderation and continued aid coupled with stern warnings against Russian intervention; the situation in Afghanistan and the Gulf, where it called for economic assistance to Pakistan and a halt to arms sales to both Iran and Iraq; Mediterranean security, urging increased assistance for the modernization of the military potential of Greece and even more urgently of Turkey; long-term space planning, the situation in the South Atlantic and South Africa, and the Law of the Sea.

NORTH ATLANTIC ASSEMBLY

All parliaments of the Alliance except Greece (absent because of national elections) were represented at the 27th annual session of the North Atlantic Assembly in Munich in October. One hundred and sixty parliamentarians took part. For the second time there was a delegation of observers from the Japanese Parliament. As had happened ever since 1978, there were also observers from the Spanish Parliament. During the year 29 parliamentarians from 11 different countries visited military installations in Canada. The proceedings opened with an address by Dr Franz Heubl, President of the Bavarian Landtag. There followed speeches by Dr Richard Stücklen, President of the Bundestag, by Dr Franz-Joseph Strauss, Minister-President of the Bavarian Free State, by the Hon. Jack Brooks (USA), president of the North Atlantic Assembly, and by Dr Peter Corterier, German Minister of State for Foreign Affairs.

Among the resolutions adopted, the Assembly urged the governments of the Alliance to improve cooperation in order to combat terrorism; to reiterate firmly their protests about human rights violations at the Madrid Conference; to continue to press the Soviet Union for a political settlement respecting Afghan rights. More baffling was a call to facilitate a just and peaceful settlement in the Middle East in accordance with Camp David agreements and the unanimous Venice declaration of the EEC Governments.

The Assembly re-elected Mr Jack Brooks (USA) as president and Mr Robert Laucournet (France) as treasurer. The three vice-presidents were from West Germany, Greece and the United Kingdom. Mr Philippe Deshormes (Belgium) was re-elected secretary general for a further two years.

EUROPEAN FREE TRADE ASSOCIATION

Like WEU (see p. 356) Efta sought to establish parliamentary links with the European Community. (see p. 356) Following initial contacts in the summer, a first working meeting between MPs of Efta countries and members of the European Parliament took place in Geneva on 13 November. Both sides expressed their commitment to the European free trade system and its progressive development, with particular concern for elimination of technical barriers to trade; supported wider economic cooperation between Efta and the EC on a pragmatic basis; and felt that parliamentarians should play a key role in shaping the future policies of both organizations.

Efta countries shared the effects of world economic recession, showing a rise of only 0·5 per cent in aggregate output in 1981; unemployment rose comparatively slowly, but inflation faster than the OECD average. Both imports and exports of the group fell, the latter less sharply than the former. At a meeting of the Efta Council at ministerial level on 26-27 November Ministers expressed concern at the economic situation, especially the volatility of exchange rates, which added to the general uncertainty and thus hampered productive investment and employment. They saw structural adaptation as a key element in policies for restoring non-inflationary growth. To their renewed commitment to multilateral free trade they added a call for enhanced trade with less developed countries and an early start for the global negotiations adumbrated by the Cancún summit.

New loans totalling $22 million were approved by the Efta industrial development fund for Portugal. At the same time Efta took an understanding view of Portugal's desire to join the EEC, which would leave Efta with only six members.

ORGANIZATION FOR ECONOMIC COOPERATION AND DEVELOPMENT

'Science, technology and innovation in the 1980s; national and international perspectives' was the theme of a meeting in March of OECD science Ministers. A Declaration they adopted stressed the need to integrate science and technology policies with other aspects of government activity, particularly economic, social, industrial (including energy), education and manpower policies.

Over 100 parliamentarians from OECD countries took part on 10-11 April in a symposium on the theme: 'Energy challenge to policy-makers: changing energy supply, the consequences for the economy and policy response.' This was the first gathering of parliamentarians with a central role in formulating their countries' energy policies. Particular stress was laid on energy conservation and on the need for effective stock policies to restore calm in the market in the event of any future crisis such as that caused by the Iran-Iraq war.

In 1981, the OECD's Environment Committee entered into its second decade of work. This was marked, in April, by a special session on 'The OECD and policies for the '80s to address long-term environment issues'. A special panel studied all forms of policy, ranging through economics, energy, aid, trade and other fields.

The importance of further international harmonization of chemicals control was underlined by the OECD Council on 12 May when it agreed to extend the Organization's chemicals programme for a further three years. A decision was adopted stating that test data on chemicals produced in one country would be accepted as valid in all other OECD countries for purposes of assessment of chemicals, or for other purposes relating to the protection of health and the environment.

On 16 and 17 June the OECD Council met at ministerial level. Attention was concentrated on 1) member countries' economic prospects and policies, 2) current trade problems, 3) the energy situation, and 4) relations with developing countries. On 1), Ministers emphasized that in the present circumstances curbing inflation and reducing unemployment must be of prime concern. To bring this about the need for balanced use of a range of available policy instruments was recognized, taking account of the interdependence among countries and the need to find the right combination of action directed to conjunctural and structural problems, the demand and supply sides and the short and medium run. On 2), they reaffirmed their determination to implement fully and effectively the commitments made in the multilateral trade negotiations and the importance of action to improve and liberalize the conditions of international trade. On 3), Ministers stressed the danger of complacency during the present easing of the market and the need to continue strong efforts to reduce the vulnerability of the world to any future supply disruptions. On 4), they surveyed economic relations with developing countries in all aspects, including the importance of wide-ranging dialogue which would take into account the diversity of the problems, needs and responsibilities of participating countries as well as their common interest.

International Energy Agency (IEA) Ministers met on 15 June to address short-term oil market issues as well as the achievement of structural change in the medium and longer term. They expressed satisfaction that policies adopted earlier had contributed to avoiding serious market disturbances in the second half of 1980 and in 1981. There was unanimous agreement that progress in achieving structural change in IEA countries' energy economies was as urgent as ever.

During October a symposium was organized on 'rural change and public management', aimed at contributing to government efforts to promote economic and social developments in rural areas and to tackle critical employment situations by determining sectors in which investment could be encouraged.

Again in October, senior government officials met to discuss prospects and policies relating to access to higher education systems and the different facets thereof—changes in student demands and in the relationship between higher education and working life; new patterns of authority, notably autonomy and participation; financing; and redeployment of resources.

NORDIC COUNCIL

The 29th session of the Nordic Council was held in Copenhagen between 2 and 6 March 1981. The Council passed 32 recommendations for action by the Council of Ministers, the most important being these: that the Council of Ministers implement measures to stimulate cooperation on Nordic export 'project-packages', that they conclude the revised 1955 social security convention giving the five countries' citizens full cover in any Nordic country, extend the Nordic common labour market to cover new groups of health workers, conclude a Nordic language convention permitting Nordic citizens to use their own language when dealing with the authorities of other Nordic countries, and implement measures to reduce youth unemployment. The Council also recommended that the Council of Ministers produce a definite proposal on the controversial television satellite project NORDSAT in time for the 1982 session.

The main themes of the general debate were energy and industrial cooperation, the recession, and foreign and security policy issues. An example of Nordic energy and industrial cooperation was announced during the session. This was a twenty-year Norwegian-Swedish agreement (signed on 25 March) under which Norway would sell oil to Sweden in exchange for electricity. The agreement also provided for a jointly-financed industrial fund to help finance common projects, and the Governments promised to remove legal and other obstacles to cooperation between their national firms. This type of bilateral agreement was described by Norway's Prime Minister, Mrs Gro Harlem Brundtland, as a 'building-block' in Nordic cooperation, in that it was capable of being extended beyond the original signatories and thus offered a way forward to greater general cooperation.

Referring to the recession, some speakers expressed their fears that increased Nordic unemployment (up from 130,000 to 400,000 between

1973 and 1980) could undermine confidence in democracy's ability to master the crisis. There was general agreement that the main task facing the members in this time of structural adaptation was to preserve the Nordic social model, essential features of which were the individual's right to work and to economic and social security.

Foreign and security policy issues were raised by a Communist-left-Socialist proposal that the Nordic Council organize a between-session seminar for parliamentarians on the idea of a Nordic nuclear-free zone. Denmark's Prime Minister, Mr Anker Jørgensen, was ready to discuss ways in which such issues might be debated in the Nordic Council without altering its character. Finland's Prime Minister, Mr Mauno Koivisto, speaking to journalists, even suggested a separate plenary debate on foreign and security issues, arguing that, as such issues always arose anyway, they could at least be discussed in an orderly fashion and without the debate being dominated by extreme views. However, such a formal inclusion of foreign and security policy questions in the Council's debates was opposed by other influential politicians, such as Norway's Mr Kåre Willoch (Prime Minister after October) and Denmark's Mr K. B. Andersen.

COMECON

Three factors drove the member states of Comecon into further measures of economic collaboration during 1981. The most important consideration was the decline in trade with the West and the increase in their debts. Both Soviet and Eastern European sales to the developed market economies declined in volume: East Europe cut its imports relatively more sharply than exports to carry the high burden of debt service, whereas the USSR had to increase its imports, notably to buy grain. The group's gross debt in convertible currencies reached some $95,000 million. Poland failed to honour its commitments and at the end of the year both it and Romania were still in negotiation for rescheduling. The Soviet Union did not exercise the 'umbrella' role ascribed to it by some Western financial circles, but assisted both of the countries in difficulties with supplies which they would otherwise have had to pay for in convertible currencies (in the case of Poland with credits). The Soviet Government's power to extend such support, or to venture into more buying in the West, was also undermined by the decline in the world price of the two precious metals of which it is the second largest producer and exporter—gold and platinum. At the year-end, both sold for half the price reached at a peak in September 1980.

The second inhibition on trade with the West, the obverse of which was encouragement of intra-Comecon trade, was the Western embargo.

The United States, at the change of Administration, had lifted restrictions on grain sales to the USSR, but had reimposed them, together with severe limits on technology transfer, after the December coup in Poland. The Western summit meeting at Ottawa in June had agreed to extend the list of embargoed items, and a draft was agreed by the Coordinating Committee for Multilateral Export Controls (CoCom) for presentation to a high-level conference of participant states (Nato, less Iceland, plus Japan) in January 1982.

The third element was the suspension since October 1980 of all institutional contact with the EEC (see AR 1980, p. 363). The prospect of a treaty favouring trade and other flows between members of the two groups had wholly receded. Such must have been among the conditions which gave further impetus to measures of Comecon integration during 1981.

The XXXVth session of the Council (Sofia, 2-4 July) was, as usual, attended by the Prime Ministers of member states (save for Cuba and Vietnam, from which Deputy Premiers came); there were observers from Afghanistan, Angola, Ethiopia, Laos, Mozambique, the Yemen PDR and Yugoslavia. As the host, the Chairman of Bulgaria's Council of Ministers presided. Two themes dominated the formal speeches: first, the contrast between the maintenance of economic growth in member states and recession among capitalist economies, and, secondly, socialist economic integration under the Complex Programme of 1971, the tenth anniversary of which was duly observed; they merged in the consideration of members' five-year plans to 1985, all of which had been published (at least in draft, though none at all from Poland) since the previous annual session.

The session reviewed the work of its agencies in coordinating those plans (which for some branches of the economy comprised targets for further ahead to 1990) and approved a 'Concerted Plan of Multilateral Integration Measures' for 1981-85 which comprised three fields of collaboration, namely, multilateral joint projects, specialization agreements, and the coordination of aid to the three developing countries within its membership: Cuba, Mongolia and Vietnam. As a progress report on the first field, the session noted the completion in 1979-81 of the Soyuz gas pipeline spanning seven member states, and of the Kiembai asbestos works, the first section of the Ust-Ilimsk paper and pulp plant and the Novovolynsk plant for electrical engineering equipment; in Cuba, nickel mining and refining; and in Mongolia, copper and molybdenum mining and concentrating. Whereas these projects and the Long-term Target-oriented Cooperation Programme (see AR 1979, p. 363) had been individually conceived as collaboration schemes, those planned for the future would, the session resolved, be more closely woven into national five-year plans.

Specialization agreements on production and the forecasting of aggregate consumption covered energy, electronics and engineering. The 98th meeting of the executive committee (13-15 January) reviewed the work of Comecon's linked electricity grid and the XXXVth session approved work on an aggregate balance of energy to 1990 and beyond. The practical work on such forward estimations was embraced by Comecon's Committee for Cooperation in Planning, which met on 4 July in Moscow, immediately after the session. The reported 10 per cent cut in the Soviet plan for the sale of oil to other members for 1982 must have been on the agenda. At the previous year's session, the Soviet delegation had promised 400 million tonnes of crude oil to members during 1981-85, so the reduction for 1982 must have been unanticipated as well as unwelcome. A specialization scheme was adopted for electronics (especially micro-electronics) at the 99th Executive meeting (12-14 May) and two sets of recommendations were formulated for engineering—on machine-tools at the 98th, and on high-technology engineering at the 101st (13-15 October). The other Executive meeting of the year, the 100th (4 July) did no more, according to its communique, than follow up the decisions of the Council session. The session itself dealt with aid to all three less-developed members, notably to Cuba for the development of citrus-fruit growing; the 98th and 99th Executives both discussed aid to Vietnam. Negotiations in various fields of technological collaboration resulted in an agreement at the session on joint research into corrosion in tropical climates.

A significant innovation was a discussion at the session about the intentions of member governments on economic reform. The contemporary stalemate in Poland, where drafts for economic decentralization proliferated without any implementation, and the greater Soviet determination to press further with the modest reform of 1979 (as was later made plain at a Party Central Committee meeting of 16 November), must have been in view. A plan of research during 1981-85 for the organization's International Institute for the Economic Problems of the World Socialist System (located in Moscow) was approved by the 98th Executive, but without publication of even its broad content.

While continuing to concern itself chiefly with production, the organization also dealt with measures directly affecting the consumer. The 98th Executive called on the conference of Ministers of domestic trade of Comecon member states to extend its collaboration on the broadening of the variety of goods on the retail markets of their countries. Modest arrangements had long been in force whereby those ministries could by-pass the tight intergovernmental contracts of normal foreign-trade channels in order to barter consumer goods among themselves. Since retail shortages (worse in 1981 than in any year of the past twenty or so) were not of the same goods in each country, product 'swaps' could only improve matters. The other consumption field was health care; the same executive approved a research plan for inter-member specialization running to 1990 which identified as principal areas cardio-vascular and viral diseases, cancer and transplant surgery. The journal of the Comecon secretariat carried a series of articles on the health service in member states.

The banks with membership identical with Comecon took only some $500 million from the Western financial market in 1981; no Euro-currency bond issue had been made by any entity within Comecon since the first half of 1980. The International Bank for Economic Cooperation (IBEC) lent Poland $2,200 million in transferable roubles 'as a financial credit to cover a trade deficit', to which the Soviet Bank for Foreign Trade and the International Investment Bank (IIB) added a further $780 million; the USSR, in August, agreed to hold over $2,200 million of its bilateral debt. Since neither IBEC nor IIB had much convertible currency to lend to its members, the latter had recourse to bank loans and supplier credit (the channel arranged in November for the gas pipeline from Yamburg in northern Siberia to West Germany). A non-financial route to avoid further borrowing was increasingly used: an OECD study pub-lished in November estimated that one-fifth of Western exports to Comecon members was covered by barter provisions. Hungary and Poland applied in November for membership of the International Monetary Fund in the expectation of borrowing up to their quota; a proposal that the Bank for International Settlements lend $500 million to Poland had just been rejected. The communique issued after the 54th meeting of the IBEC Council (Budapest, 22 October) was, as always, un-informative, noting that the operational plan for 1982 and the draft plan for 1983 had been approved; any realistic projection would have indeed been gloomy.

Chapter 6

AFRICAN CONFERENCES AND INSTITUTIONS—ASSOCIATION OF
SOUTH-EAST ASIAN NATIONS—CARIBBEAN ORGANIZATIONS—
ORGANIZATION OF AMERICAN STATES

AFRICAN CONFERENCES AND INSTITUTIONS

THE 18-year-old Organization of African Unity (OAU) seemed, as ever, to survive by the skin of its teeth. It became heavily committed in the Chadian imbroglio, in a fashion that aroused some deep misgivings about its fate should the operation come unstuck.

The ministerial council, held in Addis Ababa in February, approved an 'austerity budget' for 1981-82 involving a 10 per cent drop in real income; for although the budget had risen by over 10 per cent to $19½ million that would not cover half the average price rise in the African continent. Arrears amounted to nearly $25½ million, less than 60 per cent of contributions having been paid in 1979-80. Persistent defaulters, it was reported, would be deprived of voting rights.

The annual summit, held in Nairobi from 24-28 June under the chairmanship of President Arap Moi of Kenya, was preceded by a week-long meeting of the ministerial council. The summit drew a high level of attendance of heads of state, although the Nigerian President, Alhaji Shehu Shagari, dropped out at the last minute in protest at the way the OAU secretariat had handled the Nigeria-Cameroon frontier incident in May in which five Nigerian soldiers were killed (see p. 234).

The major issue, as in the previous two years, was that of the recognition by the OAU of the République Arabe Sahraoui Démocratique (RASD) in the Western Sahara. After the secretary-general, Edem Kodjo, had reported that, despite the recognition of the Polisario Front by 26 states, the OAU Charter required adherence to the 'simple majority procedure' for the RASD to be admitted, the summit was startled by a major new initiative from Morocco. King Hassan II arrived late and announced: 'We have decided to envisage a procedure of controlled referendum, of which the procedures would simultaneously respect the latest recommendations of the *ad hoc* committee'—the so-called Committee of Wise Men—'and the conviction which Morocco has of its legitimate rights'. The *ad hoc* committee (composed of Guinea, Mali, Nigeria, Sudan and Tanzania) had recommended OAU and UN supervision of a referendum, as well as a ceasefire with a return to barracks, on both of which points King Hassan was silent.

His speech was applauded by the Libyans, not the Algerians, although President Benjedid Chadli recognized that it marked a step forward towards peace and stability. Mauritanian criticism of Moroccan involvement in an attempted coup in March (see p. 239) caused King Hassan to walk out, but he and the Mauritanian President were reconciled at a meeting in Saudi Arabia after the conference.

The summit set up an action committee to ensure the implementation of the *ad hoc* committee's recommendations. The new committee would have the same membership as the old plus Sierra Leone and Kenya. It met in Nairobi in August and, after interviewing in turn King Hassan, President Chadli, President Haidalla of Mauritania and the secretary-general of Polisario, adopted a number of proposals. The referendum was to offer a choice between independence and integration with Morocco. The committee rejected the King's proposal that the poll be restricted to the 73,497 Sahraouis counted in the last Spanish census, and decided that refugees in neighbouring countries should also be enfranchised, so there could be more than 200,000 voters. On the other hand they rejected Polisario's proposal for a total withdrawal of Moroccan troops and civil administration before the referendum. The OAU and the UN would conduct the poll, in collaboration with an 'impartial interim administration' aided by a UN peacekeeping force. Moroccan and Polisario troops would be confined to bases.

There were doubts, however, of Moroccan willingness really to prosecute this plan, in spite of official acquiescence. In Nairobi the King had refused to accept any direct contact with Polisario. When on 13 October Polisario launched a heavily-armoured attack on the isolated Moroccan base of Guelta Zemmour, apparently with Libyan support, King Hassan's statement that the action 'restores to us our total freedom of action' put the whole OAU plan on ice, although Morocco remained officially committed to a referendum (see also pp. 218 and 220).

On Chad the summit kept alive the proposal for an OAU peacekeeping force, and required an undertaking from neighbouring states not to engage in sabotage or destabilization; but there was no criticism of Libya and it was accepted that the removal of Libyan troops was a question for the Chad President, who had invited them to come. President Nimairi of Sudan denounced Libya's presence and used strong diplomatic pressure to prevent the OAU 1982 summit from being held in Tripoli. This was finally agreed despite many reservations and the absence of Colonel Qadafi.

In October it transpired that, on a French initiative, a number of African countries, including Nigeria and Senegal, had agreed to participate in a joint peacekeeping force, to be sponsored by the OAU. Nigeria's decision, apparently negotiated between Presidents Mitterrand and Shagari at the Cancún summit, was a key factor, as were the acceptance by President Oueddeye and the French to pay most of the cost of the force. President Oueddeye requested withdrawal of Libyan troops and Colonal Qadafi announced that he was complying. His troops were entirely withdrawn in two weeks from the end of October, but the OAU force was not in place before mid-December. This gave time for Habre forces to consolidate a position in eastern Chad (see p. 243). At the end of the year there were contingents of 1,000 troops from Nigeria and 600 each from Senegal and Zaïre under the command of General Geoffrey Ejiga of Nigeria. Togo, Benin and Guinea having changed their minds, Zaïre declared itself willing to increase its contingent to 2,000. The US and British also expressed willingness to assist the operation, but anxiety remained as to the pitfalls for the OAU implicit in the whole exercise.

Although the Franco-African summit in Paris was dominated by the Chadian question, it was also an occasion for the African countries to

Press Association

A new British political party is formed: the 'gang of four' ex-Labour Cabinet Ministers (left to right: Mr Roy Jenkins, Dr David Owen, Mr William Rodgers, Mrs Shirley Williams) launch the Social Democratic Party on 26 March 1981.

Rex Features

A picture that scarcely needs a caption: Korchnoi unsuccessfully challenges Karpov for the world chess championship, November 1981.

Four European political figures prominent in the news of 1981: above, Andrea George Papandreou and François Mitterrand, socialist victors in the Greek and French elections; below, General Wojciech Jaruzelski, Prime Minister of Poland, and President Orho Kekkonen of Finland, who resigned on 27 October after 26 years in office.

Among the eminent people who died in 1981 were, above, President Ziaur Rahman of Bangladesh and President Anwar Sadat of Egypt, both assassinated; below, Cardinal Stefan Wyszynski, Primate of Poland, and Moshe Dayan, Israeli soldier and statesman.

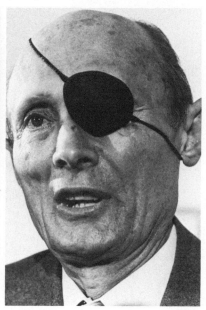

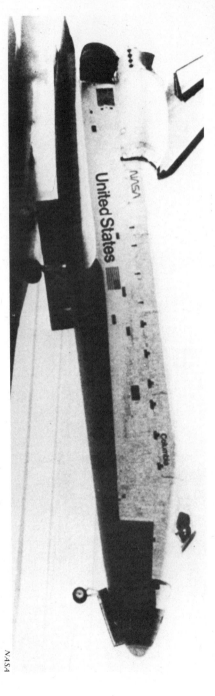

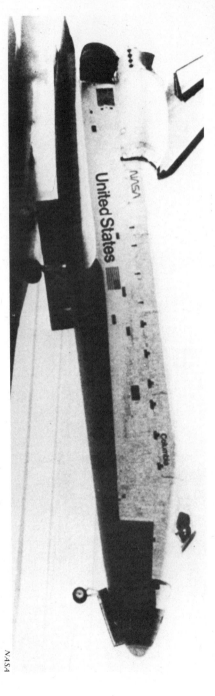

Triumph and disaster: above, the American space shuttle *Columbia* makes a perfect landing, 14 April 1981; below, a Soviet submarine aground near the Swedish naval base of Karlskrona, 29 October 1981.

N.A.S.A

Press Association

demonstrate their enthusiasm for the new French regime. One evidence of this was the higher-than-ever attendance: 29 African countries (more than half the OAU) took part, ten of which had observer status, including Somalia, Sierra Leone, Tunisia and, for the first time, Egypt, Sudan, São Tome and Angola, President Giscard having already opened the doors beyond the francophone countries. The meeting discussed economic issues, and appealed for the regulation of prices of raw materials and of essential commodities imported by developing countries. The summit had been switched to Paris from Kinshasa, ostensibly because President Mitterrand did not wish to travel to Africa so soon, in fact to avoid his being a guest of President Mobutu, whom he had denounced as a tyrant during his election campaign.

Of African regional organizations, those in West Africa seemed to be in the best health. The 16-nation ECOWAS (Economic Community of West African States) and the 6-nation francophone CEAO (Communauté Economique de l'Afrique de l'Ouest) consolidated their largely complementary positions. Both held summit meetings: the CEAO summit in Dakar in December was followed by two other summits involving some of the same members: those of ANAD (Accord de Non-Aggression at d'Assistance en Matière de Défense), involving the CEAO members—Senegal, Ivory Coast, Mali, Mauritania, Upper Volta, Niger—plus Togo; and of UMOA (Union Monétaire Ouest-Africain) covering CEAO minus Mauritania plus franc-zone Togo and Benin. The main UMOA decision was to postpone the membership of Mali, which although in the franc zone had its own currency. Although the Manyo River Union (Sierra Leone, Liberia and Guinea) had been quiescent since the 1980 coup in Liberia, the establishment of the Senegambia confederation (see p. 236) introduced a more closely-knit grouping than any other.

Observing the progress made by its brainchild ECOWAS, the UN Economic Commission for Africa (ECA) encouraged other parts of the continent to pursue the path of regional unity, with some success in Central Africa, where the annual summit in December of UDEAC (Union Douanière et Economique de l'Afrique Centrale, comprising Gabon, Cameroon, CAR and Congo) not only accepted the requested re-integration of Chad, which had left in 1968, but also agreed in principle to set up a Central African Economic Community, involving the three countries of the CEPGL (Communauté Economique des Pays des Grands Lacs), Zaïre, Rwanda and Burundi, as well as São Tome and Angola. Another ECA-inspired plan, for a 22-nation free trade area in East and Central Africa, fell on stonier ground. A summit to establish the proposed pact, held in Lusaka just before Christmas, was boycotted by seven of the countries concerned, including Tanzania, whose tense relations with Kenya were a hangover from the dissolution of the East

African Community. The nine-nation SADCC (Southern African Development Coordination Conference), set up the previous year, seemed a much sounder proposition.

SOUTH-EAST ASIAN ORGANIZATIONS

Asean continued its efforts to bring pressure on Vietnam to end the occupation of Kampuchea. The Association was successful in strengthening support for its position in the Non-Aligned conference in Delhi in February and in the United Nations in the autumn. It was hampered in these endeavours by the widespread detestation of the policies and conduct, when in control of Kampuchea, of the Khmer Rouge regime, which, however, still provided the main military resistance to the occupation, was well as having claims to legitimacy. Khmer Rouge effectiveness in harrying the Vietnamese increased noticeably during the year, as did that of the largest non-communist resistance group, the Kampuchean People's National Liberation Front (KPNLF) led by Son Sann.

Vietnam insisted that the situation it had created in Kampuchea was irreversible and tried to divide the Asean countries and at the same time to force recognition of the indissoluble unity of Laos and Kampuchea with Vietnam. On 28 January Vietnam stated that it was prepared to withdraw some troops from Kampuchea when Thailand stopped providing bases, food and weapons to Khmer guerrillas—which Thailand denied that it did—but would consider a complete withdrawal only when 'the threat from China' no longer existed. It proposed a conference between the three Indochinese countries, attending as a bloc, and Asean. Asean rejected these proposals as unacceptable, but Hanoi continued to press them.

In 1980 the UN General Assembly had proposed the convening of an international conference on the Kampuchean problem. This was to secure the withdrawal of foreign troops from Kampuchea and free elections under UN supervision, as well as guarantees against foreign intervention. The proposal was described as 'entirely unacceptable' by Vietnam, supported by the Soviet bloc. The conference was nevertheless held in July and was attended by nearly 80 countries. It called for a cease-fire, a rapid Vietnamese withdrawal, free elections and measures to ensure law and order pending the establishment of a government. The conference also made plain that China adopted a much harder attitude towards the Vietnamese than did Asean.

In September the number of countries voting in the UN General Assembly to accept the credentials of the Khmer Rouge regime showed a further increase. In October the General Assembly passed a resolution approving the proposals adopted at the July conference, deciding that this conference should be reconvened in due course and authorizing the establishment of an *ad hoc* committee to promote dialogue on the issues before the conference met again. The resolution, which was supported by 100 countries, also reiterated the points made in previous years.

In order to consolidate Khmer resistance to the occupation the Asean countries pressed for the formation of a coalition between the Khmer Rouge, the KPNLF and Moulinaka, a non-communist group formed by supporters of Prince Norodom Sihanouk. The attempt to form a coalition was hampered by the dislike of the Khmer Rouge leaders by both Sann and Sihanouk, the conviction that the Khmer Rouge would revert to their former policies if given the slightest chance of regaining power and the fear that association with them would alienate the Kampuchean people.

Agreement was nevertheless reached between the three parties that a coalition should have Sihanouk as head of state and Sann as Prime Minister, with a Khmer Rouge Deputy Prime Minister. Below this level the Khmer Rouge wished their existing governmental structure to remain intact and legitimate, enabling them to resume control once the Vietnamese had withdrawn. Asean, however, proposed a looser coalition Government with only six members, two each from the three parties, including the head of state, Prime Minister and Deputy Prime Minister. This Government would concentrate on coordinating the military and political struggle against the Vietnamese occupation and would be dissolved after a Vietnamese withdrawal, so that the Khmer Rouge governmental structure would have no status. The Khmer Rouge leaders also appeared to fear that the arrangement would assist the building-up of KPNLF armed forces and that Sihanouk and Sann, once installed as head of state and Prime Minister, would erode such popular support as the Khmer Rouge retained. At the end of the year, therefore, the Khmer Rouge were resisting the Asean coalition proposals and appeared to have Chinese support in this.

CARIBBEAN ORGANIZATIONS

A critical report by a group of experts on the future of the 8-year-old Caribbean Community (Caricom) was submitted to the Caricom Council of Ministers at its 19th meeting and was being studied. The Council supported Guyana in its dispute with Venezuela, expressed its determination that the living marine life of the Caribbean should be exploited for the benefit of its peoples, expressed concern over the British Nationality Act, denounced the 'economic aggression' of the US against Grenada, and set up a small working party on the 'zone of peace' concept for the Caribbean. The question of establishing a quick-disbursing aid programme for rehabilitation and reconstruction was raised with Western aid donors in Washington. A united Caribbean front on President Reagan's Caribbean Basin initiative emerged and was essentially critical of early aspects of the proposal. The Caribbean Development Bank rejected an offer of US$4 million because the US Government specifically excluded Grenada from its use. The Bank took the opportunity to fulminate against the growing practice among donors of dictating aspects of aid use by creating a multiplicity of hard-to-disburse 'special funds', of which there were now more than twenty.

THE ORGANIZATION OF AMERICAN STATES

In January news of the outbreak of fighting between troops of Ecuador and Peru (see p. 82) led to the convening of the Permanent Council of the OAS in Washington. The Council convened on 29 January and urged both sides to accept the creation of a commission of investigation, a proposal which was accepted by Ecuador but rejected by Peru on the grounds that only the four guarantor powers of the Protocol of Rio de Janeiro of 1942 were competent to mediate in the dispute. The Peruvian representative subsequently abstained, together with the representatives of Guatemala and El Salvador, when the Council adopted by 20 votes to nil the Ecuadorian request for a meeting of Foreign Ministers the following week. The representatives of the guarantor powers, Argentina, Brazil, Chile and the United States, met at Brasília two days later, and after twenty hours arrived at proposals acceptable to both sides in the dispute, so that happily when the Foreign Ministers of seven members of the OAS met in Washington on 2 February a ceasefire had already been established. The Foreign Ministers resolved to call upon both sides to cease military operations and to demobilize their forces, and expressed satisfaction that both Governments had agreed to 'establish and consolidate peace'.

The General Assembly of the OAS met in Castries, St Lucia, on 5 December. On behalf of the United States, General Alexander Haig launched an attack on the Provisional Government of Nicaragua, who, he claimed, were building up a considerable armed force which was a threat to peace in the area. The Nicaraguan delegate rejected the charges, saying that his country's forces were only for self-defence. Discussing the continuing civil war in his own country, Dr Fidel Chávez Mena, Foreign Minister of El Salvador, repeated charges of Nicaraguan interference in the conflict, and denounced the French and Mexican Governments for recognizing the guerrillas (see p. 88). After a long debate, the Assembly on 8 December accepted a resolution presented by the Governments of El Salvador, Costa Rica and Honduras, rejecting the Franco-Mexican position, and condemning all acts that constituted a 'violation of the principle of non-intervention'. The motion was passed by 22 votes to 3, the minority votes being those of Grenada, Mexico and Nicaragua. Panama, St Lucia, Suriname and Trinidad and Tobago abstained.

Chapter 7

THE NON-ALIGNED MOVEMENT

FOLLOWING the Soviet intervention in Afghanistan, it had been agreed that the regular triennial Foreign Ministers meeting of the Non-Aligned, originally scheduled for mid-1981, would be brought forward by six months (see AR 1980, pp. 374-5). When the meeting was held from 9 to 13 February in New Delhi, the question of Afghanistan was still high on the agenda. Neither the Cubans, currently holding the chairmanship of the Movement, nor the Indians, who produced a bland draft statement on the issue, wanted to condemn the Soviet Union. However, the majority made sure that the conference 'urgently called for a political settlement on the basis of the withdrawal of foreign troops' from Afghanistan. The other main dispute was over Kampuchea, which had caused great bitterness at the 1979 Havana summit (see AR 1979, p. 373), but now with minimal objection from Singapore, Malaysia and Indonesia it was decided to maintain a policy of keeping Kampuchea's seat in the Movement vacant. At the same time, after long debate, the conference also called for 'the withdrawal of all foreign forces' in Kampuchea, as an attack upon Vietnam's intervention.

Although Iran had boycotted the Islamic Conference summit in January, both Iran and Iraq were represented in Delhi and subjected to intense pressure to negotiate over their border war. The seven-member 'goodwill committee' appointed in October 1980 had been unable to proceed (see AR 1980, p. 375), but a smaller group of Cuba, India, Zambia and the PLO was accepted at Delhi. It set to work immediately afterwards with meetings in Geneva and Beirut, but made no substantive progress during the year.

On the Middle East there was a distinct shift in the Non-Aligned position. Blanket opposition to the Camp David agreements was watered down, while opposition to the provisions for the West Bank was spelt out more strongly. Nineteen Arab countries revived the attempt, begun in Havana, to suspend Egypt from membership of the Movement, but resolute resistance from the African countries again produced a decision to postpone the issue. It seemed that Egypt's seat was secure, so long as concessions were not made to the Israelis in the negotiations on Palestinian autonomy.

South Africa's disruption in January of the Geneva negotiations on implementing the UN plan for Namibian independence (see pp. 326-7) caused great concern at Delhi and unified support for Swapo, which was a member of the Movement. The 35th session of the UN General Assembly, resuming in March, passed ten resolutions on Namibia, including one calling on the Security Council to impose full sanctions on South Africa. As decided at Delhi, in mid-April there was a special ministerial meeting of the Non-Aligned Coordinating Bureau on Namibia in Algiers, which authorized 24 members to take part in the Security Council debates on behalf of the Movement. In May, after four sanctions resolutions had been vetoed by Britain, France and the United States, an initiative from the Havana summit of the Non-Aligned came to fruition with the holding of a UN conference in Paris on the practical problems of implementing sanctions. Initially the Western countries boycotted the conference, but the Socialist victory in the French elections led to their participation, with an announcement that French policy would change to support for sanctions. As agreed at Delhi, the Non-Aligned campaign continued when they convened in September an Emergency Special Session of the UN General Assembly. No advance was made during the year on bringing sanctions into effect, but the initial moves by the Reagan Administration to improve US relations with South Africa were reconverted into American pressure for progress towards Namibian independence.

The Economic Declaration produced by the Foreign Ministers in Delhi conveyed an air of desperation and despair at the worsening economic conditions of the developing countries, compounded by the intransigence of the major developed countries towards the 'global negotiations'. The damage done to the Non-Aligned Movement's own economic Action Programme by the 1979 decision to abolish annual ministerial meetings of the Bureau was shown when at Delhi only six of the 18 groups of coordinating countries had reports to offer on work in the previous eighteen months. Nevertheless, the groups were urged to continue and three new ones were set up, to cover industrial harmonization, education and housing.

Despite the problems over Namibia and over economic development, the February meeting saw the Non-Aligned in a highly critical mood towards the Soviet Union and at their least anti-Western for several years. By September, at their annual meeting of delegations to the General Assembly, President Reagan had so antagonized them on all their main concerns that they produced their most anti-Western communique for many years. The American ambassador to the UN, Jeane Kirkpatrick, responded to negative mentions of the United States 'nine times by name and dozens of times by implication' by sending an angry letter, denouncing 'fabrications and vile attacks', to 58 of the 97 Non-Aligned members. She particularly objected to allegations of

American aggression in the Gulf of Sirte incident (see p. 71) and destabilizing pressure by the USA on the Governments of Grenada and Nicaragua. At the end of October US Senator Moynihan proposed an amendment to the Foreign Assistance Act to cut off funds to those countries which failed to dissociate themselves from the communique. The amendment was withdrawn but a milder version, asking the President to take the matter into account when allocating aid, was passed unanimously. The Non-Aligned made no public response individually or collectively.

The September meeting endorsed the candidature of Salim Salim of Tanzania to be Secretary-General of the UN. He succeeded in securing the withdrawal of Kurt Waldheim, but failed to be elected because of American vetoes. However, the compromise candidate, Sr Perez de Cuellar of Peru, who was elected, was also from a Non-Aligned country.

During the year the Non-Aligned Movement increased from 94 to 97 members, St Lucia and Ecuador moving up from 'observer' status and Belize becoming a full member on attaining independence. The Saudi Arabians, who had boycotted the Havana summit, also returned to active membership in 1981. In both Delhi and New York the twentieth anniversary of the Movement was celebrated.

Chapter 8

THE CANCÚN SUMMIT

A SUMMIT conference of heads of state or government from 22 selected developing and developed countries was held in Cancún, Mexico on 22-23 October. Officially designated the International Meeting on Cooperation and Development, it took place some 20 months after the idea for such a mini-summit, to give new impetus to seeking solutions for urgent global economic problems, was first proposed in the Brandt Commission's report (see AR 1980, p. 499). The summit was initially sponsored by Austria and Mexico.

In March 1981 the Foreign Ministers of 11 co-sponsoring countries— Austria, Canada, France, West Germany and Sweden from 'the North' and Algeria, India, Mexico, Nigeria, Tanzania and Yugoslavia from 'the South'—met in Vienna. At American urging they agreed to postpone the conference from June to October to ensure the attendance of the US President. They drew up a list of countries to be invited, seeking a regional balance as well as a cross-section of major interests. Besides the co-sponsors, Saudi Arabia and Venezuela from Opec, Guyana, Brazil, the Ivory Coast, Bangladesh, the Philippines and China, together with Britain, Japan and the United States, were invited and agreed to attend.

American attendance was conditional, however, on Cuba's absence; though currently chairman of the Non-Aligned Movement, Cuba was later persuaded not to attend. The USSR declined its invitation.

The 22 Foreign Ministers met in Cancún in August. They confirmed that the summit would be deliberative, not decision-taking, and, largely at American insistence, that it would not have a formal agenda or produce a final communique. They named the themes for discussion—food, energy, trade and monetary and financial issues—and decided that the aim would be to facilitate agreement on how to proceed with global economic negotiations. They also agreed to invite the UN Secretary-General to the summit.

Brandt Commission members, meeting in West Berlin in May, had urged that the summit should in particular seek agreement on how best to approach the most serious economic problems affecting developing countries. The summit, however, achieved little. The concluding summary issued to the press by co-chairmen Mexican President Portillo and Canadian Prime Minister Trudeau revealed that participants could agree only to informal talks in the UN on launching global economic negotiations. Developed countries still opposed negotiations held entirely within the UN—as envisaged by developing countries—on the grounds that they would undermine the autonomy of the Northern-controlled IMF and World Bank. No agreement was reached on the content or purpose of the global negotiations.

American opposition prevented unanimous support for setting up a World Bank energy affiliate to promote energy production in developing countries. The key to elimination of hunger—given high priority for international cooperation—was said to lie in the internal efforts of developing countries combined with effective international technical and financial support, not in food aid. But no specific proposals for cooperation to increase food self-sufficiency in developing countries found general acceptance. On trade and financial issues, no new proposals were unanimously considered to provide a basis for future cooperation between rich and poor countries.

XII RELIGION

THE POPE. On 13 May Pope John Paul II was shot and seriously wounded as he was being driven in an open jeep among 10,000 pilgrims in St Peter's Square, Rome. Two bullets hit the Pope in the abdomen, right arm and left hand, and two American tourists were also wounded. The Pope was rushed to hospital for a five-hour operation to remove part of his alimentary canal. He returned to the Vatican on 2 June but further surgery was needed in August and he finally left hospital for a long convalescence. A papal visit to Switzerland was cancelled and the Pontiff's full activity was not resumed until October.

The Pope's assailant, who was immediately arrested, was Mehmet Ali Agca, aged 23, from Turkey. Convicted of murder in 1979 he had escaped and in a letter to a Turkish newspaper had threatened to kill the Pope, whom he called 'commander of the masked crusaders', if his 'untimely visit' to Turkey later that year was not cancelled. No such attempt was made, and Agca escaped from Turkey, travelling widely in Europe before reaching Italy; many people asked where he had obtained forged passports and money for expensive hotels. On 22 July Agca was charged with attempted murder of a head of state at Rome Court of Assizes and sentenced to life imprisonment, extradition to Turkey being refused.

In February the Pope had visited Pakistan, where a bomb exploded shortly before his celebration of Mass, the Philippines, the only Asian country with a Christian majority, and Japan, where Christians were less than one per cent of the population. He beatified the first Filipino martyr, Lorenzo Ruiz, and visited the Japanese Emperor Hirohito, the peace memorial at Hiroshima and the slums of Manila. But His Holiness strongly condemned the artificial contraception which the Government of the Philippines promoted.

In Italy an anti-abortion campaign, Movement for Life, was described by the Pope as a 'holy cause', defending human rights and the commandment not to kill. But in referendums on 17-18 May two-thirds of Italian voters rejected proposed restrictions on abortion laws, yet also vetoed proposals by the Radical Party to remove all restraints on abortion. On 15 December the Vatican issued a papal exhortation, *Familiaris Consortio*, attacking 'a certain panic' in estimates of population growth, branding contraception as manipulation of the divine plan, and civil remarriage of divorcees as 'an evil', though such Catholics were urged to attend Mass without receiving Communion.

UNION AND DIVISION. The wedding of the Prince of Wales and Lady Diana Spencer in St Paul's Cathedral on 29 July was an ecumenical occasion, with prayers by Cardinal Hume and the Moderator of the Church of Scotland, the lesson read by the Methodist Speaker of the House of Commons, the service introduced by the Dean and the formal words and sermon spoken by the Archbishop of Canterbury, Dr Robert Runcie. 'The Christian faith', said the Archbishop, saw 'the wedding day not as the place of arrival but the place where the adventure really begins'. The traditional 1662 Prayer Book service was used, omitting the bride's pledge to 'obey' her husband.

The General Synod of the Church of England in February voted overwhelmingly for recognition of the sacraments of the Free Churches and of their women ministers. In November the Synod agreed that Anglican women might be ordained deacons though not yet priests. But in December an English deaconess, Miss Elizabeth Canham, went to Trinity Cathedral, Newark, New Jersey, to receive American Episcopalian ordination as priest, in a service in which the former Bishop of Southwark, Dr Mervyn Stockwood, took part. To help towards unity with the Anglican Church the Methodists in July agreed for the first time on the appointment of their own bishops in the United Kingdom. But the new Bishop of London, Dr Graham Leonard, enthroned at St Paul's in September, opposed both female ordination and unity schemes with the Free Churches.

On 24 August the Salvation Army withdrew from the World Council of Churches, of which it had been a founder member, because support for guerrilla movements appeared to be 'motivated by politics rather than the Gospel' (see AR 1978, pp. 360-1). In September the World Council allocated £319,000 to 47 groups, the largest award going towards legal and administrative costs of the South West Africa People's Organization, and a small grant to the British magazine *Searchlight*, which monitored extreme right-wing and racist organizations.

In February the Templeton prize of £90,000 for progress in religion was awarded to Dame Cicely Saunders, founder of St Christopher's Hospice in south London for the very ill and dying. Some of the largest anti-nuclear demonstrations ever seen in Europe were organized by the churches, notably in West Germany and the Netherlands. In December 20,000 young people from Europe met in London on a pilgrimage of peace and reconciliation, organized by the Taizé Community in France.

'Creationism' versus evolution was argued across the United States in many forums and court cases. Kelly Segraves, Baptist head of a creation-science research center in San Diego, argued in court at Sacramento that children's religious freedom was infringed by the teaching of Darwinian theories of evolution in state schools. In June the judge, Irving Perluss, gave his written decision that 'in a discussion of origins in science texts, dogmatism should be changed to conditional statements'. At a court in Arkansas an education professor, Larry Parker, claimed that to teach evolution without creation was 'tantamount to indoctrination', but the American Civil Liberties Union contended that to teach both theories in school violated the constitutional separation of church and state.

STRUGGLE. On 2 June the Archbishop of Canterbury began a visit to Northern Ireland, where he met Cardinal Tomas O'Fiaich and knelt with him in Armagh Cathedral to pray for peace. Dr Runcie condemned the hunger strike in the Maze prison, suggested there might be some new initiative to break it, but ruled out granting political status to prisoners. On 17 June the Roman Catholic bishops' conference at Maynooth implored 'the hunger strikers and those who direct them to reflect deeply on the evil of their actions and their consequences. The contempt for human life, the incitement to revenge, the exploitation of the hunger strikes to further a campaign of murder, the intimidation of the innocent, the initiation of children into violence, all this constitutes an appalling mass of evil'. In November Cardinal O'Fiaich condemned the IRA as sinful, saying that 'participation in the evil deeds of this or any other paramilitary organization . . . is a mortal sin which will one day have to be accounted for before God in judgment.'

Cardinal Stefan Wyszinski, Primate of Poland, died of cancer on 28 May (see OBITUARY). President Jablonski and Prime Minister General Jaruzelski paid tribute to the Cardinal as priest and patriot; official mourning was announced throughout Poland, with flags at half-mast and theatres and cinemas closed.

On 7 July the Pope nominated Bishop Josef Glemp, aged 52, of Warsaw, a specialist in civil and canonical law, as Primate of Poland. After the imposition of military rule in December it was reported that General Jaruzelski had asked for a meeting with Archbishop Glemp, but he had refused unless the trade union leader Lech Walesa was present and this had been turned down. On 20 December a message from the Primate was read in all Polish churches stating: 'We are helpless, confronted by sufferings and evil. But . . . we beg you in the name of God not to raise an arm filled with hatred against one another. Keep calm, do not drive our country to a still greater disaster.' The military regime granted an entry visa to a special envoy from the Pope, Mgr Luigi Poggi, though he was not allowed to see Lech Walesa, but later the Polish episcopate set up a team to try mediation between the military authorities and trade union leaders.

Unprecedented numbers of religious victims throughout Latin America led to increasing protests. In May, 500 priests, including Cardinal Aloisio Lorscheider of Brazil, published a statement in Mexico City denouncing 'the terrible situation of the people of El Salvador under

an oppressive Christian Democrat military junta responsible for exter-
mination, genocide, kidnappings and disappearances' (see AR 1980, p.
378).

In August evangelical churches and Muslim mosques were closed in
northern Ethiopia, their leaders arrested and blamed for spending too
much time in prayer and being thereby responsible for poor farming and
famine. In December it was reported that 600 Ethiopian Christian and
Muslim leaders had been executed.

FRINGE RELIGION. Britain's longest libel action ended in March,
brought by the Unification Church, organization of Sun Myung Moon
(see AR 1977, p. 359), against the *Daily Mail*. The *Mail* had alleged that
this church used 'sophisticated mind control techniques' on recruits,
resulting in a 'perpetual vapid smile', that it 'broke up families', Mr
Moon lived 'in splendour while his followers were in forced penury', and
his church controlled vast funds derived from dubious activities. The
jury gave a unanimous verdict for the defendants, implying they found
these charges true. The charitable status of the Unification Church was
questioned but the Charity Commissioners decided not to take action.

Shree Bhagwan Rajneesh had an ashram at Poona at which red-robed
devotees chanted the founder's synthetic teachings and engaged in sexual
'encounter' sessions. After critical description by the BBC it was reported that Bhagwan had disappeared and his ashram broken up, some
members becoming religious beggars and others returning to Europe and
America. But in August Bhagwan's 'meditation center' paid $6 million
for a cattle ranch of over 100 square miles in Oregon.

JEWISH DEBATE. Excavations below the walls of the Old City of Jerusalem, in hope of finding the original city of David, provoked violent
demonstrations in August. The ultra-orthodox Natorei Karta sect
claimed the site was an ancient cemetery and should not be disturbed.
The Chief Rabbi, Shlomo Goren, demanded revocation of the licence to
dig under threat of religious sanctions, but public opinion was on the side
of the archaeologists, 75 per cent being opposed to rabbinical intervention. Orthodox protests against traffic on the Sabbath continued,
religious forces in the coalition Government urging closing Sabbath bus
services, airports and entertainments (see AR 1977, p. 358).

Proposed amendment of the Law of Return recognized only Orthodox conversions, causing dissent from Reform and Conservative Jews.
In the United States, Reform Jews in the Union of American Hebrew
Congregations decided in December to end a four-century ban on prose-
lytization. Converts would be sought in the conviction that 'Judaism is a
living, meaningful, spiritual religion that welcomes all who wish to
embrace it'. Children of a mixed marriage would be regarded as Jewish,

against the former tradition that Jewishness depended on the mother (see AR 1970, p. 372).

ISLAMIC ACTION. An Islamic summit meeting, representing 38 countries, met in Saudi Arabia in January with opening prayers in the Grand Mosque of Mecca. There was agreement on a *Jihad* (holy war) to recover Israeli-occupied territories and warnings of the dangers of foreign ideologies, east and west.

In Pakistan measures continued to bring the legal code and public practice into accordance with Islamic *shariat* law. From 1 January it was forbidden to serve alcoholic drinks on Pakistan International Airlines, foreign embassies were asked to serve soft drinks only to Pakistanis at receptions, judges and civil servants were ordered to wear Islamic dress in their offices, women students were to be veiled and Islamic studies were made compulsory for all students seeking bachelor degrees. Interest-free banking was introduced to enforce the Islamic ban on usury, and *zakat* (alms tax) was imposed on deposits and savings, with exception for the Shia who protested that *zakat* should be voluntary.

In Iran radical Mujaheddin issued a statement in July holding Ayatollah Khomeini personally responsible for murder of revolutionaries. Rejecting his title they asserted; 'We see Mr Khomeini's arms are covered with the blood of the Iranian people.' He thought he was 'deputising for Muhammad the 12th imam', but his organization was 'Satan's party'. Violent clashes with the authorities preceded and followed this attack.

On 27 February three British Anglican missionaries who had been arrested the previous August were allowed to leave Iran after documents accusing them of spying were proved false. Dr John and Mrs Audrey Coleman, Miss Jean Waddell and four Iranian Anglicans were released, but the Anglican church was forbidden to continue work in Iran, centres and clinics having been closed after attacks by Muslim extremists (see AR 1980, p. 379).

The 300,000 Bahais in Iran, the largest minority religion, came under increasing pressure. Some 100 leaders had been executed and thousands were homeless or fled the country. Accused of political plotting, those executed were heads of local Bahai communities and were said to have been offered reprieves if they renounced their religion. Bahais outside Iran appealed to the United Nations Commission on Human Rights.

Continuing struggles between Muslim fundamentalists and Coptic Christians in Egypt, as well as opposition to the Government, caused President Sadat to order widescale arrests in early September (see AR 1980, p. 379). The Coptic Pope, Shenouda III, was stripped of temporal power, replaced by a committee of five bishops and exiled to a desert monastery. Following the example of Iran, Muslim revivalists opposed westernism, demanded veiling of women and bans on alcohol, and were alleged to have plotted the assassination of the President (see pp. 192-3).

CHINA. Articles in official publications defending the policy of religious toleration suggested both support for religion and some opposition (see AR 1980, p. 380). On 1 March *Red Flag* reported that 'at present quite a large number of people in China believe in religion. We must respect this objective fact.' Among Chinese 'nationalities' it named ten that were Islamic, Tibetans and Mongols who were Buddhists, and 'extensive influence' of Christians among the Miao, Yu and Yi.

On 6 June the Roman Catholic Bishop Deng Yiming was appointed by the Pope as Archbishop of Guangdong province, the first papal episcopal appointment in China for 25 years. But the Chinese Patriotic Catholic Association described this action as 'illegal' and 'a rude interference in the sovereign affairs of the Chinese Church'.

On 7 April the Protestant Bishop Ding Guangxun reported that the number of Protestants in China had increased from 700,000 in 1949 to a million. Over 100 churches had been reopened and there were many other house churches, attracting large numbers of young people, and 130,000 copies of the scriptures had been printed. Chinese missionary work was planned but foreign missions were discouraged. The old denominations had been replaced by unity in the Self-Patriotic Movement.

On 13 August over 6,000 Muslims celebrated the feast of Id ul-Fitr after Ramadan at two mosques in Peking, and a third mosque was reopened in October. A new translation of the Koran, the first in modern standard Chinese, was in the press.

BOOKS

Priestland's Progress, by Gerald Priestland, religious affairs correspondent of the BBC, was a series of 13 programmes on Radio 4 exploring Christianity today. Published as a book in December, 10,000 copies sold out at once and the author was chosen by radio listeners as second only to the Prince of Wales as most popular man of the year. Personal religious struggles were also recorded in selections from the diaries of Malcolm Muggeridge, *Like It Was,* and in Philip Toynbee's *Part of a Journey.* More theological stringency came from two Anglican brother professors, Anthony Hanson of Hull and Richard Hanson of Manchester, in *Reasonable Belief.* In *The View from Planet Earth* Vincent Cronin found that the improbability of the universe's coming into being by blind chance led him to a Christian outlook, but Arthur Koestler in *Kaleidoscope* rejected a creator who allowed universal cruelty. In *The Pope's Divisions* Peter Nichols challenged Stalin's dismissal of Roman Catholicism, showing its modern vitality and universal extent, but finding widespread rejection of 'the Vatican's disciplines on sexual teaching'.

Cyril Williams in *Tongues of the Spirit* described ancient glossolalia and linked them with modern charismatic movements, while *Medusa's Hair* by Gananath Obeyesekere examined Hindu and Buddhist ecstatics in Sri Lanka. Leslie Howard in *The Expansion of God* urged the need to adjust Christian thought to religious teachings of Asia. In *Flowers of Emptiness* Sally Belfrage described disillusionment with Shree Bhagwan Rajneesh, and V.

S. Naipaul's *Among the Believers* considered Islamic revival in Iran, Pakistan, Malaysia and Indonesia as a throwback to medieval times. Edward Said in *Covering Islam*, following his volumes on *Orientalism* and *The Question of Palestine*, criticized ignorance and misrepresentation of Islam in the Western press, also accusing academics of a conspiracy of silence or of being agents of Western power. Ernest Gellner's *Muslim Society* was an ambitious title for careful limited anthropological research in the Moroccan Atlas, and *The Politics of Islamic Reassertion*, edited by Mohammed Ayoob, stressed the diversity of Islamic movements in different cultural contexts.

XIII THE SCIENCES

Chapter 1

SCIENCE, MEDICINE AND TECHNOLOGY

SPACE. After delays, the first American space shuttle, *Columbia*, made its maiden flight into space and back again from 12 to 14 April. This was the first flight of a reusable manned space vehicle. It demonstrated that the American National Aeronautics and Space Administration could do what it had set out to do: build a reusable spaceship which would allow scientists, engineers, technicians and even spectators and journalists to go into space easily without years of training, work in a comfortable atmosphere and return.

There was some concern about the loss of 13 of the 30,000 heat-resistant tiles which protected the spacecraft from the heat of re-entry into the Earth's atmosphere. Unexpectedly severe vibration followed the ignition of the two reusable solid-fuel booster rockets which helped the shuttle off the ground. Delay of the launch was caused by problems in communication between the shuttle's five computers. But the problems were recognized as minor. Engineers echoed commander astronaut John Young's exuberant verdict, 'It's better than advertised', as *Columbia* glided to a stop after a faultless landing.

Columbia's second flight ended on 14 November three days early. The planned five days in orbit had been cut to only two, mainly because of leaks in the fuel cells which supplied the shuttle with power and drinking water by combining hydrogen and oxygen. This launch had also been delayed and questions were asked about the reliability of such a complex vehicle, since it was intended to be used as a space workhorse, with a planned one hundred successive flights per shuttle at intervals of only two and a half weeks.

However, it was not really surprising that something went wrong on only the second flight of much the most complex flying machine ever to be built. The first forty flights of *Columbia*, and its sister shuttles *Challenger* and *Discovery* which were under construction, were already fully booked with 86 scientific payloads. Four of these payloads were for the US Department of Defense, while construction of the American air force's own shuttle base for military reconnaissance flights was well advanced.

The shuttle was still some way from fulfilling its builders' promise of cutting satellite launch costs by a factor of ten. And during 1981 it became clear that it had a real rival for the increasingly lucrative launchings of commercial communications satellites, worth many millions of pounds in the decade ahead. This rival was Ariane, the co-operative European space rocket which had failed in its second test launch in 1980 but was twice successfully launched in 1981.

Ariane's third test launch placed the European weather satellite Meteosat 2 and the Indian communications satellite Apple into geo-stationary orbit. The fourth and final test firing, from the launch base at Kourou in Guyana, orbited the one-ton British-built maritime communications satellite Marecs (Maritime European Communications Satellite). By the end of the year Ariane had won orders for satellite launches and had demonstrated that, for the next few years at least, until the American shuttle programme gathered momentum, Ariane would be a real commercial rival.

A British educational satellite UOSAT (University of Surrey Satellite), designed and built entirely by university engineers, was successfully orbited on 5 October. It worked well for the rest of the year, transmitting TV pictures of the Earth and voiced messages in English, and investigating the properties of the ionosphere for the benefit of short-wave radio enthusiasts, who were themselves able to receive data from the satellite. UOSAT demonstrated that complex satellites could be built for a fraction of the cost of earlier such spacecraft.

Further away from Earth, Voyager II flew close by Saturn at the end of August and added much in the way of pictures and data to what had earlier been returned by its sister spacecraft, Voyager I, in November 1980 (see AR 1980, p. 391). Voyager II had taken four years to reach Saturn in a long, curving path which had taken it past Jupiter in July 1979 and would, it was confidently hoped, take it on to Uranus and then Neptune over the next eight years.

The pictures of Saturn showed that the weather on the planet had changed substantially since the previous fly-past. Voyager II's pictures showed hurricanes raging, with belts of cloud moving in opposite directions at different latitudes and wind speeds up to 1,800 km per hour. Voyager II examined the planet's rings closely by observing a star through the rings and counting the rings as they successively cut off the star's light. These studies revealed that the rings seen from Earth are made up of thousands of individual ringlets, giving an appearance like a grooved gramophone record seen from close at hand. The rings appeared to be made of dirty ice, possibly the debris of a shattered moon.

Voyager II also took a close look at five of Saturn's 17 known moons. The most intriguing was the largest, Titan. Data from Voyagers I and II showed that Titan's atmosphere contained clouds of methane and ammonia which formed complex organic molecules—acetylene, ethylene, propane, hydrogen cyanide—on and around Titan's surface. These were the building-blocks composing the much more complex protein molecules found in living things. Titan thus appeared to possess the same sort of primeval 'soup' as that out of which it was believed life on Earth had evolved. Unfortunately the soup on Titan was too deep-frozen, at temperatures of around minus 180 degrees Centigrade, for there to be any chance of life having evolved there.

The pictures and data concerning Venus, Mars, Jupiter and Saturn made it possible to compare the weather on those planets and the events in their upper atmospheres with parallel events on Earth. But the effects of the Sun's radiation and the solar wind of charged particles thrown out from the Sun and blowing over the Earth, causing the glowing effect seen as the Aurora Borealis or Northern Lights, still remained largely unknown.

To investigate these effects further was the aim of EISCAT (the European Incoherent Scatter radar), a system of enormously powerful radar transmitters and receivers set up in northern Finland, Sweden and Norway at a cost of about £13 million and formally inaugurated by the King of Sweden in August. The aim of EISCAT, working in conjunction with satellite- and rocket-borne experiments, was to probe the iono-sphere, the layer of charged particles in the atmosphere, with beams of very high-frequency radar which, as the name implied, were scattered rather than reflected back to Earth. Most of the charged particles res-ponsible for the Aurora were created by the effects of solar radiation on the upper atmosphere. Some actually came from the Sun in the solar wind. Both kinds were channelled down towards the Earth in the extreme north by the lines of force of the Earth's magnetic field, which bend down to Earth in that region. So EISCAT's studies of the Aurora and the charged particles causing it also provided data about the effects of all the energy being transferred to the Earth by the Sun.

The Sun itself was probed in a new way by Dr George Izaac and his colleagues in Birmingham University. They analysed the way in which shock waves travelled across the interior of the Sun from one part of its surface to another, and from these measurements deduced things about the Sun's interior, including the fact that the centre of the Sun was rotating up to seven times as fast as its surface. The techniques were similar to those used to search for new oilfields on Earth and provided the first reliable method for gaining information about the Sun's interior and, for the future, the interiors of other stars.

FUNDAMENTAL PHYSICS. The first months of the year saw the start of work using the world's first purpose-built Synchrotron Radiation Source at the government-financed laboratory at Daresbury in Cheshire, which had been formally inaugurated in the autumn of 1980. The SRS provided intense radiation at a very wide range of wavelengths, from hard, short-wave X-rays to long infra-red. This was achieved by accelerating electrons near to the speed of light and holding them in a circular path using magnetic fields, thereby producing intense radiation which could be directed to particular experimental areas. The SRS could enormously speed up, for example, the analysis of big protein molecules in living cells as well as metallurgical and solid-state research. Similar machines were being purpose-built in the USA, West Germany and Japan during the year.

There were several important developments in the field of fundamental particle physics. In October and November physicists used the Super Proton Synchrotron at the headquarters of the international CERN organization near Geneva to collide particles of matter with particles of anti-matter head-on, when the protons and anti-protons annihilated each other, releasing up to one hundred times as much energy as had ever been released before in particle accelerators.

The aim was to try to simulate the conditions which had occurred in the Universe in the first fraction of a second of its existence after the supposed Big Bang. At that time, physicists increasingly believed, the four separate forces which held matter together—gravity, electromagnetism, the weak nuclear force and the strong nuclear force—could have been recognized as what they really were, different aspects of one universal force. Theorists had already inferred that electromagnetism and the weak force were two extremes of the same thing. It was hoped that the violent matter-antimatter collisions would prove sufficiently energetic to reveal the particles, known as W and Z particles, which carried the weak force in the same way as photons carried the electromagnetic force, thus confirming the close relationship between the two forces. In December CERN's governing body approved the construction of a new machine, to be called the Large Electron Positron Collider (LEP), for collisions between electrons and anti-electrons(-positrons), with the same target of unification in view.

In May a report in *Nature* revealed that physicists in India had detected, for the first time ever, events which might represent protons decaying. If this was confirmed, the implication was that one kind of matter, that represented by quarks, the ultimate particles out of which protons and other nuclear particles were built up, could be transmuted into the other ultimate form of matter, represented by leptons, particles such as the electrons which orbit around atomic nuclei. This would represent another step towards the physicists' dream of unifying all forms of matter and the forces holding it together.

Another manifestation of the same exciting progress came in October when physicists at Stanford University collected several instances of the apparent creation of particles nicknamed 'glueballs' because they were made out of the strong force, dubbed 'glue', which held quarks together in atomic nuclei. This was a clear example of the interchangeability of matter and energy. Quarks themselves remained firmly locked up inside protons, but the 'glueballs' suggested that quarks might, after all, occasionally be able to escape from protons, not singly but in pairs, called diquarks.

In order to unify concepts of matter and energy completely it would be necessary, cosmologists contended, theoretically to recreate the first quantum of time after the Big Bang—the first tick of the cosmic clock. In this first 10^{-43} seconds of time quarks had been unconfined and the strong nuclear force would have appeared as basically the same as the weak and electromagnetic forces. Even gravity could be fitted into the same scheme of unification at that time if it could be shown to be, like the other forces, discontinuous—in other words, if a theory of quantum gravity could be created.

While, however, the grand unified theory which had eluded Einstein for the second half of his life seemed almost within reach, horrible suspicions were beginning to arise that physicists had not after all really reached the end of the road in their search for the ultimate constituents of matter. Six different kinds of quarks and six leptons were known and were arranged in symmetrical patterns. These patterns resembled those formed by larger particles, which had first led physicists to surmise that such patterns could best be accounted for by supposing that the particles were really clusters of smaller particles, the quarks. The suspicion that some particle more fundamental than the quark existed was hard enough for the hypothetical particle to have been given a name, the rishon.

The Nobel prize for physics was shared by two Americans and a Swede. Professors Nicolaas Bloembergen of Harvard and Arthur Schawlow of Stanford won their share for their development of laser spectroscopy, in which laser light is used in chemical analysis. Professor Kai Siegbahn of Uppsala won his share for his development of high-resolution electron spectroscopy, enabling phenomena such as corrosion and catalysis to be studied with the aid of X-ray beams probing surface phenomena by means of the electrons emitted when the X-rays strike the surfaces.

MEDICINE AND BIOLOGY. A great deal of medical research effort continued to be focused on the possible value of interferon, one of the human body's natural defences against virus infections, now being produced in quantity outside the body by genetically-engineered bacteria. The clinical trials of interferon against cancer were at too early a stage for doctors to conclude much beyond the fact that interferon seemed likely to be a valuable accessory to existing therapy for some forms of cancer, though by no means all, but that it would certainly not provide a 'miracle cure'. However, research reported from the UK Clinical Research Centre and Common Cold Research Centre showed that interferon was actively involved in combating 'flu infections and that children who caught continual successions of colds were often deficient in interferon production; the clinical implications were obvious.

During the year the government-backed UK biotechnology group Celltech began to market anti-interferon, a very specific reagent of the type known as a monoclonal antibody, which made it possible to purify interferon to a very high extent in a single-step process, thus speeding up manufacture greatly. Anti-interferon had been developed at the Medical Research Council's molecular biology laboratory at Cambridge and was one of the first-fruits of a contract whereby Celltech was allowed commercially to develop the pioneering research of scientists supported by the Medical Research Council.

Also in the UK researchers in ICI's corporate laboratory succeeded in artificially synthesizing the complete gene for a form of interferon, a remarkable biotechnological feat since the gene contained no less than 514 sub-units (bases) which had to be strung together in exactly the correct order.

A new use of biotechnology, in the shape of genetic engineering, being developed in 1981 was the supply of blood components for transfusions. Speywood Laboratories received £4 million of government and private investment to fund continued development of techniques to allow the vital protein compounds required in blood transfusions to be manufactured by bacteria, by inserting genes for the proteins involved into the bacteria by genetic engineering, with the long-term aim of making it unnecessary to collect blood plasma from donors.

Research at the Princess Margaret migraine clinic in London indicated that the basic cause of the severe headaches, nausea and other symptoms of attacks of migraine was an abnormality of the blood cells called platelets. The research showed that, whereas normal platelets released an active compound known as 5HT at a constant rate when stimulated by the release of stress hormones, those of migraine sufferers released much larger quantities of 5HT than normal in response to all kinds of stress. This abnormally high release was, it was shown, responsible for the fact that attacks of migraine could be brought on by widely varying forms of stress at certain times but not at other times.

At the Hammersmith Hospital in West London, tests with the prototype Nuclear Magnetic Resonance (NMR) scanner installed there for testing and development showed that the scanner was much more effective than the CAT scanning technique in showing up brain damage in multiple sclerosis, and was also more effective in some important ways in differentiating between the soft tissues of other organs. While CAT scanning worked by projecting X-rays into a patient from all around his or her head or body, and using a computer to construct a cross-sectional view from the results of these X-rays, NMR scanning used beams of radio waves which stimulated molecules in living tissues themselves to give out radio waves, which were picked up and used as data by a computer to construct cross-sectional views.

NMR scanning had the advantage over CAT and other X-ray techniques that the radio wavelengths used were completely harmless, so that as many repeated scans as were needed could be made with none of the health risks involved in repeated X-rays. This and the clarity and detail of the images obtained at the Hammersmith Hospital pointed to a valuable complementary role for NMR, alongside CAT scanning.

In November American doctors at Rochester University published research showing a strong link between the posssession of certain genes and abnormal susceptibility to severe depression and manic depression. This was the strongest evidence yet for a genetic factor in mental illness and suggested how more effective drugs might be developed to treat depression.

A new approach to the problem of defects in unborn babies was used at Denver University in the USA, where doctors inserted a valve into the skull of an unborn baby to relieve the pressure of fluid due to hydrocephalus, an abnormal accumulation of fluid in the brain. The operation was successful, preventing the enlargement of the skull usually found in hydrocephalic babies who were normally treated after birth. In another pioneering operation at the Moffitt Hospital in California doctors removed a baby from the womb to remove an obstruction of the urinary tract and then replaced the baby to develop normally.

At the Westminster Hospital in London, doctors successfully treated children suffering from normally progressive and fatal disease caused by genetic defects, by implanting bone marrow grafts taken from close relatives. The implanted bone marrow produced the missing enzymes needed to begin to reverse the symptoms of the disease. There was an outcry when the leader of the surgical team involved, Professor John Hobbs, revealed that children were dying while on his waiting list for the operation. Substantial gifts following press publicity went some way towards remedying the situation.

Meanwhile another surgical team, at Guy's Hospital in London, attempted a new approach to the same problem, using a transplant of amniotic membrane to provide the missing enzymes. Amniotic membrane, part of the protective bag which surrounds the foetus, would not be recognized as foreign. This gave it substantial advantages when used as a transplant for any purpose, since unlike bone marrow and virtually any other transplants it caused no rejection problems.

Toward the end of the year at least twelve of the 120 women who had been treated at the private Cambridge clinic of Mr Patrick Steptoe and Dr Robert Edwards were expecting 'test-tube' babies and about ten such babies had been born in Australia. The technique offered an average ten per cent chance of motherhood to women who were infertile because of a blockage of some kind in their Fallopian tubes, these being bypassed by external fertilization of egg cells removed artificially from the ovaries.

Doctors and others pointed out certain urgent ethical problems involved. It was becoming possible for a rich woman's fertilized egg to be implanted in a poor woman's womb for growth and birth; or to replace the nucleus of a fertilized egg cell with a nucleus from another individual before implanting the egg cell in the womb, so that a genetic 'carbon copy'—a clone—of the person from whom the nucleus had been removed would be produced. It was already theoretically possible for fertilized egg cells to be kept alive in deep freeze indefinitely before being implanted to develop in the womb of any foster mother. Responsible doctors and others were concerned that public opinion and legislation had not yet caught up with these problems.

Some medical advances, however, were greeted with unqualified approval. Among these was the technique of diaphragm pacing, in which regular electrical stimulation of the nerves supplying the diaphragm replaced the use of iron lungs and other ventilators for people paralysed from the neck down. First introduced experimentally, by the end of the year diaphragm pacing had been used in more than fifty patients at Yale University's department of medicine and was being introduced elsewhere. Diaphragm pacing offered paraplegic patients much greater freedom to move, using mouth-controlled wheelchairs.

Equally beneficial, and potentially for a larger number of people, was the technique of cryoanalgesia, first introduced on a large scale during the year by surgeons at the Colindale Hospital in North London, for the relief of post-operative pain. The technique involved freezing the nerves which carried the sensation of pain within the chest by placing an intensely cold probe on the nerves while the chest wall was still open after major chest surgery. Cryoanalgesia used in this way had been shown, in more than 150 patients, to have big advantages in pain relief and in reducing the need for special care after surgery.

There were important though not spectacular advances in anti-cancer therapy. A new drug, Razoxame, was shown in clinical trials to halve the death rate from bowel cancer after surgery. American research produced drugs which completely suppressed the symptoms of violent nausea and vomiting associated with some of the most effective forms of cancer chemotherapy. This made it possible for higher doses to be used and encouraged patients to return for treatment rather than abandoning it because of the excessively unpleasant side-effects. In general, these and other improvements in chemotherapy involving the use of several different drugs continued to offer the biggest improvements in cancer treatment, with interferon on the way as another.

A discovery with great possible significance for the future was made by doctors at Duke University, USA, that of a substance known as TPA which transformed cancer cells not merely into normal cells but actually into macrophages, one of the classes of white blood cells which sought out and destroyed cancer cells. Strong evidence that human cancers could be caused by virus infections emerged from research at the National Cancer Institute in Maryland, where scientists who had isolated a particular kind of virus, called a retrovirus, from a patient with skin cancer identified the same kind of virus in a patient with leukaemia. Japanese researchers, still unnamed at the end of the year, had gone on to show that the same virus was able to transform normal human cells in culture into malignant, cancer cells.

Another piece of research, reported from the Imperial Cancer Research Fund's laboratories in London, suggested how such cancer viruses might have evolved. Scientists analysed the structure of a form of genetic material known as a transposon or transposable gene because it moved naturally from one part of the chromosome where it was situated to another site while performing its functions: they found an extraordinary similarity between the fine structure of the transposon and that of a type of retrovirus known to cause cancer in animals.

The 1981 Nobel prize for medicine and physiology was won by Dr Robert Sperry of the California Institute of Technology, who received half the prize, and Professors David Hubel and Torsten Wiesel of Harvard University who shared the other half. Dr Sperry was honoured for his work on so-called 'split brain' patients, in whom treatment for epilepsy which had involved severing nervous connections between the two halves of the brain had revealed that the left hemisphere was concerned with abstract thought and mathematics, while the right hemisphere was concerned with artistic expression and creativity both in music and in the visual arts. Hubert and Wiesel were joined in the award for their work in analysing the cell structure of the visual cortex of the brain.

While 'creationism', insisting that all life on Earth had been created much as it is today by God at a comparatively recent date, continued to gain popular ground as a rival to evolutionary theory in parts of the USA, the only major modifications to Darwinism propounded by serious scientists came from those who argued that the classical theory of evolution failed to explain sudden swift major changes in bodily structure. Evidence which had been put forward the previous year by two young scientists, Dr Ted Steele and Dr Reg Gorczynski, for the inheritance of characteristics acquired during an organism's lifetime was discredited to the satisfaction of other scientists. Attempts made by Professor Leslie Brent and others to repeat the crucial experiments failed completely to show any such evidence. Dr Steele, however, continued to dispute these conclusions.

While vaccines and drugs made for human medicine by genetic engineering techniques were still undergoing clinical trials, because of the need to be certain that there were no untoward side-effects, a commercial vaccine against foot and mouth disease in cattle, made by inserting viral genes into bacteria, was made commercially available by the Californian genetic engineering concern Genentech. This was the first substance made in this way to be put on the market and it was manifest that veterinary medicine stood to benefit sooner than human from genetic engineering.

During the year another new form of biotechnology, in which irradiated pollen was used to enable normally incompatible plant species to interbreed, was successfully tested at Birmingham University. The technique, pioneered by Professor John Jinks at Birmingham and developed in American laboratories as well, opened the possibility of speeding up plant breeding enormously, and of allowing breeders to bring in characteristics from species which would not normally interbreed with crop plants.

Progress towards 'green gene' engineering, the direct transfer of genes from one plant species to another, or even from animal to plant, continued to be made. At the Cambridge Plant Breeding Institute scientists showed that wheat genes responsible for photosynthesis could be transferred into bacteria, in which they could be multiplied millions of times over ready for transplanting into other plants. What had been missing was some vector to carry the genes into new plant hosts. But during the year Dr Papahadjopoulos of the California Cancer Research Institute showed that liposomes, tiny oil droplets, could be used to transfer genes into cells in culture, and that the quantities of genetic material which actually entered the cells could be increased a hundredfold by adding glycerol to the culture.

TECHNOLOGY. With financial support from OXFAM, a new unit was set up at the Royal Botanical Gardens at Kew to prepare a survey of economic plants of arid and semi-arid areas (SEPESAT). The object of SEPESAT was to bring plants and trees which had been found to be valuable in one area, for purposes ranging from fencing, animal food or fuel to soil cover or thatching, to the attention of other parts of the world where they might fulfil important needs.

Another under-exploited resource (outside China), in the view of researchers at Portsmouth Polytechnic, was sewage. They demonstrated that healthy crops, including tomatoes, sugar beet, capsicums, aubergines and sweet corn, could be grown in liquid effluent from sewage works, the sewage being treated only to separate the solids for separate disposal. Associated work by the same unit showed how microprocessor control could improve sewage treatment, how effluent could be used in aquaculture to grow seaweeds used in making food products and cosmetics and how better to make solid matter from sewage into compost. Interest in the Portsmouth work shown by visitors from the World Health Organization and the Middle East confirmed the potential value of sewage as an under-exploited fertilizer, at a time of rising prices of artificial nitrogenous fertilizers and spreading water shortages, though the risk of water-borne disease and plant poisoning by minute elements of heavy metals had always to be countered.

Rising fossil fuel costs continued to lead to investment in alternative sources of energy. In the UK, the Government announced backing for the construction of a huge windmill in the Orkneys as a pilot project; and in Cornwall the Geothermal Energy project progressed ahead of schedule, with completion of the first of two experimental shafts drilled deep into granite rocks, down which water would be pumped to be heated to over 80 degrees Centigrade.

In December the British electric Advanced Passenger Train (APT) briefly entered limited service between London and Glasgow, before being withdrawn for more modifications. It was beset, at a time of exceptionally cold and snowy weather, with a number of minor technical problems, but was still able to demonstrate the remarkable reductions in journey times made possible by the active tilting system which enabled it to round tight curves with little or no reduction in speed. Eventual success depended on Government commitment, uncertain at the end of the year, to the building of an adequate fleet of APTs and to a continuing electrification programme. Meanwhile in France the TGV (Train à Grande Vitesse) started squadron service in September between Paris and Lyons on a specially-built straight track, whereas the APT ran on the existing rail system. Over $1,000 million was being spent on railway electrification worldwide in 1981, mainly in response to diesel fuel price rises.

Another sign of the times was the appearance of the world's first electric traffic-compatible commercial road vehicle to go into quantity production. Electric milk floats had been in use for many years, but this was a full-sized electrically-powered version of a standard Dodge truck being built at the Dunstable, England, works of Karrier Motors; it was being produced at a rate of 20 per month. Estimates showed that for most duties the electric truck was already more than competitive with the equivalent diesel- and petrol-powered versions of the truck and their similar competitors.

Two technological innovations promised to be of special value in safeguarding the environment. One was the commercial launch of a system, developed by the Cambridge, England, company Topexpress, for silencing loud low-pitched noise such as that caused by jet aircraft on the ground or gas turbines used to compress gas, using beams of 'anti-noise'—sound at exactly the same frequencies as those of the noise to be silenced but broadcast back precisely out of phase so that the noise and anti-noise cancelled each other. Trials showed the technique was cheaper and more effective than conventional sound muffling for low-pitched noise.

Another innovation was the so-called 'Eagle' system, developed by ICI and marketed commercially during the year, which used beams of light from two identical lasers to detect air pollution with greater sensitivity than had hitherto been possible. One laser beam was tuned to the precise wavelength of light absorbed by whatever pollutant chemical engineers were on the watch for in the atmosphere. The other laser was tuned to a slightly different wavelength. After reflection both beams were picked up by sensitive detectors and their relative intensities measured. If the beam tuned to the wavelength absorbed by the pollutant became slightly less intense than the other, the presence of the pollutant was revealed.

The Nobel prize for chemistry was shared by Professor Kenichi Fukui of Japan and Professor Roald Hoffman, born in Poland and working in the USA, who had independently developed the same theory by which it could be calculated whether hypothetical chemical reactions would or would not be possible in reality. Their work showed that, when two atoms became joined together by a chemical bond, then their consequent sharing of the outermost electrons in orbits around each atom was characterized by the conservation of symmetry. In other words, symmetrical features found in the outer orbital electrons before such reactions would still be found after the reactions. If symmetry could not be conserved in this way, then a reaction could not take place. Using powerful computers, this theory had made it possible to predict the feasibility or otherwise of many important reactions.

Chapter 2

THE ENVIRONMENT

RELIGIOUS warfare is not usually counted an environmental hazard; but during 1981 conservationists around the world were convinced that they faced the wrath of God in the unlikely person of James Watt, the new US Secretary of the Interior. Mr Watt was a fundamentalist born-again Christian. Although he denied that his religious beliefs would have any bearing on the way he did his job, which roughly corresponded to that of the British Secretary of State for the Environment only with vastly more power, most of his actions since taking office early in the year suggested that he had meant what he said when, in one of his few public utterances on the subject, he mentioned his 'responsibility to follow the scriptures, which call upon us to occupy the land until Jesus returns'. He did not know, he added, 'how many future generations we can count on'.

The Interior Secretary administers almost one-third of the land area of the United States, most of it in the mineral-rich Western states, including all the national parks, wildlife reserves and wilderness areas. He also runs the Bureau of Reclamation, responsible for dams and other hydrological works, and controls oil leases and mineral rights on federal land.

In his first year in office Mr Watt proposed so many drastic changes in environmental policy that the coalition of conservation groups anxiously compiling petitions for his removal hardly knew where to turn. He declared his intention of reversing government bans on mountaintop mining and on offshore drilling near four of California's most beautiful beaches and two marine reserves. He proposed that land acquisition for national parks be halted and that private companies operating catering and souvenir concessions in the parks should have a say in running them. He started a programme of staff cuts that threatened to reduce the regulatory Office of Strip Mining by almost half, attempted to remove the regulations that require mine operators to re-landscape, and was instrumental in rewriting clean-air legislation to free individual states from strict federal timetables.

The word 'stewardship' recurred in discussion with and about Mr Watt; but clearly he and his opponents defined that word very differently. In the Interior Secretary's view, a steward would oversee a rational use of his domain; to the environmentalists, stewardship implied the inviolability of its object. Cynics were not slow to point out that, in the conflict between these differing attitudes towards the use of natural resources, the quasi-religious fervour of the conservationists had at last met its match.

International interest in the squabble was more than merely a reflexive response to any threat to any environment anywhere. Conservationists and development experts who spent their days lobbying in the bureaucratic corridors where power resides were keenly aware of how severely other nations could be affected by any shift in the American wind. It was no coincidence, they argued, that since President Reagan took office the international Law of the Sea treaty, which had seemed on the verge of success after years of negotiations, was halted by a sudden hardening of the American attitude towards Third World interests in seabed mining (see pp. 333 and 339). Delegates to an important meeting in Delhi in February on international trade in endangered species of wildlife were shocked at the evident desire of the American contingent to cut back rather than extend existing restrictions. United States talks with Canada on common problems of trans-boundary pollution and river diversion ended abruptly, legal controls on the export of hazardous substances were relaxed almost to vanishing-point, and the United States was the only nation at a World Health Organization meeting in May to vote against an international code of conduct for the marketing of milk products for infants.

Mr Watt was hardly responsible personally for such shifts in foreign policy; but he was a convenient target for concerned outsiders, and characteristic of the Administration he served. Similarly controversial appointments were made during 1981 to other environmentally sensitive positions in the US, most notably the heads of the Environmental Protection Agency, the Bureau of Land Management, the US Forest Service and the Office of Strip Mining itself. President Reagan, presumably with the advice and consent of his Interior Secretary, also made devastating budgetary cuts in a wide range of federal environmental agencies, abolishing many of them in the process. As one writer in the British conservation magazine *Vole* put it: 'These actions are legitimate subjects for protest, but it rather stops you short when you're told that God's behind it all.' Prophetically, perhaps, *Vole* itself went out of business several issues later.

Darkly though the shadow of Watt may have coloured the thoughts of environmentalists, 1981 was not entirely a year of retrenchment: 1982, after all, was to be the tenth anniversary of the Stockholm declaration, and the initiatives set in motion at that great creative burst of bureaucracy continued to develop as smoothly and remorselessly as ever.

In October the European Commission, to the surprise of some, completed its proposals for a third five-year environment action programme and submitted it to the EEC's Council of Ministers and the European Parliament for discussion and approval. In its emphasis on environmental protection, as opposed to palliative or remedial action, and its consideration of environmental action as a positive contribution to solving such economic problems as inflation and unemployment, the new programme obviously owed as much to the previous year's World Conservation Strategy as to Stockholm. Taking the enlargement of the European Community into account, the programme included extensive recommendations for the protection of the Mediterranean basin, thereby touching on the concerns of the UN Environment Programme (Unep), whose regional seas unit (its Mediterranean action plan in particular) had been an outstanding success during the past decade. Towards the end of the year, five more nations were brought into that net with the signing of an anti-pollution treaty covering the South American Pacific coast from Panama to Cape Horn.

Ironically, however, as the year drew to an end there was some confusion as to the future of Unep itself. The United States Congress—predictably, given the Reagan-Watt approach to environmental matters—seemed uncertain whether to cut its $10 million share of Unep's budget by a mere 25 per cent or altogether. As the American contribution had been 30 per cent of the total, and in convertible currency at that, Unep obviously faced hard times whatever the decision. Many conservationists, it is only fair to report, would have viewed the demise of Unep, regional seas programme notwithstanding, with equanimity. Crippled since its inception by inefficiency, nepotism and occasional scandal, the agency (it was felt) had never lived up to its Stockholm promise.

Another disappointment during 1981 was the United Nations conference on new and renewable sources of energy, held in Nairobi during the summer at a cost of some $35 million and, according to Swedish forestry experts, with enough papers (108 million pages) to account for more than 12,000 mature pine trees. The conference, granted the rebarbative acronym 'Unerg', seemed in the end to have more to do with North-South politics than with environment. In its favour, it did provide an opportunity for a review of the many and growing categories of real or potential alternative energy sources.

In the United Kingdom that most unreliable of energy sources, oil, was the subject of some unexpected good news from the Royal Commission on Environmental Pollution. In its report on oil pollution of the sea, undertaken initially in response to the *Amoco Cadiz* disaster of 1978, the commission came to the conclusion that the long-term effects of oil pollution were far less serious than had been feared. 'We have found no ground for concern that oil may constitute a threat to the marine ecosystem or, indirectly, a threat to man', the report said, comparing the relatively insubstantial threat from oil with the effects of heavy metals or radioactivity. Although oil pollution could have serious economic consequences, and caused great offence to the public, the commission was convinced that the marine environment 'eventually recovers from even the most serious oil pollution incident'.

Whether the British Parliament would ever recover from its marathon consideration of the Wildlife and Countryside Bill, which attracted a record number of amendments before receiving Royal Assent on 30 October, was another matter. The final product was useful primarily as a codification of legal principles, new and old, governing the protection of wild birds, animals and plants, conservation of countryside, including natural habitats, and public rights of way in the countryside. Above all, perhaps, the exercise was a salutary reminder to politicians of the breadth and depth of public concern over wildlife issues.

Public feeling also ran high in connection with the meeting of the International Whaling Commission in Brighton. While Friends of the Earth, Greenpeace and other pressure groups marched through the streets with their placards and inflatable whales, the meeting arrived at two useful decisions: bans on the hunting of sperm whales and on the use of the cold harpoon from 1982. It was questionable whether the ban on sperm whaling could be enforced completely; but the replacement of the cold harpoon (which had been used only to take the small minke whales) by more humane explosive devices was considered a breakthrough.

Finally, in a year during which the mighty World Wildlife Fund celebrated its 20th anniversary, fate produced three felicitous birthday presents: the yellow-fronted gardener bowerbird, the black-footed ferret and a new species of crested iguana. The bowerbird, never before seen alive by scientists, was sighted in the Foja mountain region of New Guinea; the ferret, presumed extinct since 1978, was captured in Wyoming, and the as yet unnamed iguana had the distinction of appearing, quite fortuitously, on location in Fiji with Brooke Shields in the American film *Blue Lagoon*.

XIV THE LAW

Chapter 1

INTERNATIONAL LAW—EUROPEAN COMMUNITY LAW

INTERNATIONAL LAW

IN the International Court of Justice, the UN Security Council and General Assembly elected Abdallah El-Khani (Syria) and Stephen Schwebel (USA) to replace the two Judges who had died in 1980 (see AR 1980, p. 398). In August the President of the Court, Sir Humphrey Waldock (UK), died (see OBITUARY); Sir Robert Jennings (UK) was elected to replace him. Guy Ladreit de Lacharrière (France) and Keba M'Baye (Senegal) were also elected to the Court, and Nagendra Singh (India) and José-Maria Ruda (Argentina) were re-elected. Judge El-Erian (Egypt) also died later, but the General Assembly deferred until 1982 its choice of a replacement.

Pursuant to the agreement between the US and Iran on the return of the US hostages and other matters (see p. 64) proceedings in the *Case concerning US Diplomatic and Consular Staff in Tehran* (see AR 1980, p. 398) were discontinued. Proceedings continued in the case concerning the delimitation of the continental shelf between Tunisia and Libya (see AR 1978, p. 384). Malta had sought to intervene on the ground that the judgment of the Court might be relevant to its own boundary dispute with the two litigants. However, it had stipulated that intervention was not to have the effect of putting in issue its own claims; in the light of this consideration in particular, the Court unanimously dismissed the application on the ground that Malta had no 'interest of a legal nature' at stake in the proceedings. Oral hearings in the main action were concluded in October. Two new cases were brought before the Court. In one, review of a decision of the UN Administrative Tribunal regarding repatriation grants for UN officials was requested; the other was the submission, to a chamber of the Court, of a US-Canadian dispute regarding the delimitation of the maritime boundary in the Gulf of Maine area.

The European Court of Human Rights gave a number of important judgments. Potentially the most important in the long-term was that in the case of *Young, James & Webster*. The three applicants had been dismissed by British Rail, which had entered into a closed-shop agreement in 1975, for having refused on grounds of principle to join one of the three recognized unions. Under the Trade Union and Labour Relations

Act 1974, as amended in 1976, such objections (unless based on religious grounds) were ineffectual and the dismissal was to be treated as fair. Article 11(1) of the European Convention for the Protection of Human Rights and Fundamental Freedoms provides that 'everyone has the right to freedom of peaceful assembly and to freedom of association with others, including the freedom to join trade unions for the protection of his interests'. Whilst stressing that it did not have to consider the legality of the closed shop generally, the Court held, by 18 votes to 3, that in the circumstances of the particular case compulsion to join a particular union or unions was an interference with the men's Article 11 rights. Besides its importance in the field of industrial relations, what made the case potentially so significant was the fact that the UK (Government) was held to be in breach of the Convention although the applicants were dismissed, not by an organ of the state, but by a separate state-owned entity. The involvement of the state was only indirect—Parliament had simply deprived 'conscientious objectors', other than religious ones, of the right to sue their employers for unfair dismissal, or the unions in tort. The decision could allow the development of a doctrine analogous to that of 'state action' in US constitutional law, whereby constitutional guarantees can be extended to what are essentially 'private law' relationships, provided that some involvement on the part of public authorities can be demonstrated.

During the year Gérard J. Wiarda (Netherlands) was elected President of the European Court of Human Rights in succession to Giorgio Balladore Pallieri (Italy), who died in December 1980; and Carl Aage Nørgaard (Denmark) was elected to the presidency of the European Commission of Human Rights in succession to James E. S. Fawcett (UK) who did not seek re-election after holding the post since 1972 but who remained a member of the Commission.

The slow progress of the third UN Conference on the Law of the Sea suffered a serious setback when the new US Administration announced that it was reviewing its position on the draft convention. It was particularly unhappy about the proposals regarding the regime governing exploitation of deep-sea-bed resources in areas beyond national jurisdiction. At the end of the year the General Assembly decided to convene a final decision-making session of the conference in the spring of 1982, but it was still not clear whether the demands of the US and others could be satisfied, or whether the 'package' would fall apart. In the meantime, the UK and a number of other Western industrialized nations followed the lead of the US in making 'temporary' legislative provision for the licensing, etc., of deep-sea mining by those subject to their jurisdiction.

In the Annual Register 1979 (pp. 402-3) it was reported that the immunity of foreign states from the jurisdiction of the English courts in respect of their commercial and similar activities awaited clarification by the House of Lords. It was substantially provided by the decision in *I Congreso del Partido*,[1] where the House unanimously upheld the restrictive theory of sovereign immunity, according to which no immunity exists in respect of private, as opposed to governmental, acts. Whereas the impact of this judgment would be largely confined to cases not covered by the provisions of the State Immunity Act 1978 because it was non-retrospective (see AR 1978, p. 386), another decision—*Buttes Gas & Oil Co. v. Hammer*[2]—was potentially of more wide-ranging effect. Broadly speaking, the rules of sovereign immunity do not apply in proceedings between non-sovereign entities, unless they are acting as agents or instrumentalities of a foreign state. However, in *Buttes* the House of Lords unanimously 'restated' a further doctrine of English law, whereby the English courts will not adjudicate on or review the actions of foreign states, even if those actions are relevant to litigation between private parties.

EUROPEAN COMMUNITY LAW

The year 1981 will be remembered for the significant increase in confidence of the European Court of Justice. The Court seemed to acquire a new strength of will which enabled it to tackle several difficult problems without flinching and to produce a large number of leading judgments.

This may have been not unconnected with a dramatic change in its composition. For the long campaign to increase its numbers finally succeeded, and an extra Judge and an extra Advocate-General were authorized by the Council. At the same time Greece's new Judge joined the Court; a new President took office; his predecessor resigned and was replaced by a new German Judge; and both British and French Advocates-General were changed. The year began, therefore, with a new President, a larger 11-man Court a quarter of whom were new, and five Advocates-General of whom three were new. It was agreed that the 11th Judge would come from France and the post would then rotate among the larger member-states; while the 5th Advocate-General would be appointed from the smaller member-states, starting with the Netherlands.

Of great constitutional significance was the judgment against the UK in case 804/79, one of several involving fisheries. The Court had held against the coastal states' powers in a long line of cases, but it was always careful to restrict its rulings to the facts and leave open a loophole on the fundamental issue. But this time it took the plunge and held unequivocally that the EEC had completely taken over all power in the field of

[1] [1981] 2 All ER 1064.
[2] [1981] 3 WLR 787.

fishery conservation, and that the member-states are 'no longer entitled to exercise any power of their own in this matter and may henceforth only act as trustees of the common interest' (and then only where there is no relevant EEC legislation). Never has the Court declared an 'occupied field' so firmly and utterly, not even in customs matters. The purely legal basis for that conclusion was circumstantial and equivocal; but the result was made the more inevitable because of the ambivalence of the UK Government's brief, resulting in its failure to argue the constitutional issue and shown in its nakedly nationalistic approach to fisheries management and legislation.

This case appeared likely, in its result if not in its reasoning, to enter the constitutional law books on a par with *Costa* v. *Enel* or with the early US case of *McCulloch* v. *Maryland*. It did not, however, stem the flow of fisheries litigation—several more cases were entered on the register by the year's end. Political solutions were no nearer attainment either, the British presidency in the latter half of the year having failed to achieve agreement in the Council on final legislative settlement of a revised common fisheries policy. Indeed, there were several hints that the French Government was deliberately blocking progress until 1983, when the UK's accession powers to retain coastal fishery monopoly would expire.

The case law on free movement of goods continued to receive firm support, and the reservations of industrial property lawyers were not allayed in *Merck* [1981] 3 C.M.L.R. 463, which held that a patentee who himself marketed his goods in Italy, where they had no patent protection, could not then stop their parallel import into Holland, where he held the Dutch patent. In *Pfizer* v. *Eurim-Pharm* [1982] 1 C.M.L.R. 137, just before Christmas, a German trademark owner could not block parallel imports which had been repacked in transparent packets through which the original trademark was visible: it did not amount to the reaffixing of another person's trademark. And in *Musik-Vertrieb Membran* v. *GEMA* [1981] 2 C.M.L.R. 44, parallel imports of gramophone records from England, where they had paid a compulsory royalty, into Germany, where the going royalty rate was higher, could neither be blocked nor subjected to a new royalty, even to the excess over the compulsory British royalty.

On the other hand, in *Kortman*, the Court limited the value to parallel importers of its case law on health control formalities. The *Cassis de Dijon* principle continued, however, to spread its influence. In a number of cases national products, e.g. the French *brioche*, which did not generically comply with another state's technical standards, were allowed to be imported and sold nonetheless; and the Commission reiterated its intention to rely more heavily on the principle that goods lawfully marketed in one member-state should be allowed to circulate in another, notwithstanding contrary health or similar rules. Article 36 would be applied restrictively in such cases.

Of some notoriety was the decision relating to the German 'butter ships', floating supermarkets which had put out from German Baltic ports, cruised around for eight hours and then returned. The passengers would then take their purchases through customs duty-free, even though the ships had sold them 'extra-territorially' without paying import duties or tax on them, and in some cases even being paid 'export subsidies' as they had been taken outside the customs territory. The Court held that on such cruises the goods sold would have to be treated for fiscal purposes as though they were on German territory. The implications of this judgment for the whole duty-free system in inter-state air and sea travel was immediately recognized and political discussions began on what should be done.

The position of air and sea transport itself, which had always been somewhat equivocal in the Community system in view of the continental geography of the original six member-states, was the subject of notable developments. The Commission submitted to the Council draft regulations to apply the full panoply of anti-trust procedures to those hitherto semi-exempted sectors. And a British Peer, Lord Bethell, brought a 'private prosecution' against the Commission for failure to act to enforce competition in air transport; he received the support of the UK Government, which intervened in the proceedings, and which had also urged a liberalization on the political level.

Another British Peer, Lord Bruce of Donington, acquired a little niche in history by successfully fighting through the European Court an attempt by the British tax authorities to levy income tax on the lump-sum expense allowance he received as a Member of the European Parliament. The Court set out guidelines which appeared somewhat sybilline and led to some grumbling by commentators on European law, although a careful reading of the judgment revealed no real ambiguities.

Taxation was the subject of a remarkable number of cases coming before the national courts and the European Court, doubtless because the effects of the 6th VAT directive were at last being felt in practice. The London VAT Tribunal declared that it would henceforth always read the British VAT legislation together with the EEC VAT directives, giving preference to the EEC rules. On the other hand, the German Federal Administrative Court refused to apply the directives at all, claiming (wrongly) that they had no direct effect in German law and only the German implementing legislation was relevant in private litigation.

Another hitherto under-represented financial area—money and banking—began to emerge with two important keynote decisions of the Court. One held firmly that banking was subject to the competition rules of the Community and that a concerted practice by the German banks in setting fees for the conversion of foreign currency was subject to Articles 85 and 86. In the other case, faced with an Italian exchange-control prosecution of a businessman resident in Germany who had brought banknotes into Italy to make a business purchase and then, the purchase having failed, attempted to take them out again without declaring them, the Court explained in considerable detail the position of the free movement of capital in the Community system at the present time.

After the strong activity the previous year, the Court produced little of note in the field of restrictive practices law except for one dramatic but in reality minor case. The Commission had been investigating IBM for some years and finally sent it a long 'statement of objections'. IBM, instead of merely attending the oral hearing before the Commission to argue its case, and then appealing the subsequent decision to the European Court, decided to go into the attack first. It therefore appealed to the Court against the statement of objections itself, claiming that it was a decision and that there were procedural irregularities. The Court robustly dismissed the action, and the procedure was left to pursue its normal path within the Commission.

In the autumn the Commission, which had been exceptionally quiet during the rest of the year, doubtless absorbing both a new Commissioner (Mr Andriessen) and a new Director-General (Dr Schlieder having resigned), produced an important batch of anti-trust decisions which demonstrated a firmness in the new team. Major export bans (champagne, Hasselblad cameras) led to large fines. An evasive answer by the French importer of Matsushita products, indicating that no export bans were applied, resulted in a finding of 'false information' and the imposition of the maximum fine possible. Other major decisions related to the rights of foreign performing artistes in Germany to share in the benefits of the German Performers' Rights Society and to the grant of loyalty discounts.

On a more individual level, the major event was the inclusion of the self-employed in the Community social security system. This had been urged for many years by the UK and had been creeping into a number of national systems. Two regulations were enacted by the Council amending the basic social security regulations 1408/71 and 574/72 to include the self-employed in the definition of protected persons. On equal pay, most of the action was still to come. Two decisions in the spring, both on references from England, held that a technical aspect of the British Rail staff pensions scheme discriminated against young women employees and that lower pay for part-time work might be discriminatory depending on the circumstances. Both judgments were very cautious. Others were awaited shortly after the end of the year, together with argument on the mass 'prosecution' brought by the Commission against several of the member-states for failure properly to implement the sex-discrimination directives.

The Commission also brought actions against six member-states for

failure to implement the 2nd Company Law directive (several years overdue) and showed signs of taking a much tougher line against such failures
in the future.

All the signs were that Community law was beginning to bite in practice and that the Community organs (Commission and Court) had shed
any reluctance to hasten that process.

Chapter 2

LAW IN THE UNITED KINGDOM

THE most controversial legislation enacted in 1981 was the British
Nationality Act, which radically altered the old *jus soli* rule by requiring
that, in addition to birth in the UK, a person must have one parent born
or settled in this country (see also pp. 32-3). The Act was criticized for
giving virtually unfettered power to the Home Secretary to determine
who is British. The Contempt of Court Act, described by Lord Hailsham
L.C. as 'his little ewe lamb', was the Government's response to the 1979
Sunday Times (thalidomide) decision in the European Court of Human
Rights and the 1974 Phillimore report. The ultimate supremacy of the
administration of justice over free speech was maintained, with the
balance tilted to the latter, and blanket bans were imposed on obtaining,
disclosing or soliciting jury-room deliberations and on the use of tape-
recorders in court without express permission.

The Supreme Court Act consolidated existing provisions on jurisdiction and procedure and provided (a) that the defence of self-
incrimination may not be invoked in civil proceedings for infringement
of intellectual property rights or passing off, and (b) that trials may be
heard by a judge alone if likely to be lengthy and inconvenient for jurors.
This clause was added as a result of an unsuccessful 100-day libel action
brought by the Unification Church against the *Daily Mirror*, which had
strongly denounced the sect, commonly known as the 'Moonies' (see p.
378). The Criminal Justice Amendment Act amended the law relating to
reporting of committal proceedings where there were two or more
accused, and the Criminal Attempts Act replaced the much criticized
offence known as 'sus' with a new offence of vehicle interference and
made it possible to convict a person of an attempt notwithstanding that
unknown to him the offence was impossible to commit (e.g. picking an
empty pocket). A Private Member's Bill became the Indecent Displays
(Controls) Act which created a new offence of publicly displaying
indecent matter, but shops and places where charges were made for
admission and adequate warning notices were displayed were exempted,
as were art galleries, plays, cinematograph and television programmes.

The Matrimonial Homes and Property Act enabled orders for sale to be made under the Matrimonial Causes Act 1973 and made it clear that, for the purposes of the Matrimonial Homes Act 1967, a spouse was entitled to occupy the matrimonial home notwithstanding that it was mortgaged. The Companies Act implemented the European Community's Fourth Directive on company accounts, enabled companies to purchase their own shares, tightened and extended the law on disclosure of interests, and extended the powers of the court to disqualify those committing fraud or misconduct. An Insurance Companies Act made special provision for regulating the insurance business. The Disabled Persons Act imposed duties on highway and local authorities, and the Wildlife and Countryside Act dealt *inter alia* with animals, as did measures on Control of Dogs, Pet Animals, Animal Health and Zoo Licensing.

The most noteworthy case coming before the courts concerned the power of the Greater London Council to carry out the local Labour Party's election pledge to reduce tube and bus fares and recoup the deficit by a supplementary rate (see p. 34). The House of Lords, upholding the Court of Appeal but overruling a unanimous Divisional Court, ruled that the action was an abuse of powers and *ultra vires* since the reduction had been made arbitrarily without regard to ordinary business principles, and there had been a breach of the Council's fiduciary duty owed to ratepayers. Following *Prescott* v. *Birmingham Corporation* (1954), the Court held that the Greater London Council could not further a particular social policy by a thriftless use of ratepayers' money.[1]

Some important tort and criminal cases were reported. In *Whitehouse* v. *Jordan*[2] the House of Lords upheld the Court of Appeal's view that a forceps delivery resulting in brain damage did not result from negligence on the part of an obstetrician, but rejected Lord Denning M.R.'s distinction between error of judgment and negligence. Merely to say that a surgeon committed an error of clinical judgment, their Lordships declared, was wholly ambiguous since such an error could still be negligent. The case, which involved the upsetting of a finding of fact by the justices, was thus an expensive and pointless exercise and an argument for jettisoning the fault principle in cases of this sort and implementing the Pearson report on compensation for personal injuries. In *Gammell* v. *Wilson*[3] the House regretfully reached a decision it considered neither 'sensible nor just' in claims arising out of two accidental deaths. It called for legislation to overturn the 1980 decision in *Pickett's* case and to implement the Pearson recommendation that claims for pecuniary loss in respect of 'lost years' should not survive for the benefit

[1] *Bromley London Borough Council* v. *Greater London Council* [1982] 1 All E.R. 129.
[2] [1981] 1 All E.R. 267.
[3] [1981] 2 W.L.R. 248.

of a deceased's estate; in February the Solicitor-General announced that a Bill similar to the Damages (Scotland) Act 1976 would be introduced.

In an important *obiter dictum* the House suggested that where economic loss consists of liability to pay damages to the ultimate consumer for physical injuries it may yet be held to be recoverable by a distributor from the manufacturer.[1] It also held that, where the purpose of respondents in agreeing to contravene a Rhodesian Sanctions Order was to further their own interests rather than to injure the appellants, there was no claim in conspiracy. An innominate tort at the suit of a person suffering harm as an inevitable consequence of unlawful, intentional and positive acts of another was not yet part of English law.[2] Their Lordships' redefinition of 'recklessness'[3] to include inadvertent negligence was criticized by Professor Glanville Williams as 'the most serious injury inflicted on the developing criminal law since *D.P.P.* v. *Smith*' and he described Lord Diplock's opinions as 'going to confound judges and juries, be a bane to law students, and add to the incomes of practitioners, for some time to come'.[4] Lord Diplock also raised eyebrows by commenting, in a case where a police officer was held not to be entitled to enter private premises without consent or express statutory authority, that once again the ingenuity of defence lawyers had enabled the breathalyser law to be frustrated.[5] In *Cunningham*[6] their Lordships held that a person who unlawfully kills another intending only to do him grievous bodily harm is guilty of murder, rejecting the contrary view in *Hyam* (1975). The use of a credit card to obtain goods when the holder's limit had been exceeded was held to constitute the offence of obtaining pecuniary advantage by deception under the Theft Act 1968 even if the firm was not induced to complete the transaction by any false representation.[7]

Of particular interest to land lawyers was *Midland Bank Trusts Co.* v. *Green*,[8] where a father conveyed land to his wife for an inadequate sum in order to defeat a son's option to buy which had not been registered. The House held that this was a valid conveyance and that it was not fraud to rely on legal rights conferred by Act of Parliament. An important point involving natural justice was settled in a case where a person was held to be entitled to adequate notice and an opportunity to be heard before a judicial order was made against him.[9] The House also

---

[1] *Lambert* v. *Lewis* [1981] 1 All E.R. 1185.
[2] *Lonrho Ltd.* v. *Shell Petroleum* [1981] 2 All E.R. 456.
[3] *R* v. *Caldwell, R* v. *Stephen Lawrence* [1981] 2 W.L.R. 509, 524.
[4] [1981] C.L.J. 252, 283.
[5] *Finnigan* v. *Sandford* [1981] 2 All E.R. 267.
[6] [1981] 2 All E.R. 863.
[7] *Lambie* [1981] 2 All E.R. 776.
[8] [1981] 1 All E.R. 153.
[9] *R* v. *Brighton M.L. ex p Hamilton,* The Times, 18 June.

described the Copyright Act 1956 as 'labyrinthine and tortuous'[1] and tolled the death-knell of certain artificial tax avoidance schemes.[2]

In the Court of Appeal it was held that the Central Electricity Generating Board was entitled to use self-help to remove those obstructing a survey for a nuclear power station site.[3] Lord Denning took the novel view that a breach of the peace occurred whenever a person who was lawfully carrying out his work was unlawfully and physically prevented by another from doing it. In another case it was said that there could not be a breach of the peace unless the act done or threatened either actually harmed a person, or, in his presence, his property, or was likely to cause such harm or fear of it.[4] The Court also held that it was not an offence to set fire to one's own property notwithstanding an inchoate intent to defraud an insurance company.[5] Lord Denning spoke of the 'unacceptable face of British justice' when a technical error in a legal aid form caused loss to an innocent defendant, and called for reform of the Legal Aid Act 1974.[6] It was held not to be in the public interest that it should be a defence to assault arising out of a fight (other than a sport) to claim that the other consented, if actual bodily harm was intended.[7]

One interesting case decided that husbands and wives can be liable for the tort of conspiracy *inter se*. Lord Denning said that, although medieval lawyers had held that spouses were one person in law and the husband that one, that had been a fiction then and was a fiction now and he would reject it.[8] Lord Denning made similarly forthright remarks in *Home Office* v. *Harman*,[9] a case where the legal officer of the National Council for Civil Liberties had released to the press documents disclosed on discovery in litigation. Despite the fact that the documents had been read out in open court, Miss Harman's conduct was not 'extremely trivial' as *The Times* had claimed but a 'serious contempt'.

A person adding sleeping-tablets to another's milk bottles was guilty of administering a 'noxious thing' since this included quantity,[10] and the disconnection of a life-support system by doctors was held not to be a defence to a murder charge against the original assailant.[11] The scope of the duty of care was limited as a matter of policy in two important negligence cases, one on 'nervous shock' and the other on the extent of the

---

[1] [1981] 1 All E.R. 1057.
[2] *W. T. Ramsay Ltd.* v. *I. R. C.* [1981] 1 All E.R. 865.
[3] *R* v. *Chief Constable of Devon and Cornwall,* The Times, 21 October.
[4] *R* v. *Howell* [1981] 3 All E.R. 383.
[5] *R* v. *Denton* ibid.
[6] *R. & T. Thew Ltd.* v. *Reeves,* The Times, 7 May.
[7] *A.G's Reference (No. 6 of 1980)* [1981] 2 All E.R. 1057.
[8] *Midland Bank Trust Co. Ltd.* v. *Green* (no. 3), The Times, 10 June.
[9] [1981] 2 All E.R. 349.
[10] *R* v. *Marcus* [1981] 2 All E.R. 833.
[11] *R* v. *Malcherek* [1981] 2 All E.R. 422.

liability of a local authority whose operations caused a house to subside, whereupon squatters moved in and caused further damage.[1]

In the Divisional Court the Environment Secretary was held to have exceeded his discretionary powers by reducing the rate support grant payable to local authorities without listening to their representations,[2] and a breach of natural justice occurred when a prison officer failed to acquaint a board of visitors with the name of a witness supporting a prisoner's account of an incident even though the visitors themselves were blameless.[3] A case where a justices' clerk prosecuted and gave evidence when two men were charged with absconding, having been seven minutes late in surrendering bail, was described as a 'legal pantomime' and full of irregularities,[4] and a prison governor was held guilty of contempt for stopping an application to the court for leave to issue proceedings against him.[5] A qualified woman judo referee was unlawfully discriminated against on grounds of sex when prevented from refereeing men's national competitions,[6] and the Employment Appeals Tribunal decided that it was unlawful for an employer to have a policy against employing women with children.[7]

Notwithstanding *Re B (a minor)*,[8] where the Court of Appeal ordered an operation to save the life of a Down's Syndrome baby, a jury in a later case acquitted a paediatrician of attempted murder, thus concluding that he had not taken 'active steps' to bring about the child's death (see p. 40). This demonstrated (to some) the reason for retaining jury trials. A plea for manslaughter by reason of diminished responsibility in the 'Yorkshire Ripper' trial (see p. 39) was rejected by the judge, and the defendant was duly convicted of murder. The Attorney-General later gave three reasons for having agreed to accept a plea of guilty to manslaughter; (i) the medical evidence of four doctors as to the diminished responsibility of the accused (Sutcliffe) was unanimous; (ii) the judge would have been able to impose a sentence of life imprisonment in any case; (iii) the families of the victims would be spared many days of press coverage and detailed knowledge of the horrific injuries inflicted.

In October the Director of Public Prosecutions, after earlier refusing to intervene, was granted a voluntary Bill of Indictment to commit three prison officers for trial for murder (see p. 40). In June the Scottish

---

[1] *McLoughlin* v. *O'Brien* [1981] 1 All E.R. 809; *Lamb* v. *L.B. of Camden* [1981] 2 All E.R. 408.
[2] *R* v. *Secretary of State for the Environment ex. p.L.B. of Brent*, The Times, 29 October.
[3] *R* v. *Board of Visitors of Blundeston Prison*, The Times, 29 October.
[4] *R* v. *Gateshead J.J.*, The Times, 2 April.
[5] *Raymond* v. *Honey* [1981] 2 All E.R. 1084.
[6] *British Judo Assocation* v. *Petty*, The Times, 17 June.
[7] *Harley* v. *Mustoe*, The Times, 14 March.
[8] *The Times*, 8 August.

Court of Criminal Appeal released a man who had been imprisoned for several years after investigation revealed gross improprieties by a Home Office forensic scientist.

The Report of the Royal Commission on Criminal Procedure sought to balance the interests of the community as a whole with those of the individual; its many recommendations with respect to the investigative powers of the police and interrogation of suspects[1] awaited Government action.

[1] Cmnd. 8092.

XV THE ARTS

Chapter 1

OPERA—BALLET—THEATRE—MUSIC—CINEMA—TELEVISION AND RADIO

OPERA

NEW operas in 1981 had a distinctly literary flavour. Iain Hamilton's *Anna Karenina* was a popular success at the English National Opera on 7 May. The Salzburg Festival saw Friedrich Cerha's faithful adaptation of Brecht's *Baal* on 7 August, and Cerha, hitherto known best for his completion of Berg's *Lulu*, established himself as a composer in his own right with another premiere, the more avant-garde *Netzwerk* (Vienna, 31 May). Alun Hoddinott's *The Trumpet Major*, based on Hardy, was premiered jointly by the Royal Northern College of Music and the Welsh National Opera in Manchester on 1 April. The following evening the Finnish National Opera gave the first performance of Ilkka Kuusisto's *The War for Light*, based on the *Kalevala*. On 24 April the Houston Grand Opera premiered Carlisle Floyd's *Willie Stark*, based on Robert Penn Warren's *All the King's Men*, a highly theatrical work much admired by local audiences.

Other new operas were less immediately inspired by literary sources. The action of John Metcalf's *The Journey* (Welsh National Opera, 12 June) was somewhat impenetrably based on *I Ching*, the book of choices. Philip Glass's *The Panther* (Houston, 25 April), the title-role of which was in fact taken by a cougar, took as its starting-point the poetry of Rilke, and this minimalist composer's works continued to fascinate younger, non-operatic audiences. Rilke appeared in person in Giuseppe Sinopoli's *Lou Salomé* (Munich, 10 May), whose eponymous heroine counted the poet amongst her friends. Perhaps the most ambitious premiere of the year was Stockhausen's *Donnerstag aus Licht* (La Scala, Milan, first complete performance on 3 April). The opera was part of a planned sequence of seven works, one for each day of the week, to which the composer intended to devote the next twenty years of his life. Despite a noticeable lack of dramatic shape, the work was received with awed respect by most commentators.

The centenaries of the birth of Bartók and the death of Mussorgsky were marked in various ways: most major houses mounted productions of Bartók's three stage works, and La Scala peformed a cycle of Mussorgsky's operas.

In the UK few risks were taken. At Covent Garden, highlights were a production of the complete *Lulu*, beautifully conducted by Colin Davis (see also p. 421), Gluck's *Alceste*, with Dame Janet Baker incomparable in the title-role, and Saint-Saëns's *Samson et Dalila* in an imaginative decor by Sir Sidney Nolan. The English National Opera gave Gounod's *Romeo et Juliette,* well sung but in a fustian production, and a careful staging of Charpentier's *Louise.* The success of the year, however, was *Otello*, with Charles Craig and Rosalind Plowright in a production by Jonathan Miller. Dismal stagings of *Tristan und Isolde* and *Ariadne auf Naxos* stifled whatever musical merits they may have boasted— considerable in the case of *Tristan*.

Scottish Opera having offered only an overblown version of *The Beggar's Opera* and English National Opera North still relying on borrowed productions (apart from their own lively staging of *The Bartered Bride*), the Welsh National Opera again proved itself the most adventurous company in the country, with successful and provocative productions of Strauss's *Die Frau ohne Schatten* (in English), Handel's *Rodelinda*, and Martinu's *The Greek Passion*, the last in a stunning production by Michael Geliot. In *Fidelio* and *La forza del destino*, however, given hard-line marxist interpretations by, respectively, Harry Kupfer and Joachim Herz, provocation far outweighed any theatrical merit. Herr Kupfer was also responsible for a dreary socialist-realist production of *Pelléas et Mélisande* for the ENO.

The Paris Opéra also relied heavily on borrowed productions, but mounted two stagings of *Carmen*, one a spectacle at the Palais des Sports, the other a radically-adapted version by Peter Brook at Les Bouffes du Nord. La Scala saw a wholly successful *Lohengrin*, conducted by Claudio Abbado and produced by Giorgio Strehler. The Vienna State Opera launched a visually conservative *Ring*, designed by Filippo Sanjust and conducted by Zubin Mehta, and then abandoned it halfway through. German opera houses continued to examine their recent past, with exhumations of near-forgotten works by Zemlinsky and Schreker; the most surprising, and successful, revival, in Oberhausen, was that of *Regina*, an apparently subversive opera by Lortzing, considered unperformable in the aftermath of the 1848 revolutions.

The Metropolitan Opera in New York scored successes with two triple bills designed by David Hockney, one devoted to Stravinsky (*Le sacre du printemps, Le Rossignol* and *Oedipus Rex*) the other to French works (*L'Enfant et les sortilèges, Les Mamelles de Tirésias* and Satie's *Parade*). Among noteworthy festival productions were Jean-Pierre Ponnelle's sumptuous *Tristan und Isolde* at Bayreuth (despite Vienna, the trend in Wagner was away from social-realism), Peter Hall's highly imaginative version of Britten's *A Midsummer Night's Dream* at

412 THE ARTS

Glyndebourne, and Joachim Herz's lavish if disrespectful revival of Strauss's *Die aegyptische Helena* at Munich.

Noticeable trends included numerous reinvestigations of Rossini's lesser-known works: *Semiramide* was seen in Turin, Genoa, San Francisco and Paris, there was a most satisfying staging of *Tancredi* at Aix-en-Provence, *La donna del lago* was given at Houston and Pesaro, *Adina* at Bologna, *Mosé* at Philadelphia and *Le Siège de Corinth* at Marseilles. The Donizetti revival proceeded apace, with airings for *Belisario* (Buenos Aires and London), *Maria di Rudenz* (Venice), *Fausta* (Rome), *Il Duca d'Alba* (Florence) and *L'ajo nel'imbarazzo* (Vienna).

The year's obituary list included the conductor Karl Böhm (see OBITUARY), the administrators Carol Fox and Paolo Grassi, the distinguished translator and coach Tom Hammond, the singers Rosa Ponselle, Mafalda Favero, Augusta Oltrabella, Günther Treptow, Walther Ludwig, Harold Blackburn and Neil Warren-Smith, and Sergeant Martin, linkman at Covent Garden and a familiar, imposing yet much-loved figure there since 1946.

BALLET

The year was remarkable for its anniversaries, each of which brought its own celebrations and commemorative books. For the centenary of the birth of Anna Pavlova the Museum of London mounted a special exhibition of photographs and relics with appropriate music. It was also the 50th anniversary of Ninette de Valois's Sadlers Wells (now Royal) Ballet and of the reopening of Lilian Baylis's Sadlers Wells Theatre, for which galas were held at that theatre and at the Royal Opera House, Covent Garden, which itself was celebrating the 250th year since it was first built.

The Royal Ballet's major production *Isadora*, a full-length ballet about the life of Isadora Duncan, was choreographed by MacMillan to commissioned music by Richard Rodney Bennett and decor by Barry Kay. It was immensely spectacular but found little favour because it made a figure of ridicule of an artist whose influence on the art of dance was immense. Merle Park danced the eponymous role, spoken and acted by an actress, Mary Miller.

The company suffered by the departure of Lynn Seymour, who left to form a rock group (but did not succeed), and by the loss to America of Anthony Dowell, together with injuries to Stephen Jefferies and David Wall. Norman Morrice continued his excellent policy of bringing forward his younger dancers to principal roles, giving Bryony Brind *Swan Lake* and *Afternoon of a Faun,* Karen Paisey *Symphonic Variations* and, in *Afternoon of a Faun,* Ashley Page, David Peden and

Ravenna Tucker. The Royal Ballet also made its first visit to New York for five years, where its success, though great, was less than had been hoped. At the end of the year Ashton's *Illuminations* (originally created for the New York City Ballet in 1950) came into the repertoire and was no longer found shocking.

It was Peter Wright's Sadlers Wells Royal Ballet which had the greater public appeal during the year. His team of young, bright dancers (Nicola Katrak, Sherilyn Kennedy, Marion Tate, Susan Lucas and others) charmed audiences wherever they went (and this included Monte Carlo, Yugoslavia and the Far East), and their season culminated in his new production of *Swan Lake* which was so lavish that it could be shown only in large opera houses, not in their own theatre. Galina Samsova joined the company as prima ballerina.

London Festival Ballet battled successfully with its financial problems and by forming a little 'educational' group under its archivist John Travis had tremendous success in making young audiences understand and appreciate ballet, thereby assuring the company's future.

Scottish Ballet had a setback when the Scottish Arts Council refused to allow them to appear outside Scotland (though they did manage a week in Brighton). Northern Ballet Theatre produced two more full-length ballets (*Sylvia*, choreographed by Richard Glasstone, and *Midsummer Night's Dream* by de Warren to Mendelssohn's music). The company also appeared in Catania, Sicily—indeed they spent more time away from Manchester than in it. The Dublin City Ballet had to trim its finances and become a small modern group; its former director, Janet Lewis, left and formed the London City Ballet, which in turn came to an end through lack of funds. However, another small classical company, the London City Ballet (directed by Harold King), flourished and enlarged, took Beryl Grey on its board and engaged Maina Gielgud as its ballet mistress.

In Russia the distinguished old dancer Konstantin Segueyev mounted a *Joan of Arc* at the Moscow Stanislavky Theatre (with Drosdova as Joan), and Vladimir Vassiliev choreographed a rock-opera (the first in Moscow), *June and Perchance*, based on a Russian naval expedition to San Francisco in 1906. The Bolshoi dancers continued to complain against their director, Yuri Grigorovitch, for his hard-line, old-fashioned policies—to no avail. The publication of a book, *Divertissement* by Vadim Gayevski, highly critical of the state and direction of the Bolshoi Ballet, caused a big scandal and a disciplining of the publishers, and soon it became unobtainable, but not before it had reached many cities in the free world. Yuri Grigorovitch was also the editor-in-chief of a very fine *Encyclopaedia of Ballet* published in Moscow during the year. Well produced and illustrated, it covered world ballet with great accuracy, but it could not be considered a work of true scholarship, for it lacked all reference to Russia's greatest living dancers, Nureyev, Makarova, Baryshnikov and the teacher Sulamith Messerer, and without considerable study it is impossible to say if the whole work is similarly politically slanted and the truth suppressed.

The 'ballet-explosion' in the United States continued apace, with companies proliferating and Balanchine's New York City Ballet still in the lead. A major event was their Tchaikovsky Festival in New York. Baryshnikov became director of American Ballet Theatre and retained the services of Antony Tudor and Nora Kaye. However, he disbanded the ABT School (previously one of the USA's leading ballet schools) except for a handful of highly selected students. Natalia Makarova's group 'Makarova and Company' continued in an uncertain way in spite of its galaxy of guest stars—Anthony Dowell (who was hardly seen in London at all), Bujones, Cynthia Gregory, Karen Kain and others. The Joffrey Ballet presented two ballets by a choreographer of considerable promise, Choo San Goh, and gained much publicity from having a son of President Reagan as a member of the company. Three American companies appeared in Britain—Violette Verdy's Boston Ballet at the London Coliseum (presenting *Swan Lake* with Nureyev) and the San Francisco Ballet at the Edinburgh Festival, where Dan Wagoner and Dancers also performed.

In Germany, Pina Bausch's company at Wüppertal continued to fascinate the critics with her tortured, obscure and decidedly unballetic creations (her *Ariel* had the dancers splashing about on a stage inches deep in water). A major creation of the Hamburg Ballet was John Neumeier's *Matthew Passion*—Bach's great choral work danced out before the altar of St Michaelis-Kirche, with choir and full orchestra in the north transept—a most moving experience in this setting but a little tedious when transferred to the Opera House. The Danish dancer Egon Madsen, who made a distinguished career in the Stuttgart Ballet, became director of the ballet in Frankfurt and invited Peter Wright to mount his well-considered version of *Giselle* (already performed by several European ballets). Wright also had a great success with his version of *Sleeping Beauty*, produced for the Dutch National Ballet in Amsterdam. The Munich Ballet had an uneventful first year under the direction of Edmund Gleede, a dramaturg from Berlin and not a ballet specialist. West Berlin was dominated by the Panovs. Valerie Panov created *War and Peace* (Tchaikovsky) in June and the company presented Tolstoy's *The Idiot* (Shostakovitch) with Valerie and Galina Panov and Eva Evdokimova in the leading roles.

The ballet scene in Australia was overshadowed by a strike of the dancers of the Australian Ballet who complained of over-work (236 performances) and the spartan regime imposed by their financial director, on account of rising costs which made the future of the company uncertain. In Canada the National Ballet had a tremendous success with their full-length *Napoli*, mounted for them (and danced) by Peter Schaufuss.

A curious feature of the year was the number of ballets created on the theme of Tchaikovsky and his suicide in the shade of approaching scandal over his affair with a young Russian prince. It was done by various choreographers in Düsseldorf, Warsaw, Nuremberg, Munich and, most notably, Charleroi (Belgium) by the Ballet Royal de Wallonie, choreographed by Jorge Lefèbre.

At the Paris Opéra Heinz Spoerli of Basle mounted a version of *La Fille Mal Gardée* (music Hérold and Hertel), and Nureyev produced his version of *Don Quixote* with Pontois and Atanassoff in the leading roles. Nureyev was offered the directorship of this difficult company for the following season, but by the end of the year had not made up his mind.

As a tribute to the Royal Ballet on its attaining its fifty years, the Theatre Museum mounted an exhibition in the Victoria and Albert Museum called Spotlight, bringing together a remarkable collection of ballet costumes worn over four centuries and of ballet costume designs and lithographs; the catalogue remains a valuable source of reference.

Among the deaths recorded were those of Lydia Lopokova (see OBITUARY), Felia Doubrovska, Paul Petroff, George Skibine and Edward Caton.

THEATRE

A critic who had ended 1980 ritually lamenting the dearth of interesting new drama would have been pleasantly surprised by 1981. At least four works were likely to be remembered and, perhaps, revived in times to come: *Passion Play*, which some thought Peter Nichols's best effort to date; *Translations*, by Brian Friel, which *The Times* proclaimed a 'masterpiece'; *Quartermaine's Terms*, by Simon Gray; *Good*, by C. P. Taylor, a gifted and undervalued playwright whose premature death occurred in December. To that list might be more tentatively added *Goosepimples*, a play improvised by its cast and shaped and scripted by Mike Leigh, Edward Bond's *Restoration* and Tom Stoppard's adaptation of Nestroy, *On the Razzle*.

Passion Play, staged by the Royal Shakespeare Company (RSC), gave a contemporary twist to a subject long fallen into critical disfavour, the eternal (or interminable) triangle. Nichols was concerned less with sexual immorality *per se* than with the human damage inflicted by deception and betrayal upon both the deceiver and the deceived; and he found a strikingly fresh way of expressing this. Both husband and wife acquired living, breathing *alter egos* to represent their hidden desires, guilts, resentments, angers and anguishes. The result had both psychological richness and emotional force, chronicling nothing less than the spiritual destruction of two people.

Translations, by comparison, seemed a somewhat cerebral piece, set in an Irish 'hedge school' in the early nineteenth century and using the appearance of military cartographers from England to mount a wide-ranging debate on matters cultural and linguistic. It was dense yet sensitive, and not without its rueful relevance to Anglo-Irish relations today; and it clearly merited its transfer from Hampstead Theatre Club to the National Theatre. Some, however, thought it flawed on the emotional level. When a cross-cultural love-match burgeoned between a peasant girl and a young lieutenant—each speaking only in his or her own language, like the Mortimers in *Henry IV Part One*—the play lapsed into a kind of energetic cliché.

Quartermaine's Terms was another of Gray's studies of withdrawal, detachment, this time represented by an amiable but ineffective language-school teacher exploited by his colleagues, despised by his pupils, and finally sacked by his principal: a sympathetic, touching picture brought to shambling life by that admirable actor, Edward Fox. And *Good* also offered a remarkable performance, perhaps the most remarkable of the year. Alan Howard, previously known mainly as a trumpet-tongued classical actor, was asked to chronicle the transformation of a young German intellectual into one of the powers at Auschwitz; and he brought off this improbable feat with a sly, subtle awareness of the inner geography of temptation and corruption. The play—showing with sympathy and sorrow the tenacity with which some people cling to moral self-regard against all the odds—was convincing proof of the loss the British theatre sustained in C. P. Taylor.

Goosepimples, which transferred from Hampstead to the Garrick, suffered from flaws frequently found in 'improvised' plays, namely dull patches and a tendency on the actors' parts to patronize the characters they have invented; but its description of the humiliation of a visiting Saudi by English car-salesmen did at least give theatrical expression to a growing national prejudice, against 'rich' Arabs. In *On the Razzle*, Stoppard's exuberant wit made his audiences laugh, as always; but one felt he was squandering his verbal imagination on too trivial a subject, the farcical misadventures of 'country mice' in the big city. And the serio-comic *Restoration*, about an outrageous fop's abuse of the servant classes, was spoiled by the moralizing tenor, the ideological explicitness, that has marked Bond's recent work, most notably *The Worlds,* which also arrived in London in 1981. This last, a tale of striking workers and kidnapped executives, also showed how willing one prominent playwright of the left had become to endorse terrorism as a means of accomplishing social change.

It was a little worrying that the year's most memorable work came from established playwrights aged over 40. There was scant sign of fresh talent emerging. Indeed, the best-received play by a 'new' dramatist in 1981—*Steaming*, a celebration of female solidarity in a municipal bath threatened with closure—was by Nell Dunn, who already enjoyed an established reputation as a novelist. The nearest to a genuinely 'promising' playwright to appear was Hanif Kureishi, a young Englishman of Pakistani origin and the author both of *Outskirts*, about the social and economic pressures conspiring to produce a British fascist, and of *Borderline*, about the travails of Asian immigrants in West London. The plays received the imprimatur of productions by the RSC and Royal Court respectively, and they undeniably had their stirring moments. However, both also suggested that Kureishi, like so many contemporary playwrights, felt an overriding obligation to be politically responsible, socially significant, and they left one wondering if this burden was not distorting his true talent.

In some ways 1981 was a curious year. Who could have predicted that an Italian trotskyist, Dario Fo, would have three pieces simultaneously running in London mainstream theatres—or six, if one counted all four of his feminist *One Woman Plays* at the National? And even if *Can't Pay? Won't Pay!* and *Accidental Death of an Anarchist* scored their respective successes because they were funny, rather than because they were politically subversive, they at least demonstrated that things were continuing to change in and around that supposed citadel of middlebrow, middle-class taste, Shaftesbury Avenue.

Soaring costs and stayaway audiences had made life very difficult for commercial managements in recent years, and some had become abjectly dependent on the subsidized theatre's cast-offs for their own more prestigious successes. The presence in the West End at the year's end of *Children of a Lesser God* (transferred from the Mermaid), *Amadeus* (from the National), *The Mitford Girls* (from Chichester) and *Steaming* (from Stratford East) showed that this parasitism still flourished in 1981. Nevertheless, there were signs that the impresarios were recovering some of the initiative. A booth in Leicester Square selling cut-price tickets to West End plays more than justified itself, as did several first-hand productions, notably a powerful revival of Arthur Miller's *All My Sons* at the Wyndhams, the musical *Cats* at the New London, and *Quartermaine's Terms* at the Queens.

The fortunes of the subsidized theatre itself were mixed. The Old Vic Company, after several frankly mediocre productions, collapsed in the spring, leaving one of our more historic theatres without a tenant or, it seemed, a purpose. The Mermaid reopened in the well of a Blackfriars office-block with a revival of *Eastward Ho!* so critically and commercially unsuccessful that it, too, was obliged to 'go dark' temporarily. The

Royal Court had a generally disappointing year, though it did give house-room to a lively improvised play about the vicissitudes of 'show-business', *Four in a Million*, and to yet another interesting piece by the prolific Brian Friel, *Faith Healer*. Too often its authors and directors failed to give imaginative life to the socially committed drama in which that theatre specializes. More consistently enjoyable work was to be found at less prestigious addresses: Hampstead, Greenwich, the Bush, Riverside Studios, the Half Moon and, out of London, the Royal Exchange, Manchester. The worst anxieties about the level of government funding turned out to be unjustified, since an increase of eight per cent in the Arts Council's drama budget was announced at the year's end.

The undeclared contest for supremacy between the two major national companies ended, it seemed, as the RSC again failed to attain quite the heights it achieved in the early 1970s, while the National sustained its recent artistic improvement. The year at Stratford-upon-Avon was uneven, though John Barton's *Merchant of Venice,* with David Suchet a baleful, cackling Shylock and Sinead Cusack an unusually sentient Portia, and Trevor Nunn's inventively Edwardian revival of *All's Well* did much to compensate for a disappointing *Midsummer Night's Dream* and a miscalculated double-bill of *Titus Andronicus* and *The Two Gentlemen of Verona*. The programme at the RSC's main London house, the Aldwych, proved more consistently alluring, even if it did include yet another season of the eternal *Nicholas Nickleby* and several transfers from the previous year's Stratford season. *Richard II* glistened with intelligence and historical excitement. Solzhenitsyn's *Love Girl and the Innocent*, receiving its overdue British premiere, proved a more powerfully theatrical picture of *gulag* life than its seemingly cluttered text had suggested. *Passion Play* has already been noted.

For the RSC, 1982 promised to be a particularly difficult year, since it would be moving into a spanking new auditorium in the Barbican Arts Centre, marooned in the City of London. The National Theatre had certainly taken its time adjusting to a less obviously traumatic move, 300 yards from the Old Vic to its tailor-made building on the South Bank. Indeed, 1981 was probably the first year one could sit back in any of its three auditoria, confident of the company's own self-confidence, consistently sure of its artistic consistency. It offered fine revivals of Shaw's *Man and Superman*, complete with the Don Juan dream-sequence, Calderon's *Mayor of Zalamea* and (especially) Dekker's *Shoemaker's Holiday*, a model example of how sensitive direction, here provided by John Dexter, could bring to life a classic more than usually of and about its period. Indeed, its fault, if it was one, was perhaps an excess of sensitivity, at any rate where poverty, war, affliction and sickness were involved. The characters' facial and vocal response to such things tended to be more contemporary than Jacobean. By contrast, an example of the kind of over-slanted revival too frequent in recent years was a *Measure for Measure* performed by black actors and transformed into a study of political corruption in the modern Caribbean, briefly on offer in the National's Lyttelton auditorium.

The National's year was one more of revivals than of new plays. Indeed, the only British premiere of note there was that of Arnold Wesker's *Caritas*, a bleak picture of a despairing medieval anchoress not greatly liked by reviewers. But by the year's end some critics were too overwhelmed to complain very loudly. In late November, the most remarkable, if not the most successful, production the decade had so far seen, Aeschylus's *Oresteia*, adapted by Tony Harrison, was staged in the well of the Olivier amphitheatre by the National's artistic director, Peter Hall. It was performed in masks, which added to the visual excitement but did make some passages hard to hear. And Harrison's translation, a curious amalgam of contemporary colloquialism and Beowulf pastiche, itself turned out to be something of a mask, cutting off the audience from direct contact with Aeschylus. It was a testimony to the energy and skill of the all-male cast, the imagination of Jocelyn Herbert's designs, and the precision with which Hall choreographed the movements both of chorus and principals, that the production was still compulsory viewing. When could the British theatre expect again to see anything so genuinely audacious and ambitious?

New York Theatre

Among the felicitous events of 1981 were the emergence of a clutch of talented new playwrights, notably Beth Henley with a first play, *Crimes of the Heart*, displaying prodigious skill with macabre humour; Wendy Kesselman's *My Sister in this House*, based on an actual incestuous incident in France in the 1930s, echoing Genet's *The Maids*; Christopher Durang's evening of one-act plays, *The Actor's Nightmare*, and *Sister Mary Ignatius Explains it All for You*, an honest, witty yet vengeful attack on Roman Catholicism; Bill C. Davis's *Mass Appeal*, which dealt affectionately and profoundly with clerical weakness; and finally and most original David Henry Hwang, a Chinese-American born in Los Angeles, with no less than three plays produced during the year—*Fob, The Dance and The Railroad* and *Family Devotions*, all dealing essentially with aspects of immigrants' struggle with absorption into US civilization. After some previous respectable attempts at playwrighting, Jules Feiffer, the accomplished cartoonist, this year succeeded with a laudably amusing and bitter play, *Grown Ups*.

The habitual British imports included Ronald Harwood's *The Dresser* with Tom Courtenay repeating his original title role, and Paul Rogers adding his great strength to the role of Sir. The Royal

Shakespeare Company's thundering, riotous, sprawling production of *Nicholas Nickleby* filled houses despite the highest-priced tickets in history, $100 for both parts—a fee which was slowly approached by other productions. More brief-lived was Andrew Davies's *Rose,* starring Glenda Jackson in the title role and Jessica Tandy in the minor role of her mother, overwhelming the critics with her exceptional expertise. Other returning seniors illuminated the year: Katherine Hepburn, still alluring if not stunning in Ernest Thompson's *West Side Waltz*; Claudette Colbert, effortlessly charming in the feeble *A Talent for Murder* by Jerome Chodorov and Norman Panama; Eva Le Gallienne in a fruitless *To Grandmother's House We Go* by Joanna M. Glass; and Rex Harrison in his original role in *My Fair Lady*. Other welcome stars chiefly from films were Elizabeth Taylor in Lillian Hellman's *The Little Foxes*; Joanne Woodward, intelligent as *Candida*, but poorly supported; and Nicol Williamson in his original role in *Inadmissible Evidence*. Brian Friel's local premiere of *Translations* had an impressive performance by veteran Bernard Hughes.

Among established companies, The Negro Ensemble Company received an Obie (Off Broadway award) for 'sustained achievement' in its past seasons, and produced a splendid new work filled with rich characterizations and profound social and historical vision, *A Soldier's Play* by Charles Fuller, an Obie awardee for his previous play, *Zooman and the Sign*. La Mama, Ellen Stewart's experimental theatre, celebrated its twentieth year, chiefly with revivals from its impressive past, e.g. Tom Eyen's *Why Hanna's Skirt Won't Stay Down,* and Leonard Melfi's *Birdbath*. The Classic Stage Company had notable success with a two-part *Peer Gynt* and Büchner's rarely-performed *Woyzeck* and *Leonce and Lena*. The Roundabout Theatre continued its policy of classic plays using mainly British stars—among others, Susannah York as *Hedda Gabler*. Uptown at Lincoln Center the large Beaumont Theatre closed after poor productions of *Macbeth*, disastrously directed by Sarah Caldwell, the skilled opera conductor and stage director, and of a pedestrian new play by Woody Allen, *The Floating Light Bulb*. The smaller theatre there, the Newhouse, suspended operations after its first presentation of new one-act plays organized by Edward Albee. He must also be included in a list of distinguished failures this year with his muddled adaptation of Nabokov's *Lolita*; the list included Simon Gray's *Close of Play* at the highly-professional Manhattan Theatre Club; Tennessee Williams's memoirs adapted by Gray, *Something Cloudy, Something Clear*; Neil Simon's *Fools*; Tom Kempinski's *Duet for One* from London was directed by film director William Friedkin who, despite the outstanding cast, Anne Bancroft and Max von Sydow, proved incapable of solving the play's weaknesses; and Stephen Sondheim's musical setting of Kaufman and Hart's *Merrily We Roll Along*, with book by George Furth, had a very brief run.

The musical scene, however, celebrated two outstandingly superior works: *Lena Horne, The Lady and her Music,* much more than the title suggests—a recounting of the life of an outstanding woman whose struggles and contribution to society went far beyond her singing career; and a new Michael Bennett study of battles for and with success in the theatre, *Dreamgirls* (book and lyrics by Tom Eyen, music by Henry Krieger). Director Wilford Leach spruced up Gilbert and Sullivan's *Pirates of Penzance* with daring freshness to the delight of critics and audiences. A collage of Duke Ellington's music, *Sophisticated Ladies,* was elegantly mounted; Jane Lapotaire scored a personal success in Pam Gems's *Piaf* from the RSC; and duty compels reporting Lauren Bacall's appeal in *Woman of the Year,* a weak updating of a Hepburn-Tracy film. However, two small musicals charmed—*Pump Boys and Dinettes,* a revue, and *March of the Falsettos* by a new composer, William Finn, with an unlikely book dealing with a man who leaves his wife and child for a male lover.

Among musical revivals were Cole Porter's *Can Can* with Zizi Jeanmaire; a lacklustre *Camelot* with Richard Harris; a fine presentation of Webber and Rice's *Joseph and his Amazing Technicolor Dreamcoat*; and, among some disasters, an attempt to adapt Dickens's 'David Copperfield' (*Copperfield*); a sequel to *Bye Bye Birdie* (*Bring Back Birdie*); additional collages of the music of Sondheim and of Vincent Youmans; and an unsuccessful attempt at the dramatic story of baseball's Jackie Robinson (*The First*).

A unique work, *Behind the Broken Words,* a compilation of song and poetry edited and performed by the accomplished black actor Roscoe Lee Browne and Anthony Zerbe, who occasionally played the guitar, should have laid to rest the myth that US actors cannot speak or perform verse drama at the level of other native English-speakers.

The theatre world mourned the closing of the Chelsea Theatre Centre after 16 years of producing more than 100 plays and garnering five Tony Awards and 20 Obies, and the deaths of playwrights Paul Green and Sidney (Paddy) Chayevsky, who won three Oscars for film writing.

MUSIC

Covent Garden's production of the recently-completed three-act version of Berg's *Lulu* early in 1981 was an event whose importance far transcended the world of opera; it was an international performance, of the sort that characterizes London at its best. The year closed on a more dismal note, with Covent Garden's introduction of a new work for children by the Scottish composer Thea Musgrave, a setting of Dickens's *A Christmas Carol,* remarkable for its academic construction and its complete avoidance of melody. Between these two extremes (Berg and Musgrave), the established repertoire made up far the greater part of the musical fare, not only in the theatre but in other areas of music.

South Bank concerts in 1981 followed much the same pattern as that of previous years. The orchestras, including visitors, pursued a conservative course. This was evidently the case the world over; in an article in the *New York Times* the American composer Lester Trimble pointed out that major symphony orchestras prefer the European classics to the music of their own day, and that American orchestras ignore American composers just like their British counterparts. It is a process, he wrote, of 'reverse chauvinism amounting to a cultural death-wish'. Certainly in London, signs of imaginative programming were isolated: the London Symphony Orchestra gave Panufnik's *Concertino* and repeated the Tippett *Triple Concerto*, which was such a success the previous year; the Philharmonia under Riccardo Muti introduced some new works alongside the familiar favourites. But no particular theme was apparent. Mahler enjoyed something of a vogue, perhaps because 1981 marked the 70th anniversary of his death; and Mendelssohn was well represented. Radu Lupu played the Beethoven piano concertos. Apart from such standard concerts, one noticed a larger number than usual of 'light music' concerts, 'Viennese Evenings' and entertainment by such pseudo-cabaret groups as 'The King's Singers' and 'Instant Sunshine'.

Generally speaking it was the smaller ensembles and solo performers who were more adventurous. Many found accommodation on the South Bank in 1981. One put on Boulez-Gehlhaar-Xenakis; another was so rash as to perform all the Berio *Sequenzas* in one concert. Such acts of abandon were normally met by row upon row of empty seats; the rift between contemporary music and the established repertoire was plainly apparent. The most successful recital was given by the virtuoso Maurizio Pollini, who combined Beethoven with Webern and Boulez for his Festival Hall recital in October; for him the hall was about two-thirds full.

The BBC had a lean and somewhat grey musical year. Its Festival Hall concerts set out to be, and succeeded in being, off the beaten track; they did not succeed, however, in breaking any new ground artistically, lacking apparently any clear policy or purpose. The chief novelty in the BBC's Promenade Concerts was John Tavener's *Akhmatova Requiem*, a lament for the victims of Stalin's terror. The composer was received into the Russian Orthodox Church in 1977, and the work was sung in Russian —which many found an obstacle to enjoyment. Both in the London concert and at the Edinburgh Festival, where it was heard a week earlier, public indifference was reflected in a small audience. Tavener's static, ritualistic style was already familiar from his earlier works.

Most British composers received short shrift in their native land in 1981; some, however, were given more favourable treatment in the

United States. André Previn played some British music with the Pittsburgh Orchestra, and directed a 'British Music Festival' in New York. Among the composers commissioned by the Boston Symphony for its centennial were two Britons—Maxwell Davies (*Symphony No. 2*) and Michael Tippett (*The Mark of Time*)—who encompassed the twin poles of British music, the avant-garde and the traditional. The week of contemporary music at Tanglewood, privately patronized by Paul Fromm, also included the *Third Symphony* by the younger Oliver Knussen.

If American composers received little recognition from American orchestras in 1981, and the New York season resembled London's in its heavy reliance on classical works, one or two striking events suggested that the rebuilding of the broken lines of communication between the composer and his audience, largely through the use of melody and greater simplicity of construction, was being treated as a priority by some American composers. Among them was John Harbison, who had several successful performances in the year and was commissioned by the Boston Orchestra to write a centennial piece.

Another composer who achieved something of a breakthrough with a mass audience in 1981, in a different style, was Philip Glass, whose opera *Satyagraha* was a deliberate attempt to reverse the intellectual academicism of so much contemporary music, in favour of sensuous melodies, simple harmonies and repetitive, hypnotic rhythms. What might sound like a recipe for the most banal popular style was redeemed, first, by Glass's technique, secondly by the sustained structure of the work. The opera, sung in Sanskrit, the language of the Mahabharata, is concerned with Gandhi's struggle against racial discrimination in South Africa between 1893 and 1914. It was originally commissioned by the City of Rotterdam, and was a triumphant success when it was first heard in America in 1981.

Perhaps the most important worldwide event in 1981 was the celebration of the Bartók centenary. In Budapest itself there were daily radio performances of his music, and in October an international conference of musicians and scholars to consider many different aspects of his work. Elsewhere there were numerous performances of his works, and some fine commemorative recordings were issued. Among the most notable were those by the young virtuoso pianist Zoltán Kocsis, by the Berlin Philharmonic under Lorin Maazel, by the Tokyo String Quartet (whose performance of the six quartets set new standards of ensemble playing), by the composer's widow Ditta Bartók-Pażstory, and by Murray Perahia, Homero Francesch and Gyorgy Pauk.

Another product of international cooperation, mainly Anglo-American, was the publication in 1981 of the latest edition of *Grove's Dictionary of Music and Musicians*, edited by Dr Stanley Sadie. Over

2,400 contributors wrote over 22,500 articles for this lexicon, which extended to 20 volumes and cost £850. This could indeed be called the testament to our Alexandrian age, the pinnacle of musicology today. Most of the articles were written by music critics or academics of the English-speaking world. Reviewing such a gigantic production clearly presented problems; who could be expected to read, even in a lifetime, all these volumes? So it is little wonder that in-depth reviews were few and far between. From the handful that appeared, such as one by Charles Rosen in the *New York Review of Books*, and some articles in *Performance*, it seemed that, as well as numerous accolades, there were reservations in those areas where journalists and academics are not best placed to have the last word, and where composers or performers would have had more to say (See also p. 445).

The different compartments of music remained distinct in 1981. Pop music continued unabated (called by Anthony Burgess, in an article in *The Times*, 'a moronic sub-art'), and one well-known group defied its obituary notices of 1978 by reappearing in 1981 for another American tour. The Rolling Stones, with a reformed, middle-aged Mick Jagger, presented themselves to a new generation of teenagers, yet unborn when the Stones first hit the pop music trail.

On the other side of the cultural divide, Early Music continued to appeal to many audiences, and the cult of 'authenticity', both of instruments and of performance, continued to excite controversy. One protagonist in this field was Nikolaus Harnoncourt, whose editions, productions and recordings of the Monteverdi operas and madrigals proved highly successful.

The record industry remained in spate in 1981, despite the recession. Patterns were changing, as keen competition came from small, independent companies (some 50 in America, the same number in Europe), challenging the large international corporations. Although the world's most famous musicians continued to be heard under the prestige labels of the great companies, much more music, of greater variety and, to many collectors, of greater interest, was to be heard from these other quarters. Apart from the Bartók records, among the countless releases of 1981 two giant projects might be singled out: the 31-disc centennial edition of Stravinsky's works from CBS, and the 30-disc set of French organ music from Calliope. Among the many opera recordings (always a favourite with record companies), Wagner fared particularly well in 1981; some might say excessively so. The complete *Ring*, recorded at Bayreuth by Boulez, was released by Philips, while DG countered with *Parsifal*, in a magnificent performance under Karajan. As for *Tristan*, no fewer than three versions appeared, under Kleiber, Bernstein and Goodall respectively. There were also many other opera recordings, and a host of classical releases.

Those who died in 1981 included the oboist Janet Craxton, the Swedish-born composer Gunilla Lowenstein, the German organist and conductor Karl Richter, the eminent Russian conductor Kyril Kondrashin, the Polish composer Tadeusz Baird, the American composer Samuel Barber, and, in the pop world, Bill Haley, doyen of 'rock and roll', and Hoagy Carmichael, the immensely successful American songwriter. (For Barber and Haley, see OBITUARY).

CINEMA

Cinema attendance in Britain declined in 1981 to a midsummer level of 1·58 million a week; nevertheless it came as a shock when the Rank Organization decided in June 1981 to close a further 38 of its theatres, reducing its circuit to 231 from its 1950 maximum of some 600. The largest chain in Britain remained Thorn-EMI's ABC circuit of 342 theatres.

Indigenous British production was described as 'a mere trickle', and film-makers claimed that television, showing old features on a massive scale while paying as little as £15,000 an hour for the privilege, accounted for decreased theatre attendance; ITV had shown 328 cinema films in 1980, and the BBC over 60 during the Christmas period. In June the announcement of Lord Grade's heavy loss on his $35 million production, *Raise the Titanic*, shook the industry in spite of the considerable profits his company, Associated Communications Corporation, had made in the previous year out of their first Muppets film. Notable successes in British production included EMI's *The Elephant Man* and 20th Century-Fox's *Chariots of Fire* (budget $6 million). *Chariots of Fire* was sponsored by Goldcrest Film International, of which a leading partner was the publishing group Pearson Longman. Goldcrest also placed a substantial stake in Sir Richard Attenborough's production, *Gandhi* (budget $22 million). EMI announced investment of up to £35 million in production, their sponsorship including Lindsay Anderson's latest feature, *Britannia Hospital* (a low-budget film costing £1,500,000). Another success was Karel Reisz's *The French Lieutenant's Woman*. No less than 15 new British productions were presented in the London Film Festival in November; this was due to the resurgence of lively, low-budget productions of a strictly indigenous nature, like Chris Petit's *An Unsuitable Job for a Woman* and Bill Forsyth's *Gregory's Girl* (budget £189,000). British studios also continued to give outstanding support to outside work, contributing substantially to such American successes as *Clash of the Titans* and *Excalibur*, as well as *Star Wars, Superman* and their successors. The British Film Institute's production division dispensed some £900,000 in sponsorship money during 1981, and the choice of Sir

Richard Attenborough as chairman of the Institute's governing board in 1982 should increase its interest in production.

Hollywood's parallel to the *Raise the Titanic* disaster was Michael Cimino's *Heaven's Gate* (United Artists). After its initial failure, this 3-hour 40-minute film was withdrawn and reissued in April with some 50 minutes pruned away. American feature production in 1980 numbered some 200 films with an average cost of $9,380,000 per picture. Inflation, strike action or the threat of it, instability in management and the need for constant adjustment to new technologies appeared to be the principal threats to production, together with the gradual spread in America of cable-tv and the availability of comparatively recent feature productions on video-cassette or video-disc. New technologies entice new outlooks, and the traditional industry shivered as company after company came under sometimes 'whizz-kid' managements. MGM bought out United Artists suddenly in the summer. The image in Hollywood became increasingly that set by Coppola, Lucas, Spielberg, Scorsese, Redford and the like, many of them former students from the American film schools. However, many of the better films, and the most successful, were produced on comparatively low budgets—for example *Ordinary People* ($6·3 million) and *Kramer versus Kramer* ($6·6 million).

Australia continued to be a success story. Backed by federal aid and tax incentives, nurtured by the founding of the Australian Film Commission, combined with the establishment some ten years earlier of the Australian Film and Television School, that country produced an increasing number of internationally successful features. Among the growing number of younger 'New Wave' film directors were Bruce Beresford (*The Getting of Wisdom, Breaker Morant, Puberty Blues*), Peter Weir (*The Last Wave, Gallipoli*), Gillian Armstrong (*My Brilliant Career*), Fred Schepisi (*The Chant of Jimmy Blacksmith*) and Philip Noyce (*Newsfront*).

For the English-language cinema, 1981 was a thin year for high quality films. Outstanding among British productions were two adaptations from literature, Roman Polanski's Franco-British *Tess* (impressively visual, but too far from Hardy) with Natassia Kinski, and Karel Reisz's *The French Lieutenant's Woman* (Meryl Streep, Jeremy Irons), excellently acted. In another Franco-British film, *Quartet* (with Isabelle Adjani, Maggie Smith, Alan Bates), James Ivory achieved unique atmosphere in portraying Paris in the 1920s, while expatriate Yugoslav director Dusan Makavejev made an Anglo-Swedish film, *Montenegro*, in which an upper-class Swedish housewife murders her working-class Yugoslav lover. Another adaptation, Just Jaeckin's Franco-British *Lady Chatterley's Lover,* relapsed into 'soft porn' rather than portraying Lawrence's ritualized male sexuality. *Chariots of Fire* (Hugh Hudson, with Ben Cross, Ian Charleson) enjoyed success as a dual biographical drama concerning two diverse Olympic runners of the 1920s. Indigenous on a more modest scale were such films as *Gregory's Girl* (already mentioned) and David Gladwell's adaptation from Doris Lessing, *Memoirs of a Survivor* (Julie Christie). The twelfth Bond subject, *For Your Eyes Only* (John Glen, with Roger Moore), relied wholly on the expertise of the British studio technicians supplying the special effects, as did Terry Gilliam's *Time Bandits*, a comic-strip fantasia from a child's imagination in which stars from Sean Connery to Ralph Richardson appeared to enjoy their 'bit' roles.

The specifically American films of the year that involved specialist forms of spectacle included John Boorman's personal vision of Malory, *Excalibur*; spectacular, too, was Michael Cimino's ill-fated *Heaven's Gate*, in its way highly significant for its social implications as an epic Western, starring Kris Kristofferson, John Hurt and Isabelle Huppert. But the most important genre was domestic and psychological, led by *Ordinary People* (Robert Redford, with Donald Sutherland, Mary Tyler Moore, Timothy Hutton), but also including Dennis Hopper's *Out of the Blue*, Tony Ritt's directorial debut with a film about adolescent violence, *My Bodyguard*, L. J. Carlino's *The Great Santini* (Robert Duvall), Martin Scorsese's *Raging Bull* (Robert de Niro) and Ken Russell's American film, *Altered States* (William Hurt in various self-induced, hallucinogenic conditions that rival the metamorphosis in 'Dr Jekyll and Mr Hyde'). Turning to crime, Sidney Lumet's *Prince of the City* dealt with the intricacies of drug surveillance as it affects the police. Many of the psychologically slanted films were also crime thrillers: the multiple killers in Larry Cohen's *Demon*, the woman (Gena Rowlands) who desperately shoots her way free of the 'mob' in John Cassavetes' *Gloria*, the successive shootings and other acts of violence in Elliot Silverstein's *Nightmare Honeymoon*, Peter Yates's *The Janitor*, Mark Reichart's *Union City* (not unlike Hitchcock), John Huston's *Phobia,* with its cumulative deaths, and Ulu Grosbard's *True Confessions* (with Robert De Niro as a Catholic priest and Robert Duvall as his brother, a retired policeman), all culminating in James Glickenhaus's *The Exterminators* and the hideous but well-made successor to *The Texas Chainsaw Massacre, The Funhouse* (Tobe Hooper), with its horrific mutant killer. *The Postman Always Rings Twice*, the fourth version of James M. Cain's novel, directed by Bob Rafelson, gained not only in sophistication but also in violent sexual action, polished by Sven Nykvist's magnificent cinematography.

Several American films centred on real-life personalities. While Michael Ritchie's *Divine Madness* gave Bette Midler a chance to display her diversely vulgar powers, the dead were raised in the 'bio-pics', *Melvin and Howard* (Jonathan Demme, with Jason Robards as Howard Hughes), *Marilyn, the Untold Story* (based on the book by Norman Mailer, with Catherine Hicks as the star, and with actors portraying Arthur Miller, Billy

Wilder, Montgomery Clift, Jack Lemmon and even Laurence Olivier), and *Mommie Dearest* (with Faye Dunaway as Joan Crawford).

Perhaps more sociological in purpose were *Nine to Five* (Colin Higgins, with Jane Fonda, Lily Tomlin), a comedy (almost a burlesque) about three office girls' response to sexual harassment, presented with a strong feminist slant, and Robert Aldrich's film of corruption in the women's wrestling industry, *The California Dolls*. Two notable films by women directors, *Head over Heels (Joan Macklin Silver, with John Heard, Mary Beth Hurt)* and *It's My Turn* (Claudia Weill, with Jill Clayburgh), were more concerned with tangled love relationships between people of the professional class, the former in particular an accomplished work. Ralph Bakshi's *American Pop* exposed the corruption in the American 'pop' industry, and Frederick Wiseman's two-hour documentary, *Model*, showed the hazards of the modelling profession.

Films made by Continental European directors were led by four made in English—Louis Malle's successor to *Pretty Baby, Atlantic City USA*, a study in the illusion and disillusion of dreams conjured by life in such a city as Las Vegas, Alain Tanner's *Light Years Away*, an imagistic film set in the year 2000 AD, Bertrand Tavernier's science-fictional *Death Watch* and, more specialized, Nicholas Ray's and Wim Wenders's *Lightning over Water,* a strange projection of the dying Ray's philosophy made during the weeks preceding his death from cancer in 1979.

Most notable of foreign-language films distributed were Truffaut's *The Last Metro*, set in Paris during the Nazi occupation, Blier's parody of *film noir, Buffet Froid,* Pialet's *Loulou*, Fellini's idiosyncratic *City of Women*, Antonioni's *The Oberwald Mystery* (a new version of Cocteau's *The Eagle has Two Heads*), Rohmer's *The Aviator's Wife*, which initiated a new series, *Comédies et Proverbes*, Bergman's West German production, *From the Life of the Marionettes,* a stark study of a compulsive murderer, Fassbinder's *Lili Marleen,* the tragi-comedy of the famous singer of Nazi Germany, and Alexander Kluge's *The Patriot*, debating an original approach to German history; while István Szabó's Hungarian film *Mephisto* recreated the emergence of Nazi Germany through the portrait of a star actor of the period. A unique trio of films came into collective distribution from Poland's leading film-maker, Andrzej Wajda—*Man of Marble* (1977), *Rough Treatment* (1978) and *Man of Iron* (1980), each in one way or another profoundly concerned with the implications, deceits and moral pressures, as well as the significant silences, that surrounded Poland's dissident movement. The Russian Andrei Tarkovsky's *Stalker* (1979) offered a fable of the search for some form of socio-political liberation.

The year was darkened by the deaths of many celebrated personalities of the cinema: the directors René Clair (see OBITUARY), William Wyler, Raoul Walsh, Alan Dwan and Jean Eustache, and the stars Bernard Lee,

Nigel Patrick, Richard Boone, Beulah Bondi, Melvyn Douglas, Jack Warner, Jessie Matthews, Vera-Ellen, Robert Montgomery, William Holden and Natalie Wood.

TELEVISION AND RADIO

In a year which in Britain saw BBC television licence fees increased by 35 per cent, the birth pangs of four newly-constituted ITV companies and the gradual shaping of a fourth television channel, the development that claimed widest attention was the threatened curtailment of British broadcasting to the rest of the world.

In June the Government announced that, to save £3 million a year, seven languages would be dropped from the list of 39 regularly broadcast (besides English in the World Service) by the External Services of the BBC. The cuts would also mean the end of the BBC transcription service, which made 36,000 hours of radio tapes available annually to more than 100 countries. At the same time a capital development programme amounting to £100 million over ten years would be inaugurated to provide badly-needed new transmitters and relay stations. In the House of Commons the Prime Minister, Mrs Thatcher, stated: 'We think it better that 33 language services should be properly heard, rather than 40 languages improperly heard.' The languages affected were French, Italian, Spanish for Europe, Portuguese for Brazil, Maltese, Burmese and Somali.

The proposals, coming less than two years after an earlier plan to lop the External Services (which, unlike BBC domestic television and radio, are funded directly from Whitehall), caused an immediate outcry. Some 170 MPs of all parties signed a motion opposing the cuts. In the House of Lords the Government was defeated by 82 votes to 45 when its plans were debated. The BBC pointed out that wavelengths once abandoned could almost certainly never be recovered, and that the contraction would come at a time when other world services, notably Moscow's, were being stepped up. The shock waves of dismay reverberated among BBC listeners round the globe. In Spain, for instance, 350 leading journalists petitioned against the closure of the Spanish service. Faced with the serious possibility of a defeat in the Commons, the Government bowed to the storm and on 26 October announced that only three languages (Maltese, Italian and European Spanish) would disappear, while French and Brazilian Portuguese would be curtailed, halving the proposed financial saving. This solution was denounced by the Labour opposition as 'a shabby and ridiculous compromise'. Ironically, the Government decision coincided with the publication of a survey claiming that the BBC, only sixth in the world 'league table' in terms of broadcasting hours, commanded the highest audience of 100 million.

In December, following a vigorous year-long campaign for a £50 licence, the BBC was rewarded with an immediate increase in the colour television fee to £46, to last for a minimum of three years. The previous fee of £34 had been fixed at the end of 1979. Monochrome fees were raised from £12 to £15, leaving them still by far the cheapest television licences in Europe. At the same time the Home Secretary, Mr Whitelaw, announced the introduction of schemes for payment by instalments. The BBC appeared satisfied with the new licence level, which it was estimated would yield £673 million in a full year, compared with £545 million at the old rate. The director-general, Sir Ian Trethowan, said that the BBC's priorities in disposing of its enhanced income would be to reinforce individual programme budgets, and reduce the proportion of repeats and American imports. Shortly before Christmas it was announced that Sir Ian would be succeeded on his retirement on 1 August 1982 by Mr Alasdair Milne, managing director of BBC Television.

The altered pattern of ITV franchises produced by the IBA decisions of 28 December 1980 (see AR 1980, pp. 426-7) left a trail of problems for some of the programme companies. In the south of England the new franchise-holders, Television South, had difficulty in persuading their predecessors, Southern Television, to sell the TV studios in Southampton. Agreement was finally reached for a rumoured price of £11 million at the end of April. Two other companies, Yorkshire TV and Central Independent TV (successor to ATV), encountered unexpected setbacks in attracting regionally-based shareholders as required by the IBA. The three new companies (Central, TV South and the Plymouth-based Television South West) were due on air for the first time on 1 January 1982.

Detailed planning for the 1982 launch of the fourth television channel went ahead with the recruitment of senior staff and the acquisition of London premises. No fewer than 6,000 people applied to fill six posts as the channel's 'commissioning editors'. Speaking at the Edinburgh Television Festival in August, Mr Jeremy Isaacs, the chief executive, said that TV-4 would screen the best American comedy shows, past as well as present, and a high proportion of feature films, besides more specialist fare. The IBA revealed that it would be seeking a loan of £49 million to pay for the channel's initial stages.

Britain's first Pay-TV service since the late 1960s was launched unobtrusively on 9 September by Rediffusion, one of five contractors licensed by the Home Office. About 2,000 initial subscribers in five centres paid between £7·95 and £11·95 per month to see programmes of feature films. Services in six other areas were due to follow. Earlier in the year, on 1 August, a new BBC Charter, formally permitting the Corporation to compete in the subscription and satellite fields, took effect.

A guide to spoken English published by the BBC in October recom-

mended that network broadcasters should base their pronounciation on
that of 'a person born and brought up in one of the Home Counties' and
'educated at one of the established southern universities'. The booklet,
compiled by a three-man committee under Dr Robert Burchfield, chief
editor of the Oxford English Dictionaries, included contrary views expressed by northern broadcasters. 'People on Merseyside would wonder
what the newsreader was about if he pronounced *mandatory* and
municipal as recommended,' one commented.

Easily the most talked-about British television production of 1981
was Granada TV's dramatization of the Evelyn Waugh novel *Brideshead
Revisited*. The 13-hour serial made news long before it reached the screen
on 12 October because of the 1979 ITV strike which sent costs rocketing
to £5 million. Filmed in locations which included Castle Howard (home
of BBC chairman George Howard) and the liner QE2, its superb pictorial
and dramatic quality attracted critical superlatives and set new standards
for fidelity to an original literary work.

It was something of a vintage year for 'series' drama. Southern TV,
one of the ITV companies extinguished on 31 December, contributed
Winston Churchill: The Wilderness Years, a well-researched account of
the Churchillian inter-war doldrums distinguished by Robert Hardy's
title performance. Another major British statesman was celebrated in
The Life and Times of David Lloyd George from BBC Wales. In June
BBC-1's ratings soared in response to an outstanding Australian series
based on Nevil Shute's *A Town Like Alice,* shown on four successive
evenings. The BBC also screened seven more plays in its Shakespeare
marathon, including *Othello, Troilus and Cressida* and the rarely-
performed *Timon of Athens*, and an almost comically misjudged saga of
fourteenth-century papal Italy, *The Borgias*.

Documentary series included two almost simultaneous programmes
about Ireland, *The Troubles* (ITV) and *Ireland: A Television History*
(BBC). The BBC-2 cultural blockbuster of 1981 was *The Making of
Mankind*, a (more or less) popularized view of archaeology presented by
Richard Leakey. Malcolm Muggeridge became the first person to achieve
an eight-part television autobiography in *Muggeridge: Ancient and
Modern*, a retrospective of his many works for the medium, and London
Weekend TV completed a remarkable triple win at the Prix Italia with
their affectionate documentary tribute to Sir William Walton, *At the
Haunted End of the Day*. At Christmas an outstanding *Pygmalion* from
Yorkshire TV competed with *Gone With The Wind*, which the BBC had
bought in a telephone auction against ITV for £4·4 million.

A major broadcasting event during the year was the televising of the
royal wedding on 29 July: 81 broadcasting organizations in over 50
countries, including seven American networks, took the BBC's coverage,
and the worldwide audience was estimated at over 700 million.

In France the inauguration of the Mitterrand Administration had widespread repercussions for the state broadcasting institutions. A number of top-level Giscard appointees, including Maurice Ulrich, president of Antenne-2, and Claude Contamine, head of FR-3, resigned. In contrast to Giscard's attempts to repress the mushrooming 'pirate' radio stations, President Mitterrand's Minister of Communications, M George Fillioud, announced that jamming would cease in exchange for certain guarantees of conformity. These included the dropping of advertising and the reduction of transmitter power to a radius not exceeding seven miles.

In October the Government published the report of the Moinot commission advocating radical changes in the structure of French broadcasting established by President Giscard d'Estaing in 1974. It proposed bringing the two main television channels, TF-1 and Antenne-2, under a single organization, setting up 31 regional broadcasting councils as part of the Government's policy of decentralization, and placing all broadcasting under the ultimate control of a nine-member council, or *Haute Autorité*. The Moinot proposals were to be placed before the National Assembly early in 1982.

Broadcasting development in the United States was marked by the increasing spread of cable television in various forms. In May the electronics and entertainment group RCA went into partnership with the Rockefeller Centre to set up the first nationwide cable channel, expected on air in 1982. Unlike existing cable enterprises, it proposed to offer a full service of drama, films, arts and children's programmes, of which 40 per cent would come from the BBC. Later in the year seven cable groups bid a total of £49 million for long-lease transmission time on the Satcom IV satellite, due for launching in January 1982. It was estimated that one-quarter of American homes, a total of over 19 million, received their television programmes by cable in 1981, and that nine million subscribed to Pay-TV sources. In some parts of North America viewers could exercise a 60-channel choice.

The comedy series *Soap*, enormously popular with British viewers, was dropped by ABC because of falling ratings at home. Walter Cronkite, America's best-known and most trusted broadcaster, retired at the age of 64. American academics continued to sound dire warnings against the effect of television on children.

Belgian radio and television, hitherto financed from licence fees and government grants, planned to take advertising for the first time in the 26-year history of BRT (Belgische Radio en Televisie). But as 65 per cent of viewers were receiving French, German, Dutch and Luxembourgeois TV via cable, the only effect of continuing an advertising ban would be to divert advertising revenue to foreign agencies.

Italian television imparted a new meaning to 'actuality' programming with a film showing a French prostitute entertaining her clients. Made by an all-woman team for the second Italian channel, it was shot via a two-way mirror. Two attempts to prevent transmission were made by parliamentary and legal authorities before it reached the screen. In June it was estimated that a total of 636 private television companies, transmitting on 800 channels, were in operation in Italy.

In the year when Spanish television celebrated its 25th anniversary, the director-general, Fernando Castedo, an appointee of former Premier Adolfo Suarez, resigned after allegations that the media had been subject to too much 'left-wing' influence. Despite opposition, a revealing BBC documentary about King Juan Carlos was screened in the early hours of a Saturday in February and attracted a large audience.

South Africa's second television channel, aimed at the majority black population, came into operation on 31 December with programmes in the five main African languages (Xhosa, Zulu, Tswana and two varieties of Sotho). Estimates put black ownership of TV sets at less than 250,000, but this was expected to grow with the arrival of electrification schemes in black townships.

An 18-month enquiry into the Australian Broadcasting Commission (the Dix report) published on 10 June recommended programme sponsorship by private companies, less sports coverage and the disbanding of six orchestras. In general the report praised the ABC's programme output but criticized its financial management.

The Canadian Broadcasting Corporation was involved in the largest known international programme sale when it bought 728 episodes of British ITV's *Coronation Street*, to be shown on five nights a week for three years.

Chapter 2

ART—ARCHITECTURE—FASHION

ART

AMID the encircling economic gloom, the West continued on a seemingly implacable course of promoting block-buster exhibitions. Behind the scenes the art market was unsettled, and the baroque intricacies of the battles between the art and antique dealers and the major auction houses over the latter's introduction, in a gloomy market, of buyer's premiums and other financial devices continued to proliferate. At the close of 1981, the Office of Fair Trading asked the dealers for their documentation concerning alleged complicity between Christie's and Sotheby's over the introduction of the buyer's premium. Christie's reduced its buyer's premium, Sotheby's did not, and the out-of-court settlement between the dealers, themselves divided, and the auction houses showed severe strain.

For the spectator, several trends in the fine arts became apparent. Hunger for the arts continued unabated. The National Gallery counted over 2·7 million visitors in 1981, more than ever before, even in the Jubilee year 1977.

Perhaps anticipated economies meant that more and more museums and galleries in the public sector concentrated on the appropriate display of objects and items drawn mainly from their own resources. Thus the winter opened with a breath-taking exhibition at the Victoria and Albert simply called *Drawing: Technique and Practice*, with over 200 examples from the 15th century to the present, from British collections: from Mantegna, Leonardo and Rembrandt to the first scribble by Joseph Paxton that led to the design for the Crystal Palace, and Issigonis's ideas for the Mini motor car. *Goya's Prints* at the British Museum celebrated the Tomas Harris gift of 1979 with as inclusive a survey of them as has probably ever been attempted. The revelatory exhibition of Poussin at the National Gallery, Edinburgh, united for the first time the surviving Sacrament paintings: those of the Duke of Sutherland, on long loan to Edinburgh, and those of the Duke of Rutland, from Belvoir Castle. After very difficult negotiations, the multi-million-pound gift of Old Master drawings and paintings from Count Seilern to the Courtauld Institute, London University, finally went on public view (July) at the Courtauld galleries; the permanent home for the Seilern Bequest, now called the Princes Gate Collection, had not yet been decided.

A marvellous exhibition, shown at the Toronto Art Gallery, Canada, the Yale Center for British Art, New Haven, and finally at the British Museum, *Turner and the Sublime*, devised by Andrew Wilton, also author of a substantial volume on the subject, typified several aspects of major exhibitions: the outstanding quality of accompanying catalogue-books, the intellectual basis behind many a visual essay, and, some commentators noted, a new interest in realism. For in the 1960s Turner had been acclaimed as a precursor of abstract painting, just as in the 1970s Monet's late paintings were specifically linked to abstract expressionism; now Turner was seen as a realist.

Realism indeed became the vogue word, trends towards realism combining with a return to painting (as opposed, let us say, to assemblage, installation, performance, conceptual art) in the contemporary area. There was an urgent attempt to rehabilitate 19th-century Salon realism with a huge exhibition *The Realist Tradition 1830-1900*, shown at the Cleveland Museum of Art, Ohio, then at the Brooklyn Museum, New York, the St Louis Museum, Missouri, and finally the Glasgow Art Gallery. The exhibition vitiated its case by overstatement and a lack of rigour in selecting exhibits. Nearer our own time, the French re-examined the art of the 1930s, defined as *Realism between the Wars*.

Meanwhile, yet another form of realism was touted. In Cologne, *Westkunst*, a gigantic exhibition culled from America and Western Europe, attempted nothing less than an overview of the entire postwar period, with introductory material from 1939 on. It was a hugely ambitious and eye-opening anthology, which recreated, as far as was possible, influential exhibitions and even competitions, such as that of 1953 for the Monument to the Unknown Political Prisoner. The overwhelming impression was of the sheer quality of the Old Masters of modernism, from Henry Moore's shelter drawings to Mondrian's New York paintings, and the sheer vitality of Picasso, while such innovators as Jackson Pollock impressed with their energetic inventiveness. It also became apparent that one of the major strands in 'modernism' was pluralism and eclecticism: anything could enter and has entered the domain of art.

It seemed, though, that in some respects the 1980s were set to be a period of imaginative consolidation, with 'realism' and 'painting' as key concepts. This was exemplified by a new movement in art, promoted by dealers, museums and critics, which had its first substantial airing at the Royal Academy, under the title *A New Spirit in Painting* (January–March). The contents were heavily weighted towards youngish American, German and Italian painters who concentrated on recognizable subject-matter, much quotation from the history of art, and an expressionist, heavy use of paint. After the exhibition, many of the artists were given major one-man shows in important commercial galleries in Europe, Britain and America. The influential critic Hilton Kramer of the *New York Times* heralded the number of younger European artists now being shown in New York as indicative of a new vitality in contemporary art which was challenging American supremacy in the contemporary field.

The passionate interest in Picasso may also be indicative of a new interest in painting: after the record-breaking show at New York's Museum of Modern Art in 1980, *Picasso's Picassos,* a selection of his work from his own collection, was magnificently displayed with a specially sensitive arrangement of the work from July to October at London's Hayward Gallery. Another appropriate, even symbolic event which occurred in 1981, the centenary of Picasso's birth, was the return to Spain of his major political painting, *Guernica*, which Picasso vowed would never return to Spain until democracy did. *Guernica,* long housed in New York's Museum of Modern Art, and depicting in symbolic form the bombing of the civilian population of the town Guernica during the Spanish civil war, is now on view in a specially-built section of the Prado, Madrid. Spain, too, is hungry for art: while in 1982 the first modern art fair was planned for Madrid, the summer of 1981 saw the largest exhibition of Henry Moore's work to take place anywhere since the huge exhibition in Florence nearly a decade ago, open to huge acclaim and large crowds in beautifully converted buildings in the Buen Retiros park in the centre of Madrid.

Another area of 20th-century art increasingly under scholarly and commercial scrutiny was that of the Russian avant-garde that flourished from about 1908 to 1930. Curiously, the Russians were the inventors of various forms of abstraction; more, the innovators were conscious of attempts to make design and art serve the state. Their effervescent energy in attempting to reconcile the demands of the individual sensibility and serving those of society as a whole, doomed finally by the purges of the 1930s, appear in retrospect ever more heroic. In an extraordinary coup, the Guggenheim Museum showed hundreds of works of the period from the George Costakis collection. Costakis, a Greek born in Moscow, was said to possess the finest collection of Russian avant-garde art in the world. Costakis left Moscow for Athens in 1977, donating four-fifths of his collection to the Tretiakov Gallery, Moscow, and bringing much art out to the West as well—in fact some 1,200 items, of which 275 works, from the period 1908-32, were shown at the Guggenheim.

Another interesting emphasis in 1981 exhibitions was on sculpture. The largest exhibition ever devoted to Auguste Rodin, *Rodin Rediscovered,* was seen in the summer at the National Gallery, Washington, mammoth in scope as it celebrated with scholarly exactitude the sculptor's protean energy. The Art Gallery of Ontario, which already housed the largest collection of large-scale Henry Moore plasters, put on a major sculpture exhibition called *Gauguin to Moore,* the first to examine primitivism as used by sculptors in the modern period. The Fondation Maeght in the south of France put on a major anthology of 20th-century sculpture, *Tradition et rupture,* which dealt with the period 1900-45, included only two Americans (Alexander Calder and David Smith) and devoted much space to the Russians and the French, including the major painters who were also major sculptors—Degas, Matisse and Picasso. In Britain, a major rehabilitation was performed by an exhaustive two-part survey of 20th-century British sculpture at the Whitechapel Art Gallery, which brought forward much major work by minor masters, while underlining the quality of the few internationally famous sculptors, such as Henry Moore, Epstein and in the post-1945 period Anthony Caro, Eduardo Paolozzi and Phillip King. Phillip King himself had a major retrospective in the spring (Hayward), while a big piece of public sculpture by King, called *Clarion,* was installed in Fulham, London, sponsored by Romulus Construction. In London new exhibition spaces included Riverside Studios, Hammersmith, which opened in January with an exhibition of drawings by Leon Kossoff;

coincidentally, paintings by Kossoff inaugurated later a doubling of space at Oxford's Museum of Modern Art.

Throughout the year major exhibitions examined contributions to architecture and design, heralding an accelerated increase of interest in such related subjects as the role of the designer, architect and artist in society. Thus, William Morris led the field with major exhibitions and publications devoted to his work, followed by exhibitions devoted to such figures as Voysey and C. R. Ashbee, and a fine exhibition called *Architect-Designers* devoted to the period at the Fine Art Society. The climax came with the spectacular showing at the Hayward Gallery, London, of the work of the man who dominated British architecture in the first part of the 20th century, Sir Edwin Lutyens (1869-1944). In terms of exhibition design, the exhibition broke new ground in immediacy, with the skilful work of Piers Gough. Some thought the show a highly political affair with its implicit criticisms of some of the excesses of modernism, in both architecture and art.

The Royal Academy had a unique showing, in two parts, of art from the Edo (Tokyo) period of Japanese art, entitled *The Great Japan Exhibition (1600-1868)*. This, the largest compilation anywhere of the fine and applied and decorative arts of the period ever attempted, was accompanied by a substantial catalogue which was the most authoritative survey in English yet published. The British Museum reopened its Egyptian Galleries, which had been closed for several years while substantial rearrangements took place, allowing us now to see its unparalleled holdings with new clarity.

In New York, the death was reported of Alfred H. Barr, Jr. (b. 1902), the first director of the Museum of Modern Art in New York, who had rightly been called 'The museum man of the century'; the Museum itself, stamped by his creative scholarship and 'eye', has been described as a 'walk-through encyclopedia of art, architecture, design, photography and film as they had developed' during this century. Yet our passion for the past was unslaked, and the Victoria and Albert reported unprecedented attendances for an exhibition called *Splendours of the Gonzaga* which reported on art and patronage during the Renaissance in Mantua, from Mantegna to Rubens, and which was also accompanied by a substantial and interesting catalogue.

The winners of the 1981 Mitchell prize for the history of art were Sir John Pope-Hennessy, for *Luca Della Robbia* (Phaidon/Cornell), and, uniquely, for a 'first' book, Martin Kemp's *Leonardo: The Marvellous Works of Nature and Man*. The CINOA prize for art history was won by Norman Bryson, for *Word and Image*, a study of French 18th-century painting (Cambridge University Press).

ART BOOKS OF THE YEAR: *Leonardo: The Marvellous Works of Man and Nature,* by Martin Kemp (Dent/Harvard); *Taste and the Antique,* by

Nicholas Penny and Francis Haskell (Yale); *Michelangelo and the Language of Art,* by David Summers (Princeton); *David,* Anita Brookner (Chatto); *English Art and Modernism 1900-1939,* by Charles Harrison (Allen Lane); *Sebastiano del Piombo,* by Michael Hirst (Oxford); *The Paintings of Eugène Delacroix,* by Lee Johnson (Oxford).

ARCHITECTURE

Architects' hopes for an increase in new commissions, and the building industry's for an uplift in work-load, were justified in the UK in 1981. There was a small improvement in both; but architects' earnings fell. The previous slowdown began to show in fewer numbers of important buildings completed.

The Barbican Centre for Arts and Conferences in the City of London, which included concert hall, theatre and cinemas, by architects Chamberlin, Powell and Bon was opened to the public in July. It had changed little since the 1956 design was revised in 1959. Morecambe's Leisure Park by architects Faulkner Brown Hendy Watkinson, costing £3 million, and grant-aided by the EEC, was opened in the same month. An unusual feature of the scheme was an oval-shaped six-lane swimming pool with waves, surrounded by sunbathing terraces. In June the first part of a library and museum building was completed for Milton Keynes New Town by the corporation's own architects. The accommodation included libraries, exhibition space and a non-denominational church in a modest steel-framed structure clad in light brown brickwork, sited next to the civic offices. A new church and presbytery, Holy Innocents Catholic Church, Orpington, by architects Michael Blee Whittaker Partnership, dedicated in September to serve a new housing estate, was visually unusual and very adaptable. Rooms for various purposes were separated from the body of the church by a cloister. They were lit by roof lights, not by windows. The steeply pitched main roof was shaped like a wigwam with its peak above the altar.

In July James Stirling's design for a new L-shaped extension to the Tate Gallery, London, endowed by the Clore Foundation and designed to contain the Turner Bequest collection, pleased the gallery's trustees. Towards the end of the year the Government decided, after a non-public inquiry in 1980, to allow the demolition of the east gallery of Alfred Waterhouse's Natural History Museum, South Kensington, a grade I listed building, and its replacement by new exhibition and research space designed by Robert Matthew Johnson Marshall & Partners. The proposed new accommodation had been revised to meet all the criticisms made at the inquiry; objects would be better displayed and maintained, but no more of the museum's vast collection placed on view.

Town planning was dominated, as in 1980 (see AR 1980, p. 436), by the problems of Thames-side redevelopment in London. Fresh proposals by Abbot Howard for European Ferries on the so-called 'Green Giant' site, downstream from Vauxhall bridge on the South Bank, were rejected by Lambeth borough council in March. European Ferries appealed, but in the summer withdrew their appeal and appointed architects Morgan Karn & Partners of Hove to prepare a fresh scheme. Meanwhile the public inquiry into the scheme by Arunbridge on the upstream site from Vauxhall Bridge, belonging to Effra Ltd, was commenced then postponed. In December, provided agreement was reached with the Greater London Council, an architectural competition was to be promoted by Arunbridge for an integrated scheme covering the Effra and 'Green Giant' sites and the Nine Elms cold-store site. If the subsequent winning design was approved by the Environment Secretary, the scheme would be allowed to go ahead without further planning consent.

The public inquiry into Richard Rogers's Coin-street proposals (see AR 1980, p. 436) for Greycoat Commercial Estates opened in April, and promptly had to be postponed because vociferous objectors protested at the revised scheme of glass-enclosed galleria and office blocks, the heart of the project. The Association of Waterloo Groups (AWG) protested strongly because their own planning application for housing and light industry on the site was not to be considered at the inquiry, an omission repaired when the hearing restarted in September. The Richard Rogers scheme was criticized for the lack of a theatre square at the west end of Coin-street to act as a point of arrival for the National Theatre on its east side.

Results of the Hay's Wharf public inquiry, opened in May, were still unrevealed when, in July, Parliament approved the idea of a Development Corporation including within its authority the Hay's Wharf site, the Courage Brewery in Southwark and St Katherine's Dock in Tower Hamlets.

A great aesthetic and engineering achievement came to completion in July when the new suspension bridge, some 2,200 metres long, over the river Humber by engineers Freeman, Fox & Partners was opened by HM the Queen.

Among the buildings in England newly listed during the year were the Dorchester Hotel, the Savoy Hotel and Broadcasting House in London, and Guildford Cathedral in Surrey.

In June the International Union of Architects held their 14th world congress in Warsaw, Poland, and their assembly in Katowice. The congress theme, Architecture—Man—Environment, was discussed by some 2,000 delegates, about half from Poland and other East European countries.

The 1981 Royal Gold Medal for Architecture was awarded to architect Sir Philip Dowson in recognition of his role in founding and directing the multi-disciplinary practice of Arup Associates, which had produced many fine buildings. The American Institute of Architects 1981 Gold Medal was awarded to José Luis Sert, one of the founders in the 1930s of the International Congresses of Modern Architecture (CIAM). The American Institute of Architects 25-Year Award went to the late Mies van der Rohe's last residential work, the Farnsworth House in Plano, Illinois. Built in slender reinforced concrete and glass, the house looked as elegant in 1981 as it did when built in 1956. The first Aga Khan Awards for architecture in modern Islamic society were presented in Lahore, Pakistan, to 15 winning projects from 200 nominations representing 12 countries. The winners shared $500,000 in prize money. In Britain the Concrete Society nominated the Goodwood racecourse grandstand by architects Howard Lobb Partnership and structural engineers Jan Bobrowski and Partners for its 1981 award. From 68 entries the assessors of the *Financial Times* Industrial Architecture Award were unable to find an overall winner.

The work of British architects overseas was particularly noteworthy in 1981. In Hong Kong a striking design by Foster Associates for the Hong Kong and Shanghai Banking Corporation's new premises on Statue Square, overlooking the waterfront, the winner in a limited competition, was made public in February. The tower block, in three bays of 28, 35 and 41 storeys, had floors suspended between eight steel pylons, conspicuous on the outside. The interior office floor-space was thus unimpeded. The new European Investment Bank by architects Denys Lasdun, Redhouse & Softly was completed in the spring on a wooded site overlooking a ravine towards the city of Luxembourg. The building's office and ceremonial wings, faced in precast concrete, stepped gracefully down the hillside in a mixture of horizontal indoor and outdoor terraces, typical of Sir Denys Lasdun's style. In West Berlin architects Maguire & Murray won a limited competition for a guestworkers' building.

In preparation for the 1984 International Architecture Exhibition in Berlin, in which real constructions and urban spaces were to form a live exhibition with the theme 'Living in the City', British architect James Stirling's science centre, Gustave Peichl's purification plant and Moore Ruble Yudell's design for a cultural, residential and recreation complex were selected for construction on a lakeside site in Tegel, a weekend resort in Berlin's suburbs.

In the USA, I. M. Pei & Partner's west wing of Boston's Museum of Fine Arts was opened in the summer. Occupying some 80,000 square feet it was built of the same granite as the old building designed by Guy Lovell about 1909. On the first floor was a skylit galleria developed from Pei's east building of Washington's National Gallery of Art. Another building for the arts, still under construction, was Richard Meier's High

Museum of Art for Atlanta, to house historic art prints dating from Early Italian and Renaissance periods through to the 20th century.

In Houston, Texas, a 56-storey office development, the Republic Bank Centre by Johnson/Burgee, made public in the summer, illustrated once again the return of modern architects to earlier forms of design. In this example the glass and Swedish red granite building, ascending in three setback segments with steep stepped roofs, seemed to borrow from both Dutch and Renaissance architecture. The setbacks made floors of different areas possible within the total office floor-space of up to 2 million square feet, with retail floor space and underground parking in addition. An office design of quite a different kind was the first of six blocks of commercial and office complexes, the Oxford Centre, Pittsburgh, by New York architects Hellmuth, Obata & Kassabaum. The design was a cluster of towers rising to 46 storeys. The lower five floors of commercial space had floor-to-ceiling glass fronts. The towers were connected by bridges on one level.

At year's end a row developed in New York over plans to build a 59-storey office tower behind St Bartholomew's Episcopal Church, a Byzantine-styled building designed by Bertram Goodhue and built around 1919. The office building, by Edward Durrell Stone and Associates, was sheathed in mirrored glass to reflect the church and the nearby Waldorf Astoria hotel.

Two important exhibitions added their weight to historic architectural revival. The Altes Museum, Berlin, recently restored, devoted the whole of its main floor to the mainly neo-classical work of the Museum's architect, Karl Friedrich von Schinkel (1781-1841). The second exhibition, opened at the Hayward Gallery, London, in November, showed the extensive works of Sir Edwin Lutyens.

Jacob B. Bakema died in February aged 67. He formed a link between the early Modern Movement in architecture in his native Netherlands and later modern work. Bakema's work since World War II included the well-known Lijnbaan shopping centre in reconstructed Rotterdam. Albert Speer, who among other things was Hitler's official architect, died aged 76 (see OBITUARY). Marcel Breuer, head of the Bauhaus at Dessau, Germany, before he joined Walter Gropius in the USA in 1937, died aged 79 (see OBITUARY).

FASHION

At the beginning of the year frilled trimmings on clothes became the biggest current fashion trend, cascading round necklines, cuffs and hemlines on day and evening wear. This pretty addition to the previous classic look became a major fashion when Lady Diana Spencer, bride-tobe of the Prince of Wales, wore frilly necklines and immediately became a leader of the popular fashion. After the royal wedding in July, the Princess of Wales continued to set trends with her delightful fashion sense, wearing, among other new styles, the big cape-coat and full-skirted, romantic ball gowns, and returning the hat to favour.

Culotte skirts, Bermuda shorts, trousers and knickerbockers were frequently worn in all classes of society, and during the summer skirt-lengths remained modestly at knee length. The mini and mid-calf skirt-lengths were adopted by the more avant-garde women and girls, but their real success had not yet blossomed by the end of the year.

Knitwear was an important choice at all price-levels, from mass-production collections to costly hand-knitted garments. Waistcoats formed an essential part of the *femme sportive* look and were widely worn during autumn and winter. The trouser suit, too, reappeared after a rest of some years, its high fashion status starting in the USA. These classic clothes were worn with frilled blouses rather than with strict shirts.

The duffle coat, another old favourite, also returned with high fashion rank, inspired by leading Paris designer Yves Saint Laurent. It was soon in general use, made by mass-production firms in tweeds, leather, nylon and the original Loden cloth.

The natural fibres, including wool and silk, retained a strong grip on the fabric market, but many clothes were made in mixtures of natural and synthetic fibres which gave them a hardwearing quality.

Despite bad economic conditions, the year closed with a rush of glamorous party clothes, made with frills, tiers and yards of fabric. Sparkling metallic thread and golden cloth were particularly popular. This unexpected movement was apparently inspired by the influential and far-reaching effect the romantic royal wedding had on the fashion industry and its customers. That the country was in post-wedding-party mood until the end of the year was clearly demonstrated by a desire to dress up, especially at the top end of the market, where money spent bordered on extravagance.

David and Elizabeth Emanuel, a young husband-and-wife design team, created the ivory silk taffeta and lace wedding dress worn by the Princess of Wales at her wedding in St Paul's Cathedral. The train stretched for 25 feet and the bridal veil was embroidered by the famous firm of S. Lock with 10,000 mother-of-pearl sequins. The five brides-maids wore dresses, also designed and made by the Emanuels, very similar in style to that worn by the bride. The two young pages wore full-dress Royal Navy cadets' uniforms of 1863.

Chapter 3

LITERATURE

IN literary terms, 1981 was a good year in Britain, particularly because of the production of a substantial number of novels by new writers. While the sale of most 'literary' novels remained relatively small, some titles had substantial success. More importantly, 1981 was described as the year 'when publishers went sane'. The number of titles published in Britain fell for the first time since 1976 and by just over 10 per cent from the staggeringly large total of books published in the previous year. Even so, at 43,083, of which 9,387 were new editions, mostly in paperback, the total was higher than in any year other than 1980, some 10,000 more than ten years earlier and 25,000 more than 30 years earlier.

The year before had seen publishers in something of a panic—many of them were making substantial losses—and in an effort to keep up turnover figures in a depressed market an absurdly large number of books were published. In 1981 many publishing firms, having pruned their staffs and made themselves more efficient in other ways, found that their financial position had improved more decisively than that of many other manufacturing industries. Few of the expected failures or amalgamations took place, and at the end of the year the majority were looking forward with reasonable confidence, though a little warily.

In its twelfth year, the Booker McConnell prize for fiction fulfilled the expectations of its sponsors in that not only was there wide acceptance that the best novel, *Midnight's Children* by Salman Rushdie, had been chosen but the publicity accorded to the prize also ensured that the book thereafter became a bestseller. It had been published much earlier in the year to considerable critical acclaim but to only lukewarm public interest. Rushdie's novel, part realistic and part fantasy, described the fate of a number of people born at the precise moment when the British Government handed over power in India. Unlike many winners of the Booker McConnell prize, it was a long book and by no means an easy read.

There was the customary surprise over the award of the Nobel prize for literature in that none of the favoured candidates was chosen, the selectors preferring to give the award to Elias Canetti, a Hungarian-born Jewish writer living in England whither he came as a refugee from Nazi oppression. His readership in his adopted country was small—none of his books were in print at the time of the award, though this situation was being remedied as the year ended—but he was widely read in Europe, particularly by Germans in whose language he always wrote. The Prix Goncourt went to Lucien Bodard for his novel, *Ann-Marie*.

Among the British novels, the most highly acclaimed, after *Midnight's Children*, was D. M. Thomas's *The White Hotel,* like *Midnight's Children* a second novel. While the praise for this novel, a case-study of a hysterical woman, presented partly in direct narrative but also in her erotic poems and diaries and fantasies, was considerable, it was disliked as forcefully by some people. Two major novels came out of South Africa—Nadine Gordimer's *July's People* and Alan Paton's *Ah! But Your Land is Beautiful.* Mrs Gordimer provided a powerful story set in the future when civilization as imposed by the Europeans had come to an end in South Africa, and a surviving family of whites had to turn to the Africans for help in survival. As always, this author's writing was not approved in her own country. Also critical of the South African system, though much gentler in tone, Paton's first novel for 25 years examined through a large cast of characters the knock-on effect of intolerance; while it might trouble someone very little, the same process could totally destroy another.

William Boyd's *A Good Man in Africa*, which won the Whitbread award for a first book, was reminiscent of the early Evelyn Waugh novels set in Africa. It was a black comedy about the misadventures of a junior diplomat at odds with his seniors and with the corrupt local government. The title was ironic in that few of the characters were in any way 'good'; the only one with the possibility of being so called was killed. Paul Theroux's *The Mosquito Coast* also had a tropical setting (Central America). It examined the fate of a man determined to go back to nature, taking his family with him. The experiment was not a success.

The short list for the Booker McConnell prize produced few surprises, though the absence from it of Mrs Gordimer's novel and Brian Moore's best book for a number of years, *The Temptation of Eileen Hughes,* was surprising. Muriel Spark's lively novel of literary life, or love among the biographers, *Loitering with Intent,* and Molly Keane's *Good Behaviour* (the first book she had published under her own name, having used the pseudonym M. J. Farrell for earlier books), a novel about growing up in an Anglo-Irish family, were natural choices for the short list. The inclusion of Ian McEwan's second novel, *The Comfort of Strangers*, an uncomfortable story of the destruction of innocents in a fictional Venice, aroused more controversy; some critics thought that it might have been better handled in McEwan's customary *genre*, the short story. The others on the list were the third volume of Doris Lessing's continuing science-fiction work, *The Sirian Experiments*, and Ann Schlee's *Rhine Journey*, a gentle story set in the 19th century.

There was more interest in three posthumously-published works. For long British readers had been waiting for a new version of *Remembrance of Things Past*; for it was known that the original translation of Marcel Proust's novel, published in the 1920s and 1930s, had been based on a bowdlerized text. Terence Kilmartin put this right, though modestly keeping the names of the original translators on the title page. John Kennedy Toole's savage, sad American novel, *A Confederacy of Dunces*, appeared some ten years after the author's suicide. Numerous publishers had turned down the neo-Joycean work, and it was in despair that Toole killed himself. Fortunately for the many who enjoyed the novel, his mother continued the struggle to get the book into print, and finally succeeded. G. B. Edwards would probably have found a publisher for *The Book of Ebenezer Le Page* without difficulty during his lifetime but he was never satisfied with it and insisted on continuing to tinker with his panoramic novel of life in Guernsey. Other novels that aroused interest were Maurice Leitch's *Silver's City*, set in Northern Ireland, which won the Whitbread award for fiction, A. N. Wilson's *Who Was Oswald Fish?*, Piers Paul Read's *The Villa Golitsyn*, John Gardner's *Freddy's Book* and Michael Moorcock's *Byzantium Endures*.

The Queen's Gold Medal for poetry was awarded to D. J. Enright, in the year when his *Collected Poems* was published. There were few new poetic voices to be heard from between the covers of books, though a number of established poets published new volumes, among them Douglas Dunn with *St Kilda's Parliament*, Peter Porter with *English Subtitles* and R. S. Thomas with *Between Here and Now*. The continuing interest in Sylvia Plath, represented by an even more comprehensive edition of her *Collected Poems*, remained obvious, though there were signs that the posthumous adulation for this poet who committed suicide in her early thirties was ending. In America, her native country, critics were looking much more sharply and less appreciatively at her work.

Undoubtedly the most important work published during the year was the new edition of *Grove's Dictionary of Music and Musicians*. Originally it had been compiled in four volumes more or less single-handed by Sir George Grove and published over a period of years starting in 1878. There had been numerous revisions, some better than others, but the latest one, edited by Dr Stanley Sadie, appeared to be an entirely new book. It had been expanded by a large team of writers into a work of 20 volumes and took in various forms of folk music from all parts of the world in a way that would have totally bemused Grove. (See also p. 423).

Although the most comprehensive biography of the year, *Monty: the Making of a General* by Nigel Hamilton, dealt with a military figure, the greatest interest was in literary biographies. Hamilton, who was virtually an adopted son of the Field Marshal, was the first to have full access to all the papers. He produced a work so vast that the first volume only took Montgomery's life up to the battle of El Alamein. Perhaps the most accomplished of the literary biographies was the second volume of James Lees-Milne's life of *Harold Nicolson*. The first volume had proved fairly easy, describing the untrammeled story of Sir Harold's youth and career as an unusual diplomat, but the second, dealing with his happy but eccentric marriage (he retained his homosexual attachments while his wife, Victoria Sackville-West, retained her passionate friendships with Virginia Woolf and others) and his career as politician and a literary journalist, was a far more difficult task. Mr Lees-Milne accomplished it well. Of another leading literary figure of the 1930s, Edith Sitwell, many efforts had been made to paint a portrait in words but none so successfully as that by Victoria Glendinning in *Edith Sitwell: a Unicorn among the Lions*. Jean Strouse provided what must surely be the definitive portrait of *Alice James*, Henry James's unbalanced sister who furnished so much of the material for biographies of members of this polymathic family.

Thackeray's daughter Anne, a popular novelist in her own right, was a great literary hostess and formed an excellent subject for Winifred Gérin in *Anne Thackeray Ritchie*. Sad to say, Mrs Gérin died two days before the publication of her book. Anne Ritchie's contemporary, Christina Rossetti, had taxed several biographers in that there was very little to write about this somewhat reclusive poet. Georgina Battiscombe, using new material, managed, in *Christina Rossetti: a Divided Life*, to make the poet a much more interesting figure than had usually been thought. Violet Powell provided a workmanlike biography of a late Victorian and Edwardian writer, almost forgotten today, *Flora Annie Steel: Novelist of India*, who besides being a writer who influenced Kipling was also an important figure in Indian education.

It was a good year for books about crime novelists. There were James Brabazon's over-emotional *Dorothy L. Sayers: Portrait of a Courageous Woman* (her courage was a little difficult to discern, though her cantankerousness was readily apparent), and *Shadow Man: the Life of Dashiell Hammett* in which Richard Layman did his best to make coherent the rather wasted life of the creator of the hardboiled American thriller. *The Selected Letters of Raymond Chandler* gave unwittingly a picture of Hammett's chief rival as a jealous and dissatisfied man.

Outstanding among the autobiographies was a first instalment of the life of a playwright, *A Better Class of Person: an Autobiography* by John Osborne. It contained a chilling portrait of his mother, who was extremely protective in his youth but whom he had come to loathe. Not since Edmund Gosse's *Father and Son* had there been such an outspoken description of a family relationship. Mrs Osborne appeared to be mildly put out by her son's version of her behaviour during his childhood. That she was a somewhat less ogreish character than the one portrayed by her son was suggested by the fact that she took no action to prevent publication of his book. A much more gentle autobiography of a writer was *As I Walked Down New Grub Street* by Walter Allen. Mr Allen, writer, university teacher and critic, had known most of the successful and, more interestingly, unsuccessful writers from 1930 onwards, and in an anecdotal way provided a large number of footnotes to literary history. One of the disappointments of the year was the autobiography of the Nobel prizewinning novelist Patrick White, *Flaws in the Glass*. While he was prepared to give a reasonably full picture of his childhood in Australia and England and of his discovery of his homosexuality, the second half of the book degenerated into a travelogue of trips to Greece and fulminations about his hatred of publicity.

Lord Harewood, a cousin of the Queen, wrote in *The Tongs and the Bones* of his upbringing in palace circles and his later fascination with music, which led him to become an administrator, running for a time the Edinburgh Festival and later the English National Opera company. In Philip Ziegler's *Diana Cooper* the author's difficult task, which to a large degree he accomplished, was to put on the page a woman whose only claim to fame was her charm and beauty.

Among the literary studies two stood out, though neither could be said to be in the mainstream of normal lit. crit. One was a deeply researched and splendidly written account of the lives and attitudes of the great 19th-century historians, *A Liberal Descent*, which rightly won for John Burrow one of the Wolfson prizes for historical writing. The other, more limited in scope, was *Abroad: British Literary Travelling between the Wars* in which Paul Fussell analysed the urge of British writers to seek inspiration by travel in the 1920s and 1930s, shedding new light on W. H. Auden (also the subject of a well-received critical biography by Humphrey Carpenter during the year), Christopher Isherwood, Evelyn Waugh and others, including such almost-forgotten names as Robert Byron who proved to be the father of so much travel-writing in that period.

One of the most strident of academic controversies of 1981 concerned the failure of the Cambridge University English faculty to appoint a structuralist scholar to a lectureship, an event which brought into public discussion this relatively new school of criticism. One of its most able expositors, David Lodge, gave examples of the system, in a more readable and assimilable form than shown by some of its practitioners, in *Working with Structuralism*.

It was not a particularly distinguished year for historical writing, though it did contain the long-awaited English translation of Fernand Braudel's *Civilization and Capitalism, 15th-18th Centuries, Volume I*, a work that underlined the author's theory that historical evidence found in the everyday life of people was quite as valuable as that found in state documents and published accounts. The most striking general history was Kenneth O. Morgan's *Rebirth of the Welsh Nation, 1880-1980*, though a work that came so close to its own time of writing inevitably contained an element of polemic. That the Wars of the Roses retained their inevitable fascination was displayed in important lives (in that they altered the established picture of the kings concerned) of *Henry VI* by

Bertram Wolfe and *Richard III* by Charles Ross. The equal fascination with the peripheries of World War II was displayed by F. Kerraudy's *Churchill and de Gaulle*, analysing the difficulties the two great leaders had in communicating, and Martin Gilbert's indictment of the Western nations' callousness towards the plight of the Jews, *Auschwitz and the Allies*.

In addition to Mrs Gérin, historical writing lost Dame Frances Yates and Professor J. A. W. Bennett, and literary studies were the poorer for the death of Professor Harry T. Moore, Mrs Q. D. Leavis and the critic and novelist Philip Toynbee. Among the novelists whose deaths were announced were Pamela Hansford Johnson, A. J. Cronin, William Saroyan, David Garnett, Eugenio Montale (see OBITUARY), Robin Maugham, Gwyn Thomas and Alec Waugh. Desmond Stewart, the Arabist and historian, Marshall McLuhan, who achieved some notoriety in the 1960s for his forecast of the death of the book, and the maverick journalist Claud Cockburn also died. It was sad to learn also of the death of Nadezhda Mandelstam, the widow of the Russian poet, who wrote such poignant accounts of tyranny in the Soviet Union.

Among the interesting new books published during the year were:

FICTION: *Other People* by Martin Amis (Cape); *Walking Naked* by Nina Bawden (Macmillan); *A Good Man In Africa* by William Boyd (Hamish Hamilton); *If on a Winter's Night a Traveller* by Italo Calvino (Secker); *Bliss* by Peter Carey (Faber); *The Book of Ebenezer Le Page* by G. B. Edwards (Hamish Hamilton); *The Hill Station* by J. G. Farrell (Weidenfeld); *Freddy's Book* by John Gardner (Secker); *July's People* by Nadine Gordimer (Cape); *The Company of Women* by Mary Gordon (Cape); *The Hotel New Hampshire* by John Irving (Cape); *The Christmas Tree* by Jennifer Johnston (Hamish Hamilton); *A Breed of Heroes* by Alan Judd (Hodder); *Good Behaviour* by Molly Keane (Deutsch); *Silver's City* by Maurice Leitch (Secker); *The Syrian Experiments* by Doris Lessing (Cape); *The Comfort of Strangers* by Ian McEwan (Cape); *Lantern Lecture* by Adam Mars-Jones (Faber); *The Death of Men* by Allan Massie (Bodley Head); *Byzantium Endures* by Michael Moorcock (Secker); *The Temptation of Eileen Hughes* by Brian Moore (Cape); *Ah! But the Land is Beautiful* by Alan Paton (Cape); *Remembrance of Things Past* by Marcel Proust, translated by Terence Kilmartin (Chatto); *The Villa Golitsyn* by Piers Paul Read (Secker for Alison); *Funeral Games* by Mary Renault (Murray); *Zuckermann Unbound* by Philip Roth (Cape); *Midnight's Children* by Salman Rushdie (Cape); *Rhine Journey* by Ann Schlee (Macmillan); *Gorky Park* by Martin Cruz Smith (Collins); *Loitering with Intent* by Muriel Spark (Bodley Head); *Mosquito Coast* by Paul Theroux (Hamish Hamilton); *The White Hotel* by D. M. Thomas (Gollancz); *The Confederacy of Dunces* by John Kennedy Toole (Allen Lane/Penguin); *Gemini* by Michel Tournier (Collins); *Beyond the Pale and Other Stories* by William Trevor (Bodley Head); *The Death of Robin Hood* by Peter Vansittart (Owen); *The Collected Stories of Eudora Welty* (Boyars); *Who Was Oswald Fish?* by A. N. Wilson (Secker).

POEMS: *Church Poems* by John Betjeman (Murray); *Poems* by Paul Celin (Carcanet); *St Kilda's Parliament* by Douglas Dunn (Faber); *Collected Poems* by D. J. Enright (Oxford); *Continuous* by Tony Harrison (Rex Collings); *Collected Poems* by Sylvia Plath (Faber); *English Subtitles* by Peter Porter (Oxford); *The Apple Broadcast* by Peter Redgrove (Routledge); *Between Here and Now* by R. S. Thomas (Macmillan).

LITERARY CRITICISM: *The Short Story in English* by Walter Allen (Oxford); *Me Again: the Uncollected Writings of Stevie Smith*, edited by Jack Barbera and William McBrien (Virago); *Shakespeare and Tragedy* by John Bayley (Routledge); *A Liberal Descent* by

John Burrow (Cambridge); *John Donne* by John Carey (Faber); *History of the Nonesuch Press* by John Douglas (Nonesuch/Bodley Head); *Red Shelley* by Paul Foot (Dempsey); *Abroad: British Literature Travelling Between the Wars* by Paul Fussell (Oxford); *Working with Structuralism: Essays and Reviews on 19th and 20th century Literature* by David Lodge (Routledge); *The World of Franz Kafka* by J. P. Stern (Weidenfeld).

BIOGRAPHY: *Orpen: Mirror to an Age* by Bruce Arnold (Cape); *Christina Rosetti: a Divided Life* by Georgina Battiscombe (Constable); *Dorothy L. Sayers: Portrait of a Courageous Woman* by James Brabazon (Gollancz); *The Rise and Fall of a Regency Dandy: the Life and Times of Scrope Beardmore Davis by T. A. J. Burnett (Murray); W. H. Auden: a Biography* by Humphrey Carpenter (Allen & Unwin); *Gwen John* by Susan Chitty (Hodder); *Lord Randolph Churchill: a Political Life* by R. F. Foster (Oxford); *Anne Thackeray Ritchie* by Winifred Gérin (Oxford); *Edith Sitwell: a Unicorn among the Lions* by Victoria Glendinning (Weidenfeld); *P. G. Wodehouse: a Literary Biography* by Benny Green (Michael Joseph); *Monty: the Making of a General* by Nigel Hamilton (Hamish Hamilton); *K: a Biography of Franz Kafka* by Ronald Hayman (Weidenfeld); *The Little Field Marshal: Sir John French* by Richard Holmes (Cape); *Matthew Arnold: a Life* by Park Honan (Weidenfeld); *Saki: the Life of Hector Hugh Munro* by A. J. Langgurth (Hamish Hamilton); *Harold Nicolson: a Biography,* Vol. 2, *1930-1968* by James Lees-Milne (Chatto); *George Orwell* by Peter Lewis (Heinemann); *Flora Annie Steel: Novelist of India* by Violet Powell (Heinemann); *Alice James* by Jean Strouse (Cape); *Diana Cooper* by Philip Ziegler (Hamish Hamilton).

AUTOBIOGRAPHY AND LETTERS: *As I Walked Down New Grub Street* by Walter Allen (Heinemann); *Anyone Here Been Raped Who Speaks English* by Edward Behr (Hamish Hamilton); *The Selected Letters of Raymond Chandler* edited by Frank McShane (Cape); *Last Waltz in Vienna* by George Clare (Macmillan); *A Better Class of Person:* an autobiography by John Osborne (Faber); *Letters of Charles Dickens,* Vol. 5, *1847-1849* edited by Graham Storey and K. J. Fielding (Oxford); *Within the Whirlwind* by Eugenia Ginzburg (Collins/Harvill); *The Tongs and the Bones: the Memoirs of Lord Harewood* (Weidenfeld); *Guardian Years* by Alastair Hetherington (Chatto); *Henry James Letters,* Vol. 6, edited by Leon Edel (Macmillan); *The Gates of Memory* by Geoffrey Keynes (Oxford); *Like It Was: The Diaries of Malcolm Muggeridge* selected and edited by John Bright-Holmes (Collins); *Freedom's Battle: Byron's Letters and Journals,* Vol. 11, *1823-1824,* edited by Leslie A. Marchand (Murray); A Better Class of Person by John Osborne (Faber); *Towards the Mountain* by Alan Paton (Oxford); *Siegfried Sassoon: Diaries, 1920-1922,* edited by Rupert Hart-Davis (Faber); *Letters of J. R. R. Tolkien* edited by Humphrey Carpenter (Allen & Unwin); *Part of a Journey: an Autobiographical Journal, 1977-1978* by Philip Toynbee (Collins); *Flaws in the Glass* by Patrick White (Cape).

HISTORY: *Civilization and Capitalism, 15th-18th Centuries,* Vol. 1, by Fernand Braudel (Collins); *Bismarck* by Edward Crankshaw (Macmillan); *Auschwitz and the Allies* by Martin Gilbert (Michael Joseph); *God's Fifth Column: a Biography of an Age* by William Gerhardie (Hodder); *The Return to Camelot: Chivalry and the English Gentleman* by Mark Girouard (Yale); *Charles I* by Pauline Gregg (Dent); *The Voyage of the Armada* by David Howarth (Collins); *Uprising* by David Irving (Hodder); *Churchill and De Gaulle* by F. Kerraudy (Collins); *The Cheka: Lenin's Political Police* by George Leggett (Oxford); *Buckingham* by Roger Lockyer (Longman); *Athleticism in the Victorian and Edwardian Public School* by J. A. Mayor (Cambridge); *Rebirth of a Nation: Wales, 1880-1980* by Kenneth O. Morgan (Oxford); *Among the Believers* by V. S. Naipaul (Deutsch); *Venice: the Greatness and the Fall* by John Julius Norwich (Allen Lane); *Richard III* by Charles Ross (Eyre Methuen); *Grove's Dictionary of Music and Musicians* edited by Stanley Sadie (Macmillan); *Stalin's Secret War* by Nikolai Tolstoy (Cape); *Joan of Arc* by Martin Warner (Weidenfeld); *MI5: British Security Operations, 1909-1945* by Nigel West (Bodley Head); *Henry VI* by Bertram Wolfe (Eyre Methuen).

XVI SPORT

ASSOCIATION FOOTBALL

QUALIFICATION for the 1982 World Cup finals in Spain was the major preoccupation of international teams throughout the world. There being 24 final places, instead of the usual 16, available for the first time, there was more scope for success. Nonetheless, some notable teams failed to make it, including the Netherlands, runners-up in the world championship in both 1974 and 1978, and Uruguay, winners of the first World Cup competition in 1930 and of a 50th anniversary tournament among all the previous winners (except England) early in the year.

England were very lucky to qualify in a season in which only two of nine internationals were won. Fortunately both victories were in World Cup games against Hungary, which compensated for unexpected defeats by the two 'minnows' in their group—Norway and Switzerland. It was the first time England had managed to qualify since the 1962 finals—they appeared as hosts in 1966 and holders in 1970. Scotland, under their new manager, 'Jock' Stein, made the finals for the third successive time, and Northern Ireland also won through, for the first time since 1958. Cameroon, Algeria, Kuwait and New Zealand qualified for the first time, the last-named scoring on the way a World Cup record 13-0 victory over Fiji.

The year of the 100th FA Cup Final saw two unusual events associated with the world's oldest football knock-out trophy. After a 1-1 draw between the two finalists, Tottenham Hotspur and Manchester City, in the first match, there was an unprecedented replay at Wembley stadium which Tottenham won 3-2. When the 1981-82 competition got under way in the autumn, Mrs Elizabeth Forsdick, aged 28, made history by becoming the first woman to officiate in the Cup's history. The only woman Class One referee on the Football Association's books, she was appointed a 'linesperson' in a third-round qualifying match between Burgess Hill and Carshalton Athletic in October.

Aston Villa won the Football League championship for the first time in 71 years, but it was Second Division Queens Park Rangers who made history by installing the first synthetic turf pitch for professional matches in Britain. It proved a particularly successful innovation when severe weather caused the wholesale cancellation of other matches in December.

Other English clubs continued recent successes in European competitions. Ipswich Town won the UEFA Cup 5-4 on aggregate against the Dutch club AZ Alkmaar, and Liverpool the European Champions Cup for the third time (and the fifth successive victory by an English club),

beating Real Madrid 1-0 in the final in Paris. This crowned the remarkable career of Liverpool manager Bob Paisley, who in less than seven
years had won ten major honours—four League titles, three European
Cups, one League Cup, one UEFA Cup and one European Super
Cup—more than any other manager in the League's history. Apart from
World War II service, Paisley had been at Liverpool since 1939, as
successively player, trainer, physiotherapist and assistant manager
before taking over the reins from Bill Shankly, who himself had won six
trophies in his 15 years as manager of the club. Shankly, 67, died in
September after a heart attack.

ATHLETICS

Although they never actually raced against each other on the track,
British athletes Sebastian Coe and Steve Ovett continued their duel over
the middle distances with another series of record-breaking performances. Coe began in February with a world-best 1 min 46·0 sec indoor
800 metres in an international match against East Germany. On 10 June
in Florence he broke his own world record for the same distance
outdoors, with 1 min 41·72 sec. On 19 August in Zürich he shaved
27-100ths of a second from Ovett's world mile record in 3 min 48·53 sec,
but on 26 August, in Koblenz, Ovett regained this title in 3 min 48·40
sec. Two days later, in Brussels, Coe retorted with 3 min 47·33 sec in
winning the IAAF's Golden Mile event. Between them Coe and Ovett
had broken the record five times since July 1979.

But a bigger phenomenon was the increase in mass marathon
running, following the popularity of jogging as a keep-fit exercise in the
past decade. New York, birthplace of the 'public' marathon, attracted
over 16,000 runners from all over the world for its 1981 event, which
resulted in a time beating the world best that had stood since 1969, when
Alberto Salazar, a Cuban-born American, covered the 26 miles 385 yards
in 2 hr 8 min 13 sec. London had its first mass marathon on 29 March
when 6,700 runners, plus an estimated 1,000 unofficial entries, pounded
the capital's streets between Greenwich and Constitution Hill. Dick
Beardsley of the USA and Inge Simonsen of Norway finished hand-in-
hand in 2 hr 11 min 48 sec, the fastest time ever recorded in England. Mrs
Joyce Smith, a 43-year-old housewife from Watford, Herts, recorded the
fastest British and Commonwealth times for a woman in 2:29:56. The
course was also completed by a blind man and a 78-year-old great-
grandfather, Bob Wiseman, who took over six hours for the run. Police
estimated that over 100,000 people watched the race. A month later
Greater Manchester staged the biggest event in Europe with 8,753 taking
part and some 250,000 spectators.

East Germany swept the board in the European athletic champion-ships, taking both the men's and the women's titles, the latter for the sixth successive time with victories in ten of the 15 events. East Germany's women also won the World Cup, but the men were beaten into second place by an All-European team.

BOXING

When, at the height of his career, Muhammad Ali kept insisting 'I am the greatest' his claim to be the best world heavyweight champion of all time did not impress those who remembered Joseph Louis Barrow in his prime. On 12 April, Joe Louis died at the age of 66 (see OBITUARY), only a few hours after attending a world title fight between Larry Holmes and Trevor Berbick. The esteem in which he was held was marked by his burial among other national heroes in Washington's Arlington National Cemetery. Louis, son of a poor Alabama sharecropper, won the world title in 1937 and defended it successfully 25 times. But, his record apart, what most people admired about the man and the boxer was what the *New York Times* called 'his simple dignity'. Joe Louis eschewed all flamboyance in and out of the ring in good times and in bad. He was a master craftsman—modest in victory and generous in defeat.

Ali made yet another attempt at a comeback, his third, at the age of 39 but suffered his fifth defeat in 61 fights, on a unanimous points decision after 10 rounds against Berbick, who had earlier been beaten by Holmes for the title. Sugar Ray Leonard won the undisputed world welterweight title with a knockout of Thomas Hearns in 14 rounds, but Scotland's Jim Watt's two-year reign as world lightweight champion ended in June with a points defeat by Alexis Arguello of Nicaragua.

CRICKET

Sensational headlines flowed thick and fast from all the major playing areas of the world, beginning in January in the West Indies when Roland Butcher became the first West Indian to play for England in the country of his birth. A month later Australia's captain Greg Chappell was censured by his own Cricket Board of Control following an unprece-dented instruction to his younger brother Trevor in a World Series game against New Zealand. Greg made Trevor bowl the last ball of the innings under-arm and along the ground to prevent the New Zealand batsman attempting to hit a six needed to tie the match. A week later, in Mel-bourne, India avoided defeat for the first time in a Test series against Australia by bowling out the opposition for a total of 83 when they needed only 143 for victory.

England had already been thrashed in the first Test in the West Indies when the series was almost abandoned in early March. This followed the serving of a deportation order by the Guyana Government on Robin Jackman—making his first tour with England—when the party arrived in Georgetown for the second Test. Jackman had spent many years playing and coaching in South Africa (and Zimbabwe) during the English winter. Although the second Test was not played, assurances from the other Caribbean countries hosting the tour that no similar action was planned saved the series.

West Indies went on to win the third Test handsomely and to have the better of the draws in the two others, while England were further dispirited in the middle of the tour by the sudden death of their popular assistant manager Ken Barrington in Barbados. Barrington had been forced to retire as a player in the middle of a distinguished career after a heart attack while on tour in Australia in 1968.

England's problems, particularly those of out-of-form captain Ian Botham, seemed to multiply when the touring Australians won the first Test in England and drew the second. Mike Brearley, the most successful of recent England captains, was recalled from self-imposed Test retirement to lead the side in the third Test at Leeds; but that, too, seemed lost when, at 135 for 7, England needed 91 runs to avoid an innings defeat. But, in an exhilarating attack, Botham struck 149 runs from 148 balls, leaving Australia needing 130 to win on the last day. They were destroyed in an astonishing spell by fast bowler Bob Willis, who took 8 wickets for 43 in 15·1 overs, and were beaten by 18 runs. It was the first time this century—and only the second in cricket history—that a team had won a Test match after following on their first innings. England went on to win the fourth Test when Botham took the last five Australian wickets for one run in 28 balls after they had reached 114 for 5 chasing a winning total of 151.

There was another Botham-inspired reversal in the fifth encounter at Manchester. After establishing a first innings lead of 101, England were struggling in their second knock at 104 for 5 when Botham strode to the wicket. When he left, 123 minutes later, he had hit 118 runs, including a century in 86 balls, out of a stand of 149. He struck six sixes—the most ever in an innings in the history of England-Australia matches—and his century was the fastest in these encounters since Gilbert Jessop's in 1902. England won this Test and, after drawing the last match, took the series 3-1.

Botham's big hitting extended to domestic cricket when he hit a century in 61 minutes—the fastest ever in limited-over cricket—for Somerset against Hampshire in a Sunday League game. But it was the 60-over NatWest Trophy which provided most excitement. Derbyshire won through to the final against Northants only after beating Essex in the semi finals with a single off the last ball to tie the scores, Derbyshire having lost fewer wickets. They won the final—and their first honour for 35 years—in exactly the same way. After nearly nine hours of play, Derbyshire again needed one run off the last ball to tie the scores but to win the match on fewer wickets lost, and again they scraped through.

England cricket authorities had to take a firm line when politics threatened the tour of India. Objections were made by some Indians to the selection of both Boycott and Cook for the England party because of their activities in South African cricket. But both players were finally accepted, after the issue had been considered by India's Prime Minister, Mrs Gandhi, and in the third Test in Delhi, on 23 December, Boycott became the highest scoring batsman in Test history, beating West Indian captain Sir Garfield Sobers's aggregate of 8,032 runs (scored in 160 innings in 93 tests) during his 190th innings in 107 Tests.

Four days later, on 27 December in Melbourne, Australian fast bowler Dennis Lillee became the top wicket-taker in Test cricket history, taking his record-breaking 310th wicket in the first Test against West Indies. Lillee needed only 58 Tests to reach the record compared with 79 by the previous holder, West Indies off-spinner Lance Gibbs.

GOLF

Records were broken at both ends of the scale in the British Open Championship at Royal St George's in July. Jack Nicklaus, three times winner, began with an 83—his highest ever in 19 years of open championship play. But next day he equalled the course record of 66 just before it was broken by one stroke by former England amateur international Gordon Brand. However, the title eventually went to Texan Bill Rogers, four strokes ahead of West German Bernhard Langer. Apart from becoming the first German to win the German Open in its 70-year history, Langer emerged as the most successful and consistent player on the European circuit with record earnings of over £81,000.

But Langer and others from Europe could not stem the tide of Ryder Cup defeats in the first match in which Continental players joined those from Britain and Ireland in a European challenge to the USA. They were defeated 18½ to 9½ after taking an unexpected lead on the first day. Britain continued to fight the Walker Cup alone, but again went down to defeat 15-9 in Monterey, California.

Peter Tupling, 30, scored a world record four-round total of 255 (63, 66, 62, 64), beating the previous best by USA's Mike Souchak in the 1955 Texas Open by two strokes when winning the Nigerian Open in Lagos—his first major victory in 12 years as a pro.

RUGBY FOOTBALL

Anti-apartheid demonstrators surpassed themselves during the South African Springboks' tour of New Zealand, beginning with the destruction by fire of a grandstand at the Christchurch ground, where the first Test was due to be played. Between 7,000 and 8,000 protestors battled with police at Wellington, scene of the second Test, and an aircraft was used to launch flour bombs on the field during the final Test in Auckland (see also Pt. X, Ch. 2).

The series was won 2-1 by New Zealand, but the rugby took second place to events off the field. The selection by South Africa of the first coloured player, Errol Tobias, to represent them in a rugby international, against Ireland in May, did not pacify the militants in any way. In the aftermath of the Springboks' reception in both New Zealand and the USA (where they played one match in extraordinary cloak-and-dagger secrecy) the Welsh RU subsequently cancelled a planned tour of South Africa in 1982.

Scotland also toured New Zealand in June, but could not overcome their record of never having beaten the All Blacks in 76 years of matches between the two countries. In fact, in the second Test Scotland went down to their heaviest defeat ever by the All Blacks by 40-15, the first time New Zealand had scored 40 points against a major opponent.

The rise of Argentina as a major rugby-playing nation was confirmed when England awarded caps for the first time to players appearing in two internationals during a seven-match tour of South America in May. Argentina drew the first Test 19-19, and England had to be at their best to win the second 12-6.

France scored their third Grand Slam victory in the international championship, thanks partly to a mistake by Scottish referee Alan Hosie, who allowed France to score a try and conversion from an illegal line-out on their way to beating England 16-12 in the final match at Twickenham.

The Twickenham authorities were accused of spoiling the 100th University match by failing to clear the pitch of snow. Neither side was able to play up to its potential or provide the spectacle the occasion demanded. However it proved more of a memorable occasion for Cambridge who won 9-6 (all the points came from penalties) to take the lead 44-43 in the series for the first time ever.

TENNIS

The reign of Bjorn Borg as Wimbledon champion was brought to an end by the American John McEnroe, appropriately on 4 July, when he won the men's singles title for the first time 4-6, 7-6, 7-6, 6-4. It was Borg's first defeat in 42 consecutive singles matches at Wimbledon and ended his bid to win the title for the sixth successive year. Unfortunately, McEnroe's achievement was spoiled by his attitude towards and arguments with court officials during the tournament, which resulted in his being fined and disciplined three times. He was also not given the traditional award to a winner of honorary membership of the All England Club.

But there was no denying McEnroe's power on the courts. He beat Borg in four sets again at Flushing Meadow, New York, in September to add the centennial US Open singles to his titles, and in December rounded off a good year for US tennis by winning all his three matches in the Davis Cup final to give his country a 3-1 victory over Argentina. Borg's only major success was in winning the French Open for the sixth time. The French women's title was won by the rising Czech star Hana Mandlikova, who also reached the Wimbledon women's final; she lost to America's Chris Lloyd, who became the first to take the title without dropping a set since Billie Jean King in 1967.

Miss Mandlikova's ex-Czech compatriot, Martina Navratilova (who became a US citizen during the year), was beaten in the US women's singles final by 18-year-old Tracey Austin after winning the first set 6-1 in 26 minutes. Miss Austin won the last two, 7-6, 7-6 and the match went on for two hours 42 minutes.

MOTOR RACING

The international governing body, FISA, and the Formula 1 manufacturers' association (FOCA), who had been in dispute for much of 1980, settled their differences in time for most of the 1981 world drivers championship to be run as scheduled, but not before further dispute had vindicated the forecast of *The Times* correspondent that the new agreement was 'built around technical rules which are about as watertight as a colander'.

Nelson Picquet of Brazil, driving a Parmalat Brabham, won the world title by one point from Carlos Reutemann of Argentina in a TAG Williams car. The 1980 champion Alan Jones was third, but announced his intention to retire to concentrate on cattle-ranching in Australia.

Arguments about track rules also nearly brought about the first disqualification of a winner in the 65-year history of the Indianapolis 500 race. Bobby Unser, 47, the oldest winner in history, was disqualified from the 24 May race after allegedly infringing caution rules as he left the pits. It was not until the following October that Unser finally won his appeal and was reinstated as winner.

THE TURF

Once again the Aintree Grand National had an epic ending. It was won by a horse and jockey who had both recovered from crippling and near fatal illnesses. Eighteen months before the race, jockey Bob Champion was undergoing treatment for cancer, one result of which was the loss of all his hair. One thought which kept him going through a long and painful treatment was that of riding Aldaniti in the 1981 Grand National. But the horse went lame for the second time and with a broken leg among his history of injuries should 'by all the rules of science be a cripple' according to expert Lord Oaksey. However, both horse and rider had recovered sufficiently by 4 April to lead the field of 39 (12 of whom finished) over most of the National course and win by four lengths from the favourite Spartan Missile, ridden by John Thorne, at 54 the oldest jockey ever to finish on a placed horse.

Shergar rewrote the Epsom Derby record books with a 10-length victory, the longest winning distance in the classic's history. He also gave 19-year-old jockey Walter Swinburn victory in his first Derby ride. Shergar went on to win the Irish Sweeps Derby, this time ridden by Lester Piggott, at 3-1 on, the shortest starting odds in the history of that race. With Swinburn back in the saddle in July, the horse swept through the field of the £180,000 King George VI and Queen Elizabeth Diamond Stakes. Not surprisingly, his owner the Aga Khan headed the prize money list for the Flat season with a total of £441,654.

Piggott won his tenth jockey's championship at the age of 46, riding 179 winners to 114 of his arch-rival Willie Carson. However, Carson had looked set to retain the title he won in 1980 until he suffered severe injuries, including a fractured skull, when his mount, Silken Knot, fell in a race at York in mid-August. Carson was out for the rest of the season. But Piggott had also suffered injury and said he was lucky to be alive when his mount at an Epsom meeting suddenly squeezed underneath the front of the starting stall, nearly ripping off one of the jockey's ears in the process.

In America Willie Shoemaker was still way out in front at the age of 49. On 27 May at Hollywood Park he rode his 8,000th winner, eleven years after beating the previous best winning record of 6,032 by Johnny Longden—and that remained the second highest total. Panamanian-born Jorge Velasquez, aged 35, became the first jockey in New York history to ride six winners out of six mounts in a single day at Belmont Park, Long Island. But the richest prize of all time—the new Arlington Million International, run for the first time at Arlington Heights, Illinois, on 30 August, was won by Shoemaker on John Henry from a field of 12. The winner earned his owner $600,000.

OTHER EVENTS

Baseball. A players' strike paralysed the US professional leagues for 50 days—the longest walkout in American professional sports history— and forced the cancellation of 580 games. Essentially the dispute concerned the right of the players to 'free agency' and the compensation due to clubs losing players in the annual free-agent re-entry draft, but a number of side issues were added as the dispute dragged on. When play resumed on 10 August it was decided to have a 'split' season—the first in the sport's 112-year history. In the World Series, Los Angeles Dodgers won the last four games after losing the first two, to beat New York Yankees.

Rowing. Susan Brown, a 22-year-old undergraduate reading bio-chemistry at Wadham College, became the first woman crew-member in the 152-year history of the University boat race when she coxed Oxford to an eight-lengths victory on 4 April. Women crews from Britain, Canada and the United States also rowed at Henley for the first time in the regatta's 142-year history. The honour of being first women winners past the post fell to American sisters Judy and Carly Greer, who won the invitation double sculls.

Olympic Games. Two women, Pirjo Haggman, 30, a Finnish athlete in three Olympics, and Flor Isava Fonseca, 60, a former horsewoman, of Venezuela, became the first women to be elected members of the International Olympic Committee. The IOC also made significant relaxation of its amateur Rule 26 by introducing a bye-law enabling athletes to take part in advertising provided that all financial arrangements are made through international federations or national Olympic Committees.

Swimming. John Erikson, a 26-year-old physical education teacher from Chicago, became the first to complete a three-way swimming of the English Channel. He landed at Cap Gris Nez, France, on 13 August after spending a total of 38 hours 27 minutes in the water. East Germans won all 14 women's events in the European championships in Split, Yugoslavia, but finished second to the Soviet Union on overall medals tally with 29 to 32. Britain's women swimmers were third with eight medals.

Skiing. Phil Mahre, 23, of Yakima, Washington, became the first American to win the Alpine skiing World Cup after finishing in second and twice in third position in the seasons since 1978.

XVII ECONOMIC AND SOCIAL AFFAIRS

Chapter 1

RIVAL ECONOMIC STRATEGIES

THE combination of high unemployment and high inflation (commonly called stagflation) from the mid-1970s onwards forced the Governments of all major industrialized countries to reassess their economic policies. By 1981 a variety of approaches had emerged, reflecting not only differing political circumstances in the various countries but also the breakdown of the post-war economic consensus among economists themselves. In particular, the USA (and to a lesser extent the UK) and France adopted markedly contrasting economic strategies, at least in theory, though in practice the results turned out to be not so divergent as their political leaders claimed.

The initial response to the large oil price rise of 1979-80 reflected, however, a considerable degree of unanimity among the large Western countries about what should be done to avoid the same poor performance as followed the first oil price shock in 1974-75. Communiques after meetings of Finance Ministers all stressed the need to tighten policies aimed at aggregate demand. The object was to ensure that the rise in the price of oil was not built into the domestic wage-price spiral and to prevent a squeeze on profit margins of the kind seen in 1974-75. However, as the OECD's *Economic Outlook* pointed out in December 1981, 'even where reasonably good progress had been made in containing inflation, some Governments had to continue with tight policy in order to protect their exchange rates so as to avoid higher imported inflation'.

The starting-point was the argument that many of the economic problems of the 1970s, notably the persistently high rates of inflation, could be attributed to the expansionary fiscal and monetary policies of the previous decade. Economists maintained that attempts to manage the economy through fine adjustments in budgetary policy had led to instability rather than stability and had created an excessively large public sector. The result was widespread attempts by Governments to reduce the size of public sector deficits and the scale of state operations generally. Some countries reduced direct tax rates in order to boost incentives. This action was coupled with setting monetary targets to contain the expected growth of nominal Gross National Product (GNP), a policy frequently leading to high real interest rates (that is, after adjusting for inflation).

The two countries where this mixture of fiscal and monetary policies was pursued with the greatest vigour were the UK and the USA. Their experiments became known as Thatcherism and Reagonomics after the appearance of right-wing Administrations in May 1979 and January 1981 respectively. In both countries the strategies were based on a common belief that governments by themselves could not create jobs and end recessions. Indeed, on this view, the public sector destroyed jobs and enterprise in the private sector, since high public expenditure tended to mean both high taxation and high public sector borrowing, and hence rapid inflation. Consequently, it was necessary to cut back the public sector in order to reduce both budget deficits and taxation. Lower taxes should provide enterprise and workers with incentives, while lower budget deficits should reduce the rate of monetary growth, leading in turn to a lower rate of inflation.

In practice, however, there were considerable differences between the strategies of the two countries. In the UK the Budget introduced after the election in summer 1979 attempted both a restrictive monetary and fiscal policy and tax cuts, benefiting the highly-paid in particular. Yet when it quickly became clear that public spending was proving to be more difficult to control, let alone cut, than had been hoped the programme of tax cuts was halted, indeed put into reverse. Both the 1980 and the 1981 Budgets increased the personal tax burden, through increases in indirect tax rates and a failure to adjust income tax allowances and thresholds to compensate fully for inflation. By the end of 1981 anyone with up to twice average earnings was paying a higher percentage of his or her income in tax and national insurance contributions than immediately before the 1979 election.

In the words of Mr Nigel Lawson, then a junior Treasury Minister, fiscal rectitude had preference over tax cuts. The emphasis was on the need to contain public sector borrowing, coupled with a recognition that public expenditure would be higher than originally planned because of the recession. The ensuring complications on the monetary side are described in Chapter 4 below.

The attempt to secure lower monetary growth by way of relatively high interest rates contributed to the sharp rise in the sterling exchange rate in 1979-80. Together with a rapid rise in wages this aggravated the pressure on the competitiveness of British industry. The monetary squeeze was therefore blamed by many for the severity of the recession. Indeed, by the end of 1981 some influential economists who favoured monetarism were admitting that the squeeze might have been too tight in view of the damagaing effects of the rise in sterling on manufacturing industry. In practice, the strategy was being interpreted more flexibly, though still with a determination to hold down public borrowing.

In the USA a moderately restrictive policy had been adopted by the

Carter Administration, but there was a marked change of course when President Reagan took office (the details are discussed in Chapter 3 below). The Reagan Administration went further than Mrs Thatcher's in asserting that it was possible both to impose a tight fiscal and monetary policy and to embark on an immediate large-scale programme of tax-cutting.

In addition to monetarism, this approach reflected what became known as 'supply side' economic theories. These asserted, *inter alia*, that the impact of income tax cuts on incentives would be so large and rapid that any immediate consequent loss of government income (and hence higher borrowing) would be quickly recouped from the tax revenue produced by a faster rate of economic growth. This view was clearly distinct from that of the Thatcher Government, which argued that the benefits of income tax cuts would take time to affect economic effort and national income. Consequently, any tax reductions should go hand in hand with cuts in public spending.

The first Reagan Budget attempted to bridge this gap by assuming a rapid rate of economic growth and hence higher tax revenue, leading to a steady reduction in the budget deficit, despite the large cuts in tax levels. The programme soon ran into problems because of the rise in the defence budget and the failure to secure sufficient expenditure savings elsewhere to match the tax cuts. In addition, the US economy was weaker than had been hoped, and there was a considerable gap between the initial optimistic projections and actual experience. The result was a sharp rise in the expected size of the federal budget deficit both for the current and for later fiscal years. As 1981 ended, this project was not only putting upward pressure on interest rates but also leading to calls for increases in taxation to limit borrowing, though there were yet no signs that this would happen.

In France, a directly contrary approach was adopted after the election of President Mitterrand in May. The main objective of the previous Administration, like that of other industrialized countries, had been to contain inflation as a means of restoring competitiveness and creating the conditions for an improvement in employment. The Mitterrand Administration changed the priorities, saying that its objective was directly to reduce unemployment by boosting economic growth and by introducing special employment subsidies. In simplified terms it adopted a broadly Keynesian approach of expansion rather than the monetarism of the UK and the USA. The immediate measures included raising the lowest wages and social benefits, boosting public and private investment, increasing expenditure in the public sector and reducing the working week.

The French programme, like the others, soon faced difficulties—notably on the foreign exchange markets, where pressure on the French franc led to a tightening of exchange controls and a rise in interest rates. After a realignment of currencies in October, measures to combat inflation were announced, involving temporary and partial price controls or freezes. By the end of the year cutbacks in public expenditure were being planned for 1982. Monetary policy also had to face the conflicting objectives of stabilizing domestic demand and of defending the franc.

By the end of 1981 it was too soon to reach any more than a tentative judgement on the comparative US and French experiments. There were, however, signs that, despite the divergent ideological stances, pressures were pushing actual policies in the same direction. The need to control inflation and hold up the exchange rate acted as a check on the scale of expansion in France, while the persistence of high unemployment and high levels of public spending limited the extent of retrenchment in the USA.

The evidence pointed, in particular, to the problems of overruns in public expenditure during a recession. The OECD's *Economic Outlook* for December 1981 pointed out that, despite the widespread intention to cut public expenditure and stabilize or raise personal taxation, the results did not show any marked decrease in the ratio of government deficits (including local and state borrowing) to Gross Domestic Product (GDP).

GOVERNMENT FINANCIAL BALANCES

Surpluses (+) or deficits (−) as a percentage of nominal Gross Domestic Product in seven major OECD countries.

	1978	1979	1980	1981
United States	0	+0·5	−1·2	−0·7
Japan	−5·5	−4·7	−4·1	−3·6
West Germany	−2·7	−2·9	−3·4	−4·4
France	−1·8	−0·6	+0·4	−2·4
UK	−4·3	−3·2	−3·5	−2·3
Italy	−9·7	−9·4	−7·8	−9·4
Canada	−3·1	−1·9	−2·1	−0·1
Total of above	−2·5	−1·9	−2·5	−2·5

Source: OECD *Economic Outlook.*

In the seven largest industrialized countries, the percentage was about 2½ per cent in both 1980 and 1981, against just under 2 per cent in 1979. However, keeping these ratios constant in face of the tendency for tax revenues to decline and government expenditure to rise during a recession required deliberate acts to cut spending and raise tax rates. The change in the relative budget deficits on such a cyclically-adjusted basis was estimated at nearly 1¼ per cent of GDP in 1980 and 1981. This tightening was most marked in the UK, Japan and Canada.

Looking at the adoption of tight policies in most countries (apart from France), the OECD concluded that the record lent 'little support to the notion that tight monetary policy can reduce inflation without a significant deflation of demand and output'. In addition, it was clear that unless policies were synchronized there could be serious distortions in the foreign exchange markets. Thus at the end of the year the combination of tight monetary objectives with a high and rising budget deficit in the USA was pushing up interest rates and the exchange value of the dollar. This in turn was causing concern in Europe both about falling exchange rates and about the implications of any consequent rise in domestic interest rates for the prospects of economic recovery. The result, as reflected in the comments of individual Finance Ministers and of the EEC collectively, was serious strains in US-European relations. At the end of 1981 a new economic consensus was still a long way off.

Chapter 2

INTERNATIONAL ECONOMIC DEVELOPMENTS

ECONOMIC developments in the major industrialized countries continued to be dominated in 1981 by the impact of high inflation and high unemployment resulting primarily from the sharp rise in oil prices in 1979-80. The rise in aggregate real Gross Domestic or National Product (GDP, GNP) in the seven major economies (the USA, Canada, France, Italy, Japan, West Germany and the UK) slackened to 1 per cent in 1980 and to just under 1½ per cent in 1981, from about 4 per cent in 1979. The slowdown was less marked than after the 1973 increase in oil prices, when the decline had occurred after an exceptional boom.

The pace of rises in consumer price levels was slightly less than in the mid-1970s—a peak annual inflation rate of 13½ per cent in the first half of 1980, compared with nearly 15 per cent in the first half of 1974. The slowdown from the peak also occurred more quickly in 1980-81 than in the earlier period, though in some countries, notably the USA, inflation rates rose above their mid-1970s levels. This restraint was attributed to the impact of restrictive fiscal and monetary policies in containing the response in the wages market. The Bank of England, in its *Quarterly Bulletin* of December 1981, observed that 'at least in the short-term these policies led to rises in real, as well as nominal, interest rates and tended to reinforce the depressive effect of the oil price increases on domestic demand and activity'.

Output and Unemployment. The main economies grew modestly in the first half of 1981. Economic activity was buoyant in the USA, Canada and Japan, while output was flat or falling slightly in the main European countries. In the seven major economies the average annual growth rate of total output in the first half of the year was 2·9 per cent.

A striking feature was that, while domestic demand weakened in most countries during that period, this was offset by a strong rise in exports to non-industrialized countries, notably the oil-producing states which were still importing on a large scale. The weak growth of internal consumption in the industrialized countries reflected a slowdown in the growth of earnings, below the rate at which prices were rising.

In the second half of 1981, however, aggregate output, as measured by real GNP, was broadly unchanged. This aggregate concealed divergent movements among different countries. In the USA, for example, output dropped sharply, whereas in Japan recovery was maintained, albeit at a slower rate, helped by buoyant exports and a pick-up in domestic demand. Activity in France continued to expand, while there were further small declines in West Germany and Italy, the result of generally restrictive policies only partially offset by favourable trade movements.

The continuing sluggish overall economic performance had a considerable impact on the labour market. In Western Europe total employment fell by 1¼ per cent in 1981 after showing no change in 1980. This decline was counterbalanced by a sharp rise in the growth of industrial employment in the USA, where the total employed workforce rose by 2½ per cent in the first half of the year before falling back by ¾ per cent in the second six months. Over 1981 as a whole, total employment in the seven major economies was static, after an increase of nearly ½ per cent in 1980. Productivity growth accelerated from just over ½ per cent in 1980 to 1¼ per cent in 1981, as output was maintained in a number of countries with fewer workers employed.

At a time when the size of the labour force of working age was growing, the result was a further sharp rise in unemployment—especially in the UK, Belgium, Denmark and Spain. By the end of 1981 total unemployment in the 24 countries in the OECD was well over 26 million—or more than 7½ per cent of their total workforce. This compared with an average of 21½ million in 1980, a rate of 6¼ per cent. Over 15 million of the total were in Europe and most of the rest in North America.

Most of the brunt fell on young people. Unemployment among the under-25s—just under one-fifth of the labour force—accounted for nearly two-fifths of the total out of work in the seven major industrialized countries. It was estimated that one in seven of this age-group was unemployed in 1981. Another significant figure was the rise in the number of people unemployed for more than six months.

World Trade. Exports by industrialized countries to the rest of the world, including the oil producers, rose sharply in the first half of 1981— at an annual rate of 14½ per cent compared with 6 per cent in the previous half-year. The volume of oil imports by the same countries fell during 1981 as a result of falling consumption, under the impact of higher prices, and destocking. Weak demand in the OECD area resulted in only a slight recovery in trade among industrialized countries themselves after the big fall in 1980. Overall, world trade was flat in 1981 as a whole, after a 1 per cent rise in 1980.

There were, however, significant shifts in the balance of trade of different countries. The current account balances of Europe and Japan improved markedly during 1981, and the total deficit of the seven major countries dropped by over $30,000 million to about $3,000 million, more than half the shift occurring in Japan. The main exception was Canada, whose deficit rose sharply. Apart from normal cyclical trends in a period of recession, the shift also reflected a speeding-up of the international adjustment process on the part of both the oil-producing and the industrialized countries.

Underlying some of these trends were important changes in the competitiveness of trade in manufactured goods. The sharp rise in the dollar caused a deterioration in the competitive position of the USA almost as large as that previously suffered by the UK. By the second half of 1981 this was reflected in the figures of trade volumes, though the current account balance was still favourably affected by the earlier exchange rate movements. Prolonged exchange rate stability (at least up to the autumn of 1981), together with divergent inflation trends, resulted in marked gains in competitiveness by West Germany and the Benelux countries.

In the world current account scene, the most important changes during 1981 were the drop in the OECD deficit and the reduced surplus of the oil producing states, the latter falling from $110,000 million to $60,000 million. The non-oil developing countries as a group incurred a slightly larger deficit. But many of them were so adjusting their import volumes as to run the maximum sustainable deficits consistent with the cost and availability of finance. The newly industrializing countries faced the same pressures after a big increase in their deficits in 1980.

Capital markets. The world's financial markets continued to be dominated in 1981 by the strength of the dollar and the fluctuations of US interest rates. The US dollar strengthened against all other currencies during the first half of 1981, when US interest rates rose above 20 per cent. By the late summer this imposed intense pressures on European currencies, notably sterling and the French franc, and there was sizeable intervention by the central banks of both countries. In contrast, the D-mark and the Swiss franc recovered after their previous declines, partly because of an improvement in the trade positions of West Germany and Switzerland from the summer onwards. The dollar also weakened during August and September. By the late summer intense pressure had developed within the European Monetary System (EMS), especially in view of the loss of foreign confidence in the French franc. The result was a major realignment of currencies within the EMS (which still excluded sterling) in early October. The Italian lira and the French franc were devalued by 3 per cent and the D-mark and the Dutch guilder were revalued by 5½ per cent.

By the end of the year some of the familiar problems had returned. Upward pressures on US interest rates and on the dollar threatened hopes of stability in the foreign exchange markets. This created a dilemma for policy-makers attempting at the same time to adhere to monetary targets and to avoid currency changes which would damage output and import inflation. As the OECD pointed out, 'resistance to increased domestic interest rates while foreign rates are rising is liable to require intervention to support the exchange rate, which can put heavy pressure on even quite high foreign exchange reserves. Conversely, if domestic interest rates are held too high in relation to foreign rates, capital inflows may induce excessive monetary expansion.'

Nobel Prize. The 1981 Nobel prize for economics was awarded to Professor James Tobin of Yale University for his 'analysis of financial markets and their relation to expenditure decisions, employment, production and prices'.

Chapter 3

ECONOMY OF THE UNITED STATES

THE economic policies of the USA changed significantly after the Reagan Administration took office, but by the end of 1981 there was no sign of any marked improvement in the underlying economic performance. The US economy weakened during the year and unemployment rose, though the inflation rate slackened slightly.

Government Policies. The Reagan Administration came into office with plans for a radical overhaul of the public sector and of taxation programmes (see also Chapter 1 above). The tax proposals were modified somewhat by Congress, and the result was a cut in personal tax rates of 5 per cent in October 1981, with further promised reductions of 10 per cent in both July 1982 and July 1983. Thereafter, the personal income tax system would be indexed to the previous year's change in the consumer price index. The cuts were intended to bring down personal tax rates at the margin from a range of 14 to 70 per cent to about 11 to 52 per cent.

Increased depreciation write-offs against business taxes were introduced and the oil windfall profits tax was eased. The longer-term impact of the tax cuts was larger than at first suggested by the Administration.

The proposed changes in expenditure were also altered by Congress. While overall expenditure plans were in line with the original proposals, major cuts in individual programmes were left unresolved, so that further decisions were required to make the details consistent with the lower totals. The gap was just under a third of the proposed cuts for the 1982 fiscal year. In particular, several proposed changes in social security were not adopted. The weakening of the economy during 1981 and the higher-than-expected level of interest payments led to a general upward revision of expenditure projections. Financial markets were worried by insufficient evidence of an emerging budget balance. Consequently, by the end of the year the Administration recognized that further measures would be needed to bring the deficit down towards previous target levels.

The extent of the problem was underlined in the turn-of-the-year reviews by the Administration. These showed that the federal deficit in the fiscal year which began in October 1981 was likely to reach a record $99,000 million compared with an original official estimate of $37,700 million. Indeed, the Congressional Budget Office estimated a deficit of more than $105,000 million for the 1981-82 financial year. This reflected higher defence spending and lower tax revenue because of the downturn in the economy. The reassessment of the likely budget deficit, and especially the effective abandonment of the goal of a balanced budget by 1984, shook market confidence. By the end of the year the many critics of the Administration were saying that the assumptions about inflation and output growth were still too optimistic. After a year in office the Reagan Administration faced as serious a fiscal problem as when it took over.

The fiscal pressures were reflected on the monetary side, where the Federal Reserve Board under Mr Paul Volcker, its independent-minded chairman, attempted to limit monetary growth in face of continuing high public borrowing needs. During 1981 the broader monetary aggregates grew at the upper end of the target ranges. Most market attention was focused on the narrower aggregates, which grew at below target rates, the difference reflecting high interest rates and institutional changes. Interest rates fluctuated sharply during the year around a historically high level, exceeding 20 per cent in the spring. This led to considerable criticism of the Federal Reserve's ability to control the money supply and tended to emphasize the potential conflict with fiscal policy.

Output and Unemployment. The US economy was growing strongly at the beginning of 1981 but soon ran out of steam. Economic activity stagnated during the spring and summer, before falling back sharply towards the end of the year as a result of the monetary squeeze and high interest rates. Over the whole of 1981 GNP probably rose by only about 1 per cent compared with 1980, while experiencing a sharp fall in the second half of the year.

Residential investment declined particularly sharply, new starts dropping from an annual rate of 1½ million units at the beginning of 1981 to well below 1 million units during its last few months. Government expenditure was also a contractionary influence in the second half of the year. However, business investment remained relatively strong, partly as a result of expenditure related to energy savings.

Consumers' expenditure was also maintained. The personal savings rate fell to slightly over 5 per cent of disposable income in 1981 compared with 5¾ per cent in 1980. This helped to offset some of the impact of falling real incomes, so that consumer spending continued to rise during the year.

The decline in output was reflected in a rise in unemployment, which accelerated towards the end of the year to a total of more than 8 million. The ratio increased to 7¾ per cent of the workforce in the second half of 1981 compared with an average of 7¼ per cent in 1980. By the end of the year the ratio was climbing towards 9 per cent.

Inflation. The inflation rate moderated somewhat during 1981, mainly because of an easing in energy, food and import prices. Food and raw material prices were restrained by the appreciation of the dollar, by increased beef supplies and a good grain harvest. And when interest rates were no longer pushing up the consumer price index the slowdown became particularly marked towards the end of 1981. The rate of growth of average earnings also slowed, though a deteriorating productivity trend kept the growth rate of unit labour costs in the 8½ to 9 per cent range. Overall, the annual rate of consumer price inflation slackened from 10¼ per cent in 1980 to 8¼ per cent in 1981.

External Finance. The competitive position of the USA deteriorated for most of 1981 as a result of the rise in unit labour costs and the rapid appreciation of the dollar in late 1980 and the first half of 1981. Coupled with the world recession the result was an adverse swing in the underlying external position. The volume of exports fell sharply during the second half of 1981, causing an overall decline of 5 to 6 per cent for the year as a whole compared with 1980. Import volume fell back fractionally in the second half of 1981 as internal demand and activity in the USA declined. Over the whole year import volume was 1 to 2 per cent up compared with 1980. But earlier favourable changes in the relative prices of exports and imports (the terms of trade) enlarged the surplus on current account of the balance of payments compared with the previous year.

Chapter 4

ECONOMY OF THE UNITED KINGDOM

THE recession in the UK at last touched bottom during the course of 1981 after the steepest and most prolonged fall in output for fifty years. By the end of the year the pick-up in activity was still limited and halting, while unemployment was continuing to rise. Moreover, average living standards were being squeezed and the inflation rate was on a plateau.

The result was intense criticism of the Conservative Government's economic policies—not only from the Labour Opposition and the new Social Democratic Party/Liberal alliance but also from within the Conservative Party (see pp. 27-9). The critics focused on doubts, first, about whether the Government's medium-term financial strategy was working within its own terms and, secondly, about whether current policies could produce any more than a weak recovery.

The all-party Treasury and Civil Service Committee of the Commons argued in a report (House of Commons paper 28, session 1981-82) that it had 'not seen any firm evidence of factors leading to a sustained level of growth in the medium-term which would significantly reduce unemployment'. Furthermore, the Committee noted general uncertainties about the money supply and public sector borrowing targets which 'must throw doubt on the underlying strategy as it was promulgated at the time of the Budget in 1980'.

Government Policy. The Conservative Government's main objective remained, in the words of Mr Terry Burns, the chief economic adviser to the Treasury, 'to reduce inflation, as a necessary part of creating the conditions for sustained growth in output and employment in the medium-term'. It remained committed to 'the underlying principle that steady but not excessive downward pressure on the rate of growth of monetary variables is an essential element in controlling the growth of money Gross Domestic Product (GDP), and inflation, over a run of years'. Yet during 1981 there were a number of important changes in the way in which the policy was operated.

The key problems concerned sterling M3, the broadly-defined money supply and the central monetary target. At the beginning of 1981 the picture was already obscured by the impact of the end of the 'corset' controls on the banks (see AR 1980, p. 470). During 1981 further distortions were caused by special factors associated with the long civil service dispute (see p. 24) which delayed tax payments. There was also a rapid expansion in lending by banks to private individuals, especially for house purchase, as well as a high level of bank borrowing by companies in response to the pressures of the recession, high wage increases and a strong pound. The result was that sterling M3 grew at an annual rate well above the target of 6 to 10 per cent increase.

The Government argued, however, that sterling M3 alone was not a good measure of monetary conditions. Narrower measures of money were growing more slowly and the depressed state of the economy generally and the strength of sterling (at least until spring 1981) were, it was suggested, indicators of a restrictive monetary policy. Consequently, the Government in practice interpreted the strategy more flexibly and based its short-term interest rate decisions not just on movements of sterling M3 but also on changes in other monetary aggregates and in the sterling exchange rate. This was reflected in the main decisions taken during 1981.

The March 1981 Budget was intended to ease the pressures on interest rates and on the sterling exchange rate. The planned level of public sector borrowing for 1981-82 was revised upwards to £10,500 million compared with the original target of £7,500 million. The change was to take account both of the increased borrowing needs of nationalized industries and of the impact of the recession on spending on unemployment and other social security benefits. There was an increase in the burden of taxation on persons (see p. 460) in order to make room for some easing in the financial position of companies by way of a reduction in interest rates. Minimum Lending Rate (MLR) was therefore cut by two points to 12 per cent.

Subsequent events did not turn out quite as hoped. Admittedly, by the end of 1981 public sector borrowing was broadly on course for the Budget target, or slightly less. There remained, however, strong upward pressures on public expenditure, reflected in the upward revision of planned spending for 1982-83 that was announced on 2 December.

The main problems arose from a sharp fall in the exchange rate, partly offsetting the appreciation of 1979-80. This resulted from a weakening of world oil prices and a sharp increase in overseas interest rates above those in the UK. MLR was suspended in August to permit greater flexibility in short-term interest rates. The Government, however, encouraged such interest rates to rise in September and October because of concern about the steepness of the fall in sterling and the strong growth in bank lending. Towards the end of the year UK interest rates fell back, and, despite rising US interest rates, the pound was relatively steady. During 1981 as a whole the pound fell by 47 cents against the dollar to $1.91, though by a smaller percentage compared with the main European currencies.

The Recession. Output was still falling sharply at the beginning of 1981. This decline continued until the second quarter of the year, when

Gross Domestic Product at constant prices was 6 per cent less than the average level in 1979. This compared with a 4 per cent drop in the 1974-75 recession. The main pressures were concentrated on manufacturing industry, where output fell by 16 per cent between 1979 and mid-1981.

Output picked up from the summer onwards, notably in manufacturing industry, mainly because of a slowdown in the previous record level of destocking by industry, which led to a revival of orders. The amount of overtime working rose and short-time working fell back. Yet by the end of the year the recovery was still hesitant. Manufacturing production was at the lowest level for nearly 15 years, while GDP in 1981 as a whole was over 2 per cent less than in 1980.

One reason for caution was the decline in average living standards, as measured by real personal disposable income, resulting from a fall in the volume of employment, a growth of average earnings slower than that of consumer prices and a rise in the personal tax burden. Consumers ran down their personal savings and so maintained their level of spending at not far from the high 1980 level in real terms.

The most dramatic impact of the recession was in the labour market. A continuing large number of major redundancies and factory closures resulted in a rise of the UK adult unemployment total by 645,000 during 1981 to 2·78 million, on a seasonally adjusted basis, equivalent to 11·5 per cent of the workforce. The numbers would have been considerably higher but for the Government's special employment subsidies. After taking into account school-leavers, the unadjusted 'headline' total was 2·94 million in December 1981 and was clearly rising towards 3 million.

Inflation and Competitiveness. The slowdown in the inflation rate during the second half of 1980 was checked during 1981, despite a relatively favourable pay round, particularly in the private sector where wage rises were held down by the recession. The annual rate of growth of average earnings slowed from over 20 per cent during 1980 to roughly 10 per cent by the end of 1981. However, the impact on prices was offset by the sharp turnround in sterling from the large appreciation of 1980 to a big depreciation which pushed up the cost of imports. In addition, the Budget measures boosted the cost of living by raising indirect taxes. The overall effect was that the 12-month rate of increase of retail prices slackened from 15·1 per cent in December 1980 to only 12 per cent by the end of the year, against a Treasury projection in March of 10 per cent by that date. A low point of 10·9 per cent had been reached in July 1981.

The rise in labour costs per unit of output in UK manufacturing industry slackened to the lowest rate for more than a decade. This reflected not only the low rise in wages in manufacturing industry, less than in the rest of the economy, but also an improvement in productivity. By the end of 1981 output per man hour was 5 per cent higher than the average level of 1979, the drop in output being exceeded by the unprecedented decline in employment and in hours worked. The result was that industrial costs in Britain were rising more slowly than abroad. After taking account of the sharp fall in the exchange rate, there was probably a 10 to 15 per cent gain in competitiveness, offsetting in part the large losses of the late 1970s and 1980.

External Finance. The UK continued to have a strong external trading position throughout 1981. The current account of the balance of payments stayed in large surplus, though detailed figures were published for only part of the period. The limited available evidence indicated that the surplus fell between the beginning and the end of 1981. This was because of a sharp rise in the volume of imports of manufactured goods as a result both of earlier losses of competitiveness and of a slowdown in destocking. Export volumes continued to rise despite the world recession.

The current account surplus was offset by large outflows on the capital account. British financial institutions invested on a record scale in overseas shares and property and there was also a deficit on banking transactions, reflecting the weaker trend of sterling and relative interest rate movements.

NOTES ON ECONOMIC AND SOCIAL DATA

The statistical data on the following pages record developments from 1976 to the latest year, usually 1981, for which reasonably stable figures were available at the time of going to press. Year headings 1976 to 1981 are printed only at the head of each page and are not repeated over individual tables unless the sequence is broken by the insertion of series of figures recording developments over a longer period than is shown on the remainder of the page.

Pages to which the point is relevant include a comparative price index, allowing the current-price figures to be reassessed against the background of inflation.

Unless figures are stated as indicating the position at the *end* of years or quarters, they should be taken as annual or quarterly *totals* or *averages*, according to context.

Tables 2, 3, 4 and 5. Statistics which are normally reported or collected separately in the three UK home jurisdictions (England and Wales, Scotland, and Northern Ireland) have been consolidated into UK series only to show general trends. As the component returns were made at varying times of year and in accordance with differing definitions and regulatory requirements, the series thus consolidated may therefore be subject to error, may not be strictly comparable from year to year, and may be less reliable than the remainder of the data.

Symbols.— = Nil or not applicable   .. = not available at time of compilation.

Sources

A. THE UNITED KINDGOM
   Government Sources
   Annual Abstract of Statistics: Tables 1, 2, 3, 4, 5, 15, 16, 21, 22, 27.
   Monthly Digest of Statistics: Tables 1, 10, 11, 12, 13, 14, 18, 19, 20, 21, 22, 23, 24, 26, 27, 28.
   Financial Statistics: Tables 9, 10, 12, 13, 17, 29.
   Economic Trends: 6, 7, 8, 9, 10, 29.
   Social Trends: Tables 2, 3, 4, 5.
   Department of Employment Gazette: Tables 23, 24, 25, 26.
   Housing and Construction Statistics: Tables 5, 15.
   Additional Sources
   National Institute of Economic and Social Research, *National Institute Economic Review:* Tables 6, 7, 8.
   Bank of England Quarterly Bulletin: Tables 11, 12.
   Midland Bank: Tables 13, 14.
   United Nations, *Monthly Bulletin of Statistics:* Table 1.
   The Financial Times: Tables 12, 14.
   British Insurance Association: Table 16.

B. THE UNITED STATES
   Government and other Public Sources
   Department of Commerce, *Survey of Current Business:* Tables 30, 31, 32, 33, 34, 35, 40, 41, 43.
   Council of Economic Advisers, Joint Economic Committee, *Economic Indicators:* Tables 34, 39.
   Federal Reserve Bulletin: Tables 36, 37, 38.
   Additional Sources
   A. M. Best Co.: Table 38.
   Insurance Information Institute, New York: Table 38.
   Bureau of Economic Statistics, *Basic Economic Statistics:* Tables 41, 42.

C. INTERNATIONAL COMPARISONS
   United Nations, *Annual Abstract of Statistics:* Tables 44, 53.
   UN *Monthly Bulletin of Statistics:* Tables 44, 47.
   IMF, *International Financial Statistics:* Tables 44, 45, 46, 49, 50, 51, 52.
   OECD, *Main Economic Indicators:* Table 53.
   Institute of Strategic Studies, *The Military Balance:* Table 48.

Chapter 5

ECONOMIC AND SOCIAL DATA
A. THE UNITED KINGDOM

SOCIAL

1. Population	1976	1977	1978	1979	1980	1981
Population, mid-year est. ('000)	55,886	55,852	55,835	55,881	55,945	..
Live births registered ('000)	675·5	657·0	687·2	735	754	..
Crude birth rate (per 1,000 pop.)	12·1	11·8	12·3	13·1	13·5	..
Deaths registered ('000)	680·0	655·3	667·2	675·6	661·5	..
Crude death rate (per 1,000 pop.)	12·1	11·7	11·9	12·1	11·8	..

2. Health						
Public expenditure on National Health Service (£ million)(1)	6,249	6,896	7,835	9,362	11,494	..
Hospitals:						
staffed beds, end-year ('000)	488·0	480·0	470·9	463·4	458	..
ave. daily bed occupancy ('000)	394·0	388·0	380·0	373·4	369·0	..
waiting list, end-yr. ('000)	722·0	715·0	801·0	809		..
Certifications of death ('000) by:						
ischaemic heart disease	180·8	179·5	184·8	179·0	..	..
malignant neoplasm, lungs and bronchus	38·0	38·3	39·0	39·5	..	..
road fatality	7·2	7·0	7·9	7·1	..	..
accidents at work (number)(2)	682	614	751	711	700	..

(1) Central government and local authority, capital and current. (2) Great Britain.

3. Education						
Public expenditure (£ million)(1)	7,408	7,881	8,697	10,061	12,199	..
Schools ('000)	35·9	36·0	36·1	36·0	..	..
Pupils enrolled ('000) in schools	11,300	11,321	11,221	11,091	10,891	..
maintained primary(2)	5,998	5,909	5,751	5,594	5,398	..
maintained and aided secondary(3)(4)	4,448	4,559	4,617	4,643	4,636	..
assisted and independent	629	623	614	615	620	..
Pupils per full-time teacher at:						
maintained primary schools	23·8	23·7	23·4	23·0	22·7	..
maintained secondary schools(4)	16·9	16·8	16·7	16·7	16·6	..
independent schools(5)	15·2	15·1	15·1	..	..	..
Further education: institutions(6)	8,046	7,073	7,110	7,185	..	..
full-time students ('000)	472	481	470	461	467	..
Universities	46	46	46	46	..	..
University students ('000)	269	294	288	296	301	..
First degrees awarded (number)	55,920	57,047	63,657	65,982	..	..
Open University graduates ('000)	6·7	6·9	6·5	6·9	..	..

(1) Central government and local authority, capital and current. Figures are for financial year: 1975 = year ending March 1976, etc. (2) Including nursery schools. (3) Including special schools. (4) 1976 estimate excludes some voluntary maintained or aided grammar schools which became independent. (5) England and Wales. (6) Great Britain.

Overall price index (1975 = 100)	*113·9*	*127·9*	*142·6*	*161·6*	*190·7*	*212·0*

4. Law and Order	1976	1977	1978	1979	1980	1981
Public expenditure (£ million)(1)	1,823	1,946	2,260	2,818	3,523	..
Police	1,149	1,221	1,397	1,691	2,100	..
Prisons	234	275	315	342	471	..
Administration of justice(2)	347	383	430	497	709	..
Police establishment ('000)(3)	130·0	130·1	130·8	131·5	132·1	..
Full-time strength(3)	122·2	118·6	119·8	124·8	129·1	..
Ulster, full-time strength	5·3	5·7	6·1	6·6	6·9	..
Serious offences known to police (4)	2,494	3,046	2,943	2,934	3,105	..
Persons convicted, all offences ('000)(4)	2,322	2,243	2,086	2,154	..	..
Burglary or robbery(5)	73	75	74	64	74	..
Handling stolen goods/receiving, theft	228	235	228	223	236	..
Violence against person	40	43	43	49	53	..
Traffic offences	1,281	1,149	1,118	1,108	1,323	..
All summary offences(4)	1,896	1,758	1,667	1,730	..	..
Prisons: average population ('000)	51·2	51·3	51·9	51·4	51·9	..

(1) Gross expenditure, capital and current, by central government (direct and by grant to local authorities) and by local and police authorities. Figures are for financial year: 1975 = year ending March 1976, etc. (2) Includes expenditure on parliament and courts. (3) Police establishment and full-time strength: Great Britain only. (4) Because of differences in juridical and penal systems in the three UK jurisdictions, totals of offences are not strictly comparable from year to year: they should be read only as indicating broad trends. (5) Specific offences: England, Wales and N. Ireland.

5. Housing	1976	1977	1978	1979	1980	1981
Public expenditure (£ million)(1)	5,106	5,085	5,258	6,135	7,156	..
Dwellings completed ('000)						
by and for public sector(2)	163·0	170	136	108	108	..
by private sector	152·2	143	153	144	130	..
Housing land, private sector,						
weighted ave. price (£/hectare)	42,260	44,342	54,334	77,637	101,991	..
Dwelling prices, average (£)(3)	12,759	13,712	15,674	20,143	23,514	..

(1) Capital and current, net of rents, etc., received, and adjusted to eliminate double counting of grants and subsidies paid by central government and expended by local authorities. Figures are for financial year: 1976 = year ending March 1977. (2) Including government departments (police houses, military married quarters, etc.) and approved housing associations and trusts. (3) Of properties newly mortgaged by building societies.

Overall price index (1975 = 100)	113·9	127·9	142·6	161·6	190·7	212·0

PRICES, INCOME AND EXPENDITURE

6. National Income and Expenditure
(£ million, 1975 prices)

	1976	1977	1978	1979	1980	1981
GDP(1), expenditure basis	97,948	99,240	101,869	102,957	100,700	..
income basis(2)	110·0	126·5	146·1	168·6	194·7	210·4
output basis (1975 = 100)	101·9	104·6	108·0	110·3	107·4	104·4
average estimate (1975 = 100)	102·8	105·0	108·3	110·2	107·6	..
Components of gross domestic product:						
Consumers' expenditure	64,815	64,583	68,222	71,485	71,477	71,467
General government						
consumption	23,213	22,948	23,435	23,834	24,216	24,290
Gross fixed investment	20,649	20,161	20,836	20,957	20,720	19,155
Total final expenditure	138,966	140,673	145,522	150,637	147,248	150,218
Stockbuilding	624	1,387	833	1,404	− 2,232	− 2,062
Adjustment to factor cost	10,786	10,874	11,895	12,398	12,411	12,164

(1) At factor cost. (2) Current prices, £ billion.

7. Fixed Investment
(£ million, 1975 prices, seasonally adjusted)

	1976	1977	1978	1979	1980	1981
Total, all fixed investment(1)	20,649	20,161	20,836	20,898	20,761	19,120
Dwellings	4,263	3,894	4,067	3,556	3,129	2,416
public	2,083	1,861	1,740	1,581	1,418	930
private	2,180	2,033	2,327	1,975	1,711	1,486
Mainly private industries & services(2)	9,559	9,607	9,823	10,753	10,660	10,701
manufacturing	3,211	3,479	3,511	3,648	3,370	2,950
other(2)	6,348	6,127	6,312	7,105	7,290	7,846
Mainly public industries & services(3)	4,039	3,687	3,489	5,483	5,424	5,305

8. Personal Income and Expenditure
(£ million, seasonally adjusted, current prices unless otherwise stated)

Wages and salaries	66,161	73,379	83,971	98,376	117,145	126,641
Current grants	12,765	15,108	17,905	20,977	25,476	31,116
Forces' pay	1,474	1,506	1,645	2,020	2,435	2,690
Other personal income(1)	20,289	22,887	27,088	33,954	38,426	41,137
Personal disposable income	84,832	96,360	113,761	136,852	160,821	174,813
Real personal disposable income(2)	73,359	72,362	78,436	83,728	84,867	83,295
Consumers' expenditure	74,952	86,001	98,947	116,717	135,403	149,965

(1) From rent, self-employment (before depreciation or stock appreciation provisions), dividend and interest receipts and charitable receipts from companies. (2) At 1975 prices.

9. Government Finance
(£ million)

Revenue(1)	42,745	48,963	54,415	65,224	80,455	95,579
taxes on income	18,864	20,333	22,461	25,098	30,888	..
corporation tax(2)	1,996	2,655	3,343	3,941	4,646	4,645
taxes on expenditure	12,050	15,175	17,572	23,777	28,987	..
purchase/value added tax(2)	3,451	3,765	4,230	4,832	8,179	10,960
taxes on capital(3)	853	866	899	1,078	1,207	..
National Insurance surcharge(4)	0	1,180	1,910	3,014	3,426	..
Expenditure(2)(5)	42,792	49,009	54,422	65,242	79,357	..
social services(6)	26,243	29,482	33,945	39,185	48,228	..
defence	6,139	6,757	7,460	8,975	11,271	..
net lending(7)	2,166	1,881	2,220	3,881	3,493	..
Deficit(−) or surplus	− 9,128	− 5,995	− 8,331	− 12,554	− 12,373	..

(1) Total current receipts, taxes on capital and other capital receipts. (2) Financial years ended 5 April of year indicated. (3) Capital gains tax and estate/death duties. (4) 1975, selective employment tax (abolished 1973). (5) Total government expenditure, gross domestic capital formation and grants. (6) Including expenditure by public authorities other than central government. (7) To private sector, local authorities, public corporations, and overseas.

Overall price index (1975 = 100)	113·9	127·9	142·6	161·6	190·7	212·0

10. Prices and Costs (index 1975 = 100)

Total home costs per unit of output(1)	113·9	127·9	142·6	161·6	190·7	212·0
Labour costs per unit of output	109·2	118·5	131·4	150·8	189·6	..
Mfg. wages, salaries/unit of output	111·8	122·7	139·2	158·9	195·0	..
Import unit values	122·1	141·5	145·0	159·5	182·2	198·7
Wholesale prices, manufactures	117·3	140·5	153·3	172·0	200·0	221·3
Consumer prices	116·5	135·0	146·2	165·8	195·6	218·9
Tax and prices	118·5	135·9	138·5	156·8	184·0	211·2

(1) Used as 'Overall price index' on all pages of UK statistics.

FINANCIAL

11. Banking(1)	1976	1977	1978	1979	1980	1981
(£ million, at end of period)						
Current and deposit accounts	163,476	178,097	204,051	243,038	286,328	398,333
Advances: to	149,964	169,324	195,698	199,590	233,371	..
local authorities	4,026	4,376	4,688	5,382	7,026	2,319
public corporations	2,693	3,301	2,880	2,065	1,799	1,317
financial institutions	4,329	4,465	5,238	6,695	7,155	10,891
companies	23,335	26,357	29,248	32,892	38,959	..
construction	1,560	1,578	1,707	1,979	2,326	2,603
personal sector	7,723	8,983	10,860	14,017	17,617	12,871
overseas residents	85,529	88,127	106,083	128,681	150,838	..
Eligible liabilities	36,876	40,850	45,003	51,647	67,462	77,651
Special deposits, cumulative(%)	6	3	3	2	2	..

(1) Unless otherwise stated, this table covers all banks in the UK observing the common 12·5 per cent reserve ratio introduced on 16 Sept. 1971 and includes the accepting houses (merchant banks), discount houses and, for deposits, the National Giro and the banking department of the Bank of England. Except in the case of overseas advances, inter-bank transactions have been omitted.

12. Interest Rates and Security Yields(1)

(% per annum, end of year)						
Treasury bill yield	13·98	6·39	11·91	16·49	13·45	15·39
London clearing banks base rate	14·00	7·12	12·50	17·00	14·00	14·50
2½% consols, gross flat yield(2)	14·25	12·32	11·92	11·38	11·86	13·00
10-year government securities(2)	13·61	12·02	12·12	12·93	13·91	14·89
Ordinary shares, dividend yield(2)	6·10	5·52	5·54	5·78	6·32	5·89
Interbank 3-month deposits	14·38	6·64	12·54	17·00	14·81	15·66
Clearing bank 7-day deposits	11·00	4·00	10·00	15·00	11·75	12·38

(1) Gross redemption yields, unless stated otherwise. For building society rates see Table 15. (2) Revised series.

13. Companies

(£ million)						
Total income	21,413	25,018	28,450	37,354	36,218	..
Gross trading profit in UK	12,248	17,424	20,588	22,459	23,080	..
Total overseas income	3,401	3,419	3,647	4,951	4,803	..
Dividends on ord. and pref. shares	1,825	2,242	2,706	3,604	3,918	..
Net profit	12,812	13,934	14,708	8,968	..	..
Companies taken over (number)	353	481	567	534	469	452
Total take-over consideration	448	824	1,140	1,656	1,475	1,144
Liquidations (number)(1)	5,939	5,831	5,080	4,537	6,891	8,607
Receiverships (number)(1)	7,207	4,485	3,902	3,500	4,038	5,178

(1) England and Wales.

14. The Stock Market

(£ million, unless otherwise stated)						
Turnover (£000 mn.)	106·4	173·3	138·8	168·9	196·3	190·7
ordinary shares (£000 mn.)	14·2	20·2	19·2	24·1	30·8	32·4
New issues, less redemptions (value)	1,114·3	926·2	819·7	738·4	773·2	1,970
Government securities	5,927	10,004	4,888	10,525	11,245	6,930
Local authority issues(1)	107·8	239·0	48·0	-170·0	-166	-157
UK companies (gross)	1,080·3	730·1	833·7	932·4	933	1,832
FT ordinary share index (1935 = 100)(2)	368·0	452·3	479·4	475·5	464·5	517·9
FT-Actuaries index (750 shares)(3)	153·04	191·91	216·68	245·52	271·32	307·7
Industrial, 500 shares	162·91	208·79	237·80	267·31	285·68	222·2
Financial, 100 shares	124·18	145·68	165·99	188·36	218·81	253·2

(1) Includes public corporation issues. (2) Average during year. (3) (1962 = 100)

Overall price index (1975 = 100)	113·9	127·9	142·6	161·6	190·7	212·0

15. Building Societies

	1976	1977	1978	1979	1980	1981
(Condition at end of financial year ended in year indicated, unless otherwise stated)						
Interest rates (%):						
Paid on shares, ave. actual	7·02	6·98	6·46	8·45	10·37	..
BSA(1) recommended, end-year	7·80	6·00	8·00	10·50	9·25	9·75
Paid on deposits, ave. actual	6·61	6·13	5·65	7·67	9·75	..
BSA recommended, end-year	7·55	5·75	7·75	10·25	9·00	9·50
Mortgages, ave. charged	11·06	11·05	9·55	11·94	14·94	..
BSA recommended, end-year	12·25	9·50	11·75	15·00	14·00	15·00
Shares and deposits, net (£ mn.)	3,405	6,099	4,822	5,769	7,159	7,060
Mortgage advances, net (£ mn).	3,618	4,100	5,115	5,271	5,722	6,207

(1) BSA: Building Societies Association.

16. Insurance(1)

(£ million)	1976	1977	1978	1979	1980	1981
Life assurance(1)(2), net premiums	3,825	4,713	5,525	6,420	7,599	..
investment income	2,230	2,620	3,070	3,800	4,297	..
benefits paid to policyholders	2,560	2,680	2,900	3,340	4,130	..
life funds, end-year	24,487	34,256	38,371	42,990	54,018	..
Non-life(1)(2), net premiums	6,114	6,600	7,071	7,618	8,281	..
underwriting profit/(—)loss(3)	− 150·5	− 52·5	− 27·0	− 216·4	− 338·8	..

(1) Companies only; excludes Lloyd's. (2) World-wide business of UK companies and authorized UK affiliates of foreign companies. (3) Including net transfers of marine, aviation and transit branch revenues to/from profit and loss accounts.

17. Money and Savings

(£ million, amounts outstanding at end period, unless otherwise stated)	1976	1977	1978	1979	1980	1981
Money stock M_1(1)	19,150	23,330	27,020	29,460	30,520	33,530
Money stock M_3(2)	44,540	48,940	56,350	63,270	74,870	88,920
Sterling M_3	40,570	44,660	51,310	57,830	68,530	78,350
Notes and coins in circulation	6,714	7,699	8,904	9,701	10,411	11,027
Domestic credit expansion	7,464	1,084	7,917	10,261	15,556	..
Personal savings ratio (%)(3)	11·6	10·8	13·0	14·7	15·8	..
National savings	8,418	9,707	11,233	10,733	12,110	..

(1) M_1 = Notes and coins in circulation with the public plus resident private sector sterling current accounts with the banks minus 60 per cent of transit items. (2) M_3 = notes and coins in circulation plus total deposits of the domestic sector. (3) Personal savings as a percentage of personal disposable income.

	1976	1977	1978	1979	1980	1981
Overall price index (1975 = 100)	*113·9*	*127·9*	*142·6*	*161·6*	*190·7*	*212·0*

PRODUCTION

18. Industrial products and manufactures, output

	1976	1977	1978	1979	1980	1981
Crude steel (million tonnes)	22·3	20·4	20·3	21·5	11·3	15·7
Man-made fibres (million tonnes)	0·62	0·55	0·61	0·60	0·50	0·40
Cars ('000)	1,334	1,316	1,223	1,070	924	953
Motor vehicles, cars imported ('000)(1)	488	1,347	807	1,021	858	827
Commercial vehicles ('000)	372	398	384	408	389	230
Merchant ships(2) completed ('000 gr.t)	1,460	1,007	1,135	707	431	216
Aircraft delivered (number)	342	353	261	179	..	..

(1) Including imported chassis. (2) 100 gross tons and over.

19. Industrial Production

(Index, average 1975 = 100, seasonally adjusted)

	1976	1977	1978	1979	1980	1981
All industries	102·0	105·9	109·8	112·6	105·3	99·6
Mining and quarrying	126·1	188·4	233·1	295·7	301·3	319·7
Coal mining	92·7	90·1	89·2	89·3	91·9	..
Manufacturing industries	101·4	102·9	103·9	104·4	95·3	89·3
Food, drink and tobacco	102·5	104·0	106·2	107·6	106·6	103·9
Chemicals	112·0	115·9	117·0	119·3	109·9	108·6
Oil and coal products	105·7	102·7	101·4	105·3	93·3	85·5
Metal manufacture	104·9	104·4	103·4	104·6	74·7	78·6
Engineering and allied	97·6	99·2	99·5	99·1	93·2	85·4
Textiles	100·8	101·6	101·3	100·0	84·1	75·6
Bricks, pottery, glass	100·6	99·6	101·4	100·9	90·8	81·6
Timber, furniture, etc.	103·3	96·8	101·3	102·8	88·8	79·5
Paper, printing, publishing	102·4	106·7	109·1	112·3	105·5	100·7
Construction	98·6	98·2	104·9	101·3	95·9	84·1
Gas, electricity, water	102·3	106·4	109·7	116·1	113·0	112·4

20. Productivity

(Index of output per head 1975 = 100)

	1976	1977	1978	1979	1980	1981
All production industries(1)	103·7	105·5	107·9	108·8	105·5	108·1
Manufacturing	105·3	107·0	108·1	109·7	105·6	110·1
Mining and quarrying(1)	94·9	92·8	94·3	96·8	97·8	..
Metal manufacture	111·7	108·1	110·8	118·3	91·7	..
Engineering	101·4	102·9	102·2	102·7	102·0	..
Textiles	104·9	107·0	109·3	109·8	100·4	..
Gas, electricity, water	102·5	108·8	113·3	118·5	115·3	..

(1) Excluding extraction of mineral oil and natural gas

21. Agriculture

(Production, '000 tonnes, unless otherwise stated)

	1976	1977	1978	1979	1980	1981
Wheat	4,740	5,274	6,610	7,170	8,470	8,410
Barley	7,648	10,531	9,850	9,620	10,320	10,320
Sugar, refined from UK beet	605	900	984	1,138	1,238	1,061
Beef and veal	1,202	1,002	1,027	1,048	1,102	1,031
Mutton and lamb	254	223	228	232	227	258
Pork	566	650	634	696	682	712
Milk, disposals (million litres)	13,128	14,400	15,096	15,120	15,180	15,084

22. Energy

	1976	1977	1978	1979	1980	1981
Coal, production (mn. tonnes)	123·8	122·1	123·6	122·4	130·1	127·5
Power station consumption (mn. tons)	77·8	79·9	80·7	88·8	89·5	87·4
Power stations' demand for oil (million tonnes coal equivalent)	17·2	18·2	19·2	18·2	11·4	8·32
Electricity generated ('000 mn. kwh.)	254·8	262·1	266·8	279·8	266·2	259·5
by nuclear plant ('000 mn. kwh.)	32·2	40·0	33·3	34·8	33·3	33·8
Natural gas sent out (mn. therms)	14,217	15,252	15,813	17,295	17,066	17,103
Crude oil output ('000 tonnes)(1)	11,678	37,884	53,376	77,796	80,472	89,388
Oil refinery output (mn. tonnes)(2)	90·3	86·3	89·2	90·6	79·2	71·6

(1) Including natural gas liquids. (2) All fuels and other petroleum products.

LABOUR

23. Employment

(millions of persons, in June each year)

	1976	1977	1978	1979	1980	1981
Working population(1)	25·52	25·68	25·77	25·80	25·70	25·44
Employed labour force(2)	24·20	24·26	24·36	24·49	24·10	22·83
Employees: production industries	9·08	9·09	9·04	8·99	8·60	7·71
Manufacturing	7·13	7·17	7·14	7·06	6·70	5·94
Transport and Communications(3)	1·45	1·45	1·46	1·47	1·48	1·42
Distributive Trades	2·67	2·70	2·72	2·77	2·73	2·58
Professional and Scientific	3·56	3·55	3·58	3·62	3·61	3·59
Insurance, Banking, financial	1·09	1·13	1·18	1·21	1·24	1·21
Public service(3)	1·58	1·56	1·55	1·57	1·54	1·53
Total employees	22·04	22·11	22·24	22·38	21·98	20·70
of whom, females	8·94	9·04	9·14	9·30	9·16	8·70

(1) Including registered unemployed and members of the armed services. (2) Including employers and self-employed. (3) Excludes employees of nationalized industries but includes British Rail and Post Office.

24. Demand for Labour

Average weekly hours worked, manu- facturing industry, men over 21(1)	43·6	43·6	43·5	43·2	41·9	
Manufacturing employees:						
Total overtime hours worked ('000)(2)	14,000	15,570	15,450	14,820	11,520	9,190
Short time, total hours lost ('000)(2)	966	856	552	767	3,916	4,174
Unemployed, excl. school-leavers, adult students (monthly ave. '000)(3)	1,358·8	1,378·2	1,375·7	1,307·3	1,667·6	2,565·8
Percentage of all employees	5·3	5·7	5·7	5·4	6·8	10·5
Unfilled vacancies, end-year ('000)	163·1	170·3	235·8	219·4	98·8	107·5

(1) October. (2) Great Britain. (3) Seasonally adjusted.

25. Industrial Disputes

Stoppages (number)(1)(2)	2,016	2,703	2,471	2,080	1,330	1,280
Known official stoppages (number)	69	79	90	82	67	
Workers involved ('000)(3)	666	1,155	1,001	4,583	830	1,437
in official stoppages ('000)	46	205	123	3,648	404	
Work days lost ('000), all inds., services	3,284	10,142	9,405	29,474	11,964	4,196

(1) Excluding protest action of a political nature, and stoppages involving fewer than 10 workers and/or lasting less than one day except where the working days lost exceeded 100. (2) Stoppages beginning in year stated. (3) Directly and indirectly, where stoppages occurred; lay-offs elsewhere in consequence are excluded.

26. Wages and Earnings

Average earnings index (Jan. 1976 = 100).						
Whole economy	106·0	115·6	130·6	150·9	182·1	205·5
Manufacturing	106·2	117·1	134·0	154·9	182·5	206·5
Average weekly earnings (1)(2)						
Men						
Manual	65·1	71·5	80·7	93·0	111·7	121·9
Non manual	81·6	88·9	100·7	113·0	141·3	163·1
All occupations	71·8	78·6	89·1	101·4	124·5	140·5
Women						
Manual	39·4	43·7	49·4	55·2	68·0	74·5
Non manual	48·8	53·8	59·1	66·0	82·7	96·7
All occupations	46·2	51·0	56·4	63·0	78·8	91·4
Average hours (3)	41·1	41·3	41·4	41·5	41·1	40·3

(1) In all industries and services, full-time. (2) April. (3) All industries and services, all occupations, men and women over 18 years.

Overall price index (1975 = 100)	*113·9*	*127·9*	*142·6*	*161·6*	*190·7*	*212·0*

TRADE
27. Trade by Areas and Main Trading Partners

(£ million; exports f.o.b.; imports c.i.f.)	1976	1977	1978	1979	1980	1981
All countries: *exports*	25,909	33,331	37,363	42,802	49,511	..
imports	31,170	36,978	40,969	48,424	51,650	..
E.E.C.: *exports*	9,197	12,152	14,103	17,876	20,825	..
imports	11,386	14,171	16,584	20,874	20,802	..
Other Western Europe: *exports*	4,287	5,606	5,710	7,017	8,129	..
imports	4,579	5,576	6,991	8,100	8,162	..
North America: *exports*	3,137	3,821	4,245	4,837	5,450	..
imports	4,225	4,948	5,341	6,207	7,489	..
Other developed countries: *exports*	1,967	2,110	2,334	2,477	2,665	..
imports	2,119	2,698	2,834	2,912	3,367	..
Oil exporting countries: *exports*	3,144	4,374	4,767	3,793	4,937	..
imports	4,207	3,800	3,470	3,385	4,349	..
Other developing countries: *exports*	3,381	4,261	5,033	5,473	5,293	..
imports	3,514	4,362	4,385	5,319	4,418	..
Centrally planned economies: *exports*	730	911	1,070	1,186	1,317	..
imports	1,110	1,371	1,300	1,533	1,435	..

28. Terms of Trade
(index 1975 = 100)

	1976	1977	1978	1979	1980	1981
Volume of exports(1)	109·7	118·9	121·5	125·6	127·8	..
manufactures	109·0	117·0	116·0	116·0	117·0	..
Volume of imports(1)	105·6	107·3	112·8	425·6	119·0	..
food	102·0	102·0	101·0	103·0	96·0	..
fuels	102·0	83·0	80·0	78·0	66·0	..
Unit value of exports(2)	120·9	142·6	155·4	171·8	192·9	..
manufactures	121·0	143·0	157·0	171·0	191·0	..
Unit value of imports(2)	121·8	141·3	146·5	161·9	185·9	..
food(3)	113·0	132·0	142·0	145·0	151·0	..
fuels(3)	131·0	148·0	139·0	175·0	248·0	..
Terms of trade(4)	99·2	100·8	105·6	106·1	103·8	..

(1) Seasonally adjusted; f.o.b. (2) Not seasonally adjusted. (3) c.i.f. (4) Export unit value index as percentage of import unit value index, expressed as an index on the same base.

29. Balance of Payments
(£ million: current transactions seasonally adjusted; remaining data unadjusted)

	1976	1977	1978	1979	1980	1981
Exports (f.o.b.)	25,424	32,184	35,070	40,687	47,376	..
Imports (f.o.b.)	29,013	33,891	36,643	44,184	46,199	..
Visible balance	− 3,589	− 1,709	− 1,573	− 3,497	− 11,177	..
Invisible balance	2,452	2,115	+ 2,280	+ 1,867	+ 1,560	..
Current balance	− 1,137	406	+ 707	− 1,630	+ 2,737	..
Current balance (unadjusted)	− 1,137	406	+ 707	− 1,630	+ 2,737	..
Capital transfers(2)	—	—	− 1,839	− 2,306	− 2,107	..
Official long-term capital	− 158	− 291	− 336	− 384	− 56	..
Overseas investment in						
UK public sector	203	2,182	− 99	+ 882	+ 413	..
UK private sector	2,063	3,096	+ 2,640	+ 2,849	+ 2,564	..
UK private investment overseas	− 2,156	− 2,167	− 4,414	− 6,573	− 6,870	..
Longer-term data (£ million)						
Current surplus (+)/deficit (−)	− 1,060	− 206	+ 707	− 1,630	+ 2,737	..
Overall surplus (+)/deficit (−)	− 3,927	− 2,278	− 1,573	− 3,497	+ 1,177	..
Official reserves, end of year	2,426	10,715	7,689	10,129	11,487	..
Foreign liabilities(2), net, do.	8,320	9,404	7,765	6,555	5,012	..
Overall price index (1975 = 100)	*113·9*	*127·9*	*142·6*	*161·6*	*190·7*	*212·0*

B. THE UNITED STATES

30. Population	1976	1977	1978	1979	1980	1981
Population, mid-year est. (mn.)	214·12	216·82	218·72	220·58	227·64	229·81
Crude birth rate (per 1,000 pop.)	14·7	15·3	15·3	15·8	16·2	..
Crude death rate (per 1,000 pop.)	9·0	8·8	8·8	8·7	8·9	..

31. Gross National Product
('000 million current dollars)

Gross national product	1,718	1,918	2,156	2,413	2,626	2,922
Personal consumption	1,084	1,205	1,349	1,511	1,672	1,858
Gross private domestic investment	258	322	375	416	395	451
Net exports, goods and services	13·8	−4·2	−0·6	13·4	24·2	25·0
Government purchases	362·1	394·5	432·6	473·8	534·6	591·3

32. Government Finance
('000 million dollars, seasonally adjusted)

Federal government receipts	331·4	375·1	431·5	494·4	540·8	625,·6
from personal taxes(1)	146·8	170·1	194·9	231·4	257·8	296·2
Federal government expenditure	385·2	421·5	460·7	509·2	601·6	688·3
Defence purchases	86·8	94·3	103·0	115·0	132·8	154·4
Grants to state/local govts.	67·1	67·5	77·3	80·4	88·1	87·2
Federal surplus or (−) deficit	−53·6	−46·4	−29·2	−14·8	−61·2	−62·2
State and local govt. receipts	264·7	296·2	327·7	351·2	384·1	417·8
from indirect business tax(1)	127·1	140·0	150·3	159·0	171·7	189·9
State and local govt. expenditure	246·2	266·6	299·8	324·5	355·0	380·4

(1) Includes related non-tax receipts on national income account.

33. Balance of Payments
(millions of dollars)

Merchandise trade balance	−9,306	−30,873	−33,759	−27,346	−25,342	−27,843
Balance on current account(1)	+4,383	−14,110	−14,078	+1,412	+3,725	..
Change in US private assets abroad(2)	−43,865	−31,725	−57,279	−56,858	−71,456	..
Change in foreign private assets in US(2)	18,897	14,167	30,804	51,845	34,769	..

(1) Includes balance on services and remittances and US government grants other than military. (2) Includes reinvested earnings of incorporated affiliates.

34. Merchandise Trade by Main Areas
(millions of dollars)

All countries: *exports* (f.o.b.)	106,157	113,323	143,662	181,802	220,705	..
imports (c.i.f.)	192,984	128,872	171,978	206,327	241,195	..
Western Europe: *exports*	30,874	35,901	43,608	53,617	66,817	..
imports	21,200	23,640	37,985	43,548	46,352	..
Canada: *exports*	21,744	24,106	28,374	33,096	35,395	..
imports	21,747	26,238	33,525	38,099	41,024	..
Latin America/other western hemisphere:						
exports	15,670	15,487	20,185	26,257	36,030	..
imports	16,840	13,228	18,556	24,782	29,916	..
Japan: *exports*	9,563	10,144	12,885	17,579	20,790	..
imports	11,268	15,504	24,458	26,243	30,866	..
Dollar purchasing power (1967 = 100)	*58·7*	*55·1*	*51·2*	*46·0*	*40·6*	*36·7*

35. Merchandise Trade by Main Commodity Groups

(millions of dollars)	1976	1977	1978	1979	1980	1981
Exports:						
Machinery and transport equipt.	49,501	50,248	59,255	70,404	84,553	..
Motor vehicles and parts	10,949	11,796	13,237	15,077	14,590	..
Electrical machinery	9,278	10,285	6,967	8,635	10,485	..
Food and live animals	15,710	14,116	18,311	22,245	27,744	..
Chemicals and pharmaceuticals	9,959	10,812	12,618	17,308	20,740	..
Imports:						
Machinery and transport equipt.	29,824	36,407	47,590	53,678	60,546	..
Motor vehicles and parts	13,104	15,842	20,631	22,074	24,134	..
Food and live animals	10,267	12,538	13,522	15,171	15,763	..
Petroleum and products	31,798	41,526	39,104	56,046	73,771	..
Iron and steel	4,347	5,804	7,259	7,466	7,364	..

36. Interest Rates

(per cent per annum, annual averages, unless otherwise stated)

	1976	1977	1978	1979	1980	1981
Federal Funds rate (1)	5·05	5·54	7·93	11·19	13·36	16·38
Treasury bill rate	4·99	5·27	7·22	10·04	11·51	14·02
Government bond yields: 3-5 years	6·94	6·85	8·30	9·58	11·51	14·34
Long-term (10 years or more)	6·78	7·06	7·89	8·74	10·81	12·87
Banks' prime lending rate(2)	6·84	6·84	9·06	12·67	15·27	18·87

(1) Effective rate. (2) Predominant rate charged by commercial banks on short-term loans to large business borrowers with the highest credit rating.

37. Banking, money and credit

('000 million dollars, outstanding at end of year, seasonally adjusted)

	1976	1977	1978	1979	1980	1981
Money supply M1-A(2)	305·0	328·4	351·6	369·7	387·7	364·4
Money supply M1-B(3)	307·7	332·5	359·9	386·4	414·5	440·9
Money supply M₃(1)	1,299·7	1,460·3	1,623·6	1,775·5	1,963	2,188
Currency	80·7	88·7	97·6	106·3	116·4	123·1
Deposits of commercial banks	844·3	941·4	1,009·9	1,073·2	1,239·9	1,288·4
Advances of commercial banks	576·0	632·1	747·8	849·9	915·1	975·0
Instalment credit	211·0	254·1	273·6	312·0	313·4	..
Motor vehicle contracts	66·1	82·9	101·6	116·4	116·3	..
Mortgage debt	889·2	1,023	1,169	1,327	1,452	..

(1) Demand deposits at banks, currency in circulation, deposits at mutual savings banks, and savings capital of savings and loan associations. (2) Currency plus demand deposits. (3) M1-A plus other checkable deposits.

38. Insurance

($million, unless otherwise stated)

	1976	1977	1978	1979	1980	1981
Property-liability, net premiums written	60,813	72,397	81,690	90,122	95,600	..
Automobile(1)	25,255	30,700	33,218	36,640	39,153	..
Underwriting gain/(−) loss(2)	−2,189	1,111	−1,296	−1,301	−3,300	..
Combined ratio(2)	102·4	97·1	000·0	000·0	..	..
Automobile(1)	103·9	95·6	000·0	000·0	..	..
General liability(3)	107·9	95·1	000·0	000·0	..	..
Life insurance, total assets, end-year	321,552	350,506	389,92	432,28	479·21	..

(1) Physical damage and liability, private and commercial. (2) After stockholder and policy-holder dividends and premium rebates. (3) Sum of ratios of losses and loss expenses to earned premiums, and underwriting expenses to written premiums.

	1976	1977	1978	1979	1980	1981
Dollar purchasing power (1967 = 100)	58·7	55·1	51·2	46·0	40·6	36·7

39. Companies(1)
('000 million dollars)

	1976	1977	1978	1979	1980	1981
Net profit after taxes	102·5	120·0	140·3	167·8	163·2	155·3
Cash dividends paid	37·4	39·9	44·6	50·2	56·0	63·1

(1) Manufacturing corporations, all industries.

40. The Stock Market
(millions of dollars, unless otherwise stated)

	1976	1977	1978	1979	1980	1981
Turnover (sales), all exchanges	194,969	187,203	249,257	299,973	475,934	..
New York Stock Exchange	164,545	157,250	210,426	251,098	397,670	..
Securities issued, gross proceeds	113,297	120,027	120,399	120,808	..	..
Corporate common stock	8,304	8,034	7,937	8,709	18,881	..
Stock prices (end-year):						
Combined index (500 stocks)(1)	107·46	95·10	96·11	107·94	135·76	122·55
Industrials (30 stocks)(2)	1004·65	831·17	805·01	838·74	963·99	875·00

(1) Standard and Poor Composite 1941-43 = 10. (2) Dow-Jones Industrial (Oct. 1928 = 100).

41. Employment
('000 persons)

	1976	1977	1978	1979	1980	1981
Civilian labour force(1)	94,773	97,401	100,420	102,908	104,719	108,691
in non-agricultural industry	84,188	87,302	91,031	93,648	93,960	97,033
in manufacturing industry	18,958	19,682	20,476	21,062	20,363	20,262
in agriculture	3,297	3,244	3,342	3,297	3,310	3,368
unemployed	7,288	6,855	6,047	5,963	7,448	8,290
Industrial stoppages(2) (number)	5,600	5,590	4,200	4,800	4,500	..
Workers involved ('000)	2,508	2,296	1,600	1,700	1,500	..

(1) Aged 16 years and over. (2) Beginning in the year.

42. Earnings and Prices

	1976	1977	1978	1979	1980	1981
Average weekly earnings per worker						
(current dollars): mining	274·78	302·88	332·88	365·50	396·1	437·40
contract construction	284·56	295·73	318·69	342·99	367·78	395·60
manufacturing	208·12	226·90	249·27	268·94	288·62	317·60
Average weekly hours per worker						
in manufacturing	40·0	40·3	40·4	40·2	39·7	39·8
Farm prices received (1977 = 100)	102	100	115	132	134	138
Wholesale prices (1967 = 100)	182·9	194·2	209·3	235·6	268·8	293·4
Petroleum products	276·6	307·9	321·0	444·8	674·7	805·8
Consumer prices (1967 = 100)	170·5	181·5	195·3	217·4	246·8	272·4
Food	180·8	192·2	211·4	234·5	254·6	274·6

(1) Based on changes in retail price indexes.

	1976	1977	1978	1979	1980	1981
Dollar purchasing power (1967 = 100)(1)	58·7	55·1	51·2	46·1	40·6	36·7

43. Production

	1976	1977	1978	1979	1980	1981
Farm production (1967 = 100)	113	116	000	000		
Industrial production (1967 = 100)	129·8	138·2	146·1	152·5	147·0	151·0
Manufacturing	129·5	138·4	146·8	153·6	146·7	150·4
Output of main products and manufactures						
Coal (million tons)	665·0	670·1	671·3	781·1	829·7	..
Oil, indigenous (million tons)	443·7	472·9	550·8	545·7	..	..
Oil refinery throughput (mn. tons)	656	618	616	612	..	..
Natural gas (million cubic metres)	559·9	630·0	637·0	646·8	..	..
Electricity generated ('000 mn. kwh)	2,108	1,926	2,204	2,247	2,286	..
Steel, crude (million tonnes)	116·3	124·9	137·0	136·0	111·8	120·0
Aluminium ('000 tonnes)	4,984	5,166	4,804	5,023	5,130	..
Cotton yarn ('000 tonnes)	1,676	1,939	2,605	3,422	..	..
Man-made fibres (million lbs.)	7,317	8,201	9,526	1,029	..	..
Plastics/resins ('000 tonnes)	9,785	1,124	1,410	1,356	..	..
Motor cars, factory sales ('000)	8,497	11,040	9,165	8,419	6,400	..

C. INTERNATIONAL COMPARISONS

44. Population and GDP, Selected Countries	Area '000 sq. km.	Population (millions), mid-year estimate		Gross Domestic Product (1) US$ mns (2)	
		1979	1980	1979	1980
Argentina	2,777	26·73	27·06	..	..
Australia (3)	7,695	14·42	14·62	121,404	140,159
Belgium	31	9·85	9·86	111,225	119,104
Canada	9,976	23·69	23·94	228,530	253,528
China	9,561	970·9	982·6	215,434	242,258
Denmark	34	5·12	5·12	65,752	66,378
France	552	53·48	53·71	573,369	651,893
Germany, Western (incl. W. Berlin)	248	61·34	61·56	760,489	819,112
India (incl. India-admin. Kashmir)	3,268	650·98	663·60	120,236	138,047
Irish Republic	69	3·36	3·40	14,814	17,337
Israel (excl. occupied areas)	21	3·78	3·87	17,549	20,196
Italy	301	56·91	57·04	324,552	393,954
Japan	370	115·87	116·78	999,626	1,036,163
Kuwait (4)	18	1·27	1·36	23,111	..
Netherlands	34	14·03	14·14	149,058	160,153
New Zealand (4)	104	3·10	3·10	21,387	23,281
Norway	324	4·07	4·09	46,747	57,295
Portugal	92	9·84	9·93	20,096	24,076
Saudi Arabia	2,150	8·11	8·37	74,250	116,194
South Africa (incl. S.W. Africa)	1,221	28·48	29·29	56,532	79,974
Spain	505	37·18	37·43	196,976	..
Sweden	450	8·29	8·31	101,491	123,681
Switzerland	41	6·36	6·37	95,327	101,499
Turkey	781	44·24	44·92	70,209	57,696
USSR	22,402	263·42	265·54	..	..
UK	244	55·88	55·95	403,974	519,695
USA	9,363	225·06	227·66	2,370,100	2,576,500

(1) Expenditure basis. (2) Converted from national currencies at mid-year exchange rates. (3) Years beginning 1 July. (4) Years beginning 1 April.

45. Central Bank Discount Rates (per cent per annum, end of year)	1976	1977	1978	1979	1980	1981
Belgium	9·00	9·00	6·00	10·50	12·00	15·00
Canada	8·50	7·50	10·75	14·00	17·26	14·66
France	10·50	9·50	9·50	9·50	9·50	9·50
Germany, West	3·50	3·00	3·00	6·00	7·50	7·50
Italy	15·00	11·50	10·50	15·00	16·50	19·00
Japan	6·50	4·25	3·50	6·25	7·25	5·50
Sweden	8·00	8·00	6·50	9·00	10·00	11·00
Switzerland	2·00	1·50	1·00	2·00	3·00	6·00
UK	14·25	7·00	12·50	17·00	14·00	
USA(1)	5·25	6·00	9·50	12·00	13·00	12·00

(1) Federal Reserve Bank of New York.

46. World Trade(1)

(millions of US dollars. Exports f.o.b.; imports c.i.f.)

	1976	1977	1978	1979	1980	1981
World(1): exports	907,000	1,030,500	1,191,500	1,508,100	1,865·8	..
imports	923,200	1,059,000	1,233,600	1,546,200	1,920·8	..
Industrial Countries: *exports*	598,040	678,639	813,871	1,056,900	1,243·9	..
imports	633,182	720,501	839,224	1,141,900	1,369·1	..
USA: *exports*	114,997	121,212	143,659	181,802	220,706	233,739
imports	129,565	157,560	183,137	218,927	252,997	273,352
Germany, West: *exports*	101,977	118,091	142,295	171,887	192,861	176,091
imports	88,209	101,475	121,820	159,711	188,002	163,912
Japan: *exports*	67,167	81,126	98,415	102,299	130,435	..
imports	64,748	71,328	79,900	109,831	141,291	..
France: *exports*	57,162	64,997	79,205	100,691	116,016	..
imports	64,391	70,497	80,909	107,008	134,874	..
UK: *exports*	46,300	58,165	71,711	91,016	115,137	..
imports	55,981	64,551	78,592	102,949	119,910	..
Other Europe: *exports*	35,160	41,987	48,718	26,880	33,830	..
imports	56,890	66,744	70,331	47,910	58,600	..
Australia, NZ, S. Afr: *exports*	23,800	26,537	30,946	41,769	53,132	..
imports	22,830	23,305	26,828	31,723	47,200	..
Less Developed Areas: *exports*	246,370	312,100	330,400	341,506	346,640	..
imports	210,870	292,900	342,900	357,031	377,069	..
Oil exporters: *exports*	130,500	145,304	141,400	207,740	293,530	..
imports	66,600	83,105	37,834	101,620	133,380	..
Saudi Arabia: *exports*	35,622	41,164	37,935	57,616	102,503	..
imports	11,759	14,656	19,068	24,021	30,171	..
Other W. Hemisphere: *exports*	38,290	45,068	49,550	64,370	85,720	..
imports	50,312	52,392	59,270	79,270	107,680	..
Other Middle East(2): *exports*	8,030	9,022	9,877	11,930	15,980	..
imports	17,660	20,516	23,990	24,780	29,520	..
Other Asia: *exports*	52,550	62,891	76,240	96,900	120,320	..
imports	57,660	69,561	87,907	117,460	150,420	..
Other Africa: *exports*	15,180	20,078	28,473	41,500	52,460	..
imports	18,500	24,608	32,205	37,080	54,990	..

(1) Excluding trade of centrally planned countries (see Table 47). (2) Including Egypt.
(3) Unweighted average of IMF series for US$ import and export prices in developed countries.

World trade prices (1970 = 100)(3)	216·1	235·3	258·7	284·5	336·0	..

47. World Trade of Centrally Planned Countries

(millions of US dollars)

European(1): *exports*	85,200	99,200	113,500	136,149	157,371	..
imports	96,700	105,900	118,372	134,278	154,159	..
USSR: *exports*	37,168	45,161	52,219	64,762	76,481	..
imports	38,109	40,817	50,546	57,744	68,523	..
China: *exports*	6,915	7,072	10,120	13,784	19,782	..
imports	5,975	5,744	10,316	14,379	19,416	..
Cuba: *exports*	3,684	3,571	3,537	4,456	..	..
imports	4,218	4,188	4,687	5,000	..	..

(1) Except Yugoslavia and Albania.

48. Defence Expenditure

	Expenditure or budget (US $ mn.)				$ per capita	% of GNP
	1978	1979	1980	1981	1981	1980
Egypt	..	2,168	..	..	..	..
France	17,518	18,776	20,220	26,008	483	3·9
Germany, East	4,238	4,762	4,790	6,960	415	6·1
Germany, West (incl. W. Berlin)	21,355	24,391	25,120	25,000	405	3·2
Greece	1,523	..	1,770	..	..	5·1
Iran	9,942	3,974	4,200	..	..	..
Israel	3,310	4,932	5,200	7,340	1,835	23·2
Japan	8,567	10,083	8,960	11,497	98	0·9
Portugal	568	587	890	944	94	3·8
Saudi Arabia	13,170	14,184	20,704	27,695	2,664	17·6
South Africa	2,622	2,118	2,556	..	..	..
Sweden	2,946	3,328	3,588	3,790	455	3·2
Turkey	2,286	2,591	2,921	3,106	67	4·2
USSR	..	..	..	..	..	12-14
UK	13,579	17,572	24,448	28,660	512	5·1
USA	113,000	114,503	142,700	171,023	759	5·5
World trade prices (1970 = 100)	258·7	284·5	336·0	..		

49. Industrial Ordinary Share Prices (Index 1975 = 100)	1976	1977	1978	1979	1980	1981
Amsterdam	95	86	86	76	66	71
Australia, all exchanges	124	119	135	166	248	258
Canada, all exchanges	104	93	101	147	200·1	195
Germany, West, all exchanges	106	105	110	106	101	102
Hong Kong (31 July 1968 = 100)(1)	444	387	496	879	1,580	1,406
Johannesburg	100	93	107	144	213	210
New York	100	112	110	119	139	149
Paris	99	79	104	133	152	128
Tokyo	112	121	133	144	152	177
UK	120	154	173	197	210	237

(1) Hang Seng index for Hong Kong Stock Exchange only: last trading day of year.

50. Exchange Rates
(middle rates for overseas settlements end of year, unless stated)

	Currency units per US dollar					per £
	1977	1978	1979	1980	1981	1981
Australia (Australian dollar)	0·8761	0·8692	0·9046	0·8469	0·8866	1·6940
Austria (schilling)	15·14	13·37	12·43	13·80	15·89	30·07
Belgium-Luxembourg (franc)	32·94	28·80	28·05	31·52	38·46	73·40
Canada (Canadian dollar)	1·0944	1·1860	1·1681	1·1947	1·1859	2·266
China (yuan)(1)	1·73	1·58	1·50	1·53	1·75	..
Denmark (krone)	5·778	5·085	5·365	6·015	7·325	13·94
France (franc)	4·705	4·180	4·020	4·516	5·748	10·88
Germany W. (Deutschemark)	2·105	1·828	1·732	1·959	2·255	4·29
Italy (lire)	871·60	829·75	804·0	930·5	1,200	2,292
Japan (yen)	240·00	194·60	239·70	203·0	219·90	419·5
Netherlands (guilder)	2·280	1·969	1·906	2·130	2·469	4·70
Norway (krone)	5·14	5·02	4·93	5·18	5·81	11·07
Portugal (escudo)	39·86	45·80	49·78	53·04	65·25	124·5
South Africa (rand)	0·8696	0·8696	0·8268	0·7461	0·9566	1·8285
Spain (peseta)	80·91	70·11	66·15	79·25	97·45	183·75
Sweden (krona)	4·670	4·296	4·147	4·373	5·571	10·54
Switzerland (franc)	2·000	1·615	1·580	1·761	1·796	3·435
USSR (rouble)(1)	0·734	0·659	0·654	0·667	0·753	1·357
UK (£)(2)	1·919	2·042	2·224	2·385	1·908	..

(1) Official fixed or basic parity rate. (2) US dollars per £.

51. Prices of Selected Commodities
(index 1975 = 100)

	1976	1977	1978	1979	1980	1981
Aluminium, (Canada)	102·5	131·7	152·5	178·4	217·0	..
Beef, Irish (London)	102·5	107·3	139·9	171·0	199·3	197·5
Copper, wirebars (London)	113·9	106·4	110·6	161·0	177·6	141·1
Cotton, Egyptian (L'pool)	105·5	115·3	107·1	118·1	118·6	117·5
Gold (London)	77·5	91·7	120·0	190·4	377·5	285·5
Newsprint, S. Quebec	107·3	113·9	118·9	130·7	156·0	166·9
Petroleum, Ras Tanura	107·4	115·7	118·5	158·3	267·4	303·2
Rice, Thai (Bangkok)	70·1	75·0	101·2	92·0	119·5	133·0
Rubber, Malay (Singapore)	137·6	144·7	174·4	224·3	252·1	..
Steel bars (W. Germany)	112·4	101·2	106·5	106·5	114·9	..
Soya beans, US (R'dam)	105·0	126·8	121·8	135·0	135·0	131·0
Sugar, f.o.b. (Caribbean)	57·0	39·9	38·6	47·6	140·9	83·3
Tin, spot (London)	111·5	157·5	187·4	225·5	245·5	..
Wheat, (Canada No. 2 CW)	81·9	63·3	74·0	95·2	106·0	..
Wool, greasy (Sydney)	108·6	124·5	128·8	139·5	165·7	..

52. Consumer Prices, Selected Countries
(index 1975 = 100)

	1976	1977	1978	1979	1980	1981
Argentina	543·2	1,499·6	4,131·4	10,721	21,524	44,012
Australia	113·5	127·4	137·6	150·1	165·4	..
France	109·2	119·6	130·6	144·8	164·1	186·0
Germany, West	104·5	108·6	111·4	115·6	122·0	129·2
India	92·2	100·0	102·5	109·0	121·5	..
Japan	109·3	118·1	122·6	127·0	137·2	143·9
South Africa	111·3	123·6	136·2	154·2	175·3	201·9
Sweden	110·3	122·9	135·1	144·9	164·7	184·7
UK	116·5	135·0	146·2	165·8	195·6	218·8
US	105·8	112·7	121·2	134·9	153·1	169·0

	1976	1977	1978	1979	1980	1981
World trade prices (1970 = 100)	*216·1*	*235·3*	*258·7*	*284·5*	*336·0*	..

53. World Production
(index 1975 = 100)

	1976	1977	1978	1979	1980	1981
Food (1)	104·1	108·1	111·9	115·3	..	..
Industrial production (2)	108·1	113·2	118·7	124·2	124·0	..
OECD	109·1	115·4	117·7	123	123	124
EEC (3)	107·8	109·7	111·4	118	117	115
France	109	111	113	118	118	..
Germany, West	109	111	112	117	117	116
Italy	112	114	114	121	128	125
UK	102	106	111	115	108	103
Japan	111	116	123	133	142·0	146
Sweden	99	94	92	98	98·0	94
USSR	105	111	116	120	124	..

(1) Excluding China. (2) Excluding China, USSR, Eastern Europe. (3) Community of ten.

XVIII DOCUMENTS AND REFERENCE

SOVIET-POLISH RELATIONS

Partial text of the communique issued after a meeting between President Brezhnev, Mr Stanislaw Kania (Prime Minister of Poland) and General Jaruzelski in the Crimea on 14 August 1981.

The situation (in Poland) remains very complex and difficult. The industrial output and national income are lowering, there are considerable shortcomings in supplies to the population.

All this is the consequence not only of past mistakes but also of various subversive actions of the forces hostile to socialism. These forces seek to aggravate the difficulties and use them against the Party and the people's power. Strikes and demonstrations that were held in the recent weeks, as well as numerous facts of anti-state and anti-Soviet propaganda, create a serious threat to the security of the state, its independence, and the vital interests of the Polish people.

In these conditions, the Polish United Workers' Party and the Government of the Polish People's Republic see their priority task in pooling all the patriotic forces for the sake of national salvation of the motherland, averting a profound crisis, establishing the normal functioning of the entire national economy, putting a barrier to the manifestations of anarchy with the aim of resolute struggle against the threat of counter-revolution. All this must ensure the development of socialist Poland and its strengthening as a firm link of the Socialist community of states and peoples.

In view of the difficult economic situation of the Polish People's Republic, the Soviet Union is giving it considerable material assistance. It has been decided at present to defer the payment of Poland's debts to the Soviet Union to the next five-year period, to supply additionally raw materials for light industry and certain consumer goods.

There are obvious attempts to interfere in the internal affairs of socialist states. This is the only way to view the recent resolution of the House of Representatives of the United States Congress concerning the domestic situation in Poland. The Soviet Union wholly supports the stand taken by the Polish People's Republic on this issue. These facts of interference in the affairs of other states introduce new complications into the present-day tense international situation.

MILITARY TAKEOVER IN POLAND

Text of the proclamation issued in Warsaw on 13 December 1981 by the Martial Council for National Redemption.

Poles, citizens of the Polish People's Republic.

The Martial Council of National Redemption is addressing you. Our country is threatened by mortal danger.

Anti-state, subversive activities of forces hostile to socialism have pushed the society to the brink of civil war. Anarchy, lawlessness and chaos are ruining the economy, render the country powerless, endanger the sovereignty and biological existence of the nation.

The already open preparations for a reactionary coup, the threat of terrorism, can lead to bloodshed.

The efforts of the Sejm of the Polish People's Republic, the Government and organs of the state administration have proved ineffective. Appeals for patriotic prudence and all acts of good will are ignored. Aggressiveness of the anti-socialist forces, often inspired and financially supported from abroad, hit out at the constitutional principles of the system, torpedo national agreement. The forces from under the banner of Solidarnosc (Solidarity), the independent and self-governed labour union, are deliberately boycotting the initiatives which can contribute to leading the country out of the crisis.

It is time to abandon the road of disaster, to prevent national destruction.

It is time for determined actions in the name of supreme necessity. The implementation of and respect for the decisions of the legal authorities and state organs, discipline, law and order must be immediately ensured.

Guided by the supreme national interest and the gravity of the historic moment, the Council of State, on the strength of Article 33, Item 2 of the Constitution of the Polish People's Republic has declared martial law on the territory of the entire country as of December 13, 1981.

The restrictions resulting from martial law are indispensable for the transitional period. This will be understood by anyone who wants to prevent the dismantling of the state and make it possible to continue the reform of the execution of authority and the economic system, who wants socialist renewal.

Fellow countrymen,

The Martial Council of National Redemption was constituted in the night of December 13, 1981. Its chairmanship was assumed by Army General Wojciech Jaruzelski.

Having the armed forces of the Polish People's Republic behind it, counting on the trust and support of all patriotic and progressive social forces, the Martial Council of National Redemption is determined to ensure internal peace and security of the country.

The council is a provisional organ which will act until the situation returns to normal. It is composed of senior officers of the Polish Army. It does not infringe upon the competence of and does not relieve any link of people's power of their duties. The task of the council will be to frustrate the attempt on the state, stabilize the situation, ensure and execute, within the law, the performance of efficient activities of the organs of administration and economic units.

The council declares the maintenance of our political-defensive alliances, and also the implementation of international agreements and obligations, concluded and adopted by the Government of the Polish People's Republic.

The council supports the creation of conditions for the development of socialist democracy. It will favour the realization of the economic reform according to the main assumptions adopted so far.

The council, having law and the good of the working people in mind, will combat with full severity, through proper organs, speculation, wastefulness, the enrichment of individuals at the cost of the society, will root out delinquency, disruption of public order and malicious shirking of work.

The Martial Council of National Redemption is acting through ministerial, voivodship, city and rural plenipotentiaries—commissars of the country's defence committee appointed on the basis of Article 15 of the Law on the General Duty to defend the Polish People's Republic of November 21, 1967.

The Martial Council of National Redemption appeals to all:

—Representative organs of state authorities to understand that the extraordinary situation renders impossible their normal functioning. The council will make every effort to bring about as soon as possible conditions allowing them to resume regular work.

—Legal political and social organizations to strenuously act in favour of stabilizing life in Poland. The authorities of these organizations become responsible for the duty of exacting from subordinate cells and members decisions contained in the statutes and official programmes of activity.

—Organs of state administration to timely and consistently implement tasks and ventures stemming from the state of emergency. Simultaneously, the council warns about the consequences of failing to fulfil the duties and reminds about the principle of personal responsibility. The issue of primary importance to everybody at present is the ensuring to the population basic supplies of food, means of health protection and the easing of the effects of winter.

The conditions of martial law entail the necessity to suspend the activity of trade unions. The council voices a conviction that they will be able to resume their statutory activity shortly in the interest of working people.

The Martial Council of National Redemption desires and intends to eliminate the danger of the fall of the state and its losing sovereignty, to step up the overcoming of the crisis and to ease the difficulties weighing down on the conditions of life of all the citizens.

Poland needs above all strenuous, productive work, a great and universal civic effort. Peace is indispensable. It is no time for animosities and disputes.

The society and the state can no longer tolerate the freedom of subverters, troublemakers and adventurists. They must be isolated until they are brought to reason.

Justice must be finally dispensed to people responsible for bringing the country to the state of August 1980, for misappropriation of social means. Before this act is fulfilled by appropriate organs these people should not enjoy freedom.

The various other punishable acts that have not been judged so far can and should in this critical situation be unconditionally forgiven and forgotten on the power of the abolition decree adopted by the council.

Persons guilty of acting against the interests of the socialist state and the interests of working people will from now on be punished with all the severity, with the help of all measures and powers stemming from the martial law.

The historic moment has come for the Polish nation and the last chance to make order in its own home with its own forces. This chance must not be wasted.

LIMITATION OF NUCLEAR ARMAMENTS

I. EXCHANGE OF LETTERS BETWEEN THE PRESIDENTS OF THE USA AND THE USSR

1. President Reagan to President Brezhnev

The full text of President Reagan's personal letter of 24 April 1981 to President Brezhnev has not been published. The following passage is an extract from the official text of a speech by the United States President to the National Press Club in Washington on 18 November 1981 in which he quoted parts of his letter. Upon this partial publication, Mr Brezhnev released the text of his reply.

Back in April while in the hospital I had, as you can readily understand, a lot of time for reflection. One day I decided to send a personal, hand-written letter to Soviet President Leonid Brezhnev reminding him that we had met about 10 years ago in San Clemente, California, as he and President Nixon were concluding a series of meetings that had brought hope to all the world. Never had peace and goodwill seemed closer at hand. I would like to read you a few paragraphs from that letter.

'Mr President: When we met I asked if you were aware that the hopes and aspirations of millions of people throughout the world were dependent on the decisions that would be reached in your meetings. You took my hand in both of yours and assured me that you were aware of that and that you were dedicated with all your heart and mind to fulfilling those hopes and dreams.'

I went on in my letter to say: 'The people of the world still share that hope. Indeed, the peoples of the world, despite differences in racial and ethnic origin, have very much in common. They want the dignity of having some control over their individual destiny. They want to work at the craft or trade of their own choosing and to be fairly rewarded. They want to raise their families in peace without harming anyone or suffering harm themselves. Government exists for their convenience, not the other way around. If they are incapable, as some would have us believe, of self-government, then where among them do we find any who are capable of governing others?

'Is it possible that we have permitted ideology—political and economic philosophies—and governmental policies to keep us from considering the very real, everyday problems of our peoples? Will the average Soviet family be better off or even aware that the Soviet Union has imposed a government of its own choice on the people of Afghanistan? Is life better for the people of Cuba because the Cuban military dictate who shall govern the people of Angola?

'It is often implied that such things have been made necessary because of territorial ambitions of the United States; that we have imperialistic designs and thus constitute a threat to your own security and that of the newly-emerging nations. There not only is no evidence to support such a charge, there is solid evidence that the United States, when it could have dominated the world with no risk to itself, made no effort whatsoever to do so. When World War II ended, the United States had the only undamaged industrial power in the world. Our military might was at its peak—and we alone had the ultimate weapon, the nuclear weapon, with the unquestioned ability to deliver it anywhere in the world. If we had sought world domination then, who could have opposed us?

'But the United States followed a different course—one unique in all the history of mankind. We used our power and wealth to rebuild the war-ravaged economies of the world, including those nations who had been our enemies. May I say there is absolutely no substance to charges that the United States is guilty of imperialism or attempts to impose its will on other countries by use of force.'

I concluded my letter by saying: 'Mr President, should we not be concerned with eliminating the obstacles which prevent our people—those you and I represent—from achieving their most cherished goals?'

2. President Brezhnev to President Reagan

The following text of President Brezhnev's reply, first released by the USSR embassy in the United States, appeared in Soviet News *on 24 November 1981.*

I have given careful thought to your personal letter to me and want to respond to it in the same personal and frank manner.

Just as you do, I recall our brief conversation at the reception given by President Richard Nixon at Casa Pacifica in June 1973. Today, as we did at that time, everyone in the Soviet leadership and I myself commit our hearts and minds to realizing the hopes and aspirations of all the peoples of the world for peace, a tranquil life and confidence in their future.

At the recent Congress of our Party it was with all emphasis stressed once again that not war preparations, which doom the people to senseless squandering of their material and spiritual wealth, but the preservation and consolidation of peace and, thereby, the implementation of the foremost right of every person—the right to live—that is the key to the future.

I noted that, recalling the year 1973, you indicated that peace and goodwill among men had never seemed closer at hand. And indeed, it was precisely in those years that our two countries took the path of reaching agreements which marked a radical turn for the better, not only in Soviet-American relations, but in the international situation as a whole. Those were the years when the USSR and the USA actively, and with some success, set about accomplishing the task of limiting arms, first of all strategic arms, when they started seeking common solutions to acute international problems, and when mutually-beneficial bilateral ties and cooperation between our countries in a variety of fields were developing fruitfully.

Why, then, did hitches begin to appear in that process? Why did it pause and even find itself set back? To answer this question correctly, one thing is necessary—to take an objective, unbiased look at the course of events.

And then, Mr President, we shall recall that even at that time, when Soviet-American relations were developing for the better, the voices resounded in the USA of those who did not like such a development and who stubbornly tried to slow down and disrupt this process. And later on their efforts became even more active. Those were the efforts that were pulling back to confrontation, efforts embodied in quite a number of concrete steps aimed directly against the improvement of relations between the USSR and the USA, against the relaxation of international tension. On the other hand, nothing of the sort was taking place in the Soviet Union.

We have differences of opinion between us of a philosophical and ideological nature, and it could not be otherwise. But when it comes to the events of international life, whether pertaining to the present day, or to the recent or more distant past, then an objective approach is not only possible, but necessary. Otherwise it is easy to take a wrong step and plunge into serious errors.

Here, for example, it is said in your letter that after the Second World War the USA had the capability to dominate the world but, deliberately, as it were, made no use of that capability. Let me say straight away: it is hard to find many people among those who are familiar with that time through their own experience or who have seriously studied it, who would share such an affirmation.

Actually, the USA did the most it could, using a wide array of military, political and economic means, to achieve what American leaders themselves called the *Pax Americana,* in other words, to restructure the world in the way the USA wanted it to be. But this proved to be beyond its possibilities—and this is the way it was. Even the possession during a certain period of time of what you call 'the ultimate weapon' did not make the USA omnipotent.

To follow your logic we, in our turn, could have said that after the defeat of Hitler's Germany and, incidentally, even before the American atom bomb emerged, the Soviet Union was in a position to do much of what it did not do, being guided by its principled convictions, remaining true to its word and respecting its commitments as an ally. However, I would not like to go deeper into this subject now and to discuss events that did not take place.

You are saying that the policy of the USA has never constituted a threat to anyone else's security. Let us go back to the facts again. Hardly three years had passed after the end of the war when the USA set about creating Nato—a closed military bloc. One must wonder what the need for that was. After all, fascist Germany had been routed and militarist Japan destroyed. The keys to peace were in the hands of the allied powers of the anti-Hitler coalition. Who was the target of the Nato military bloc and the numerous overseas American bases? No secret was ever made in the USA of whom that was directed against.

You made mention of the postwar American economic assistance programmes. The USA really did give assistance. But who was the recipient? It was only those countries which chose to submit their policy to foreign interests. On the other hand, the states belonging to a different social system and the peoples which did not agree to submit their policy to outside *diktat* did not receive American assistance. That is how matters stood. In essence, that is precisely how they stand at the present time.

If we are to take the most recent years, when after a period of improvement the relations between our countries began to deteriorate, and deteriorate sharply, it is known that the lion's share was contributed to this by the Carter Administration. That was done consciously and purposefully, but in the final analysis, let us be frank, it brought no laurels to Carter. Isn't that so, Mr President?

However, for some reason or other, the new US Administration too, has decided to continue on the same path. Try, Mr President, to see what is going on before our eyes. Attempts are being made to revitalize the US-made military and political alliances. New bases are being added to those which already exist thousands of kilometres away from the USA and are aimed against our country; the American military presence abroad, in general, is being increased and expanded; large areas of the world are being declared spheres of 'vital interest to the USA'.

Nobody even asks if the people inhabiting those areas wish to be under the patronage of other countries. Attempts are being made to tell some other peoples what to do with their natural resources, threatening them otherwise with all kinds of punitive actions.

For all their differences, however, the peoples have the same right to be masters of their own destiny. There should be no double standards in this respect. One must not believe that if something is good for the USA, then it also has to be good for others. After all, is it good, for instance, for the average American family, not to mention the family of a peaceful Afghan peasant, when the intention is openly announced in Washington to go on supplying arms to the bands carrying out incursions into Afghanistan's territory from the outside?

It is not for the sake of polemics that I am sharing my thoughts with you, Mr President. I would like them, on the one hand, to give you a better understanding of what actually constitutes the policy of the Soviet Union and, on the other hand, to help clarify how we and, indeed, others as well, perceive certain actions of the USA, especially those of recent times.

The main idea, though, that I would like to convey through my letter is that we do not seek confrontation with the USA nor do we wish to infringe upon legitimate American interests. What we seek is different: we want peace, cooperation, a sense of mutual trust and benevolence between the Soviet Union and the USA. Guided by this sincere desire, we propose now to the USA and other Western countries honest and constructive negotiations, as well as a search for mutually acceptable solutions for practically all major questions existing between us—be it restraining the arms race, eliminating the most dangerous sources of tension in various areas of the world or measures for confidence-building and developing mutually beneficial cooperation. Those proposals of ours contain no ruse nor any ulterior motives. And I would like you to accept them precisely in this way and with no bias.

Thus our policy is a policy of peace. We will never build up the fire of war. You know very well, as we do, what such a fire would lead to. I want to believe in the wisdom of your people, and also in your personal wisdom, not to permit anything that would push the world towards catastrophe.

These are some of the general considerations which I wanted to convey to you, Mr President, in connection with your letter. Maybe it was not possible to express everything in sufficient detail. An exchange of correspondence has its limitations, and in this sense a private conversation is better. In this regard, concerning the possible meeting between us, I would like to say that it is also my view that such a meeting should be well prepared. We could still return to the question of its timing, I believe, at a moment acceptable to both of us.

II. PRESIDENT REAGAN'S PROPOSAL

Below is the continuation of President Reagan's speech to the National Press Club on 18 November 1981, an extract from which is printed above as Mr Reagan's letter to Mr Brezhnev.

Some young people question why we need weapons—particularly nuclear weapons—to deter war and to assure peaceful development. They fear that the accumulation of weapons itself may lead to conflagration. Some even propose unilateral disarmament.

I understand their concerns. Their questions deserve to be answered. But we have an obligation to answer their questions on the basis of judgment and reason and experience. Our policies have resulted in the longest European peace in this century. Would not a rash departure from these policies, as some now suggest, endanger that peace?

From its founding, the Atlantic alliance has preserved the peace through unity, deterrence and dialogue. First, we and our allies have stood united by the firm commitment that an attack upon any one of us would be considered an attack upon us all; second, we and our allies have deterred aggression by maintaining forces strong enough to ensure that any aggressor would lose more from an attack than he could possibly gain; and, third, we and our allies have engaged the Soviets in a dialogue about mutual restraint and arms limitations, hoping to reduce the risk of war and the burden of armaments, and to lower the barriers that divide East from West. These three elements of our policy have preserved the peace in Europe for more than a third of a century. They can preserve it for generations to come, so long as we pursue them with sufficient will and vigor.

Today, I wish to reaffirm America's commitment to the Atlantic alliance and our resolve to sustain the peace. And from my conversations with allied leaders, I know that they also remain true to this tried and proven course.

Nato's policy of peace is based on restraint and balance. No Nato weapons, conventional or nuclear, will ever be used in Europe except in response to attack. Nato's defense plans have been responsible and restrained. The allies remain strong, united and resolute. But the momentum of the continuing Soviet military build-up threatens both the conventional and the nuclear balance. Consider the facts.

Over the past decade, the United States reduced the size of its armed forces and decreased its military spending. The Soviets steadily increased the number of men under arms. They now number more than double those of the United States. Over the same period the Soviets expanded their real military spending by about one-third. The Soviet Union increased its inventory of tanks to some 50,000 compared to our 11,000. Historically a land-power, they transformed their navy from a coastal defense force to an open ocean fleet, while the United States, a sea-power with transoceanic alliances, cut its fleet in half.

During a period when Nato deployed no new intermediate range nuclear missiles, and actually withdrew 1,000 nuclear warheads, the Soviet Union deployed more than 750 nuclear warheads on the new SS-20 missiles alone.

Our response to this relentless build-up of Soviet military power has been restrained but firm. We have made decisions to strengthen all three legs of the strategic triad—sea, land and air-based. We have proposed a defense program in the United States for the next 5 years which will remedy the neglect of the past decade and restore the eroding balance on which our security depends.

I would like to discuss more specifically the growing threat to Western Europe which is posed by the continuing deployment of certain Soviet intermediate range nuclear missiles.

The Soviet Union has three different missile systems—the SS-20, the SS-4 and the SS-5—all with a range capable of reaching virtually all of Western Europe. There are other Soviet weapons systems which also represent a major threat. The only answer to these systems is a comparable threat to Soviet targets—in other words, a deterrent preventing the use of these Soviet weapons by the counter-threat of a like response against their own territory.

At present, however, there is no equivalent deterrent to these Soviet intermediate missiles. And the Soviets continue to add one new SS-20 a week. To counter this the allies agreed in 1979, as part of a two-track decision, to deploy, as a deterrent, land-based Cruise missiles and Pershing II missiles capable of reaching targets in the Soviet Union. These missiles are to be deployed in several countries of Western Europe. This relatively limited force in no way serves as a substitute for the much larger strategic umbrella spread over our Nato allies. Rather, it provides a vital link between conventional, shorter-range nuclear forces in Europe and intercontinental forces in the United States. Deployment of these systems will demonstrate to the Soviet Union that this link cannot be broken.

Deterring war depends on the perceived ability of our forces to perform effectively. The more effective our forces are, the less likely it is that we will have to use them. So, we and our allies are proceeding to modernize Nato's nuclear forces of intermediate range to meet increased Soviet deployments of nuclear systems threatening Western Europe.

Let me turn now to our hopes for arms control negotiations. There is a tendency to make this entire subject overly complex. I want to be clear and concise.

I told you of the letter I wrote to President Brezhnev last April (*see above*). Well, I have just sent another message to the Soviet leadership. It is a simple, straightforward, yet historic message: the United States proposes the mutual reduction of conventional, intermediate range nuclear, and strategic forces. Specifically, I have proposed a four-point agenda to achieve this objective in my letter to President Brezhnev.

The first, and most important, point concerns the Geneva negotiations. As part of the 1979 two-track decision, Nato made a commitment to seek arms control negotiations with the Soviet Union on intermediate range nuclear forces. The United States has been preparing for these negotiations through close consultation with our Nato partners. We are now ready to set forth our proposal.

I have informed President Brezhnev that when our delegation travels to the negotiations on intermediate range land-based nuclear missiles in Geneva on the 30th of this month, my representatives will present the following proposal: the United States is prepared to cancel its deployment of Pershing II and ground-launch Cruise missiles if the Soviets will dismantle their SS-20, SS-4 and SS-5 missiles. This would be an historic step. With Soviet agreement, we could together substantially reduce the dread threat of nuclear war which hangs over the people of Europe. This, like the first footstep on the moon, would be a giant step for mankind.

We intend to negotiate in good faith and go to Geneva willing to listen to and consider the proposals of our Soviet counterparts. But let me call to your attention the background against which our proposal is made. During the past six years, while the United States deployed no new intermediate range missiles and withdrew 1,000 nuclear warheads from Europe, the Soviet Union deployed 750 warheads on mobile, accurate ballistic missiles. They now have 1,100 warheads on the SS-20, SS-4 and SS-5 missiles and the United States has no comparable missiles. Indeed, the United States dismantled the last such missile in Europe over 15 years ago.

As we look to the future of the negotiations, it is also important to address certain Soviet claims which, left unrefuted, could become critical barriers to real progress in arms control. The Soviets assert that a balance of intermediate range nuclear forces already exists. That assertion is wrong. By any objective measure, the Soviet Union has an overwhelming advantage, of the order of six-to-one.

Soviet spokesmen have suggested that moving their SS-20s beyond the Ural mountains will remove the threat to Europe. The SS-20s, even if deployed behind the Urals, will have a range that places almost all of Western Europe, the great cities—Rome, Athens, Paris, London, Brussels, Amsterdam, Berlin and so many more—all within range of these missiles, which incidentally are mobile and can be moved on short notice.

The second proposal I have made to President Brezhnev concerns strategic weapons. The United States proposes to open negotiations on strategic arms as soon as possible next year. I have instructed Secretary Haig to discuss the timing of such meetings with Soviet representatives.

Substance, however, is far more important than timing. As our proposal for the Geneva talks this month illustrates, we can make proposals for genuinely serious reductions but only if we can take the time to prepare carefully. The United States has been preparing carefully for resumption of strategic arms negotiations because we do not want a repetition of past disappointments. We do not want an arms control process that send hopes soaring only to end in dashed expectations.

I have informed President Brezhnev that we will seek to negotiate substantial reductions in nuclear arms which would result in levels that are equal and verifiable. Our approach to verification will be to emphasize openness and creativity—rather than the secrecy and suspicion which have undermined confidence in arms control in the past.

While we can hope to benefit from work done over the past decade in strategic arms negotiations, let us agree to do more than simply begin where these efforts previously left off. We can and should attempt major qualitative and quantitative progress. Only such progress can fulfil the hopes of our own people and the rest of the world. Let us see how far we can go in achieving truly substantial reductions in our strategic arsenals. To symbolize this fundamental change in direction, we will call these negotiations 'START'—Strategic Arms Reduction Talks.

The third proposal I have made to the Soviet Union is that we act to achieve equality at lower levels of conventional forces in Europe. The defense needs of the Soviet Union hardly call for maintaining more combat divisions in East Germany today than were in the whole allied invasion force that landed in Normandy on D-day. The Soviet Union could make no more convincing contribution to peace in Europe—and in the world—than by agreeing to reduce its conventional forces significantly and constrain the potential for sudden aggression.

Finally, I have pointed out to President Brezhnev that to maintain peace we must reduce the risks of surprise attack, and the chance of war arising out of uncertainty or miscalculation. I am renewing our proposal for a conference to develop effective measures that would reduce these dangers. At the current Madrid meeting of the Conference on Security and Cooperation in Europe, we are laying the foundation for a Western-proposed conference on disarmament in Europe. The conference would discuss new measures to enhance stability and security in Europe. Agreement on this conference is within reach. I urge the Soviet Union to join us and the many other nations who are ready to launch this important enterprise.

All of these proposals are based on the same fair-minded principles: substantial, militarily significant reductions in forces; equal ceilings for similar types of forces; and adequate provisions for verification. My Administration, my country and I are committed to achieving arms reductions agreements based on these principles. Today I have outlined the kinds of bold, equitable proposals which the world expects of us. But we cannot reduce arms unilaterally. Success can only come if the Soviet Union will share our commitment; if it will demonstrate that its often-repeated professions of concern for peace will be matched by positive action.

Preservation of peace in Europe and the pursuit of arms reductions talks are of fundamental importance. But we must also help to bring peace and security to regions now torn by conflict, external intervention and war. The American concept of peace goes well beyond the absence of war. We foresee a flowering of economic growth and individual liberty in a world at peace.

At the economic summit in Cancún, I met with the leaders of 21 nations and sketched out our approach to global economic growth. We want to eliminate the barriers to trade and investment which hinder these critical incentives to growth. And we are working to develop new programs to help the poorest nations achieve self-sustaining growth.

Terms like 'peace' and 'security' have little meaning for the oppressed and the destitute. They also mean little to the individual whose state has stripped him of human freedom and dignity. Wherever there is oppression, we must strive for the peace and security of individuals as well as states. We must recognize that progress in the pursuit of liberty is a necessary complement to military security. Nowhere has this fundamental truth been more boldly and clearly stated than in the Helsinki accords of 1975. These accords have not yet been translated into living reality.

Today I have announced an agenda that can help to achieve peace, security and freedom across the globe. In particular, I have made an important offer to forego entirely deployment of new American missiles in Europe if the Soviet Union is prepared to respond on an equal footing.

There is no reason why people in any part of the world should have to live in permanent fear of war or its specter. I believe the time has come for all nations to act in a responsible spirit that does not threaten other states. I believe the time is right to move forward on arms control and the resolution of critical regional disputes at the conference table. Nothing will have a higher priority for me and for the American people over the coming months and years.

Addressing the United Nations twenty years ago, another American President described the goal we still pursue today. 'If we all can persevere,' he said, 'if we can . . . look beyond our own shores and ambitions, then surely the age will dawn in which the strong are just and the weak secure and the peace preserved.' He did not live to see that goal achieved. I invite all nations to join with America today in the quest for such a world.

III. COUNTER-OFFER BY PRESIDENT BREZHNEV

Text of a speech by Leonid Brezhnev, general secretary of the central committee of the Communist Party of the Soviet Union and President of the Presidium of the USSR Supreme Soviet, at the dinner given in his honour in Bonn on 23 November 1981, by the Federal Chancellor of the Federal Republic of Germany, Helmut Schmidt (from Soviet News, 24 November 1981).

Last time I was in Bonn in springtime. I remember the rays of the May sun, playing even on people's faces. Now it is autumn, the season of falling leaves, and it seems that even human faces have become more serious. The cause of this, evidently, lies not only in the change of the seasons of the year. Everywhere alarm has grown over the destinies of peace.

But people want to have greater confidence in the future. We know this both from meetings with our compatriots and with foreign representatives. People want to work peacefully, to bring up their children, and peace is necessary for this.

You, Mr Federal Chancellor, probably feel these sentiments as well. This is understandable. The peoples of our states went through such grim sufferings during the years of the Second World War that it is no wonder that the very idea of a new war, and still more so, a nuclear war, seems criminal to them.

There are situations in politics when a single wrong step may become a fatal one. The same holds true now. The point is in what direction events on the European continent will develop in the near future: towards consolidating the fundamentals of peace, as was decided at Helsinki, or towards their destruction.

We have discussed this subject in great detail with the Federal Chancellor today, including, certainly, the question of the medium-range nuclear weapons in Europe. And I expressed the Soviet point of view in all sincerity.

We consider the situation to be alarming. The West's biggest power is out to cause the arms race to spiral still further. This includes the adoption of new and gigantic programmes for the deployment of strategic and other weapons; it also includes a start on the production of neutron weapons. But using them would mean leaving Europe without human beings, turning it into a tombstone to itself.

Things have gone so far that assertions are being made about the possibility and all but the advisability of 'limited nuclear wars'. Doesn't the stubborn reluctance to assume on a mutual basis the commitment not to be the first to use the nuclear weapon, as is proposed by the Soviet Union, speak for itself?

It emerges that the possibility of using nuclear weapons in the 'European theatre of military operations' is being elevated to the status of a military doctrine. As if Europe, where hundreds of millions of people live, were already doomed to become a theatre of military operations. As if it were a box of little tin figures, which do not deserve a better fate than that of being melted in the flames of nuclear explosions.

It is bitter and painful to speak of such things. But it is our duty, especially to young people, to tell the whole truth about war. Not only about the tragedy of the past, but also about what a nuclear war may mean.

Whatever may divide us, Europe is our common home. A common fate has linked us through the centuries, and it links us today, too.

We are deeply convinced that the plans to deploy in Western Europe, and above all on the territory of the Federal Republic of Germany, the new US nuclear-missile weapons targeted on the USSR are creating for the whole continent a formidable danger, such as has never before existed. People are keenly aware of this danger and, of course, expect that everything will be done to eliminate it.

The question of nuclear weapons in Europe will, as is well known, be the subject of the Soviet-American talks which are to open in Geneva shortly. It would, of course, be naive to surmise that the very fact of the start of the talks is already enough to resolve a problem of such concern to the peoples of Europe. The outcome of the talks will depend on both sides. The Soviet Union goes to the talks with the firm intention to achieve positive results. As regards the other side, however, we are of the view that signs abound which are capable of putting one on one's guard.

In the USA, as well as in some other Nato countries, one frequently hears statements that bear witness to a desire to spare no effort to deploy new US missiles in Europe, rather than to a desire to seek a balanced agreement. These apprehensions are only enhanced by the contents of the recently-published proposal of the US Administration on how to solve the problem of medium-range nuclear weapons in Europe.

How do we assess this proposal? If one is to speak frankly, then, in our opinion, its sponsors turn upside down the very notion of fairness and reciprocity in a question affecting the interests of security and the very lives of hundreds of millions of people. And, of course, there is already no question whatsoever of any 'zero option' in it.

It is being demanded of us that we should unilaterally disarm, while hundreds of land-based and sea-based missiles trained on our country and our allies, aircraft with nuclear bombs, all this formidable arsenal now in the possession of the United States and other Nato countries in the region of Europe is to remain intact. In other words, if at present the ratio between the medium-range nuclear means of the two sides in Europe is expressed quite accurately by the figure of one to one, the USA would wish to change it to about two to one in favour of Nato.

It is clear that the Soviet Union will never agree to such a variant. We call on our partners in the coming talks to adopt a more objective approach to the question and to seek, together with us, a solution which is really acceptable to both sides and useful for the cause of peace and universal security.

To facilitate the dialogue and to create a favourable atmosphere for it, we have put forward this proposal: that while the talks continue, both sides should abstain from deploying new, and modernising existing, medium-range nuclear means in Europe. As you can see, there is no question here of any perpetuation for all time of the present level of medium-range nuclear means.

Besides, as we have informed the Federal Chancellor today, should the other side consent to the moratorium I have just spoken about, the Soviet Union would be prepared not only to discontinue a further deployment of its 'SS-20' missiles. We would go even further.

As an act of good will, we could unilaterally reduce a part of our medium-range nuclear weapons in the European part of the USSR. In other words, engage in some anticipatory reduction, moving towards that lower level which could be agreed upon by the USSR and the USA as a result of the talks. This is a new and substantive element in our position.

In the course of the talks with the United States we shall resolutely advocate radical cutbacks in the medium-range nuclear weapons maintained by each side in Europe. It stands to reason that specific figures should be worked out in the course of the talks themselves. But speaking of ourselves we would be prepared to carry out reductions not by dozens, but by hundreds of units of weaponry of that class. I repeat, by hundreds of units. This is our approach.

If our partners display readiness to reach agreement on the complete renunciation by both sides—the West and the East—of all types of medium-range nuclear weapons aimed at targets in Europe, we stand for this.

Generally speaking, we stand for Europe becoming eventually free from nuclear weapons, both medium-range and tactical ones. That would be a genuine 'zero-option' which would be just for all the sides.

The Soviet Union and the Federal Republic of Germany have different social systems. Each of us has his own friends and allies. We have largely disparate political views, and we have our differences. But we believe that they should recede into the background before our common main task, that of safeguarding peace, this supreme treasure of mankind.

The short remainder of President Brezhnev's speech did not deal with nuclear disarmament.

ANGLO-IRISH RELATIONS

Joint communique issued after a meeting between the British Prime Minister and the Taoiseach of the Irish Republic on 6 November 1981

1. The Prime Minister, the Rt. Hon. Margaret Thatcher, MP, had discussions today at 10 Downing Street with the Taoiseach, Dr Garret FitzGerald, TD. The Prime Minister was accompanied by the Rt. Hon. The Lord Carrington, Secretary of State for Foreign and Commonwealth Affairs, the Rt. Hon. James Prior, MP, Secretary of State for Northern Ireland, and the Rt. Hon. Nigel Lawson, MP, Secretary of State for Energy. The Taoiseach was accompanied by the Tanaiste and Minister for Industry and Energy, Mr Michael O'Leary, TD, and the Minister for Foreign Affairs, Senator James Dooge.

2. The meeting was the first between the Prime Minister and the Taoiseach since Dr FitzGerald took office. They discussed a number of international questions and a range of issues arising in the European Community which are to be considered at the European Council in London on 26 and 27 November.

3. The Prime Minister and the Taoiseach affirmed the importance which their two Governments attached to the maintenance and development of close Anglo-Irish relations.

4. The Prime Minister and the Taoiseach agreed on the need for efforts to diminish the divisions between the two sections of the community in Northern Ireland and to reconcile the two major traditions that exist in the two parts of Ireland. Such a development could come about only on the basis of mutual respect as between those traditions, to the achievement of which the Taoiseach has made a public commitment.

5. The Taoiseach affirmed that it was the wish of the Irish Government and, he believed, of the great majority of the people of the island of Ireland, to secure the unity of Ireland by agreement and in peace. The Prime Minister affirmed, and the Taoiseach agreed, that any change in the constitutional status of Northern Ireland would require the consent of a majority of the people of Northern Ireland. The Prime Minister said that, if that consent were to be expressed as a result of a poll conducted in accordance with the Northern Ireland Constitution Act 1973, the British Government would of course accept their decision, and would support legislation in the British Parliament to give effect to it. The Prime Minister and the Taoiseach agreed that both Governments were ready to join in promoting arrangements which might help to reduce tensions between and to reconcile the peoples of the two parts of Ireland.

6. The Prime Minister and the Taoiseach reiterated their resolute opposition to violence, and commended the level of cooperation between the security forces of the two countries. They noted with approval the efforts now being made under the criminal law jurisdiction legislation to ensure that those who committed crimes in one country should not be able to escape prosecution and conviction by seeking refuge in the other, and invited the British and Irish Attorneys-General to consider what further improvements to that end might be possible.

7. The Prime Minister and the Taoiseach received a joint report (annexed to this communique) on studies made by officials from both countries of possible new institutional structures, citizenship rights, economic cooperation and measures to encourage mutual understanding. (*The report and the papers on which it was based were published on 11 November: Cmnd. 8414. For security reasons the study on security matters was not published*).

8. Recognizing the unique character of the relationship between the two countries, the Prime Minister and the Taoiseach have decided to establish an Anglo-Irish Intergovernmental Council through which institutional expression can be given to that relationship between the two Governments. This will involve regular meetings between the two Governments at ministerial and official levels to discuss matters of common concern. The Prime Minister and the Taoiseach agreed that it would be for the Parliaments concerned to consider at an appropriate time whether there should be an Anglo-Irish body at parliamentary level comprising members to be drawn from the British and Irish Parliaments, the European Parliament and any elected assembly that may be established for Northern Ireland. They also agreed to work towards the establishment of an advisory committee associated with the Anglo-Irish Intergovernmental Council on economic, social and cultural cooperation, with a wide membership.

9. The Prime Minister and the Taoiseach noted that each country afforded the other's citizens most of the rights and privileges available to its own. The Taoiseach indicated that the arrangements for the grant of voting rights at parliamentary elections to British citizens resident in the Republic were well advanced and that he hoped to have the necessary legislation introduced soon.

10. The Prime Minister and the Taoiseach agreed on the need to intensify economic cooperation between the two countries and between the two parts of Ireland. They expressed the hope that such cooperation would make a contribution towards the improvement of the economy throughout the two countries and that the practice of economic cooperation would, in itself, generate further cooperation. They gave special consideration to the question of cooperation on energy matters. They noted that assessments of the possibility of the supply of natural gas from the Kinsale field to Northern Ireland had suggested that such a project might be viable, and that discussions of the terms on which gas might be supplied were now in train. They agreed on the desirability of restoring electricity interconnexion between the two parts of Ireland. They also agreed that economic and technical studies should be pursued on the possibility of an electricity link across the Irish Sea.

11. The Prime Minister and the Taoiseach looked forward to holding their next meeting in the spring of next year in Dublin in the framework of the new institutional arrangements agreed upon at this meeting.

ANGLO-IRISH JOINT STUDIES: JOINT REPORT

1. At their meeting in Dublin on 8 December 1980, the Prime Minister and the then Taoiseach commissioned joint studies covering possible new institutional structures, citizenship rights, security matters, economic cooperation and measures to encourage mutual understanding, in order to assist them in their special consideration of the totality of relationships within these islands. These joint studies were undertaken by senior officials of the two governments. In carrying out their task officials bore in mind the already close relations between the two countries and their common membership of the European Community. The outcome of the studies, other than that on security matters, is as follows.

Possible New Institutional Structures

2. Officials noted that the unique relationship to which the two joint communiques of May and December 1980 referred was the result of geography, history and population movements. The joint studies brought out the variety of contacts between the two countries. They confirmed that in many fields relations and cooperation were closer and more extensive than between other countries in Europe where a particularly close relationship had been given specific institutional expression. Officials agreed that, over a very wide range, these relations involved common interests and mutually beneficial exchanges but recalled that the communique of 8 December 1980 had recorded agreement that the full development of the links between the two countries and their peoples had been put under strain by division and dissent in Northern Ireland.

3. Officials considered how the development of the unique relationship between the two countries might appropriately be enhanced by giving it more comprehensive institutional expression, without impeding the many informal links; and in this context examined the following possibilities—

i. the establishment of an Anglo-Irish Intergovernmental Council to provide the overall framework for intergovernmental consultation, at head of government, ministerial and official levels, on all matters of common interest and concern with particular reference to the achievement of peace, reconciliation and stability and the improvement of relations between the two countries and their peoples; and what might be the component elements of the structure, its functions and certain aspects of its operation;

ii. how the parliamentary links between the two countries might most appropriately be developed as the natural and desirable complement to the establishment of a new intergovernmental body;

iii. the establishment, as an adjunct to the proposed intergovernmental Council, of an Advisory Committee on economic, social and cultural cooperation, with a wide membership reflecting vocational interests;

iv. the establishment as an interim measure, pending the creation of an Advisory Committee as at iii, of an 'Anglo-Irish Encounter' organization under the direction of an Executive Board composed of independent public figures of repute and ability and government representatives, with the major function of organizing high-level conferences on the Koenigswinter model.

Citizenship Rights

4. Officials reviewed the rights and privileges on the one hand, and the obligations and duties on the other, of citizens of each country residing in the jurisdiction of the other. The areas looked at were eligibility to vote and to stand for elective offices; employment in the civil and armed services; legal rights and obligations (including jury service); social rights; consular protection; and freedom of movement.

5. It was noted that, in the absence of a written constitution on the British side, the various rights and obligations are defined by specific Acts of Parliament, which Parliament being sovereign can later amend. The role of the Courts in this context is to interpret legislation. On the Irish side, by contrast, there is both specific legislation covering a similar range of subject-matter and a written constitution guaranteeing fundamental human rights. Proposals to alter the Constitution must be approved not only by Parliament but also through a referendum. The Courts have power to strike down legislative Acts held by them to be inconsistent with the Constitution.

6. It was further noted that each of the two countries maintained provisions which ante-dated the requirements of their common European Community membership and afforded in different ways privileged treatment to the citizens of the other. Indeed, each accorded the other's citizens virtually all the rights and privileges available to its own. At the same time a number of differences were identified, notably in respect of the two countries' practices in relation to the control of movement of non-citizens; and in respect of the qualifications for local elections in Northern Ireland as compared with Great Britain.

7. Officials noted the decisions of the Irish authorities to extend voting rights in national elections to resident British citizens. Officials also reviewed possibilities for do ̣ ̣with other differences; but made no agreed proposals for doing so.

Economic Cooperation

8. Officials considered a wide range of existing and potential areas of economic and technical co-operation, both bilateral and in the context of the two countries' common membership of the European Community, and made recommendations as to how these might be encouraged and developed. They agreed that the machinery of Anglo-Irish Economic Cooperation (AIEC) had proved effective within its terms of reference in fostering the development of economic and technical matters of mutual interest. If a new intergovernmental institution were established as envisaged in their work on institutional structures, the Steering Group on AIEC (and its subordinate groups) or a comparable official level body might appropriately be placed under the aegis of that new institution.

9. Among the subjects considered were—

—future cooperation on energy, in particular the possibilities for electricity interconnexion (both across the land border and across the Irish Sea) and for the supply of gas from the Kinsale field in Northern Ireland and the exploitation of new energy technologies;

—the exchange of information on pollution of the Irish Sea and coordination of responses to pollution emergencies;

—broadcasting of television and radio programmes direct to the home from a satellite;

—cooperation in the field of animal and plant health;

—the facilitation of economic development in Lough Foyle, Carlingford Lough and the nearby offshore areas;

—industrial development, particularly of small and craft industries;

—trade promotion;

—industrial training;

—tourism;

—continuing cooperation in the economic development of border areas;

—science and technology.

10. Officials believed that further work in this field would make a contribution towards the improvement of the economies of these islands and that the practice of economic cooperation would in itself generate further cooperation.

Measures to Encourage Mutual Understanding

11. Officials analysed the reasons for misconceptions in each country over attitudes and Government policies in the other, and considered measures that the two Governments might appropriately take, jointly or separately, to remove such misconceptions and improve mutual understanding.

12. It was recognized that, as between Britain and the Republic, the problem appeared to be more one of knowledge than of misconception. This might be remedied by efforts aimed at a more intensive exchange of information. As between North and South in Ireland the problem went deeper. In this context the issues which were relevant were the constitutional 'claim' and the 'guarantee'; and Church/State relationships. Action to reduce misunderstanding of these matters would clearly be needed. Institutional arrangements were also required, deliberately framed to reduce suspicion and distrust, together with measures to make more effective the prosecution of offenders who seek to evade justice by crossing from one side of the border to the other. Moreover, greatly increased contacts and joint endeavours in appropriate fields, as well as intensified information exchanges, might all offer some hope of progress.

13. Officials noted that there existed already a welcome multiplicity of contacts and that it was desirable that these should continue and be developed. In this context they considered a range of possibilities including:

increased contacts between officials concerned with youth and sport activity and the scope for increased cooperation between sporting organizations in both parts of Ireland;

the development of the already considerable contacts between vocational and community relations groups in both parts of Ireland;

in the field of education, increased exchanges between teachers and inspectors as well as between pupils and students; particularly the potential for more use by students from the South of tertiary education facilities in Northern Ireland;

the active pursuit of cooperation between the Open University and the proposed Distant Study Unit of the National Institute for Higher Education in Dublin;

the establishment of a formal scheme for interchange of officials;

the encouragement and expansion of close cooperation and contacts between the Arts Councils, North and South, in Ireland; and between both of these Councils and the Arts Councils in Great Britain.

THE MELBOURNE DECLARATION

The Declaration below was attached to the final communique of the Commonwealth heads of government meeting in Melbourne, Australia, from 30 September to 7 October 1981

We, the Heads of Government here assembled, drawn from five continents and representing a quarter of the world's entire population:

1. Affirm our strong and unanimous conviction that all men and women have the right to live in ways that sustain and nourish human dignity;

2. Believe that this right imposes obligations on all states, large and small, not only in respect to their own people but in their dealings with all other nations;

3. Assert that the gross inequality of wealth and opportunity currently existing in the world, and the unbroken circle of poverty in which the lives of millions in developing countries are confined, are fundamental sources of tension and instability in the world;

4. As a consequence, assert our unanimous conviction that there must be determined and dedicated action at national and international levels to reduce that inequality and to break that circle;

5. Believe that for all these reasons it is imperative to revitalize the dialogue between developed and developing countries;

6. Declare that this will require a political commitment, clear vision and intellectual realism which have thus far escaped mankind and to all of which the Commonwealth can greatly contribute;

7. Believe that the dialogue must be conducted with a genuine willingness to accept real and significant changes commensurate with the urgency of the problems we now face;

8. Firmly believe that the choice is not between change and no change but between timely, adequate, managed change and disruptive, involuntary change imposed by breakdown and conflict;

9. Maintain that success will only be achieved as states recognise and give due weight to the essential inter-dependence of peoples and of states;

10. Declare that, while the most urgent humanitarian considerations demand action, self-interest itself warrants a constructive and positive approach to these great human problems by all governments;

11. Recognize that in the process of negotiations, nations must cast aside inhibitions and habits which have thwarted progress in the past and find new ways of talking constructively to one another so as to reach agreement of effective joint action;

12. Note that, as well as technical economic considerations, it is imperative that states keep in the forefront of their attention the larger moral, political and strategic dimensions of what is at stake;

13. Maintain that while the problems are formidable, they are not of such a weight that they will defeat our purpose, given political will and an understanding of the needs of different countries and groups;

14. Assert that what is at stake—in terms of how hundreds of millions will live or die; of the prospects for cooperation or conflict; and of the prospects for economic advance or stagnation—is of such vital importance in human terms that it would be an indictment of this generation if that political will and the readiness to find a creative compromise were not found;

15. Firmly believe that the issues are so important that they require the personal commitment and involvement of political leaders who, representing the will of their people, have the greatest power to advance the common cause of mankind;

16. Attaching the highest importance to the principles and objectives of this document, recognising the mutual interests and interdependence of all nations, declare our common resolve: to end the present impasse: to advance the dialogue between developed and developing countries: to infuse an increased sense of urgency and direction into the resolution of these common problems of mankind: and solemnly call on all leaders of all countries to join us in a commitment to taking prompt, practical and effective action to that end.

Canberra, 3 October 1981.

THE UNITED KINGDOM CONSERVATIVE ADMINISTRATION

(as at 5 January 1981 after changes on that day)

Prime Minister, First Lord of the Treasury and Minister for the Civil Service . . .	Rt. Hon. Margaret Thatcher, MP
Secretary of State for the Home Department	Rt. Hon. William Whitelaw, CH, MC, MP
Lord Chancellor	Rt. Hon. The Lord Hailsham of Saint Marylebone, CH, FRS
Secretary of State for Foreign and Commonwealth Affairs and Minister of Overseas Development	Rt. Hon The Lord Carrington, KCMG, MC
Chancellor of the Exchequer . .	Rt. Hon. Sir Geoffrey Howe, QC, MP
Secretary of State for Industry . .	Rt. Hon. Sir Keith Joseph, Bt, MP
Chancellor of the Duchy of Lancaster, Paymaster General and Leader of the House of Commons	Rt. Hon. Francis Pym, MC, MP
Lord President of the Council and Leader of the House of Lords	Rt. Hon. The Lord Soames, GCMG, GCVO, CH, CBE
Secretary of State for Employment . .	Rt. Hon. James Prior, MP
Secretary of State for Defence . .	Rt. Hon. John Nott, MP
Lord Privy Seal	Rt. Hon. Sir Ian Gilmour, Bt, MP
Minister of Agriculture, Fisheries and Food .	Rt. Hon. Peter Walker, MBE, MP
Secretary of State for the Environment .	Rt. Hon. Michael Heseltine, MP
Secretary of State for Scotland . .	Rt. Hon. George Younger, TD, MP
Secretary of State for Wales . . .	Rt. Hon. Nicholas Edwards, MP
Secretary of State for Northern Ireland .	Rt. Hon. Humphrey Atkins, MP
Secretary of State for Social Services .	Rt. Hon. Patrick Jenkin, MP
Secretary of State for Trade . .	Rt. Hon. John Biffen, MP
Secretary of State for Energy . .	Rt. Hon. David Howell, MP
Secretary of State for Education and Science .	Rt. Hon. Mark Carlisle, QC, MP
Secretary of State for Transport . .	Rt. Hon. Norman Fowler, MP
Chief Secretary to the Treasury . .	Rt. Hon. Leon Brittan, QC, MP

MINISTERS NOT IN THE CABINET

Ministers of State, Ministry of Agriculture, Fisheries and Food	The Earl Ferrers
	Alick Buchanan-Smith, MP
	Jerry Wiggin, TD, MP
Minister of State, Civil Service Department .	Barney Hayhoe, MP
Minister of State, Ministry of Defence .	The Viscount Trenchard, MC
Ministers of State, Department of Education and Science	The Baroness Young
Minister with responsibility for the Arts .	Rt. Hon. Paul Channon, MP
Minister of State, Department of Employment .	The Earl of Gowrie
Minister of State, Department of Energy .	Hamish Gray, MP

Ministers of State, Department of the Environment:	
Minister of Local Government and Environmental Services . . .	Rt. Hon. Tom King, MP
Minister for Housing and Construction .	John Stanley, MP
Ministers of State, Foreign and Commonwealth Office	Hon. Douglas Hurd, CBE, MP
	Hon. Nicholas Ridley, MP
	Peter Blaker, MP
Minister for Overseas Development . .	Neil Marten, MP
Ministers of State, Department of Health and Social Security	
Minister for Health	Dr Gerard Vaughan, MP
Minister for Social Security, with special responsibility for the disabled . .	Hugh Rossi, MP
Ministers of State, Home Office . . .	Timothy Raison, MP
	Patrick Mayhew, QC, MP
Ministers of State, Department of Industry .	Kenneth Baker, MP
	Norman Tebbit, MP
Ministers of State, Northern Ireland Office .	Michael Alison, MP
	Hon. Adam Butler, MP
Minister of State, Scottish Office . .	The Earl of Mansfield
Ministers of State, Department of Trade:	
Minister for Consumer Affairs .	Rt. Hon Sally Oppenheim, MP
Minister for Trade . . .	Cecil Parkinson, MP
Financial Secretary to the Treasury .	Rt. Hon. Nigel Lawson, MP
Ministers of State, Treasury . .	Peter Rees, QC, MP
	The Lord Cockfield
Parliamentary Secretary to the Treasury .	Rt. Hon. Michael Jopling, MP

LAW OFFICERS

Attorney-General	Rt. Hon. Sir Michael Havers, QC, MP
Solicitor-General	Sir Ian Percival, QC, MP
Lord Advocate	Rt. Hon. The Lord Mackay of Clashfern, QC
Solicitor-General for Scotland . .	Nicholas Fairbairn, QC, MP

THE UNITED KINGDOM CONSERVATIVE ADMINISTRATION

(as at 31 December 1981, following Government changes on 14 September)

Prime Minister, First Lord of the Treasury and Minister for the Civil Service . .	Rt. Hon. Margaret Thatcher, MP
Secretary of State for the Home Department .	Rt. Hon. William Whitelaw, CH, MC, MP
Lord Chancellor . . . '. .	Rt. Hon. The Lord Hailsham of Saint Marylebone, CH, FRS
Secretary of State for Foreign and Commonwealth Affairs and Minister of Overseas Development	Rt. Hon The Lord Carrington, KCMG, MC
Chancellor of the Exchequer . .	Rt. Hon. Sir Geoffrey Howe, QC, MP
Secretary of State for Education and Science .	Rt. Hon. Sir Keith Joseph, Bt, MP
Lord President of the Council and Leader of the House of Commons . . .	Rt. Hon. Francis Pym, MC, MP
Secretary of State for Northern Ireland .	Rt. Hon. James Prior, MP
Secretary of State for Defence . .	Rt. Hon. John Nott, MP
Minister of Agriculture, Fisheries and Food .	Rt. Hon. Peter Walker, MBE, MP
Secretary of State for the Environment .	Rt. Hon. Michael Heseltine, MP
Secretary of State for Scotland . .	Rt. Hon. George Younger, TD, MP
Secretary of State for Wales . .	Rt. Hon. Nicholas Edwards, MP
Lord Privy Seal	Rt. Hon. Humphrey Atkins, MP
Secretary of State for Industry . .	Rt. Hon. Patrick Jenkin, MP
Secretary of State for Trade . .	Rt. Hon. John Biffen, MP
Secretary of State for Transport . .	Rt. Hon. David Howell, MP

Secretary of State for Social Services . .	Rt. Hon. Norman Fowler, MP
Chief Secretary to the Treasury . .	Rt. Hon. Leon Brittan, QC, MP
Chancellor of the Duchy of Lancaster and Leader	
of the House of Lords . .	Rt. Hon. The Baroness Young
Secretary of State for Energy . .	Rt. Hon. Nigel Lawson, MP
Secretary of State for Employment . .	Rt. Hon. Norman Tebbit, MP

MINISTERS NOT IN THE CABINET

Ministers of State, Ministry of Agriculture, Fisheries and Food . . .	Rt. Hon. Alick Buchanan-Smith, MP
	The Earl Ferrers
Minister of State, Civil Service Department .	Barney Hayhoe, MP
Ministers of State, Ministry of Defence .	Peter Blaker, MP
	The Viscount Trenchard, MC
Minister of State, Department of Education and Science:	
Minister with responsiblity for the Arts .	Rt. Hon. Paul Channon, MP
Minister of State, Department of Employment .	Michael Alison, MP
Minister of State, Department of Energy .	Hamish Gray, MP
Ministers of State, Department of the Environment:	
Minister for Local Government and Environmental Services . .	Rt. Hon. Tom King, MP
Minister for Housing and Construction .	John Stanley, MP
Ministers of State, Foreign and Commonwealth Office	Hon. Douglas Hurd, CBE, MP
	Richard Luce, MP
Minister for Overseas Development .	Rt. Hon. Neil Marten, MP
Ministers of State, Department of Health and Social Security	
Minister for Health . . .	Dr Gerard Vaughan, MP
Minister for Social Security, with special responsibility for the disabled .	Hugh Rossi, MP
Ministers of State, Home Office . .	Patrick Mayhew, QC, MP
	Timothy Raison, MP
Ministers of State, Department of Industry .	Norman Lamont, MP
Minister for Industry and Information Technology	Kenneth Baker, MP
Ministers of State, Northern Ireland Office	Hon. Adam Butler, MP
	The Earl of Gowrie
Paymaster General . . .	Rt. Hon. Cecil Parkinson, MP
Minister of State, Scottish Office . .	The Earl of Mansfield
Ministers of State, Department of Trade:	
Minister for Consumer Affairs .	Rt. Hon Sally Oppenheim, MP
Minister for Trade . .	Peter Rees, QC, MP
Financial Secretary to the Treasury .	Hon. Nicholas Ridley, MP
Ministers of State, Treasury . .	Jock Bruce-Gardyne, MP
	The Lord Cockfield
Parliamentary Secretary to the Treasury .	Rt. Hon. Michael Jopling, MP

LAW OFFICERS

Attorney-General	Rt. Hon. Sir Michael Havers, QC, MP
Solicitor-General	Sir Ian Percival, QC, MP
Lord Advocate	Rt. Hon. The Lord Mackay of Clashfern, QC
Solicitor-General for Scotland . .	Nicholas Fairbairn, QC, MP

OBITUARY

Abdul-Hadi, Ibrahim (b. 1899), was Prime Minister of Egypt 1948-49. A sentence of death by a revolutionary tribunal was commuted to life imprisonment, and he was later freed. Died 18 February

Alice, HRH Princess, Countess of Athlone (b. 1883), was the last surviving grandchild of Queen Victoria. Her father, Duke of Albany, died of haemophilia when she was a year old; her mother was a Princess of Waldeck-Pyrmont. She married in 1904 Prince Alexander of Teck, a title he forsook in 1917 to become Earl of Athlone, and accompanied him on his governor-generalships of South Africa 1923-27 and Canada 1940-45; after his death in 1957 she succeeded him as Chancellor of London University until 1971. Died 3 January

Auchinleck, Field Marshal Sir Claude, GCB, GCIE, CSI, DSO (b. 1884), was Commander-in-Chief in India for six months in 1941 and from 1943 to 1948, and GOC-in-C Middle East (between Wavell and Alexander) in 1941-42. As an Indian Army officer he served in Egypt and Mesopotamia in World War I and he commanded a brigade in action on the NW Frontier in the early 1930s. Early in World War II he commanded the forces in northern Norway of the ill-fated Narvik landing; a short-lived tenure of Southern Command was followed by his brief but successful first term as C-in-C in India, a post he exchanged with Field Marshal Wavell in July 1941. In command in the Middle East, he organized the offensive which raised the siege of Tobruk and drove the enemy back west into Cyrenaica, with the loss of 20,000 prisoners, the first great victory in North Africa. Strongly reinforced, Rommel counter-attacked, retook Tobruk and drove the British forces back to El Alamein, as Auchinleck warned would happen for lack of armour in Libya. At Alamein he took personal command of the battle, halted Rommel and saved Egypt. His defence and counter-attack paved the way for the victories of Alexander and Montgomery later in 1942. In his second term as C-in-C India he had the task, not of fighting the Japanese—the role of S-E Asia Command—but of maintaining and supplying a vast army, and eventually of demobilizing a large part of it. The end of the war brought him deep into the political maelstrom—over the Red Fort trials of Indian POWs who had defected and had committed crimes against their fellow soldiers, over the role of the C-in-C under a political regime, over the partition of India and consequently of its armed forces, and over the military consequences of the mass migrations and the struggle over Kashmir. Though it was a bitter period for him, his sympathy with Indian aspirations, joined to his loyalty as a soldier, held the respect of the politicians and the affection of all ranks of the army. Died 23 March

Bahonar, Muhammad Javad (b. 1933), was Prime Minister of Iran for the last month of his life, having previously served as Minister of Education in the Government of his long-time friend Muhammad Ali Rajai, *q.v.* An intimate of the Ayatollah Beheshti (*q.v.*), whom he succeeded as leader of the Islamic Republican Party, he had been prominent in the resistance to the Shah's regime. Killed by a bomb explosion 30 August

Barber, Samuel (b. 1910), American composer, displayed his talent at a very early age, winning the American Prix de Rome and a Pulitzer prize for music in 1935; in the following year the premiere of his *Adagio for Strings* was conducted by Toscanini, who later recorded it. Another milestone was the performance of his *Second Symphony* by the British Symphony Orchestra in 1944. Among his later works the most enduring included the *Capricorn Concerto* (1944), the ballet music

Medea (1946) and the opera *Vanessa* (1958, libretto by Menotti). Died 23 January

Beheshti, Ayatollah Muhammad, was the leader of the dominant Islamic Republican Party (IRP) in Iran, Chief Justice and, at his death, a member of the presidential council, after Ayatollah Khomeini the most powerful political figure in the regime. A doctor of theology of Teheran University, he returned from Germany, where he was spiritual adviser to the Iranian Islamic centre in Hamburg, to conduct anti-Shah demonstrations in the last year of the monarchy. After the revolution he founded the IRP, which came to dominate the Majlis and had a fundamentalist whip-hand over his rival President Bani-Sadr, whose downfall he engineered. Assassinated 28 June

Betancourt, Rómulo (b. 1908), President of Venezuela 1959-64, had spent all his adult life in radical left but democratic and anti-marxist politics (though in his youth he was for a short time a communist). Twice in his 30s he had to flee the country, which was governed by a right-wing dictatorship. He was one of the founders of Accion Democratica (AD), which took office after a coup d'état in 1945 and made him provisional President, but in the presidential election of 1947 he supported the victorious Romulo Gallegos. A military coup, followed by another dictatorship, drove him again into exile for a decade, but when its leader Perez Jimenez was overthrown AD took over and Betancourt was elected President. He introduced a number of radical agrarian and social reforms but was strenuously opposed to the contagion of Castro's communism after the Cuban revolution. His legacy to Venezuela was not only a more equitable division of wealth (augmented by oil) but also a well-tried structure of democratic government. Died 28 September

Böhm, Karl (b. 1894), Austrian conductor, became Generalmusikdirektor of the Dresden Opera in 1934 after working in Munich, Darmstadt and Hamburg. His most favoured composers were Mozart, Wagner and Richard Strauss. He was music director of the Vienna State Opera 1943-45 and 1955-56. Thereafter he was principally associated with Bayreuth and Wagnerian opera, though his love of Mozart was reflected in some memorable recordings. Died 14 August

Bradley, General of the Army Omar N., Hon. KCB (b. 1893), commanded 12 Army Group in the invasion of Normandy in 1944 and was responsible for the swift breakthrough from the Cotentin peninsula into Brittany and the south and the elimination of the German 7th Army. His generalship in the advance to the Rhine, including the Ardennes counter-offensive when Montgomery characteristically stole the limelight, was equally successful. Previously he had commanded the 2nd US Corps in North Africa after its failure at the Kasserine Gap and in Sicily after its triumphant link-up with British 8th Army. His pre-war career had been largely as an instructor in infantry tactics, an art which he was to apply with such success in the field. He was administrator of veteran affairs 1945-47, chief of staff of the army 1948-49, and chairman of the joint chiefs of staff 1949-53, a period which included the Korean war. In retirement he became chairman of the Bulova Watch Company. Died 8 April

Breuer, Marcel (b. 1902), Hungarian-born American architect and designer, was a student and colleague of Walter Gropius at the Bauhaus 1921–28, during which time he invented tubular steel furniture, with which he equipped the Bauhaus buildings. Under the Nazi regime he migrated to Switzerland, Britain and eventually to the US (1937), where he joined Gropius at Harvard University. In 1946 he moved his architectural practice to New York. Though he was responsible for many buildings in America, much of his distinctive work was elsewhere, including apartment buildings in Zurich (with the Roth brothers, 1935), the Unesco headquarters in Paris (with Zehrfuss and Nervi, 1958), the Bijendorf department store in Rotterdam and the American embassy at The Hague. He won the gold medal of the American Institute of Architects in 1968. Died 1 July

Boyle of Handsworth, Lord, CH (b. 1923), British Conservative politician, had been a member of the Cabinet at such an early age and was so widely respected, above all in the Tory Reform wing of his party, that he was seen by some as a potential Prime Minister; but in 1970 he deserted party politics to become a Life Peer and vice-chancellor of the University of Leeds. There he was immensely successful, while in national public life he continued to earn respect (though not always the agreement of politicians) as chairman 1971-80 of the Review Board which advised on the remuneration of judges and high officers of the civil and armed services. Elected to Parliament as Sir Edward Boyle, Bt., at the age of 27, he held junior ministerial office until joining the Cabinet as Minister of Education (1962-64). Died 28 September

Caroe, Sir Olaf, KCSI, KCIE (b. 1892), British administrator, had been the foremost expert on the affairs of the North West Frontier of India (of Pakistan since 1947). Joining the ICS after army service in World War I, from 1923 he alternated between work in the frontier province and important central government posts. He was secretary of the External Affairs Department 1939-46 and Governor of the NWFP 1946-47, accepting premature withdrawal under pressure on the Viceroy by Congress leaders who falsely accused him of partiality. In retirement he wrote important books, including *Wells of Power* (1951), a study of the oilfields of Iran and Arabia, and *Soviet Empire* (1952), and became a champion of Tibetan rights. Died 23 November

Clair, René (b. 1898), French film director, scored huge international success with his delicious comedies *The Italian Straw Hat* (1929), *Sous Les Toits de Paris, Le Million, 14 Juillet, A Nous la Liberté, The Ghost Goes West* (with Korda). In Hollywood 1940-46 he made, among other films, *Flame of New Orleans* (with Marlene Dietrich) and *Forever and a Day*. Back in France after the war, his works included *Les Belles de Nuit, Porte des Lilas, Les Grandes Manoeuvres* and *Les Fêtes Galantes* (his last film, in 1965). Died 14 March

Darlington, Professor Cyril Dean, FRS (b. 1903), British scientist, exerted a highly constructive influence on the development of biological and evolutionary studies, primarily through his epoch-making book *The Evolution of Genetic Systems* (1939). Ten years earlier he had virtually launched the systematic science of cytology with his *Recent Advances in Cytology*. Later the application of his ideas on genetics and evolution to historical human populations, notably in *The Evolution of Man and Society* (1969), led him into controversial fields of race differences, and his work was criticized for the very qualities of imaginative synthesis which had made it so important. He was director of the John Innes Horticultural Institute 1939-53, Sherardian Professor of Botany and Fellow of Magdalen College, Oxford 1953-71. Died 26 March

Dayan, Moshe (b. 1915), Israeli soldier and politician, left two indelible marks on the turbulent history of his country. In 1967, already honoured for his role in the occupation of Sinai during the 1956 Suez escapade (which, as he revealed in his memoirs, he had helped to plot with the British and French Governments), he became a national hero when, as Minister of Defence, he initiated and completed the victorious six-day war in 1967. In 1977-78 he played a crucial role in the negotiations leading to the Camp David peace treaty with Egypt. Between these triumphant episodes his reputation had been debased by the responsibility placed on him by the public for the bitter losses of the Yom Kippur war of 1973. He was a notable changer of sides. A member of the illegal Haganah self-defence force under the mandate, he was enlisted by the British as a temporary policeman in 1936, but was sentenced in 1939 to ten years' imprisonment for militant anti-government activity, from which he was released in 1941 to serve in the British forces against the Vichy French regime in the Lebanon, where he lost an eye. In the 1948 Arab-Israeli war he led dramatically daring actions as a Haganah field officer. In 1956 he was Israel's army chief of staff, but gave up a military career for academic studies and politics as a Labour member of the Knesset and held office under Mr Ben Gurion's leadership. With Ben Gurion he left Labour to form the Rafi party, and was in opposition when Ben Gurion's successor enlisted him as Defence Minister just before the Israeli pre-emptive strike in 1967. The 1973 debacle led to his being dropped from Mr Rabin's Cabinet in 1974. Not the least extraordinary U-turn was his joining Mr Begin's Likud Government as Foreign Minister, but in pursuit of his lasting objective of peace he opposed Mr Begin's forward policy in the West Bank, resigned his office and in March 1981 formed a new centre party. Died 16 October

Delbrück, Professor Max (b. 1906), shared the Nobel prize for medicine with Dr Alfred Hershey and Dr Salvador Luria in 1969 for their work on molecular genetics. German by birth, he migrated to the US in 1937 as professor of biology at the California Institute of Technology, and took American citizenship in 1945. Died 9 March

Donskoi, Mark (b. 1901), Russian film director, won international fame with a trilogy, *The Childhood of Maxim Gorky, My Apprenticeship* and *My Universities* (1938-40), based on Gorky's autobiographical works.

He transmuted Soviet realism by a subtle artistry and a sense of poetry. He continued to produce notable films into the 1970s. Death reported 24 March

Euwe, Dr Max (b. Amsterdam, 1901), was world chess champion 1935-37 and president of the international chess federation 1970-78. By profession a student and teacher of mathematics, he remained in effect an amateur for most of his career. He was chess champion of the Netherlands 12 times. In 1935 he beat Alekhine in a world title series, but two years later was defeated in a return match. The war and the occupation of the Netherlands interrupted his playing career, and, although he had some brilliant successes thereafter, by 1948 he had bowed out as a great international champion. Alekhine once said of him: 'He never made a faulty combination.' Died 26 November

Fawzi, Dr Mahmoud (b. 1900), was Minister of Foreign Affairs of Egypt 1952-58 and of the abortive United Arab Republic 1958-64, Deputy Prime Minister 1964-67, Vice-President 1967 -68, Prime Minister 1970-72 and again Vice-President 1972-74. Educated partly in Europe and the USA, he joined the Egyptian foreign service in 1924 and mounted the diplomatic ladder from vice-consul in New Orleans to Egypt's representative at the UN Security Council from 1946 and ambassador to Britain in 1952. Surviving the regimes of King Farouk and Colonel Nasser into that of Anwar Sadat, he preferred the conduct of diplomacy and foreign policy to internal politics and was unhappy as Prime Minister. Died 12 June

Fraser of North Cape, Admiral of the Fleet Lord, GCB, KBE, (b. 1888), was First Sea Lord 1948-52, but his most distinctive service to the Royal Navy was rendered during World War II as Controller of the Navy 1939-42, responsible for the vast expansion of its *matériel*, as C-in-C Home Fleet 1942-44, when his great exploits in northern waters included the sinking of the battleship *Scharnhorst,* and as C-in-C British Pacific Fleet 1944-47, welding the Commonwealth contribution with the vast US Navy and coping with the fearful post-war problems of the Pacific area. Died 12 February

Frederika, Queen (b. 1917, daughter of the Duke of Brunswick), as a Princess of Britain and Hanover, granddaughter of the German Kaiser, married to the Crown Prince, later King, of Greece, was typical of the links that made the crowned heads of Europe an international family distinct from the rival nationalisms of their native or adopted countries. She married Prince Paul of Greece in 1938, and suffered exile after the German invasion, returning in 1946 with her husband, who succeeded to the throne in the following year. She was suspected of being a powerful backstage influence both during his reign and after the succession of her son Constantine in 1964, and in spite of her good works and courage became an unpopular figure. After the 'colonels' coup' in 1967 she went into exile in Rome. Died 6 February

Gance, Abel (b. 1889), French film director, earned the description of 'the Victor Hugo of the French cinema'. He began as an actor and made his first film, *Le Masque d'Horreur,* in 1912. Spectacular war films followed, then *La Roue,* an emulation of Griffith's Hollywood epics, and in 1927 his most famous product, *Napoléon,* with a score by Honegger. Of his later films the uncharacteristic *Paradis Perdu* (1939) and *La Tour de Nesle* (1955) were among the most notable. Died 10 November

Gopallawa, William (b. 1897), was Governor-General of Ceylon 1962-72 and Sri Lanka's first President 1972-78. His public service had been in local politics until he was appointed Ceylon's ambassador to China 1958-61 and then to the US, becoming Governor-General a year later. His succession to the Presidency of the new Republic in 1972 was natural and unopposed; himself austere and non-political, he made way for a politically powerful successor six years later. Died 30 January

Gundelach, Finn Olav (b. 1925), Danish diplomat, was a member of the European Commission 1973-81, and vice-president in charge of agriculture from 1977. He had been his country's permanent representative at the UN office in Geneva 1954-59, a senior official of the GATT secretariat 1959-67, and then Danish ambassador to the EEC, experiences uniquely qualifying him as Danish member of the Commission, where he became a powerful figure. Died shortly after his appointment for a third four-year term, 13 January

Hailwood, Mike (b. 1940), British motor-cycle racer, won nine world championships in 1961-67 and a tenth in 1978. In between he took up motor racing and won the 1972 European Formula Two championship. In 1973 he was awarded the George Medal for bravery in rescuing a competitor from a blazing car during the South African Grand Prix. Died 21 March

Haley, Bill (b. 1925), American singer, was the first apostle of 'rock and roll'. His recording *Rock Around the Clock* (1954), though almost unnoticed when first issued, became the world-wide anthem of the 'pop' youth of the time after its use in the film *Blackboard Jungle* (1955). He and his group 'The Comets' made other million-selling records like *See You Later, Alligator* before his fame waned in the 1960s, but the earlier 'rock' records remained universally popular. Died 9 February

Hassel, Professor Odd (b. 1898), Norwegian chemist, shared with Professor Derek Barton the Nobel prize for chemistry in 1969, for his work on the three-dimensional geometric structure of molecules. Until 1964 he was director of the physical chemistry department of Oslo University. Died 11 May

Jackson of Lodsworth, Baroness, DBE (b. 1914), was best-known as Barbara Ward, her maiden name under which from an early age she exerted great influence as a writer on economics and politics and participant in public affairs. After Oxford and a university extension lectureship, her real career began as assistant editor of *The Economist* from 1939, later foreign editor, and during World War II she also wrote copiously for American journals and became a highly effective broadcaster both at home and in the US. In 1950 she married Commander (later Sir) Robert Jackson, from whom she separated five years later. An active supporter of the Labour Party, she became a governor of the BBC, also of Sadler's Wells and the Old Vic. From 1957 her base was Cambridge, Massachussetts, as a visiting lecturer and director of research at Harvard and Radcliffe. Her interest, stimulated by much travel, became focused on problems of economic development and the relations between rich and poor countries. In 1967 she was appointed one of the first members of the Pontifical Commission for Justice and Peace; a devout Christian, she had been one of the founders of 'The Sword of the Spirit'. Her many books included *India and the West, Rich Nations and Poor Nations* and *Only One Earth*. Died 31 May

Krebs, Sir Hans, FRS (b. in Germany 1900), shared the Nobel prize for medicine with Fritz Lippmann in 1953. After four years of research at the Kaiser Wilhelm Institute for Biology he taught and practised medicine in a Freiburg clinic. Fleeing from Nazi Germany, he continued in Cambridge, England, his research, financed by the Rockefeller Foundation, into the cyclical metabolic pathways of biological chemistry, which remained the prime and highly successful field of study of his whole career. In 1935 he became lecturer in pharmacology at the University of Sheffield and in 1945, after

wartime service in nutritional research, professor of biochemistry there. From 1954 to 1967 he was Whitely Professor of Biochemistry at Oxford. Died 22 November

Lopokova, Lydia (b. Lopukhova, 1892), Russian ballerina, married Maynard Keynes (later Lord Keynes) *en deuxième noces* in 1925, and thereafter, living in England, danced little though sometimes taking secondary parts on the legitimate stage. Trained at the Imperial School of Ballet in St Petersburg, she danced at the Mariiusky Theatre before a highly successful debut with Diaghilev in Paris in 1910. In and out of the Diaghilev company from 1915 to 1925, she played leading roles in some of his most famous productions, her acting ability and enchanting personality triumphing over her lack of classical perfection. Died 8 June

Louis, Joe (b. 1914), American part-negro boxer, won the world heavyweight title in 1937 and defended it 25 times (including a triumphant defeat of Max Schmeling who had knocked him out in 1936) before retiring undefeated in 1949. Tax debts forced him into an unsuccessful come-back, but after his defeat by Rocky Marciano in 1951 he quit the fighting ring for good. He remained, however, the respected hero of millions of boxing fans, especially his fellow coloured citizens of the United States. Died 12 April

MacDonald, Rt. Hon. Malcolm, OM (b. 1901), began his public life in the shadow of his father, Ramsay MacDonald, the first Labour Prime Minister of Britain, but in later life earned a unique personal reputation as overseas representative of his country. Elected a Labour MP in 1929, he followed his father into the National Government camp, and entered the Cabinet as Colonial Secretary in 1936 (for a time being also Dominions Secretary). He was Minister of Health 1940-41, then found a new métier as high commissioner in Canada 1941-46, Governor-General of Malaya

1946-48, commissioner-general for the UK in SE Asia 1948-55, high commissioner in India 1955-60, Governor (later Governor-General) of Kenya 1963-64, and high commissioner in Kenya 1964-65. In all these posts he displayed not only great diplomatic ability as an envoy but also natural sympathy with the views and aspirations of the peoples among whom he worked, whether Canadians, Africans or Asians. In 1961-62 he was largely responsible, as head of the British delegation, for the success after year-long negotiation of the Geneva conference on the future of Laos. Other favourable developments that owed much to his skill, patience and charm included the transition of Kenya to stable democratic independence and the continued cohesion of the Commonwealth in the late 1960s when the Rhodesian crisis threatened to split it; he was appointed by Prime Minister Wilson roving envoy in Africa 1965-70. Modest and informal, he loved to study birds, about which he wrote several books. Died 11 January

Montale, Eugenio (b. 1896), was described in a London *Times* obituary as 'perhaps the greatest Italian poet since Leopardi'. Soldiering in World War I arrested an intended career as an opera singer, and thereafter his life was devoted to literary criticism and poetry. His first volume of poems, *Le occasioni* (1939), was published a year after he had been dismissed as director of the Vieusseux Library in Florence for refusing to join the fascist party. After World War II he became literary editor of the Milan newspaper, *Il corriere della sera,* and his international fame rested as much on his literary criticism as on his poetry, which ranged from limpid sea and love poems to intense and enigmatic verse. Often likened to T.S. Eliot because of their concern for the meaning of words and their attraction to 'waste lands', Montale differed in his pessimistic philosophy and his idealization of 'divine indifference'. English translations of his poems were published by Edinburgh University Press (1964) and

New Directions, New York (1965). He was awarded the Nobel prize for literature in 1975. Died 12 September

Oldfield, Sir Maurice, GCMG (b. 1915), British intelligence chief, was head of MI6 1973-78. Destined for an academic career (he became a Fellow of Manchester University in 1938), he enlisted in the army in World War II and swiftly showed his aptitude for intelligence, rising from the ranks to a lieutenant-colonelcy. After the war he served in a succession of intelligence posts in the Foreign Service, including that of liaison between MI6 and the CIA in Washington 1960-65, until in 1973 he was appointed as 'C', the head of the secret intelligence service, where he discouraged 'special operations' and concentrated on counter-intelligence. Retiring five years later, he was called back to be security coordinator in 1979 but resigned for health reasons in the following year. Died 11 March

Parri, Ferruccio (b. 1890), leader of the radical anti-fascist Action Party, was the first post-war Prime Minister of Italy, June-November 1945. An ardent opponent of fascism, he was several times imprisoned, once for his share in organizing, in 1926, the escape of the prominent Socialist Filippo Turati. In 1943-45, he played a leading part in organizing military partisan resistance in north Italy and in negotiations with the Allies. His brief premiership in late 1945 ended when he and his small party were pushed aside by the three mass parties. He was appointed a life Senator in 1963. Died 8 December

Pella, Giuseppe (b. 1902), was Prime Minister of Italy for a brief period in 1953, but his main political career had lain in the Ministry of Finance, where for many years under different Christian Democrat Premiers he conducted an austere policy that gave his country a sound basis for economic expansion. He became a Senator in 1968. Died 31 May

Rajai, Muhammad Ali (b. 1933), Prime Minister of Iran from August

1980 to July 1981 and thereafter President, joined the resistance movement against the Shah's regime and suffered imprisonment and torture for his activities in the 1970s. A dyed-in-the-wool Islamic fundamentalist, he became Minister of Education in the first revolutionary Government headed by Mehdi Bazargan. Then and as Prime Minister under the presidency of Mr Bani-Sadr he followed a stridently anti-Western line, backed by the Islamic Republican Party whose swelling power brought about Bani-Sadr's dismissal and his own election as President. Killed by a bomb explosion 30 August

Russell of Liverpool, Lord (b. 1895), who was Assistant Judge Advocate-General 1951-54, became known all over the world as the author of *The Scourge of the Swastika*, an account of German Nazi crimes. The Lord Chancellor having indicated that its publication was incompatible with his judicial office, he resigned and devoted his time to writing: his books included *The Knights of Bushido*, about Japanese atrocities, and *Deadman's Hill*, a study of a controversial British murder case. He had served with distinction in both World Wars, in the first as an infantry officer, in the second as a military lawyer, having been called to the Bar in 1931. Died 8 April

Sadat, Muhammad Anwar al (b. 1918), President of Egypt from 1970, was indelibly associated with the Camp David negotiations and the Israeli-Egyptian treaty of March 1979. His visit to the Knesset in Jerusalem in November 1977 to launch his peace initiative was an extraordinary act of faith which, unhappily for him and for Egypt, was not matched by an equal response from Israel and Mr Menachem Begin. In the subsequent negotiations, direct and with the mediation of Washington, Sadat was forced to give way on two vital points on which he had insisted in his speech to the Knesset, self-determination and statehood for the Palestinians and a comprehensive peace including all

Israel's neighbours, besides complete Israeli withdrawal to the 1967 frontiers; nevertheless he did secure large territorial recovery for Egypt, including the oil-bearing region, and the peace brought a substantial improvement to the weak Egyptian economy. Egypt became virtually isolated in the Arab world and Sadat himself faced rising popular discontent, much of it channelled into a Muslim fundamentalist movement. In his last days, although overall he had held to his objective of giving Egypt more democracy, he took a number of repressive measures against his political opponents. Much of the esteem in which he was held by Egyptians for the recovery of the Suez Canal Zone in 1973, as well as the euphoria that greeted his peace initiative, had evaporated. By profession a soldier, he had taken part in various subversive activities, including the coup which ousted King Farouk and created the republic, before entering politics in 1954. Patronized by President Nasser, he held various posts of greater political than administrative importance, ending with the Vice-Presidency, from which he was elevated, more or less as a stop-gap, to the supreme office upon the death of Nasser in 1970. War and peace apart, from the outside world's point of view his most decisive act as President was the dismissal of the Soviet military mission and cancellation of all Soviet military and naval facilities in July 1972. At home his policies were generally liberalizing and economically progressive but his most dramatic strokes of defence and foreign policy could not overcome the discontent based on mass poverty and ill-distributed wealth. Assassinated 6 October

Saroyan, William (b. 1908), American short-story writer, novelist and dramatist, was perhaps best known internationally for his collection *The Daring Young Man on the Flying Trapeze* (1934), though other books like *The Trouble with Tigers* also gained him a great reputation. His work for the theatre included *My*

512 OBITUARY

Heart's in the Highlands (1938), *The Time of Your Life* (1939), *Pal Joey* (1942) and *Sam, the Highest Jumper of Them All* (1960). Died 18 May

Seper, H. E. Cardinal Franjo (b. 1905), was Prefect of the Congregation for the Doctrine of the Faith (formerly known as the Holy Office) 1968-80. Born in Croatia and educated at the Gregorian University in Rome, he was ordained priest in 1930 and became a bishop in 1954. In 1960 he succeeded Cardinal Stepinac, whose auxiliary bishop he had been, as Archbishop of Zagreb. In his Vatican post he disappointed hopes of a liberal change from the policies of his predecessor Cardinal Ottaviani. Died 30 December

Sheares, Dr Benjamin Henry, FRCOG (b. 1907), was President of Singapore from 1971 to his death. He had been professor of obstetrics and gynaecology at King Edward VIII College of Medicine, Singapore, 1945-47, and at the University of Malaya in Singapore 1950-60, and thereafter occupied in private practice. Died 12 May

Shehu, Mehmet (b. 1913), was Prime Minister of Albania 1954-81. He shared absolute power with Enver Hoxha, the Communist Party leader, throughout most of his political career. After fighting in the Spanish civil war on the republican side, he returned to Albania in 1939, and organized and commanded the Albanian communist resistance movement during World War II. When the communists came to power after the war, he became chief of the general staff of the army and subsequently Minister of the Interior. Suicide reported 18 December A.L.

Soong Ch'ing-ling (b. 1890), as widow of Dr Sun Yat-sen for 56 years, occupied a very special position in communist China as a living symbol of the legitimate succession of the regime to the first Chinese republic established by the revolution of 1911 which Sun Yat-sen had led. Previously his secretary, she married him in 1915; he died ten years later. The daughter of a

Chinese Methodist, and educated partly in America, Soong Ch'ing-ling was converted to communist views under the influence of Mikhail Borodin, Soviet adviser to the Kuomintang in the mid-1920s, and after the break between the Kuomintang and the communists she spent most of the rest of that decade in exile in Moscow, a focus of opposition to Chiang Kai-shek's Nationalist Government. Although she returned to China during World War II, and occupied honorific posts under the Nanking Government, she continued to attack the Kuomintang for its betrayal, as she saw it, of the revolutionary cause. After the communists took power in 1949 she was made a vice-chairman of the People's Republic and later served on several diplomatic missions, but her influence did not compare with her symbolic status. Died 29 May

Speer, Albert (b. 1905) was a man without whose drive and efficiency Nazi Germany could hardly have fought World War II for nearly six years. From 1942 to 1945 he was Minister for Armaments and Ammunition and head of the Todt organization (named after his predecessor) for employing conscript workers from German-occupied Europe. An architect by profession, he displayed such foresight and administrative skill that production of aircraft and munitions was first greatly enlarged and then sustained despite vast destruction by Allied bombing. An ardent admirer of Hitler as a young man, by 1935 he had become the Führer's personal friend, one who was nevertheless always frank with him. Yet in February 1945, when the end was in sight, Speer took part in a plot, accidentally frustrated, to assassinate Hitler. At the Nuremberg trial he admitted his guilt, and he served his full term of 20 years' imprisonment for war crimes. Died 1 September

Sut Yat-sen, Mme, *see* Soong Ch'ing-ling

Thomas, Lowell (b. 1892), American writer and broadcaster, became world-famous as a purveyor of travel experiences and descriptions. His immensely successful book *With Lawrence in Arabia* was a product of his commission from President Wilson to make an historical record of the fighting in World War I, which took him to all the principal fronts. Travel in far countries and hazardous places remained the main material of his many books, broadcasts and films (he was a pioneer producer of Cinerama, the wide-screen novelty of the 1950s), but he also became in 1930 the first American radio newscaster with a national following. His journeys and his accounts of them continued into his old age. Died 29 August

Torrijos Herrera, Brig.-Gen. Omar (b. 1929), was Chief of Government of Panama 1972-78, having been effective national leader for the previous four years after leading a military coup against the regime of Dr Arnulfo Arias Madrid. While effecting important economic and agrarian reforms, his greatest achievement, largely personal, was the conclusion of two new treaties ending US control of the Panama Canal (see AR 1977, pp. 65 and 73). Died 31 July

Trippe, Juan T. (b. 1899), pioneer of American civil aviation, founded Pan American Airways in 1927 and remained its chief executive for over 40 years; he was honorary chairman 1968-75 and thereafter an honorary director. Learning to fly while at college, he served in the US navy air force in World War I, and in 1922 launched his first airline. In 1926, as general manager of Colonial Air Transport, his second venture, he won the first American airmail contracts. His most crucial decision as executive head of Pan Am was to buy 45 jet aircraft in 1955, inaugurating a new era in worldwide air transport. Died 3 April

Urey, Professor Harold (b. 1893), American chemist, was awarded the Nobel prize for chemistry in 1934 for his work in isolating deuterium, the heavy isotope of hydrogen. He taught chemistry in the universities of Montana, California, Johns Hopkins and Columbia, where he became full professor in 1934. In World War II he was director of the War Research Atomic Bomb Project and played a large part in the scientific research leading to the first nuclear detonation. He returned to academic work as a professor at the University of Chicago 1945-58. Died 5 January

Ürgüplü, Ali Suat Hayri (b. 1903), was briefly Prime Minister of Turkey in 1965. A lawyer by profession, he was a People's Party member of the National Assembly 1939-46 and Minister of Customs and Monopolies 1943-46. Switching to the Democratic Party, he was re-elected to the Assembly in 1950 but was then enlisted as a diplomat and became (1950-60) vice-president of the Council of Europe and Turkish ambassador successively in Bonn, Washington, London and Madrid, before returning as a member of the Senate (Speaker 1961-63). Died 26 December

Waldock, Sir Humphrey, CMG, OBE, QC (b. 1904), was a judge of the International Court of Justice 1973-79 and from 1979 its president. He had been Fellow and law tutor of Brasenose College, Oxford, 1930-47, with a five-year break of civilian war service in the Admiralty, and then Chichele Professor of International Law at Oxford 1947-72. Meanwhile he had taken part in the settlement of many quasi-judicial international disputes (Italo-Yugoslav, Sino-American, Swedish-Finnish, Swedish-Swiss, Swedish-Turkish, German-Swiss, US-Danish, Chilean-Italian, Danish-Norwegian, Swedish-Spanish) and was the principal draftsman of the Convention on the Law of Treaties (Vienna 1968-69). He was a member of the UN International Law Commission 1961-72 (president 1967), of the European Commission of Human Rights 1954-61 (president 1955-61) and of the European Court of Human Rights 1966-74 (president 1971-74). Died 15 August

Ward, Barbara, *see* Jackson of Lodsworth, Baroness

Williams, Rt. Hon. Dr Eric (b. 1911), was the first Prime Minister of Trinidad and Tobago from its independence in 1965 until his death, having been Chief Minister under colonial rule 1956-64. A first-class honours graduate of Oxford, professor of political science at Howard University, Washington, D.C., he became in later years the model of an intellectual autocrat, governing through democratic forms, a Salazar of the Caribbean. Entering Trinidad politics only in 1955 from a staff post on the Caribbean Commission, he founded the People's National Movement and led it to electoral victory in the following year. Thereafter its power and his were scarcely challenged for twenty years. A wave of industrial unrest in 1965 provoked him into declaring a state of emergency and carrying an Act which virtually outlawed strikes, and a decade later he countered moves to unite a fragmented opposition by imposing a statutory obligation on MPs to resign on changing party: but he preserved the rules of parliamentary democracy and maintained his rule by pragmatic policies and astute manoeuvre. He encouraged foreign investment and saw his country grow dollar-rich, though employment-poor, through exploitation of its oil and other resources. He was a prolific author, mainly of books on Caribbean history, his original academic vocation. Died 29 March

Wyszynski, H. E. Cardinal Stefan (b. 1901), Primate of Poland, was the heroic saint of Catholic survival and renaissance under the communist regime. While accepting the facts of communist power, and constantly urging calm, he fought implacably for the rights of religious freedom, which merged into general human rights, and demanded a full price in those terms for his cooperation, which became more and more indispensable to the Politburo as popular respect for him grew and identified his cause with the historic national spirit of the Polish people. A brilliant scholar of poor parentage, he studied in Rome, France and Belgium as well as Poland before becoming professor at the Wloclwawek seminary 1931-39. Identified with the Catholic workers' movement, he was active in the underground resistance in World War II. He was Bishop of Lublin 1945-49 before being elected Primate as Archbishop of Warsaw and Gniezno, when his great role as spiritual father and advocate of the Polish people began. He was arrested in 1953 for denouncing the show trial of a fellow bishop, but was later released. After strongly defending the worker victims of counter-repression in 1976, he gave valued counsel and support to the Solidarity movement in 1980, while still striving to avert violent internal or external conflict. Theologically he was conservative, and an adherent of the Latin Mass. Died 28 May

Yukawa, Professor Hideki (b. 1907), won the Nobel prize for physics in 1949 for his work on the sub-atomic particle the meson, whose existence he had deduced as early as 1933. He was professor of physics at Kyoto 1939-53 and director of the Kyoto research institute for fundamental physics 1953-70. Died 8 September

Ziaur Rahman, General (b. 1935), was Chief Martial Law Administrator of Bangladesh 1976-77 and President from April 1977 to his death in a violent insurrection. Previously, after the murder of Sheikh Mujib in August 1975 he had wielded effective supremacy as chief of army staff in the military Government. His assumption of the presidency was ratified by a referendum and confirmed by an election in June 1978. In 1979, after parliamentary elections which gave his Bangladesh National Party an overwhelming majority, civilian parliamentary government was restored and President Zia retired from the army. Holding the rank of major when Bangladesh revolted in 1971, he played a key part in the operations against West Pakistani forces. In office he pursued a policy of non-alignment, mended fences with Pakistan, and attempted important economic and social reforms. Died 30 May

CHRONICLE OF PRINCIPAL EVENTS IN 1981

JANUARY

1 Greece admitted as tenth member of European Community.
3 Government of Zimbabwe announced formation of Zimbabwe Mass Media Trust to take over South-African-controlled press.
5 In UK, Mr St John Stevas replaced as Leader of the House by Mr Francis Pym who was succeeded at Ministry of Defence by former Trade Secretary Mr John Nott (see 14 Sept.).
  In Portugal, Dr Francisco Pinto Balsemão, PM designate, presented Cabinet to President Eanes.
6 M Gaston Thorn succeeded Mr Roy Jenkins as President of European Commission.
  US President-elect Reagan held talks with Mexican President Lopez Portillo.
8 In UK, Report of Royal Commission on Criminal Procedure included proposals for some extension of police powers to stop and search.
10 In Zimbabwe, Mr Nkomo demoted to Minister of Public Service; Mr Tekere (acquitted of murder in Dec. 1980) dismissed.
11 Three-man British team led by Sir Ranulph Fiennes completed longest and fastest crossing of Antarctica reaching Scott base in 75 days after travelling 2,500 miles.
13 UN-sponsored conference on Namibia at Geneva failed to agree ceasefire and implementation of UN plan for Namibia's independence.
  Polish trade union leader Lech Walesa led Solidarity delegation on 7-day official visit to Rome; 15 Jan. received by Pope John Paul II.
18 In UK, thirteen young black people died in house fire at Deptford; 13 May, inquest jury recorded open verdict.
20 Mr Ronald Reagan inaugurated as 39th President of USA.
  Iran released all 52 US embassy hostages following signing of agreement in Algiers and transfer of frozen Iranian assets from USA to account at Bank of England.
21 Former Stormont Speaker Sir Norman Stronge and son shot dead by IRA gunmen at home in S. Armagh.
22 In UK, Fowzi Nejad, only surviving terrorist of Iranian embassy siege in London in April 1980, gaoled for life.
23 In S. Korea, President Chun Doo Hwan commuted death sentence on Opposition leader Kim Dae Jung to life imprisonment.
24 In UK, special Labour Party conference at Wembley voted for electoral college of MPs, constituency parties and trade unions to elect party leader.
25 In UK, four former Labour Cabinet Ministers (Messrs Rodgers, Jenkins and Owen and Mrs Williams) announced formation of Council for Social Democracy (see 26 March).
  In China, suspended sentences of death passed on Jiang Qing and Zhang Chunqiao; others received long gaol sentences for treason and other anti-state activities.
26 In UK, Industry Secretary Sir Keith Joseph announced £990 million government aid for British Leyland investment programme.
  In South Africa, 120 died in severe flooding in Laingsburg, Western Cape.
27 In Indonesia, 500 died when passenger ferry sank in Java Sea.
  In UK, Chancellor of Exchequer announced introduction of 20p and £1 coins in 1983.
29 Senor Adolfo Suárez resigned as PM of Spain (see 10 Feb.).
30 In UK, Miss Susan Hurley elected first woman fellow in 542-year history of All Souls College, Oxford.

FEBRUARY

2 Peru and Ecuador agreed ceasefire on disputed frontier after five days of fighting.
3 Dr Gro Harlem Brundtland elected Norway's first woman PM following resignation of Mr Odvar Nordli (see 13 Sept.).

In Spain, King Juan Carlos received rough reception in Basque towns Bilbão and Guernica.

5 37th Franco-German summit conference opened in Paris.

6 In N. Ireland, Rev. Ian Paisley paraded 500 'loyalist' men claiming they were prepared to take action to prevent union with the Republic.

9 General Wojciech Jaruzelski succeeded Mr Josef Pinkowski as PM of Poland (see 18 Oct., 13 Dec.).

10 In Spain, King Juan Carlos named Sr Leopoldo Calvo Sotelo PM. Cabinet named 26 Feb., first since 1939 with no generals.

12 In Zimbabwe, PM Mugabe ordered air force and army into action as rival Zipra and Zanla forces clashed in Entumbane; 16 Feb. Mr Nkomo persuaded Zipra ex-guerrillas to lay down arms.

13 In UK, a deal was concluded for the sale of Times Newspapers Ltd by the Thomson Organization to Mr Rupert Murdoch's News International Ltd with immediate effect.

14 In Irish Republic, 49 young people died in fire at club in Dublin.

16 Pope John Paul II began 10-day visit to Pakistan, Japan and Philippines.

17 In UK, HRH Princess Anne elected Chancellor of London University, defeating Mr Jack Jones and Mr Nelson Mandela in controversial poll.

18 In UK, Government and National Coal Board agreed to withdraw plan for 23 pit closures and increase state aid to avert threatened national coal strike.

In USA, President Reagan's first budget contained largest package of tax cuts and spending curbs ever proposed by a US Administration; $90,000 million increase in defence spending proposed over next 4 years (see 29 July).

20 USA claimed communist powers were attempting overthrow of El Salvador Government in effort directed through Cuba.

23 26th Congress of Soviet Communist Party opened in Moscow, ending 3 March.

In Spain, 200 civil guards led by Col. Tejero Molina stormed Cortes and held 350 MPs at gunpoint in attempted coup; 24 Feb. civil guards surrendered following denunciation by King Juan Carlos.

In Kuwait voters went to polls to elect 50-seat National Assembly suspended since 1976.

24 In UK, the engagement was announced between HRH The Prince of Wales and Lady Diana Spencer (see 29 July).

25 Mrs Thatcher in Washington for 4-day official visit.

In UK, ICI announced biggest-ever fall of profits and cut dividend for first time since World War II.

27 Three Anglican missionaries detained in Iran since Aug. 1980 released.

MARCH

1 In Central African Republic, Mr David Dacko confirmed as President in first election since overthrow of Emperor Bokassa (see 1 Sept.).

2 In UK, 12 MPs resigned Labour Whip to form Social Democrat grouping in House of Commons; 9 Labour peers did likewise.

Terrorists of militant Al-Zulfiqar organization hijacked Pakistani plane with 148 passengers aboard and forced it to fly first to Kabul then to Damascus; 15 March, all hostages released after Pakistan freed 55 political prisoners.

3 In UK, report of Security Commission, *The Interception of Communications in Great Britain (Cmnd. 8191), found controls on telephone tapping satisfactory.*

5 Mrs Thatcher on visit to N. Ireland said there would be no change in constitutional position of Province and gave reassurance about talks with Irish PM Haughey.

6 Twelve new Ministers appointed in major political reshuffle in China; Deputy PM Geng Biao became Minister of Defence.

9 In UK, civil servants began series of strikes and other disruptive action in pursuit of pay claim (see 30 July).

10 In UK, a harsh Budget; income tax allowances unchanged; MLR reduced 2 per cent to 12 per cent; windfall tax on bank profits; new tax on North Sea oil; excise duties up, including 20p per gallon on petrol; aid for small businesses; government spending for 1981-82 forecast at £104,000 million; PSBR set at £10,500 million.
   President Reagan in Ottawa for two days of talks with Canadian PM Trudeau.
11 In Chile, President Pinochet sworn in for 8-year term as constitutional President.
17 President Shagari of Nigeria began 4-day state visit to UK.
22 Warsaw Pact manoeuvres in Poland extended because of political situation in country; ended 7 April.
23 Two-day summit conference of EEC heads of government opened in Maastricht, Netherlands.
   Great Train Robber Ronald Biggs taken into custody in Barbados after abduction from Brazil; 23 April, Biggs won appeal against extradition to Britain and returned to Brazil.
26 In UK, Social Democratic Party officially launched; twelve major points of policy included incomes policy, proportional representation, support for Nato and membership of EEC.
   In UK, Mrs Thatcher said in House of Commons that investigation in 1974 concluded there was no ground for believing that Sir Roger Hollis had worked for KGB as alleged in *Daily Mail* article (23 Mar.); announced Security Commission inquiry into selection procedures for security services.
27 USSR issued strong statement attacking Polish trade union Solidarity as counter-revolutionary.
   Mr John Louis named US ambassador to UK.
29 In UK, Sir Harold Wilson confirmed *Sunday Times* report that coup against his Government had been planned in late 1960s but denied involvement of late Lord Mountbatten.
   In UK, 6,700 runners competed in first London marathon.
   Lieut.-Gen. Roberto Viola sworn in as President of Argentina (see 22 Dec.).
30 In USA, President Reagan and three presidential aides shot and injured in Washington; John Hinckley arrested and charged.
   Three terrorists and one passenger killed when troops stormed hijacked Indonesian airliner at Bangkok.

APRIL

1 Western banks and governments assembled massive package of food and financial aid for Poland.
   In Lebanon, heavy fighting broke out in Beirut and Zahle between Arab peacekeeping force and Lebanese right-wing militia.
4 In UK, Oxford won University Boat Race by 8 lengths, coxed by a woman, Miss Sue Brown; Aldaniti won Grand National at 10-1.
6 Czechoslovak Communist Party Congress opened in Prague, attended by President Brezhnev.
7 In Philippines, voters overwhelmingly approved new constitution giving sweeping powers to President Marcos (see 16 June).
9 In N. Ireland, Robert Sands, IRA hunger striker in Maze prison, won by-election in Fermanagh and South Tyrone, in 87 per cent poll (see 5 May, 20 Aug., 3 Oct.).
11 In UK, 114 police and 192 civilians injured in violent rioting in Brixton; violence continued for 4 nights causing millions of pounds of damage (see 25 Nov.).
12 In USA, Nasa launched space shuttle *Columbia* on maiden flight with two astronauts aboard; 14 April, *Columbia* made perfect landing at Edwards air force base.
14 In Canada, Parti Québécois under M Lévesque won 80 out of 122 seats in election for provincial legislature.
15 Mrs Thatcher, PM of UK, began week's visit to India, Saudi Arabia and Gulf States.
17 In Poland 3·7 million private farmers won legal right to form independent union.
   Mr Nguza Karl I Bond resigned as PM of Zaïre.

23 In UK unemployment topped 2·5 million (10 per cent of work-force) for first time since 1930s.
27 In New Zealand, Royal Commission exonerated crew for crash of DC-10 airliner in Antarctica in 1979 in which 257 died, accusing Air New Zealand of 'an orchestrated litany of lies'.
29 In South African general election (white voters only), National Party returned to power with reduced majority.
30 In Poland, session of Central Committee of Communist Party endorsed Mr Kania's programme of realistic and moderate reforms.

MAY

5 In N. Ireland, Robert Sands became first of 10 IRA hunger strikers to die in Maze Prison (see also 9 Apr., 30 Oct.).
6 In UK, the Prince of Wales and Lady Diana Spencer obtained injunction preventing publication of transcripts of allegedly tapped telephone calls from Australia; tapes later found to be forgeries.
 USA expelled all Libyan diplomats because of Libyan Government's support for international terrorism.
7 In UK local government elections Labour made widespread gains from Conservatives.
8 US special envoy, Mr Philip Habib, began peace mission to Middle East in effort to defuse crisis over Syrian missiles in Lebanese border area; recalled to Washington 27 May.
9 In UK, IRA bomb exploded at Sullom Voe where HM the Queen was opening new £1,200 million oil terminal; no one hurt.
10 In second round of French presidential election, M François Mitterrand (Socialist) defeated President Giscard d'Estaing.
 In Germany, Social Democrats lost elections in West Berlin for first time since World War II; 11 June Herr Richard von Weizsäcker (Christian Democrat) elected Chief Burgomaster.
11 Mr George Chambers elected PM of Trinidad and Tobago in succession to late Dr Eric Williams.
 W. German Chancellor Schmidt at Chequers for two days of talks with Mrs Thatcher.
12 President Benjamin Sheares of Singapore died in office.
13 Pope John Paul II seriously wounded by gunman in St Peter's Square (see 22 July).
15 UN Committee published list of international sportsmen alleged to have participated in sporting contacts with South Africa in defiance of UN resolution.
 President Datuk Hussein Onn of Malaysia announced his retirement (see 19 July).
18 43 reported dead, 100 injured after two days of shelling by Syrian troops in Christian sector of Beirut.
19 In N. Ireland, 5 soldiers died in landmine explosion in S. Armagh.
21 M Mitterrand installed as President of France; named M Pierre Mauroy as PM.
 Chancellor Schmidt of W. Germany in Washington for talks with President Reagan.
22 In UK, Peter Sutcliffe ('The Yorkshire Ripper') gaoled for life at Old Bailey after conviction on 13 counts of murder.
24 President Jaime Roldós Aguilera of Ecuador killed with 7 others in terrorist-directed air crash; 25 May, Sr Osvaldo Hurtado sworn in as President.
 In Spain, police stormed a Barcelona bank and released some 250 hostages held for nearly 2 days by terrorists.
 General election in Cyprus; President Kyprianou remained in office with support of Akel Party.
26 In Italy, Government of PM Arnoldo Forlani resigned following scandal surrounding alleged activities of Masonic Lodge P2.
 General election in Netherlands; PM Van Agt's coalition lost parliamentary majority; 11 Sept. new Government under Mr Van Agt sworn in.
28 Cardinal Wyszynski, Primate of Poland for 30 years, died; 31 May, funeral relayed by radio and television and attended by head of state Jablonski; 7 July, Mgr Jozef Glemp nominated Primate.

29 Mr Peng Soran elected Secretary-General of People's Revolutionary Party of Kampuchea.
30 President Ziaur Rahman of Bangladesh assassinated.

JUNE

2 Archbishop of Canterbury, on one-day visit to N. Ireland, condemned violence and the
  hooded men.
3 In UK, Shergar won the Derby by biggest margin this century.
4 In UK, British Nationality Bill, creating three new categories of citizenship, received
  third reading in House of Commons.
6 In India, between 1,000 and 3,000 people feared dead when train crashed into river in
  Bihar.
8 Israeli planes bombed £140 million nuclear plant being built for Iraq near Baghdad by
  France; 19 June, UN Security Council voted unanimously for resolution condemning attack.
9 King Khalid of Saudi Arabia began three-day state visit to Britain.
11 General election in Ireland; PM Haughey's Fianna Fail failed to win overall majority;
   30 June, Dail elected Dr Garret FitzGerald Taoiseach at head of coalition of Fine
   Gael and Labour Party.
   In Iran, at least 2,000 feared dead in earthquake in Kerman province.
12 In Poland, PM Jaruzelski sacked five Cabinet Ministers and proposed major reconstruction of Government to tackle severe economic crisis; 3 July, 8 Ministers dismissed in extensive Government reshuffle.
13 In UK, man fired blank cartridges at HM the Queen at Trooping of Colour ceremony;
   14 Sept. Marcus Sarjeant gaoled for 5 years.
16 In UK, Liberals and Social Democratic Party issued joint statement of principles, *A
   Fresh Start for Britain* (see 16 Sept.).
17 The Prince of Wales encountered hostile pro-IRA demonstrators during one-day visit
   to New York.
21 In second ballot of French general election, voters gave Socialist Party landslide victory;
   Communist Party seats halved.
22 In Iran, Ayatollah Khomeini dismissed President Bani-Sadr, Parliament having voted
   for his impeachment; 29 July, Bani-Sadr granted political asylum in France.
   In Spain, Lower House of Parliament gave approval to law legalizing divorce (banned
   by General Franco).
25 In UK, White Paper *The United Kingdom Defence Programme: The Way Forward*
   (Cmnd. 8288), published.
28 In Iran, 74 died, including Chief Justice Ayatollah Beheshti, in bomb attack on headquarters of Islamic Republican Party.
   In Italy, Signor Giovanni Spadolini (Republican) became PM of first coalition Government not headed by a Christian Democrat for 35 years.
29 Two-day summit of EEC heads of government opened in Luxembourg (see 6 July).
   In China, Central Committee of Communist Party elected Hu Yaobang Chairman; Hua
   Guofeng became a Party Vice-Chairman.
30 In Israeli general election, results were indecisive; 5 Aug. Knesset approved new coalition led by Mr Begin.

JULY

1 Mr Alden Winship Clausen succeeded Mr Robert McNamara as President of World
  Bank.
2 In UK, N. Ireland Secretary of State Atkins outlined Government proposals to set up an
  advisory council for Northern Ireland.
6 In UK, violent rioting continued for third successive night in Toxteth district of Liverpool: millions of pounds worth of damage as youths attacked police (who sustained
  extensive injuries) and set fire to buildings.

British Foreign Secretary in Moscow to put EEC proposals for conference on Afghanistan; Mr Gromyko said proposals unrealistic in present form.

8 London hit by rash of street violence as other major cities continued to be affected by rioting and looting in worst violence seen in UK this century.

14 Extraordinary Congress of Polish Communist Party opened in Warsaw; adopted 8-point programme to provide general guidelines for Party and approved new Party constitution; Central Committee elected new enlarged Politburo.

16 In UK, by-election in Warrington won by Labour with greatly reduced majority; Mr Roy Jenkins, in first electoral test for Social Democratic Party, polled 42·4 per cent of vote.

17 In Lebanon, more than 100 died when Israeli jets bombed Palestinian areas of Beirut; 24 July, Israel and PLO agreed ceasefire ending two weeks of hostilities on border.

In UK, HM the Queen officially opened new Humber bridge, longest single-span bridge in world.

19 South African Springboks rugby team arrived in New Zealand at start of controversial 8-week tour which was accompanied by violent anti-apartheid demonstrations.

In Malaysia Datuk Sri Mahathir Mohammed named new Government.

In USA, 111 died when Hyatt Hotel, Kansas, collapsed.

20 Two-day summit conference of seven Western nations opened in Ottawa.

21 In UK, England beat Australia in Headingley Test Match by 18 runs; first time in 87 years a side had won a Test after following on.

22 In Italy, Mehmet Ali Agca gaoled for life for attempted murder of Pope.

24 Muhammad Ali Rajai achieved 88 per cent of vote in Iranian presidential election (see 30 Aug.).

In China, over 700 died in floods in Szechuan province; 1·5 million homeless and £500 million of damage.

27 In UK, PM announced £500 million package aimed at reducing unemployment.

28 In Iran, 1,000 died in earthquake in Kerman.

In UK, MPs, in free vote, approved motion in favour of compulsory use of car seatbelts.

29 In UK, marriage of The Prince of Wales and Lady Diana Spencer at St Paul's Cathedral seen by 750 million television viewers around world.

In USA, Congress approved President Reagan's Bill giving 25 per cent income tax cuts over three years.

30 In UK, civil servants ended 5-month strike (longest national pay dispute since 1926) after acceptance of 7½ per cent offer (see 9 March).

Sir Dawda Jawara, President of Gambia, unseated in military coup while in London; restored to power 5 Aug. with aid of Senegalese troops (see 14 Nov.).

AUGUST

3 President Sadat of Egypt began tour of London, Washington and Vienna.

4 US court ordered striking air traffic controllers back to work and New York judge imposed $2·4 million per day fine on Professional Air Traffic Controllers' Organization for duration of strike.

7 In UK, Court of Appeal ruled that 10-day old mongoloid baby must have life-saving operation against parents' wishes (see 5 Nov.).

9 In USA, President Reagan announced decision to proceed with manufacture of neutron bomb.

13 In UK, 13 died in Britain's worst-ever helicopter crash in North Sea.

East Germany celebrated 20th anniversary of building of Berlin wall.

16 Communique of summit conference of Soviet and Polish leaders in Moscow announced that USSR had agreed to postpone repayment of credits by Poland and increase supplies of raw materials and consumer goods.

17 In Iran, Majlis overwhelmingly endorsed new Government of Muhammad Javad Bahonar (see 30 Aug.).

19 US fighter planes shot down two Libyan SU22 fighters attempting to intercept two US fighters participating in naval exercises in Gulf of Sirte (see 1 Sept.).
   In Turkey, trial opened in Ankara of 587 rightists accused of attempting to seize power by force in violence preceding military coup in Sept. 1980.
20 In by-election in Fermanagh and South Tyrone, N. Ireland, Mr Owen Cannon (hunger-strike supporter) won seat vacated by Mr Bobby Sands (see 5 May).
23 Soviet Politburo issued communique urging Polish Communist Party to rebuff anti-Socialist forces and stressed importance of adherence to leninist standards.
25 US spacecraft Voyager II sent back most detailed pictures of Saturn yet available.
26 South African PM Botha confirmed that South African troops had been fighting Angolan forces in southern Angola in continuing operations against terrorists.
   OAU committee meeting in Nairobi agreed programme for ceasefire in Western Sahara.
28 Sebastian Coe regained world mile record (broken two days earlier by Steve Ovett) in Koblenz in 3 min 48·40 sec.
30 In Iran, PM Bahonar and President Rajai among some 15 dead in bomb explosion at PM's office in Teheran.
31 In Johannesburg, Mr Edward Heath warned that South Africa should not assume that West would stand by her so long as apartheid remained.

SEPTEMBER

 1 In Uruguay, General Gregorio Alvarez succeeded President Aparicio Mendez.
   In Central African Republic, President David Dacko overthrown in military coup; General André Golingba assumed power.
   In Libya Colonel Qadafi threatened to create an 'international catastrophe' by attacking US nuclear bases in Mediterranean if US again entered Gulf of Sirte (see 19 Aug.).
 2 In Iran, Majlis approved appointment of Hajatoleslam Muhammad Reza Mahdavi-Kani as interim PM (see 29 Oct.).
 4 Soviet forces began largest military exercises in Baltic since World War II.
   In Egypt, Muslim fundamentalists staged massive demonstrations in Cairo following government crackdown on religious extremists.
 5 In Poland, first national congress of Solidarity opened in Gdansk, ending 10 Sept.
 7 In UK, TUC congress opened in Blackpool.
 9 Israeli PM Begin in Washington for talks with President Reagan.
   French Government announced intention to nationalize 36 private banks and 11 leading industrial groups.
10 President Mitterrand of France in London for two days of talks with Mrs Thatcher.
11 Picasso's masterpiece *Guernica* returned to Spain from New York for first time since Civil War for permanent display in Prado museum.
13 In Norwegian general election Labour Government of Mrs Brundtland defeated.
14 In UK, major Cabinet reshuffle; Mr James Prior moved to N. Ireland office and replaced at Employment by Mr Norman Tebbit.
15 In UK, Liberal Assembly opened in Llandudno; 16 Sept. overwhelmingly voted in favour of alliance with Social Democratic Party.
   Pope John Paul II published encyclical on *Human Work*.
18 French National Assembly voted in favour of abolition of guillotine and capital punishment.
20 Belize achieved independence from Britain.
21 World Council of Churches announced £67,000 grant to Swapo as part of programme to combat racism.
25 Mrs Sandra Day O'Connor sworn in as first-ever woman judge of US Supreme Court.
27 In UK, Mr Denis Healey narrowly defeated Mr Tony Benn in vote for deputy leadership of Labour Party.
28 World financial markets swept by panic as share prices collapsed in Hong Kong, Tokyo and London.
30 Conference of Commonwealth heads of government opened in Melbourne, ending 7 Oct.

OCTOBER

1 Master spy Günter Guillaume released from gaol in West Germany and returned to East Germany.
2 In Iran, Hojatoleslam Ali Khameini overwhelmingly elected President.
3 In N. Ireland, hunger strike at Maze prison, which had claimed 10 lives, ended.
4 In UK, Social Democratic Party assembled in Perth for first national conference, moving later in week to Bradford and London.
6 President Sadat of Egypt assassinated by soldiers; 10 Oct. funeral attended by many Western leaders and Israeli PM Begin.
  In UK, woman died, 40 injured in IRA nail bomb explosion in London.
12 In UK, Director of Public Prosecutions announced police inquiry had found no evidence of financial irregularities and criminal conduct alleged against Mr John De Lorean, head of Belfast-based sports-car company.
13 In UK, Conservative Party conference opened in Blackpool.
14 Mr Husni Mubarak confirmed as President of Egypt in national referendum.
  Nobel peace prize awarded to UN High Commission for Refugees, Geneva.
16 In Japan, 94 died in mining accident at Yubari.
18 In general election in Greece, Mr Andreas Papandreou's Panhellenic Socialist Movement (Pasok) defeated ruling New Democracy Party; 21 Oct. Papandreou sworn in with first Socialist Government in Greek history.
  In Poland, PM General Jaruzelski succeeded Mr Kania as First Secretary of Polish United Workers' Party.
19 In UK, Government announced projected sale of majority stake in North Sea oil.
21 HM the Queen and Duke of Edinburgh began 5-day visit to Sri Lanka.
22 A two-day North-South summit conference attended by 22 world leaders opened in Cancún, Mexico, but failed to reach agreement on ideas for reducing poverty in the Third World.
  In UK, by-election at Croydon NW won by Liberal candidate (in alliance with SDP) from Tories.
23 Presbyterian Church of S. Africa instructed clergy to marry people of different races in defiance of apartheid laws.
24 Massive anti-nuclear demonstrations took place in many European cities; 150,000 attended rally in London.
25 In USA, 16,000 participated in New York City marathon won by Alberto Salazar in world best time 2hr 8min 13sec.
27 Prince and Princess of Wales began three-day visit to Principality.
  President Kekkonen of Finland resigned; powers transferred to PM Koivisto pending election in Jan. 1982.
28 Soviet submarine ran aground in Swedish territorial waters; 6 Nov. Swedish officials released vessel after protests to USSR and discovery that submarine was probably armed with nuclear warheads.
  US Senate rejected attempt to block Administration's plans to sell 5 AWACS radar planes and associated defence equipment to Saudi Arabia.
  In Uganda, British-born Bob Astles, former aide to Idi Amin, acquitted of murder.
29 Mr Hosein Musavi confirmed as 5th PM of Islamic Republic of Iran.

NOVEMBER

1 Antigua and Barbuda achieved independence from Britain.
  In Tunisia, first multi-party elections since 1959; Government-backed National Front won all seats amid claims of cheating.
3 Lord Carrington in Saudi Arabia on behalf of EEC to discuss 8-point plan for settlement of Middle East conflict put forward by Prince Fahd (see 25 Nov.).
4 In UK, state opening of Parliament; Queen's Speech foreshadowed Bills to curb local authority rate rises, to further limit trade union immunities and to bring private investment into British National Oil Corporation.

Polish Primate, Lech Walesa and PM Jaruzelski held unprecedented discussions on country's labour and economic crises.

5 In UK, Dr Leonard Arthur acquitted of attempted murder of 3-day old Down's syndrome baby by prescribing 'nursing care only'.

6 Second Anglo-Irish summit conference held at 10 Downing Street. British and Irish Governments agreed to establish Anglo-Irish Intergovernmental Council.

8 General election in Belgium; 14 Dec. M Martens (Flemish Social Christian) formed coalition after 5-week deadlock.

9 General San Yu elected President of Burma in succession to General Ne Win.

14 In N. Ireland, Rev. Robert Radford, Official Unionist MP for Belfast South, shot dead by IRA gunmen.

Gambia and Senegal formed a confederation to be known as Senegambia, headed by Senegal President Abdou Diouf.

15 In presidential election in Bangladesh, Acting President Abdus Sattar achieved overwhelming victory over Awami League candidate Dr Kamal Hossain (see 30 May).

18 President Reagan offered four-point programme to cancel plans to deploy Pershing and Cruise missiles in Europe if USSR dismantled all its SS-20 and other medium-range missiles targeted against W. Europe.

20 West Germany signed agreement with USSR for supply of 40,000 million cubic metres of Siberian natural gas.

Anatoly Karpov retained world chess championship following 18-match championship game against Viktor Korchnoi in Merano, Italy.

In UK, Dr Paul Vickers convicted of murdering his wife by administration of poisonous drugs.

22 In Spain, 200 people reported to have died during year from contaminated cooking oil.

23 President Brezhnev began two-day summit conference with Chancellor Schmidt in Bonn; arms control was principal topic.

In N. Ireland, thousands of Protestants brought much of heavy industry to standstill in loyalist day of action organized by Rev. Ian Paisley.

24 President Eanes of Portugal began first official visit to former colony of Mozambique.

25 Twelfth Arab Summit Conference opened in Fez, Morocco, but quickly abandoned because of deadlock over Saudi Arabian Midde East peace plan.

In UK, publication of *The Brixton Disorders 10-12 April 1981*: Report of an inquiry by Rt. Hon. Lord Scarman, OBE (Cmnd. 8427).

26 In UK, by-election at Crosby; Mrs Shirley Williams became first-ever Social Democrat elected to Parliament.

EEC heads of government began two-day summit conference in London.

Seychelles troops foiled attempted coup by foreign mercenaries.

28 In general election in New Zealand, Government of Mr Muldoon left with no clear majority; Social Credit Party held balance of power.

29 In Syria, 64 dead, 135 injured in terrorist bomb explosion in Damascus.

In presidential election in Honduras, Liberal Party swept to victory; Dr Roberto Suazo Cordova to take office in Jan. 1982, ending 17 years of military rule.

30 President Mitterrand began two-day visit to Algeria.

DECEMBER

1 174 died in air crash in Corsica.

Soviet-US talks on nuclear arms limitation opened in Geneva.

2 In UK, Chancellor of Exchequer announced package of economic measures including increases of £5,000 million in public expenditure in 1982-83, higher national insurance contributions, rents, rates and prescription charges.

Canadian House of Commons overwhelmingly passed resolution to patriate Canadian constitution from Britain.

7 South Africa admitted that its air and ground forces conducted raids into southern Angola in November.

8 General election in Denmark; 29 Dec. PM Joergensen presented new minority Social Democrat Cabinet despite heavy losses at polls.

9 Lisa Alekseeva granted permission to leave USSR after 17-day hunger strike by her mother and stepfather Dr Andrei Sakharov.

11 West German Chancellor Schmidt in East Germany for talks with Herr Honecker, ending 13 Dec.

12 In general election in Malta, Mr Dom Mintoff's Labour Party returned for third term of office.

13 In Poland, General Jaruzelski announced imposition of martial law; civil liberties and trade union activities curbed; thousands detained.

14 In Israel, Knesset voted 63-21 to approve extension of Israeli law to Golan Heights territory conquered from Syria in 1967 war.

15 At least 35 died in bomb explosion which destroyed Iraq embassy in Beirut.

17 In UK, Law Lords ruled that Greater London Council cheap fares policy was illegal.
    In Poland, Warsaw radio reported 7 miners killed by security forces in Katowice.

18 Albanian PM Mehmet Shehu reported to have committed suicide.

19 In UK, 16 died, including 8 lifeboatmen, when coaster *Union Star* ran aground off Cornish coast; subsequent appeal for lifeboatmen's families raised £2·7 million.

20 Polish ambassador to USA granted political asylum in USA.

22 General Leopoldo Galtieri sworn in as President of Argentina; President Viola had resigned because of ill-health.

29 President Reagan announced programme of economic sanctions against USSR because of its role in imposition of martial law in Poland.

31 In Ghana, civilian Government of President Limann overthrown in military coup led by Flt.-Lieut. Jerry Rawlings.

INDEX

AUSTRIA, 164–6; economy, 165; foreign affairs, 165–6; Polish refugees, 165–6; political changes, 164–5; USSR and, 165
AVEROFF, Evangelos, 179
AWOLOWO, Chief, 233
AZINAS, Andreas, 181

BACCOUCHE, Taieb, 216
BACO CARBO, Ing. Raúl, 83
BADAWU, General, 192
BAGAZA, Jean-Baptiste, President of Burundi, 247
BAHAMAS, THE, 97
BAHONAR, Mohammad Javad, 268; obit., 504
BAHREIN, 206–7, 209–10; security agreement with Saudi Arabia, 203
BAI HUA, 300
BAIRD, Tadeusz, 425
BAKALI, Mahmut, 127–8
BAKEMA, Jacob B., death, 441
BALBIN, Ricardo, 78
BALLET, 412–15
BALSEMÃO, Francisco Pinto, 172, 174, 352
BANDA, Dr H. Kamuzu, President of Malawi, 254
BANDARANAIKE, Anura, 280
BANDARANAIKE, Sirimavo, 280
BANGLADESH, 277–9; coup, 278–9; presidential elections, 279; South Talpatty island claim from India 278, 279
BANI-SADR, Abol Hassan, 140, 267, 268
BARBADOS, 93–4; extradition of Ronald Biggs denied, 40–41. 94
BARBER, Samuel, death, 425; obit., 504–5
BARCIKOWSKI, Kazimierz, 114
BARCO VARGAS, Dr Virgilio, 82
BARKAT, Gourat Hamadou, 224
BARR, Alfred H., Jr., death, 437
BASNAYAKE, Hema, death, 281
BATTEK, Rudolf, 120
BAUMEL, Jacques, 356
BAYERO, Ado, 233
BEGIN, Menachem, 70, 140, 186, 187
BEHESHTI, Ayatollah, 267; obit., 505
BELAÚNDE TERRY, Fernando, President of Peru, 84
BELGIUM, 150–2; coalition Governments, 151, 152; economy, 150–1, 152, 464; general election, 151–2; steel industry bankrupt, 150, 151; television, 432; treaty of economic union with Luxembourg, 154; Zaïrean exiles and, 245
BELIZE, 96; Commonwealth membership, 335–6; independence, 76, 89, 96, 329; map, 92; UN and, 329
BELL, Terrel, 57
BENIN, 241
BENN, Tony, MP, 15, 19–22, 49
BENNETT, Professor J. A. W., death, 448
BERLINGUER, Enrico, 148, 150
BERMUDA, 99
BERROUET, Edouard, 87

BETANCOURT, Rómulo, 86; obit., 505
BETANCUR, Belisario, 82
BETHELL, Lord, 176
BHAGWAN, Shree Rajneesh, 378
BIBÓ, István, 123
BID, Salim al, 205
BIFFEN, John, MP, 27, 28, 36, 44, 274
BIGGS, Ronald, 40–41, 94
BINAISA, Godfrey, 230
BIRD, V. C., 336
BIRENDRA, HM King of Nepal, 281
BISHARA, Abdullah, 207
BLACKBURN, Harold, death, 412
BLAZEY, Ces, 318
BLIZ, Hans, 331
BLOCK, John, 57
BLOEMBERGEN, Professor Nicolaas, 386
BLUNT, Anthony, 41
B'NEIJARA, Sidi Ahmed Ould, 239
BODARD, Lucien, 443
BÖHM, Karl, death 412; obit., 505
BOHMAN, Gösta, 162
BOLIVIA, 78–9; coup, 76, 78; relations with USA, 79
BOLKIAH, Sultan Sri Hassanal, 288
BONDI, Beulah, death, 429
BONGO, Albert-Bernard, President of Gabon, 242
BONNER, Elena, 106
BOONCHU ROJANASATHIEN, 292, 293
BOONE, Richard, death, 429
BORAN, Professor Behice, 183
BORG, Bjorn, 455–6
BOTHA, P. W., 262–3, 266
BOTHA, R. F., 260, 261
BOTHAM, Ian, 453
BOTSWANA, 261
BOUABID, Abderrahim, 220
BOUTEFLIKA, Abdel Aziz, 218
BOUTERSE, Daysi, 100
BOUMÉDIENNE, Houari, 218, 219
BOYCOTT, Geoffrey, 454
BOYLE OF HANDSWORTH, Lord, obit., 506
BRADFORD, Rev. Robert, MP, 54
BRADLEY, General Omar N., obit., 505
BRANDT REPORT, summit conference, Cancún, Mexico 6, 46, 374
BRAZIL, 79–80; abertura, 76, 79; 'Southern Cone' bloc rejected, 78
BRENT, Professor Leslie, 390
BREUER, Marcel, death, 441; obit., 505–6
BREZHNEV, Leonid, birthday (75th), 101, 102; disarmament policy, 65, 66, 109, 111, 145, 490–7; Jordan, King of, visit, 194; peace offensive 344, 345, 490–7; Polish crisis, 108, 120, 341, 489
BRITISH INDIAN OCEAN TERRITORY, 284–5
BRITTAN, Leon, MP, 27
BROCK, William, 57
BROCKLEBANK-FOWLER, Christopher, MP, 15
BROOKS, Jack, 357